I0112994

ERECTED
BY THE
STATE OF DELAWARE
TO COMMEMORATE THE SETTLEMENT
ON THIS SPOT OF THE FIRST
DUTCH COLONY UNDER DE VRIES
A. D. 1631

SOME RECORDS OF SUSSEX COUNTY DELAWARE

Compiled by

C. H. B. Turner

HERITAGE BOOKS
2019

HERITAGE BOOKS
AN IMPRINT OF HERITAGE BOOKS, INC.

Books, CDs, and more—Worldwide

For our listing of thousands of titles see our website
at
www.HeritageBooks.com

A Facsimile Reprint
Published 2019 by
HERITAGE BOOKS, INC.
Publishing Division
5810 Ruatan Street
Berwyn Heights, Md. 20740

Originally published
Philadelphia
Allen, Lane & Scott
1909

— Publisher's Notice —
In reprints such as this, it is often not possible to remove blemishes from the original. We feel the contents of this book warrant its reissue despite these blemishes and hope you will agree and read it with pleasure.

International Standard Book Number
Paperbound: 978-1-55613-249-0

PREFACE.

Some of the records in this book have been published before, but in a form inaccessible to most people.

Previous to the settlement of the dispute between Lord Baltimore and Penn Sussex County was only 30 miles long and 12 miles wide. That is the portion referred to in these records.

I am deeply indebted to the Rev. Sadler Phillips, Chaplain to the Bishop of London, and the Rev. and Mrs. P. T. Mignot of Guernsey for many kindnesses shown me when searching for records in Europe.

To Mr. William M. Marines' "Bombardment of Lewes," I owe most of my information about that important event.

C. H. B. T.

Lewes, Del., November 5, 1909.

SOME RECORDS OF SUSSEX COUNTY.

"There is probably no State in the Union where one would find less material for writing its history than in Delaware," says the American Historical Association in its report for 1906.

Let one attempt to write the history of any portion of Delaware and the statement of the American Historical Association will be found only too true.

Where Lewes now stands the Indians had a village called Sikoness, or Sikeoyness. We can imagine the astonishment of the savages as on August 28th, 1609, Henry Hudson sailed into the bay opposite the village.

From that time until 1631, when the expedition called Devries' expedition sailed into what is now called Delaware Bay and planted the Colony on a point of land above Lewes, which the colonists called Swaanendael, the Indians saw very few, if any, white persons.

The VanRenssalaer Bowier papers give us some account of the doings at Swaanendael until the colonists were massacred by the Indians. It is as follows:—

> "With the de Walvis, they, in 1631, took possession of the bay of the South River in New Netherland, occupying the place of their colony with twenty-eight persons engaged in whaling and farming, and made suitable fortifications, so that in July of the same year their cows calved and their lands were seeded and covered with a fine crop, until finally by the error of their Commis all the people and the animals were lamentably killed, whereby they suffered incalculable damage, which damage the remonstrants attempted to repair in the year 1632 with the former ship den Walvis and besought the Company to lend a helping hand, who neither by word or deed would render any assistance."

Samuel Godjn, Patroon of Swaandael, sold out to the West India Company, July, 1634.

There had been considerable friction between Kilian* and the West India Company, because Kilian wanted colonists to till the land, and the West India Company were opposed to having the land cleared and settled, as it caused a scarcity of fur-bearing animals.

---

* Van Renssalaer.

The VanRenssalaer Bowier papers say:—

"During the two years when the late Mr. Godijn and his people were trading in Swanendael, the Company received from the South River, through their servants, a no less quantity of skins than in former or later years, but he obtained his furs in addition to these by bartering with other tribes.

"This caused so much jealousy that the Company sent a Commis there, trading close by the people of Godijn, deprived him in one year of over 500 skins in Swanendael alone."

Again Kiliaen VanRenssalaer says: "We are trying to populate the land and in time to spread the teaching of the Holy Gospel by many people, while they (the West India Company), on the contrary, employing only a few people, look solely for the profits of the fur trade."

The Swedes do not seem to have attempted to colonize what is now Sussex County.

Secretary Van Tienhoven, writing from The Hague, February 22d, 1650, says: "The further progress of the Swedes could be prevented and neutralized by planting a Colonie at Swaanendael, otherwise called the Whorekil, on the West side of the Bay."

And he also says: "Send a clergyman, or, in his place provisionally, a Comforter of the Sick, who could also act as Schoolmaster."

While records are lacking that would tell us many things to the credit of the Dutch, the above record sets forth in a few words that they had a care for men's souls, as well as for their minds and bodies.

The Hoorn Kil, the name given these parts by the Dutch settlers, unfortunately spelled Horekil, Whorekill, and so many other ways, suggests the love of David Pietersen de Vries for his native place the municipality of Hoorn.

Vice-Director Alrichs, writing to Amsterdam, Holland, from New Amstel, on the South River, August 13th, 1657, says: "I have already stated that there is a fine and excellent country called the Whorekil, abounding very much in wild animals, birds, fish, &c., and the land is so good and fertile that the like is nowhere to be found. It lies at the entrance of the Bay, about two leagues up from Cape Henlopen."

Lord Baltimore's people were giving the Dutch on the South River much uneasiness by their claims to all the territory occupied by the Dutch, from New Amstel to the Whore Kil.

The Marylanders were threatening New Amstel and the Whore-Kil; New Amstel, being the more important place, the Dutch "did resolve to quit the Whore-Kill, thinking it better to quitt that place then to run the hazard of weakening New Amstell. The English then came out of Maryland, from a part now called Somersett County and drew neere the Whorekill, tradeing with the Indians. Whereupon it was reported that the said English men began to build and settle in that part of the country.

"A Commander and sixteen men were sent to the Whorekill to take possession againe, but another 'resolucôn' was taken a short time after to call the said soldiers back, and soe the Whorekill was left againe.

"There was likewise a boate dispatched to the Whorekill and there plundered and tooke possession of all effects belonging to the Citty of Amsterdam, as alsoe what belonged to the Quaking Society of Plockhoy to a very naile, according to the letter written by one of that company to the City of Amsterdam, in which letter complaint was made that the Indians at the Whorekill had declared they never sold the Dutch any land to inhabitt."

The Dutch placed buoys in the Bay, 1658. The same year the Whore Kil was annexed to New Amstel.

In 1657 the Indians near Lewes, or the Whore Kil, had captured some shipwrecked English.

Word was sent to Vice-Director Alrichs at New Amstel. In a letter from Alrichs to Mr. Petrus Stuyvesant, Director-General of New Netherland, dated Fort New Amstel, October 29th, 1657, he says: "Since writing the foregoing I have tried in several ways, as for instance dispatching first Capt. Flaman, to go to the Horekil, to release the English, who were shipwrecked there with two boats, but he, Flaman, has come back, without having accomplished anything on account of the loss of an anchor; I then have sent Michiel * * * there, who, after an absence of 14 days ransomed the remaining Englishmen from the Indians and brought them here together * * *, to the number of 14."

One of the earliest settlers in the Whore Kil was Halmanius Frederick Wiltbank, to whom was granted 800 acres of land, July 28th, 1676. There were grants to others at the same date: Henry Stricker, Timothy Love, (Rehoboth Creeke), Randall Reveille, John King, Robert Winder,

Daniel Harte, John Roods (Roads), Daniel Brown, Alexander Molestine, Abraham Clemmy, and Otto Wolgast.

As we shall see later Wiltbank played a more important part in the history of Lewes than did the others named above.

Order Appointing a day of General Fasting and Prayer:

"HONORABLE, DEAR, FAITHFUL

"Although the most merciful God, rich in grace and compassion, hath, notwithstanding our unworthiness, watched over us hitherto and daily gives us abundant cause to proclaim His praise and to bless His august name for the innumerable benefits and favors exhibited from time to time, in granting peace and quiet both with our neighbouring Christian nations and the Indians, the natives of the country, as well as in bestowing a bountiful harvest, having certainly blessed our basket of bread and staff of life, wherein His goodness and beneficence are clearly manifest.

"Yet, considering that the righteous God hath visited many and divers inhabitants of this Province, not only this summer, with painful and long, lingering sickness, but, moreover, also, that His kindled anger and uplifted hand threaten with many and divers punishments, especially with a devastating Indian war, which is no other than a just punishment and visitation of our God for our enormous sins of unbelief, dilatoriness in God's service, blaspheming His holy name, desecrating the Sabbath, drunkenness, lasciviousness, whoredom, hate, envy, lies, fraud, luxury, abuse of God's gifts, and many other iniquities. And because we run counter to God in our sins, God, in His threatenings will oppose us with punishments, unless we turn to Him, (whom, in our iniquities we have abandoned) in sincere humility and true contrition of heart that He may turn aside His wrath from us, and assist and bless us with His favor, therefore, we have considered it necessary, to that end, to proclaim Wednesday, the 15th October of the current year, a day of Universal Fasting and Prayer, and, accordingly, notify and command all our officers and subjects that they prepare themselves on the aforesaid day to appear, at the time aforesaid, with changed heart, at the usual place in the usual place in the general meeting, not only to hear God's word, but also, unanimously, with an humble and penitent heart, solemnly to call on the Lord's name that it may please His Divine Majesty to remove from our road His just plagues, wherewith we are already stricken, and to divert His rod, which flourishes over us, and to pour down His wrath upon the Heathen who know not His name; to take this budding Province into His fatherly protection; to maintain it against the efforts of all evil-minded men who seek its ruin; merciful to visit the inhabitants of this Province with corporeal and spiritual blessings, that the Word of Truth may be proclaimed and spread among many people, and that their rulers may be as lights among this evil and perverse generation; that to this end God may vouchsafe to send forth faithful laborers into His harvest to proclaim unto Jacob his sins and unto Israel his transgressions; particularly that God may be pleased to endow our Magistrates and regents of this land with understanding, wisdom, foresight and godliness, that they may resolve, design and valiantly execute whatsoever may be of service to the happiness of the country and welfare of the inhabitants both in body and soul. In order that it may the better be put into practice, we interdict and forbid, during divine service on the day aforesaid, all exercises and games of tennis, ball-playing, hunting, fishing, ploughing, sowing, and, moreover, all other unlawful practices, such as dice, drunkenness, on pain of the corporeal correction and punishment thereunto already affixed; in like manner are all servants of the Divine Word, within our government, hereby admonished to direct their preaching and prayers to this end.

"Thus done and concluded in our Council, in Fort Amsterdam, in New Netherland, the 30th September, 1659.

"Signed P. STUYVESANT

"C. VAN RUYVEN, Secretary.

"Delivered the writing to Domine Welius on the 10th of this October, 1659."

At this date Lewes, or the Hoorn Kil, was part of New Netherland, and the inhabitants were obliged to observe this, the first Fast Day, of which there is any record.

October 16th, 1659, Director Alrichs was made very angry by a statement of two of the Commissioners of the Director General of New Netherland, that the Fort at the Horekil or Sikonesse was "apparently built more for private designs than for the good of the Country."

Alrichs said: "We demand hereby further explanation and interpretation of these words, for it will not do to blurt out every thing bad and to make honest people suspected by their Masters and Principals without foundation and reason. * * * We say we could not do else, but what we have done until now, 'nor that we know to have promised the recall of the garrison from the Horekil, as your Honors say,' but only of a few men, according to your Honor's advice, who were really ordered up, but afterwards remained for some reason there."

At a court-martial held in New Amstel November 3d, 1659, to try one Samuel, a Corporal, who "while very drunk did not obey the order to go into arrest, because he had beaten his own wife, whereupon the Lieutenant struck him with his ratan, Samuel tore the same from his hand, the Lieutenant then drew his sword and struck him with the flat side of it and drove him, with the assistance of the Sergeant into the guardhouse. The Lieutenant said that he abused him meanwhile very much."

The Sheriff Van Sweeringen demanded that Samuel be shot.

Samuel's wife came to Vice-Director Beekman, "saying that her husband had been condemned last Wednesday or the 5th inst. to be banished the Colony for 6 months, but that as yet he was kept in chains and that now another resolution had been taken to send him with three men to the Horekil, about which she was very grieved."

The conditions of the Horekil must have been quite different from the Lewes of the present day, for banishment to Lewes would be considered a reward rather than a punishment.

In 1660 the aforesaid Samuel was carried away from the Horekil by Michiel Carman, who got in trouble for the act.

A ferry between Cape May and Lewes was established very early in the history of the Horekil for we read, July, 1660, that "the sail-boat or ferry at the Horekil has been cast ashore and badly damaged; the garrison have sent me word, (Beekman, at New Amstel) several times and complained that they are victualled very sparingly."

Word was received by Beekman at New Amstel, 1662, "that the Horekil was to be abandoned and the City's soldiery here (Hoorn Kil) to be disbanded."

This did not happen, for the ship St. Jacob,* skipper Peter Luckassen, which arrived at New Amstel July 28th, 1663, with about sixty farm laborers and girls, had left "41 souls with their baggage and farm utensils at the Horekil."

1663. May 12th. Herry Petefar, Englishman, and Jacob Jansen, Dutch sailor, make a declaration at request of Peter Alrick, commander of the South River, that without his and the people's assistance no goods could have been saved from the bark "King Charles," stranded on April 12th, last, near Cape Hinlopen. Witness, Jurien Blanck and Michiel Taeleus.

The English having taken New Amsterdam, 1664, the "ffrygotts, the Guinney, and the William and Nicholas, and all the souldyers which are not in the Fort" were ordered to proceed to the Delaware as speedily as possible to capture the towns, &c. Thus ended the Dutch rule for some years.

The English granted Mr. Peter Alrichs "liberty to Trade or Trafficke either by himself, or his Deputy with the Indyans or any others, in or about Hoare Kills in Delaware Bay, for Skins, Peltry or what other Commoditye those parts shall afford."

---

* Plockhoy came in this ship. See page 34.

THE FORT.

In 16$\frac{69}{70}$ "there was no officer at ye Whore-Kill to keep the Peace."

William Douglass was sent to New Castle for trial. It was charged against him that he had "behaved himself ill at ye Whore-Kill." The Court ordered "hee shall bee Continued in Prison, untill farther Order, but that his Irons bee taken off. However if hee can give security not to returne to ye Whore-Kill &c hee may bee Discharg'd."

Very early in the history of Sussex County the inhabitants protested against tariff, and the Governor, Sir Francis Lovelace, and his Council ordered: "Whereas, I Received a Petition from ye Inhabitants at ye Whorekill in Delaware Bay wherein is represented unto me ye great Inconvenience of ye late Imposition of 10 P. Cent upon all furres & peltry exported from thence, The wch hath no way redounded to a publique good as was proposed, &c & I have thought fitt to remitt & abolish ye late ord^{r} for custumes there October 22, 1670."

William Tom and Peter Alricks wrote Governor Lovelace, March 9th, 167$\frac{0}{1}$, of the "intention to build a blockhouse 40 foote square wth 4 att every for fflancks in the middle of the Towne the Fort not being fitt to be repaired and if repaired of noe defence lying at the extreme entrance of the town and noe garrison therefore wee beg that wee may libty to pull itt downe and make use of the tiles bricks and other materials for the use of o^{r} new intended fortificacion wch if wee have noe occasion for, as wee fear wee shall, will be convenient for a Courthouse notwithstanding."

This fort was destroyed before 1773, as an Act of the Assembly, for that year, for erecting a bridge over Lewes Creek, states that the bridge is " to begin at or near the place where the fort in the said town stood."

Trouble had been brewing between the people of Maryland and the people of the Hore Kil for some time. It was the trouble about Lord Baltimore's grant, as to the boundaries North and East.

A letter from the Hore Kil, April 27th, 1672, signed by Will Tom, Pieter Alricks, Walt^{r} Wharton, Ed. Cantwell, states: "This morning appeared before us Harmen Cornelius ent John hyshebon who informe that a certain prson by name Mr. Jenkins who rane into the Horekill and thus surveyed severall lands in the bay by p'tended commission from the Lord Baltimore threatening the Inhabitants that denyeth his power that they shall be sent for into Maryland there to be punished whether he has commission or noe is uncertayne these we thought fitt to acquaint yo[r] hon[r] to wayte y[r] hon[rs.] further order."

Richard Perrot, of Virginia, asks for a grant of land on the Horekil.

"May it plese your Honour

"In May last my selfe with some other Gentlemen of Vergeney came over to Delieware to see the plase and liking the plase wee made choise of severall tractes of Land for our Selfes and nabores and had made bold to have given your Honor A visitt had not one of our Company falen ill so that wee implied Mr. Walter Wharton ffor to paten our Land: now may it plese your Honor about four days before I came to seete [settle], the Mareland men Have sarvaed it again in the Lordes name I much fear it will disharten the Rest of the gentlemen from cuming vp at the falle and severall more of our nabores that would cume vp at the fale of the lefe very Honest-men and good House Keepers they desired me to take them vp sume Land, which I am doutfull to doue unless your Honor will bee plesed to give me permission for it.

"I dout not but to se the plase well seted in tow or three years at the * * * and a trade from London, the plase is good and helthy and wanteth nothing but peple I was in good Hopes I should have had the hapines to have got vp before your Honore left deliware but my hopes was in vaine I Hope your honor will bee plesed to honor me with A line or two whoe is youre faithful and obedient servant unknowne

"From the Horekil "Richard Perrot.

"June 21, 1672."

This P. S. is added to the above letter.

"If your Honore plese to grant us all the land to us Vergenianes that lieth betwene the Horekil and the Mortherkill wee shall take spedey care fore the seating of it, as may bee expected at so great a distance when Layed out according to menes familise what good Land there may bee found in the distance. I know not at present wee Have A desire to be neare together as the plase will aforde I intend Vergeney for sum occasione of bisnes and send up my sonn. "R. P.

"These ffor the Honored ffransis Loulis, Esqr. Governor and Captain Generall of new Yorke pr with Care."

At a Council held at Fort James, New York, July 1st, 1672, among other cases to be tried was that of Daniel Brown who had been arrested at the Horekil and sent, prisoner, to New York.

The court ordered Daniel to enter into a Recognizance of £20 for his good behavior on his return to the Horekil, and that Daniel was to ask pardon of the Magistrates at the Horekil on his return.

At the same court this order was made:

"The Request of ye Magistrates at the Whore-Kill being taken into Considercon, wherein they desire reperacon of the Damages & Losses they susteyned by the Privateers the last Winter, they may be permitted to lay an Imposition upon strong liquo[rs].

"It is allowed of & consented unto, and the Magistrates there have hereby power to levy & receive upon each Anchor of strong liquo[rs] spent of disposed of amongst them the value of foure Guild[rs] in wamp[m], & this to continue for one year only after this shall come to the said Magistrates hands, untill the Conveniency or Inconveniency thereof shall better appear."

One Jones with a number of companions from Maryland attacked the Whorekil and plundered the inhabitants. Word having been sent to the Governor at New York, Lovelace, he wrote the following letter to Governor Philip Calvert of Maryland, August 12th, 1672:—

"Sr. I thought it had been impossible now in these portending boysterous times, wherein all true hearted Englishmen are buckling on their Armo[rs] to vindicate their Hono[r] & to assert ye imperial Interests of his Sacred Majesties Rights and Dominions, that now (without any just ground either given or prtended) such horrid Outrages should be committed on his Ma[ties] Leige subjects, under ye protection of his Royall Highness Authority as was exercized by one Jones, who wth a party as dissolute as himself, took ye paines to ride to ye Whore Kill, where in Derision and Contempt of the Dukes Authority bound ye Magistrates, and Inhabitants, despitefully treated them, rifled, and plundered them of their Goods; and when it was demanded what Authority, hee acted, answered in noe other language than a Cockt Pistol to his Breast, wch if it had spoke, had forever silenced him.

"I doe not remember I have heard of a greater Outrage & Riott committed on his Majesties Subjects in America, but once before in Maryland.

"Sr you cannot but imagine his Royall Highness, will not bee satisfied wth those violent proceeding, in wch ye Indignity rebounds on him; Neither can you but believe, It is as easy an Undertaking for mee to retaliate the same Affront on Jones his Head and Accomplices as hee did to those indefensible Inhabitants.

"But I rather chuse to have first a more calme Redress from you, to whom I now appeale, and from whom may in Justice expect that Right in ye Castigation of Jones cum Socys, that yo[r] Nature and Law has provided for: Otherwise I must applye myselfe to such other Remedyes as the Exigence of this Indignity shall perswade mee to. Thus leaving it to your Consideracion I still remaine

"Yo[r] very humble servant "Fr Lovelace.

"Fort James in New York
"Ye 12th day August 1672."

Captain John Carr writes the following letter from New Castle to Gov. Lovelace:—

"SIR:—According to your Honors orders we sent those papers to the Horekil by Mr. Wharton where they found noe reception. I need not give your Honor the reasons, for your Honor will find them in the papers inclosed taken by Mr. Wharton, the number of men and horse that came to the Horekil was about thirty, but they were sixty halfe way, where meeting Mr. Parrot goeing to Acamahe and soe to Virginia and understanding by him there was noe other forces from your Honor but the Inhabitants of the Horekil thirty horse was sent back to Maryland, this Mr. Parrot is a gentleman seated near Horekil by your Honor's patent, the Horekil boat is come heere with fower of the inhabitants and desiers to take a tract of land up the river near your Honors land, they say before they came from thence Harmanus and Sanders was returned from St. Maries, who brings news that in Maryland they are levieing a considerable force to bring this place &c. to their obedience. "JOHN CARR."

Answer to Carr's letter:—

"CAPT CARR:—The Lett[r] you sent by Express over Land came safe to my hands wth the enclosed Relacion and Papers concerning the Whore Kill, & the Marylanders forcible possessing themselves of the Place, as also of the Goods and Estates of some of the Inhabitants of w[ch] wee had some Rumo[rs] before, but did not give much Credit to it, supposing what was done before to bee the rash Action of some Private person, not thinking the Authority of Maryland would invade his Royall Highness Territoryes w[ch] he hath been possest of for near 8 yeares &c. &c.

"Yo[r] very Loving Friend FR. LOVELACE.

"FORTE JAMES IN NEW YORK
"the 7th day of Octob[r] 1672".

Captain Cantwell to Governor Lovelace about the affairs at the Whorekil:

"N. CASTLE ye 10 of December 1672

"RIGHT HONORAB[LE] S[R]:—Yo[r] Hono[r] writt Mr Aldrichs of my not writing to yo[r] hono[r] I had writt to Capt. Nicholls att Large of what I heard and saw in Maryland.

"I thought Capt. Nicolls would have informed yo[r] hono[r] of all I heard so much that my Lorde thus intend for to keepe ye Whore kill.

"I saw Jones procure and seas all Indyan goods or skins att ye Whorekill and one Smith ye Judge of ye Co[rt] att ye Whorekill tould me that my Lorde Baltemore gave him order for to drive a 20d naile in ye touchhole of ye greate gun and seas ye guns and millstones att ye Whorekill.

"His Commmission was so Large as yo[r] hono[r] can imagene, when I came to St. Mary's Jones wen't to ye Governo and he writt upon ye backside of his Comission that he would maintain his Comission.

"I tould them that itt was folly for them to strive against yo[r] hono[r]'s power and tould them if yo[r] hono[r] gave but order for to beatt a down all ye servants would come away from them, ye most part of ye people thus fear that theire servants will run away from them all ye people will be glade submitt themselves under yo[r] hono[rs]

Government and they plainly say that they will not Resist yors honors power nor will have noting to doe with what my Lorde has done &c &c

"To Command "ED CANTWELL."

Order for the Administration of the Horekil Precint:—

"At a Council in New York April 14, 1673 It is Ordered, That a Commission be sent to ye Officers & Magistrates at Delaware to goe to ye Whore-Kill, there to keep a Court in his Maties name, & to make inquiry of all Irregular Proceedings, & to settle the Govermt and Officers there as formerly under his Maties Obedience, & the Protection of his Royall Highness, for the wch there shall likewise be sent particular instructions."

The Dutch having retaken New Netherland there was Council held at New York September 12th, 1673, at which the Deputies from the South River appeared and presented their credentials.

It was decided that "The court for New Amstel shall have jurisdiction over the inhabitants of the east and west side of Christina Kil as far as Boomtieshook" and "The court for the inhabitants of Hoere Kil, to have provisional jurisdiction over the people on the east and west side of Cape Hinlopen and northward to Boomties Hook."

Pieter Alrigs was made Schout and Commander of the South River of New Netherland.

Appointment of Magistrates for Horekil District:—

"28. 9bre. His Honor the Governor, has selected, upon the nomination by the inhabitants of the Horekil, the following persons to be Magistrates there for the next year:

"Mr. Harmanus Wiltbank
"Sander Maelsteyn
"Doctor Jan Roots (Rhoades)
"Willem Claessen."

The Dutch having ceded New Netherland to the English, Governor Andross issues an order November 2d, 1674, for the reinstatement of all officers who were in the English service before the occupation by the Dutch, "Excepting Peter Alrick, the Bayliffe, he having proferrd himself to ye Dutch at their first coming, of his own Motion and acted very violently (as their cheife Officer) ever since."

Commissioners of the Colonie on the South River to the Burgomasters of Amsterdam, 1663.

"Your Worships will also please give orders about maintaining possession of Ciconicing or Whorekil, inasmuch as by the discharge of the soldiers, it runs the risk of being occupied by the English, since it is very fertile and well prepared land, and lies on the sea at the mouth of the river."

J. Alrichs writing from New Amstel, August 16th, 1659, to Amsterdam, says:

"A new fortification and settlement were made at the Whore or Sickoneysincks Kil, which have been daily visited.

"In respect to the 3 persons sent as Councillors, the first hath asked for and obtained his discharge; the third, who was Commissary, is dead, and his place still vacant.

"The second should command at the Sickoneysincks Kil, in order to establish possession and government firmly there."

Letter.

Helmer Wiltbank to Governor Andros; Lord Baltimore about to renew his claim. Rebellion in Virginia.

"Richt Honoble Governeur,—Yours receaved the 18th of this Instand month wear in wy understand your great Cear & diligenth of us wich my durender to your Honor menny tanks wear in wy doe inform your Honor that wy ar in good Helt Lickwise thear is good Hops of success & situatie of this plaets by menny persons both out of Virginnia & Merryland & heave also reseaved ohn halfe barrel of powder which youe thet sent by your schaloop & given alsoo menny tanks to your Honor for your good instruction and schal mack as good jus af them as possibelly Lays in our pour & Schayl how that your Honor thet deseir af occasion thet requeir a piloot for your Honors Schaloop; thear was non keapabele her & your Honors Schaloop meester thet not much question his gohin well.

Wy doe hereafulger raport from the Commun people in Merrylandt that the Lord Baltomore thus ar immagine to Heave this pleats again but wy doe wenset & wy thacht fit to give your Honor notis af at.

Lickewise her is dayly severale persons Cummin out of Virginia which brings news that the rebellion thus Continue still against thear gouverneur & gouverment & Lick to be wors which is a great dishartening to all payes & sober meyndeth people. Not else but your Honors servant to Commaund & pray for your Honors good helt & success in your gouverment. "Helms Wiltbank.

"167$\frac{6}{7}$ this 26th of February at the Whorekil.

"Her is prsent news out of Accumacke that ther is twoo fregats is Com in & that the heave brought the Contre to a pays again & moor thy my Lord Baltomore heave gott a grant from his Majesty fors is land & that the seam scud follow fourtnight after the fregats thet seth outh.

"These for the right Honoble Gouverneur Ed. Androsz at New York."

At a special Court held at Horekil, March 19th, 167$\frac{6}{7}$, Mr. Helm. Wiltbank, Mr. Edwd. Southrin, Capt. Paul Marsh, Mr. Alex. Molestine, and Mr. John King, Justices, being present, John Stevens petitoined for a resurvey of some land he had purchased from William Willoughby and Robert Dicks.

At a Court held May 14th, 1677, William Planer for confirmation of title to land on Slater Creeks claimed by Randell Revell.

A letter from John Audrey, the Horekil, September 10th, 1677, to Governor Andros:

"MY LORD:—I Am At present in A very weeke Condishion And have not ben out of my hous this siks wekes having And still have a fever Every Day In as much I cannot goo on hundred yardes from my hous If it would save my life.

"The holl pepell of the plas knows it your owner knows the thing That I am broute Thether Is nothing Consernin me but It lies between Peter Groondike And docter Smith And Allsoo what I did was to the best of my knowledg not having and consenting with on of them mor then the other soo humbelly Craven your owner to Conider my Condishon I shall Ever Remain your owners most humble servant.

"JOHN AUDREY.

"MY LORD:—The intent of Mister Smith was to have Com with me in my boat And had it not ben for Mr. Helmanus Willbank for he toulld me he was intended to Com to the falls in his own boat which was the occashun I Left him be hind me. "JOHN AUDREY."

HELMER WILTBANK TO GOVERNOR ANDROS.

"WHOOREKILL Sept. 18. 1677.

"HONORABLE SIR: Whereas by accidentiall of sum sickness of body by feavor & ague and Lameness of my one Legg Cannot by no possibility appear at the High Court of assize please yor Honor to pardon mee.

"Have but this onely to say for my selfs that up the Relacions of Peter Groenendike in the matters between the sd Groenendike & Henry Smit I apprehend & understood at that time with rest of the Jury buth Groenendike afterwards goth Abraham Clement with a petition that wy migt Recalle our verdict & Groenendike spoocke himself to mee sum time whit treatning that the Jury hath given his monny away & further sayeth that of so bey wy would petition to the Court I may have Rehearing this would bee the easiest way and the least Chardge & so I tocht the Jury may have him done wrang not noying & of soo bie the Court would give rehearing what is that to the Jury being from thear oath & the writtens out of thare aknowledge which being to mee understanding to have Rehearing on a Reexamination as being not perfect to Distinguish the Circumstanges of many English woords or speaches by which Referr myselfs unto yor Honor favor, futher acquainting yor Honor of one Major John West out of Accumacks in Virginia whom hath writ unto mee about a Considerable quantity of Land for himselfs & sum partners of him which Land being Just to the Northward of the supposed Cabo Hinlopen seperating itself from itselfs from the sd Cape with one Inlett and a Creeke Comly called by the Indians Assawarnon the which I have mentioned unto your Honor In my former Lettr that they of Merrylandt have made sum certaine survays by thiere prtended Right, the which sd Land the sd Major West affirmes by his Lettr to settle Immediately In his R. H. right soe he the sd Major West may obtaine good Incorredgement and bee protected by yor Honor hee being a very able prson with a vast Estate to which End I have answered his lines that what soever previledges & Incorredgement might or could be Expected from yor Honor should not bee wanting therefor of yor Honor pleased to Express any particulars in such a Concerne to setle the utmost bounds and Limitts of the government Refer the same unto yor Honors wisedome & discretion, otherwise it is lukly to be settled by them of Merryland these winter as far as I Can understand.

"One favor shall request of yor Honor that whereas it was your Honors pleasure the last yeare to depute mee for one of the Magistrates for these partes which now the time of Limitation thereof being Expired therefore hereby begg yor Honor may be pleased to discharge mee by Writ of Ease shall Humbly thank yor Honor for the same Being but little learnet and weak of apprehension & understanding of the Lawes; have no more at prsent to acquaint yor Honor onely take leafe to Conclude & Remaine with all due Love & Respect

"Your Honrs humble Servant to Command

"HELMS. WILTBANK."

Wiltbank and the other Magistrates to Governor Andros November 13th, 1677. "A petition from Thomas Wellburne, merchant, In behalfe of himself and partners and William Anderson of Accomack County Virginia."

These petitioners had had their land surveyed by Cornelius Verhoofe; Verhoofe sent the certificates to Captain Edward Cantwell, General Surveyor, to register and sign. Cantwell erased the names of the lawful owners of the grants, Welburn and others, and substituted names of his, Cantwell's, friends, Henry Streeter and Abraham Clements.

CIVIL AND MILITARY APPOINTMENTS FOR HOREKIL.

November, 1674.

Capt. paull Mash, Lieut & prsident of the Court;
Mr. Helmanus Wiltbanck, Justice, Sheriffe & Collectr;
Mr. Alexander Molestede, Justice;
Mr. John Kipharen, Justice;
Mr. Otto Wolgast, Justice;
Mr. Daniell Browne under Sheriff & Constable.

1675, June 25.

Mr. John Avery, Lieut, & prsident of the Court;
Mr. Edward Southrin, Justice.

"At a Court held for the Whorekill The 11th day of June 1678. Mr. Helms. Wiltbanck: Concerned

"Com: Mr. Henry Smith, Mr. Alex. Molestine, Mr. Edward Southrin, Mr. John Roades, Present. Concerned.

"John Roads Plt, Helms Wiltbank Deft.

"By reason of the Death of Mr. John Backstead & Absence of Capt. Paul Marsh there was not magistrs for a Court, therefore by Consent of both parties & the magistrs it is Referred to the next Genll Assizes at New York for tryall.

"Vera Copia.

"Test. CORNELIS VERHOOFE Cl. Co. Whorekill."

More trouble with Avery. Letter to Governor Andros.

"WHOOREKILL ye 30th June 1679

"HONNORED SR:—Yor Honnor hath beene pleased to Joyne mee in Commission with others As a Magistrate for this County, which I have ever sence bene both willing and radye to sarve you and my Countrey to the best of my Judgement and having that Trust reposed in me I Looke upon myself oblidged to Inform your Honnor of suc miscariges and misdemeanors as happen or fall out that cannot be rectified here; And that is the Grose Abusses that hath bene committed by Capt John Avery presedent of this Cort. both relating to the Trust reposed in him and otherways.

"1st. That when the rest of the Magistrates could not consent to doe and determaine things as he would have it; Contrary to our Judgement he have in greate Rage and feury went out of Court Cursing and swaring, Calling of the rest of the Court ffooles, Knaves and Rouges; wishing that if ever he satt amongst us againe, that the devil might com and fetch him away, and also threeting and prently after did strik one of the Magistrates with his Kane, and had he not bene prevented by the spectatours, might a done much damage that way.

"2 Hee Tooke upon himself to Marry the widdow Clament to one Bryant Rowles, without publiquecation notwithstanding she was out aske at least a Month to another man, namly Edward Cocke; The which when the said Cocke hard that she marryed to another man said that it would be his death And presently went home fell sick and in forty eight hours dyed; he left it on his death that her marrying was the cause of his dyeing.

"3d Hee took upon him to grant a Licence to Marry Daniel Browne to Susan Garland widdow, without any publiquecation, which Marrige was effected, notwithstanding it is Generally knowne or at Least the said Daniel confesses that he knows no other but that he have a wife living in England.

"4thly One Judith the wife of Thomas Davids being subspected to have stoole sume goods from severall persions the goods being found in her Custidy was held in examination by me and at ffirst she did Confidently Affirm that she brought the sd. goods out of Mary Land and that thay ware hur owne Lawfull goods, but well knowing that it would be proved otherwise, did soone Confess that she did steale them and from whom, upon hur Confession made hur * * * and Commited hur to the Custidy of the Constable till the next Court then following; but soon after Capt. Avery sent a noote by hur Husband to the Cunstable requiring him to give hur hur Libierty threetening both me that had Commited hur and the Cunstable that did detaine hur soe that the Cunstable being subprised with fear did discharge hur out of his Custidy.

"In short he the said Capt. Avery is an Incouriger and upholder of Dronkingnes Theeft Cursing, swaring, and ffighting to the Affrighting, Amazing, and Terifienge of his Majties quiet and peacable subjects: Whoes grose weelkedness and Unhuman conversation, if a timely stop be not put to it, may justly be expexted to bring downe Gods Heavey Judgment upon this place.

"5thly. I goeing into the house of Helmanus Wiltbank on the fifteenth day of this Instant June being the Lords day whare the said Capt. Avery was drounk, whoe soone after brooke out in a greate Rage and feurey (without any provocation) Calling me beagerly Rouge and theefe with many more reflexting speachess, saying that he would prove me Rouge and Theefe and that I was not worth one grot. I did till him that if he would not give me satisfaction for the Abusse he had Cast upon me that I would sue him, To which hee replyed, The he would faine see any Magistrate, that would dare to signe a warrant or sumeance Against him, And that what he had said he would not be accountable to any Court, but onely to the Governor and that he is above any power here; soe that the other Commisoners have Refeused tó to signe a sumeance Against him: he Curses and swares at such A rate, that he ffrights all others from doeinge any thing in order to bringing him to Justice, &c &c &c

"Your Honnors Obedeant and ffaithful Servant

LUKE WATTSON."

"At a Court held for the Whorekill, July 12, 1679.
"(Capt John Avery)

"Comrs: Mr. Francis Whitwell, Mr. Alex Molestine, Mr. John Kipshaven, Mr. Luke Wattson, Mr. John Roades, Mr. James Wells, Prsent.

"John Richardson petitioner.

"Whereas the petitioner hath made Appeale By the Evidence of John Bridgs there unto sworne and Mr. Francis Whitwell Confirming the same that hee the said petitionr was by his Tenant Thomas Crompton the first Setler In Building Clearing and manuering the said Land according by a Certificate Bearing Date July 18, 1676. The said tenant Silently Departed by which one John Stevens or his order having taken possession of the said house & Land which said Clayme and possession taken by said John Stevens, Doth not as yet Appeare to the Court to bee the said Stevens his Just Rights &c.

"CORNELIS VERHOOFE Cl. Co. Whorekill."

At a meeting of the Court July 25th, 1679, the above decision was reversed and John Stevens was put in possession of the land. In 1676, August 18, John Richardson and Thomas Crumpton, of Dorchester County, Maryland, had entered into an agreement about a piece of land on the West side of Delaware Bay called Duck or Duke Creek.

In 1678, Captain Nathaniel Walker, had had a grant of six hundred and eighty acres at a place called Cedar Neck, between "Rehobah Bay and the Indyan Inlett to the Southward."

Secretary Matthias Nicolls wrote to Captain Avery, 1679, to see to it "that Capt. Walker may no longer bee delayed, about his patent."

The decision of the Court in giving John Stevens possession of lands in dispute does not seem to have satisfied Stevens, for we find September 10th, 1679, that he had written to Edmund Cantwell, at New Castle, asking whether Cantwell have authorized one Thomas Phillips to grant warrants for land.

Cantwell said that he had not and he did not give John Richards or Richardson a warrant for more than three hundred acres of land. Cantwell had only seen Richards or Richardson once at the house of John Edwardson in Chaptonke.

Richards used both names Richards and Richardson.

John Stevens was living on Thomas Crompton's land July 7th, 1677.

"Commission to the Justices at ye Whorekill Oct. 8, 1678: John Avery, ffrancis Whitwell, Alexander Molestein, John Kippshaven, Luke Wattson, John Roades, James Wells."

October 30th, the Court at Whorekill granted a piece of land to Walter Dickeson. The land was on St. Jones' Creek.

John Stevens has more trouble, having ejected one John Glover.

Griffith Jones was attorney for Glover and on the twenty-sixth day of January, 1678, had made a deed for the land from John Richardson of Dorchester Co. to the said Glover. Samuel Styles had formerly lived on the place.

The case was tried February 10th, 11th, 12th, $16\frac{79}{80}$.

The pannell of ye Jury:—Mr. Edward Southrin, Samuell Gray, Otto Wolgart, Helms Wiltbanck, Daniell Browne, George Young, William Firtcher, John Hackister, Richard Levick, Charles Johnson, Richard Peaty, Thomas Howard.

A copy of a land warrant dated July 18th, 1676, and signed by Thomas Phillips, Deputy Surveyor, read as follows:—

"Laid out for me John Richardson and James Shackleday & John Richardson Senor a tract of land &c.

"The Deposicon of William Watson aged 34 yeares or there abouts Sayth yt in ye yeare 1676 Sometime in ye month of August or thereaboute he came in companey of Jno Richardson to Thomas Phillips his house wth some others and ye sd Thomas Phillips Jno Richardson & others did goe to ye branches of Duck Creeke and there did see a howse upon a branch side and ye Thomas Phillips and Jno Richardson did say yt hee ye sd Jno. Richardson did build ye same &c &c.

"Sworn in open Court December 10, 1679.

"Christopher Jackson aged 30 year. Edward Ryan aged 36 years and Peter Bawcombe.

"The last one, Bawcombe heard Robert Dick and William Willoughby say that they Never would come up to seate their land if they could have given all ye land in thes parts for ye Plague and trouble of ye muscitesh and would sell their land to yor Depont for a pr of shoos apeece."

Census For Cedar Creek, 1680.

Robt Hart, 3 in family;
upon Joseph Cowdree plantation, 3 in family;
Mr. Bowman, 2 or 3 in family;
George Collens, on Shackelys plantation;
Jno Curtis, 4 in family;
Jno Richardson, 6 in family;
Thomas Groves, 2 in family;
Thomas Heiffer, 2 in family;
Alexander Ray, 2 in family;
Thomas Williams and John DeShaw, 2 in family.

At a Court held at Horekil, June 7–18, 1680.

Walter Dickson (Dickinson) plt., Barnard Hodges deft.

"Samwell Stiles aged 44 deposed that John Richardson came with severall other persons to the house, that John Stevens seated him upon neare Lettle Creeke in the Whoorekill precents; and demanded him to give the sd Richardson possession of the howse and Land &c. Verdict for the Plaintiff."

Luke Watson, John Roades, John Kipphaven, William Clark, and Otto Wolgart, Magistrates, to Gov. Andros relative to a Prison and Court House, Surveys and Settling of Land.

"Honorble Governor: The commission wee have received And in obedeance there unto have proceeded &c. whereas there have heatherto bene a neglect in geting A prison here; for want of which there have bene not long sence a prisoner for debt, whoe was A stranger made his Escape; which may prove damage either to the County or Sherife; for the preventing of the like for the futter: we have ordered A prisson stocks and wheeping post, forth with to be built, which will cost between three or four thousand pounds of tobacco; here is also a greate want of a Court house, which will cost five thousand pounds of Tobacco; our request is that thee will be pleased to Impower us to make a Tax; to Leavy the same on the Inhabitants; There was sume Certain Land formerly laid out by Capt Cantwell for a Towne; which was to be devided into Lots of 60 foot in breadth and 200 foot in Leingth; and the Land and woods that lye back was to be common; for food for cattle and firwood, it being in all about 130 Acres of Land; Sence which time Armainas Wiltbank have got the said land survayed; but we doe not understand that he have any pattent for it; hee demands a bushell of winter wheat a yeare of any person that shall build upon the said Towne lots; which is soe high a rent that it gives noe Incouragement for any to build; we should think one-halfe of that rent would bee anouffe; but that we leave to thy ordering and to whom the rent shall be paid; whether to the duke of York or to Armianas Wiltbank; here is a greate marsh that lyes at the north west side of the Towne, which if it should be at any time here after taken up by any perticolar person it would be a great Inconvenancy to those that doe or shall here after live here; as also the Cape, whare there is good pin Trees for building; the Land Lettes worth; both which wee desier may Lye in common for the use of the Towne; It hath bene spoake here as if thee ded intend as an Ease to the Court to Impower the survayor to grant warrants to Lay out land to such persons as shall Come to take it up; But wee being senceable of the Ill Consequence that will attend that, doe desier that thee would be pleased to forbear giving him any such power; for our precents is now but small; And he for the Lucker of geting the more money will lay out such Large tracts of land for a perticolar person, that might sarve many famileys to live Comfortably upon; theare have been Expearance of the like; As when Capt. Cantwell had the same power he survayed Three Thousand Acres of princable land at prime hook for Henry Smith; And others of the like nature might be mentioned; And wee have good cause to resolve for the time to Come tó grant less Tracts of Land to perticolar persons then have been formerly granted; for this County as it is now divided is not above halfe soe big or Large as St Jones; nor will not hold halfe so many people; neither is the Land soe generally good as that is; And this being the Anciantest place wee thinke with submission might a bene continowed at least Equil with the others; which if thee please may be redressed in the next commission or sooner, which may be by deviding by Murther Creeke and soe downe wards; when Capt Avery was in commission he ded petition the Court for three Thousand Acres of Land for three persons living in Acomack, which the court ded grant to be taken up in any part of these precents that was not allready survayed and taken up; sence which Cornelous Verhoofe have at the request and procurement of the said Captain Avery and one of the three persons of Acomack survayed and Laid out the said three Thousand Acres of land at prime Hook; most of it being the land that was taken up and seated by Henry Smith; now, wheather or noe thee will Allow the said Henry Smith the three Thousand Acres of land by him taken up and seated; wee doe not in the least dispute; But how ever wee humbly conceave that no part of it ought to a bene survayed for any person what soever without a speacell warrant obtayned from thy Honr; It hath bene too much in use here for sume persons to sall land before they make any plantation or Settlement thereon Espeacally by Capt Avery, who have sold severall parcells of land; by which he have gotten greate quantitys of Tobacco; wee would bee willing to have thy positive order as to that Concerne; whether thee allow of such things or not; Thee were pleased to send a Caske of powder heather for the service of this place; which powder hath bene all sold and Imbarseled away by Capt. John Avery to the Indians and others, and if there should be an occasion for powder here, there is not any to be got here for money.

"Wee having as in duty bound laid these things before thee, doe deseir that thee will be please to give such order and direxions therein as in thy greate wisdome shall seeme most meete; the which wee shall bee rady to observe and follow &c.

"TRUE SERVANTS."

When the above letter was written the County of St. Jones, now Kent, had been taken from the Whore kil, leaving the Whore Kil thirty miles long and twelve to fourteen miles wide.

The Courts were still held at the Whore Kill, now Lewes, and the people for St. Jones County had to bring all their legal matters to the above Court. It would be bad enough now for the people of Kent Co. to have to attend the Court at Lewes, but it was far worse in that day.

They petitioned the Governor, "Sr. Edmond Andros, Knt Seigneur of Sausmarez, Lt. and Governor Generall under his Royal Highness James Duke of York," as follows:—

"Wee whose names are hereunto subscribed living and ambitious to abide under the sunshine of yor Honrs Govermt Inhabiteinge in the upland part of the Whorekill County.

"In all humble manner shew unto yor Honor the great greivances, Hazards and perills both by land and water that wee undergoe in goeing to the Whorekill Court nott onely the distance being to some of us 50 some 60 miles want of Comodacons of man and beast there, butt the unpassable dangerous waies by reason of perillous Creeks which many tymes cannot bee past over by man or beast the hazardous large Marshes and myreous and difficult branches &c.

"Yor Honor will be graciously to order authorize &c a Court to be held in some convenient place in St Jones Creeke &c that all persons Inhabiteinge from the North side of Cedar Creeke to the South side of Blackbird Creeke be ordered &c and deemed within the Jurisdiction of the said Court &c &c.

"And wee as in duty bound shall ever pray for Yor Honors health and happiness That Age may Crowne your Snowy haires with Cesar's Honors and with Nestor's yeares.

Griff Jones	John Walker	Wm. ———
John Glovear	Walter M Powel	Robt ffrances
Robert Porter	George Martens	Alexander Humphrey
Arthur Alstone	Jafeth N Goesen	John Brinklo
Henery Plomer	Isaac Balsch (?)	Gabriel Jonses
Robert Millen	Thomas Bolsticke	Christopher Jecsons
William Millen	Simon Frounsen	David Margin
John Dawson	John Brigs	Abram brate
Henry H. Stevens	William Berry Jr	Isack Webe
John hilard	John Lloyd	John Webster
Richard Griffin	John C Barrett	Thomas Heffer
John R. Richeson	his marke	Allesxander Raey
Robt. R Pernatry	John Barton	William Spartes
marke	Daniel Jones	Thomas Cliford
John Rechardson Jr	Wm W———	John Getes
A. Alston	Eauan Dause	Robert bedewel
ffran. Whitwell	John Conely	Richard Louicks
Petter Bawcom	Ed Prince	John Cortes
John Baswell B his marke	Jno. Dishaa	Thomas William
Daniell Arnestead	Benoni Barnes	Thomas Grover
E. Pack	L. Orema	Thomas Hill
	Robert Johnson	Jno. Haye

The shipe goeing away wee had nott time to gitt ye rest of there names butt wee think there may bee about 100 tithabel.

A notice dated June 21st, 1681, was sent from New York to the Justices, &c., residing in the New Province of Pennsylvania, releasing them from their allegiance to the Duke of York.

An order from New York, dated August 15th, 1681, directed the Magistrates at Deale, alias Horekil, Del., to search for the records, retained by Cornelis Verhoofe, the former clerk.

Verhoofe had been dismissed for various misdemeanors and he refused to turn over the records to William Clarke who was appointed to succeed him. By an order dated New York, November 21st, 1682, the "Magistrates and other officers att New Castle St Jones Deale als Whore kill att Delaware" were notified to "Submitt and Yeald all due obedience and Conformity to the Powers Granted to the said William Penn."

This separates the three counties from New York and annexes them to Pennsylvania.

Settled by the Dutch, captured by the Swedes, recaptured by the Dutch, captured by the English, recaptured by the Dutch, ceded to the English as a part of New Netherland, separated from New York and annexed to Pennsylvania all in the space of fifty years.

Perhaps the people of Delaware were getting very tired with the many changes and had quite made up their minds to run the State or Three Lower Counties, as an independent body.

At a "Councell of the Province of Pensilvania, and Territories Thereunto belonging" held at Philadelphia March 10th, 1682, John Vines who had been Sheriff before the Hore Kil or Deal had changed hands is reappointed "Sherif of the County of Sussex." The name of the County is changed to its present title. The members of the Assembly from Sussex County were William Firtcher, John Kipshaven, Alexander Molestine, Robert Bracy, Senior Thomas Bracy, John Hart, John Clowes, Luke Watson and Cornelius Verhoofe, &c. There were "12 Deligates out of each County with power to act as the Provinciall Councelours & General Assembly, and it being proposed to the elected members aforesaid if they were chosen to serve in both those capacities, they answered they were; That is to say, three of each Twelve for the Provinciall Councill, and the remaining Nine of each Twelve to constitute the General Assembly." March 29th, 1683, William Clarke represented Sussex County in the Council and Luke Watson in the Assembly. There was an appeal from a decision of the Sussex County Court at this Council; John Bellamy, plaintiff, and Luke Watson, defendant.

It was about land at Prime Hook bought by defendant from Captain Henry Smith. It was ordered that "the plaintiff pay to the defendant for his improvements, &c., adjudge by three Commissioners appointed by this board, Jno. Roads, Robt. Brasey and Alexander Draper of the said County, or any two of them."

As Bellamy had not paid for any part of the improvements October 27th, 1683, the Council order "ye said Luke Watson, do Peacebly Enjoy the sayd Plantation till ye said John Bellamy hath payd or given sufficient Security to pay the same."

The Council sent two letters to Kent and Sussex concerning the meeting of the General Assembly to be held at New Castle, May 10th, 1684.

At a Council held at Sussex August 14th, 1684, Luke Watson and John Bellamy agreed before "ye Govr & Councill as followed" Luke to continue upon the three hundred acres at Prime Hook, "whereon are his improvements, together with the 200 acres adjoining thereto * * * John Bellamy to have 457 Acres as p. Pattent, being formerly the lands of One Wm Canes, and seated by —— Prentice."

At a meeting of the Council in Philadelphia, September 28th, 1685, Philip Russell was granted a "Lycense" to keep an Ordinary or Inn at Lewis.

This Inn was located at the South corner of Mulberry or Knitting St. and Second St. The house is still standing and is occupied by the widow of the late Charles Marshall. John Hill was made Sheriff January 9th, 1685, and Henry Bowman was made Ranger for the County of Sussex. Joshua Barkstead was appointed "Atturney Genall for ye County Sussex," April 9th, 1686.

In 1686 Luke Watson was notified by the Assembly "to forbear to give his attendance until further Order." Luke had threatened the life of his brother-in-law, Henry Smith, and the Council thought best to exclude Luke until the matter was looked into.

Henry Bowman came before the Council May 12th, 1686, and declared that "Luke Watson's Brother-in-law (one Smith) told him yt the Difference between him & Luke Watson was ended."

John Roades kept an Ordinary in Sussex County, 1686. The same year William Clark was elected to serve in Council for the next three years; Samll Gray, John Vines, Hen Bowman, Norton Claypoole, Albert Jacobs, Hen Stricher, for the Assembly.

August 5th, 1686, at the Council Room in Philadelphia Justices Commission "be fortwith drawn to Commissionate Wm Clarke, Jno. Roads, Tho. Langhorne, Tho. Price, Robt Clifton, Samll Gray & George Young."

March 31st, 1687, Major William Dyer* presented his credentials as member of the Council from Sussex County.

"The Councill Expressed their Genll Dissatisfaction and unwillingness to permitt him, and Desired to Desist, Declareing yt they Could not in Duty and Respect to ye King, nor with Security to ye Province, take such into ye Councill who had not discharged the Office of ye Kings Collr of his

* Son of Mary Dyer of Boston.

Customs within this Governmt with faithfulness and a good Report."

John Redwood presented a petition to the Council, May 18th, 1687, asking "for Releef against an Execution Surreptitiously obtained against him at ye Sute of Richard Hogbean at ye County Court of Philadelphia." Council ordered as follows: Redwood was "to give Security to pay ye Debt in Sussex County, where the Creditor lives, &c. Therefore this board's Opinion is, that ye Creditor Richd. Hoggbean's behaviour in this is Litigious and Vexatious."

March 31st, 1688, Luke Watson "Presented himselfe as a member of Councill, Chosen ye last Election, for ye County of Sussex, but no Returne being made Could not be admitted."

"The Complaint of ye Major part of ye free-holders of Sussex County against ye Sheriff, for not returning a Member they had Chosen to serve in Provll Council," was read.

John Hill presenting "ye Complaint" was Called in, and answer given him that it "should have a Due Consideration, and Justice Don to ye County."

"Orded That franc Cornwell, Sheriff of Sussex County, be Orded to appear before ye Govr and Council ye same day ye next Genll Assembly is to meet, to answer ye Complaint above."

The minutes of the Assembly for April 10th, 1688, say "The Returne of ye members for Sussex County was Read and allowed."

Adam Johnson appealed to the Council February 19th, $168\frac{8}{9}$, for protection against Peter Ludgar. Peter has been arrested, tried and imprisoned for theft and the Sheriff had allowed him to be at liberty. "The Sheriff ffrancis Cornewell to forthwith apprehend the prisoner and keep him in the Common Gaol or Workhouse of the County."

Francis and William Smith were ordered to be imprisoned, also, for a debt due Charles Pickering. They complained "that there was no bed lye on." The Sheriff acquainted the Board that he might bring in his beds to the prison, and should have them again when discharged.

November 2d, 1689. The Council sent copies of the proclamation declaring William and Mary to be King and Queen of England.

Thomas Clifton was returned as member of the Provincial Council 1690, to serve three years. Eight months later (he was elected in March), Thomas "was gon to England" and they had to have another election.

Let us go back to 1689. The Court sitting at Lewes, June 5th, of that year, has left us the following record:—

"The Court considering what few inhabitants there is in the town of Lewes, and being willing to Incurage people to live in the said Town and to seat and improve the back part of the said Town are willing to grant Larger Lotts then hath been usually granted, and for that the clearing the back parts of the said Town, will be covenant and benefic all to bring a vew to the front of the said Town, they do order that whosoever shall take up any back Lotts, shall not suffer any Tree or Trees to grow thereon to the hight of Twenty feet, and whosoever plants any frute Trees, or other Trees thereon, shall not plant them nearer than forty feet asunder, and keep their Lotts Continually Clean of brush or other wood, and also to keep the Streets afore their Lotts Clean of brush, and all the trees in the Streets to be grubed up, the said back Lotts to be four acre Lotts, with a square in the middle of the Town, for any publick use or uses that the Court shall think fitting, the pond on the backide of Author Starr's to be dreaned and remain for Common to Come down the Valley, the where the Ship is building into the River Lewes, and that he builds and Clears first shall have the first Lotts next to the Town."

The "Valley" is now Camomile Street, and where the ship was building is called Shipcarpenter Street.

"A list of Several Receitels of Sundry Deeds Down from a patent granted by Sir Edmond Andross At New York unto Andrew Deprea for 400a of land Called Timber Neck Dated the 12th day of August A. D. 1679 or a breef State of the Title Down from the afores'd pattent To the Present owner of the said land posser of the same.

"first Andrew Dupreas Patent of 400 acres of land granted by Sir Edmond Andross In New York bearing Date the 12 day of August Anno Domini 1679.

"2dly Andrew Deprea of the County of Sussox planter did convey by his Deed of Sale 400a of land unto John Deprea of the aforesd Cooper Dated the 13th day of the 12th month Called February the whole Tract 1682.

"3ly County Sussox.

"James Askew did Convey by his Deed of Sale a 140a of land unto John Coe of the Same place a part of Timber Neeck a part of 400a of the within Tract Dated the 6 day of February 1698.

"Sussex County.

"John Coe Did by his Deed of Sale Convey a 140a of land unto Joseph niell now part of the within 400a of land Dated the 4 day of September 1699.

"Edward Nixson of the County afors'd Did Convey by his Deed of Sale a 140a of land unto Sary Clifton widow of the Town of lewis & County afors'd part of aforsd Tract of 400a of land Dated the 20th day of July 1703.

"And at the Death of Sary Clifton widow of Lewis Town the aforsd 140 acres of land Decended unto her Son Robert Clifton as heir at law.

"And whereas Robert Clifton Son of the aforsd widow Deceast did by his last will & Testament bearing Date the 10th day of May 1720 Did order his Executors to Sell the Said land of 140a above s'd if Need bee who was John Foster & Ann his wife.

"The abovesd John Deprea did leave & bequeath his last will and Testament the afores'd Tract of 400a of land unto his Two Sons to wit William & John Deprea dated 1 day of october 1706.

"William Deprea and his mother mary deprea widow & Relockt of John Deprea deceast did Convey by there Deed of Sale 100a of land part of the abovesd 400a Tract of land unto Richard hinmon Esquire Dated th 5th day of May 1720.

"C. Richard Hinmon did Convey by his deed of Sale 100a of land part of the abovesd 400a of land unto Peter marsh the grandfather of y Said Peter marsh dated the 7th day of August 1722.

"John Foster of the aforsd County black Smith and Ann foster his wife executors of the last will & Testament of Robert Clifton of the Town of lewis & County afors'd did Covey by their deed of Sale a 140a of land unto Peter marsh of Rehoboth & County afors'd part of the aforsd 400a Tract of land dated the 14th day of october 1721.

"County of Sommerset.

"John Deprea of the Province of maryland planter did Convey by his deed of Sale a 160a of land unto Richard hinmon of the County of Sussex gentelman part of the Tract of 400a of land afors'd Dated 6th day of August 1735.

"And the afors'd Richard hinmon did by his last will & Testament bequeath unto his Two grand Sons to wit Hinmon Rhoades & John Rhoads the aboves'd 160a of land part of the aboves'd 400a of land dated 13 day of January 1741 and Hinmon Rhoads dying without Ishu the land fell to his younger brother John Rhoads And John Rhoads & his wif Ellenor Rhoads by their deed of sale Conveys the aboves'd 160a of land or all the Residue of the afors'd Pattent of 400a of land unto Peter marsh the younger now In the Possition of the same as by the Deed dated the 7th day of march 1769."

Elon (Ellen) Hazzard's Will, Book D, No. 4, page 387. Date 9–7–1790, mentions her children Cord, David, James and John Hazzard, and speaks of her son Hinman Rhoads, and Grandson John Rhoads, and daughter Margaret Rhoads.

As Elon (Ellen) died the widow of David Hazzard, she must have been the widow Rhoads when she married Hazzard.

September 23d, 1726.

Complaint Against a Magistrate, 1726.

"The Petition of Alexander Molliston, most humbly sheweth,

"Whereas your Petitioner begs leave to represent to your Honour a difference that did arise, together with the Judicial Proceedings thereon, (under the Administracon of Sr William Keith, our late

Govern'r) that happened between William Till, Esq., and your Petitioner; the Sum of the Difference, so far as I can impartially remember, is briefly thus:

" First. Your petitioner having a Sute Depending in the County Court for Sussex, Judgment passed against your Petitioner, Execution immediately by my Antagonist was threatened. William Till, Esq., owing your Petitioner a small Debt on Account, going out of town, Your Petitioner went to said Till being on horse-back and calling him aside, asked him for the Debt, he replied that if I would prove my Account he would pay it, and turned about & called to Simon Kolluck Esq., standing some Distance off, and desired Mr. Kolluck to answer so much on acct. to your Petitioner, which the said Mr. Kolluck promised to do.

"William Till further proceeded and asked your Petitioner what Day of the Month it was, your Petitioner said, the Seventh, then replied Mr. Till You must come to me for Licence or I will demolish your House. Your Petitioner made Answer that he would not go to the said Till for Licence, but go to his master, then William Till called yr. Petitioner Rogue and Rascal with other abuses and threatened to put your Petitioner in the Stocks, Your Petitioner bid him do if he dared, and further said he was neither Rogue nor Rascal any more than William Till, but was as honest a man as himself and so esteemed among my Neighbour. Then William Till called the Constable standing by, and commanded the Constable to put Your Petitioner in the Stocks; the Constable at the first not willing to answer his command. Then William Till again called the Constable and, and said, damn you, Dog, do your office or I will commit you, then the Constable followed your Petitioner as he was going home, and put your Petitioner in the Stocks, who there remained during the pleasure of the said William Till. Which Punishment together with the Infamy thereof, yr Petitioner (with humble Submission) doth conceive would have been a sufficient Atonement for such an offence, considering the cause thereof did arise from a Difference in their own private Affair; altho' whatever words might fall or escape from your Petitioners Lips, was caused by the rash Expressions and threatening Words of the said William Till, with out any Design or Affront to the person of the said Till, or the Commission that he bears, or any Disregard or Contempt in the least to ye Authority of our Sovereign Lord the King. But yet the Punishment of your Petitioner for the aforesaid Offence did not cease there; but in a short time afterwards the said William Till came into Town and bound over your Petitioner by Recognizance to his good Behavior, without the Concurrence of any other Justice of the Peace, and when I demanded a copy of the said Recognizance, put it in his pocket, refusing either a Sight or a copy of it,—and then Your Petitioner desired of the said William Till a Licence, but he would not give it to your Petitioner.

"2d. And then contrary to an Act of Assembly of this Government, made against such as shall speak in Derogation of Courts, write or speak slightingly of any Magistrate in the duty of his office, which provides that such Offendors shall be fined Fifty Shillings; On which said Act of Assembly, afterwards (To Wit) on the 3d Day of November, in the Year of our Lord 1724, at a Court of Quarter Sessions of our Lord the King, held at Lewis Town, before the Justices of our Lord the King, an Information was exhibited in the said Term by Francis Allen especially appointed by the Justices aforesaid for that purpose to prosecute for our Lord the King, as by a Copy of the said Information duly certified may appear, On which Information it was so far proceeded, that your Petitioner was forced to plead thereto, and was destitute of Council, and could not get a Lawyer or Council to speak in your Petitioner's Behalf, and also threatened that if an Attorney should presume to appear in Behalf of your Petitioner he should be thrown over the Barr; whereon a verdict of 12 Men did pass against your Petitioner and by the Justices aforesaid was fined in the sum of Twenty Pounds; and your Petitioner still being bound afresh finding good security for his Good Behavior, And tho' then your Petitioner for the aforesaid Time was not immediately committed to close prison, yet was desired by the sheriff not to go any great distance out of the County, but first acquaint him with it, and in this Circumstance yr Petitioner remained for the Space of about Nine Months, and then the aforesaid fine was levied by Execution on the House that yr Petitioner lived in; (As by a Transcript of the Records of the proceedings thereof may also appear) to the most grievious Hurt and Damage of yr. Petitioner; Contrary to the aforesaid Act of Assembly, Your Petitioner was forced to plead to an Information illegally exhibited, and for an Offence which requires no such Proceeding, being not an Offence against the Government, but only a few Words in Passion, for which the Law makes another Provision by binding the Party to his good Behavior. So that yr. Petitioner was utterly deprived of his then calling and ever since in that capacity disabled in getting of his and his Family's Bread. And yr. Petitioner doth further beg your Honour's patience, to lay before your Honours another Grievience of yr. Petitioners which is thus: On the first Day of January, in the year 1724, in the absence of yr. Petitioner, the aforesaid William Till (by a pretext of a purchase which he said he made of three Bushels of Salt from one Abraham Depister, loged in your Petitioners Custody, and promised by ye Petitioners Wife to be delivered to the said William Till,) did obtain a warrant from Samuel Rowland Esq., one of his Majesty's Justices of the Peace for the County of Sussex aforesaid, By Virtue of said Warrant yr Petitioners Wife was brought before the said Samuel Rowland to answer the Premises; and Judgment was obtained against yr. Petitioners Wife without any Proof, altho' your Petitioners Wife offered to swear, and bring Evidence to prove, that she had not one Bushel of Salt of the said Abraham Depister's in her Custody; Yet notwithstanding, the Evidence was denyed and rejected and Execution granted, by Virtue whereof the Constable, with several raised Men, in his Majestys Name, were ordered (with audible voice) to break open the doors of Your Petitioners House; on the hearing of this, your Petitioners family opened the Doors, and the Constable with the raised Men aforesaid, opened the Cellar Door, after that he was forewarned, and there did bear away three Bushels of Salt, with four & Six Pence of Yr. Petitioners Goods for the said William Till was extorted and taken away from yr. Petitioners Wife, When in Truth and in Fact, no such Salt was lodged in yr. Petitioners Custody on that Account, nor did yr. Petitioners wife make any such Promise.

"And now since your Honours happy Arrival to this Goverment yr. Petitioner made application to the Court (for a Recommendation to yr. Honour in order to obtain a Licence from your Honour) which hapned in the absence of William Till Esq., the Court would not grant the aforesaid favor without the Concurrence of William Till, the said Justices producing this Reason, that they were certainly informed by William Till that the sd William Till did affirm to the Court aforesaid that he had received particular Instructions from yr. Honour that if I did not make my Application to the sd William Till and get him to sign my Recommendation that yr. Honour had promised him that yr. Petitioner never should have any Licence; Altho' his Majestys Justices did say they had nothing to alledge against me.

"And tho' I have not enumerated all the Calamitys and Hardships that yr. Petitioner has sustained and laboured under in the course of the above said Proceeding, yr. Petitioner fearing to be too tedious, and that I have already trespassed on yr. Honours Patience, shall leave it, And humbly desire yr. Honour would be graciously pleased to take these things into yr. Honours Consideration & give me some Relief, as yr. Honour in yr. Wisdom shall judge meet. And yr. Petitioner as in Duty bound Shall ever pray, &c.

"ALEXANDER MOLSTON."

CIVIL AND MILITARY APPOINTMENTS FOR HOREKIL.

November, 1674.

November, Capt. Paull Mash, Lieut. and president of the Court.

Mr. Helmanus Wiltbank, Justice, Sheriffe & Collector.

Mr. Alexander Mosestede, Justice.

Mr. John Kipharen, Justice.

Mr. Otto Wolgast, Justice.

Mr. Daniel Browne, under-Sheriffe & Constable.

1675, June 25th,

Mr. John Avery, Lieut. and president of the Court.

Mr. Edward Southrin, Justice.

Mr. Alexander Molestede, Justice wish non abler.

Mr. John Kiphaven, Justice, well to take.

Mr. Otto Wolgast, Justice good ordinary planter.

Mr. Daniel Browne, under-Sheriffe and Constable.

Cornelis Verhoofe, Clerke Deputy Survr. & Collectr.

167$\frac{5}{6}$, January 4th, Mr. Daniel Browne being Discharged of the Constables office and Simon paling Ellected. In the sd office.

Dito: Jury of Inquest as followeth:—Hermanus Wiltbank, foreman; Abraham Clement, petit; John Collison; William Prentice, Simon Paling, Robert Murdick

List of the names of persons in Horekil:—Henry Smith, John Avery, Edward Southrin, John King, Pauell Mash, Sander Mollesten, Hermanes Wildbank, Thomas Phillips.

In 1670, January 12th, James Mills purchased a neck of land from the English Commissioners by consent of the Governor at New York. It is described as "Lyeing to the Southward of ye Towne at ye whorekill in Delaware Bay."

There was a Council held in Fort James, New York, May 17th, 1672, to consider the pretended claim of Lord Baltimore to the Whorekill.

The first Court was established at the Hoour Kil in 1673. "And whereas it is necessary for the maintenance of good order, police, and so forth, that the inhabitants of the South river be provided with some courts of justice, we have therefore deemed it necessary to order and instruct the inhabitants of said river to nominate by plurality of votes, for each court, eight persons as Magistrates whose jurisdiction shall provisionally extend as follows:

"One Court of Justice for New Amstel &c One Court of Justice for the inhabitants of Upland &c.

"One Court of Justice for the inhabitants of the Whorekil, to which shall provisionally resort, the inhabitants both on the East and West sides of Cape Hinloopen, unto Boomties Hook."

The Governor selected as Magistrates, November 28th, 1673, Mr. Harmanus Wiltbanck, Sander Maelsteyn, Doctor John Roots, William Claesen. These same magistrates were ordered to send "2 millstones lying idle in the Whorekil which heretofore belonged to the city's colonie on South river" to New Amstel "as the garrison at New Amstel hath need of them."

Letter from Halmanius Wiltbank to Governor Andros, Lord Baltimore about to renew his claim for the Hore Kil, and a rebellion in Virginia.

"Richt Honoble Gouverneur:—Yours receaved the 18th of this Instand month wear in wy understand your great Cear & diligenth of us wich wy durender to your Honor manny tanks wear in wy doe inform your Honor that wy are in good Helt Lickewise thear is good Hops of success & situatie of this plaets by menny persons both out of Virginnia & Merryland & heaue alsso reseaved ohn halfe barrel of powder which youe thet sent by your schaloop & given alsso menny tanks to Your Honor ffor your good instruction and schal mack as good jus af them as possibelly Lays in our pour & Schal how that Your Honor thet deseir af occasion thet requeir a piloot for your

Honors Schaloop; thear was non keapabele her & Your Honors Schaloop meester thet not much question his gohin well

"Wy doe hereafulger raport from the Commun people in Merrylandt that the Lord Baltomore thus are immagine to Heave this plaets again but wy doe wenset & wy thacht fit to give your Honor notis af at

"Lickewise her is dayly severale persons Commin out Virginia which brings news that the rebellion thus Continue still against theare Gouverneur & gouverment & Lick to be wors which is a great dishartening to all payes & sober meyndeth people

"Not else but your Honors servant to Commaund & pray for your Honors good helt & success in your gouverment

"167$\frac{6}{7}$ this 26th of February at the Whorekil

"HELMS WILTBANCK

"Her is prsent news out of Accumache that ther is twoo fregats is Com in & that the heave brought the Contre to a pays again & moor that my Lord Baltomore heave gott a grant from his Mastre fors is land & that the seam scud follow fourtnight after the fregats thet seth outh

"These for the right Honoble Gouverneur Ed. Androsz at New York."

It is to be hoped that the Governor was not a profane man.

In another letter dated Whoorekil, September 18th, 1677, from Halmanus Wiltbank to "Major Edmond Andros," he speaks of being too unwell to appear at the meeting of the High Court, he has fever and is lame in one leg. There was a case before the jury about Peter Groenendick and Henry Smit. The suit went against Groendick and he wanted Judge Wiltbank to have a rehearing of the case.

Wiltbank speaks of not being "perfect to Distinguish the Circumstanges of many English woords or speaches by which Referr myself unto Yor Honors fauor."

John West of Accomack County, Virginia, had written Wiltbank about getting a quantity of land for himself and "sum partners," "which Land being Just to the Northward of the supposed Cabo Hinlopen seperating itself from itself from the sd Cape with one Inlett & a Creeke Comly called by the Indians Assawarnon, &c."

November 13th, 1677, Helm. Wiltbank, Edward Southrin and Alexander Molestine send a complaint and petition to Sr. Edmund Andros, charging Captain Ed. Cantwell, Surveyor, with erasing the names of Thomas Wellburne and his partners and the name of William Anderson from certificates for lands surveyed by Cornelius Verhoofe.

Thomas Wellburne was a merchant; and all the parties petitioning were from Accomac County, Va Cantwell erased the names of Wellburne and partners and wrote his own name in place of erasure together with Henry Streeter and Abraham Clements. In place of William Anderson's name he put the names of Samuel Styles and Robert Anderson. Wellburne had named his tract Welburne's Wilderness, and Anderson called his place Anderson's Delight.

Commission of Captain John Avery to be Justice at Horekil, Del.

"SR EDMUND ANDROSS KT. &c: By vertue of his Maties Lettr Pattents & the Commission and Authority unto mee, given by his Royall Highness, I doe hereby in his Maties Name Constitute, appoint and Authorize you John Avery, Francis Whitwell, Alexander Molestine, John Kiphaven, Luke Wattson, John Roades and James Wells, to be Justices of the Peace at the Whore-Kill and Dependency in Delaware Bay, and any foure of you to be a Cort of Judicature, and In Case of Sicknesse absence or Otherwise of the first &c. the next in Commission to preside Giveing & Granting unto you and every of you full power to act in sd Employmt according to Law Regulacon and former practice, of which all persons concerned are to Take Notice & give you the due respect & Obedience belonging to yor Places in Discharging yor Dutyes. This Commission to bee of force for the Space of one yeare after the date hereof and takeing Yor Oathes and Places for the Same or till farther Order. Given under my hand & Seale of the Province in New Yorke, this 8th of Octobr in the 30th yeare of his Maties name Annoq Domini 1678.

"Examined by mee "E. ANDROSS.

"MATTHIAS NICOLLS Secry."

Henry Smith declares "That the time that Helmanus Wiltbank was questioned for Treason was when the Whorekill was under Maryland. The persons that accused him were Dr. John Roades and William Prentice. The accusacon was made to Mr. Francis Jenkins a Justice of peace in Maryland who committed him to prison for the space of about a week & as is reported hee was cleared by the sd. Jenkins by giving him a Bribe.

"That afterwards the sd. Jenkins was questioned for taking a bribe to cleare sd. Wiltbank and taken into Custody as a prisonr by order of Dr. Roades on that acct., but in few days was releas't; Whereupon Dr. Roades came to the above Mr. Smith complaining of the Fact, but he having newly had his Writt of Ease directed him to goe to my Lords to St. Maryes which he did accordingly, but what the Issue of it was there, hee knowes not.

"As to the discourse of Edwd Southrins conversacon with the devill, Hee knowes nothing but what hee & divers others have heard from his own Mouth, talking often extravagantly in that nature.

"As to Cor: Verhoofes being guilty of keeping false Records; The same hee saith hath beene proved in Cort."

Captain Nathaniel Walker, formerly from Boston, lately from Virginia, Eastern Shore, was granted land in Cedar Neck on Rehoboth Bay, 1679.

"HOREKIL ye 14th, 3d mo called May 1679.

"GOVERNOR ANDROS:—Since thee ware pleased when I was at Yorke to aske me if there was anything I knew that related to this place for thee to settle or order doth Imbolden me to Lay one thing before thee, which I observe to bee a greavance and that which does prevent the better seating of this County, and that is thay that have land here are not at any Certainty what they must doe for survaying itt: The planters that come out of Maryland are and have been in an expectacion that they should pay no more then is paid for survaying there &c &c "WM CLARK."

William, we see, was a Quaker.

1679, May 19th, Governor Nicolls, at New York, appointed John Vine to be Sheriff of the Horekill.

William Penn continued him in office.

Magistrates at ye Whorekil Oct. 8, 1678: John Avery, ffrancis Whitwell, Alexander Molestein, John Kippshaven, Luke Wattson, John Roades, James Wells.

"Court held at the Whorekil 10, 11, & 12th Dayes of February Ao. 167$\frac{9}{80}$.

"John Richards or Richardson, plt., John Stevens, Deft. Trespass & Ejectant.

"Jury: Mr. Edward Southrin, Samuell Gray, Otto Wolgast, Helms. Wiltbanck, George Young, Daniell Browne, William Firtcher, John Hackister, Richard Levick, Charles Johnson, Richard Peaty, Thomas Howard, Cornelius Verhoof, Clk."

John Richardson was the son of John Richardson, Senr., of Dorchester County, Maryland.

John Richardson and James Shackleday had taken up land on Duck Creek.

Thomas Crompton was from Dorchester County, also.

1680. Census of the responsible housekeepers & their families residing in Muther Creek, Cedar Creek, &c.

In Cedar Creek:

Robt Hart........................3 in family
Upon Joseph Cowdree plantation......3 " "
Mr. Bowman....................2 or 3 " "

George Collins, on Shackerly's plantation
Jno. Curtis..........................4 in family.
Jno. Richardson......................6 " "
Thomas Groves........................2 " "
Thomas Heiffer.......................2 " "
Alexander Ray........................2 " "
Thomas Williams and John De Shaw....2 " "

Contract for the Conveyance of Mennonists to the Delaware River. See pages 285-288:—

"Burgomasters and Regents of the City of Amsterdam.

"Whereas we remain, at all times, disposed to advance this city's Colonie in New Netherland, therefore have we, with the knowledge and consent of the XXXVI. Councillors, resolved to enter into the following agreement to that end with Pieter Cornelisz Plockhoy, of Zieriksee, viz. He, Pieter Cornelisz Plockhoy, undertakes to present to us, as soon as possible, XXIIII. men, who, with him, make a Society of XXV persons, shall bind themselves to depart by the first sailing ship or ships to the aforesaid city's Colonie to reside there and to work at the cultivation of the land, fishing, handicraft, etc. and to be as diligent as possible not only to the end that they should live properly by such labor, but that provision may thereby be made for other coming persons and families.

"Therefore the aforesaid Society of XXV. male persons, whether the same be more or less, according as they may increase or diminish, shall, for the whole, and, moreover, each member of said society for himself individually, have the privilege of selecting, taking up and appropriating as much land, the property of no other person, whether in the Whorekil or in any other part of the district of this Colonie wherever it may lie, as they shall be willing and able to cultivate and pasture.

"Which lands, both divided and undivided, the aforesaid Society and Colonists respectfully shall occupy in full property, to do therewith as to them shall seem good.

"And the aforesaid Colonists, for the peace, union and welfare of their Society, such rules and orders shall be empowered to e act as they shall think proper, provided, nevertheless, that each person who may consider himself wronged shall be at liberty to appeal to the Magistrate there or here.

"The aforesaid Society, and each member thereof in particular, shall, for their further encouragement, be granted freedom from Tenths and all other imports, howsoever they be named, for the term of XX years.

"And there shall be paid, likewise, to each of the aforesaid 25 persons, by form of a loan, a sum of one hundred guilders to provide himself therefrom with necessaries according to pleasure, on condition that such sum is understood to include his passage money only, and not those of his wife and children, who shall be conveyed over at the expense of this city, conformably to the printed Conditions.

"Therefore the aforesaid XXV Colonists promise and bind themselves, in solidum, the one for the other, to repay the aforesaid 2,500 guilders, in order to return hither, he shall be at liberty to do so, on condition of leaving to the Society the undivided land, cattle and all other common property, and taking with him only his own particular goods, so that the repayment may be effected by the remaining Colonists.

"Therefore the passage money of such Colonist and family as have gone away shall be paid by the Society out of the common stock in return for his contributed labor.

"And if any person will go over, or make the voyage at his own expense and yet wish to save or even sell his share in the common fund, he shall be at liberty to do so, on condition that he previously put one in his place or sell to such a one as the Society respectively shall approve of, in order to help to have a strict eye over the common labor and other things besides.

"The aforesaid Society and the individual members thereof remaining further bound to observe, in all other respects, the aforesaid printed articles. In like manner, also, the explanation of whatever should herein be found to demand further interpretation remains reserved unto the Burgomasters of this State.

"In testimony whereof we, the Burgomasters and Regents aforesaid, the seal of this city affixed to these presents the 9th of June A° 1662 "Signed WIGBOLT SLICHER."

"Having a seal impressed in Green Wax.

At a meeting of the Council September 25th, 1688.

"Margaret ffisher, of ye County of Sussex, Complayning that shee having appealed from ye Judgement of ye County Court of Sussex, where shee had Indicted one John Barker of ye said County, for robing her and her son Thomas ffisher of three head of Cattle, and that shee was Come up according to her Security Given, to have it reheard in ye Provll Court, but ye Court not sitting, nor ye said Barker appearing in Philadelphia, she very much feared y^t Said Barker would, before ye next Provll Court, make away with ye said Cattle

"Ordered that ye Secretary Send to ye Justices of Sussex County, in behalfe of Widdow ffisher, yt they doe her what right ye Law will allow to Secure the Cattle or the value, till it be reheard next Provll Court, in Regard there were no Court at this time."

At a meeting of the Council Philadelphia Feb. 26, 168$\frac{8}{9}$.

"The Goverr not satisfied with ye behaviour of ye high Sheriffe of ye County of Sussex, proposed some other might be named by some of ye members present, ffor as much as himselfe was wholly a stranger there whereupon Wm. Rodeney was nominated by Wm. Clark, and Recommended by Griff Jones & Wm. Darrall, as the ffitest person they Could think off ffor ye present."

William Rodney had returned to Kent County, May 15th, 1693, and "had the oaths and Test, and oath of Clarke of the County of Kent, administered to him."

List of persons, old and young, living at the Hore Kil, Del., May 8, 1671.

Helmanus Frederick Wiltbank, his wife, two sons and a man servant;
Alexander Moelsteen, his wife, two sons, and a man servant;
Otto Wolgast, his wife, one son, and a man servant;
Willem Klassen with two daughters and a child;
Jan Kipshaven, his wife and daughter;
James Weedon, his wife, one daughter, one son and four servants;
John Rods, his wife and five children, three sons and two daughters;
Daniel Breen, his wife and his partner, John Colleson;
Jan Michiels, Anthony Pieters, Abraham Pieters, Pieter Smith, Pieter Gronedick, Anthony Sander, Herman Cornelisson, Herman Droochestraeder;
There are on Capt. Martyn Cregiers sloop "Bedfort" five persons.
On small boat of Pieter Alrichs from New Castle two persons.

Edward Southrin was also accused with having conversed with the Devil. Henry Smith stated that "Hee (Smith) knowes nothing but what hee and divers others have heard from his (Southrin's) owne mouth, talking often extravagantly in that nature."

Cornelis Verhoofe was proven guilty keeping false Records. William Clark, a Quaker, lived in the Whorekill. He wrote a letter to Governor Andros dated:—

"WHOREKILL YE 14th $\frac{mo}{3}$ called May 1679

"GOVERNOR ANDROS:—Since thee ware pleased when I was at York to Ask me if there was anything I knew that related to this place for thee to settel or order doth Imbolden me to Lay one thing before thee, which I observe to bee a greavance and that which does prevent the better seating of this County, and that is thay that have land here are not at any Certainty what thay must doe for the survaying itt; The planters that come out of Maryland are and have bene in an expectacion that thay should pay no more then is paid for surveying there, which is one hundred pounds of Tobacco, for the first hundred acres, and fifty pounds for the second hundred Acres, twenty five pounds for every hundred Acres after to thousand Acres; soe that the survaying of one thousand Acres comes to but 350 pounds.

"But insteade thereof some have paid here Two Thousand pounds of Tobacco for survaying one thousand Acres &c., &c."

The following letter was sent by Governor Andros to the Magistrate of the Whorekill:

"In the matter between Helmanus Wiltbanck & Cornelus Johnson Concerning the which the Court have certified their Report The same is to be allowed by order of the Governour & to be confirmed to the sd Halmanus Wiltbanck: In answer to the peticon of Cornelys Verhoofe to your Court, about his being Confirmed Clarke, about a Regulation of Fees there, the which is Certifyde to be granted by sd Court: Upon their Recommendation there of to the Governor, the same is allowed by him, & that the fees of Extraordinary Courts bee Ascertained, & all fees (as in other places) to be collected in the nature & as by execution: In answer to a former Request from the sd Cor. Verhoofe; upon the Courts choice and Recommendation of him to bee surveyor at the Whore kill, the Go; orders him to bee confirmed till further order; Upon a peticon of John Kipphaven to his honour the Go.; for a piece of wast land neare some other land which hee hath purchased, being his only passage into the wood, The Governour hath granted the same & to bee Surveyed in order to a patent, your Certificate whereof will be Requested; Upon an other peticon to his honour from John Vine that he may officiate as Sheriffe at the Whore kill & precints, The Go: returned the Following answer: Upon Security & Courts Choice allowed & confirmed for the yeare as the Court is; Upon a Letter or Addresse of Wm. Clarke from your place to the Governour concerning the uncertainty of the Surveyors Fees in sd parts, Its his honour's order that the price of surveys bee at the Whore Kill &c as in Virginia & Mary Land, money or value; There is yet one thing I have in Charge to acquaint you from his honour which is an unadvised Act of Mr. Guilaine Verplank one of the magistrates of this city, in taking an oath here of William Tayler the pretended Surveyor, concerning Severall Fees by him claymed for Surveying the Whore kill, the which likewise sd to bee demanded by Capt. Cantwell that employed him &c. &c.

"New York June 6, 1679."

Mr. Alexander Molestede, Justice, wish non abler.
Mr. John Kiphaven, Justice, well to take.
Mr. Otto Wolgast, Justice, good ordinary planter.
Mr. Daniell Browne, under Sheriffe and Constable.
Cornelis Verhoofe, Clerke Deputy Survr. & Collectr.

167$\frac{5}{6}$, January 4th.

Mr. Daniell Browne bing Discharged of the Constables office & Simon paling Ellected. In the sd office Dito: Jury of Inquest as followeth: Hermanus Wiltbanck, foreman; Abraham Clement, petit; John Collissen, William Prentice, Simon Paling, Robert Murdick.

A letter to the Magistrate at the Horekil from New York:

"By Informacon from Mr. Peter Groenendyke (the bearer hereof) to the Councell, That a certaine piece of Land granted to Wm Plainer, whereof he was in possession twelve months, was by misinformacon or mistake afterward given & granted by patent to Randall Revell, who neither sought after nor ever had pretence to the same, Concerning the wch no order being left his honor, It will be convenient to Let the matter rest as it is untill his Return, and in meane time Wm Playner not to bee dispossest, This I give you as the opinion of the Councell, being "Gent, Yor humble servt

"M. N

"(Secretary Nicolls)."

One John Hillyard petitioned Sir Edmond Andros about some land at the Whorekill, July 30th, 1678. He says:

The humble petition of John Hillyard Humbley sheweth that wheare as youre pettr obtained a warrant of ye worshipfull Courte of ye Whorekil for eight hundred acceres of Land in the presinks of Dellayway Bay wheare upon youre peeticoner sould his Land & Cattill at a verey under rate by Reason of ye greate distance I lived from youre honners goverment & in October last I adventured with three of my family in a verrey small boat through ye mane sea & come to ye Whorekill.

"John not finding a surveyor and hearing that there was plenty of land at Duck Creek, set out for that place arriving there December 24."

He was not very fortunate there in obtaining land. A friend of Hillyard's, George Merten, asked for a grant adjoining the said Hillyard's land at the date above and was as unsuccessful, as he found one Whitwell had a patent for the same.

The old times, in colonial days, were not better than these times, as is very evident to one looking over the records of the Courts. The following petition of Edward Southrin to Gov. Andros about John Avery shows that there were some very lawless people living in Lewes in the seventeenth century. Southrin says:—

Whereas it was your Honors good pleasire to put and Consigne mee though a person unworthy of soe high a Calling to bee a magistrate at the Whorekilles in which office and Calling I have Indeavoored by the help of God to so Discharge my Concience before God and man to the best of my skill and Knowledge without favor or Affection to any prson and soe Doeing I have Received many Abusess both from Mr. John Avery and Mr. Henry Smith and for noe other cause nor reason as I know off but for doeing my office which I humbly conseave to bee my duty to doe when Lawfull called there to by any of his magesties subjects and not to be called Roague & beggerly Roague with many such like abusess Speaches saieing Sarra you pettyfull Lousy Raskell lett mee know you Ever grant any attachmt or warrants againe and you had better be hanged and if the Governor Doth Lett such pettifull Raskels to bee in comission I will not sitt for I hold it beneath mee to sitt with such a pettyfull fellow as thou art it is not onely mee but others of the Comission whom they will not be Conformable to his unreasonable will for Mr. John Kipphauen because hee would not Draw him a Bottell of Rom for an Indian, hee had hired on the Sabbath Day in the like termes and for noe other Cause that I know of Unreasonably abused by Mr. John Avery. And as for Mr. Henry Smith his abuses to the Court and the book of Lawes are not Inferior to the Rest for if wee doe act any thing Contrary against Mr. Smith his will then wee are called Roagues and a Confedeadrate with Roagues and with other threatening words which as I Humbly Conseave not to be omitted therefore thought it my Duty to inform yor Honor with it for if I Issue forth a Summons or a warrent In his magisties name to warren in any prsons who are Liveing in Mr. Smith his howse Either the warrant is not Excecuted or if Excecuted not obeyed for hee Doth prtend They are his Servants and not to answer noe warrant or Summons without his Leave but I humbly Conseave though they where Mr. Smith's his Servants which I know not such thing for to my knowledg they were both freeman not long since yet they where as Lyable to his Ma[ties] Lawes as Mr. Smith or any other prson if they bee good Subjects this being part of the Irregular proceedings I humble beseech yor Honor to give mee the patient prsell hearing hereof for should I take a penman to writt and yor Honors Eares to heare an Like yor Honor I send alle the proceedings that I have done in my office and place which I hope yor Honor will pruse and find whether I have deserved these abuses or no and wholy Rely upon yor Honors good pleasure Either to Justifie mee or Condem mee as yor Honors wisedom shall think fitt, Soe hoping yor Honor in yor good time will rectifie Both these and all others misdemeanours by whosoever Committed one thing I humbly begg it of yor Honor nott that I am worthy to give advice, but onely begg it of yor Honor Both for the good of the people and the good of the place that yor Honor will bee pleased to Constitute sum wise Discreet sober minded Gentleman that may lead the people into obedience for the safety of a King or Chief governor Consistes in obedient people, for hee that knoweth not how to obeye neither knowes how to Command for which cause I humbly beseech yor Honor to make choyse of a Cheife Commander according to yor Honors Discretion for this partes and that yor Honor will bee pleased to discharge mee from this and all other offices of trust which is the Humble Request of yor Honors servant to Command, soe hoping &c. "EDWARD SOUTHRIN.

"From the Whorekill,
"Sept. 18, 1678."

Avery seems to have been a turbulent fellow and a disturber of the peace, yet through some influence, we find Governor Andros issuing a commission to Captain John Avery to be Justice at the Whore Kill. As it is dated October 8th, 1678 (New York), and Southrin's petition is dated September 18th, 1678, Andros may not have received Southrin's letter when he issued the commission for Avery to be Justice.

He was in New York when the Commission was issued October 8th, and took the Oath as Magistrate October 12th, 1678, and was authorized to administer the Oath to the other Justices, Francis Whitwell, Alexander Molestine, John Kiphaven, Luke Wattson, John Roades and James Wells.

These gentlemen seem to have had plenty of work to do, for Henry Smith makes a declaration: "That the time that Helmanus Wiltbank was questioned for Treason was when the Whorekill was under Maryland." The persons that accused him were Dr. John Roades, and William Prentice.

The accusation was made to Mr. Francis Jenkins, a Justice of Peace in Maryland, who "committed him to prison for the space of about a week and as is reported hee was cleared by the sd. Jenkins by giving him a Bribe." That afterwards "the sd. Mr. Jenkins was questioned for taking a bribe to cleare the sd Wiltbank and taken into Custody as a prisoner by order of Dr. Roades on that Acct.; but in a few days was releas't; Whereupon Dr. Roades came to the above Mr. Smith complaining of the Fact, but he having newly had his writt of Ease directed him to goe to my Lords to St. Maryes which he accordingly did, but what the Issue of it was there, hee knowes not."

November 21st, 1690.

The members of Sussex County set forth yt. one ye members of Councill ffor their County viz: Thomas Clifton was gon to England.

May 8th, 1693.

Nehemiah Field had oaths & Test, with the oath of Clarke of the Countie of Sussex, administered unto him.

Nehemiah Field was returned as member of the Assembly May 10. 1697.

March 6th, 1694.

"The Court gives Liberty for a Ditch to be Cutt through the most Convenient place of the Town of Lewes into the Creek for the Convenency of Dreaning the Savanah on the back part, next to the Second Street Lotts, and order that the Vacant Ground that lies between the Lott of Nehemiah Field, (Behind the Second Street and fronting on Mulberry Street) and the four acre Lott of Captain Thomas Pemberton, adjoining upon Richard Holloway, be Reserved for a Market Place, and the vacant peace of Land next Adjoining on the Southwest side of John Miers, his Lott, to the Block House pond, and between the Block House Field and that be used as a Common Burying Ground."

The ditch was made to run down the Southwest side of Mulberry Street, and up what is now Third Street. The Market House would have been between Mulberry and Camomile Streets, and Third, and Church Streets.

Later on we see that the Court changed its mind, for we read, "September 6, 1696, Whereas at a Court held the sixth and seventh days of March 1694 a Certain peace of Land In the Town of Lewes, In the Mulberry Street, Lyeing and being between the 4 acres of Captain Thomas Pemberton, and the Lott of Nehemiah Field was ordered to be reserved for a Market place the Court upon a second Vue thereof Do find the same not to be convenient as was expected, and so order the same to be free, to be granted out unto Town Lotts 60 foot in breadth and 200 foot in Length.''

May 20th, 1695.

Wm. Clark. Thomas Pemberton & Robert Clifton were returned as members of the Assembly for Sussex County.

September 3d, 1698.

The Lt.-Gov. acquainted the Council yt he had received a Lre from ye Justices of Sussex County, & desired ye Secrie to read it, which hee did viz: may it please yor Honor, This to or sorrows, but according to our dutes, is to inform, That on friday last, in the afternoon, a small snug-ship & a sloop came to wtin our Cape, not not wholly undesired, but little dreaded of being an enemy or french, both which they proved & yesterday morning Landed about 50 men, well armed & came up ye town & plundered almost every house yrin, Committing great spoil, breaking open doors & chests, and taking away all money or plate to be found, as also, all manner of goods & merdize worth any thing, together with ruggs, blanketting, & all other bedd Covering, Leaving scarce any thing in ye place to Cover or wear.

They brought two English prisoners on shore wt. ym bound, one of ym known to be Jno Redwood, of philadelphia, His Boy, with whom they would suffer no Converse, but wee suppose ye sd sloop to be said Redwood's taken coming out of Cinnepuxon Inlett; They all went on board last night; killed several sheep and Hogs. They continue still at anchor in ye birth, as neer in the bay opposite to this town as they well can find water to ride in, & its doubted they will be on shore again before night for more Cattle, if not to burn ye houses; but we shall endeavor to scare ym. They Ly ready for all mischief inwards or outwards by land or water, and Have pilots any way.

They are now in Chasse Inwards of a Briganteen with their sd sloop.

The briganteen outsails ym, & wee Hope in God, will escape.

They are begarly Rogues, and will pillage for a trifle, and do think they tarry long enough untill ye man of warr att York may have speedy notice.

They took about eleven of ye Chief of our town prisoners, & when they had made them help on board their plunder, dismist all except one man, Capt. Watson's Carpenter.

This place is verie open to danger, & verie naked for defence.

Mr Clark's House & Goods hath Sufficiently shared in ye villany.

Wee hope wee need not repeat ye Calamities aforesaid, nor ye great terror yt must needs here attend all Sexes & Sizes;—By Sir yer Humble Servants—Luke Watson, John Hill, Tho. Oldman, Jonat Baily.

May 11th, 1698.

Representatives returned for Sussex County Thomas Oldman, Jonathan Bayley, Cornelius Wiltbank, & Luke Watson Jr.

June 27th, 1693.

Edward Burch set forth, That having Sailled from Barbadoes in the barkenteen Ann, George Stiles, Mr. & onlle one man and a boy more belonging to her, the petitioner and his servant being to have their passage for their Labour; that the Mr, to the Southward of the Cape Henlopen, was casually knockt over board and Lost, to the hazard of the Shipp, goods & passengers, and that att the desire of the people on board, the petitioner, with great hazard of his life, went ashoare, & for saving the Life of the people, & for preserving the vessell & cargoe, did agree with a person to pylot her to some safe harbour, and to give him twentie pounds, and having had an easie & speedie passage into the whorekills, the said pylot was willing to take ten pounds sterling.

June 15th, 1695.

Order to the Justices of the Peace at Lewes that a watch by two men, be kept a Cape Henlopen, to watch for the French enemies, from 5 Oclock in the morning to Seven Oclock at night.

William Massey was made collector of the Customs at Lewes November 21, 1696.

Thomas Pemberton, Roger Corbet & John Miers members of the Assembly for Sussex Co. Oct. 26, 1696.

September 10th, 1696.

John Stoaklie, Thomas Oldman, Joseph Booth, Henrie Malleston, James Peterkin, & Jonathan Baylie were members of the Assembly, for Sussex Co.

April 12th, 1700.

The pror. & Gov. acquainted ye Council yt hee had Late intelligence yt Wm. Orr. Geo. Thompson peter Lewis Henry Stretcher & Diggerie Tenny, inhabitants of ye town of Lewis in Sussex Countie, had gone on board Capt. kidd, ye privateer, (who in July last Lay some days before Cape Henlopen,) and had Corresponded wt him, & received from him and his crew some muslins, Calicoes, monies & other goods wch. wer East India, & prohibited goods, & yt they had brought ym on shore hid, sold, & given away most of ym, wtout acquainting ye. govrmt, or ye king's Collr of ye port of Lewis wt. ye same, wch hee lookt upon to be, if not piracie, at Lest Confederating wt ym, and accessories & promoters of illegal trade, & yrfor desiring ye Councill's advice yrin. Itt was the opinion of the Gov. & Council, The ——————— Lawman, Collector of port Lewis, should be attested as solemnlie as if he took an oath to declare ye truth as farr as hee knows &c.

August 16th, 1703.

Samuel Rowland of Philidia, mariner, having yesterday arrived with his sloop from Lewis, in Sussex, & brought advice, That there was a certain ship lately arrived there wch they had some reason to suspect was on no honest design; the Council meeting upon that occasion, sent for the said Rowland and examined him, and upon his solemn attestation he declares

Wn He, the said Rowland, and ye Collector of ye said Port, (viz H. Brooke) having been a few miles out of ye town of Lewis, & returning thither on Wednesday last, ye 11th instant, they perceived a ship ride off ye sd Port, and enquiring in the town concerning her, they were told she was either a ffrench Ship or Prize, and found some of her men landed, two of whom particularly they met with, and ye said Collector Inquiring of them whether they belonged to that vessel they answered yes; ye Collectr then asked what papers they had to show, upon wch they produced a Copy of a Commission wch they said was their Capts; That presently after they mett with three more of ye men, who had come ashore & staid wth them near three hours, that ye two they first mett with prest ye other three to goe on board with water they came ashore for, but they refused, and that ye said two earnestly urged the others not to lett their fellow Souldiers perish, calling them Barbarous Dogs for their Inhumanity, & that it would be kinder to pistol them then to lett them die for thirst Upon wch this Informant offered that in Case one of ye sd two men (who were ye most genteel) would stay on shore as a pledge for him he would carry them water on board, and accordingly one staid, & he carried them four anchors of water, of wch they drank up two He thinks before he left them; That they called ye Capt. Burgess, & said ye ship was a french prize, loaden with wheat, came from Callary within ye Straights, Was taken ye Canaries by Capt. Pullen, Companion to Capt. Dampier, on his intended expedition to the South Seas; that ye men said they were ordered by Capt. Pullen to come with the said ship into these parts to Sell her, & when sold he would meet them in this river; That they said they had but 15 men in all; That they had 12 great Guns, & Seemed to be about 120 Tuns; that according to their own accot they had Tenn Thousand Bushels of wheat aboard.

That ye said Informant going on board with only two of the 5 men (viz) one sailor and another of ye two first, they saw the Capt. who seemed much disturbed, his men were not come aboard, But that he that was left a pledge wrote a letter to ye Capt. by ye other person, upon wch the Capt was satisfied; that ye Capt after some words, resolved himself to come on shoar, wch he accordingly did;

That meeting those of his men that were on the shoar, and menacing them they submitted & promised to goe on board, being sent to gett some water & Provision they ran away, and that one of the other two who came ashoar wth the Capt., said he would do the same when he could.

That hereupon the Capt took occasion to threaten this Informant as the cause of his men running away, that he attempted to draw upon him but that he was disarmed by the Company, as as also the Capt's Companion Charleton by name, Upon wch the Sherif Secured ye Boat, and was consulting with ye Collector to raise ye Posse of ye County & took ye Capt into Custody That ye Informant further adds, that inquiring earnestly of some of the men to know what they were, One of them told him that their then Capt who was Lieutenant to Capt Pullen, had been 3 days in irons some time before they parted from the sd Pullen.

He further adds, that upon a lighted match, accidently touching one of the men's legs, who Complained of ye pain, the Capt asked him how he would have bore what their Boatswain did, to have matches burn between his fingers, upon which the other swore the Boatswain was a stout fellow, suffered bravely, without divulging any thing.

That there was none of the prisoners on board of when the ship was taken, of wch being asked ye Reason, they said she was taken in the night near ye shore, & that the men gott off in their boats & escaped, and that those who were on shoar said, that if they who were on borrd could gett-on shoar, at least 8 or 10 of them would desert her. There was a commission issued to Capt Thomas Braines to proceed to Lewes seize the ship and bring it to Philada.

August 24th, 1703.

Information being made to this board, That ye Collector of Lewis was come upon to this town & made Complaint to Judge Clark, & the Secry of Jonathan Bailey, the Sherif of the County of Sussex, that he was remiss in Discharging his duty, & giving him the sd Collectr necessary assistance in apprehending ye Commandr & Sailors of ye ship that had lately come in and anchored before that port, being the Prize taken by Capt Pulleyn, and ye said Judge Clark, the Supream officer of ye said County, directing the said Complaint to ye Board, & accusing him of great remissness & stubborness in his office in general.

It was ordered, that ye said Jonathan Baily's Commission should be superseded, & the place granted to Luke Watson, senr, who had formerly petitioned for the same.

July 9th, 1709.

Richard Westly of Lewis, in Sussex, arriving here early this morning, with an express sent from thence by him, in a Boat & 4 Oars, by the Govr. now there, to give notice to the Govmt, here, that on ye 6th & 7th instant, a french Privateer had Endeavoured to Land at Lewis aforesaid, but being prevented by the opposition made to him, stood up the Bay where the said Westly, on coming up did pass him; Whereupon (as he further informs), he according to the Govr's Orders to him, which was the principle Design of sending him by water, had given notice to all ye outward bound Vessels, yt he could possibly come to speak with, that they might avoid the danger, and the sd Westly Desiring to be satisfied for his own & his Companions Trouble herein.

March 6th, 1704.

Cornelius Wiltbank, Brother in Law to Jno. Williams, who hanged himself at Lewis, having waited on the Govr & acquainted him that he desired & requested Letters of administration on the said Defendts Estate, & the Govr acquainted him with the orders made Concerning that Estate, the sixth of last month.

The said Cornel. Wiltbank appeared at this board and pleads that his Brother in Law was not *Compos Mentis* at the time of making himself away, and that it plainly appears to be so by the Inquest then past upon him.

November 9th, 1709.

Richard Westly of Lewis, having produced to the Govr, a letter from Capt. Cook, Commandr of the Garland, certifying that the said Westly had served 21 days on board her Majesty the Queen's Ship, as Pilot, while she was in our Bay, for which service this Govmnt ought to consider him.

They allowed him 21 Dollars.

April 20th, 1704.

Commission of ye Peace, & for ye County of Sussex was filled up & directed to Willm Clark, John Hill, Tho. Pemberton, Luke Watson, Tho. ffisher, Tho. ffenwick, James Walker, Phil Russel, Jno. Waltham, & Willm Bagwell, Esqrs, and commission renewed to Luke Watson, senr, for Sherif & Nehemiah ffield, for Clerk of ye said County, & a *Dedimus Potestatem*, directed to Geo. Lowther, for qualifying ye said Justices.

October 21st, 1708.

The following members withdrew from the Assembly in Philada, for form a separate body in the Three Lower Counties

Thos. ffisher Suss	Philip Russell	Sussex
Rich. Empson Newc	Willm ffisher	
Corns Wiltbank Suss	Nichos Grainger	
James Booth Kent	Ad Johnson	

November 23d, 1721.

The Govr acquainted the Board, That as they were all sensible he had, with their Advice and Approbation, in pursuance (as He had understood) of the late Proprietor's Inclinations when here, ever since his Administration, observed some kind of an Equality or Proportion in his appointment of the subordinate officers of Govnmt., between those who profess themselves Members of the Church of England and the People called Quakers. He had no reason to doubt but that the Board was well satisfied the same method should be observed in the Council. He had some time ago made mention to most of the members now present of Henry Brooke, Esq., Collector of his Majesty's Customs at Port Lewis, within this Government, and of late a useful magistrate in the County of Sussex, as a fit person to supply the place of Jasper Yeates, Esq. a member of this Board, lately deceased; To which the Governour was more particularly induced from this consideration, that it had been usual, and is still expected by the Inhabitants of the lower Counties, that there should be always at least two members in the Council from those Counties: Wherefore, He now proposes that with the consent of this board, the said Henry Brooke should be admitted a member thereof.

All the Members present being sensible of Mr. Brooke's great Knowledge, Ability, and Worth, unanimously agree that He be admitted accordingly as soon as the Governour thinks fit.

July 25th, 1726.

Henry Brooke & Jonathan Baily Esqs of Sussex were appointed Judges of the Supreme Court.

September 23d, 1726.

The Govr acquainted the Board, that one Alexander Molliston of the County of Sussex had seven or eight days since brought him a petition, complaining of some abuses he had received in that County—the said Petition was read setting forth sundry abuses the Petitioner had suffered from William Till, who as magistrate, & by his Influence on the Court of the County, had admitted divers arbitrary acts, by means of which the Petitioner was utterly disabled from following his Employment & providing Bread for his Family.

After reading Petition, one of the Members likewise informed the Board, that the same Justice William Till had some months agoe broke open & Kept up a Letter wrote & sent by James Steel of Philada. to Robert Shankland, Surveyor of the County of Sussex, inclosing some copies of an Address from a late Assembly of the lower Counties to the Governour Sir William Keith, in the Beginning of his Administration, which were thought proper to be distributed for the Proprietors Service, that the said William Till had most contumeliously treated the said James Steel on that occasion, tho' he had acted therein for the Proprietor's Service only, & as his officer, and had not given either the said William Till, or any reasonable Person, any just occasion to be offended with his Proceedings in that affair.

Another Member likewise, that in a late Assembly of the three lower Counties, Mr Till had used most indecent & disregardful Expressions of the Proprietary Family.

William was relieved of his office, A new Commission of Peace being to be issued for the said County, the following Persons are agreed on to be inserted in the same, vizt: Henry Brooke, Richard Hinman, Philip Russel, John Roades, Woolsey Burton, Samuel Rowland, Jeremiah Claypoole, Jacob Kollock, John Jacobs, Samuel Davis, Joseph Cord, Robert Shankland, George Walton & Enoch Cumings.

October 4th, 1726.

For Sussex County Rives Holt, & Peter Adams being returned for Sherifs, & Samuel Davis & Edmund Naws for Coroners, Rives Holt is appointed Sherif & Samuel Davis Coroner.

October 4th, 1727.

For Sussex County: Rives Holt & Peter Adams being returned for Sherifs, and Samuel Davies and John Russell for Coroners, Rives Holt is appointed Sherif & Samuel Davies Coroner.

October 3d, 1728.

For Sussex County: Rives Holt & Robert Smith being returned for Sherifs, & John Jacobs & Samuel Davis for Coroners. Rives Holt is appointed Sherif, John Jacobs Coroner.

October 4th, 1729.

For Sussex County. Rives Holt & John Jacobs returned for Sherifs, & Joseph Pemberton & John Roades for Coroners, Rives Holt is appointed Sherif & John Roades Coroner.

October 6th, 1730.

For Sussex County: James Fenwick & Simon Kollock being returned for Sherifs, & Robert Smith & Cornelius Wiltbank for Coroners, Simon Kollock is appointed Sherif & Cornelius Wiltbank Coroner.

October 6th, 1731.

For the County of Sussex: Simon Kollock & James Fenwick being returned for Sherifs, & Cornelius Wiltbank & John Clowes for Coroners, Simon Kollock is appointed Sherif & John Clowes Coroner.

October 4th, 1733.

For the County of Sussex: Simon Kollock & Robert Smith being returned for Sherifs, & Joshua Fisher & John Clowes for Coroners, Simon Kollock is appointed Sherif, & Joshua Fisher Coroner.

October 5th, 1734.

For the County of Sussex: Robert Smith & Cornelius Wiltbank being returned for Sherifs, and Joshua Fisher and John Roades for Coroners, Cornelius Wiltbank is appointed Sherif and Joshua Fisher Coroner.

October 3d, 1735.

For the County of Sussex, Cornelius Wiltbank & John Shankland being returned for Sherifs, and Daniel Nunez & William Selthuge for Coroners, John Shankland is appointed Sherif, and Daniel Nunez Coroner.

October 3d, 1740.

Commissions made out to Cornelius Wiltbank as Sherif of Sussex County, & John Wynkoop as Coroner of said County.

October 5th, 1745.

Commissions to William Shankland Esq. Sherif, & Robert Gill, Gentm. Coroner of the County of Sussex.

October 4th, 1746.

William Shankland Sheriff and John Molliston Coroner of Sussex County.

July 13th, 1747.

A letter by Express from New Castle:

"GENTLEMEN:—This Moment Thomas Quant & a son of Mr Nandins informs me a Company of French or Spaniards, to the number of One hundred or thereabouts, has Robb'd & Plunder'd the Houses of James Hart & Edmund Liston, and carried off all the valuable part of their Negroes & other Goods, and its supposed they have done so all the way to Lewis Town.

"DAVID WETHERSPOON."

September 14th, 1747.

The Capt. of a Pilot Boat, Despatched as an Express from Lewes Town last Saturday, delivered to the President this morning the following Letter directed to the President & Council:

"SIR & GENTLEMAN:—On Tuesday last 2 Sloops went up the Bay with a Pilot Boat tending in each of them; on Wednesday evening they returned & anchored with the said boats in Lewes Road, which hath kept our Watch upon hard Duty Day and Night.

"One of the said Vessels we imagine to be gone over to Cape May, the other took in our sight last Night a Ship outward Bound, and her Pilot Boat another Ship this morning that was coming in, and is now in Chace of a third ship, which we fear will fall into her hands in an hour or two.

"These things we judged proper to immediately communicate, and hope the Merchants & Traders at Philadelphia will pay this Express £3, being the sum agreed for to convey it.

"Sir & Gentlemen Your obedt, hble Sevts

"RS HOLT
"JACOB KOLLOCK
"JACOB PHILLIPS."

This Assembly "could only lament their & the good People of Lewes Town's unhappiness in being thus remedilessly exposed to any Attempts the Enemy should please to make."

They paid the Express £3.

September 21st, 1747.

"Information being given that several Vessells belonging to this and other Ports were lately taken by a French Privateer of the Capes of Delaware, and that some of the Pilots & People who were on board at the time of Capture were in Town, they were sent for, and Mr. Kelly & Luke Shields, one of the Pilots who had the charge of the Privateer, attending without, they were examined."

September 25th, 1747.

"William Kelly being sworn on the holy Evangelists of Almighty God deposeth and saith, that he being a Passenger on board the Sloop Elizabeth, Pyramus Green Commander, bound from Providence to Philadelphia, on or about the 28" day of August last he was taken off the Coast of North Carolina by a French Privateer Sloop called the Marthel Vodroit, Capt. Lepay Commander, belonging to Cape Francois, who had taken three English Prizes before as this Deponent was informed; that after they had taken the said Sloop Elizabeth they stood to the Northward, and on their cruise took six more English Prizes, to wit, a Brigantine and two Ships off the Capes of Virginia, and a Sloop about fifteen Leagues off the Capes of Delaware, one Newbold Master, & two Ships in the Bay of Delaware, one of them called the Bolton, Oswald Eves Commander, and the other called the Delaware, —— Lake Commander, this Deponent being at the times of the taking of the said six Prizes, a Prisoner on board the said French Privateer.

"That the said French Privateer was a Vessel of about Ninety or one hundred tons, and carried fourteen Carriage Guns, sixteen Swivels. and six Swivel Blunderbusses, and had when he left Cape Francois, as this Deponent was informed, about one hundred and seventy men, but at the time of this Deponent's being taken, had but one hundred & thirty men belonging to her.

"That this Deponent took some of the Privateer's Crew to be English, some Irish, and some Scotch, but the most part of them were Frenchmen & Spaniards.

That the first land they made off Delaware was Cape May; that the Privateer hoisting English colours, one William Flower, a Pilot, came off from the said Cape and came on board the Privateer, that when the said William Flower came on board, the Commander of the Privateer, by a Linguist, ordered him to take Charge of the said Privateer & to carry the said Privateer where the Shipping lay; that the said William Flower at first misunderstanding the said Commander's Orders, as this Deponent imagines, made answer that there was water enough there, pointing towards the Sea, but upon being told that that was not what the Commander meant, he the said William Flower asked if they meant that he should carry the Privateer up the River, to which the said Commander answered, Yes, and then the said William Flower took Charge of the said Privateer and was carrying her round towards Cape Henlopen, when Luke Shields, another Pilot, came on board from Cape Henlopen, the said Privateer being under English Colours, that the said Commander of the said Privateer was very Inquisitive concerning Philada. and asked William Flower how Matters stood at Philadelphia, and what Shipping was coming down. William Flower answered that he could not tell as he had not been to Philadelphia for seven or eight days; that upon Luke Shields coming on board, the Commander of the Privateer asked him the like questions, and Luke Shields answered, that as he had not been at Philadelphia for a great while, he could not tell, but that his Man knew as he had been there lately.

"The Man being asked, answered that the Privateer Trembleur was then coming down, and that he believed the Pandour was fitting out.

"That after Shields coming on board the care of the Privateer was committed to him in conjunction with Flower, that this Deponent acquainted Shields that Flower had promised this Deponent to carry the Privateer within less than a Mile of Cape Henlopen, to the end this Deponent might swim on Shore in the Night, which this Deponent had resolved to do in order to obtain his Liberty and inform the People of the said Privateer, and this Deponent made it his request to the said Shields that he would assist this Deponent in his Design by bringing the said Privateer so near the shore that this Deponent might swim on shore with safety, but the said Shields refused to do it, & said he would carry the said Privateer where she might meet with the most Prizes; upon this Deponent asking him why he would do so, he answered that the Privateer came for Prizes and would not go away without them, and by this Means he should sooner get his Liberty; That the said Pilot brought the said Privateer to an anchor somewhere about the Brown, but it blowing hard she afterwards came to an anchor within two leagues of the pitch of the Cape; That the Day after the taking of the last Prizes, the English Prisoners to the number of about seventy, were permitted to go on shore in three Pilot Boats which the Enemy had taken."

"Bernard Martin of Philada, Mariner, late Commander of the Ship Mary of London, Being within a mile of Cape Henlopen, and a signal for a Pilot being out on Tuesday the fourteenth Day of July 1747) about seven o'Clock in the Morning, this Deponent was hailed by a Privateer Sloop of about ten Guns, but as this Deponent had verything ready for an Engagement, the Privateer made off without making an attack.

"That about Eight o'Clock the same morning this Deponent saw a Pilot Boat coming towards him, which this Deponent well knew as the Pilot who this Deponent saw upon Deck; that this Deponent taking it to be an English Pilot permitted it to come along side of his ship; that thereupon a number of French & Spaniards, to the amount of Thirty Five or thereabouts, instantly boarded this Deponents Ship, and this Deponent offering to make some Resistance, he, this Deponent, was shott at by three of the Enemy, and one of the Balls grazed this Deponent's Cheek, and another his arm & side, and immediately afterwards this Deponent was knocked down; and then they tacked the Ship and stood out to Sea, but did not crowd Sail; and the next morning they tack'd again and stood in for the Bay, and at about four o'Clock in the Afternoon on Wednesday they put this Deponent and seven of his men into the Pilot Boat and discharged them, and then stood off with the Ship with an Intention, after they had got provisions and other Things necessary (as this Deponent heard some of them say) to cruize between this Bay, the Capes of Virginia, and Cape Fear. That this Deponent understood the People on board the Pilot Boat who took this Deponent did belong to the Privateer Sloop which this Deponent had seen in the morning of the Day he was taken. That the Captain's name was —— Barnard, a Frenchman, & had a French Commission which he shewed to this Deponent; that about half his Company were French and about half Spaniards. That among the said Privateers there was one Englishman who this Deponent was told was a Boston Man, he having owned the same to one of this Deponent's Mariners as this Deponent was informed; that he spoke very good English, and like an Englishman, and told this Deponent he knew Philadelphia.

"That the Captain Barnard told this Deponent he did not doubt but he should be up at Philadelphia in Six Months. That from the scarcity of Provisions among the said Privateers this Deponent verily believes they intend to make a Descent in order to procure more, that what little Provisions they had they were very lavish of, washing their feet in fresh Water and throwing their offal Victuals overboard; that this Deponent understanding Spanish and French heard the said Privateers talking among themselves, and understood from them that they intended to make a Descent somewhere for provisions—this Deponent being in his Hammock he supposes they imagined he was asleep. "BERNARD MARTIN.

"Sworn the 17th July, 1747 before

"JOS. TURNER."

April 11th, 1748.

A Petition from the Pilots using the Bay & River of Delaware was read in these words, viz:

"To the Honourable Anthony Palmer, Esqr., Presid[t] of the Government of the Counties of New-Castle Kent, and Sussex, on Delaware, & Province of Pennsylvania,"

"The humble Petition of the Pilots, Inhabitants of the County of Sussex, on Delaware.

"Whereas, Your Petitioners. as well Pursuant to an Act of General Assembly of this Government as Your Honour's late Proclamation, are prohibited going on board any inward bound vessell in the Bay & River Delaware, which said Act & Proclamation your Petitioners are fully convinced are justly Calculated for the safety of this Government, and therefore willing to pay all due obedience.

"And Whereas, The Pilots that dwell in the Government of New Jersey (from a false Representation of Your Petitioners having Lycence to Cruise for Vessells & go on board the same as Pilots) are not restrained by any Law of that Government, but, as Your Petitioners are informed have leave to Cruize and go on board vessells as Pilots, & daily do the same within the Bay & River aforesaid, which in its Consequence may prove prejudicial to this Government and likewise prevent Your Petitioners acquiring a Competent support for their Familys, for Your Honour may be assured that no inward bound Vessell will call at Lewes for a Pilot when any other may be had Cruizing off.

"Your Petitioners therefore humbly entreat your Honours Interest and Friendship with the Government of the Jersey for restraining the Pilots of that Government in such manner and by such measures as may be thought most expedient, not only for the safety of this Government but that Your Petitioners may have an Equal Chance for their Livelyhood in their proper Employments; And Your Petitioners shall ever pray.

"Wm. Field,
"Luke Field,
"Samuel Rowland,
"Samuel Rowland, Jun.
"Wm. Rowland,
"Simon Edwards,
"John Baily,
"John Maull,
"John Adams."

June 2d, 1748.

The President & Four Members sign'd a Commission to Abraham Wiltbank to Command an Intelligence Boat & wear a Flagg.

"By the Honable, the President and Council of the Province of Pennsylvania.

"To Abraham Wiltbank of Lewis Town, Pilot, Greeting:

"Whereas, by reason of the Bay and River Delaware being now greatly infested with the Enemie's Privateers, we have judged it necessary that some fit and proper Persons shall be forthwith employed and commissioned to observe and give us constant intelligence of the Motions and Designs of the said Privateers; and we have thought you fitly qualified for that purpose & confiding in Your Loyalty, Vigilance, & Integrity, Do hereby Grant Commission to Authorize and appoint You the said Abraham Wiltbank to fit out and Command an Intelligence Boat for the purposes aforesaid, & therewith immediately to proceed and continue to pass & repass down & up the said River & Bay (During our Pleasure) in order to discover, observe, and get force, & designs of the said Privateers or other his Majesty's Enemies, & from time to time bring or transmit to Us with the utmost Expedition full Accounts and Advice thereof, Hereby giving & granting to you License & Authority during your acting and continuing in the same service to hoist & wear in Your said Boat A Red Pendant with two white Cresses, and for so doing this shall be your warrant.

"Given under our Hands in Council & the Lesser Seal of the Said Province, at Philadelphia, the 3d of June, in the Twenty-first Year of His Majesties Reign, Annogz Domini, 1748.

"ANTHONY PALMER."

Another of the same Tenor was Signed to John Maule, authorizing him to wear an English Jack.

May 31st, 1748.

Abraham Wiltbank, Commander of one of the Government Pilot Boats, bringing advice that he had been for a day or two off the Capes & met with no Enemies Vessells—the Embargo was taken off.

October 4th, 1755.

[Jacob Kollock, Jun, Sheriff Paynter Stockley, Cor^r^. Sussex County.

October 5th, 1756.

John Rodney, Sheriff
Wrixam Lewis, Cor^r^. } Sussex Co.

"Resolved that Mr. Samuel Morris Junr wait on Mr. William Rechards, Captain Falconer, and Captain Reed, and inform them they are (with any other person they may fix on) appointed a Committee to fix up proper signals in the River and Bay of Delaware, to give the most speedy intelligence of any Enemy Ships that may arrive at or within the Capes of Delaware The Committee appoint James Maul with his Boat

"Whereas Captain William Bradford and Thomas Pryor report to this Board that Angus McBean made application yesterday to Nehemiah Maul for his Pilot Boat to go on board the Man of War, now in our Bay, with the assurance that he had the consent of this Committee &c McBean guaranteed £130 in case Man of War detained him. March 31, 1776."

April 15, 1776.

"A Pilot allowed the Sloop Congress provided the Captain of her will promise and engage to go down the Cape May Channel and land his Pilot there."

May 24, 1776.

"Lt George Ball, belonging to the Roebuck Man of War, taken in a Pilot Boat at Cape Henlopen some time past. Paroled."

September 19, 1776.

"James Maul appointed Pilot to carry vessels through the chevaux de frise, in room of Daniel Gordon, deceased."

October 15, 1776.

"Mr. Nesbit directed to pay James Thomson for 35½ gallons of Rum, and 4 quarts of Molasses, for use of Col. Miles Battlion* while at Lewes Town, to be charged to Congress. £18."

CHEVAUX DE FRIZE PILOTS.

Michael Dawson........................October 11, 1775
Joseph Gamble........................October 11, 1775
Daniel Gordon........................October 11, 1775
William Marshall........................October 11, 1775
Nehemiah Maul........................October 11, 1775
William Molleston........................October 11, 1775
James Roberts........................October 11, 1775
William Ross........................October 11, 1775
John Schnieder........................October 11, 1775
James Maul........................February 20, 1776
Nathan Storey........................February 20, 1776
Michael Dean........................June 26, 1777

John Marshall was pilot on the fire ship "Hecla" July 21st, 1777.

---

*REV. C. H. B. TURNER, LEWES, DEL.

It appears from the official records that Captain David Hall's Company and Captain Charles Pope's Company of the Delaware Battalion (or Regiment) of Continental troops, commanded by Colonel John Haslet, was in barracks at Lewes (or Lewis) Town April 11, 1776; and that a part of Captain Latimer's Independent Company, Delaware, was "On station at Lewes by order of the House of Assembly or Council of Safety of this Government" April 29, 1776. No original records of those organizations are on file in this office, but, from correspondence with the Secretary of State of Delaware, it appears that some records of those organizations are on file in his office.

From such an examination of the incomplete collection of Revolutionary records on file in this office as it has been practicable to make, it has been impossible to ascertain whether any other organization was quartered or stationed at Lewes, or in Sussex County, Delaware, during the Revolutionary war.

No record of any Colonel Miles' Battalion of Delaware troops in that war has been found on file in this office.

F. C. AINSWORTH,
The Adjutant General.

COURT RECORDS.

[This begins with 2d entry in Record Book, the first being well faded out.]

DEALE COUNTY.

JUNE 15TH, 1681.

A patton of Land Acckowlidged in open [Court] by John Kiphaven and Bartree his wife to William Clark; and by william Clark and Honnor his wife to nathanil walker.

A patton of Land Accknowlidged in open Court by Elizabeth Parling and nathanil walker unto william Clark.

The Court fine nathanil walker ffifty pounds of Tobacco; for smoking of Tobacco in the Court.

The Court Grant unto Phillip Morrise foure hundred Acres of Land; warrant Given out 15th Insnt for these Lands.

The Court Grant unto John Dickerson foure hundred Acres of Land; warrant Given out the 15th, 2 mo, 1681.

The Court Grant unto Richard w[illiam] foure hundred Acres of Land; Richard william warrt given [torn].

John Kiphaven have a Grant from the Court of the third Towne Lott to the front from the Land of nathanil walker; he paying the Rent which shall be ordered by the Governor yearly.

The Court order and Grant unto John Hagester ffoure hundred Acres of Land; A warrant given out the 26th, 11 mo, 1681.

Halmanias wiltbanck peticoner Agt John vines shreife. The peticoner sett forth that the shreife have taken upon Execu- Henry Harmon at the suit of the peticoner; And that the said shreife doe Contrary to Law suffer his prissoner to goe at Larg; the shreife pleade that he have no prison provided to keepe his prissoners in at present; The Court doe there for order that the shreife shall confine these prisoners to the house and yards whare the sd shreif do or shall Live untill the said prisoner shall be Leagally discharged by the plt; and that in the mean time the plt shall A[llow] the prisoner Two shillings and six pe[nce] a week for his maintance; And the Like order that the Court doe make for all other pe[rsons] that shall be upon Execution for debt; u[ntill] there Can be a prison built and provid[ed] for that purpose.

[Two entries omitted, mostly torn away, only a few words remaining.]

The Court Grant unto Yoakim Goyl[torn] by his Atturney Henry Bowman; ffoure hundred Acres of Land; warrant Given out 26th day 5 mo, 1681.

The Court Grant unto John ffinch by his Atturney Henry Bowman six hundred Acres of Land; warrant Given out 26th day 5 mo, 1681.

The differences that are depending betwene Capt John Avery & Peter Groundyk Concerning the Account of Capt Avery over Charging the said Peter Groundyk, [etc., etc. Signatures torn].

I Mary Simons doe here in the presence of the Lord and you his people declare and depose upon my Corperall oath that I am free and Clear from being under the bonds of Mattrimony to any person now Liveinge whatsoever. In wittnes & Testamoney wharof I have hereunto sett my hand this seaventh day of the Moneth Called July Anno; Dm; 1681; signed MARY SIMONS
Sworen befor me

WM: CLARK.

Thomas Howard And Mary Simons ware Joyned Together in Marrig by me william Clark one of the Kings Justices of the peace for deale County [July 17, 1681, after due publication and in presence of several witnesses, not named].

[Ard Johnson van Kirk and Grace Bundock married by William Clark one of the Kings Justices of the peace, July 28, 1681, after due publication "and in presence of several wittneses."]

SEPT. 13 & 14th.

Att A Court held at Deale for the Towne and County of Deale; by the Kings Authori[ty] the 13th and 14th days of the Moneth Called September Anno; Dm; 1681; Commoners present; Luke Wattson John Roades John Kiphaven William Clark.

An Action of the Case Refered from the Last Court [etc. etc.] John Hagester plt, Harmon Corneling deft.

Alexander Moulston John Hagester Cornelius verhoofe & John vines Complantants Halmainas wiltbanck deft To be Tryd by bill and Answer as A Cause of Equeity.

Action of Traspass. John Depree plt, Will footcher deft, Corverhoofe sworen. Jureymen—Alex Draper Alex Moulston Cor Johnson Mil Chambers will Troter Hen Stracher Robt Johnson Will Townsend will prantices Rich williams John Oakey Robt Traile.

The Court order and Appoint Alex Draper fachl Gray & william footcher to be Survayors of the High ways and bridges; and doe hereby order Impower and Authorize them or any or either of them to sumame In the Inhabitents of this County to mend make and repaire the High ways Roades and bridges with in this County; as soone as may be.

The Court Grant unto Richard Stevens by his Atturney Edward Southrin six hundred Acres of Land; warrant Given out the 14th, 7 mo, 1681.

The Court Grant unto Nortton Claypoole by his Atturney John Hill five Hundred Acres of Land; warrant Given out 25th, 11 mo, 1681.

The Court Grant unto Thomas wellborn by his Atturney Henry Bowman Eighte hundred Acres of Land; warrant Given out the 10th day of the 3 month 1683.

The Court Grant unto Robert Twelley by his Atturney John vines foure hundred Acres of Land.

The Court fine George young Cunstable for not giveing his Attendance in Court Two hundred pounds of Tobacco.

The Court fine John Roades one of the Justices of the peace for this County for his absence from Court the 14th day of September 1681; the sume of foure hundred pounds of good Marchantable Tobacco (in Caske);

NOVEMBER 8th & 9th, 1681.

Att a Court Held at Deale for the Towne and County of Deale by the Kings Authority the 8th & 9th days of the Moneth Called november Anno; Dm: 1681; Comisconers presents: Luke Wattson John Roades William Clark.

An Action of Debts. Henry Bowman plt, Joseph Browne Deft. In Sept. Court the deft being out of the Govermt And his Atturney Capt John Avery being sick peticoned the Court for a Reference; the Court there for Grant the deft A reference untill the next Court; in novmber Court the plt declare &c., and brought in there verdict; that they finde that the deft have paid and satisfied the 1000lb Tob by Capt Averys Ingaging for the paymt of it; and there for finde for the deft wt one shill damag and Cost of suit; the Court passe Judgmt According to the verdict of the Jurey Alias Execution. Jurey Men Alexander Draper William ffootcher Daniell Browne John Smith William Emitt John King Simon Parling

An Action of Debt. Henry Bowman plt, Joseph Browne & Andrew Depree defts. John Smith Will Emitt Ri[ch] Williams John King Rich Gill Tho Davids Elij Cartle. In Sept Court the defts being out of the County And there Atturney Capt John Avery being sick peticoned the Court for A Referance the Court there for Grant the deft A Referance untill the next Court; now in novmber Court the plt declare that the defts stands Indebted unto him in one Thousand pounds of Tobacco wone of the defts at a horse Race the defts pleaded that they wone and Craved A Jurey to Try the Cause; which being Granted the bussines was debated on both sides and severall wittneses Excamined After which the Jurey went out and brought in there verdict that they finde for the deft; with Cost of suit; & six pence Damages; the Court passe Judgmt According to the verdict of the Jurey; Alias Executcion; Alexander Draper William ffootcher Daniell Browne Simon Parling Henry Stracher Thomas Pinder Robert Bracey Jurey Men.

An Action of Trespass. Thomas Haward & Wight Haward plts. Nathanil Walker deft. Jurey finds for the deft and gives him Twelve pence Damages and the Court order Judgmt to be entered according to verdict of the Jurey. norton Claypoole Alexander Draper Henry Bowman James Welles John Smith Halmainas Wiltbanck William ffootcher Robert Bracey John Hill [S]amwell Gray Thomas Pinder Daniell Browne Jurey Men.

An Action of the Case. Andrew Depree plt, Thomas Denison deft.

An Action of the Case. Capt John Avery plt, Ben Coudrey Deft.

Attachment. Alexander Draper plt, Robert Millenor Deft.

An Action of the Case. ffrancis Gunby plt, Capt John Avery Deft.

An Action of the Case. Bryant Rowles plt, Harmon Cornelison deft.

An Action of the Case. Henry Bowman plt, John Newall Deft.

An Action of the Case. Henry Bowman plt, James Welles & John Newall defts. Jo Croper Tho Pinder Robt Johnson Will Rodeney & Will Keene. The plt declare that the defts did Contract & Agree wt him to Run A horse Race for three Thousand pounds of Tobacco; and that he the said plt ded wine; the deft pleaded that the Contract was not Confirmed the Cause being debated on both sides and severall wittneses Excamined the Cause was Refered to a Jurey; wch went out and brough in there verdict; that they finde for the plt with Cost of suit and one shill Damages; and the deft's arest the Judgmt of the Court & Craved an Appeale to have the Cause to be Tryd at the next Gennarall Court of Assisses at new york befor the Honorable Governor and Councell; the vallow being under Twenty pounds the Court Could not agree wheather it was Appealeable or not; and soe refered the same untill the next Court; there being sume thing dubous in the Testament of the wittneses [The following names are on the margin—] Alexander Draper Samwell Gray Nathanil Walker Daniell Browne John Smith Nathanil Bradford Henry Stracher.

An Action of Debt. John Roades plt, Richard Adkinson deft; with drawen by order of the plt.

An Action of Debt. John Roades plt, Richard Gill Deft. "with drawen."

An Action of Debt. William Clark plt, Robt Williams Deft—"refered."

An Action of Debt. William Clark plt, Thomas Davids Deft—"with Drawen."

An Action of the Case. William Clark plt, Richard Gill Deft—"with Drawen."

An Action of Debt. William Lewis plt, ffrancis Gunby Deft—"with Drawen." by order of James Welles the plts Atturney.

Peticon Henry Harmon Halm Wiltbanck. The peticoner setting forth in his peticon that whareas Halm wiltbank recovered Judgment of this Court Agt him for Twenty Thousand pounds of Tobacco; for the not giveing him the sd Halm wiltbanck possession of the house plantacon Land and premisses that Cornelie Johnson live upon According to Contract; and that the sd Halm wiltbanck had no right to let the Land to the peticoner; but that befor that time the sd Halm had sold and delivered it to John Kurk there for the peticoner Craved a rehearing in the sd Cause; the Court order that it be rehard tomorrow and that Halm wiltbanck have nooties of it this night; the next dae upon the request of the sd Halm wiltbanck the Cause is refered to by Tryd the next Court.

The Court Grant unto John Davids by his Atturney Thomas Davids Two hundred Acres of Land.

The Court Grant unto John Croper One Thousand Acres of Land; warrants Given out the 6th 12 mo, 1681.

A Deede of sale Accknowlidged in open Court by Edward Southrin Atturney to John Outim unto Henry Bowman of A plantacon house and Land Lyeing and being near Ceeder Creeke.

This day Elizabeth Carter the Late wife of Otto Woollgast deceased peticoned the Court to be Admited to Adminnister on the Estate of hur deceased Husband; for that the Executrx Appointed in the Will by the said Otto Woollgast have nedglected to Adminnister for the space of six Moneths and upwards Afer the death of the said Otto Woollgast all though they had sone after his death nooties there of given unto them and a Copie of the said will; for which Reasons the Court doe grant Letters of Adminnistracon unto William Carter and Elizabeth his wife; They puting in sufficent securety to the Court to give in a true Inventory of all the Estate goods and Chattels that the said Otto Woollgast was possessed of at the time of his Death or just befor; and to be accoumptable for the same and pay and satisfie the debts and Leigeses of the said Otto Woollgast According as the Law directs in that Case. William Carter and Elizabeth his wife have this day in open Court proved the Last will and Testament of Otto Woolgast deceased being in writinge; which is by the Court ordered to be recorded; Justices Luke Wattson John Roades Wm; Clark signed the dockett.

December [1]3th.

Att A Court Held for the Towne and County of Deale by the Kings Authority the 13th day of the Moneth Called December Anno Dm 1681. Commisconers present: Luke Wattson John Kiphaven; William Clark.

Plea upon the Case. Capt John Avery plt, Peter Groundyk deft.

An Action of the Case upon An Attachment. Alex Draper plt, Robert Millener deft.

An Action of the Case. Henry Bowman plt, James welles and John newall defts; Wittneses Jo Croper Tho. Pinder Robt Johnson Will Rodeney & Will Keene. In Novmb. Cot. Jurey Men: Alex Draper Samll Gray Nat Walker Danil Brown Jo Smith Nathanil Bradford Henry Stracker.

An Action of Debt. William Clark plt, Robt Williams Deft; "refered" and finally "with drawen."

Peticon. Henry Harmon Agt, Halm wiltbanck deft; Wittneses Ed Southrin Cor Johnson and his wife. The peticoner setting forth in his peticon that whare as Halm wiltbank Recovered Judgment of this Court Agt him for Twenty Thousand pounds of Tobacco for the not giveing him the said Halm wiltbanck possession of the house plantacon Land and premisses that Cornelis Johnson Lives upon According to Contract; And the peticoner setts forth that the sd Halm Wiltbanck had no right at that time to Let the said Land to the peticoner; But that befor that time the said Halm Wiltbanck had sold and delivered the Land and premisses to one John Kurk; therefor the peticoner Craved a Rehearing of the said Cause the Court ordered that the Cause be Rehard the next day that the shreife doe give nooties thereof to the said Halm Wiltbanck that night; the next day upon the Request of the said Halm the Cause is Refered to be Tryd or Rehard the next Court; In december Court it was proved by the oath of Edward Southrin Cor Johnson and his wife; That the said Halm Wiltbanck had sold and delivered possession of the said Land and premisses by Tufe and Twig unto the sd John Kurk; befor the sd Halm Wiltbanck Let to the peticonr the Judgment of the Court therefor is that the said Halm Wiltbanck had no Right or power to Let the said Land to the peticoner; And therefore doe order that the Judgment obtained formerly in this Court Agt the peticoner at the suit of the said Halm Wiltbanck be void and the peticoner sett at Libirty from his Imprisonment; and that the said Halm Wiltbanck doe pay the peticoner his damiages sustayned; with Cost of suit; Alias Executcion;

Alexander Moulston plt, Henry Harmon deft—An Action of the Case with drawen by order of the plt.

Thomas Davids plt, Anthony Enlose deft—An Action of defamacon with drawen by order of the plt.

An Action of the Case. Capt John Avery plt, ffrancis Gunby deft; wittneses, Thomas Pinder John Barnett & Jane Holiway. [*In re.* to purchase of a horse]. Jury men: Norton Claypoole Daniell Browne Cornelis Verhoofe Capt Marsh Robert Bracey William ffootcher John Hill. [Jury men's names written on margin].

An Action of the Case. Capt Avery plt, fra Gunby deft. [*In re.* to purchase of "A Clorth of silver peaty Coat" Eleaver or Twelve years since].

An Action of the Case. Capt Jo Avery plt, Ben Coudrey deft.

An Action of the Case. Alex Moulston plt, Thomas Davids deft; "with drawen" by order of the plt.

An Action of the Case. Alex Moulston plt, Rich Gill Deft; "with drawen" by order of the plt.

An Action of Debt. William Clark plt, Robert Johnson deft; "Refered."

An Action of the Case. Richard Gill plt, Alex Moulston deft.

An Action of the Case. Richard Gill plt, Alex Moulston deft: non suit.

An Action of the Case. Robert Williams plt, Richard Gill deft; "with drawen."

An Action of the Case. Jacob Shattham plt, Thomas Davids deft; "refered."

An Action of the Case upon A Repleavey. Peter Groundyk plt, Halm Wiltbanck deft. The plt. declare that he Left in the Custidy of the deft fiftye three dutch Ells and a halfe of duffells or Trading Clorth to sell for the plt [etc.].

Halm Wiltbank plt, Peter Groundyk deft; "refered."

An Action of the Case upon an Attachment. Peter Groundyk plt, William Carter Adminst, "refered."

An Action of defamacon or Slander. Mathias Everson plt, John oakey & his wife deft; Wittnes william prentice.

An Action of ——. ffrancis Rumbolt plt, William Carter Administ to otto woollgast Estate deft.

An Action of the Case. ffrancis Rumbolt plt, Harmon Cornelison deft; "refered."

An Action of Debt. John Kiphaven plt, Richard Patte deft; "with drawen."

An Action of Debt. Thomas Atthow plt, Henry Stracher & William Clark defts; "Refered."

An Action of Debt. Capt Marton Creagor plt, Anthony Hamen* Alias Haverly deft; "Refered."

Attachment. Harmon Cornelison plt, the Estate of John Shackley deceased in the Custidy of Alex Moulston deft; The Court refer Judgment.

A patton of foure Hundred Acres of Land Accknowlidged in open Court by James Welles and William Emitt Authorized by Mary his wife unto George Young and to his heires and Assignes for ever.

The above patton of foure hundred Acres of Land was Accknowlidged in open Court by Georg Young unto John Jenings and to his heires and Assignes for ever.

---

* This name sometimes seems to be *Hamen* and at others like *Hancen*.

A patton of one Thousand Acres of Land Accknowlidged in open Court by John depree to Henry Bowman; and to his heires and Assignes for ever.

A deede of Conveyance of the above said parcell of one Thousand Acres of Land was this day in open Court signed sealed & delivered from John depree to Henry Bowman; upon Condition that the said Henry Bowman ded befor the Court Consent and Agree that he his Executors Administrators or Assignes; should never here after expect or Compell the said John Depree his heires Executors Administrators or Assignes to make the said Land Cleare or free any further then his right or any Claiming under him; any thing Contained in the deede of Conveyance to the Contrary notwithstanding.

Peticon. Joane Streate Agt William Clark.

A patton of three Hundred Acres of Land Accknowlidged and Assigned over in open Court; by William Clark and Honnor his wife unto William Durnall; and to his Heires and Assignes for ever.

The Court Grant unto Luke Wattson Jüner upon A peticon put into this Court for that purpose; the three Hundred Acres of Land that was James Leyes; he paying for the patton; he the said James Leyes never seating or Improving any part of the said Land; absenting himself out of the Country; if Clear from the Lawfull Claim of any other.

The Court Grant unto William Durnall [Durvall?] of the Citty of New York, Merchant One Thousand Acres of Land; warrant Given out ye 10th 12 mo; 1681.

The Court Grant unto John Savidge Eighte hundred Acres of Land; warrant Given out the 10th, 12 mo; 1681.

The Court Grant unto Abraham Potter three Hundred Acres of Land; warrant Given out the 22th 11 mo; 1681.

The Court Grant unto William Butler Thurty Acres of Land Adjoyning to his Land allrady taken up; wart Given out ye 6th, 4 mo; 1682.

Henry Bowman peticoning the Court and setting forth that he have Lost Two warrant that he had to take up six hundred Acres of Land for John Finch and foure hundred Acres of Land for Yoakom Goylack the Court doe order the Clark to give him the peticoner Two new warrants upon Conditcon that the other Two which are said to be Lost be void and of no Effect; & to be given unto the Clark when found if ever thay be.

This day John Kiphaven proved by his oath that the Estate of otto woollgast deceased standeth Justly Indebted unto him as followeth; [etc.].

Luke Wattson John Kiphaven Wm; Clark Signed the Dockett.

Janwary 10th, 1681.

Att A Court Held for the Towne and County of Deale By the Kings Authority the 10th day of the Moneth Called Janwary Anno; Dm; 1681; Commiconers present Luke Wattson John Roades John Kiphaven William Clark.

Plea upon the Case. Capt John Avery plt, Peter Groundyk deft; the Court Cause an non suit to be entered Agt the plt with Cost of suit Alias Execution.

An Action of the Case. Capt John Avery plt, Beniamin Coudrey deft; Robt Hart senr wittnes & Halm Wiltbanck.

An Action of Debt; [Tobacco] William Clark plt, Robt Johnson deft; Execution given out 10th, 12 mo; 1681.

[Debt 15½ "Bushells" of Indian Corn.] Jacob Shaltham plt, Thomas Davids deft.

An Action of the Case upon a Repleavey. Peter Groundyk plt, Halm Wiltbanck deft; [In re. to same piece of "Clorth" mentioned previously.]

Halm Wiltbanck plt, Peter Groundyk deft. In december Court the deft not being here and there not being A full Court of Justices without the defts Atturney; the Cause was Refered unto this Court; the plt declare that he sent seaven Beavers and A halfe by the deft to be delivered unto Capt Mountveale at new york; which the deft owne that he ded not deliver them; According to the plts order the Court therefor passe Judgment Agt the deft for the seaven Beavers and a halfe with Cost of suit Alias Execution.

An Action of the Case upon an Attachment. Peter Groundyk plt, William Carter Adminstrator to otto Woollgast Estate deft; with drawen."

An Action of the Case. ffrancis Rumbolt plt, William Carter Administrator to otto Woollgast Estate deft. In december Court the plt not being here and there not being A full Court of Justices without the plts Atturney being John Kiphaven the Cause was Refered untill this Court the plt declars that otto Woollgast was Indebted unto him upon Account in the year 1674; In the sume of one hundred sixty six gilders. But the plt not proveing any Lawfull demand in all that time of the said sume; and the deft pleades the statute of Limentaticon the Court there for order an non suit to be entered Agt the plt with Cost of suit Alias Execution.

An Action of the Case. ffrancis Rumbolt plt, Harmon Cornelison deft. * * * The plt declars that the deft stands indebted unto him upon Account in the yeare 1674; In the sume of 128 gilders to be paid in Beaver * * * [This case is similar to the preceding one.]

An Action of Debt. Thomas Atthow plt, Henry Stracher & William Clark defts. In december Court there not being a full Court of Justices without one of the defts the Cause was Refered untill this Court The plt declare by his Atturney John Hill that the defts stands Justly Indebted by there obligacon under there hands and seales in forteene Thousand pounds of Tobacco; Conditioned for the makeing a good tittel of the Land & premisses that Henry Stracher one of the defts now Live upon unto the plt or his Assignes the defts Craves a Referance untill the next Court which the Court Grant them.

An Action of Debt. Capt Marton Creagor plt, Anthony Hamen Alias Haverly deft. "Refered."

Attachment. Harmon Cornelison plt, The Estate of John Shackley deceased in the Custidy of Alex Moulston deft. In december Court the plt declare that the Estate of John Shackley deceased stands Justly Indebted unto him in seaven hundred sixty five pounds of Tobacco Two Beavers in Peltrey And fortye gilders all upon A Judgmt obtained in this Court the 13th day of April 1680; Agt the Estate of the sd John Shackley deceased as by the records it doth Appear

* * * The Court doe still refere passing Judgment for the plt untill the next Court.

An Action of the Case. Samwell Gray plt, Cornelias Creagor deft; with drawen by order of the plt.

An Action of the Case. John Kiphaven plt, William Carter deft; with drawen by Consent and the deft to pay Cost of suit.

An Action of Debt. Richard Bundock plt, William Davids deft; with drawen by order of the plt and deft.

An Action of Debt. Peter Groundyk plt, Halm Wiltbanck deft; * * * the defts pleads payment and Craves A Referance untill the next Court to prove the same which the Court Grant.

Upon the Complaint of Parritt the Indian Shackamacker Alleadging that Henry Bowman and others takes his Lands and gives him no satisfacon for it; the Court doe therefor order that every person that seate any Land shall pay unto the Indian proprietor for every parcell of Land of six hundred Acres or under one Match Coote and if a bove six hundred Acres Two Match Cootes; And that at the time of the Indian Receiveing the Coote or Cootes to Convey the sd Land to the person that he receive the sd Coote or Cootes of; And if any person doe or shall refuse to pay the Indians for the Land as a forsaid; Executcon to be given out for the same directed to the shreife to Execute and pay to the Indian.

William Townsend peticon Agt Halm Wiltbanck. The peticoner setts forth that he moved brought and sett up 450 Logs on the Towne Lotts Intending to fence and plant there by the defts sence which the deft have carried the Logs or part of them away & Converted them to his own use; the peticoner therfor Craves order of this Court for his Labour; it is agreed by the peticoner and the deft that he shall have what he sold to William [donneall?] and no more.

The Court fines John Barnett fifty pounds of Tobacco for smocking Tobacco in the Court.

The Court Grant unto William Clark five hundred Acres of Land; warrant Given out the 6th, 12 mo, 1681.

The Court Grant unto Thomas Pemberton Eighte hundred Acres of Land; warrant given out the 6th, 12 mo, 1681.

The Court Grant unto Phillip Morrise one hundred Acres of Land more then what he had a grant for befor; warrant Given out 10th 11 mo, 1681; for the whole.

The Court Grant unto william page foure hundred Acres of Land; warrant Given out the 11th 11 mo, 1681.

Luke Wattson John Roades John Kiphaven Wm. Clark Signed the Dockett.

Ffebruary 14th, 1681.

Att a Court Held att Deale for the Towne and County of Deale by the Kings Authority the 14th day of the Moneth Called ffebruary Anno; Dm; 1681. Commisconers present: Luke Wattson, John Roades, John Kiphaven, William Clark.

An Action of Debt. Thomas Atthow plt, Henry Stracher & William Clark defts. In December Court there not being a full Court of Justices without one of the defts; the Cause was refered untill Janwry Court at which time the plt declared by his Atturney John Hill That the defts Stands Justly Indebted unto the plt by there obligacon under there hands & seales in forteene Thousand pounds of good sound Merchantable Tobacco in Caske; Conditconed for the Makeing good tittel of the Land & premisses that Henry Stracher one of the defts now Live upon; unto the plt or his Assignes; the defts Craves a referance unto this Court which the Court Granted them; this Court the defts promiseing to Asure and Convey the said Land befor the next Court the Cause is therefor by the Court refered untill the next Court.

An Action of Debt. Capt Martton Creagor plt, Anthony Hamen alias Haverle deft. [By Consent of plt, refered from Dec. Court to Jan., and from Jan. Court to March Court.]

An Action of Debt upon An Attachment. Harmon Cornelison plt, the Estate of John Shackley deceased in the Custice of Alex Moulston deft. * * * the Court ded Refere passing Judgmt untill this Court whare the Administrator was three times called and he or they not Appearing the Court passe Judgment for the plt Agt the Effects of the said John Shackley deceased that is in the Custidy of the said Alex Moulston being one Thousand one hundred and fortye pounds of Tobacco Alias Executcon.

An Action of Debt. Peter Groundyke plt, Halm Wiltbanck deft.

An Action of Debt. ffrancis Gunby plt, Richard Lawes deft; ["non-suit"].

An Action of ye Case. Halm Wiltbanck plt, Anthony Hamen deft; ["refered untill the next Court"].

An Action of the Case. Anthony Hamen plt, Cornelis Johnson deft; the plt and deft being prevented from Coming by reason of bad weather the Court order that the Cause be refered untill the next Court.

An Action of the Case. Nortton Claypoole plt, John Oakey Deft; ["refered untill the next Court"].

An Action of the Case. Richard Bundock plt, Cornelis Johnson deft; ["with Drawen"].

An Action of Debt. Nortton Claypoole plt, John Johnson Senr Deft; ["Judgmt for the plt * * * with Cost of suit Alias Execution"].

Action of the Case. William Carter Adminstrator to the Estate of Otto Woollgast deceased Plt, Robert Johnson Deft; [Judgmt for the plt * * * with Cost of suit Alias Execution;"].

An Action of Trasspasse upon the Case. Luke Wattson Plt, Henry Skidemor deft; wittnes Hen Smith & Hen Bowman. The plt declare that he was possessed of a Tract of Land on Slatter neck; and that the deft ded Cutt his trees and timber and Committed A Trasspase on the Plts Land to the daimag of the Plt five and Twenty pounds sterl money the deft by his Atturney Edward Southrin pleads that the sd Lands is the defts, the Cause is put to the triall of A Jurey which went out and after debate Brought in there verdict that they find for the Plt with Twelve pence daimg and Cost of suit the Court passe Judgmt for the Plt According to the verdict of the Jurey Alias Execution. Jurey men—Halm Wiltbanck Samwell Gray John Hill Edward Williams William Carter Alex Moulston William Rodeney.

An Action of Trasspasse upon the Case. Henry Bowman plt, Alexander draper deft; wittnes Cor verhoofe Henry Smith Junr

Harmon Cornelison. The plt declares that the deft have Committed a Traspass upon his Land by Cutting his trees and Timber; the deft pleades that the Land is his the Cause is put to a Jurey which went out and brought in there verdict; the plt being three times Called in Court and not Appearing suffered an non suit; Jury men Halm wiltbank Sam Gray John Hill will Carter Alexander Moulston John depree William Rodeney.

An Action of Debt. Henry Smith Plt, daniell Browne deft; ["refered untill the next Court;"].

An Action of Debt. Henry Smith Plt, Will Clark deft; ["refered untill the next Court'"].

The Court fines William Rodeney fifty pounds of Tobacco for smocking Tobacco in the Court.

The Court Grant unto James Gray one Thousand Acres of Land warrant given out the same day.

The Court Grant unto John Maccomb five hundred Acres of Land; warrant Given out the same day.

The Court Grant unto Alex Moulston five hundred Acres of Land; warrant Given out the same day.

John Roades have to this day pay due to him for foure woolfes heads.

The Court Grant unto Thomas Hassold foure hundred Acres of of Land; warrant Given out ye 25 12 mo, 1681.

The Court Grant unto Robert Warrin three hundred Acres of Land warrant Given out 15th Insint.

The Court Grant unto Thomas dunton six hundred Acres of Land warrant Given out the 15th Insint.

The Court Grant unto John Hill Two Hundred Acres of Land to be aded to his former grant of three hundred Acres; wart given out the 24th 12 mo, 1681.

The Court Grant unto John Kiphaven five hundred Acres of Land warrant Given out the same day.

The Court Grant unto William Rodeney five hundred Acres of Land warrant Given out the same day.

* * * unto Nortton Claypoole—500 acres—warrant 27th 12 mo, 1681.

* * * unto Robert Hudson—500 acres—warrant 31th 11 mo, 1682.

* * * unto William Trippoth—300 acres—warrant 31th 11 mo, 1682.

* * * unto Samwell Gray—500 acres—warrant 6th 11 mo, 1682.

* * * unto Richard Lawes—200 acres—warrant 24th 12 mo, 1681; ["to be Aded to his former Grant of three hundred Acres;"].

A deede of Conveyance of 150 Acres of Land in Kickoutneck past and Accknowlidge by Anthony Inlose unto John Kiphaven and to his heires and assignes forever.

A deed of Conveyance of three hundred Acres of Land in Kickout neck past and Accknowlidged by Alex Moulston & Robert Trayle unto John Kiphaven and to his heires and Assignes for ever.

* * * unto Edward Williams—500 Acres—warrant 24th 12 mo, 1681.

"A patton and Conveyance" of 196 Acres "this day Assigned by Luke Wattson unto Samwell Gray," etc., "being the Land Called

St Giles Lyeing in a neck Called Parritts neck Adjoyning unto the Land of Daniell Browne near Pagan Creeke;"

Upon the peticon of Henry Skidemor for a new Trial in the Cause that was this day trid betwene Luke Wattson and the petr the Court doe grant order that if the peticoner please he may have a new trial the next Court.

Ordered by the Court that the Certivecates that Cornelis verhoofe this day presented to the Court to be signed Allowed by the Court being now in the Custidy of the Clark; be Certified and signed save onely that of Nathanil Walker that hath took in the house plantacon and Land that Thomas and night Haward Live upon seated and have a patton for it and one of Stephen whetmans that doe take away the previlidg of John Kiphaven goeing to the Marsh onely excepted.

Luke Wattson the presedent of this Court enters his desent as to the order of a non Trial betwene himselfe and Henry Skidemore.

Luke Wattson John Roades John Kiphaven William Clark, Signed the Dockett.

The persons under named ware fined by the Court for not working in the High ways after Leagaly warned there unto as followeth;

	Tobacco.		Tobacco
William Durvalls man	100 ℔	Will Page	050 ℔
John Roades	100	Cornelis Johnson	050
John Kiphaven	100	Richard Patte	050
William Clark	100	Daniell Browne	050
Alex Moulston	100	Thomas denison	050
Nortton Claypoole	100	Thomas Streacher	050
Henry Bowman	100	Robert Johnson	050
John Hill	100	Barnwell Jackson	050
William ffootcher	200	ffrancis Gunby	050
Will Emitt	050	Thomas Hassold	050
Mathias Everson	050	Robert Mudock	050
Richard Shoulter	050	Thomas Haward	050
	1150		600

MARCH 14th, 15th, 1681.

Att A Court Held at Deale for the Towne and County of Deale By the Kings Authority the 14th and 15th days of the Moneth Called March Anno Dm: 1681-82; Justices present; Luke Wattson John Roades John Kiphaven William Clark.

An Action of Debt. Thomas Atthow plt, Henry Stracher and William Clark defts. [Cause refered from December Court last past untill Janwary Court; * * * when the defts Craved A referance untill febuary Court. * * * In Feburey Court the defts promising to Asure and Convey the sd Land befor or at the next Court; the Cause was therefor by the Court Refered untill this Court; at which time the said Land and premisses was Conveyed & Asured unto nortton Claypoole the Assignes of the plt; whare for the plt Atturney with drawes the Action; in open Court; by Consent of the defts.]

An Action of Debt. Capt Marton Creagor Plt, Anthony Hancen Alias Haverly deft. [Refered from December Court untill Janwary Court; then untill March Court; and in March Court the sd Cause was by Consent of the Plt Atturney Cor Verhoofe Refered untill the next Court.]

An Action of Debt. Peter Groundyk plt, Halm Wiltbanck deft. The Cause having been refered from both the "Janwary" Court and the "febuary" Court, is now-in the March Court "refered untill the next Court."

An Action of the Case. Halm Wiltbanck Plt, Anthony Hamen deft. * * * the deft being prevented by bad wheather from Coming to [the February] Court; the Court refered the Cause untill this Court [when it was tried by Jury—verdict—the plt had no Cause of Action—and Should pay Cost of suit]. Alias Execution. Jurey men—[E]d williams Jos Barsteede Danll Browne [H]en Stracher will Rodeney Andrew depree [J]ohn depree.

An Action of the Case. Anthony Hamen Plt, Cornelis Johnson deft. In febuary Court the Plt and deft being prevented from Coming to the Court by reasion of bad wheather * * * [refered untill this Court] * * * Court order an non suit to be entered for the deft Agt the plt wt Cost of suit Alias Executon.

An Action of the Case. nortton Claypoole Plt, John oakey deft. [Referred from Feb. Court to this Court; the Action now "with drawen."]

An Action of Debt. Henry Smith Plt, Daniell Browne deft. In febuary Court the deft being out of the County his wife Craved A Reference untill this Court and this Court the plt declared by his Atturney Thomas Hassold that the deft stands Indebted unto him in one Thousand seaven hundred and fiftye pounds of pork; the deft promise to pay the sd sume by the next Court and Craved a referance untill then which the Court Granted.

An Action of Debt. Henry Smith plt, William Clark deft. [From Feb. Court, and now withdrawn.]

An Action of the Case. Halm Wiltbanck Plt, ffrancis Gunby deft. [Judgment for the Plt Agt the deft for the said sume of 876℔ of Tobacco with Cost of suit; Alias Execution.]

An Action of the Case. William Trotter Plt, Edward Southrin deft; the plt declare that the deft dĕd stop and detayne his working Tooles and a Cart wheale & other goods the Court doe order that the deft doe forth with deliver unto the plt his said Tooles wheale and other goods with Cost of suit Alias Execution.

An Action of the Case. ffrancis Gunby plt, Halm wiltbanck deft; * * * the Court therefor passe Judgment for the plt Agt the deft for the said sume of 940 ℔ of Tobacco with Cost of suit Alias Execution.

Henry Skidemore plt or peticoner Agt Luke Wattson; * * * the Court order an non suit to be entered Agt the plt with Cost of suit Alias Execution.

An Action of the Case. Capt John Avery plt, Richard Patte deft; ["with drawen in open Court"].

An Action of the Case. Halm wiltbanck Plt, Henry Bowman deft; [non suit entered].

An Action of Debt. William Clark Plt, John Hagester deft; [Judgment for plt].

An Action of the Case. William Darvall Plt, Cornelis Johnson deft; [Judgment for plt].

An Action of the Case. Halm Wiltbanck Plt, William Townsend deft; [with drawn in open Court].

An Action of the Case upon an Attachment. William Clark Plt, James Welles Estate in Custidy of Alex draper deft.

An Action of the Case upon An Attachment. William Darvall Plt, James Welles Estate in Custidy of Alex Draper deft; ["with drawen"].

An Action of Trasspase and Ejectment. Henry Bowman Plt, Alex Draper deft; ["with drawen"].

An Action of the Case upon an Attachment. William Clark Plt, Daniell Browne Estate in the sd Plts hands deft; * * * the Cause is refered untill the next Court.

An Action of Debt. John Hagester Plt, William Emitt deft. Refered untill the next Court.

The Court Grant unto William Keninge three hundred Acres of Land; wart Given out the 11th 2 mo, 1682.

The Court Grant unto Jacob Shattain Three hundred Acres of Land; Warrant Given out the 15th Insint.

* * * unto William Wargent, 300 Acres; Warrant 2 2 mo, 1682.

* * * unto William Dunton, 400 Acres; Warrant 18 1 mo, 1682.

* * * unto Daniell Darby, 600 Acres; Warrant 11 2 mo, 1682. renewed ye 11th 7 br, 86.

* * * unto Thomas Hall, 600 Acres; Warrant 11th 2 mo, 1682.

* * * unto John vines, 400 Acres; Warrant 2th 2 mo, 1682.

* * * unto Jeffrey Sumerford, 300 Acres; Warrant 2th 2 mo, 1682.

* * * unto Richard Tendall, 400 Acres; Warrant 2th 2 mo, 1682.

* * * unto Samwell Heights, 400 Acres; Warrant 2th 2 mo, 1682.

* * * unto Robert foster, 900 Acres; Warrant 18th 1 mo, 1682.

* * * unto Robert Burtton, 600 Acres; by Baptis newcomb; Warrant 5th 2 mo, 1682.

* * * unto Abraham Potter, 300 Acres; Warrant 4th 2 mo, 1682.

* * * unto Henry Moulston, 500 Acres; Warrant the same day.

* * * unto John Barrows, 400 Acres; Warrant same day; Wart given out 18th 1 mo, 1682.

* * * unto Harcklos Sheepard, 300 Acres; Wart 16th day of same mo.

* * * unto Richard Harvey, 300 Acres; Wart 2th 8 mo, 1682.

* * * unto John Townsend, 500 Acres; Wart same day.

* * * unto Thomas Besent, 500 Acres; Wart same day.

The Court Grant unto Edward Southrin the three hundred Acres of Land that was Edward Cooks if free from the Lawfull Claime of all other persons; warrant Given out the same day.

* * * unto John Roades, five hundred Acres; wart 18th 1 mo, 1682.

* * * unto Michell Chambers, 300 Acres; wart 10th 2 mo, 1682.

* * * unto Francis Gunby, 400 Acres; wart 4th 2 mo, 1682.

* * * unto John Depree, 300 Acres; wart 9th 3 mo. 1682.

* * * unto Jacob Depree, 300 Acres; wart 9th 3 mo, 1682.

* * * unto Halm Wiltbanck, 500 Acres; wart 18th 1 mo, 1682.

The Court Grant unto William Planer one Thousand Acres of Land upon Slatter neck whare Henry Skidemore now Live on Condition that he takes into his survey no Land that any other person have any Lawfull Claim unto; Warrant given out the 5th 8th mo, 1683.

* * * unto Cornelis verhoofe, 1000 Acres; Warrant 2th 2 mo, 82.

* * * unto Henry Stracher, 800 Acres; Warrant 18 Insint.

A patton & Conveyance of Land being six hundred Acres Accknowlidged in open Court by John depree unto John Saviadge and to his heires and Assignes forever.

John oakey Peticoner. The peticoner sett forth that severall persons are Indebted unto him for sarveing of warrt when he was Constable and Craves that the fees that are due to him may be taken By distrase; which the Court Grant; According to the Laws of the Goverment.

Joshua Barsteade Peticoner Agt John vines Shreife. The peticoner setting forth that he was unJustly Accused & Imprisoned for being A Confeaderate with Trayters And A Concealer of Treasion for which Crimes he was Cleared by the Court from being Guilty; not withstanding John vines Shreife doe threaten to distrayne for his prison fees upon the debate of the matter the Court find that the warrant that the peticoner was committed upon was not According to Law the Court doe therefor order that the sd Shreif doe not take any fees of the peticoner for his said Imprissonment.

Wm. ffootcher Peticoner Agt John Johnson Junr. The peticoner sett forth that he disbursted five hundred pounds of Tobacco for the deft to save him from Corporall ponishment the Last year; and that he ran the Hasard of Looseing it if the said deft should a done other ways then well; the Court doe therefor order that the deft doe pay unto the plt six hundred pounds of Tobacco with Cost of suit Alias Execution.

A patton and Conveyance of Land Accknowlidged in open Court by Halmainas Wiltbanck unto Nortton Claploope [sic]; the sd Land Lyeing and Being Betwene the Land of william Clark and Luke wattson at the Towne of Deale; And at the same time nortton Claypoole doe promise and Ingage to Convey and a sure unto Anthony Hamen Alias Haverly Twenty Acres of the afor said Land; which was sold by Henry Stracher and is now in the possession of the sd Anthony Hamen alias haverly.

Robert Hignett Peticoner Agt william footcher. The peticoner sett forth that he put his sun An Apprantices with william footcher for Tenn yeares and that the deft was oblidgd and did give unto his said Apprantices an Heffer; and that the said Apprentices being sence dead the peticoner Craves an order for the said Heffer to be and remayne to the next Heires at Law, and the deft refusing to give his oath that he gave the Heffer to the sd servant the Court doe order that the peticoner shall have his request and that the deft doe deliver the said Heffer to the peticoner for the use of the next Heire at Law being the sd sarvants youngest Brother with Cost of suit and the sd Heffer and hur encrease to be to the onely proper use and behoofe of the sd heire at Law for ever.

The Grand Jurey present Barnwell Jackson and william Trotter for falling A Tree in the Kings High ways for which the Court fine them ffiftye pounds of Tobacco; Betwene them.

The Grand Jurey present John oakey for haveing a strang Child at his house which is not Certainly knowen whoes it is; Henry Bowman doe Ingage to save the County Harmless from being put to any Charge for the maintaining of the said Child.

It is agreed and Concluded upon by the Court and Alexandr Moulston as followeth; that from the first day of this moneth the said Alexandr Moulston shall have to his owne proper use all the Amacements that doe from that day becom due to the Court for one whole yeare; and that the said Allix Moulston doe Ingage to find and allow the Justices of this Court for the time being and there freinds and strangers with house roome and diett And one gallon of Rum and wine for every Court during the said year.

April 11th, 1682.

Att A Court Held at Deale for the Towne and County of Deale by the Kings Authority the 11th day of the Moneth Called April Anno; Dom; 1682, Commiconers present Luke Wattson John Roades John Kiphaven William Clark.

An Action of debt. Capt Marton Creagor plt, Anthony Hamen Alias Haverla deft. [The Cause refered from month to month since December and now until the June Court. Plts Attorney—Corn verhoofe.]

An Action of Debt. Peter Groundyk Plt, Halm Wiltbanck. [Refered from the different Courts since January. Now "with drawen".]

An Action of Debt. Capt Henry Smith Plt, daniell Browne deft. [Since "febuary Court." Alias Execution.]

An action of the Case. William Clark Plt, daniel Browns Estate in the defts hands deft; [referred until June Court].

An Action of Debt. John Hagester Plt, William Emitt deft; ["with drawen"].

An Action of the Case. Halm wiltbanck plt, Henry Bowman deft; * * * the deft not being well and the weather not being fitt to Travile in; the Court grant the deft Referance untill the next Court.

An Action of the Case. William footcher Plt, Robert Hignett deft; * * * but the weatther not being fitt to Travile in; the Court Grant the deft A referance untill the next Court.

Traspasse of the Case. Baptis newcomb Plt, John Daniell deft; Wittneses Cor verhoofe Robt Bracey Junr Rich Shoulter. The plt declares that the deft did on or about the 21th day of the Moneth Called March Last past make a forceable Entrey into the plts house and by force of Arms hath and still and still doth keepe the plt out of his house and from making A Crop on the said Land; to his damiag fortye pounds sterl money; The Plt proved by the oath of Cornelis verhoofe that he surveyed the sd Land by vertue of A warrant from this Court for the Plt on or about the —— and the other Two wettneses Robt Bracey Junr and Rich Shoulter swore that the Deft did by force keepe the plt out of his said house; the deft pleaded by his Atturney Capt John Avery that his Master nathanil Bradford have A right to the sd Land, and Craved a referance untill the next Court to prove the same.

An Action of the Case upon an Attachment. Capt Tho. dellavall plt, Capt Henry Smith deft. The Plt declare by his Agent William Rodeney * * * ["with drawen"].

An Action of the Case. Peter Groundyk Plt, Corn verhoofe deft. The Plt declares that the deft stands Justly Indebted unto him in one Thousand nine hundred fiftye one gilders and fifteene stivers of wampon upon Account produced in Court the deft Craved A Referance untill the next Court; the Court grant the deft A refernce untill the next Court; with drawen.

An Action of the Case. Peter Groundyk plt, Corn verhoofe Deft. The Plt declares that the deft stand Justly Indebted unto him in six Cows with Calfe or Calves by there sides; which the deft sold for the Plt Att a vandue as vandue master and that the deft hath not paid the Plt for the same or given him any Account to whome the same ware sold; the deft plead that he have not his wittneses in a radynes to Answer this Court, and there for Craves a referance untill the next Court; which the Court Grant; with drawen.

An Action of the Case. William Darvall Plt, Henry Bowman deft. The Plt declares that the deft stand Justly Indebted unto him in Twenty foure pounds Dutch waight of dear skins and in [money or peltrey, in Indian Corn, Pork and Tobacco] * * * the Court granted a referance untill the next Court; at the deft request by his potcion [being ill].

An Action of debt. Cornelis verhoofe Plt, Peter Groundyk deft; Wittnes John vines & Halmanis Wiltbanck. The Plt declars that the deft stands Indebted unto him in three hundred nintye Two pounds of Tobacco; by soe much the deft received of the Plt of John Roades and past his bill to bring or send the produce in Linen from new York * * *.

An Action of debt. Capt nathanil Walker, Assine of Henry Able Plt, Peter Groundyk deft. The Plt declare by his Atturney Cornelis verhoofe that the deft stands Indebted unto him in * * * as Assine of Henry Able by bill then produced in Court. * * * the Court order an nonsuit to be entered Agt the Plt with Cost Alias Execution.

An Action of the Case. Halm Wiltbanck Plt, Henry Bowman deft. With drawen by order of the Plt and the shreife it being a mistake in a resting the deft upon Two wretts for one and the same debt.

An Action of the Case. Henry Stracher Plt, Peter Groundyk deft; [referred until next Court].

An Action of the Case. John King Plt, Will ffootcher deft. The Plt declars that the deft stands Indebted unto him in foure Cows and the encrease of them for seaven years; the deft deneys it; and the Plt not proveing his declaracon or any part of it the Court order an non suit to be entered Agt the Plt with Cost of suit Alias Execution.

An Action of the Case. Edward Williams Plt, Halm Wiltbanck deft. * * * The Court ordered an non suit to be entered Agt the Plt with Cost of suit Alias Execution.

Peticoner. William ffootcher Agt John King. The peticoner sett forth that the deft did promise and agree to Asure and Convey unto the Plt the three hundred Acres of Land that the peticoner Live upon ye deft haveing received satisfacon for the same; the deft not Appearing the Court refer the Cause untill the next Court; with drawen.

Cornelis verhoofe Agt Peter Groundyk by way of fire facous; ["refered untill the next Court"].

An Action of the Case. Halm Wiltbanck Plt, francis Gunby deft; ["referance untill the next Court;" "with drawen"].

An Action of the Case. ffrancis Gunby Plt, Halm Wiltbanck deft; ["Refered * * * untill ye next Court, with drawen"].

An Action of the Case. Halm Wiltbanck Plt, Peter Groundyk deft. The plt declars that the deft stands Indebted unto him in six hundred sixty six pounds of Tobacco; by taking and Converting to his owne use soe much of the plt Tob; of and from the plantacon that Cornelis Johnson now Live upon being about Two years Last past; * * * ["Refered"].

The Court Grant unto Simon Parling five hundred Acres of Land; Wart Given out 13th 2 mo, 1682.

* * * unto Thomas Hasell, 300 Acres; Warrant 17th Insint.

* * * unto Charles Spooner, 300 Acres; Warrant 12th Insint.

The Court Grant unto Capt John Avery the Island Lyeing in Rehover Bay Adjoyning unto the land that the sd Capt Avery now Live upon & to be surveyed and Aded to his Land he live on; wart given out the 16th Insint.

The Court Grant unto Joseph Lowe three hundred Acres of Land; wart Given out the 7th 7 mo, 1682.

* * * unto ffrancis Henry, 500 Acres; Warrant 12th 3 mo, 1682.

* * * unto Mathew Taylor, 500 Acres; Warrant 9th 3 mo, 1682.

* * * unto Rich Kockshall, 300 Acres; Warrant 16 Insint.

* * * unto Stephen Whetman, 600 Acres; Warrant "the same day."

* * * unto david Corsey, 300 Acres; Warrant "the same day."

Cornelis verhoofe peticon the Court that he may have an order of Court to Attache the Estate of Rich dawson for his Clarks and surveyors fees which are due to him; which the Court Grant unto the peticoner.

Nathanil Bradford peticons that he may have A warrant to survey the Twelve hundred Acres of Land into one survey that he bought of John Hagester which the Court Grant unto the peticoner; wart given out 13th 4 mo, 1682.

* * * unto Thomas Hassold, 200 Acres "to be Aded unto his former grant; wart Given out 12th Insint.

* * * unto William Emitt, 400 Acres; Warrant 12th Insint.

* * * unto William Simons, 300 Acres; Warrant 11th 3 mo, 1682.

* * * unto John Clark, 500 Acres; Warrant 17th Insint, to John Townsend.

* * * unto Henry Eubanck, 300 Acres; Warrant 17th Insint, to Tho besent.

The Court Grant unto Peter Groundyk A Calld Court to be held to morrow the 12 Insint to Try & determin the 2 Causes that are depending Betwene the said Peter Groundyk plt and Cornelis verhoofe deft that ware this day refered to the next Court.

The Court order the Clark to draw up An Account of the Amacements that are due to the Court; and to deliver it to the shreife and the Court doe order the shreife forth with After it Com in to his hands to take the same by disstrase; or other ways to take the severall parsons bills for the payment of the severall sumes the 10th day of october next.

April 12th, 1682.

Att A Calld Court Held at Deale by the Kings Authority the 12th day of the Moneth Called April Anno: Dm; 1682. Commiconers present, Luke Wattson, John Roades, John Kiphaven, william Clark.

An Action of the Case. Peter Groundyk plt, Cornelis verhoofe deft. The plt declars that the deft stands Indebted unto him in one Thousand nine hundred fiftye one gilder and fifteene stivers of wampon * * * the Court pass Judgmt for the plt * * * Alias Execution; Execution given out same day Agt the body of the deft.

An Action of the Case. Peter Groundyk plt, Cornelis verhoofe deft. The plt declars that the deft tooke upon him selfe to sell six Cows of the plts for him as vandue Master which the deft have given the plt no Account or satisfacon for the said Cattell; the deft pleads that the Cattell that he sold at A vandue was none of the plts but that they ware at that time Capt John Averys. The plt proved by the oath of John vines shreife that five of the Cows that was sold at the vandue by the deft; was the Cattell of the plts. * * * [Judgment for the plt.]

May 10th, 1682.

Att A Calld Court Held at Deale by the Kings Authority the 10th day of the Moneth Called May Anno; Dm; 1682. Commiconers present Luke Wattson John Kiphaven William Clark.

An Action of the Case. Cornelis verhoofe plt, Peter Groundyk deft. The plt declare that the deft stands Indebted unto him in seaven hundred ninty three gilders and Twelve stivers by an Account produced in Court. * * * [Judgment for the plt.]

An Action of the Case. Cornelis verhoofe plt, Peter Groundyke deft. The plt declars that the deft stand Indebted unto him in seaven hundred ninty one gild upon Account produced in Court Agt the deft; being mostly for Atturneys fees and work done a bout his sloop; the deft haveing nedglexted to take A Copie of the said Account from the Clark; Craves of the Court that he may have Two or three hours time to vew the said Account befor he pleads to it; which the Court Granted unto the deft; and the deft had the Account delivered to him According to his request and after he had vewed it returne into the Court and pleaded that the plt promise that he would not take any Atturney fees of the deft for the manigmt of his affairs and that for the worke he had done about the defts sloop he had pd the plt for it; but did not prove his plea; the Court finding that the plt have Charged to much in his sd Account for Atturneys fees; the Court Allow him onely foure hundred Gilders for his Atturneys fees; and the rest of the said Account being fiftye one Gilders the plt swaring to it; the Court passe Judgment for the plt. * * * with Cost of suit Alias Executcion.

An Action of the Case. Cornelis verhoofe plt, Peter Groundyk deft. The plt declare that the deft stands Indebted to him * * * [Tobacco, part of which being an Assigned bill of Henry Able to nathanil walker * * * Judgment for plt * * * with cost of suit; Alias Execution.

An Action of the Case. Cornelis verhoofe Plt, Peter Groundyk deft. The Plt declare that the deft Imployed him to sell at A vandue severall Cows; and that the deft sued the Plt in this Court and recovered Judgment of Court Agt the Plt for the Effects that the sd Cows ware sold at; being fine Cows; and the deft tooke out Execution upon the sd Judgment of Court and Charged the same on the body of the plt; not withstanding the deft have received of John Hill Eighte hundred Twenty one pounds of Tobacco at halfe a peney ℔ lb. in part of payment of one of said fine Cows which was sold for fortye seaven shillings; and one of the said fine Cows the deft bought at the vandue himselfe at 33 shill both which the deft owne in Court; the Court therefor passe Judgment for the Plt Agt the deft for the said sumes of Eighte hundred Twenty one pounds of Tobacco at halfe peney ℔ lb. and one pound thurteene shill with cost of suit Alias Execution.

The Court fine Peter Groundyke for smoking Tobacco in the Court fiftye pounds of Tobacco.

The Court fine Cornelis verhoofe for smoking Tobacco in Court fiftye pounds of Tobacco.

The Court fine Mathias vandehyden for smoking Tobacco in the Court fiftye pounds of Tobacco.

The Court order Cornelis verhoofe to receive of Peter Groundyk the Amacemts due to the Court from the said Peter Groundyk in the time that the said Cornelis verhoofe was Clark of this Court And upon non payment on demand Execution is to Issue out Agt the said Peter Groundyk for the sd Amacements of Court; Alias Execution; and the sd Corn verhoofe to be Accountable to the Court for what he shall receive.

Cornelis verhoofe produceing in Court An Account Agt Peter Groundyk for Clarks fees being the sume of one Thousand three hundred Twenty seaven gilders due to him for fees in the time that he was Clark of this Court; and Craves an Execution Agt the said Peter Groundyk for the said sume; (the Court Excamining the peticlors Charged in the said Account for Clark fees) doe order that if the said Peter Groundyk doe not pay the said sume on demand that then Execution shall be given out Agt the said Peter Groundyk for the said sume of one Thousand Three hundred Twenty seaven gilders.

JUNE 13th, 14th, 1682.

Att A Court Held at Deale for the Towne and County of Deale By the Kings Authoritye the 13th and 14th days of the Moneth Called June, Anno; Dm; 1682. Commiconers present: Luke Wattson John Kiphaven William Clark.

An Action of Debt. Capt Marton Creagor Plt, Anthony Hamen Alias Haverla deft; [Cornelis verhoofe the Plts Atturney. "The Cause was refered" from the December Court, appearing each month, and now is "Refered * * * untill the next Court"].

An Action of the Case. William Clark Plt, Daniell Browne Estate in the Plt hands Deft; [Carried over from March Court, and now "Judgment is Refered untill September Court"].

An Action of the Case. Halm Wiltbanck Plt, Henry Bowman Deft. In April Court * * * the deft not Being well and the weather not being fitt to Travile in; the Court Grant the deft A Referance untill June Court; and in June Court the Plt ordered that the Action be with drawen.

An Action of the Case. William footcher Plt, Robert Hignett Deft. In Ap Court * * * the weather not being fitt to Travil in the Court Grant the deft A Referance untill this Court. * * * soe that the Court passe Judgmt for the Plt * * * with Cost of suit Alias Execution.

An Action of Traspass of the Case. Baptis newcomb Plt, John Daniell Deft. Wittneses Robt Bracey senr Robt Bracey Junr John Johnson senr Rich Shoulter Mathias Everson. In April Court the Plt declared that the deft did on or about the 21th day of Moneth Called March Last past make a forceable entery into the Plt house and by force of Arms hath and still doth keepe the Plt out of his house; and from makeing A Crop on the said Land to the Plt damiag ffortye pounds sterling money; the Plt proved by the oath of Corn verhoofe that he surveyed the said Land by vertue of A wart obtained from this Court for the Plt on or about the moneth of December Last past; And the other Two wittneses Robt Bracey Junr and Richard Shoulter sware that the deft did by force keepe the Plt out of his sd house; the deft pleaded by his Atturney Capt John Avery that his master nathanil Bradford have a right to the said Land; And Craves A Reference untill the next Court to prove the same which the Court Granted; In June Court the deft prove by the oath of Richard Shoulter that nathanil Bradford did Clear part of the said Land and did plant sume Corn on the said Clear Land; And did hire sume men to build A house on the said Land; which men did deceive him; Mathias Everson sware that he did worke foure days on the said Land by order of nathanil Bradfor [sic] Towards the geting A frame for A house; the Plt proved by the oath of Robert Bracey senr that the Plt built the first house on the said Land; and Robert Bracey Junr sware that there never was any Corn Tended on the said Land by the said nathanil Bradford or his order; but that there was About one hundred Corn hills made on the said Land the Cause was Left to A Jurey of Twelve men and debated on both sids [sic] after which the Jurey went out and brought in there verdict that they finde for the Plt Twelve pence daimage with cost of suit; the Court passe Judgmt According to the verdict of the Jurey Alias Execution; Jurey men nortton Claypoole Alexander Draper Samwell Gray Halmaines wiltbanck Richard Lawes Henry Stracher William Carter Anthony Hamen william Kening George Young Henry Bowman John depree.

An Action of the Case. Henry Stracher Plt, Peter Groundyk deft. [From April Court * * * In June Court the Cause was put to A Jurey—verdict for plt. with cost of suit.] Jurey men—N Claypoole Alex Draper Hal Mainas Will Carter Will Kening Geo Young Hen Bowman Jo Depree.

Cornelis verhoofe Agt Peter Groundyk by way of searifacous. [From April Court, the deft. to shew cause for not paying "the Plt. the Clarks feese that are due to him in a Cause formerly depending in this Court; Betwene the deft and Capt John Avery;" * * *]

An Action of the Case. Halm Wiltbanck Plt, Peter Groundyk deft. Wittnes Anthony Hamen Corn Johnson & Hen Stracher. [From April Court. At this Court left to a Jury, who find for the Plt. "with

Twelve pence damiag and Cost of suit."] Jurey men nortton Claypoole Alexander Draper William Carter william Kening George Young Henry Bowman John Depree.

An Action of the Case. William Darvall Plt, Henry Bowman deft. [From April Court, when "the deft beinge prevented from Coming to Court; by reasion of Ellnes And the badnes of the weather to Travile in; the Court Granted * * * A reference untill this Court" * * * Judgment for the plt Agt the deft with Cost of suit Alias Execution.]

An Action of the Case. Richard Lawes Plt, Samll Showell deft; the plt oath [Debt of Tobacco. Judgment for Plt, with Cost of suit. Alias Execution].

An Action of the Case. Henry Stracher Plt, Peter Groundyk Deft; the Plts oath. The Plt declare that the deft received of the Plt by the hands of Alexander Moulston five hundred pounds of Tobacco * * * [verdict of Jury "for Plt and gave him five hundred pounds of Tobacco wt Cost of Suit"]. Jurey men nortton Claypoole Samwell Gray George Young Alexander Draper William Carter William ffootcher william Keninge.

An Action of the Case. John vines Plt, Peter Groundyk deft. Refered at the Request of the deft untill the next Court.

William ffootcher Plt, John King deft. Wittneses Peter Groundyk Corn verhoofe will Taylor Capt Avery Capt [Cantreel?] John Crew Robt Hignet Robt Bracey Senr Rich bundon. The Plt declare that the deft did Agree to Convey unto the Plt the three hundred Acres of Land that the Plt now live upon And that he had satisfied the deft for the same; the Cause was Left to A Jurey and After being pleaded to on both sides and the wittneses sworen and excamined; the Jurey went out and brought in there verdict; that they finde for the Plt with Cost of suit; the Court passe Judgment According to the verdict of the Jurey Alias Execution. Execution given out the 2th Eleaventh Moneth 1682. Jurey men nortton Claypoole Alexander Draper Samwell Gray Halmainas Wiltbank Rich Lawes Henry Stracher William Carter Anthony Hamen Will Kening Georg Young Hen Bowman John Depree.

John King Plt, Will footcher deft wittnes Arin Biship Robert Hignett. The Plt declare that Elias Hartle did give unto the Plt Mother & hur heires A Cow and Calfe with there encrease for a stock for the Plts Mother and hur heires; And that the deft have Long sence possessed himselfe with foure Cows being of the encrease of the said Cow and Calfe; the Cause was Left to A Jurey * * * verdict that they finde for the deft with Cost of suit * * * Jurey men nortton Claypoole Alexander draper Samll Gray Halmainas wiltbank Rich Lawes Hen. Stracher Will Carter Anthony Hamen will Kening Georg Young Henry Bawman [sic] John depree.

An Action of the Case. William footcher Plt, John King deft; "with drawen."

An Action of the Case. Alexander Draper Plt, John Dickerson deft; "with drawen."

An Action of the Case. John Crew Plt, John Johnson Junr deft; "with drawen."

Whare As William Clark did buy of Capt John Osborne of Sumersett County in the provience of Mary Land An negor man Called or knowen by the name of black Will for and during his natrill Life; Never the Less the said William Clark doe for the Incourigment of the sd neagor servant hereby promise Covenant and Agree; that if the said Black Will doe and shall well and Truely sarve the said William Clark his Executors Administrators or Assignes five years from the Twentieth day of May Last past; that then the said Black Will shall be Clear and free of and from Any further or Longer sarvicetive or slavery; After he have sarved the said five years As A for said as wittnes my hand this Thurteenth day of the Moneth Called June Anno; Dm; 1682;

Signed, Test. LUKE WATTSON
his mark
JOHN K. KIPHAVEN

WM: CLARK.

The Court Grant Samwell Jones three hundred Acres of Land; wart Given out 19th Inst.

* * * unto John Booth, five hundred acres; wart 19th Insint.

* * * unto ffrancis Bateson five hundred acres; wart 14th 4 mo, 1682.

* * * unto Mathew osborne, 300 acres; wart 24th Insint.

* * * unto John Barnett, 300 acres; wart 9th 2 mo, 1683.

* * * unto ffrancis Williams, 400 acres; wart 31th 5 mo, 1682.

* * * unto Robert Richards, 400 acres; wart 31th 5 mo, 1682.

* * * unto Thomas Grimdyk and francis Henry, 500 acres; wart 12th 6 mo, 1682.

Peter Groundyk peticon the Court that he may have the Cause That was this day Tryd betwene Henry Stracher Ant this peticoner; to be Tryd in Equiety the next Court by bill and Answer As is use in the Court of Chancrey in England which the Court would A perswaded him to A dissisted in it; and rest himselfe satisfied in what was allready done; but through his perswading the Court Grant the peticoner his request; provided that the proceeding be put in in due time According to Law.

John Crew as Atturney to John Savidge did this day Accknowlidg A deede of Conveyance And Patton of six hundred Acres of Land unto John Depree in open Court; to have and to hold unto the said John depree and to his heires and Assignes for ever.

Parrit the Indian Shackamacker doe Accknowlidg in open Court that he have sold unto Henry Bowman the Indian right of the Thousand Acres of Land that the said Henry Bowman purchised of John Depree Lyeing on the neck of Land Betwene Slater Branch and Ceeder Creeke for which he Accknowlidge to have received full satisfacon for the same.

Parrit the Indian Shackamacker doe Accknowlidg in open Court that he have sold unto Henry Bowman the Indian right of the seaven hundred Acres of Land that was Lately in differance Betwene the said Henry Bowman and Alexander Draper Lyeing betwene the Land of the said Alexander Draper; and the Land that the said Henry Bowman Bought of John Depree; for which he Accknowlidg to have received full satisfacon for the same.

Henry Stracher doe Except of A Cow at six hundred Twenty five pounds of Tobacco; which sd Cow was not Long sence taken upon Execution from the said Henry Stracher at the suit of Peter Groundyk.

The Court Grant unto Thomas Silby six hundred Acres of Land; wart given out 19th 4 mo, 1682; another wart Given oute ye 26th 12 mo, 1685 the first being lost.

The Court order Alexander Moulston to Receive of Peter Groundyk Twenty one Shilling in three Causes that he was Cast in this Court; being for the Jurey feese.

The Court order Alexander Moulston to receive of John King sixteene shilling for the Jurey feese in the Cause he was Cast in this Court.

The Court order Bapties Newcomb to pay unto Nortton Claypoole forman of the Jurey Twelve Shillings for the Jurey feese in the Cause that he was Plt in this Court.

The Court order William footcher to pay unto Nortton Claypoole forman of the Jurey Eighte Shillings for the Jureys feese in the Cause that he was Plt in this Court.

The Court Grant unto John Smith Two hundred Acres of Land; warrant Given out the 11th 6 mo, 1682.

The Court is AdJurned untill the second Tusday of September next ensueing. Test WM; CLARK JJ Cl.

SEPTEMBER 12th, 13th, 1682.

Att A Court Held at Deale for the Towne And County of Deale By the Kings Authority the 12th and 13th days of the Moneth Called September Anno; Dm; 1682; Commisconers present: Luke Wattson John Roades John Kiphaven William Clark.

An Action of debt. Capt Marton Creagor Plt, Anthony Hamen Alias Haverla deft. [Refered from Court to Court beginning with December. Now,—"the Plt not Appearing by him selfe or by his Atturney to prosecute his suit" the Court grant "An non suit Agt the Plt with cost. * * *]

An Action of the Case. William Clark Plt Daniell Browne Estate in the Plts hands deft. [From the March Court—"And at September Court the Cause was refered untill Novmber Court to see if the deft would Com and make defence in the said Cause."]

An Action of the Case. John vines Plt, Peter Groundyk deft. [Refered from June Court * * * "Att Septemb Court the deft produced An order from the Comander in Cheife and Councell to stop the proceedings Agt the deft; which the Court submitted to."]

An Action of Debt. Nortton Claypoole Plt Henry Bowman deft. Witnes Jo Hill; [* * * "the deft not being here the Court refere the Cause untill the next Court."]

An Action of Traspase. William Kening Plt Robert Bracey senr deft. wittnes Capt Avery Corn verhoof Baptis newcomb Hen Stracher John oakey, sepene. The Plt declare that the deft Caused part of the Plts Land to be surveyed for his owne use and Cutt and marke severall of the Plts trees; the Cause was put to a Jurey; the Plt prove by the oath of Cornelis verhoofe that the deft had as he thought surveyed part of the Plts Land * * * the Jurey * * * finde for the Plt with one shilling damag and Cost of suit * * *. Jurey men Norton Claypoole Will footcher Alex Draper Geo Young Antho Hamen Rich Patte Roger Gum John Depree Hen Stracher Rich Lawes John Smith Bryt Rowles sworen.

An Action of Traspase. Georg Young Plt, ffrancis Williams deft. wittnes Rich Shoulter Stephen Whetman Anthony Parsley, Sepene

The Plt declare that the deft Cutt sold and distroyd his Tmber on A parcell of Land of the Plt Lyeing Betwene Rehower bay and the Indian River; the deft pleads that the Land is William Burton and John Baggwell whoe sett him at work on the said Land; And Craved A referance untill the next Court to prove the same; which the Court Granted.

An Action of the Case. John Kurk Plt Halm Wiltbanck deft. With drawen by order of the Plts Atturney.

An Action of the Case. William Beaverly Plt. William Davids deft. wittnes Rob Williams James Hews, sepened. The Plt declare that the deft did in the night time sease upon his person and bind him with Cords, and doe other harmes to his body in the plt hired house; the deft did Confess that he did binde the plt; the Cause was put to A Jurey which after being pleaded unto by the plt and the deft the Jurey went out and brought in there verdit that they finde for the plt and give him Twelve pence damiag and Cost of suit the Court pass Judgmt Accordingly Alias Execution. Jurey men Nor Claypoole Will footcher Alex draper Geo Young Ant Hamen Rich patte John Smith Roger Gum John depree Hen Stracher Rich Lawes Bry Rowles sworen.

An Action of the Case. Thomas Rogers Plt, John Barnett deft. The Plt declare that the deft stands Indebted unto him one new pair of men franch fall shoes which the deft owne; and therefor the Court passe Judgment for the plt Agt the deft for one pair of shoes as A for said with Cost of suit Alias Execution.

An Action of defamacon. Cornelis Johnson Plt Barnwell Jackson deft; "with drawen."

Samwell Showell Plt, Richard Lawes deft; "with drawen."

An Action of Debt. John Beaman Plt, William Bourne deft. The Plt declare by his Atturney Capt John Brigs that the deft stands Justly Indebted unto him in Ten Thousand pounds of Tobacco Conditconed for the payment of five Thousand pounds of Tobaccc on demand; the deft pleads that he was A prisoner at the suit of the Plt when he passed the bill and that he did signe it to get his Libirty; not that he was so much Indebted unto the Plt; And that he did give the Plt order to receive more Tobacco that is due to the deft in Mary Land then the five Thousand pounds Com to; and Craves A referance untill the next Court to prove the same; upon which the Court Granted the deft a Referance untill the next Court.

An Action of debt. Nichols Greenbury Plt, William Bourne deft; [similar to preceding case, with Capt John Brigs "Atturney"].

An Action of Traspase. John Bellamey Plt, Henry Smith Junr deft; Wittnes Sepene, Henry Skidemore. The Plt declared that the deft did Cart and Carrie a way a bout A Cart Load of Clap boord of from the Plt Land Lying in prince Hook neck and did hinder and obstroct his Carpender from proceeding in his work; the deft pleads that the Land is his father and that what he did was by his fathers order; the deft haveing had but a short time to prove his father tittle to the sd Land sence he was A rested Craves A Referance untill the next Court wch the Plt Consented unto.

An Action of Traspase. John Bellamey Plt, Luke wattson senr deft; wittnes, sepene, Henry Skidemore. The Plt declare that the deft did hinder obstroct and mollest his Carpender by for warning him from working on the Plts Land at prince hook neck and by falling of Trees on the Carpenders work; the deft pleads that the Land is his fathers Capt Henry Smiths* and that what he did was by the said Capt Smiths order; and the Plt and deft Agree to refer the triall untill the next Court.

An Action of debt. William Allen Plt, John Gibson deft.

Thomas Moulston Peticoner Agt William Beaverly; "with drawen."

William Bourne peticoner, Agt Nichols & Sarah Bartlett. ["Nichols Bartlett hur husband."]

The Court fine John vines shreife fifty pounds of Tobacco for smoking in the Court.

Cornelis Johnson peticon that the four hundred Acres of Land surveyed Lately for the said Cornelis Johnson Called White oak neck may be returned in the Certivecate of survey in the name of Richard Patte he haveing Given him A Consideracon for the same; which the Court Grant and this order of Court shall be A sufficient warrant for the surveyors soe doeing.

The Court Grant unto John Roades the peece of wast Land that Joynes to the new forrise being about one hundred and Twenty Acres & to be surveyed into the same. Wart given out 10th 7 mo, 82.

The Court Grant unto Josep Thorne three hundred Acres of Land; wart. 21th Insint.

Halmainas Wiltbanck Acknowlidge in open Court A patton and Conveyance of A Certaine parcell of Land Called by the name of Wilt [Witt?] Bay; Lyeing on the north side of the greate Creeke; Contayning Eight hundred Acres of Land; unto John Kurk his heires and Assignes for ever; and doe promise and Ingage to give the said John Kurk or his Assignes Quit and peaceable possession of the said Land and premisses by the Last day of october now next ensueinge the date hereof.

Ann Newcomb the Late wife of John Hagester deceased did this day proveth in Court the Last will and Testament of the said John Hagester deceased; of which said will she the said Ann is made sole Exceterce; and Letters of Administracon are by the Court Granted unto Baptis Newcomb and Ann his wife.

The Court Grant unto Baptis Newcomb A peece of wast Land Lyeing Adjoyning to the Land he now Live upon; Being about the Quantety of ffortye or ffifty Acres of Land.

The Court Grant unto John Hagester sun of John Hagester deceased three hundred Acres of Land; warrant given out the 6th 11 mo, 1682.

The Court order and Appoint Edward Southrin, George young, Henry Stracher & William Emitt to Apprize the Estate debts Goods and Chattels that John Hagester deceased was possessed with Just befor his death; And to Give in An Inventory there of under there hands unto the Clark of the Court; Betwene this and the next Court; An Account of the sd Estate debts goods & Chattells Baptis Newcomb and Ann his wife swore to give unto the Apprazer to the best of there knowlidge.

---

* When this case is called—at Court 9, 10, 11th, 11 mo, p. 93 of the Record Book —"the deft pleads that the Land is his father in Law Henry Smith" etc. a non suit was entered, etc.

Edward Southrin Ingage to the Court to be Bound with Baptis that he the said Bapties Newcomb and Ann his wife shall give in A true Inventory of the Estate debts goods and Chattels that John Hagester deceased was possessed with at the time or Just befor his death: And to perform all such things as belong to Administrator to doe and performe According to Law.

The Court Grant unto John Hill the wast Land that Lye Betwene the Land that he purchiased of Simon Parling; And Thomas Haward Land that he now Live on; Being on the north side of the greate Creeke; to be surveyed into the Land that he bought of the said Simon Parling which sd wast Land is Judged to be a bout sixty or seaventy Acres; more or Lesse.

Edward Boodle Caused John oakey to be sumance by way of searafacous * * * [debt of Tobacco].

The Court Grant unto Anthony Parsley three hundred Acres of Land; warrant given out the 2th 8 mo, 1682; the other warrt being lost another Granted the 19th 11 mo, 1686.

The Court Grant unto Thomas Grimdyk 250 acres of Land to be Added to his former Grant; wart 21th Insint.

The Court order Robert Bracey to pay unto William Clark for the Jurey fees In the Cause that he was Cast in this Court at the suit of William Kening three and Twenty Shillings; and to Alexander Moulston thurteene shillings.

The Court order William Davids to pay unto William Clark for the Jureys feese In the Cause that he was Cast in this Court at the suit of Willm Beverly foure and Twenty Shillings; and to Alexander Moulston Twelve Shillings.

The Court Grant unto John Pye 300 Acres; wart 21th Insint.

The Court order that from this day forward all declaracons shall be fild in the Clarks office Eighte days befor the Court According to the Law of this Goverment; notwithstanding Any former order of Court made to the Contrary.

The Court Adjurne untill the second Tusday of next novmber 1682. Test WM. CLARK.

WM. CLARK LUKE WATTSON JOHN ROADES JOHN AVREY HALMAINAS WILTBANCK & ALEXANDER MOULSTON:—These are to desire you to Meet me next Thursday soe Called at the Towne of New Castle Being the second Novmber; where I Intend to hold a Generall Court for the settling the Jurisdiction of these and your parts in which you will oblidge

Your Loveing friend
Signed WM. PENN.

UPLAND, the 29th 8ber, 1682.

If there be any persons of note or others that desier to be present they may Com freely with you are desired to Comunicate. W. P.

AUGUST 24th, 1682.

Know yee that James Duke of York Earle of Ulster &c. did by one deed of ffiffment dated the 24th of August 1682; pass and Convey unto William Penn Esquire Son and Heire of Sr William Penn deceased Proprietary and Governor of Pensilvania &c. And his Heires and Assignes forever from Twelve Miles southwards of New Castle Upon Dellaware River to Cape Henlopen Together with the powers and Jurisdictions there unto belonging; Resarveing unto him selfe one Moyety of the Rent thereof; where by the said William Penn Esquire Becometh Also Proprietary and Governor of the before Menticoned Tract of Land.

NOVEMBER 7th, 1682.

WILLIAM PENN ESQUIRE PROPRIETARY & GOVERNOR OF PENSILVANIA NEW CASTLE ST JAMES WHOORE KILLS ALS NEW DEALE WITH THEIR PROPER LIBERTYS:—

I doe in the Kings name hereby Constiute [sic] & Authorize you Luke Wattson William Clark John Roades John Avrey and Halmainas Wiltbanck or any three of you to be Justices of the peace And Court of Judicature for the County of Whore Kills Als New Deal; to Act in the said Imployment and Trust for the preservation of the peace and Justices of the provience; Hereby willing and Charging all persons within the said Limitts to take notice hereof; And Accordingly to yeild you all due and Just obedience in the discharge of your said Trust, And this Comicon to be of force for the space of one whole year from the date hereof; or untill further order; Given under my hand and seal In New Castle this 7th day of Novmb 1682;

WM. PENN.

To My Loveing ffriends; Luke Wattson; Wm. Clark; John Roades; John Avery; Malmainas [sic] Wiltbanck.

NOVEMBER 14th, 1682.

Wee Luke Wattson William Clark John Roades John Avery & Halmains Wiltbanck Being by William Penn proprietary and Governor of Pensilvania & Territories there unto belonging Constiuted And Authorized to be Justices of the peace And A Court of Judicature for the County of Sessex to Act in the said Imployment And Trust for the preservation of the peace and Justices of the County In Pursuance of our said Comission According to Law; Doe hereby In the presence of God declare And solemonly promise by the help of God to be Just and true to him in Managing and performing our said trust and faithfully discharge the same in obedience to our said Comission; And Act therein According to the best of our understandings wittnes our hands and seals this forteenth day of Novmber 1682;

Wittnesses present	LUKE WATTSON	(sealed)
EDWARD SOUTHRIN	JOHN ROADES	(sealed)
WM; CLARK	HALM WILTBANCK	(sealed)
JOHN HILL		
HENRY STRECTHER		

After the Justices had signed as above on the 14th day of the 9 mo; 1682; they AdJurned the Court untill the 9th 11 mo; 1682.

DECEMBER 25th, 1682.

WM: PENN PROPRIETARY & GOVERNOR OF PENNSILVANIA & TERRITORYS THEIR UNTO BELONGING.

By Virtue of the Authority derived unto me I doe hereby In the Kings name Constitute Appoint & Authorize you William Darvall Luke Wattson Norton Claypoole John Roades Edward Southrin

Robert Hart and John Kiphaven to be Justices of the Peace in the Jurisdiction of the County of the Whore Kills which my will and pleasure is shall from hence forth be Called by the name of Sussex the Extent whereof shall be from the maine branch of Mispillon Creek Called the three Runs northwards; And southwards to Asewomet Inlet; Reputed And Accounted Cape Henlopen which said Cape Henlopen I will from hence forward have Called by the name of Cape James; And you or any four of you to be a Court of Judicature; Giving you & Every of you full power to Act in the said office According to Law and the Trust Reposed in you; of which all persons are to take notice and to give you the due Respect and obedience Belonging to your places in the discharging of your duties this Comission to be of force for the space of one year After the date hereof or untill further order; Given under my hand and seal at Chester the 25th day of the 10 mo; 1682; Being the second year of my Government.

Signed WM. PENN.

JANUARY 9th, 1682.

Wee William Darvall Luke Wattson Norton Claypoole John Roades Edward Southrin Robert Hart & John Kiphaven; Being by William Penn Esquire proprietary And Governor of Pensilvania and Territories there unto belonging Constituted And Authorized to be Justices of the peace And A Court of Judicature for the County of Sessex to Act in the same Imployment and Trust for the preservation of the peace and Justices of the County In persueance of our said Comission According to Law; wee doe hereby in the presence of God declare that wee freely Accknowlidg the said William Penn to be our Rightfull proprietary and Governor; And doe solemonly promise by the help of God to be Just and true to him in Managing and performing our said trust and faithfully discharge the same in obediance to our said Comission And Act there in According to the best of our understandings; And if wee shall wittingly or willingly Act or doe any thing Contrary to Law or fidellity to our proprietary & the trust Reposed in us by him; wee doe hereby oblidg our selves to suffer and undergoe the same fine or ponishment that the matter shall in Law desarve as if wee had Activfly taken an oath; In wittnes whereof wee have hereunto sett our hands and seals the ninth day of the Eleaventh Moneth Anno; Dm; 1682.

Signed by
WILLIAM DARVALL (sealed)
LUKE WATTSON (sealed)
JOHN RHOADES (sealed)
EDWARD SOUTHRIN (sealed)
ROBERT HART (sealed)
JOHN KIPHAVEN (sealed)

Sealed signed & delivered
in the presence of
WM. CLARK
JOHN HILL.

DECEMBER 25th, 1682.

TO MY LOVEING FFRIENDS WILLIAM DARVALL LUKE WATTSON NORTON CLAYPOOLE JOHN ROADES EDWARD SOUTHRIN ROBERT HART & JOHN KIPHAVEN JUSTICES OF THE PEACE FOR THE

County of Sessex These ffriends:—Sence it hath pleased God to put the Govermt of the west side of Dellaware River and Bay into my hands; I Cannot but in good Concience Endeavor to promote Justices and Rightousness Among the Inhabitents thereof Knowing that he who is the Judg of quick and dead will Remember us for god if wee forget not him; And that A Goverment Laid and Begun by the Line of Equity and true Judgment; will not faile of prosperity; I therefor most Earnestly Recommend to you who are the Ministers of Justice for the County you Live in; Vigilancy and ffidelity, that you may neither neglect nor pervert Justice; And in order there unto That you keepe your Courts with Constancy and Gravity; and that you have your Eare open to hear all as well the poore as the Rich; And In all Cases to Judge According to the Truth of the Evidence; without fear favour Affection or Reward; That God may Bless you and the people Blesse you; which seldom faileth to be the Reward of wise Just and vertuous Magistrates; I doe Also think fitt that An Exact Catalogue be Returned to me of the names of all the people of your County; Masters Mistresses servants parents Children; Also the Number of Acres Each ffreeholder hath; And by whom and when Granted; All in distinct Columons; with a Mark on Non resident that have Claims; And if any disputes should Arise About titles of Land; they must be determined According to the Rules and orders that the Court of your County has Limited & prescribed for the seating and Improveing of Land; And soe I bid you all hartily farewell Given at Chester the 25th 10 mo; 1682; In the second year of my Government. Signed Wm. Penn.

By the Proprietary & Governor of Pensilvania & the Territorys Thereunto Belonging:—

Haveing Duely Considered the present state of your County; to the End that all obstructions to the due Improvement theirof may be Removed; And Reasonable Encouragement Given to Invite planters to settle Amongst you; I doe think fitt to order and Appoint as follows; ffirst that you in open Court shall Receive all peticons from time to time that may be made; by such persons as designe to take up Land Among you; and that you Grant them a Warrant to the surveyor to Ad measure the same; provided all ways that you Exceed not three hundred Acres of Land to A Master of A family nor A hundred Acres to A single person; At one single penny ℘ Acre; or vallue thereof in the produce of the Country which done that the surveyor make his Returne Into Court; And that the Court make theire Returne unto my secritary's office;

Secondly and because no Land shall Lye wast to the prejudice of new planters; All Lands formerly Granted and not taken up & settled within the time Limitted by the Methods of your own Court; that Granted them; shall be Accounted vacant Land and disposeable upon the termes Aforsaid; the old Claymt or pretender to have the preferance if not allrady seated owner of Above three hundred Acres; Unless allrady seated by some other person;

Thurdly that all persons for the future that shall have Grants to take up Land be also Limitted to seat it within one year After the date of the Grant; Else the said Grants to be Voyde & of no Effect;

forthly that you Endeavor to seat the Lands that shall here after be taken up in the way of Townships; As three Thousand Acres Amongst Tenn familys; if single persons one Thousand Acres Amongst Tenn of them; Laid out in the nature of A Long square five or Tenn of a side; And a way of Two hundred foot broad Left Betwene them; for an High way in the Township; this I would have you Carfull in; for the future good and great Benefitt of your Country; Given under my hand & seal at Chester the 25th of 10 mo, 1682.

Signed Wm. Penn.

To the Justices of the peace for the County of Sessex.

By William Penn Proprietary & Governor of Pensilvania & Territoryes Thereunto Belonging:—

I doe hereby order and Appoint that befor Any Land be surveyed for any other person; you doe Issue forth A warrant directed to the surveyor or his Deputy; to lay out for the duke of yorke in your County or precints Tenn Thousand Acres of Land for A Mannor; And Tenn Thousand Acres of Land for A Mannor for my selfe And I would have the duks Mannor Lye on the north side of Assn Awarmet Inlett As near to Cape James as may be; And My Mannor to be betwene the Bounds of Cedar Creek & Mispilion Creek or in the most Convenient place Towards the north side of the County; Given under my hand & seal att Chester the 26th of the 10 mo, 1682.

Signed Wm. Penn.

To the Justices of the peace of the County of Sussex.

Wm. Penn Proprietary & Governor of Pensilvania and Territoryes Thereunto Belonging:—

I doe hereby Constitute and Authorise thee William Clark of the Whoor Kills now Called the County of Sussex to be Clark of the Courts of sessions to be holden for the said County; And Register of the said County Also; to Act therein Justly and dilligently According to Law to the best of thy understanding; This Comission to be of force for the space of one year or untill further order; Given under my hand and seal at Chester the 25 day of 10 mo, 1682; In the second year of My Government. Signed Wm. Penn.

Wm. Penn Proprietary & Governor of Pensilvania New Castle St. James Whore Kills Alias new Deal with Their Proper Libertys:—

I doe hereby in the Kings name Constitute and Appoint thee John vines to be High Shreiffe of the County of Whore Kill Alls new deal Giveing thee full power & Authority to Act in the said office and Imployment According to the duty of A Sherife; and to make one or more deputy as there may be occation and to receive all the profitts and Advantages which doe or ought to belong unto the said place behaving thy selfe & being Regulated therein in all Respect According to Law; And in so doing all persons whom it may Concerne are hereby Required to bear thee due obedience as belong to a High Shreife in the Execution of thy office; this Comission to be of force for one whole year or untill further order; Given under my hand and seal at New Castle or Dellaware this Eighte day of Novmber one Thousand six hundred Eightye Two. WM. PENN.

To John vines High Sherife of the County of Whore Kills Als New deal.

WM. PENN PROPRIETARY & GOVERNOR OF PENSILVANIA NEW CASTLE ST JAMES; NEW DEAL ALLIS WHORE KILLS WITH THEIR PROPER LIBERTYS:—

These are in the Kings name to Require and Empower thee to sumon all the free holders within the precincts of thy office to meet on the Twentieth day of this Insint Moneth of Novmber and that there they Elect Chuse out of themselves seaven persons of most note for wisdome sobriety & Integrity to serve as their Deputys & Representatives In General Assembly to be held at upland in the provience of pensilvania the sixt day of December next; and then and there to Consult with me for the Comon Good of the Inhabitents of that provience and the Adjiacent Counties of New Castle St. Jones new deal Als Whore Kills under my Charge & Jurisdition of which make due and Just Returne unto me; Given under my hand and seal this Eighte day of Novmber one Thousand six hundred Eightye Two. WM. PENN.

To John vines High Shreife of the County of Whore Kills Als New deal.

WHORE KILL ALS DEAL, 21th 9 mo, 1682.

PROPRIETARY & GOVERNOR WILLIAM PENN ESQUIRE &C:—In obedience to thy warrant dated the Eighte day of this Insint to me directed; I did sumon all the free holders within this County to meet at this Towne on the Twentieth Insint to Elect and Chuse out of themselves seaven persons of most note for wisdome sobriety & Integrity to serve as their deputys & Representatives In Generall Assembly to be held at upland In the provience of Pensilvania the sixt day of December next; Att which time the free holders did then and there meet; And with A Generall vote they did Elect and Chose the persons; whose names I here Returne unto thee According to thy order; and take Leave to subscribe my selfe thy faithfull ffriend & Humble sert . Signed JOHN VINES, Sherife.

Edward Southrin, William Clark, Alexander draper, John Roades, Luke Wattson, Nathaniel Walker, Corn verhoofe.

JANUARY 9th, 10th and 11th, 1682.

Att A Court Held Att Lewis for the County of Sussex By the Kings Authoritye And by Commission from William Penn Proprietary & Governor of Pensilvania And Territoryes there unto belonging the 9th 10th & 11th days of the Eleaventh Moneth 1682. Justices present: William Darvall, Luke Wattson, John Roades, Edward Southrin, Robert Hart, John Kiphaven.

John Bellamey plt, Henry Smith Junr deft. Wittnes danill Brown Hen Stracher Henry Skidmor Will Craford Henry Skidmor Will Clork John Roades. [This case was refered from "the last seaventh Moneth Court," and at this present Court "was Left to A Jurey"] Jurey men Norton Claypoole John Richards Robert Hart Junr William Borne Alexander draper Barnard Garritt Anthony Hancen

Thomas Howard Michall Chambers Stephen Whetman Bryant Rowles Cornelis Johnson.

John Avery Plt, Richard Harvey deft. The suit falls by the death of the Plt whoe departed this Life the 16th day 9 mo, 1682.

William Clark Plt, Jacob Shattham deft. The plt declares that the deft entertayned A servant that he bought of Capt John Osborne of Sumersett County in the provience of Mary [sic] for about six weeks; the deft Confess that the said servant was at his house about that time and that he did work for the deft to the vallow of one hundred pounds of Tobacco; the Court therefor passe Judgment for the plt Agt the deft for the said sume of one hundred pounds of Tobacco with Cost of suit Alias Execution.

Halm Wiltbanck Agt Corn Johnson by way of scarifacous. The said Cornelis Johnson was sumaned to shew Cause if any he Could wherefor he doe not Give the said Halmanias Wiltbanck possession of the Land he Live upon According to An order of Court & verdict of A Jurey of Seaven men obtaind in this Court the 8th day of the 1 mo, 1681. The said Cornelis Johnson sheweth Cause by his plea delivered into the Court in writing that he had obtained in this Court a verdict of a Jurey of Twelve men for the said Land and primisses According to the Laws of England; and that the verdict of seaven men was and is Contrary to the knowen Laws of England; and that the said Halm Wiltbanck did Appeale from the verdict of the Jurey of Twelve men a for mentcioned; and that After he had Appealed he ought to have prosecuted his said Appeale; And to A [sic] had no further triall for the said Land in this Court; and for the Reasons and Cause A foresaid the deft doe refuse to deliver possession of the said Land and primisses; which I Humbly Conceive may be Judged to be sufficent Cause by this Court. The Court doe by Consent of both parties Refere the bussness untill the proprietary Com here and have a hearing of the said Cause and Give his Judgmt therein.

An Action of the Case. John Kurk plt, Halm Wiltbanck deft. The plt declare by his Atturney Edward Southrin that the deft on or about the 17th day of April 1677; did by his deed In writing signed by his own hand & seal oblidg him selfe to give the plt A good Asurance of the Land that Cornelis Johnson Live upon; and also to give the plt Quiett and peaceable possession of the same; the deft pleads that he is unjustly keept out of the possession of the sd Land and primisses and is not in A Cappasety to doe it but that as sone as he Can he will doe it; The Court therefor by the Consent of the plts Atturney and the deft Refere the Cause untill the proprietary Com Heather to hear and detarmine the same [at Court in 12 mo again referred until the proprietary come].

An Action of the Case. William Bottler plt, Henry Stracther deft. With drawen by order of the plt; by Informacon of William Emmitt depty Shriefe.

An Action of Traspasse upon the Case. Michall Chambers plt, Paul Marsh deft; wittnes Will Townsend. The plt declare that severall of his hoggs ware wounded and destroyed by dogs in the defts Corn feild; but the plt not proveing his declaracon and the deft not Confessing it; the Court order an non suit to be entered Agt the plt with Cost of suit Alias Execution.

An Action of the Case. Baptis Newcomb Administrator to the goods & Chattls of John Hagester deceased plt, Danill Browne deft; wittnes Will Emmitt. The plt declare that the deft stands Justly Indebted unto the Estate of John Hagester deceased; in five hundred and sixty three pounds of Tobacco; and prove the same to the satisfacon of the Court; the Court therefor passe Judgmt for the plt Agt the deft for the said sume of five hundred sixty three pounds of Tobacco; with Cost of suit Alias Execution.

An Action of the Case. Halm Wiltbanck plt, Agt the Estate of Samwell Jones in the hands of Henry Stracther deft. The plt declaring Agt Another person then what is in the writt; the Court order An non suit to be entered Agt the plt with Cost of suit Alias Execution.

This day the Last will and Testament of Edwd Boodle deceased was proved in open Court being in writing bearing date the 7th day of December 1682; by the Testamony of William Emmitt and Stephen Whetman; to be the Last will and Testament of him the said Edward Boodle; And Letters of Administracon are by the Court Granted unto John Kiphaven and John depree; to Administer and enter upon his Estate Lands Goods and Chattls of the deceased; they giveing security to perform the said will and save the Court Harmless.

This day the Jurey that went upon the death of John the sun of Cornelis Johnson brought their verdict into Court and say that they doe finde that he Came by his death by A dog or beast.

This day the Jurey that went upon the death of Thomas Grimdick deceased brought in their verdict Into Court that they doe finde That the said Thomas Grindick Cam to his death by A fall from his house.

Stephen Whetman peticon the Court and sett forth in his said peticon that he is the princable Craditor of the said Thomas Grimdick deceased; and prays that he may be Admitted to Letters of Administracon to Administer upon the Estate Lands Goods and Chattls of the said Thomas Grimdyk * * * [which the Court granted].

Upon the peticon of Cornelis Plockhoy the Court Grant unto him the Towne Lott that he live upon in Lewis; and the Lott next Adjoyning to that; on Condition that he Build A dwelling house on Eche of the said Lotts According to the demencons that the Governor shall order; within one yeare after this Grant; or Else to pay five pounds to the use of the publick for Eche Lott; and Lose his Lotts also.

The Court doe Chose order and Appint William Carter to be Cunstable for the year ensueing for the Towne of Lewis and to the South side of the broad Creek northwards and to the midway from hence to Rehower to the southward; and John Richards is Chose order Appointed, John Richards to be Cunstable from the north side of the brood Creek to the extent of the County northwards and William footcher is Chose order and Apointed to be Constable for the year ensueing his bound to Extend from midway betwene this Towne and Rehower unto the uttmost of the Extent or bounds of this County Southwards.

The Court order Chose and Appoint John Hill Robert Hart Junr and William Bradford to be survyrs of the High ways and Bridges for the year ensueing and that they doe warne in the Inhabitence of this County to marke Clear and mend the High wayes within this

County; and make and Repair what bridges shall be needfull within this County the said John Hills extents to be from the flat Lands southwards and to the south side of the greene branch of prime hook Creek northwards and the said Robert Hart Extent or bounds to be from the south side of the Greene branch of Prime hook south wards to the three Runs of Mispillon Creeke north wards; And the said William Bradford Extent or bounds to be from the flat lands north wards unto the Extent of the Extent of the County south wards being to Cape James formerly Called Cap hinlopen; and if any person shall Refuse there Labour after being warned thereunto; that they doe return unto the Court the names of all such persons soe Refusing to the end that they may be fined According to Law for such their nedglect.

The Court Grant unto John Kiphaven upon his peticon the Towne Lott Adjoyning to that he Live upon to the north ward; on Condition that he build A dwelling house on the said Lott within one year Afer this Grant of such demencons as the Governor shall order and direct; or Else to pay five pounds to the use of the publick; and also lose the said Lott.

Upon the peticon of William Darvall the Court Grant unto him three Towne Lotts namely that which his house stands upon and; one upon the north west side of that and the other on the south west side; on Condition * * * [as preceding Grant].

Upon the peticon of Edmond Warner the Court Grant unto him the Two Towne Lotts next Adjoyning unto William Darvall on Condition that he build * * * [as above].

Upon the peticon of Edmond Warner the Court Grant unto him three hundred Acres of Land at one penny ℘ Acre Rent to the proprietary yearly for ever; on Condition that he seate the said Land within one yeare After this Grant; wart Given out the same day.

Upon the peticon of Edmond Warner the Court Grant unto him the Land of the Cap Comonly Called Cap Inlopen Lyeing on the north East side of the Creeke formerly Called the Whoore Kills; to make Coney Warrin on and Liberty to build A house and seat A Warriner upon the said Land; upon Condiccon that the Timber and feede of the said Land and Marshes thereunto belonging be and for ever here after Lye in Common for the use of the Inhabitents of the Towne of Lewis and County of Sussex; as also free Liberty for any or all of the Inhabitents of the said County to fish Get and take of thence oyster & Cockel shells and gather plums Cranburyes and hockelbureys on the said Land as they shall think fitt; all ways provided that no person whatso ever shall not hunt or Kill any Rabbotts or harrs on the said Land without the Leave and Consent of him the said Edmond Warner his Executors Adminstrators or Assignes.

Upon the peticon of William Catter* the Court Grant unto him the Towne Lott backward Adjoyning to the Land of Nathanil Walker; and the Lott that he Live upon on Condiccon [* * * etc., as previously].

The Court upon the peticon of William Trotter Grant unto him the Towne Lott backward Adjoyning to William Carter back Lott; on Condition, etc.

[* This name was originally written Tratter, & the Tr is changed to C.]

The Court upon the peticon of John Bellamey Grant unto him the Two Towne Lotts next Adjoyning unto Edmond Warners Lotts; the one of them to be forward and the other backward; on Condiccon, etc.

Upon the peticon of John Hill the Court Grant unto him one Towne Lott on the South East Side of the blind mans Lott; on Condition, etc.

Upon the peticon of William Beverly the Court Grant unto him the Towne Lott that he is building the vessell upon on Condition, etc., & not to dispose of it.

Upon the peticon of Halmanias Wiltbanck the Court Grant unto him the Two Towne Lotts next AdJoyning to his owne Land on Condition, etc.

Upon the peticon of Henry Jones the Court Grant unto him the Two Towne Lotts next Adjoyning unto Halmainas Wiltbanck back Lott; on Condition, etc.

Upon the peticon of Robert Williams the Court Grant unto him one Towne Lott next Adjoyning unto Henry Jones Lotts on Condition, etc.

Henry Pedington peticoner, Agt the Estate of William Coudrey in the hands of Will Clark. The peticoner sett forth in his peticon that the said William Coudrey stands Justly Indebted unto him in one Cow and Calfe and A yearling Heffer due to him upon bill being for the Land that John Dickerson is now seated upon for the said William Coudrey; and proved his bill; the Court therefor order that the peticoner be paid the sd Cow Calfe and yearling Heffer out of the said William Coudrey said Land with Cost of suit Alias Execution.

John Richards pitconer [sic] Agt the Estate of William Coudrey in the hands of William Clark.

Georg Cullin peticoner, Agt the Estate of Will Coudrey in the hands of Will Clark.

Robert Hart Junr peticoner, Agt the Estate of Will Condrey in the hands of Will Clark. The peticoner sett forth in and by his peticon yt the said William Coudrey stands Justly Indebted unto him in Two hundred pounds of Tobacco; and one pair of mens shoes and proved the same by his father Testamony; the Court there for order that the peticoner be paid the said Two hundred pounds of Tobacco and one pair of mens shos out of the said William Coudreys Estate with Cost of suit Alias Execution.

Henry Stracther; peticoners & William Carter, Agt the Estate of Will Coudrey in the hands of Will Clark. The peticoners sett forth by their peticon that the said William Coudrey stands Justly Indebted unto him in one Thousand of six penny nails three hundred of single Tenns and in three bottls of rum; and proved the same; the Court therfor order that the peticoners be paid the vallow of the Thousand of six penny nails three hundred of single Tenns and three bottls of rum out of the said William Coudrey Estate with Cost of suit Alias Execution.

Where as the proprietary have wrote to the Justices of this Court therein Exprassing that he think fitt to have an Exact Account sent him of the names of the Masters Mistries Children freemen women & servants that are Resedent within this County Together with the number of Acres of Land Every peticlor person holds or Claimes with in the said County; The Court doe their for order that every person that Holds or Claimes any Land within this County; That they doe befor the next Court in the Moneth Called ffebuary bring in all their Claimes to the Clark of this Court; wheather it be by patton survey Grant of Court or other wise and the names of the persons that Live upon the said Land.

Upon the peticon of Charles Brighte the Court Grant unto him three hundred Acres of Land; on Condition that he pay one penny ꝑ Acre yearly as a rent for the sd Land and seat it within one year After this Grant; wart given out same day.

Henry Bowman peticoner, Agt the Estate of William Coudrey in the hands of William Clark. The peticoner sett forth by his peticon that the said William Coudrey stands Justly Indebted unto him in Thurty Two Shill for a Gun and one hundred and fiftye pounds of pork for A shurt and proved the same; the Court therefor order that the peticoner be paid, etc.

John Dickerson peticoner, Agt the Estate of William Coudrey in the hands of William Clark. [The Court there for order that the peticoner be paid].

Simon Parling this day Cam and in open Court Accknowlidged that he have sold unto John Hill & to his heires and Assignes for ever A plantacon with three hundred Acres of Land Lyeing and being secuated on the north west side of the broad Creek Adjoyning unto the Land of Thomas Haward; and that he have recd full satisfacon for the same.

Upon the peticon of Stephen Whetman the Court doe order and Appoint that Edward Southrin and George Young doe Apprize the Lands Goods and Chattls of Thomas Grimdick deceased and that An Inventory their of be brought into the next Court.

John Kiphaven peticoner Agt Baptis Newcomb Administrator of the Estate of John Hagester deceased.

Upon the peticon of John Barker the Court Grant unto him three hundred Acres of Land att one penny ꝑ Acre yealy [sic] rent to be paid the proprietary; on Condition that he seat the said Land within one year after this Grant; wart given out the same day.

The Court order and Appoint John Roades Norton Claypoole William footcher and John Depree to Apprize the Estate debts Goods and Chattls of Capt John Avery deceased; and that an Inventory there of be brought Into the next Court.

It is ordered by the Court that the shriefe doe forth with Collect & pay unto William Darvall for the use of his sloop Carriing the burgies up to Chester and back Againe one Thousand pounds of Tobacco; and the Burgies doe Consent by reason that the sloop was hired Cheaper then the said William Darvall Could Aford it that they will pay as followeth out of their owne Estates; Edward Southrin one hundred pounds of Tobacco William Clark Two hundred pounds of Tobacco Luke Wattson Two hundred pounds of Tobacco Alexander Draper one hundred pounds of Tobacco; Nathanil Walker one hundred pounds of Tobacco; Cornelis verhoofe Two hundred pounds of Tobacco; and John Vines one hundred pounds of Tobacco.

The Court Grant the Jurey An order for their fees In the Cause that they Try this Court betwene John Bellamey Plt and Henry Smith Junr deft.

It was publickly declared in Court this day that there was A plantacon house and foure hundred Acres of Land of William Coudrey secuate Lyeing and being on the south East side of Ceeder Creek within this County ne[ar] Adjoyning unto the Land of Alexander draper to be sold in open Court by order of Court and it was also sett up att the Court house door to give notice unto all persons whatsoever of the sale thereof to the End that the said plantacon Land and primisses might be sold to the best and most Advantidge that may be for him the said William Coudrey; it being for the bringing up the Child of the said William Coudrey Begotten upon the body of Sarah Warrin; and also for the paying his debts that he owes in this Govermt and severall persons haveing beed for the said plantacon Land and premisses Coming up to the sume of seaven Thousand pounds of Tobacco which said sume was bed by John Hill; and After that William Darvall beed seaven thousand one hundred pounds of Tobacco; After that William Clark did beed seaven Thousand Two hundred pounds of Tobacco; and it being severall times Calld to see if any person would Exceed that price and none would; soe the said William Clark is to have the sd plantacon Land and primisses by order of Court for the sd sume of 7200 ℔ of Tobacco; And to be Accountable for the sd sume unto him that shall undertake to bring up the Child and the Craditer; the Child is undertaken to be brought up by the said William Clark untill it Attayne unto the Age of one and Twenty years for nineteene hundred pounds of Tobacco.

The Court Adjurnes untill the 13th day of the 12th moneth next ensueing the date hereof.

FEBRUARY 13th, 15th, 1682.

Att A Court Held att Lewis for the County of Sussex by the Kings Authority & by Commisson from William Penn proietary [sic] And Governor of Pensilvania and the Territoryes thereunto belonging the 13th & 15th days 12 mo, 1682; Justices present: William Darvall, Luke Wattson, John Roades, Edward Southrin, Robert Hart, John Kiphaven.

Halm Wiltbanck Agt Cornelis Johnson by way of searifacous. Last Court The said Cornelis Johnson was sumoned to shew Cause if any he Could wherefor he doe not give the said Halm Wiltbanck possession of the Land and premisses he Live upon. According to An order of Court and verdict of A Jurey of seaven men obtained in this Court the 8th day of the 1th Moneth 1681; The said Cornelis Johnson sheweth Cause by his plea delivered in to Court in writing; That he had obtained in this Court befor that time A verdict of A Jurey of Twelve men for the said Land and primisses According to the Laws of England and that the verdict of seaven men was and is Contrary to the Knowen Laws of England; And that the said Halm Wiltbanck did appeale from the verdict of the Jurey of Twelve men a forementioned; And that after he had Appealed he ought to have prosecuted his said Appeale And so A had no further triall for the said Land in this Court; And for the reasions and Causes A forsaid the deft doe refuse to deliver possession of the said Land and primisses; which he Humbly Conceive may be Judged to be sufficent Cause by this Court; The Court doe by the Consent of both parties Referr the bussnes untill the proprietary Com here and have A hearing of the said Cause and Give his Judgment therin.

An Action of the Case. Mathew Scarbrough Plt, Samll Jones Estate In Luke Wattson hands deft; [the Court order an non suit].

An Action of debt. John Hill Plt, Saml Jones Estate in Luke Wattsons hands deft; wittnes Thomas Davids. The Plt declared that the deft stands justly Indebted unto him in three Cows and three Calves by bills which the Plt proved; and the deft goeing out of the County and took no Care to satisfie the Plt; the Plt Caused what Effects the deft have in the said Luke Wattson hands to be Attached; to the end that the Plt may be satisfied and paid the same with Cost of suit; the deft not Appearing the Court Refer the Cause untill the next Court befor they passe Judgment; [At a Court 14th 6 mo, 1683, refer'd till the after noon; The Court granted Judgment with Execution against the sd Estate with Cost of Suit he giveing Security to ye Court to double the Vallu of this Action that if the Judgment be reverst within a twelve mon. & a day he must answer it.]

An Action of the Case. John Hill Plt, John Smith Estate deft. [Refered untill the next Court.]

Three Actions against "Saml Jones Estate in Henry Stracther hands" being those of John Hill, John Roades and Henry Stracther].

An Action of Trasspasse. Sarah Avrey Plt, Administratrix to Capt Jo Avery deceased, Rich Harvey deft. The Plt not Appearing to present hur suit and the deft Craveing a non suit the Court order an non suit to be entered Agt the Plt with Cost of suit Als Execution.

An Action of the Case. Charles Bright Plt, Cornelis Johnson deft. Wittnes Will Townsend baptis newcomb will Troter & Henry Harmon. The Plt declare that the deft did Agree with him to make a Crop on his Land and that the plt was to have one thurd part of the Crop; which the deft deney to let the plt have to his damiadg four Thousand pounds of Tobacco and proved that he did proceed in the making of the said Crop; the Court there for passe Judgment for the plt Agt the deft for the one thurd part of the Crop that the plt Can prove was made on the said Land the Last year with Cost of suit Als Execution. Henry Harmon Testafied that he messured thurty three barrells of Indin Corn that was made on the said Land that year.

An Action of the Case. Sarah Avery Administratrix of the Estate of Capt John Avery deceased, William Traford deft. [The Plt not appearing a non suit was ordered by the Court.]

This day Richard Patte Accknowlidge in open Court the sale of foure hundred Twenty one Acres of Land Lyeing on the South East side of the broad Creeke unto Thomas Hall his heires and Assignes for ever for which he Accknowlidg to have Received full satisfacon for the said Land and premisses and Ingage to procure A patton for the same.

The Court upon the peticon of John Roades order him to be paid Twenty Shillings out of the Estate of Thomas Grindik deceased Twenty Shillings being for his fee as Crowner.

Upon the peticon of Henry Bowman the Court Grant him an order to take up soe much Land in the neck betwene Slater Branh [Branch ?] and Ceeder Creeke As it shall Appear he is short of by being Invoysed in in three severall surveys.

This day Andrew Depree Accknowlidg in open Court A patton and Conveyance of foure hundred Acres of Land unto John Depree and to his heires and Assignes for ever.

This day John Depree Accknowlidg in open Court the sale of three hundred Acres of Land unto Andrew Depree, etc.

Upon the peticon of Georg Benson the Court Grant unto him three hundred Acres of Land at one penny ℔ Acre yearly on Condicon that he seat the said Land with in one year After this Grant; wart given out the 17th Insint.

Upon the peticon of Thomas Adkinson the Court Grant him three hundred Acres of Land at one penny ℔ Acre * * * wart given out 17th Insint.

This day David Corsey Accknowlidged in open Court the sale of three hundred Acres of Land that have bene surveyed for him Lyeing Adjoyning to the Land of Thomas Pemberton and Jacob Shattham in the neck Called Winders neck unto John Hill and to his heires and Assignes for ever; and he doe Acknowlidg to have received full satisfacon for the said Land.

This day Richard Bundock Assigned over In open Court unto Norton Claypoole and his Assignes one man servant by name Mathew osborne for three years from the seaventh day of this Moneth; And the said Mathew Consented unto the said Assignment and doe Ingag to serve the said nortton Claypoole and his Assignes the said time of three years on Condition that the said Nortton Claypoole doe save his Land that the said Mathew Have a Grant from this Court for; or sell the said Land to the satisfacon of the said Mathew; the said Mathew is to Allow or sarve for the time that he shall be Imployed in seating the said Land; All ways provided that it is the Custom of Vergina for servants that are Judged in Court to sarve untill they Attayne unto the Age of foure and Twenty years.

This day John oakey Accknowlidg in open Court the sale of three hundred Acres of Land unto John Kiphaven and Alexander Moulston and to their heires and Assignes for ever which said Land Lye betwene the Land of Henry Smith and Samwell Gray and have received full Satisfacon for the same.

This day Richard Bundock proved in Court the Last will and Testament of Richard Shoulter deceased by which said will the said Richard Bundock and Nathaniel Walker are made and appointed Executors of the said will and the Court doe Grant Letter of Administracon unto them Accordingly.

This day William Trotter Accknowlidged in open Court the sale of Nine hundred Acres of Land unto William Clark and to his Heires and Assignes for ever; the said Land Lyeing on the South East side of the Cold Spring Adjoyning unto the Land of the said William Clark Henry Smith Samwell Gray and Michall Chambe[rs]. In the Dockett.

Test. WM. DARVALL.

Harklos Sheepard peticoner. The peticoner sett forth by his peticon that Capt John Avery deceased did befor the peticoner was Joyned in Marridge with Mary the wife of the peticoner and daughter of the said Capt Avery that he would give unto your peticoner with his daughter A Certaine parcell or tract of Land which was Late in the occupacon of Thomas Davids together with the plantacon house and premisses there unto belonging which said Land Lyes Betwene the Land of John Depree and the Land that the widdow Avery now Lives upon; and that the said John Avery did After the said Marridg was solmonized Give your peticoner possession of the said Land and premisses; and that he did declare the same when he Lay upon his death bead and proved the same by the Testamony of severall wittnes; the Court takeing the same Into their Consideracon and severall members of the Court haveing themselves hard the said John Avery say that his daughter Mary Should have the said Land; the Court there for passe their Judgment that the Land doe properly belong unto the peticoner and to his heires and assignes for ever.

This Day Bryant Rowle Accknowlidged In open Court A Conveyance of Two hundred Acres of Land unto Barnwell Garritt and to his heires and assignes for ever And Bartree the wife of the said Bryant Consented unto the same in open Court.

Michall Chambers Accknowlidged in open Court this day the sale of Two hundred & Twenty Acres of Land unto William Trotter and to his Heires and Assignes for ever Lyeing and Adjoyning unto the Land that the said William Trotter Conveyed in Court this day unto William Clark.

Upon the peticon of Sarah Avery the Administrix of John Avery deceased the Court is pleased to Remitt and for Give the fine of the said John Avery that is as yet unpaid being nine hundred and fiftye pounds of Tobacco.

William Borne peticoner Agt John vines Sherife. The peticoner sett forth that he sustayned foure pounds six shillings damiadg In that the Shriefe did not take security from John Brigs to prosecute the peticoner when he Caused him to be a rested at the suit of John Beaman And Nichols Greenbury; and the peticoner proveing his said damiadge the Court Grant unto the peticoner An order Agt the said John vines Shriefe for the said sume of foure pounds six Shillings with Cost of suit Als Execution.

Baptis Newcomb peticon that the Certivecate of survey of the Land that was surveyed for John Hagester deceased and by him Given to Ann his wife might be returned in the peticoners name; the Court doe there for order that the Certivecate of survey be returne by the surveyor in the peticoner name he being Married to the Late wife of the sd John Hagester deceased.

Upon the peticon of Barnwell Garritt the Court Grant unto him three hundred Acres of Land at one penny ℔ Acre yearly on Condicon that he seat, etc.; Wart Given out 1th Insint.

This day the Inventory of the Lands Goods and Chattls of Thomas Grymdyk deceased was brought into Court which Amount unto the sume of foure pounds five shillings and foure pence; And Seaven Thousand pounds of Tobacco.

This day Henry Harmon Accknowlidged In open Court the sale of six hundred Acres of Land house plantacon & premisses unto William Clark and to his heires Executors Administrators and Assignes for ever the said Land Lyeing on A neck of Land Called Kimble neck; Betwene the Land that Cornelis Johnson now Live upon and the Land that Cornelis Johnson sold unto the said William Clark that John Streate is seated upon for the said Clark.

Test. WM. DARVALL.

The Shriefe peticon and sett forth that he have suffered for there not being A prisson in the County And Craves that the Court would be pleased speedily to procure A prisson to secure those that shall be Committed to his Custidy; the Court taking the same Into their Consideracon doe therefor order that Luke Wattson be ordered forth with to build a Court Couse [sic] and prisson According to his Agreement with the Court the 1th 10 mo, 1680. Signed by William Darvall, John Roades, John Kiphaven, Edward Southrin.

This day William Lowing Accknowlidged In open Court the sale of the one halfe part of three hundred Acres of Land and primisses Lyeing Betwene the Land of John Roades and William Roades unto William Darvall and to his heires and Assignes for ever the other halfe part of the Said Land being John Simons and his heires and Assignes for ever.

This day Cam John Smith and in open Court Accknowlidged the Sale of three hundred Acres of Land unto John Hill and to his Heires and Assignes for ever the said Land Lyeing on A neck Called Kimbls neck Betwene the Land of William Clark Abraham Potter and John Vines; and did also Accknowlidge to have received full satisfacon for the said Land & premisses.

Cornelis Johnson this day Accknowlidged the sale of one hundred Acres of Land in open Court unto William Trotter and to his heires and Assignes for ever. The said Land Lyeing upon the neck Called Kimbls neck Adjoyning unto the Land of Richard Patte by the marsh side.

The Court order that John Smith doe give good securety to Appear parsonably at the next Court to be holden for this County to Answer then and there to such things as shall be objected Against him on the behalfe of the King or proprietary in the sume of fortye pounds sterl Money and in the meane time to remaine in safe Custidy; Att the request of the said John Smith Henry Bowman and Stephen Whetman doe hereby Ingage themselves Joyntly and Severally in the said sume of fortye pounds sterl money to the proprietary for the said John Smith Appearance at the next Court as a for said Als Execution.

Luke Wattson peticoner. The peticoner sett forth by his peticon that whereas he was oblidged to build a Court house and prisson; and that sence that time the Govermt is Altered and that he is much Imployed in other publick bussnes soe that it would be much to his damiadg if he should be Confined to doe the said work; the Court taking the same into their Consideracon; doe hereby order that he shall be released and discharg from the said Agreement all ways provided that this order shall in no ways Release or discharge the Said Luke Wattson from the damiadg that the Shriefe hath or shall suffer for want of a prisson to this day.

The Court Adjurne untill the second thurd day of the next second Moneth 1683.

April 10th, 1683.

Att A Court Held at the Towne of Lewis for the County of Sussex by the Kings Authority & by Commicon from William Penn proprietary and Governor of Pensilvania & Territoryes there unto Belonging the 10th day of the second Moneth 1683; Justices present Luke Wattson, John Roades, Edward Southrin, Robert Hart, John Kiphaven.

An Action of the Case upon an Attachment. Cornelis Johnson Plt, Charles Brighte Estate deft. The Plt not Appearing to prosecute his suit the Court order an non suit to be entred Agt the Plt with Cost of suit Alias Execution.

An Action of the Case. John Barker Plt, Will Bradford deft. [As above.]

An Action of ye Case. William Darvall Plt, William Borne deft; Wittnes Will Rodney & Marton Hoogland. Jureymen H. Bowman S. Gray G. Young H. Shepard J. Cullison J. Smith T. Haward W. Beverla J. Crew J. Simons M Chambers H. Strecher. The Plt declared that the deft stands justly Indebted unto him in Thurteen Thousand Eightye Two pounds of Tobacco upon Acct and proved the same by the Testamony of William Rodeney and Marton Hoogland and the deft owne Confession; the Cause was Left to A Jurey who brought in their verdict that they find for the Plt with Cost of suit and one Shilling damiag the Court passe Judgment According to the verdict of the Jurey Alias Execution.

An Action of the Case. William Borne Plt, William Darvall deft. The Plt not proceeding According to Law the Court order An non suit to be entred Agt the Plt with Cost of suit Alias Execution.

An Action of the Case. ffrancis Henry Plt, William Borne deft. The Plt declare that the deft stands Justly Indebted unto him in three hundred pounds of Tobacco for Carting of Timber to William Darvalls house at Lewis and proved the same the Court therfor passe Judgment for the plt Agt the deft * * * Execution given out the 1th 3 mo, 1683.

This day John Johnson Senr Accknowlidge in open Court the sale of Two hundred Acres of Land unto John Hill & to his heires and Assignes for ever; the said Two hundred Acres of Land being part of the Land that was John Kings which was his Mothers thurds.

John Danill Peticoner Agt Nathanil Bradford. The peticoner sett forth that he was Transported out of Burbados Into Vergina to sarve for three years and that he was Sold for the same time to the deft; and that the deft have detained the peticoner foure years & Ten or Eleaven Moneths in his services and proved the same by the Testamony of Capt John Osborne one of the Justices of the peace of Sumersett County in the provience of Maryland; the deft sun pretending that the peticoner is not yet free the Court doe therefor order that the Cause be Refered untill the next Court and that the deft sun doe in the meanetime Give his ffather notice there of to the end that he may make his defence therein if any he Can at the next Court; and that the peticoner in the meanetime shall have Libiart [sic] to procure further Testamony of what he declare; Refference. [At Court 14th 6 mo, 1683 "because neither Plt nor Deft appear'd the Action was dismist]."

The Court Grant unto Arther Star one Towne Lott Adjoyning to Pagons Creeke for to sett up A Tan office.

John Vines Shriefe & William Emmatt peticoners on the behalfe of themselves and the Inquest that sarve on the body of Thomas Grimdick deceased; and desier an order for theire feese in that Cause It being as Appeare by an Account produced in Court Three pounds nine shills and foure pence; the Court Grant an order to the peticoner for the said sume of £3 9s 4d Agt the Estate of the said Thomas Grimdick deceased in the hands of Stephen Whetman his Administrator with Cost of suit Alias Execution.

The Court Adjurne Untill further order.

Test. WM. CLARK.

May 27th, 28th, 1683.

Att A Court Held at Lewis in the County of Sussex by the Kings Authority & by Comission from William Penn Proprietary & Governor of the Provience of Pensilvania & Territories there unto Belonging; the 27th & 28th days of the Second Moneth Anno; Dm; 1683; present, Will Penn Proprietary, & Governor; Capt William Markham Deputy Governor; Justices: William Darvàll, Luke Wattson, John Roades, Edward Southrin, Robert Hart, John Kiphaven.

An Action of Trasspase & Ejectment. John Bellamey plt, Luke Wattson deft; Henry Stracther Henry Skidmore Danil Browne Will Clark John Roades Skidemore & Clark again wittneses Tho Groves; Edmond Cantwell & Will Traford. Jureymen: Halmanias Wiltbanck Will Dere Stephen Whetman Rich Law Will Kening Jo Cullison Bryant Rowles Samll Gray Robt Harley Junr Henry Bowman Baptis Newcomb Harclos Sheepard. The plt declared by his Atturney John Hill that the deft did Cutt fall and destroy severall of his Timber trees on the plts Land Lyeing at Slarter Branch on Prime hook neck; The deft plead that the Land is non of the plts but that the said Land is Capt Henry Smiths the Cause was Left to A Jurey and the above wittneses Excamined and the Cause pleaded to on both sides; And the whole matter being sumed up by the proprietary the Jurey went out and after a Long debate they brought in their verdict that they find for the deft; The plt by his Atturney Craves an Appeale to have the Cause trid befor the Governor & Provincall Council at Phelidelphia which the Court Grant unto the plt he puting in good & sufficent securety to prosecute his said Appeale.

This day Henry Jones Norton Claypoole and Alexander Draper is by the Inhabitents of this County Chosen and Appointed to be peace makers to end and detarmine all differances that shall any ways Hapen or Rise Betwene man and man if they Can; for one whole year now next ensueing from the date hereof; which said peace makers Are ordered and Appointed by the Governor & the rest of the Court to sitt about such Matters the Last thur[d] day of the week in every moneth.

Henry Jones and Alexander Draper doe solmonly promise in the presence of God in open Court; that they will to the best of their Knowlidg and understanding discharge their office of peace Makers; for one year.

The Laws of this Government was this day openly published in Court being the 28th day of the thurd Moneth about the Midle of the day.

This day John Kiphaven Alexander Moulston Halmanias Wiltbanck Cornelis verhoofe Cornelis Johnson francis Henry Cornelis Plockhoy Anthony Hamen [Hancen?] Alias Haverla haveing publiquely in open Court solmonly promised and declared in the presence of God Alleaigance to the King of England his heires and successers; And fidelity to William Penn Proprietary and Governor of the provience of Pensilvania & Territories thereunto belonging and to his heires & successers After which the Governor declared all of them to be Naterallized and as free men of this Government as any English men.

The Court is Adjurned untill the second thurd day of the 4th mo, 1683. Test. Wm. Clark.

WM. PENN PROPRIETARY & GOVERNOR OF YE PROVINCE OF PENSILVANIA & YE TREITORY'S THERE UNTO BELONGING.

These are to will & require all persons wthin ye County of Sussex that have no Pattents for the Lands or are willing to have their Pattents [ren'd?] to send up their Certificates of Survey & Old Patents by Wm. Clark Surveyor for ye Lower Counties, before ye 28th instant into my Secretaries Office, and appoint some person or other to take Patent out for them; given at Philodelphia ye 13th 4 mo, 1683.

BY WM. PENN PROPRIETARY & GOVERNOR OF YE PROVINCE OF PENSILVANIA & TERRITORIES THEREUNTO BELONGING, & COUNCILL. A PROCLAMATION.

Whereas severall complaints have been made by the freemen & indwellers of this Province against their own servants who doe imbasell & dispose of the goods & monys of their Masters & Mistris: contrary to Law & Justice to the great loss & detremt of their sd Master & Mistris. These are therefore by the Kings Authority strictly to forbid all manner of People wtsoever at any time to give lend truck sell dispose pay or receive any manner of Cloathing goods or mony to or from any Servant whatsoever without their Master or Mistris Warrant for the same, & that if any person shall at any time take receive or possess goods of any kind or monys wtsoever from any Servant as aforesd or deliver or pay to any such servant any monys or goods whatsoever wthout Order as aforesd such offenders shall be lyable to pay to ye owner of such Servant double ye vallue thereof besides ye sd goods & monys as a foresd wherefore every Justice of ye Peace are hereby strictly required and commanded & other ministers of Justice to make strict inquiery after such persons so offending & such severely to punish according to Law as they will answer ye contrary at their Peril. By Order of ye Governor & Councel.

MOORE, Secretary.

Given at Philodelphia ye 23th 3d mo 1683.

BY WM. PENN PROPRIETARY & GOVERNOR OF YE PROVINCE OF PENSILVANIA &c & PROVINCIAL COUNCILL THEREOF. A PRO CLAMATION.

For as much as there are severall unjust & unlawfull proceedings of severall persons yt have psumed to take Horses Boats & Canoies in this Province & Territories without leave from ye Owners to their great prejudice often pretending ye Horses are Strays & broken out of ye Fence as allso ye Boats &c were borrowed or runn adrift. The Governor & his Counc haveing taken this into their consideration for ye preventing of those unjust actions for ye future doe by these presents strictly charg & command all manner of persons who have ye administration of Justice in this Province & Territories thereunto belonging to punish all such offenders according to the Laws of this Province made & provided for in that behalf of wch all manner of persons are to take notice of, & so yeild All true obedience at their Peril. by Order of ye Governor & Councel

N. MOORE, Secretary.

Given at Philodelphia ye 9th 4th mo, 1683.

By Wm. Penn Proprietary & Governor of ye Province of Pensilvania &c: & Provinciall Councell thereof.
A Proclamation.

The Law of God & Man requireing Sobriety & good Manners to be propagated & maintained in all Nations & Cuntryes & haveing as in duty bound a tender respect unto Gods Honor & ye good of ye Souls of ye People & desirous that all in all stations may doe well these are therefore to charg & strictly to command the Ministers of Justice & Magistrates of ye Province & Territories to Oversee ye manner of ye People & strictly to Punish & Suppress all disorders & Debaucheries wch are or shall be committed espeacially in any Ordinary or Publique Drinking house & that without respect of Persons as you will answer the Neglect thereof at your Peril.

By Order of ye Governor & Coun.

N. Moore, Secretary.

Given at Philodelphia the 9th of 4th mo, 1683.

By Wm. Penn Proprietary & Governor of ye Province of Pensilvania &c & Provincial Councel thereof.
A Proclamation.

The Governor Provincial Councel & General Assembly haveing taken into their Serious consideration the present state & future good of this Province &c have made & provided divers good & wholesome Laws to encourage Virtue Trade & Comerce & to Punish & Suppress looseness & impiety wch distroys all Civil society it hath pleased ye Governor & Council to Quicken the execution thereof & this day do therefore strictly require & command all Magistrates & Ministers of Justice forthwith to observe & execute or cause to be executed all the sd Laws in all Points without delay favour or affection upon ye Penaltyes therein expressed & all concerned are hereby, required to take notice thereof at their Peril.

By Order of ye Governor & Councel.

N. Moore, Secretary.

Given at Philodelphia ye 9th 4th mo, 1683.

Aminadab Hanger his Cattell Mark: A Swallow Fork on both Ears & a hole on ye right Ear.

Danll Helier his Cattell Mark: A Swallow Fork on boath Ears & under bitten on ye Left.

Edward Sowthern's Brand Mark V over 4

In ye Name of God Amen

I Edward Bootle of Deal County being Sicke & Weeke yett of sound & perfect Memory * * *

Imprimus. I give & bequeath unto Mr. John Kipshaven Son John the one half of my land & plantation if it please God that I dye without Wife or Issue that is to say to him & his Heires for Ever never to be sould but to continue from Heir to heir for Ever.

Item. I give and bequeath unto John Depree & his Son Jacob Depree the other half of my Land & Plantation if it please God that I dye without Issue or Wife that is to say to them or their heirs for Ever, never to be sould but to continue from Heir to heir for Ever &

if the said John Depree should dye now or before his Son Jacob comes to age then it is my Will that Andrew Depree shall keep this Moiety of Land in his Possession untill the sd Jacob Depree doth come of Perfect Age & then to deliver the sd Jacob Depree possession of this said Moiety of Land.

Item. I give to John Kipshaven all the goods that is in my house if I dye this present.

Item. I give to John Whittman one old Sow Called Sib * * *

Item. I give unto Elisabeth Whittman Two Young Hens & a Cock * * *

Item. I give unto Martha Kipshaven one young Sow wch came of that Old Sow * * *

Item. I order 300 lb of Tobacco to be pd to Mr. Avery for Surveying the Land out of that 399 of Tobacco wch is due to me from John Oaky * * *

Item. I give to Wm. Emmatt Junr one Grisled Sow bought of John Hackester * * *

Item. I Order my great Barrow to be killed at my Funeral I order to be paid to Mathias Everson for 50 lb of Tobacco that I owe him my White faced Barrow.

Item. I order Mr. John Kipshaven to pay 60 lb Tobacco to Mr. Norton Claypoole.

Item. [Order John Kipshaven & Jacob Depree and their Heirs for Ever to pay something towards maintaining the Widdows & Fatherless Children of this County * * *

Item. Order that Mr. John Kipshaven & John Depree pay for the Pattent of my Land each of them his part * * *] I have sett my hand & Seal the Seaventh day of December, 1682.

The Mark of
EDWARD A BOATLE

the mark of
[Witnesses:—Jeffery × Summerford
the mark of
Steven S W Whitman
Wm. Emmatt

Mary Claypoole Daughter to Norton & Rachell Claypoole borne aboute the 1st Houre in the morning 10th day of the 8th Month 1682 in the presence of Edward Sowthorns wife the midwife, Katherine Hews, & her daughter Elizabeth, Honor Clark, jonica Wiltbanck Margarett Molleston, Sewsanna Grey, Sarah Stretcher, Sarah Bartlet.

WILLIAM PENN PROPRIETARY & GOVERNOR OF YE PROVINCE OF PENSILVANIA & THE TERRITORIES THEREUNTO BELONGING.

Reposeing confidence in thy Ability & Integrity I doe hereby constitute & appoint the Norton Claypoole of Lewis in ye County of Sussex to be Clark of ye Courts of Sessions to be holden for the said County to act theirin Justly & dilligently according to Law, to the best of thy understanding; this Commission to be of force for One Year or untill further Order given at Philodelphia ye 12th 3d mo in ye 35 Year of ye King, ye third Year of my Government & in ye Year of our Lord 1683.

WM. PENN.

WM. PENN PROPRIETARY & GOVERNOR OF YE PROVINCE OF PENSILVANIA & TERRITORIES THEREUNTO BELONGING.

By Virtue of the Authority derived unto me I doe hereby in the Kings name Constitute appoint and Authorise ye Alexander Moleston to be a Justice of ye Peace in ye Jurisdiction of ye County of Sussex giveing the full power to Act in ye sd Office according to Law & ye trust reposed in ye of wch all persons are to take notice & to give thee the due respect & Obedience belonging to thy place in the discharging of thy Duty this Commission is to be of Forse for ye space of One Year after the date hereof or till further Order given under my hand & Seal at Lewis in ye County of Sussex ye third day of ye third Month 1683 being ye Second Year of my Government. WM. PENN.

These to ALEXANDER MOLESTON.

WM. PENN PROPRIETARY & GOVERNOR OF YE PROVINCE OF PENSILVANIA & TERRITORIES THEREUNTO BELONGING.

TO MY LOVEING FREIND WM. CLARKE:—Greeting.—By Virtue of ye Authority derived unto me I doe hereby in ye Kings Name constitute appoint & Authorise the Wm. Clark to be a Justice of ye Peace & President of ye Court of Justice in ye County of Sussex formerly called ye Whorekill, who with any three other Justices shall be a Court of Judicature in ye sd County giveing the full Power to Act in ye sd Office according to Law & ye trust reposed in thee, of wch all persons are to take Notice & to give the due respect & obedience belonging to thy place in ye discharging of thy Duty this Commission to be in force for ye Space of One Year after ye date hereof or untill further Order.

Given under my hand & Seal at Lewis in ye sd County of Sussex the First day of the third Month 1683. Being ye Second Year of my Government. WM. PENN.

The 12th of 4 Mon: 1683. Thé Justices present at a Court held for the County of Sussex: John Roads, Edw. Southern, John Kiphaven, Alexander Mollison.

An Action of ye Case. Art Johnson Ver Kerk Plts, John Barker Deft. The Plts declares that he purchased a Sorrell Gelding of Alexander Oliver which sd Gelding Run at Jno Barkers Plantation, & yt the sd Oliver did give power unto ye Plants to take ye sd Gelding as by a bill of Sail from under the sd Olivers hand but when the Plant did goe to ye house of ye sd Barkers to Fetch away the Gelding the Deft would not suffer him bud did detain ye sd Gelding from ye Plt to his damidg. The Plt produced a bill of Sail for ye Horse the Deft said that he purchased the Horse before the bill of Sail was made, so it was referd till ye next Court. [At a Court 14th 6 mo, 1683—"The Plt not appearing the Court granted a nonsuit against the Plt with Cost of Suite."]

The Court Adjurn'd till ye 2d Tewsday 6 mo, 1683, Because they had not a Coppy of ye Laws of ye Govern.

At A Court held at Lewis in the County of Sussex the 14th 6 mo, 1683. Justices present: Luke Wattson, John Roads, Edward Southern, Alex. Moleston, John Kipshaven, Herculus Sheppard, Thomas Hart.

An Action of Debt. Harman Cornelison Plt, Art Johnson Verkerk Deft; with drawn by ye Plts Order.

An Action of Atachment. John Vines Plt, Peter Groningdike Deft. The Plt declares for Ten Pounds One Shil Six Pence due from ye sd Peter Groningdike for Sheriff Fees upon Accot. Withdrawn by Order of ye Plt.

An Action of Atachmt. Cornelius Verhoofe Plt, Richard Dawsons Estate Deft. The Plt declares for Eleaven Hundred & Twelve Pounds of Tobaco for Clarks Surveighing One Thousand Acres of Land Refer'd wth consent of ye Plant. [The case again coming before the Court] * * * Richard Dawson being deceased the Court grants a Nonsuite against ye Plant.

An Action of Debt. Hermanus Wiltbanck Plt, John Barnett Deft. The Plt declares for Eighteen Hundred Foot of Planck due upon bill. Withdrawn by ye Plant Order.

An Action of Debt due to Hen Smith. Luke Wattson Plt, Georg Martins Cattell Deft. The Plant Petitions for One Thousand Four Hundred and Eighty Pounds of Tobaco due from Georg Martin to Capt Henry Smith which was proved in Court the 11 Mo, 1677 with alowable Interest from that time. Refer'd till next Court. * * * The Deft not appearing or Cornelius Verhoof Atturney for Georg Martin pleaded against the Accot or Debt & further saith Georg Martin hath no Cattill in the hands of Baptist Newcomb, it was refer'd to the next Court.

An Action of the Case. Hermanus Wiltbanck Plant, Cornelius Johnson Deft. The Plant declares that the Deft unjustly detains from him a parcell of Land contrary to former Orders of Court & Governors approbation which our said Proprietary allso did confirm the same promisses as was done by ye Court & Governor before onely was pleased to referr to the Peace makers whether their might be any thing due to ye Deft for his Improvements or not but the Deft refused to plead before the Peace makers or have any thing to doe with them, the Plant not proving his Declaration the Court granted a Nonsuit to the Deft against ye Plant with Cost of Suite. [Brought up again 11 7 mon, 1683, when, the Court advised them to refer all differences to Men to be ended & determined betwen this and the next Court. The Plant nominated Luke Wattson & Cornelius Verhoof. The Deft nominated Henery Stecher & John Hill. In case John Hill doth not come hether before the 22nd Instant then the Deft to choose another. Then in case of differences—they to choose an Umpire.

An Action of Debt. Alexander Moleston Plant Richard Gill Deft. [Refer'd till next Court.]

An Action of the Case. Alexander Draper Plant, Robert Gillum Deft; [with drawn].

An Action of ye Case. Robert Gillum Plant, Charles Murffy Deft. The Plant declares for a bill or Note of One Thousand pounds of Tobaco payable by Edward Warner of Kent County unto the Plant which bill the Plant left in the hands of ye Deft for the use of Alexander Draper allso the Plant declares for one Coasting Coat the Deft took from the Plant & keeps it; with drawn by consent of both partyes.

An Action of the Case by Attachment. Richard Gill Plant, John Savage his Estate in ye hands of Jno Crew Deft. [Refer'd till next Court for Judgment.] [11 7 mo, 1683, again refer'd.]

Jefery Summerford Aged 43 years or there abouts & Elisabeth Johnson Aged 20 years or there abouts being examined saith that they heard Elisabeth Leveritt declare about Eight or Ten days before her departure out of this World that she did Will & Bequeath all what Estate she had unto Richard Bundick only one Cow Calf excepted which should be remaining for her son Richard Bracy at present & when Her Son Richard comes at Age the said Cow Calf with all her Increase to be deliver'd unto him by the said Richard Bundick.

A Coppy of what was Sworn in open Court concerning the last Will & Testament of Elisabeth Leveritt Sworn by Jefrey Summerford & Elisabeth Johnson. Signed JEFERY I S SUMERFORD
Signed ELIZABETH M JOHNSON

Richard Gill aged 42 years or their abouts saith yt Elisabeth Leveritt about two or three days before she Dyed did Will & Bequeath unto Richard Bundick a Mare or a Thousand pd of Tobaco in Robert Bracy's hands for the which sd Mare the said Robert Bracy did pay One Thousand ℔ of Tobaco out of the said Elisabeth Leveritts Estate & further did declare that if the sd Robert Bracy did refuse to pay the said 1000 ℔ of Tobaco it would trouble her that would come again. Sworn in open Court by Signed RICHARD X GILL

The Clarks Comition being Read, The Court Ordered ye Clarks Commition to be Recorded By Norton Claypoole [Clerricus?].

Joseph Lee Petitioner for a Town Lott which was granted upon the same Conditions of building as other's promis'd.

Thomas Edwards & Wm. Loyd Servants to John Moore in Pocoson in Virginia near York River was apprehended by Stephen Whittman & brought to Court where they confessed themselves Servants as afores'd the Court therefore Ordered them to be kept by the Sherriff till he can send to their Mr according to ye Laws of this Government.

Robert Bracy Petiti: this Court that the Bridg by Richard Bundicks may be speadily repaired the Court ordered William Bradford to gett the Bridg repaired wth speed.

John Johnson Senior was brought before the Court under suspition of Murdering his Wife, & the Deposition of Jno Oakys & Jefery Summerford was read, & the Verdict of the Jury of Twelve Women that endeavored to view the Corp's the Jurys Verdict is wee whose Names are here subscribed have endeavored to view the body of Susan Johnson and we could not discover one Sign of Murder. Jeffery Summerford denying that he saw the Roapes End strike her on the Burr of ye Ear which was one affirmation in his Oath; & the Court therefore accounted his Oath of No Vallew, & the Crowner & Jury clearing John Johnson by their Verdict the Court therefore takes John Johnson's word to appear next Court they intending to clear him if nothing more comes against him.

The Court Order'd that the Appraisers of Capt Avery's Estate should appraise it as it was when he Dyed as near as could be and if any of the 4 appraisers be wanting they may chuse another in his place & that Jno. Roads shall Swear them for the true appraising thereof.

The Court Order'd John Roads to deliver Samll Jones bill into the Clarks Office.

The Court Adjurned till the second Tewsday in the Nex Mon:.

August 31st, 1683.

Att A Special Court Called upon the Petition of Petter Adolph the 31th 6 mon, 1683. Justices present: William Clark, Luke Wattson, John Roads, Robert Hart, Alex. Moleston, Edward Southern.

An Action of the Case. Peter Adolph Plt, Hermans Wiltbanck Deft. The Plant declares that the Deft wrong fully detains & keeps from him Forty Pounds wt. of Silver Plate. The Defts Answer is that he keeps the Plate by virtue of a Contract made between them, & for the Consideration of wch Plate, the Deft is ingaged to mentain the Plant dureing his Life, the Plant produced his contract & one of ye Wettneses to Witt Will. Townsend declared that he saw the Plant sign & Seal the Contract according to the best of his knowledg but denyed to Swear possitively; John Washington declar'd as an Evidence for the Plant the day before the Contract was signed (then he was very sick and as he thincks not able to make that marke as is fixed for him to ye Contract. Petter Designy Doctor affirms to his knowledg that ye Plant was not sensible to understand such a Contract about two days before it was dated. Robert Clifton affirms the day before this Contract was signed the Plant was not sensible. John Brown declared that he brought the Plant a Chest & sett it down by him and after he saw the Chest & tooke notice of it, yett he asked him again for it, and bid him aske what he would for it and he should have it for said the Plant I shall Dye. Harmon Cornelison declared the Plant was very sick more like to dye then to live, ye day that this Contract was dated.

The Jury's Names as Follows:—Alexander Draper, John Cullison, Anthony Heverly, Baptist Newcomb, Will. Kenny, Will. Foutcher, John Depree, Stephen Whitman, Robert Bracy, Robert Richards, Fran. Williams, Rich. Laws. The Deft for want of one of his Evidences to Witt Corneli. Verhoof desired a refference untill the next Court. The Court is Adjourned till ye after Noon & Order'd ye Plant to give Security to answer it next Court else come to Tryall. Hermanus Wiltbanck Deft haveing put in Security to answer the Action next Court, the Court grants him a refference till the next Court. withdrawn the 8th of the 7 mon. by the Plant Order.

Mr. Clark & Mr. Sanders Commitions being read the Court Order'd them to be Recorded.

Baptist Newcomb hath this day agreed with the Court, to bring and deliver at the Town Landing where the Shipp is building Eighty Cyprus Logs twenty two foot Long each Log to contain at least One foot in thickness at the great End besides the Bark to be delivered between this & the twentieth day of the next 8th mon. for which the Court hath Obleidged themselves to pay unto the said Baptist or his Order the Neat Quantity of three Thousand Pounds of Tobaco to be paid betwen this & the 25th day of the next 10th mon. which said Timber is for building of a Prison & Court house.

The Court Ordered the Clark to write three Warrants to be directed one to each Cunstable Will. Carter Will. Foucher & John Richards for them to take an Accot of all the Tithables in their precincts & give in the Accounts to the next Court that is all males above 16 & under 60.

The Court Adjurn'd till the 11th day of ye next Month.

SEPTEMBER 11th, 1683.

At a Court Held at Lewis in the County of Sussex the 11th of the 7th Mon. 1683. Justices present: William Clark, Luke Wattson, Robert Hart, Alexander Moleston, Herculus Shepard.

An Action of ye Case upon Atachment. Hermanus Willtbanck Plant, The Estate of Wm. Beverly Deft. The Plant declares for Seaventeen Pounds thirteen Shil Nine Pence due upon Accounts the last Court the Deft Petiti. for a Refferance till this Court by reason that his prinsipal Evidence Henery Strecher who hath all his Writeings & Accounts are gon up the River & other of his evidences are not here which was granted till this Court, after much is put on both sides and many Objections against the said Account the Court advised them to refer it to men & accordingly the Plaintiff nominated Norton Claypoole the Defts chose Wm. Emmit & they doe declare in open Court that they doe refer all differences that are betwen them to the sd William & Norton giving them full power (if they cannot agree the said differences by or before the 20th day of this Instant) to chuse an Umpire to end & determin the sd differences & they doe promiss to Forfeit One Hundred Pounds if either of them refuseth to stand to the Award or determination of the said persons Nominated & Chosen or the Umpire which shall be chosen by the sd Norton & William.

An Action of ye Case. William Clark Plant, Edw. Southern Deft. * * * ye Plant not being here the last Court it was Refer'd by consent of the Deft till this Court, the Deft being absent upon the Publick bussiness it was refer'd to the next Court.

An Action of ye Case upon Atachment. Cornelius Johnson Plant, Charles Brights Estate Deft, in ye hands of Corn. Johnson. The Plant Petiti. last Court for one Cow & Seaven Barlls of Corn which is in the hands of ye Plant towards the satisfying of the Plant Three Thousand Five Hundred Pounds of Tobaco and by the Account unto the Plant from Charles Bright John Hill in the behalf of Henery Bowman proved that Charles Bright before his departure out of this County Sould the Cow to Henery Bowman, as for the Seaven Barlls of Corn that was refer'd to this Court the Plant not proveing that he had any such parcell of Corn in his Hands they Order'd a Nonsuite against the ye Plant.

An Action of ye Case. Hermanus Willtbanck Plant, Richard Gill Deft. [From last Court. At this Court] * * * We the Jury doe find for the Deft * * * ye Jurys Names Robert Bracy Antony Heverly Roger Gum Bap. Newcomb John Barker Wm. Kenny Will. Foucher John Depree John Simons Robert Richards Fran. Williams Stephen Whittman.

An Action of the Case. John Daniel Plant, William Bradford Deft. The Plant declares for satisfaction for near two Years Service which he hath served the Deft more than his time of servitude allso declares for freedome Mony as ye Law ℘vides. The Plant proved that he had served about one Year Nine Months more then his time of Servitude & they both refering it to the Court without a Jury the Court Order that the Deft Should pay to the Plant or his Order by and with the consent of the deft Three Thousand Pounds of Tobaco for whole satisfaction ye Deft to pay Cost.

William Emitt Deputy Coroner Plant, John Johnson senior. The Deft was oblidged last County Court to make his ℘sonal appearance before the Court to answer all & every such person that might or should appear against him on the Kings behalf to give evidence against or ꝑsecute him further on suspition of Murdering his Wife the last Court intending that if no body appeared further against him this Court & no further evidence given to sett him at Liberty ꝑclamation being made and no ꝑson appearing further against him he was cleared.

Abraham Pettors Pet. for a Town Lott being read was granted upon the same condition as Other Lotts were granted.

Thomas Edwards kept in Custody for a Runn away petitioned for his liberty the Court order him to be kept in Custody till next Court unless his Mr. comes or sends for him.

Mr. Luke Wattson signd & Seald a Conveyance of One Hundred Ninety Six Acres of Land called St. Giles to Samll Gray his Heirs Executors Administrators or Assignes for ever in open Court the 11th of the 7th Month 1683.

Will Carter Peti. that whereas his ꝑdecessors Otto Woolgast had but 300 Acres of Land Surveyed upon a grant or Warrant of 400 Acres that he may have the other hundred Acres Surveyed unto the other thre Hundred Acres.

Robert Johnson Petitioned against the Estate of Thomas Grindick for Twelve days work at 30 lb ꝑ day coming to Three Hundred & Sixty pounds of Tobaco.

William Bradford Petitioned that as the Court hath appointed him one of the Oversers of the High Ways that they will please to lett him know the bounds or Limitts of his precincts the Court Order'd he should have a Warrt. to summons in the inhabitants to help to mend the Ways and in the Warrant the Bounds of his Precincts shall be specified.

Whereas Will. Simmons had a Warrant from this Court for 300 Acres of Land which said Warrant Cornelius Verhoof doth declare he did never survey any Land upon that Warrant, therefore the Court granted that the said Simons may have his Warrant renewed.

Norton Claypoole acknowledged the Sale of One Thousand Acres of Land to John Glass & John Swain lying & being on the other side of ye Indian River whereof Wm. Kenning declared in open Court that he by Norton Claypools Order & apoyntment deliver'd them possesion by Turf & Twig.

The Jury Petitioned for there Fees according to their Summons in Petter Adolphus Cause and Hermanus Cause against Cornelius Johnson the Court therefore Order'd the Jury to have two shil a man for so many of them as appeared the Two days for Petter Adolphus & those that served but one for Petter Adolphus but 16d ꝑ man the other 8d ꝑ man & they of the Jury that were Sworn & Summon'd to serve in Hermanus his Cause to have 16d ꝑ man.

The Court Adjourn'd to the Second Tewsday of the 9th Month.

NOVEMBER 13th, 14th, 1683.

At A Court Held at Lewis for the County of Sussex by the Kings Authority & by Comition from William Penn propriator of the Province of Pensillvania and the territorys thereunto belonging the 13th & 14th days of the 9th month 1683. Justices present: William

Clark, Luke Watson, John Roades, Edward Southorne, John Kipshaven, Allexandr Molleston, Robt Hart, Herculus Shepard.

An Action of the Case. William Clark Plt, Edward Sowthorne deft; twice Referrd. Tne plt declares for two thousand foure hundred & two pounds of tobacco & one pounds sixteen shillings in Mony & three hundred pounds of porke dew upon acount; it hath bene twice Referd by Reason of the plt & deft absence being Imployed on publick buisness. The deft objected agst two articles in the plts Acount viz Stephens & Booths Grant & Warrant for Land as not dew to him to pay & allsoe agst one Article of 800 lb. tobaco of Will. Emmit's, The deft preferr'd an Acount agst the plt, the deft allsoe pretended 2000 lb. tobaco dew to him upon two parcells of Land sould unto the plt which wass in Maryland. The plt proved his Acount by his declaration & testimony of the truth of it and after pleading to on both sides the Jury went oute but had not Edward Sowthorns Acount with them; The jurye brought in theire verdict Wee of the jury doe finde for the plt with Costs Henry Bowman foreman the Court pass Judgment accordingly alias Execution Jurys Names viz Henry Bowman, John Deprey, Samwell Leonard, Halm Wiltbanck, Will. Beverly, Will Kenning, Peter Designy, Jno Barker, Robt Twilly, Robt Bracy, Jno King, Jno Symons, the Court ordered to be Entered or Recorded as followeth Edward Sowthorne did say & Affirme that the judgment of this Court is erronius agst him in this Action, The Court ordered him by fine to pay five pounds sterl. for the derogation of sentence of Court, The Court allsoe fines him ten shillings for saying or swearing * * * [The defendant was ordered to be taken from Court by the Sheriff and returned three times, Called William Clark, the president, "A Lyar," and did so much swearing that the Court imposed three fines of ten shillings each for the offense].

A prisoner by Mittimus. Abram Westrom Plt, Symon A Dutchman deft. The Mittimus declared that the prisoner or deft hath pretended himselfe to be A sorcerer or Conjuror. The Plt not Apearing to prosecute the prisoner or deft The Court ordered A nonsuite agst the Plt with Costs & that the prisoner be released oute of prison.

Cristian the Indian by way of Complaint brought two bills one whereof was against Cornelis Verhoofe & John Vines of which their apears to be remaining dew one third part of twelve botles of Indian Drinck foure duble handfulls of powder & three staves of Lead. The Court therefore orders that Cornelis Verhoofe & John Vines pay the Plt what is dew within A Month. The other bill is against the servant of Cornelis Verhoofe Called John Pye for two Matchcoates which the Court ordered he should forthwith pay unto the Plt otherwise for Not payment Execution to be granted within A Month.

John Street petitioned for one hundred & fifty Acors of Land where he may find it Cleare in this County which th Court Granted; Warrant given oute 15th 9th Month 1683.

The Court fines William Beverly & John Barker jurymen for not Attending the Court Twenty Shillings pr man.

The Court fined Cornelis Johnson for Abusing the Court & telling Luke Watson one of the justices he cared not A —— for him twenty Shillings.

William Carter petitioned the Court for three hundred Acors in this County, which the Court Granted.

The Court fined William Emmitt Twenty Shillings for saying that the Court gives the Land to Cornelis Johnson th[ ] is a diference between Halm Wiltbanck & Cornelis Johns[on] and afterward he being very peremptory giving ill Langua[ge] to the Court they fined him five pounds more.

Proclamation being made there is now to be Exposed to sale five hundred Acors of Land scituation of which by Cirtificate of Survey may Apeare & two hundred Acors m[ore] in the forke of the Cypruss Swamp belonging to the broad Kill which seaven hundred Acors of Land did belong to Thomas Grindike deceased for which Land severall persons bid mor[ ] But Mr. Griffen Jones of Phylodellphya Merchant being t[he] last & hyest bidder bought the sd seaven hundred Acors of La[nd] at two thousand three hundred pounds of tobaco to be pd between this & the next first month to Stephen Whittman Adminstrator of the sd Estate the Cirtificate of Survey was delivered to Grifen Jones above mentioned every one yt is A Creditor in the said Estate are required to bring there Acounts in to the Next Court & soe every one to have an equ[al] proportion of the Estate Acording to his Acount.

William Emmit petitioned the Court that his fine or fines might be remitted Acknowledging himselfe to be sorry for his fault therefore the Court upon his Submition ye Court hath remitted his fine of five pounds.

Henry Stretcher Peter Designy Daniell Hillyard and John Ross petitioned the Court that they might have satisfaction for their time & labour spent one day & night fetching the old boate & Apurtenances with the old tooles with A Woman & two Chilldren which they found at Cape James to this towne the Court ordered them ten shillings pr man to be pd oute of the boate & what belongs to her after the boate is sould.

Arthur Starr petitioned the Court that he might have A front Lott in the towne Instead of A back lott Which the Court formerly Granted him; This Court Grants him A lott instead of his back lott Adjoyning upon William Trottors in the second strete if Clear or elce the next lott upon Condition that he build a dwelling house by the next second Month or elce forfeit five pounds Ster.

Forasmuch as these overseers of the hyeways that hath served last yeare hath not done the worke According to their order the Court thinks fitt to continue the said overseers till the next 7th Month 1684 John Hill having Entered himselfe into the Imployment of the sosyety Samwell Gray is Chosen & Apoynted to serve in his place.

Warning being given by the Sherriff to the people to bring in their Acounts to the next Court of what they have Expended to serve the publick; the Court is Adjourned to the second twesday of the Next Month.

DECEMBER 11th, 1683.

At A Court Held at Lewis for the County of Sussex * * * the 11th day of the 10th Month 1683. Comitioners present: William Clarke, Luke Wattson, John Roades, Allexander Molleston, Herculus Shepard.

Robert Johnson petitioned agst the Estate of Thomas Grindike deceased, Twice Referrd. The petitioner petitioned last 7th Month Court against the Estate of Thomas Grindike for 12 days worke at 30lb tobaco per day coms to 360℔ tobaco, for want of Witnesses the Cause was Referrd to this Court. The petitioner proved his worke or labour performed & did Acknowledge he had receid in part of satisfaction one Gallon Rum at [and?] 100℔ tobaco. The Court judged twenty pounds of tobaco pr day to be Enough for his worke—therefore they ordered the petitioner one hundred and forty pounds of tobaco, if the Estate hold oute to satisfye all debts if not he should have his proportion.

Edward Sowthorne Acknowledged the sale of foure hundred Acors of Land which he now lives upon unto Griffen Jones of Phylodelphya Merchant, with the Apurtenances thereunto belongin acording to Articles of Agreament made & Concluded upon.

John Depree petitioned the Court that he might be allowed for two Wolves heads & Ninety five pounds of porke he lent the Burgesses which they ordered should be allowed him.

Thomas Hancock petitioned the Court for three hundred Acors of Land that is Clear in this County. The Court Granted on Condition that he should pay one penny an Acor yearely from the time of the Survey & that he shall seat build & Improve it within A yeare after the Survey.

John Browne petitioned the Court for A towne Lott Convenient to build A Sloope or Shallop. The Court Granted that he might have A towne Lott that is Cleare that Lott where the vessell is on the stocke A building Excepted the petitioner to forfeit five pounds if he doth not build A dwelling house within one yeare.

[The Court fines William Beverly twenty Shillings for Abusing the Court etc.]

The Court fines John Vines Henry Stretcher Andrew Depree & Barns Garrat fifty pounds tobaco pr man for Smoakin tobaco in the Court house [and later Allexander Molleston same amount for same offence].

The Court fines Allexander Molleston fifty pounds tobaco for smoakin in the Court house. [ditto Luke Watson].

Robert Johnson petitioned the Court that he might be allowed 10d. pr day for his 12 days worke that he did for Thomas Grindike for finding himselfe dyet during that time. The Court would not allow it, but order'd it to be Cast oute.

Robert Hignett Senior petitioned the Court for five hundred pounds of Tobaco dew to him for being Cryer of the Court for one yeare as he agread with the Court and yt he might have it pd oute of the fines or Amercements.

The Court Adjourned to the second Twesday of the 12th Month following.

FEBRUARY 12th, 13th, 1683.

At A Court Held by the Kings Authority * * * the 12th & 13th days of the 12th Month 1683. Comitioners present: William Clarke, Robert Hart, Allexander Molleston, Luke Wattson, John Kipshaw, John Roades, Edward Sowthorne & Herculus Shepard.

An Action of ye Case. Halm Wiltbanck plt, Estate of George Andrews being A Cow & A Calfe deft; once referd. The last 10th Month Court The Plt declared for two pounds foureteen shillings dew to him from Georg Andrews upon Acount; It was Referd to this Court. The Plt being dead the Action falls.

An Action of the Case. Robt Johnson Plt, William Butlor deft. The Plt declares declares for two hundred Acors of Land that he bought of the deft, & Craves Judgment of the Court that the deft May be Compelled to give him Legall posetion thereof & to ma[ke] him good title thereunto with Costs; the Deft pleaded that the Plt was obliged to make A Chimny A Clap board loft and partition Richard Laws & Joane Street declared * * * that the deft promised this Morning to make A Conveya[nce] of the said Land unto the Plt they allsoe declared that the Plt did allsoe promise to pay unto the deft foure hundred pounds of tobaco, Richard Laws Engaged the Plt should pay unto the deft foure hundred pounds of tobaco in A Month Will. Emitt engaged that the Plt should finish the house as the deft pleased & declar[ed] he was obliged to doe, that is to say A Chimny A Clap board lof[t] & partition, upon which Engagements the deft therefore did Acknowledge in open Court all his Rite & title to the tw[o] hundred Acors of Land, lyeing & being upon the great Kill unto Robert Johnson the Plt which is adjoining to the land of Otto Wulgast.

Randalph Shard Chirurgeon & Physitian agst the Estate of Cornelis Verhooft, for five pounds Ster. dew to him for his paines care & Medicins used to Cornelis Verhoofe in the time of his sickness, the petitioner proved by two Wittnesses that Cornelis did in his life time consent [to] allow him soe much, therefore the Court ordered him A judgment for the said 5lb Ster agst the sd Estate of Corne[lis] Verhoofe, with Costs; Execution given out 27 day 12 mo, 168[?].

William Cartor petitioned the Court for A towne Lott ffronting the Creek the first that hapeneth to be cleare the Court grants him that Lot next to John Roades fronting ye Creek upon Condition that he builds A dwelling house upon the sd Lott within one yeare after this day or else forfeit five pounds Ster.

William Clarke petitioned the Court for two towne Lotts upon the North side of the Cross street fronting the Kreeke the Court Grants him those two lotts on Condition that he builds two dwelling houses one upon each Lott * * *

Symon Pawlin being Chosen Cunstable did promise in the presence of God faithfully & truly to ofitiate the place or office of a Cunstable for one yeare or till another was Chosen.

John King being Chosen Cunstable did promise the same as Symon Pawlin did.

Andrew Depree petitioned agst John Oaky for the Meat of A sow of the petitioners that John Johnson junior Killed, which meat was carryed to John Oakys John Johnson senior testimony with Jeffery Summerfords was taken but not sufitient prove that John Oaky had the meate therefore the Court advised Andrew Depree to send Hue & Crye after the sd John Johnson to bring him back againe which he promised to doe.

The Court ordered the Sherriff to take Mary Oaky into his Custody till she pays five shillings for swearing in the face of the Court * * *

The Court fines Allexander Molleston five shillings for swearing * * *

John Roades petitioned the Court for A towne Lott fronting the Creek next Adjoyning to those two Lots that was Granted this Court to William Clarke which was Granted by the Court if Cleare on ye same conditions.

The Court Grants the jury an order for theire ffees in five Actions viz Luke Watson agst Walter Pomfry Estate Wm Beverly Jno Barker, Peter Designy agst the Estate of George Andrews Norton Claypoole Plt Babtist Newcome deft.

Luke Watson petitioned the Court for A towne Lott fronting the Creeke on the south side of that strete yt goes up to the place where the Court house is to be build the lot formerly granted to Wil. Darvall but now Cleare, which if Cleare the Court grants on the same conditions as to others.

John Vines Sherriff petitioned the Court for A front Lott in the towne which they Granted Next to William Cartors, on the same Conditions.

John Grantam petitioned the Court for a front Lott in the towne if Cleare or otherwise A back lott next unto the ffront, which the Court Granted on the same Conditions.

Roger Gum petitioned the Court for A front Lott they Granted him A back lott on the same Conditions.

Major Spencers letter to Mr. William Clarke desiring him with the rest of the Court to rectifye A Mistake in his Levyes he being Charged for his owne head & is above 60 yeares of Age & one of his Men gon from him before the list was taken the Court allowed his head to be abated but not his man.

John Walker petitioned the Court for 30, or forty Acors of Cleare land betwene Babtist Newcome & the Widow Hall, which the Court Granted if Cleare Warrant given oute the 15th 12th mo, 1683.

The Indian Assawmack Harmattamale Acknoledged in open Court the sale of one thousand Acors of Land to Mr Allexander Molleston which land is on the south side of the Indian Rivor.

Willam [sic] Cartor Petitioned the Court that he might [have] some Consideration or satisfaction for his time paines & troub[le] that he spent aboute taking the Levys; but the Court refused alleadging it was the Kings buisness.

William Wargent Petitioned that he might have his La[nd] Surveyed that Otto Wulgast tooke up on Mill Creeke in Cantwells Neck; which the Court Granted; the land being foure hundred Acors.

Robert Johnson petitioned the Court for one hundred & fifty Acors of Cleare land in any prt of this County; which the Court Granted; Warrant given oute 15th 12 mo, 1683.

The Court Adjourned this 13th day of the 12 month 1683 untill the second twesday of the next month.

William Bakers Eare marke for his Creetures the left Eare Crapt the Right Eare under bitten the first day of the 1st month 1683.

Robert the son of Norton & Rachell Claypoole borne the 26th day of the 11th Month 1683 aboute the 11th houre at night in the presence of Elizabeth the wife of Symon Pawlin the midwife Susanna the wife of Dennis ffisher & Elizabeth Tompson oure maid servant.

The 10th day of the first Month the freemen of this County being Assembled together did Chuse for their Dellogates or representatives for the Provintiall Counsell & Generall Assembly: Luke Watson for the Provinciall Councell; John Roades, Henry Bowman, Herculus Shepard, Samwell Gray, William Emitt, Henry Stretcher for the Assembly.

William Prentice Bill of Sale for three hundred Acors of Land to Luke Watson.

Know all men by these presents that I William Prentice of the County of Sumersett plantor hath sould unto Mr Luke Watson of Lewis one tract of Land containing three hundred Acors formerly surveyed by Mr ffrancis Jenkins, Lying of the North side of Slawtor Creek near Primehooke, to have & to hold the Aforesaid trackt of Land, to him the said Luke & his Heires for ever, from me & my heires, or any other person Claiming in thorough [sic] or by me, having recevd full satisfaction for the same as wittness my hand & seale this 30th July 1683.

Testes Hen Smith Will: Prentice
Thomas Pettly his O marke [seale]

February 11th, 1684.

At A Court Held by the Kings Authority & by Comi. from William Penn Propriator & Governor * * * at Lewis for the County of Sussex the 11th day of the first Month 1684. The Governors New Comition being read for William Clarke to be President & Luke Watson, Jno Roads John Kipshaven Robert Hart Allexander Draper & Robert Bracey to be Justices of the Peace for this County & any foure of them to keep Court Judicature in this County. This Declaration following was read:—

Wee William Clarke Luke Watson John Roades Herculus Shepard John Kipshaven Robert Hart Allexander Draper and Robert Bracy being by William Penn Esq Proprietary & Governor of Pensillvania, & territorys thereunto belonging Constituted & Authorised to be Justices of the Peace & A Court of Judicature for County of Sussex to Act in the same Imployment and trust for the preservation of the peace & Justice of the County In pursuance of oure said Comition acording to Law; Wee doe hereby in the presence of God declare that wee freely Acknoledge the said William Penn to be oure rightfull Proprietary & Governor; & doe solemnly promise by the Held of God to be just & true to him in managing & performing oure sd trust & faithfully discharging the same in obedience to oure said Comition & act therein according to the best of oure understandings; & if wee shall Wittingly or Willingly act or doe any thing contrary to Law [?] fidellity to oure Proprietary & the trust reposed in us by him: Wee doe hereby oblige oureselves to suffer & undergoe the same fine or punishment that the matter shall in Law deserve as if wee had actually taken an oath; which they Consented to withoute any objection.

Allexander Draper [seal]
Robert Bracy
his R B marke [seal]
Hercules Shepheard [seal]

The new Comition for ffrancis Cornwall & Robt Clifton to be Justices dated the 9th 2 mo, 1686, being read ye 8th 4 mo, 86 hey signed and sealed it before the Court. [F ?] Cornwall [seal]
the Marke of R Robert Clifton [seal]

There being present this Court: William Clark president Luke Watson John Roades John Kipshaven Robert Hart Allexander Draper and Robert Bracy Justices.

Thomas Winns Comition dated 13th 2 mo, 1687 was read in open Court the 3 3 mo, 1687 for him to be one of ye Justices Whereupon he declared his willingness to signe the above Declaration.

THO: WYNNE.

An Action of ye Case. Mathew Scarborow Plt, Robt Clifton Marying the Rellix & Administratrix of Capt John Avory deft. The Plt declares that Capt John Avory detained from him A Mare with her Encrease & the deft having the Estate of Capt John Avorys in his hands * * *.

An Action of the Case upon Attachment. Jonakin Wiltbanck Administratrix of the Estate of Halm Wiltbanck Plt, George Andrews Estate being A Cow & A Calfe deft. The Plt declares that George Andrews is Indebted to the Estate of Halm Wiltbanck * * * The Jury's names are Herculus Shepard, William Cartor, William ffutcher, Richard Harvey, Stephen Whittman, Thomas Howard, Richard Willis, Jacob Warren, Henry Scidmore, Richard Law, Morrice Edwards, Andrew Deprey.

An Action of the Case. Abell Portor Plt, Henry Bowman deft. The Plt declares that his servant Henry Williams A Cooper being run away & taken up in these parts the deft did Engage & promise to be security for his forth Coming upon demand, & the deft now refusing to procure or produce the said servant, the Plt Craves Judgment of this Court agst the deft for the sum of thirty five pounds ster. Mony of old England with Costs; The deft doth owne in open Court that he did promise to be security for the servants forth coming according to declaration but Craves A Refferance till next Court which the Court Granted. At Court held 4 mo, 10, 1684—The Jury's Names—William Emmitt, Babptist Newcome, Will. Cartor, Thom. Hodgkins, Will ffoutcher, Bryant Rowles, John Browne, John King, Roger Gum, Jno. Cullison, Henry Harman, & Richard Patty.

The Court ordered the Jury their ffees in two Causes viz Jonakin Wiltbanck agst Georg Andrews his Estate & Henry Stretcher agst Waltor Pomfrys Estate.

The Court fines John Barker Juryman for not Attending the Court ten shillings; John Barker pleaded that his horse being loose was going away & he went to bring him back therefore desired his fine might be remitted, upon which the Court remitted his fine.

Thomas Edwards Petitioned the Court for his liberty on which there was an Acount delivered to the Court from his Mr Jno More Amounting to ten thousand & Eighty pounds of tobaco & fouretene pounds Nineteen shillings Ster. mony agst him which he could not answer therefore consented to be sould for three yeares by the Court for satisfaction to his Mr John More. Thomas Edwards servant to John More in Virginia [is] by his owne consent sould by the Court to William Cartor, for three yeares service from this day for foure thousand six hundred pounds of tobaco for the use of ye sd John More to be pd the next fall, Thomas Edwards to have his freedome mony according to Custome when he is oute of his time. William Cartor confessed Judgment for the sd sum or m[ony] quantity of foure thousand six hundred pounds of tob[aco] to be pd next fall to John More of Yorke County in Virginia or to his Heires Executors Administrators or Assignes.

William Cartor petitioned agst the Estate of Corne[lis] Verhoofe for three hundred fifty foure Gilders ten stive[rs] dew upon Acount, The Acount being writt in dutch i[t] is suposed by Abram Clement for Otto Vulgast, Will[iam] Emmett Translated the Acount into English & did Attest it to be A true Copie of the said Acount, the Court believing the Acount to be true passed Judgment for the petitioner agst the Estate of the sd Cornelis Verhoofe for the sum of 354 Gilders 10 stivors with Costs of suite.

Nathaniell Smith petitioned for A towne Lott by [* * *] John Roades The Court Granted him A back Lott nex[t] to William Clarks Lott, the same Condition as to other[s].

William Rest petitioned for three hundred Acors of Cleare Land in this County, which the Court Granted order for.

Ann Newcome petitioned that Whereas her form[er] Husband John Haggistor did sell unto Norton Clay[poole] A Certaine parcell of Land & plantation unto wh[ich] bargaine or sale she did never Condisend nor any way yeild her rite & title of the Aforesaid Land to any person or persons therefore she Craved the Courts order for her thirds in the said Land soe far as the La[nd] shall admitt in sutch case & to order the same to be set Apart that she may peaceably posses & Enjoy the same, which petition the Court thrue away.

Richard Law petitioned that Whereas he was Charg[ed] in his Levys for James Heath, the sd James Heath being A freeman onely working with the petitione[r] upon certane Conditions the Court ordered the sd James Heath to pay his owne Levys.

Joshua Barksteads Comition for the Corroners place of this County being Read he desired it might be record[ed]:—

"William Penn Proprietary and Governor of the Province of Pensillvania & the Territorys thereunto belonging; To Joshua Barksted Greeting:—Reposing Confidence in thy Sobriety & Integrity I doe Authorise & Apoynt thee Joshua Barksted to be Corroner of the County of Sussex to Inspect the bodies of those that come untimely to their deaths & Impanell Juries upon the same, & doe what to the ofice of A Corroner belongs & to receive the fees due for the same as by Law directed: hereby requiring all persons to give thee ye Respect due to thy office, Given at Phyladellphya ye 23d 9 ber 1683.

[seale] "William Penn."

Indenture of sale of one hundred thirty two Acors of Land Sould by Samwell Gray to Randolph Shard being read in open Court before the said Samwell & Randolph it was desired by the sd Randolph it might be Recorded; which is as followeth:—

"This Indenture made the first day of 10 ber in ye year of oure Lord one thousand six hundred & Eighty three betwixt Samwell Gray of Lewis in the County of Sussex Planter of the one part & Randolp [sic] Shard Chirurgeon of the other part wittnesseth that the said Samwell Gray for & in consideration of the great care trouble & service of the sd Randolph Shard to him the sd Samwell Gray & for & in consideration of the said Randolph Shard his Charge of physick & for divers other good considerations him the sd Samwell Gray Moving hath bargained Sould Alienated & confirmed one hundred thirty two Acors of Land lying in long love Creek in the County of

Sussex & knowne by the Name of Grays Inn from him & his Heires for ever to the sd Randolph Shard * * *.

"SAMWELL G GRAY [SEALE]
his marke

"Sealed & delivered in the presence of John Cartor, John White, Gerrardus Wessels, Samwell White Samwell Gray acknoledged this to be his act & deed."

A PROTEST MADE BY BENJAMIN BLAGG MR OF THE SHIP SOC[IETY] AGST THE DETAINMENT OF A PARCELL OF OYLE & WHALE BON[E]

Sussex County belonging to the Province of Pennsillvania

Whereas the Ship Society belonging to the ffree society of traders of Pennsillvania is Expressly ordered & sent to [the] Roade within Cape James on purpose to take in & loade [A] parcell of oyle & Whale-bone belonging to & upon accoun[t of] the ffree society aforesaid, Benjamin Blagge being Mr of [the] said ship for this present voyage, have this day deman[ded] of John Hill the said oyle & Whalebone which should ha[ve] bene delivered to him by vertue of an order or Comition fr[om] the society aforesaid, for his receiving the same, the ship ly[ing] ready in the road aforesaid, for the convenient loading the sam[e] the Answer that is given me by the said John Hill is that part of the said oyle is converted by one Henry Bowman t[o] his owne use & the rest thereof is Attaiched by the said John Hill by law as allsoe the Whalebone for the societys use and Cannot have an Issue thereof in Court untill the 11th or 1[2th] day of the next Month Called June ffor which causes I Benjamin Blagg Mr of the Ship aforesaid doe here prote[st] against the detainment thereof & shall God willing proce[ed] on oure Intended voyage with oure said Ship Society According to order, This protest is made at the towne of Lewis in the County aforesaid this 3 day of ye 3 Month call[ed] May 1684 by me Benjamin Blagge in Wittness whereof I have hereunto sett my hand the Day & yeare before writte[n] with the seale of the County aforesaid;

signed in the presence of us: BENJAMIN BLAGGE.
RACHELL R C CLAYPOOLE [the County seal for Sussex
her marke
NORTON CLAYPOOLE Clerc:
Vera Copia Test. NORTON CLAYPOOLE.

JUNE 10th, 1684.

Att A Court Held * * * at Lewis for the County of Sussex the tenth day of the fourth Month 1684. Comitioners present: John Roades, John Kipshaven, Herculus Shepard, Allexander Draper, Robert Bracy, Robert Hart.

An Action of the Case. Luke Wattson Plt, The Estate of George Lacham in the hands of John Barker deft. The Plt being absent upon publick service at the Provinciall Councell the Court Referd the Cause to the next Court; with drawne by the Plts order the 6th Mo: in Court.

[In a suit for title to "house & Towne Lott"—mention is made that "Thomas Hodgins marryed the rellix & Administratri[x] of the Estate of Halm Wiltbanck" * * *]: ["Thomas Hodgkings who marryed Jane the Widow and Administratrix of the Estate of Halm Wiltbanck].

FEBRUARY 12th, 13th, 1683.

["Symon Pawlin being Chosen Cunstable" took his oath.]

John King being Chosen Cunstable did promise ye same.

The Indian Assawmak Harmatt a male Acknedged in open Court the sale of one thousand Acors of Land to Mr Allexander Molleston which Land is on the South side of the Indian River.

MARCH, 1683–4.

[A suit in which "Robt. Clifton Marying the Rellix & Administratrix of Capt. Joh Avory" is deft.] [Her name is given as Sarah].

Joshua Barksteads Comition being read twas ordered to be recorded for him to be Corroner in this County.

AUGUST 12th, 1684.

[A suit in which mention is made that "John Daniell * * * Assighned over the said bill to Katherine Vines who now is the wife of the Plt," * * * Arthur Starr.]

AUGUST 13th, 1684.

Chosen for Peace Makers William Clark Jno. Roads & Jno. Hill.

SEPTEMBER 2d, 1684.

Att the Orphans Court Held at Lewis in the County of Sussex by the Kings Authority & in the Proprietary & Governous [sic] Nane [sic] the 2 day of the 7th Month 1684. Comitioners present: Luke Wattson, John Roades, John Kipshaven, & Herculus Sheppard & Allexander Draper. The Inventories of the Estates belonging to the Orphans & other writings thereunto Appertaining being in the Registers Office & the Register of this County viz the President being gon to Phyladellphya & not left oute the writings aforesaid, this Court Could not proceed to doe any business therein, therefore this Court is Adjourned to the first tuesday in the next first Month.

[The above is followed by three items of the killing of wolves "entered by order of Court."]

NOVEMBER 11th, 1684.

John Barker is Chosen Surveyor of the hye ways in the roome of William Bradford.

DECEMBER 9th, 10th, 1684.

Samwell Gray presents for not working upon the hye ways These persons following viz Will. Emmott John Brown Richard Gill John Williams John Wocon Robert Jnoson Harmon Cornelis the delinquents are ordered to worke betwene this & the next Court what they are behind in their Work otherwise to be fined 20 ff. a day for what they are behind.

Robert Hart Surveyor of the hye ways presents for not workin upon the ways Luke Watson senior Henry Bowman Henry Smith Barnwell Jackson David Coursey Wm ffancy Wm Spencer junior Barthollmew Aplegate.

Appraisers to be Chosen William Emmot John Symons & Samwell Gray Chosen to be Appraysors for one yeare [and took oath of office].

NOVEMBER 11th, 1684.

John Barker is Chosen Surveyor of the bye ways in the roome of William Bradford.

Thomas Bocent promised to performe the office of under Sherriff for one yeare * * * [and took oath].

Babptist Newcome agread with the Court to build ye Court house & prison as is expressed elce where for 10 thousand pounds of tobaco.

FEBRUARY 10th, 1684.

Arthur Starr & Henry Vbanck being Attested declared they both heard Robt. Johnson say that he had carryed away part of the Stocks & flung it downe the banck & Arthur Starr further declared that he head [sic] the sd Jnoson say that if he had his Ax there he would cut downe the Whippin post these words was spoken as they Affirme by the sd Johnson the latter end of Octobr or In Novembr last.

MARCH 10th, 1685.

Andrew Deprey being Chosen Cunstable he was Attested to perorme the office of a Cunstable this yeare next ensuing for the precinct he liveth In According to Law & the best of his knolledge.

MAY 12th, 1685.

Henry Stretcher verbally petitioned the Court that he might take In the pond and sum upland for A pasture for the use of his ordinary on which the Court Grants that he may fence in the sd pond & upland for seaven yeares to commense the next orphans Court to be held the next 8th Month & Henry Stretcher promiseth to let any of the Inhabitants put in their Calves for 2/s ye summer that of the towne & any Inhabitant of this County to put in the horse or horsys at any time for 4d A Night Henry Stretcher allsoe promiseth that when the 7 yeares is expired to deliver peaceable and quiet possession unless he shall Agrea for Longer time the Court allsoe Grants that if the sd pond and upland be to be let oute when this seaven yeares is expired that Henry Stretcher shall have the refusing of it, he is to pay yearely to the orphans Court held in every 8th Month one Eare of Indian Corne for A yearely rent to the Court for the sd Land.

[The Court granted Arthur Starr "2 towne lotts more backward where he lives for A tanyard" * * * "for seaven yeares to begin the next 8th Month at the orphans Court he paying for a yearly rent one eare of Indian Corne to the orphans Court to be held every 8th month." * * *

MARCH 8th, 9th, 10th, 1687.

Sollomon Jones and John Williams are Chosen ffence Vewers.

Jerrimia Scott petitioned to be excused of ye Cunstables place he being Chosen by the Court his petition was not allowed and he was Attested to serve the office of A Cunstable for the yeare insuing or for soe long as he should live in the towne for ye towne precinct.

Arthur Starr petitioned to be released of the Cunstables office and the Court Chose Jerimiah Scott before inserted to serve in his Roome.

John Crew petitioned to be Excused of the Cunstables office & The Court Chose William Bradford Recited to serve.

Bryant Roles petitioned to be excused of ye Cunstables place and the Court Chose and Appointed Antony Havorly to serve in his place for this yeare next ensuing the office of A Cunstable for that precinct.

The Judgment of the Jury of Inquest upon the body of James Colle late servant to Thomas Branscom being found dead was Read in Court and ordered to be Recorded in the Booke of Records * * *.

MAY 3d, 1687.

Thomas Wynns Comition to be one of ye Justices in the Roome of Thomas Langhorne was Read viz: * * *.

[Order of "Councill" "that no undrest Deer skins be put on board any shipp Boate or Vessell with intent to transport ye same oute of this province before they have bene publickly exposed to sale * * *.

Grand Jury's presentments as followeth:—

Wee of the Grand Jury doe present Nathaniell Sikes for selling of lght [sic] bread according to Information of Albertus Jacobs and Phillip Russell. RICHARD LAW fforeman.

Wee of the Grand Jury present Babptist Newcom for Not Mending or Repairing the long bridge accordin to Information of Joshuah Barkstead. RICHARD LAW fforeman.

The Grand Jury presented the Court for Not Causing a Court house and prisson to be made. RICHARD LAW fforeman.

The Court orders Babptist Newcom to Sums in ye Inhabitants that have allready refused their Worke to mend the Long Bridg.

John Vines Corroner Returned to this Court the Verdict of the Jury of Inquest upon the death of Elizabeth the wife of James Sikes viz * * * [she "dyed suddenly on or aboute the 14th of ffeb: Ano: 1686" paper dated "this 11th day of March Ano 1686"].

JUNE, 1687.

William Kanning petitioned that Whereas he gave security A twelve month since for his good behaviour Requests that his security may be released and their bonds delivered. The Court being informed that ye Sherriff commanded him to aid and assist to put Tho. Jones in the stocks and the petitioner Refused saying if it was to put ye Sherriff in ye stocks he would help; Whereupon they would not grant his petition telling him he had as much reason to be bound to his good behaviour as fformerly therefore they would not grant it.

[* * * "The Court therefore order the said James Hardin to be Committed to the Sherriffs Custody untill he give security for his good behaviour" this was for the above offence].

"Ruith Bundick Thomas Jones Mother petitioned" * * *

JULY 21st, 1687.

The Comition from James Williams Deputy Collector Appointed by Patrick Mein Esqr to Norton Claypoole being read as ffolloweth * * * [as Genl Deputy Collector].

[Norton Claypoole Attested to discharge of above Duty 16th 5 mo., 1687.]

Norton Claypooles Comission for Deputy of ye Rolls * * * Given near Lewis the 23 4th Month 1687.

THO' LLOYD Mr of ye Rolls.

Henry Bowmans Comission for ye Navall office * * * Given at Phyladellphia the Eighth day of the sixth Month 1687.

WM MARKHAM Secretary.

SEPTEMBER 6th, 1687.

Justice Roades was soe sick that he was not able to sitt upon the bench to doe any buisness & there not being Justices enough to hold A Court withoute him the Court ordered Notice thereof to be given and the Court to be Adjourned to ye first twesday in ye Next Month which was accordingly done by proclamation.

OCTOBER 4th, 5th, 6th, 1687.

The last will & testament of John Roades was delivered to ye Court sealed up & desired by them to be publiquely opened and Read which was accordingly done as allsoe Read but the Widdow Comfort Roades desired it might not be proved till Next Court * * * untill she had A Letter of Administration * * * [this was granted].

Johnathan Baily was summoned to this Court * * * [for] violently by force of Arms Wickedly Maliciously & feloniously, oute of A sordid base Covetous desire, aboute the beginning of the last yeare 1686 * * * Contemning & despising, thy Neighbours, fence Not onely the Kings Hye way, to thy owne use, which said Hye way hath bene Made Worne & Accustomed for Many years, Neither had thy Neighbours, any other roade or hye way to ye Commons Commonly called Marshes either to ffetch Hay Looke after their Catle, or other ocations; but allsoe the onely Known Antient place of A burying ground for the towne of Lewis &ct, Notwithstanding thou hast bene twice presented for the same, Thou hast continued the use thereof to thy private advantage and benefitt and hath boldly and presumptuously in defiance of all thy Neighbours, their Right and property placed the frame of A Windmill thereon, and allsoe hast Not onely confidently & Impudently, denyed and Refused thy Neighbours the use of ye sd ground to bury their dead forbiding them or any of them to come upon the said ground but didst Cruelly in A tyrannicall and Wicked Manner threaten & [sic] the presence & hearing of severall of the Kings Leig people, that thou wouldst cutt the legs off, from those persons that would come there to Make A grave which hath bene to the great dishonor of God, contempt of Authority & to the violating the good laws of oure Sovereign Lord the King & this present Government, and to the great Terror of the Kings Leige people the Abuse of all thy Neighbours. & the Ill Example of all others offending in the like Case; * * *

Johnathan Baily being called to tryall & the petty Jury called for and aboute to be called over Mr. Wm. Clarke president being absent when the Grand Jury brought in ye sd Inditement but now being upon the bench told the Court there would be noe Need of A Jury for this buisness for to his Knowledge there was A petition delivered to the Councell aboute it, and the Councell had ordered Something in it, & how it should come ffrom the Councell to be tryed in this Court he did not know, Norton Claypoole Answered that presidt Clarke told him & ffrancis Cornwall yt the petition which presidt Loyd delivered to ye Councell aboute the burying Ground &ct was slighted by the

Councell for as much as it was not directed to them, for Indeed ye petition was directed onely to presidt Loyd when he was here hoping and believing that he would order wee should have the use of oure Antient burying ground as formerly and he told us when wee delivered ye petition that if he stayed long enough viz 3 or 4 days longer he would call A Court and have it done before he went if not ye law was open to us & told us how to proceed Presidt Clarke told the Court if they thought fitt to goe on with it he would goe off the bench ye Jury being called over before the inditement was Read presidt Clark sent for Justice Wynn off the bench and there being but three Justices left proceedings was stopt whilest Justice Wynne came againe then came Johnathan Baily with Justice Wynn & promised before the Court that he would consent that one Acor of Land to be laid oute in the same place where ye burying ground hath bene used, which gave some sattisfaction to ye Court and Country; and as for the Hye way The Court ordered that the same should be as wyde before ye said Johnathans Land as before other peoples howses in the towne Whereupon further proceedings was stopped Justice Wynn signed the said order in the dockett booke.

The Grand Jury brought in further presentments as viz, * * *. We doe Request the Court forthwith to order A Court house & A prison to be provided according to Law that the Inhabitants may not be sufferers the 4th 8 mo: 87.

℘ JOHN BELLAMY fforeman.

The Court upon the Examination of ye presentments ordered that Babptist Newcome should be sumoned to the next Court to Answer the suite of ye Court & declaration to be drawne. [I believe this has reference to the building of the Court house.]

[Norton Claypoole and others "petitioned agst ye Estate of Jno Pearce deceased."]

Wm. Emmott Requested that he might have leave to sell A tract of Land by outcrye in open Court by Inch of Candle which the Court Granted * * *.

Norton Claypoole Deputy Register for Probat of Wills and granting letters of Administration &ct shewed to the Court the Inventory of ye Estate of Henry Gitto delivered to him from Henry Smith Administrator of ye sd Estate * * *

The first day of the 9th Month 1678 [sic].

The last 8th Month Court being Adjourned to this day & Now there not being Justices enough in health to hold A Court Procclamation was made and Notice given publiquly that there not being A suffitent Number of Justices to hold a Court the buisness thereof is defered to the first twesday in the next Month.

DECEMBER, 1687.

Henry Bowman as Atturney & in the behalfe of Thomas Phillips of Newyorke Merct petitioned the Court for an order agast ffrancis Cornwall Hye Sherriff for the contents of an Execution served on the body of Henry Stretcher for fifty od pounds &ct for that he the sd ffrancis Cornwall Hye Sherriff hath suffered the said Henry Stretcher to have his liberty ever since he was taken in Execution withoute any sattisfaction of debt or Costs &ct. ffrancis Cornwall Hye Sherriff rendred the prissoner in Court and said that he had bene his prissoner ever since and he had noe better prisson to keep him in The Court having formerly made an order upon the like ocation the 4th Month 1681 upon A petition of Halm Wiltbanck deceased upon the like case viz that the Sherriff shall confine the said prissoner to the house and yards where the said Sherriff doe or shall live untill the said prissoner shall be legally discharged by the Plt and that in the meane time the Plt shall allow the prissoner two shillings and six pence A week for his Maintenance and the like order the Court doe make for all other persons that shall be upon Execution for debt untill there can be a prisson built and provided for that purpose. This Court therefore order that said recited order be renewed & Confirmed and if the Sherriff or any Sherriff hereafter untill the prisson be built and finished shall suffer any prissoner (that is under Execution for debt) to goe further then his fenced land Where his dwelling house is then he shall or may be liable to be sued for an Escape. President Clarke signed this order on the petition.

John Vines Verbally petitioned the Court for ffees dew to him as Crowner from the Estate of James Sykes deceased amounting to 2-13-6 * * * ye Heir viz Nathll Sykes * * *.

Phillip Russell petitioned agst the Estate of John Pearce deceased * * *.

The last will and testament of John Roades dated the 17th day of 7ber last past was proved * * *.

Knights Howard Sonn & Heir to Thomas Howard deceased * * *.

The Nuncative or Verball Will of James Sykes late of this County deceased being his last will and testament was proved by the Attestations of Allexander Draper and Thomas Price one of ye Justices.

It is Agread by this Court that whosoever subscribes any logs to be gotten for the use of the prison and Court house shall bring ye said logs to the place in the towne where it is to be built in forty days after the date hereof or elce forfeit double the Vallue of the said logs there is to be as followeth: 54 logs at 4/8 ps 15 foote long 1 foote over 8 Inch thick, 16 ditto at 6/8 23 foote 1 over & 8 Inch thick squard 2 sides; every person that undertakes to get any is to take 3 short to one long.

I doe undertake to get 20 logs, Wm Clarke;
and I doe undertake for 04 logs, Tho: Wynne;
I doe undertake 20 logs, Henry Stretcher;
wee doe undertake six short & two long, ffrancis Cornwall, Morrice Edwards;
ffor my selfe & Justice Gray 3 long and 15 short, Henry Mollestone and Samwell Gray;
I Babptist Newcomb doe Ingage my selfe to find Rafftors and Clabords for A prison and Cover the sd prison the Court finding Nails, Bapt: Newcomb.

Whereas severall persons have complained to this Court they know not where to Cutt their firewood the Court therefore orders that the towne Land shall be forthwith laid oute.

Margarett and Thomas ffisher Administrators of ye Estate of John ffisher dec'd * * *.

FEBRUARY 7th, 8th, 9th, 10th. 1687.

The Justices New Commission was Read, viz * * * [signed] Tho: lloyd president.

Then was Read this following obligation for the New Justices to signe Instead of an oath viz * * *.

The Inditement Agst Phillip Russell for suffering persons to play at Cards in his house, was Read to which he pleaded guilty Confessing the same saying it was the first time and much agst his will but the persons was soe Resolute he could not perswade them against it and he the said Phillip promised never to suffer the like againe the Court fined him 5/8.

The Inditement Agst Henry Strecher for playing at Cards was Read, Charles Pickering being allowed his Atturney said he must submitt to the Court the Court fined him 5/8.

MARCH 1st, 1688.

[Case in which "Charles Pickering Executor of ye last Will & testamt of Phillip ThLehamaine" is deft.]

MAY, 1688.

Phillip Russell was the last Court Indicted for selling beer at More then the laws of this Government allow; Referd.

The last Will and Testament of Major Wm. Spencer was proved by the Attestations of the Wittnesses viz: Art Jnoson Vankirk Robt Twilly, and William Emmatt.

[Thomas Ashton, who seems to be living at "Lewis," is alluded to as "late of New Yorke Soapeboyler."]

Susanna Bedwell & Thomas Bedwell Administrators of the Estate of Robt Bedwell deceased * * *.

MAY 2d, 1688.

Norton Claypoole in open Court Delivered three Matchcoats to Christian the Indian Sacamacko for the Indian Right and title of one thousand Acors of Land scittuate in Kent County on this side Dover Rivor aboute three miles from the place that Dover towne is Intended to be built and he the said Christian the Indian did then Acknowledge to have sold given and Granted the Indian Right title and Interest of the sd land being one thousand Acors according to the survey and pattent thereof from him his Heirs &c promising to defend the said Norton Claypoole from the lawfull claim of any other Indian Claiming any Right title or Interest of or to any part of the said land in Wittness Where of he the said Christian have hereunto set his hand and seale the day and yeare first above Written.

the marke X of Christian ye Indian [SEALE]

Sealed and delivered In the presence of us:

WM. CLARK,
THO. WYNNE,
HENRY MOLESTON.

Presidt William Clark Acknowledged the sale of the land mentioned in a Conveyance dated 26th day of the first month 1685 to Johnathan Baily according to the Contents of the said Conveyance save onely the burying Ground and King's hye way to be Excepted as Atturney to John Vines the which Conveyance the sd presidt delivered in open Court.

JUNE 5th, 6th, 7th, 8th, 1688.

Henry Stretcher was the last first Mo. Court Indicted by the Grand Jury for selling of Beer at More then the law directs & allows Luke Watson John Bellamy and Thomas Bessant was Attested & Tho. ffisher one of ye Jury Instead of All Draper the Petty Jury went oute upon this Cause & the other below both together and brought in their verdict Wee of ye Jury find these Indictments not to be according to law testis Jacob Warring fform.

Phillip Russell was the last first Mo Court Indicted for selling of beer at More then the law directs or allows; tried with the Cause above both together and the above Verdict Relates to this.

John Browne Shipcarpenter Acknowledges sale of two towne lots with ye houses and fences thereon * * *.

Charles Sanders and Wm Rodeney ye evidences to the last Will and Testament of Major William Dyre deceased proved the same to be his Act and deed and allsoe tested yt the sd Major Wm Dyre Acknowledged the same to be his last Will and Testament.

Upon the Request of Comfort Roades Widdow Administratrix of the Estate of John Roades that ye lands and provissions may be omitted in ye Inventory The Judgmt [sic] Court is that Whereas there is Estate suffitient to sattisfye all debts & demands besides they order that the lands and provissions for the use of the family shall be left oute and omitted in the Inventory.

Upon ye 16th Day of the Sixth Month 1688, Rachel Claypoole Widdow Haveing Desired Luke Watson Senr. and Thomas Oldman To bee Appraisers of ye Goods and Chattells Now in her possession, being ye Goods & Chattells of her Late Husband Norton Claypoole (Deceased) The Common Appraisers not being at hand Justice Thomas Wynne being present attested ye abovesaid Parties To Doe Justice To ye best of their knowledge according to Law in ye Premisses.

Testes THO WYNNE

Rachel Claypoole (Widdow) being Attested to Bring in a True acot of ye Estate Goods and Chattells of Norton Claypoole her husband Deceased did Give in an Inventorie of ye same Bearing Date as abovesaid To ye best of her knowledge As will appear by ye Said Inventorie.

Reserving to her Selfe One Bed and furniture Togather with waireing apparell and ye Plantacon She lives on.

Test THO. WYNNE
NEHEMIAH FFIELD

JUNE 6, 1694. [Court of Common Pleas.]

Robert Bracee Senr acknowledged unto his Son Robert Two hundred acres of land being Part of The Tract of Land hee now lives upon, according To Conveyance herewith Also Desired The Court would Take notice That if hee Should happen To Die without Will, That hee Bequeaths unto his Said Son Robert his Heirs & Assigns The other four hundred acres which hee Calls and Reckons To bee his home Plantatcon and Two hundred acres more which belongs To ye Said Tract which is in all 800 Acres, hee also Gives and bequeaths unto his Said Son his Heirs and Assigns if the law Can Recover it hee having made ye Said 200 Acres over in Cot. to ye Children Mary and Elisabeth.

his
ROBT. R B BRACEE
mark

In an Acon of Defamacon. Luke Watson Senr Plt, Henry Bowman deft. The Suit ffell by ye Deft Death.

In an acon of ye Case. Mongo Crafford & Wm Orr in Comp Merchtts Plt, Thomas Tillton Deft; withdrawn By ye Plt.

Albertus Jacobs Coronr made Returne of ye Jurie of Inquest Verdict upon ye Death of Edward Benbrick found dead ye 29th day of May 1694 which was Thatt hee the Said Benbrick was accidentally Drowned By Riding Over ye Broad Kill Henry Strecther fforeman.

True Returne ALBERTUS JACOBS, Coronor.

The Last Will and Testamt of Cesar Godwin Deceesed was Putt into Court by ye Widow and was There Read and Proved.

SEPTEMBER 4th, 1694.

Nehemiah ffield Published his Deputacon for Dpty of ye Rolls Clarke of the Provincial and Probate of Wills and was Sworne in Open Court. The Oath administred by Capt Thomas Pemberton.

The Court appoint Woodman Stokely Overseer of ye Highwayes for ye County Bounds on ye South Side the Indian River, and Morris Edwards for Rehoboth hundred Henry Moleston for Cedar Creek Hundred And William Piles for ye Towne Hundred all ye Inhabitants belonging to Rehoboth Hundred between Bundicks Bridge and Pot hooks Creek are ordered by ye Court To assiste Woodman [sic] Morris Edwards Ordered by ye Court That The Widow ffisher Richard Law and Timothy Dowgan be hereafter Deemed 4 Inhabitants of the Towne Hundred and their Plantacons within the Precincts of the Same.

The Court Orders Thatt warrants shall be Issued out unto all ye Constables of Each Respective hundred in this County To Bringe in at December Court Next an Exact list of all the Titheables within the Same, as also by Taking from ye said Titheables own mouths what Quantity of Lands they Hold.

SEPTEMBER 5th, 1694.

Whereas There hath been some Differences and Disputes about ye Bounds of the Town of Lewis It is ordered by the Court To prevent farther such like That ye Sheriff and the Surveyor with Sutable assistance Doe forthwith Run out ye Side line That Runs along by ye Land of Abraham and Isaac Wiltbanck And ye Land of John Williams, as also ye other Side line That Runs along by ye Land of William Dyre.

[* * * Richd Paynter Iunior in the Right of his Wife Jane Executrix of William Swetnam Decesd * * *] [The name is spelled also Swetman.]

DECEMBER 4th, 5th, 1694.

Barnes Garrett and Anthony Haverley being sent for To Charles Spooner upon his Death Bed, hee ye Said Spooner Did Desire them To take notice of and To Take Care That his Wife Should have Enjoy and possess all his Estate Goods and Chattles both Real and personall to her own proper use and Disposall as She sees meet * * *.

Susanna Gray Produced in Court ye Last Will and Testament of Samuel Gray her late Husband Deceesed and Proved the Same by Saml Preston and Michael Chambers 2 Evidences to ye Same Will.

Robt Bracee appeared in Court and there produced an Indenture wherein hee had Bound his Daughter Elisabeth Bracee unto Richard Paynter Junr untill She Arrive to ye age of Seventeen Years being now according to ye tenure of the Indenture Six Years of Age which Indenture Bears Date ye 30th Day of November 1694 * * *.

The Clark Produed [sic] in Court a List of Laws which the Secretary had Sent Down which were Openly Read Over * * *.

The Said Grand Jury also Gave John Hill Six Pounds ffor ye Grand Juries Years Accomodacon And the Court house. And unto Capt. Watson Capt. Pemberton and Roger Corbett Six Pounds a peice for their this Years Service in Assembly.

MARCH 6th, 7th, 1694.

The Court Gives liberty for a Dictche to bee Cutt through the most Convenient Place Of the Towne of Lewis into the Creek for thee Conveniency of Drayning of the Sevanna On ye back part Next the Second Street Lotts: And Orders That ye Wacant Ground That lies between the Lott of Nehemiah ffield And the four Acre Lott of Capt Pemberton Adjoyning upon Richard Holloway bee Reserved for a Markett Place, And the Vacant Peice of Land Next Adjoyning on the South West Side of John Miers his Lott to ye Block house Pond And between the Block house feeld and that, To bee used as a Common burying place.

After all which the Court Caused a Letter to bee written to the Justices in Mary Land Relating to Some Difference between the Two Governments. And Ordered the Clerk to Recorde the said Letter a true Copy whereof is on the other side * * *.

JUNE 4th, 1695.

Robert Bracee Appeared in Court and Desired that hee might bee allowed and Ordered Letters of Administracon upon the Estate of his ffather Robert Bracee Sener: Deceesed upon a Will made in Open Court 6th day of June 1694 Roger Corbett Appeared for ye Widow of ye said Deceesed And produced a former Will made in ye Year 1688 under ye hand and Seal of ye Deceesed, And Pleaded that the Late Will was Nuncupative and the other a written will and So not of equal force & validitey * * * Ordered To bee Continued to the Next Court * * *.

At a Meating of the Justices On the 15th Day of July Ano Domini 1695. Justices present: William Clark, Capt Luke Watson, Capt. Thomas Pemberton, John Stokely, Thomas Oldman, Joseph Booth; An Order and Warrant from the Governor and Councill was Produced and Read Relateing to a Suspicion of A Designe of Our enemies the ffrench To Attache thes Or Some other Our Neighbouring Plantacons, wherein for safe Guard It is ordered That Two men Shall be Hired to Watche upon the Cape every day from five in the morning untill Seven att Night Untill ye first day of October next Ensueing, In Obediance whereinto The Justices Considering of Persons fitting for ye said watche Trust Did Agree and Aprove of Anthony Parssly and John Putteet therein And Accordingly Did agree with them att.

SEPTEMBER 3d, 4th, 1695.

Cornelius Wiltbanck By Peticon Acquaints The Court hee hath a Designe To Build a Water Mill In this County On that Branch Or Creek On the Broad Kill Called Mill Creek if ye Court Will Grant him the Same and Land which is Customary Adjoyning to the Same The Court Grant him the Said Streame Provided he Builde the Said Mill thereon within fifteen months from hence forward and do Attend and Minde the Same, And Doe Grinde the Graine well And in due Course as itt Comes to Mill without Respect to Persons att ye Eighth part Toll ffor wheat and Sixth ffor Indian Corne.

DECEMBER 3d, 1695.

The Court being Opened the Grand Jury were Called over * * * who haveing Received their Charge went out of Court And After some time Came in With a Paper Containing as followeth: The Grand Jury Request of the Worshippfull Court That the Road from Town to the Indian River May bee Cleared and the Bridges Repaired And that they would bee Pleased to Appoint An Overseer for that Part of the County John Miers fforeman which the Court Granted And Appointed Robert Barton Overseer in the same.

JANUARY 7th, 8th, 9th, 1695.

The Last Will and Testament of Skidmore Was Published and Read and Richard Williams peticioned The Court for thee precedency of Administracon either on the Said Will Or otherwise as the Said Will may bee Approved The Court Aprove not of the Will And Appoint ye Petitioner To Administer upon the said Estate of ye deceesed as intestate And keep the deceesed Childe, hee assuming to Give Security To pay ye Debts As for ye assetts And the plantacon to be Recorded for ye said Boy whom hee promises to keep & mentain gratis for nothing * * *.

William Clark Peticoned ye Court Thatt Letters of Administracon might bee Granted him upon ye Estate of Stephen Sargent deceed in Thatt ye said Sargent att ye time of his Death Stood Indebted unto his Majtie and the Petitionr in ye Sum of £10: And upwards for ye Custom of Tobaccoe * * * Butt ye Court thought fitt To Continue the said Peticon unto ye next Court. [The petition was granted at the Court Mar. 4, 1695.]

MARCH 4th, 1695.

* * * Return of ye Jury of Inquest upon the body of William Emmatt * * *.

Jonathan Bayly Peticoned ye Court ffor Part of ye Branch formerly Called Bundicks Branch To Build A Water mill on, which the Court Granted So far as Itt lay in their Power, But with these Condicons * * * [as in petition of Cornelius Wiltbanck on a previous page].

Whereas Daniel Hilliard Deceesed Did Dye Intestate * * * The Court Grante the said William Clarke ye priority of Administracon, And Order the Registr To grant him Letters thereof accordingly * * *.

NOVEMBER 6th, 1702.

Came Mary Goit Spinstr and the Will of Peter Goit late of this County Merchtt Deceesed Bearing Date the Tenth Day of July 1695 being read * * *.

William ffatcher Appeared in Court and Produced An Accott Agst James Walker Adminr of Henry Allen Deceesed ffor ffunerall Charges &c. * * *.

Thomas May Guardian Appointed of Richard Williams—By the Last Will and Testamt of Richard Williams His ffather Deceased, Appeared in Court And Produced the Said Will which was Read * * *.

FEBRUARY 2d, 1702.

Jonathan Starges and Honor his Wife late Widow of Jno. Kipshaven Senr. Deceased * * *.

Deborah Butler By Peticon Prayed the Court that Shee might bee allowed Satisfacon for the Trouble and Buriall of James Laytree Dec'd * * *.

MAY 4th, 1703.

Thomas Grove Appeared in Court And Produced An Accott of A Parcell of Debts that James Mathews Gave him on his Death bed the Sixth Day of ffebruary last * * *.

MAY 5th, 1703.

[Mention made that Martha Johnson, wife of Adam, was daughter of John Kipshaven, Senr.]

[Mention that Comfort Burges, wife of Ralph Burges, was dau. of Wm. Piles, dec'd.]

MAY 6th, 1703.

* * * Came Adam Johnson And Martha His Wife And Exhibitt their Bill Agst John Hill Samuel Preston and Jacob Kolluck Execrs of the Last Will and Testament of John Kipshaven Deceased, which Bill follows in these words * * * Your Orator and Oratrix Adam Johnson of the County of Sussex Yeoman And Martha his Wife That Whereas John Kipshaven late of the Said County Yeoman yor Oratrix Marthas ffather, in his lifetime was possessed of and intituled to, As well a very Considerable Real Estate in Lands and Houses, As of and in Divers Goods and Chattells householdstuff Plate Ready money Outstanding Debts Negroes Cattle and other Stock Amounting to the Value of One Thousand Pounds or upwards and being so Possessed And Interested Did Constitute and make his Last Will and Testament in Writing bearing Date the 14th Day of Janr: 1700, And in And by the Said Last Will amongst other things therein contained Did Give and Devise unto Yor Oratrx Martha The Moyety and halfe Part of his Lands in the County of Sussex During her life, And Did further Give and bequeath unto Yor Oratrix Martha the subb Moyety and halfe Part of His ℘sonall Estate Excepting A very few inconsiderable Legacies * * * John Kipshaven Soon after Departed this life * * * (the Said Testatr little or no Debts to Pay) * * * [the Executors have refused to divide the Real Estate and give possession to Adam and Martha Johnson or to Deliver the Moyety

of the Personal in Specie, and by Appraisement have undervalued the said estate perhaps one half. They] pretend that the Testatr Was much Indebted at his Death, And that A Third of his Estate belonged to Honour Kipshaven, The Widow of the said John Kipshaven, tho it is notoriously known, The Said Honr Eloped from her Husband And run him much in Debt wherever She could Obtaine Creditt, And Refused to live with him long before his Death * * * They have Suffered by Connivance the Said Widow to Sue them At Law for her thirds * * * [In the defence the Executors say] That the Said Kipshaven after hee had by his Will Given to his Grand children John and Albert Jacobs (Sons of Albertus Jacobs by His Daughtr the Said Plt Martha) The One Moyety and halfe Part of all his Estate both reall and ℘sonall Lands Goods and Chattells whatsoever within The Province of Pennsilvania & Counties Annexed hee the Said Testatr Gave unto his Daughtr the Said Plt Martha the other Moyety & halfe Part of his Lands in the County of Sussex dureing her life, But with reserve of what the Testatr by his Said Will Disposed And Ordered to bee Paid And Delivered out of both Moyeties * * * And the Said Defts, further Say That the Plts have had near, if not all their Moyety or halfe Part of the Testatrs ℘sonall Estate * * * [the widow recovered her thirds] by Judgmt of Sussex County Court After A Vigorous Defence made by these Defts or of Some of them Against her in that behalfe * * *.

MAY 7th, 1703.

[Accounts produced showing the Plts had rec'd £15 6s 4½d over their share, which was £100 15s 1½d. This Adam Johnson] Assumed in Open Court to Refunde and Pay Back to the sd Exectrs * * * they with Draw their Said Chancery Suit * * *.

MAY 2d, 1704.

* * * And the Said Grand Jury Came into Court with A Paper in Writeing in these Words following—May ye 3rd, 1704: The Grand Jury Complains that the County Wants A Prison house And that Moneys hath been Given by Two Severall Grand Juries to the Value of ffourtey Pounds for that use Wee Desire to know why the worke is not done or An Accott of the Said Money's. In Answer whereof The Court told them, Robert Cade fforeman, That the ffirst Twenty Pounds was Disposed to A very necessary use in Buildeing of Bridges in the Queens Road, which were so much wanted that People Could not Pass to and froe, without great Danger,—And the Last Twenty Pounds was forgotten to bee Assessed in ye Publick Charge, when the Last Rate was made, and Leavie Settled vizt in ffebr. Court 1702—But Should bee Remembred at the Settling of the Next Leavies.

* * * By order of the Court The Queens Road from the Town to Rehobah in Lett and the Plantacons on the Right and Left hand of itt, Extending As far As Orrs Mill (included) bee Added to ye Town hundred.

NOVEMBER 8th, 1704.

Came into Court By William ffarmer The Last Will and Testamt of the Widow Jane Potter And Was Read * * * [Executor named Richd Dobson who] absolutely Renounceth his Right of Executorship * * * [and Administracon bee Granted unto William ffarmer As Guardian of the Minor, Abraham Potter onely Son of the said Dec'd. * * *].

AUGUST 1st, 1704.

[Mention made that Jane, wife of Samuel Knowles, was formerly wife of Thomas Besent, dec'd.]

John Huling Merchtt By His Peticon Sett forth, That Whereas hee hath A house And Lott in the Town of Lewis, next Adjoyning to the Common Lotts of The Said Town, which Lotts now lies Desolate and without fence, Therefore hee being willing to promote the benefitt of the Said Town Prays liberty from the Court To fence in ye Said Lotts with his Own, which will be a Conveniency to ye Town and Security of the Grave Yarde. And upon such Grant hee will forthwith fence in the Same, And Pay Such Acknowledgmt As may Secure the Rights of the Said Lotts As they were from ye first Concession * * *. The Court Grants unto the Said John Huling His Heirs and Assigns * * *. And as to ye fencing in the burying Ground hee hath liberty to Doe it, Provided hee render up the Same when ever the Court Shall See fitt to Comande it from him * * *.

John Johnson ffree Nigroe Aged Eighty Years And Poor, and Past His labour * * * prayes the Court To Take him into the Publick Charity of the County—[Richard Laws agreed with the Court to Maintaine the Said John Johnson his life time—At ye Rate of Seaven Pounds fifteen Shillings ℘r year to bee Paid out of the Publick].

MAY 9th, 1706.

Sarah Watson late Widow & Execx of Capt Luke Watson Deced and former Widow And Adminx of Richard Paynter Senr Taylor Deced (Intestate) being Sumoned to this Court at the Complaint of her Son Richard Paynter * * * [mention made of his Eldest brother John].

William Mason and Margaret his Wife Appeared in Court And Produced An Accott of ffunerall Charges of Her late Husband James Clark Decd. * * *

JANUARY 7th, 1706.

Whereas the Grand Jury have found and brought into Court That it is absolutely Necessary for bridges to be made Over the Two Runs of Cedar Creek And Whereas the Law Impowers the Justices in Court sitting to hire Workmen To make build and Compleat the same—Mathew Parker appeared in Court and undertooke the Sd Work and That he would forthwith Goe about the same, And build Compleate & finish the Sd bridges, Substantially & Well and Sufficiently Supported in the middle the Dementions of Which Sd Two bridges is to be Governed by the Direction of ye Law in That Case. Whereupon, it was bargained and Agreed by the Justices in Open Court, And the Sd Mathew Parker That he ye sd Mathew Should have in Consideracon of Building Compleating and finishing The Sd Two bridges in manner Aforesd The Sum of ffourteen Pounds to be Raised and Paid him out of this Years Leavy List.

[In a Suit—"Henry Stretcher, Aged Sixty Seven Years or thereabouts being Deposed" said that a certain 20 acres of land in question was sold to "Peter Winster of the same Place & County Hattmaker, Who there Lived Some Time and Dyed, And Lyeth buried, att the Antient burying Place of the same Lewis" * * *].

[Another witness testifies to successive owners of the above property: "As from Johannis Winster, Son and Heir of Peter Winster Hatter Deced To Morris Edwards And from ye Sd Morris to Doctr Thomas Wynne, And from ye Sd Thomas Wynne, After the Death of him & Elizabeth his Wife To ye Sd Plt." * * *].

Rice Wolfe Peticoned the Court That Whereas he hath Intermarried with Mary the Daughter of ffrancis Cornwell (Intestate) Deced That he may be Ordered his Proportionable Part of the Sd Estate, both Reall and ℘sonal According as the Law Directs * * * [Referred to Orphans Court].

FEBRUARY 4th, 1706.

The Court Nominated and Appointed fence Viewers (Vizt) * * *.

Luke Shields by his Peticon in Open Court Read Setts forth That he have Served in the Station of a Drumer Sundry Courts Past in beating of the Drum, to Call People to Give Their Attendance at Sd Courts And is in hopes, That the Court and Grand Jury, will Allow his Sd Service therein, both Past and to Come Some Compensacon or Reward—Whereupon the Sd Peticon Was Given out to ye Grand Jury, Who Returned it back into Court (rejected). However, it was Considered, By the Court That he Continue as Drumer therein And That at the Settlemt of the Next Years Leavy Lists, They Will Indeavoure, Hee Shall Have Some Sattisfaction For his Pains.

Whereas It was Considered by the Court That Rideing of Horse Races in the Town of Lewis, Dureing the time of the Courts Sitting was Very Prejudicall and A Great Hindrance to the Dispatche of business Depending on the Same by Peoples Neglect of Attendance in Court; Wherefore it was Considered and Ordered By The Sd Court That No ℘sons Presume to Ride a Race or Races, Or Strain A horse or Horses, within the Town of Lewis, Dureing the Courts Sitting, under the Imediate forfeiture of ffive Shillings, To be Paid by the Rider or Riders, Each of Them for Every Such Offence.

John Futcher And Robert Clifton, Was Sent for, into Court by The Order of the Justices, To Thomas Smith Constable, them & Each of Them, To Answer for their Contempts, In Rideing of a Race in the Town of Lewis Dureing the Courts Sitting, Notwithstanding a Rule or Order of Court Made to the Contrary under the Penalty of ffive Shillings ℘r man for Each Such Race, To be Paid by the Riders Thereof—Whereupon the Sd Constable Returns into Court and Reports That Hee mett with Oposicon in the Discharge of his Office therein, By Mr. Luke Watson & Justice Jonathan Baily who Comanded ye Constable to Produce to him the Warrant that hee had for the Apprehension of the Sd Offendrs ffurther urging that the Court had no Power to Make Laws, And That as he was a Justice of the Peace, as well as they, he Expected the Examinacon of the Sd Matter, And Commanded the Constable to bring the Sd Riders, before him, Which ye Constable Did so,—And The Sd Justice Baily Cleared ye Sd Offendrs from the Sd Constable, Whereupon the Court Checked ye sd Constable for his Neglect and Timerousness in the Execucon of his Office, And Comanded him to Goe and fetch the Sd Robert, and John into Court, And To Comand Assistance in the Same—And Thereupon the Sd Justice Baily and Luke Watson Came into Court Togather with the Constable and the Two Offendrs, And The Said Mr. Baily Confessed he had Cleared them So That they would not, Nor Should not Pay their fines, And That he ye sd Baily Knew as much Law as any of the Court Wherefore the Court Considering the Great Contempt of their Authority Comanded The Clk fforthwith to Write A Mittimus to the Sher. To Take the Sd Robert Clifton and John ffutcher into his Close Custody And, So Keep Them untill they had Payed their Sd outmost ffines and, all Incidentall Charges and ffees, by means of the Sd Contempt. John ffutcher Also Some time After n Open Court being Attested, Declared, That the Aforesd Mr. Watson and One Bonwell, the Owner of the Horse that Run, And that the Deponant Rid,—That the Sd Watson, And Bonwell Promised faithfully to Indemnifie him for his fine, And all Damages Whatsoever That Should Arise thereby And That the Sd Mr. Watson Gave him Two Bitts, for Rideing the Sd horse and Race.

[Luke Watson gives land to his brothers John Watson and Samuel.]

[Esther Parry Widow gives land to her son John Smith and to her Son in Law Darby Collins.]

[William ffisher gives land to son John Fisher.]

March 4th, 1706.

John West & Thomas West, Joint Execrs of the Last Will and Testamt of their ffather George West Deced Came into Court And Makeing themselves Debtr by Inventary and Appraismt in the Sum of Ninety ffour Pounds ffourteen Shillings & two pence, Produced therewth an Accott of ffunerall Charges Debts and Legacies paid And other Lawfull Disbursmts Amounting in & to ye Sum of Sixty ffour Pounds Nineteen Shillings & one Peny, And prays of ye Court An Allowance of ye same * * *.

John Hagister Execr of the Last Will and Testamt of his Mother Anne Williams Deced Came into Court * * *.

Thomas Bowman Came into Court And by his Peticon in the behalfe of himselfe & brothers Sett fforth That Whereas William Clark in his Life time had Obtained Lettrs of Administracon upon the Sd Peticoner's ffather Henry Bowman Senr Decd And now the Sd William Clark is also Dead * * *.

The Widow Dunavan, and the Widow Rachael Webster, both of Musmillian Creek in this County * * * [petitioned and had their Levies remitted, owing to their Great Poverty and Charge of Children.] The Like was Granted to the Widow Mary Depray upon her ꝑsonall Applicacon, Submission, and Supplycacon in open Court, And ye Sheriff Ordered to Cease to Demand or Receive her Levy for the Year Aforesd.

Richard Hinman, in the Right of Mary his Wife Administ of the Estate of Hercules Shepheard Deced Came into Court * * *.

Frances Prittyman fformerly the Widow of Anthony Inglow's Deced And Execx of his Last Will & Testamt Came into Court * * *.

Rice Wolfe Appeared in Court And by his Petition Sett fforth That [faded out] he hath Lately Intermarried with Mary the Daughtr of ffrancis Cor [faded] Decd (Who Dyed Intestate) * * *.

"MARCH YE 27th, 1710.

"Mary Senior Widowe came to mee & Desired me to record the Age of her Daughter Frances Harding who was borne On the 23th Day of Aprill in the Yeare of our Lord 1704 soe thatt on the said 23th April next ensueing this Date she will be six Yeares of Age.

"Testr. ROGER CORBETT, Clerk.

* * * Ye Grand Jury were called over & all appeared and Gave in their Presentments Vizt: Wee of the Grand Jury thinks fitt thatt the Roade upon the bank of Lewis Creeke Layd out by the six men bee made Good by the Towne Hundred, Anderson Parker foreman. The Court thinks fitt Thatt if the ysons agt whose Land the breach of the Roade on the banke aforesaid will nott mend itt itt must Lye till further Order.

SEPTEMBER 6th, 1709.

Mary Westcott Widow & Adstratrix of Francis Cornewall Gent decd apeared and according to a former Order of Court in Sept. 1708 forthwith Devided betweene ye two Heires, Francis and Mary, by a Jury of twelve men & Captn Pemperton Surveyor * * *.

[Abigail West prays the Court for some Cattle left to Tabitha West daughter of John West & Eliz. his Wife.]

Stephen Kanning exhibits his Acct agt Eliz. Barker Widowe decd for attendance 10 days in her sicknesse & 3 dayes after death till she was buried £1 16s 0d. * * *.

[Saml Dickinson & Tho. Mariner sumoned to bring Inventory of estate of Mathew Spicer decd. of this county.]

SEPTEMBER [7th?], 1709.

Petition of Abigall West being this day read and discoursed upon the Petition setting forth &c, Justice Walker exhibits an Order of Court under ye Clarks hand, in Sept. 1708 Orphans Court for five pound for ye funerall Charges of Tabitha West daughter of John West decd to bee paid out of the Estate of the said Tabitha. Abigall West by Edward Parker prayes ye Courts Opinion whether or nott the two Children mentioned in ye petition were nott next heires att Law to ye sd Tabitha—the Court refuses theire Opinion, & putts Abigall West to prove itt. Continued to ye next adjourned Orphans Court.

SEPTEMBER 22d, 1709.

Att an adjourned Orphans Court to ye 22th Instant * * * John Haverly sonn of Anthony Haverly late of this County decd, appeared in this Court, being of the Age of nineteen yeares, three weekes before Christmas next * * *.

William Haverly aged 17 yeares Aprill ye 7th, 1709 next appeared * * *.

Andreas or Andrewe Haverly sonn of sd Anthony Haverly next appeared aged fifteen yeares in July last, and Chose Tho. Parker his Master wth him to live & dwell in the Nature of an Apprentice untill hee shall arrive att the full Age of One & twenty yeares ye sd Thomas Parker to learne him the Mistery & Arte of a Blacksmith & write & reade English to find him Meat drink &c and att the next Orphans Court to bee held in Mrch next ensueing to pay & Deliver to ye Justices of sd Court for time being the sume of One pound ten Shillings to bee disposed of att the Courts Pleasure for the use of sd Orphan & to give him att expiration according to Law.

Next appeared Daniel Haverly sonn of sd Anthony aged 12 yeares last July, & Hester Beckett daughter of Alexander Beckett aged 4 yeares in October next ensueing the Lad chose his brother Anthony for Guardian, ye Girle ye Court assigned him Guardian to * * *.

Next appeared James Haverly sonn of the aforesd Anthony ,aged 10 Yeares last July, to serve till 21 & Katherine Beckett aged 5 yeares May last the Girle to serve till 16, ye boy to bee learnt to write & reade ye Girle to reade, both bound to Mathew Parker by ye Courts Order * * *.

PROBATE RECORDS.

CHRISTOPHER TAYLOR REGISTER GENERAL OF KENT AND SUSSEX ON DELAWARE. WILLIAM CLARK, DEPUTY. 1683–1695.

Will of James Lattan; Robert Hart Administrator.

Abraham Wiltbank (son of Abram Wiltbank and Anne his wife) was borne about Twelve of the Clock at night ffriday the Tent day of ffebruary in the year of Our Lord God One Thousand Six Hundred Ninety and Nine. Their Daughter Abbigail was Borne the first day of May 1706. Jacob Wiltbank (son of Abraham and Anne Wiltbank was Borne about Twelve of the Clock att night of Monday the Sixth Day of July in the year of our Lord God One Thousand Seven Hundred and Two Registered ye 11th of September 1702.

NEHEMIAH FFIELD, Deputy Register.

Mary the Daughter of Rachell and Norton Claypoole of the Town of Lewis was borne the 10th day of the 8e month 1682 about the first hour in the morning in the presence of Mary the wife of Edward Southrine which said Mary was the midwife as allsoe in ye presence of Katherine Vines alias Hewes and her Daughter Elizabeth Hews. Honor Clarke, fonira Wiltbank, Margaret Mollestine, —na Gray, Sarah Stretcher and Sarah Bartlett.

Richard Shoulter's Will January 28′ 1682 Sussex Co. To Capt. Nathaniel Walker half the money due from said Walker unto me for my land at Rehour. Richard Bundock the other half. Presence of:—John his × B mark Barker. William Emmatt.

Abbigail Eyres Daughter of John Eyres and Abbigail his wife was Borne the Seventeenth Day of June One Thousand Six Hundred Ninety and Seven (8 years old next June) John Eyres son of the same parents was borne on the Seventeenth Day of December One Thousand Seven Hundred and Two (Two years old last December). Registered by Desire of their mother the first Day of Jan. 1704 Per me NEHEMIAH FFIELD Deputy Register.

Richard Gill Testifie in open Court that Elizabeth Leveritt deceased about Two or Three Days befor her Decad did Will and Bequeith unto Richard Bundock a Mare or a Thousand pounds of Tobacco in Robert Bracey his hands for the which said Mare the said Robert Bracey did pay one Thousand pounds of Tobacco out of the said Elizabeth Leveritt her Estate and further did declare that if the said Robert Bracey did refuse to pay the said Thousand pounds of Tobacco it would trouble her that she would Com againe. Attested in open Court.

RICHARD R GILL
his mark

[torn] 11 mo. 1683.

BANNS.

Between Daniel Jones single man and Elizabeth Roades single woman. Lewis, Del. Oct 1, 1683.

Between Abraham Westron widower and Mary Smith widow. Lewis, Del. Oct., 1683.

Susan Fisher daughter in Law to Robert Bedwell of Dover River in Kent County departed this Life the 28th Day of the Eighte moneth 1683.

Will of Cornelis Verhoofe Sick at the house of Richard Bundock in Sussex County Bequeithed to Barbara the fore daughter of Elizabeth Parling she accepted with the rest of the children of Simon Parling the Backward point next to Pagons Creeke belonging to a devedent of Land called the Ship Carpenters Yard. Unto Simon Parling so much. To Richard Bundock & his wife and etc. To John Johnson Junr etc. To Thomas Gollidge alias Jones etc. To John Betts a land in Murderkil Hundred where John Betts now lives. Halmanius Wiltbank & Peter Groundick Executors. Administrators to be careful to Transport half of Estate to Holland to my Brother-in-Law John Lilevoort (Vomb?) & my sister Eve Verhoofe. Dec. 23, 1683. Witnesses:—Randle Shard, William Emmatt.

Elizabeth Mosely Daughter of William and Hannah Mosely will be Eight years in the middle of next ffebruary That is to say she was Born in the middle of the month of ffebruary 1698. Recorded by her mothers request now the [Wife of James Richardson]. Aug, 21, 1706. N. FFIELD Clk Reg.

Elizabeth Miers Daughter of John Miers and Mary His Wife was borne on the 20th day of November 1703.

Whereas John ffoster widower and Allice Manloe widow have Obtained license to bee Joyned together in ye holy Estate of Matrimony which said License bears Even Date with Those presents These are therefore to Certify that ye said Parties did on ye Tenth Day of July 1698 Solemnly in ye presents of Almighty God and before us ye underwritten witnesses att ye house of Mr. William Clark in ye town of Lewis in County aforesaid.

JOHN FFOSTER
ALLICE A FFOSTER
her mark

Witnesses:—William Clark, Jonathan Baily, John Clark, Susanna her O mark ffreeman, Mary her un mark Miers, Mary Wolfinden, Nehemiah ffield, John Miers, Henry Strecther, Robert Corbett, William Adams, James Claypoole, William Clampitt, Peter Lewis, Wrixham White, John × Carey, Edward + Carey, Henry × Allen.

John Elme of this County Batchelor and Margaret Kelly of ye said County Spinster were married at the house of Mr. James Peterkin at the town of Lewis did solemnly Take each the other as Husband and Wife the 8th Day of September 1697.

Witnesses:—John Hill, Justice; Roger Corbett, James Peterkin, Richard Paynter, Nazareth her N mark Halloway, Margaret Simson,

Ann her X mark Seaton, Elizabeth her E mark Peterkin, Nehemiah ffield, John his H mark Haynes, Elizabeth her E mark Haynes, Jane her D mark Peterkin, John his X mark Elme, Margaret her N mark Elme.

Letter Administracon Elloner Richards County of Sussex Robert Richards deceased Day Thurteenth of January 1684.

Will of John Depree to sons of John Depree and Jacob Depree land bought of Capt. John Avery and to their brethern, sisters and etc. January 5, 1684. JOHN DEPREE.
William Emmatt, William ffootcher.

Robert Trayle of Lewis County to Alexander Mouliston etc. amounts due from John Manloe, Norton Claypoole, John Cullison, David Corsey, and for Henrick Mouliston etc. land at the fork of the great Kill Beginning at the lower end of the town.

his
ROBERT M TRAYLE
mark

John K Kiphaven, Mathias Vanderhagen, Alburtis Jacobs.

John Cullison and Barbrey his wife letter of Administracon upon the estate of Mathias Everson.

Letter of Administracon Mary Southrin upon the estate of Edward her husband.

Letter Administracon Thomas Hodgekings upon the estate of Jacob Shattham.

Letter Administracon Thomas Hodgekings upon the estate of Harmon Cornelison.

Whereas George Truitt of the County of Somersett in the Province of Mary Land Being near Related unto Paull Marsh Late of the County of Sussex.

John Tuxbury single man and Ellenor Richards widow married 5th March, 1685 at the house of John Roades take each other as husband and wife. Wm. Clark, John Roades, Harclos Shepard, Henry Strachter, John Simons, William Kennig, Moris Edwards, John Stuicbury, Ellenor Stuckbury, francis X Williams, John + Jones, Thomas X Jones, Elizabeth E Roades, widow, Johana + Simons.

Coppie of a Mortaig of Thomas Hodgkins Shallup known as the Sea Horse now riding in the Creeke of Lewis to John Wrighte. The Sloop was bought by Thomas Hodgkins & John Rodgers from John Wright and Daniel Jones 9th Day of February 1684. Thomas Hodgkins, John Vines, Henry Stracther, Alexander M Mouliston.

Georg Young single man and Mary Southrin widow married on the 24th of June 1685 at the Towne of Lewis. GEORG YOUNG
MARY MS YOUNG.

Wm. Clark, Luke Wattson, John Vines, John Hill, Wm. Emmatt, Joshua Barksteed, Will Arendeal, Morris Edwards, Salmon Jones, Thomas Besent, Arther Star, Honor Clark, Catherine Star, Rachell Claypoole, Elizabeth Pemberton, Elizabeth Hill.

Thomas Hodgkins bill of sale of a heffer to Cornelis Wiltbank 18th June, 1685. Thomas Hodgkings. John Brown, Henry Stracther, William Emmatt.

Griffith Jones bill of Sale of a heffer to Rebackah Wiltbank 16th May 1685. Griffith Jones. John Vines, Thomas Besant.

Thos. Hodgking bill of sale of a cow to Rebaekah Wiltbank 18th June, 1685. Thomas Hodgkings. John Brown, Henry Stractcher, William Emmatt.

Robert Bracey senor widdower and Ann Douglis widdow were married 30th July, 1685 at the house of William Clark in Lewis. Witnesses:—Wm. Clark, James Huling, Henry Stracther, William Rodeney, Charles Haynes, John Stuckbury, Richard Harvey, ffrancis Williams, Hornor Clark, Elenor Stuckbury, Burkee B. Kiphaven, Sarah A. Williams, Margaret her R mark Pendree,

Luke Wattsons bond to Nicholas Rideout late of Sharftbury in the County of Darcett England, 3d March, 1685. Wm. Clark, Joseph his T mark Thorne.

Alburtis Jacobs single man married to Martha Kiphaven 8th October 1685 in the house of John Kiphaven in Lewis. Beorcha Kiphaven, John Kiphaven, Wm Clark, John Roades, Henry Stracther, Moris Edwards, Nehmiah field, Henry Moulston, William Rodeney, will Emmatt, John vines, Norttron Claypoole, Arther Stare, William Carter, John Browne.

John Walker single man of Kent County married Mary Paynter single woman of Sussex County 18th October, 1685 at the house of John Kiphaven of Lewis. Richard Paynter, Sarah Paynter, Wm. Clark, John Roades, Henry Stracther, will Rodeney, Nehemiah ffield, John Browne, Arther Star, Morris Edwards, William Carter, William Emmatt, Henry Moulston, Alburtis Jacobs, Robert Holgate,

Johanias Winsteed single man married Margaret Penree single woman 18th Oct. 1685 at the house of John Kiphaven of Lewis Jane Winsteed, Wm. Clark, John Roades, Henry Stracther, Alburtis Jacobs, Wm. Carter, Morris Edwards, William Rodeney, John Browne, John Vines, Norton Claypoole, Robert Holgate, William Emmatt, John Walker, Arther Star, Nehemiah ffield.

Robert Godsell late of the Kingdom of Ireland and then of Sussex County did make his will 23d of November in favor of the following: Charles Spooner, Edward T Barrey, John White, Apalina Taylor.

Sarah Godsell's letter of Administracon on the estate of Robt. Godsell her deceased husband, 23d of November, 1685.

In the will of Robt. Hart of Cedar Creeke his wife Margaret was willed his house etc. to Robert her son etc. His daughter Margaret etc. October 4, 1685. Jonathan ffox, Ann Jennings, Symon Charles.

Margaret Hart's letter of Administracon on Robert Hart's estate 3d of December, 1685.

In the will of John ffisher made 6th of February, 1685, the property, land, etc. to his wife Margaret and children Thomas, John, James, Rachell, Sarah, and Alis Fisher. Wm. Emmatt, Richard R.C Coore, Ann S Dougdull.

Margaret's and Thomas' letter of Administracon on the estate of John Fisher, 30th April, 1686.

Marriage between John Coe Batchelor and Elizabeth Roads Spinster at the house of Mrs. Comfort Scott at Rehoboth, Delaware, June 30, 1697. Wrixham White, Peter Lewis, Richard R. Hinman, John Hill, Justice; Thos. Oldman, Thos. Besent, Samuel Dickisson, Henry H. Allen, John I Carey, Joseph O. Magnab, Comfort C Scott, Grace

× Lewis, James Walker, James Simson, Margaret Simson, Sarah Clifon, Elizabeth Hill, Eliz Stokeley.

Marriage between Charles Spooner single man and Susanna Burough single woman, December 4, 1686. Wm. Clark, Wm. Dyer, John Hill, Baptis Newcomb, Morris Edwards, Charles I Bright Robert I Murdock, Ann A. Newcomb, Elizabeth Hill, Jane O Potter, Esseble v Torbut, Lidy × Patte, Wm. Haward, Wm. P. Hignett (?), John I Webster.

Major Dyer's letter of Administracon on the estate of Capt. Nathaniel Walker formerly of New England and late of Northampton County, Virginia who died three months after July 20, 1685.

Mary the daughter of Luke and Margaret Watson was born the 28th day of the 12th month 1685 at Prime Hooke in the County of Sussex.

John the son of John Bradshaw of Kent County borne the 22d Day of December, 1686.

William the son of Robt. and Rebecka Millner born the 12th day of April, 1676.

Mercy the Daughter of Robt. and Rebecka Millner borne the 15th 12th month, 1678.

Alexander the son of Alexander and Rebecka Draper borne the 22 day of ye 9th month, 1680, Sussex Co.

Rebecka the daughter of Allexander and Rebecka Draper of Sussex County borne the 4th day of the second month 1683.

Henry the sonn of Allexander and Rebecka Draper borne the 9th day of the first Month called March 1685–6 of Sussex Co.

Elizabeth the daughter of Norton & Rachell Claypoole was borne at Lewis in ye Sussex County the 16th Day of the 3d month called May 1687 aboute ye seaventh houre in the evening in the presence of Thomas Wynne and Elizabeth his wife, ye midwife & Jane Maud her daughter Hannah Baily, Sarah Strechther Jane Hodgkins Sarah Painter and Helen Sikes.

Marriage between Henry Smith and Sarah Godsell, February 5, 1686. Henry Getto, Dorathy C Getto, Henry Bowman, Luke Watson, Junr; Thomas Tilton, Samuel Watson, Bryant Roles, John his IW marke Watson, Sarah her O marke Watson, Edward his EM marke Morgan, Elizabeth her EP marke Parsley, Richard Renords.

Banns of George Rigs & Ann Thomas Batchellor and Spinister April 17, 1687.

Mary Webb widow of Isack Webb of Kent County March 15, 1687.

A deed of Gift Henry Getto to Peter Godsell, March 5, 1687. Edward Berry, Ellinor Midleton, Henry Bowman. In the hands of Robert Turner and John Fuller for the education of Peter Godsell. If he dies before he is of age the money goes to his mother Sarah Smith. In the will of Henry Getto his wife Dorothy Getto etc. so long as she lives with his son Henry Smith to my grandchild Peter Godsell etc. March 6, 1687. Bryant B R Roales, Edward ⊕ Berry, Henry Bowman.

Marriage between George Riggs and Ann Thomas now of the town of Lewis but lately of Phyladelphya June 19, 1687. Thomas Wynn, John Roades, ffrancis Cornwall, Phillip Russell, Arthur Starr, Morrice Edwards, Norton Claypoole, Honor Clark, Adam Johnson, George

Davis, Albertus Jacobs, Philip Th Lehnmaine, Jacob Warrin, Elizabeth Wynn, Mary Cornwall, Jane Maude, Sarah Clifton.

Thomas Grove single man late of Philadelphia married Sarah Smith widow of Sussex County January 7, 1692 at the house of Sarah Smith att Prime Hook. Luke Watson, Wm. Clark, John Hill, Honnor Clark, Elizabeth Hill, Mary Bowman, Mary Wattson, Tho. Price, Henry Bowman, Peter × Godsell, Thomas Morgan, Alexr Grant, Luke Wattson, Junr; Will Rodeney, Yoems Syonsen, James Thomas.

Allexander Draper's letter of Administracon upon the estate of Jno. Pearce. 31st October, 1687.

Joane Hart in her will made 20th Janurary made her son and granddaughter her heirs, John Richards and Sarah Richards. Allexander Draper, William Emmatt.

John the sonn of John and Rachell Hilliyard of Kent County borne the 15th day of October, 1686.

Henry the son of Henry and Jane Permaine of Kent County borne the seaventeenth day of the Ninth Month, 1686.

Marriage of Isack Bowd late of Philadelphia single man to Jane Mawde of Lewis single woman or spinster. September 15, 1687, in the house of Norton Claypoole. Robt. Clifton, Justice of the Peace; Norton Claypoole, Clerk & Register; John Wynne, Adam Johnson, Henry Mollestine, John Millington, Step. Sargent, Sam. Pope, Nehemiah ffield, Johannis Winster, Joseph Alef, Mathew M. osborne, Sarah Screcther M., Sarah N Russell, Mary MOC Molleston, Margaret Mollestine, Rachell Claypoole.

John Roades will his daughter Elizabeth etc. daughter Patience land next to John Symons that he now lives on Given to Grace White etc. ajoining land of her brother Wrixham White. My son John the residence. Unto my dear and tender mother etc. Unto Nehemiah ffield etc. Unto Sarah Strechter wife of Henry Strechter. Unto John How etc. Unto my brother Richard Tull. Dear wife Comfort her thirds. Sept. 17, 1687. John Millington, Nehemiah ffield.

Verbal will of James Saykes 8th of December 1687. Affidavit of Allexander Draper of same, a daughter and son in this country and two children in England. Allexander Draper, Thomas Price.

A true Inventory of ye Eftate of John pearce deceafed

* * * The Advantage at Robert Cliftons * * *; Norton Claypooles note * * *; John Sunners bill * * *; Thomas Pembertons bill * * *. Apraysed by us ye 26th day of ye 9th month 1687

WM EMMATT
JOHN PRICE

Wm Emmatt one of ye praifers of ye Eftate of John Pearce Atteſted the 6th Xber 1687.

NORTON CLAYPOOLE deputy Regifter.

Letter of Adminiftration to Nathaniell Sikes of the Eftate of James Sikes late of ye County of Suffex.

Suffex County In the territories of penfillvania the 11th day of the 12th month Called ffebruary 1687. * * * Know yee that Nathaniell Sikes Heir Apparent of James Sikes deceafed late of the faid County of Suffex having brought unto me Norton Claypoole Deputy Regifter of the faid County the laft will and teftament of the faid James Sikes proved by the Teftimony of Allexander Draper and Thomas price and he the faid Nathaniell Sikes defiring that he might have letters of Adminiftration for the Execution of the faid Will according to the Contents thereof and the laws of this Government etc. * * * Mentions James Claypoole Late Regifter Generall of the faid province & Countys of Suffex and Kent etc. * * *.

NORTON CLAYPOOLE, deputy Regifter of ye County of Suffex.

Nuncative Will of John Badger viz Wee Robert Tomlinfon and James Hughs Doe Affirme and depofe that John Badger Deceafed did fome time before his Departure * * * difpofe of all his Eftate goods and Chattells * * * to Antony Inloyee to the truth whereof we have figned this fixth day of March Ano 1687–8

ROBERT his × marke TOMLINSON
JAMES HUGHS.

The Wittneffes * * * Attefted * * * that the faid John Badger was Compos Mentis and that he faid foe feverall times * * * Attefted the 6th day of the firft month 1687–8.

Teftis NORTON CLAYPOOLE Clerr.

Robert Tomlinson Attefted * * * that the faid John Badger told of A house and land he had in Antego. [No mention of County].

Mickell Sadler & John How Their obligation to Stephen Whetman.

Know all men by thefe prefents that wee John How and Mickell Sadler both of the County of Suffex * * * are held and firmly bound unto Stephen Whetman of ye aforefaid County of Suffex * * * in Witneff Whereof Wee have hereunto fett oure hands and feals the tenth day of ye firft Month Called March Anno Dom; 1686; The Condittion of the above obligation is fuch that if the above bounden John How and Mickell Sadler their Heirs Executors Adminiftrators or Affigns or either of them doe and fhall well and truly pay or caufe to be paid * * * at or before the 10th day of the next twelfth Month Called ffebruary withoute fraud or further delay at the towne of Lewis * * * that then the above obligation to be voyde and of no effect or elce to be and Remaine in full power force and vertue.

JOHN HOW [feal]
MICHAELL SADLER [feale]

sealed and delivered In the prefence of us

WM CLARK
WILL RODENEY.

Nehemiah the Son of Nehemiah and Rachel ffield Relicte of Norton Claypoole Deceesed was borne on the Twentieth Day of December in the year One Thoufand Six hundred Eighty and Nine, And his younger Brother William ffield Borne on the Twenty fifth of December In the year One Thoufand Six hundred Ninety and three.

Copie of Ann Rigs letter of Adminiftration.

Suffex County. In the Territories of pennfillvania the 27th day of the firft Month 1688 * * * Know yee that Ann Rigs the widdow and Rellix of George Rigs * * * deceafed having brought unto me Norton Claypoole Deputy Regifter of the fd County the laft will and Teftament of him the fd George Rigs * * * She having proved the fame before me According to Law, and fhe the faid Ann Rigs defiring that fhe might have letters of Adminiftration for the Execution of the faid Will according to the contents thereof * * * I doe therefore * * * Grant Letters of Adminiftration unto her * * * for the Ends and purpofes aforefaid; * * *

NORTON CLAYPOOLE Deputy Regifter.

Whereas Rowland Perrey of This County Widower and Esther Coore of the said County widow Have Publifhed and openly Declared their Banes and Intentions of Marriage * * * Thefe may Certifie That ye Said Parties did on ye fourteenth Day of July in ye Year of Our Lord God 1698 Att the Dwelling houfe of Jacob Kollack in ye Town of Lewis * * * Take Each The other as Hufband and Wife in manner and form following, * * *

ROWLAND R PARREY
ESTHERE PARREY.

Testes:—Jonathan Baily Juftice, John Smith, James ffifher, Richard Dobfon, James Seattonn, George Thomfon, Nathll Starr, William Adams, Ralph Norcott, Anne her H mark Seattonn, Elizabeth her X mark Moleston, Kathrine × Davies, Richard R W Williams, Roger Corbett, William Clampitt, William Dyre, Sher; Nehemiah ffield.

The laft Will & Teftament of George Rigs.

In the name of God Amen this fixth day of the fixth Month Anno qui Domini 1687, I George Riggs of Suffex County * * *. 2dly. Next I doe give and bequeath unto Ann Riggs my beloved wife all my Worldly Eftate * * *. 3dly. I doe Apoynt & Conftitute William Clark and Thomas Wynne * * * to Affift Ann Riggs my beloved wife the best that they may * * *.

GEORGE RIGGS [feal]

signed fealed and delivered in the prefence of us
BARRENTS GERRIS
DANIELL ISHELL
THOMAS BESENT

Endoffed on the back fide. Thomas Beffant one of the evidences to the within written will being legally Attefted declared the fame to be the Act and deed of George Riggs deceafed 7th day of the firft month 1687–8. Barents Gerris one other of the evidences * * * appeared before me the 26th day of the firft month 1688 * * *.

Teftis NORTON CLAYPOOLE Dep:^t Register

Certificate of Marriage ffor Thomas Oldman & Elizabeth his wife.

Thefe are to Certify etc. After due publication according to the laws etc. Thomas Oldman Batchellor of the towne of Lewis * * * Carpenter tooke Elizabeth sikes the Daughter of James Sikes deceafed fpinfter * * * to be his lawfull wife at the houfe of him the faid Thomas Oldman In the towne of Lewis Aforefaid * * * this twentyeth day of the firft Month called March 1687-8.

THOMAS OLDMAN [feal]
ELIZABETH OLDMAN [feal]

GREEN HILL LIGHTHOUSE.

Albertus Jacobs, Henry Mollefton, Norton Claypoole, Phillip Ruffell, Mofes Oboab, Nehemiah ffield, Morrice Edwards, ferrimia Scott, the mark M of William Orion, John Miers, John Redwood, Richard Daygtet, Samuel Pope, John Millington, the marke 6 of Sarah painter, Catherine Starr, Rachell Claypoole, Sarah Dyer, Mary Dyer, The mark M of Margaret Mollefton, the marke + of Martha Jacobs, the marke + of Rebecka Willaims, Sarah her + marke Stretcher.

An Inventory of the Eftate of James sikes lately Deceafed.

The laft Will and Teftament of Major Wm. Spencer.

I William Spencer Senr of Cedar Creke in Suffex County etc. Imp: I give unto my beloved wife ffrancis Spencer the plantation whereon I now life etc. during her widowhood allfo all the Eftate in Accomack that her ffather bequeathed to her; land bequeathed to Daughter Margarett Spencer; land bequeathed to fonn William Spencer; to wife land on south fide of Mifpillian Creek; property sould to William Dyer * * * well beloved fon William Spencer to be my Executor and to Adminiftrate * * * this my Eftate * * * in wittnefs whereof I have hereunto fett my hand and feal this twenty ninth day of the Ninth Month 1687 * * *.

the marke of
WM SPENCER fenr [feal]

Signed fealed and delivered In the prefence of us:

The mark of ART A JOHNSON VANKERK;
the marke of ROBERT R. TWILLEY
WM EMMATT.

The Evidences to the above Written Will appeared in open Court & * * * declared that the fame is the Act and deed of William Spencer Senr deceafed * * * the second day of the third month 1688 Wittnefs their hands WM EMMATT.
the marke of ART. A JOHNSON VANKIRK; the marke of ROBERT R TWILLY.

The laft Will & Teftament of Major William Dyre.

I William Dyre of ye County of Suffex * * * Efqr * * *

Item. I Will and Bequeath unto my Elldeft son William Dyre now at Bofton in New England all my plantation or land scittuate Lying & being in the Broad Kill In Suffex County Aforesaid Called Rumbley place, * * *

Item. I give and bequeath unto my fecond fon Edmund Dyre one plantation Lying and being upon Love Creek, In the County Aforesaid * * * formerly Called fundialls (but now Beaverwick) * * * other lands held formerly in partnership with Stephen Whettman bounded by lands of ferrimia Scott, & Thomas Branscomb * * * John Roades & William Roades * * *.

Item. I give and bequeath unto my youngeft fonn James Dyre, * * * Land lying and being upon Mifpillen Creek, In the County aforefd—other lands Lying in the forke of the Broad Kill—same county—bounded upon the Beaver dam & upon prime Hooke Creek—other land in Newcaftle County

Item. I give & bequeath unto my Elldeft Daughter Sarah Dyre land lying betweene the Cold fpring and the Cyprufs Bridge in the County of Suffex * * *.

Item. I give & bequeath unto my youngest Daughter Mary Dyre land Knowne by the name of the White horfe, lately bought of Charls pickering * * * land lying in Angola Neck * * * fometime the land of Richard Shoulfter * * *.

Item. I give and bequeath unto my Deare and well beloved wife Mary Dyre * * * Land Lying and being in Sedar Neck Suffex County * * * other land fcittuate & being Adjoyning to the towne of Lewis * * * with two towne lots * * * houfhold goods etc. * * * debt due by bond from Hendrick Van den Borgh of Newcaftle * * * one debt * * * in money or Corne due from Juftice Anderfon of the fd towne of Newcaftle * * * debt due by bond in wheat or porke due from Samuel Curtis of Allaways Creek in Weft Jarfey * * * one other debt due by accompt and bill of Capt Wm Markham * * * debt due from Wm Afsberry, due by Mortgage * * * now in the hands of Capt Stephanus Van Courtland of New Yorke * * * also land in Narraganfet Country, in New England * * * all Right & title of Inherritance to the Eftate of my Late ffather William Dyre, decd, upon Roade Ifland * * * plantation and allfoe one Ifland Called Dyres Ifland * * * also ye ballance of Mr Thomas LLoyds bond * * * Land lying at Reading in New England, and two Iflands Called the Clabboard Iflands in Gafcoe Bay in New England * * *.

Item. * * * Wife Mary Dyre and eldeft fonn William Dyre * * * sole executrix and executor * * * Sr Edmund Androfs mentioned * * * Date of will twentieth day of ffebruary 1687-8 * * * I Request my ffriends Mr. John Hill and Mr. Samuel Gray to be affifting to my wife & children In the management of their affairs in thefe parts; * * * Sr Edmund Androfs Governr Genll of New England to assist them in New England, or thereunto belonging * * * Wm Dyre [feal]

Signed fealed & delivered In the prefence of us to two:—

Charles Sanders
Will Rodeney

The Evidences * * * attefted In open Court Held for the County of Suffex the 5th day of the 4th Month Called June 1688 * *

Teftis Norton Claypoole Clerk and Deputy Regifter.

John Richards Letter of Administration on ye Estate of Thomas Moules-ton Deceast.

Suffex County * * * ye 3d day of ye 8th moth Annoq: Dom: 1688 * * * Know yee that John Richards late of Maryland * * * haveing marryed ye Relict of Thomas Molefon late of this County * * * Granted by Court to take out letters of Administration on said Estate.

Ff Cornwall, Depty Regyr of ye County Suffex.

ffrancis Cornwall son of —— & Mary Cornwall was Borne on the fourteenth day of the first moth Annoq Dom: 1687-8 * * * Att Spring houfe neare Lewis * * *.

John Molliston son of Abraham and Lidia Molliston was Borne on The Second Day of October Ano Domi 1694.

Coppey of Thomas May & Margarett Spencer there Certificate of Marriage.

These may Certify etc. that upon ye 28th day of ye 5th moth in ye yeare of our Lord 1688, there was a marryage Solemnized betweene Thomas May of Suffex County etc. Batcheler, & Margrett Spencer of ye Same County Singlewoman * * *

THOMAS MAY
MAR: her MM mark MAY

Wm. Spencer, ffrancis Spencer, Thomas Price, Luke Wattfon, Jonathan Balife, John Price, Alexr. Draper, Wm. Emmet, James Spencer, Mary Bowman, Samll. Pollard, Robert his R marke Twilleys, John Dickifon.

Certificate of Marriage Between James Carpenter and Affyance Piles.

County Suffex: This may Certify That I James Carpenter Widower And Affyance Piles Spinfter Both of This County * * * according to Law made Publicacon of Their Bains of Matrimony and Intention * * * Take each other as Husband and Wife * * * Att ye houfe of William Piles * * * The Eigth Day of Decembr 1698.

JAMES his F mark CARPENTER
AFFYANCE her E mark CARPENTER

Wittneffes: William Piles, William × Piles, Junr; John Hill, Juftice, John Miers, John Waatfon, Isaac Wattfon, Mark N Mitchell, Elizabeth E Kirwithy, Sufanah S Crowell, Isaac IW Piles, Comfort C Piles, Elisabeth × ffifher.

These Are to Certifie That Thomas Joyce of This County Batchelor and Sarah Sugars Spinftr Haveing Publifhed (as They alleage) Their Banes of Matrimony * * * Did on ye 29th Day of July Ano Domi 1697 * * * Take each other as Hufband and Wife etc.

THOMAS his T mark JOYCE

Witnesses:—Daniel Ithell, Thomas Grove, Cornelias Wiltbanck, Isaac Wattson, Henry T Tucker, Thomas Ad Morgan, William Smith, James Claypoole, Isaac his × mark Moore, Nehemiah ffield, Jane Wiltbanck, Sarah S Grove, Mary M Ithell, Elifabeth M Tucker, Elisabeth C Wiltbanck, Elifabeth × Moleston.

These may Certifie That Alexander Molefton Junr of This County Batchelor and Elizabeth Trout of ye Said County Spinftr Haveing According to Law Publifhed their Intentions of Marriage Did on ye Day and Date of Thefe presents in ye houfe of Alexander Moleston Senr in ye Town of Lewis * * * Take each ye other As Hufband and Wife * * * ye Thirtieth Day of June Ano Domi 1697.

ALEXANDER MOLESTON Junr
ELISABETH her × mark MOLESTON.

Witnefses:—Wm Clark, John Miers, James Walker, James Peterkin, Philip Rufsell, Alex Moleston, Jno E Molefton, Tho. Pemberton, Jno K Kipshaven, William M. Molefton, Johnathan Baily, Wm Dyre, James Seattoun, Cornelius Wiltbanck, Nehemiah ffield, Edward Stretcher, Elizabeth Taylor, Sarah × Sugars.

COM: SUSSEX December the 6th 1689.

Lett this Certifie whom It may Concerne That Nehemiah ffield Batchelor and Rachel Claypoole widdow Did * * * Take Each other as Hufband and Wife etc * * * NEHEMIAH FFIELD
RACHEL FIELD

Henry Strecther, Thomas Oldman, Arthur Starr, Jacob his IK mark Collock, Philip Rufsell, Will Rodeney, Katherine Starr, Elifabeth Pemberton, Elizabeth Oldman, Mary Dyre, Sarah her S mark Strecther, Sarah her S mark Rufsell, Mary her × mark Collock.

True Copy: NEHEMIAH FFIELD Dept Regiftr.

Peter Rayman and Mary Richardfon Their Certificate of Marriage.

* * * Thefe May Certifie That Peter Rayman Batchelor and Mary Richardfon Widow both of this County of Sufsex * * * Haveing Duely and according to law Publifhed their Said Banes Did in the Said Peter Raymans own houfe * * * Take Each other as Hufband and Wife * * * on the Twenty fifth Day of November in the year of Our Lord One Thoufand Six hundred Ninety and four. PETER RAYMAN
MARY her ⊕ mark RAYMAN

Tho: Pemberton, Loury Strecther, John Croutch, Richard Paynter, Richard his RH mark Harvey, Roger Corbett, Richard Parr, Peter Lewis, Nehemiah ffield, John Brearday [?], William Clampit, Samll Adams, John his I mark Deprey, Edward × his mark Williams.

True Copy, NEHEMIAH FFIELD Depty Regisr.

Copie Jane Simons Letter of Adminiftr on hur Hufbands Eftate.

Whereas Jone Simons the Late wife of John Simons of the County of Suffex * * * planter Lately deceafed Appeared before me William Clark deputy Regifter * * * defiering to take out Letters of Adminiftion upon the Eftate of the faid John Simons * * * And by Comiffion from John Blackwell Esqr Governr of the aforefaid Provience and Territories I hereby Grant Letters of Adminiftron unto the faid Jone Simons widdow of all the Eftate etc * * * Given * * * at Lewis in the faid County of Suffex the ninth day of the feaventh Month Called September in the year of our Lord According to the Englifh Account one Thoufand fix hundred Eighty nine etc.

Whereas Morris Edwards of the County of Suffex etc. appeared before me William Clark deputy Regifter etc. * * * defiering to be admitted to take out Letters of Adminiftron as one of the Princable Cradíters of the Eftate of John Millington Late of this County deceafed * * * I doe therefore * * * Grant Letters of Adminiftron unto him the faid Morris Edwards of all the Estate etc * * * Given * * * at Lewis * * * the fixt day of the Eight Moneth in the year of our Lord According to the Englifh account one Thoufand fix hundred Eighty nine etc.

Letters of Adminiftr on William Spencers Eftate.

The third day of the Tenth Moneth in the year of our Lord According to the Englifh account one Thoufand fix hundred Eighty nine

William Spencer of the County of Suffex etc. * * * Brought the Laft will and Teftament of william Spencer fenr Late of the a fore faid County of Suffex deceafed; And haveing made proofe of the fame by the Teftamony of William Emmatt And Johnfon ver Kirk and Robert Twiley wittnefes fubfcribed to the faid will, * * * I doe therefore * * * Permitt him the faid William Spencer to Adminifter upon all the Estate etc. * * * Given * * * at Lewis * * *. WM CLARK, deputy Regifter.

Sufsex:—Banns of Matrimony Between William Smith Late of Philadelphia but now of this County Widowr and Jane Smith of this County Widow, If any psons Can Show any Lawfull Cause Why These Two may not be joyned Together in the Holy State of Matrimony Lett Them under Write Thes Prsents, or Ever hereafter hold their Peace WILLIAM ye mark of W SMITH

JANE ye mark of X SMITH

LEWIS TOWN ye 17th July 1705.

Signed by me one of Her Majties Justices for this County, Philip Rufsell.

Endorced on the back of the Sd Banns as followeth, *ne* (vizt):—Septr ye 2d 1705. The within Intended Marriage was Confumated in ye prsence of us: Tho. ye mrk of T Edwards, Cornelius ye mrk of H Hide, William Drigers, Bryan ye mrk of H London, Joseph Bravan, Peter Squyre, Mary ye mrk of S Smith, Peter Ixwonboult, Rebeckah ye mrk of R Piles, Francis ye mrk of W Cornwell, Tho. ffinwick, Justice; WF, John Winch, Mary ye mrk of 3 Abchurch.

WM. ye mrk of M SMITH

JANE ye mrk of X SMITH

Will Emmatts Letters of Adminiftracon on John Vines Eftate.

The forth day of the Tenth Moneth Called december in the year of our Lord According to the Englifh Account one Thoufand fix hundred Eighty nine etc. * * * Then Came before me William Emmatt and brought the Laft will and Teftament of John Vines Late of the County of Suffex deceafed and * * * made proofe of the fame by the Teftamony of Georg dod and the name of Ben Kearl * * * wittnefes to the faid will * * * I doe therefore * * * grant Letter of Adminiftracon of the Eftate etc. * * * at Lewis.

WM: CLARK deputy Regifter.

Copie of Mary ffootcher Letters of Adminiftion on her Hufband Eftate.

Whereas Mary ffootcher widdowr the Late wife of William ffootcher of the County of Suffex etc. * * * deceafed, did the day of the date here of Appeare before me William Clark deputy Regifter * * * defiering to take out Letters of Adminiftion of the Eftate of the faid William ffootcher, * * * I doe therefore * * * Grant Letters of Adminiftracon of the Eftate * * * to the faid Mary ffootcher * * * Given * * * at Lewis * * * the three and Twentieth day of the Eleaventh Moneth in the year of our Lord etc. one Thoufand fix hundred Eighty nine * * *.

Copie of Tho Mays Letters of Adminiftion on will Spencers Eftate.

Whereas Thomas May & Margaret his wife fister to William Spencer Late of the County of Suffex etc. * * * deceafed did the day of the date hereof appeare Before me William Clark deputy Regifter etc. * * * defiering (as next of Kind) to take out Letters of Adminiftracon of the Eftate of the faid william Spencer * * * I doe therefore * * * grant Letters of Adminiftion unto them * * * Given * * * at Lewis * * * the firft day of the thurd Moneth Called May in the year of our Lord * * * one Thoufand fix hundred and ninty.

William footcher fon of William and Mary footcher was borne the Tenth day of the Twelvth Called ffebuary one Thoufand fix hundred feaventy four, five.

Sarah footcher daughter of William and Mary footcher was borne the thurteenth day of the fecond Moneth Called April one Thoufand fix hundred feaventy feaven.

Elizabeth footcher daughter of william and Mary footcher was borne the Eight day of the Twelvth Moneth Called febuary one Thoufand fix hundred Eighty one, Two.

Richard footcher fon of william and Mary footcher was borne the firft day of the forth Moneth Called June one Thoufand fix hundred Eighty four.

John footcher fon of william and Mary footcher was borne the firft day of the fecond Moneth Called April one Thoufand fix hundred Eighty feaven.

Henry footcher fon of william and Mary footcher was borne the Thurty firft day of the Eight Moneth Called october one Thoufand fix hundred eighty nine.

Aminadab Hanser the fon of Aminadab and Rofe Hanser was born the Twenty thurd day of the Eleaventh Moneth Called Janawary one Thoufand fix hundred Eighty eight, nine.

Copie of Sarah Smiths Letters of Administracon on Hen Smiths Est.

Whereas Sarah Smith of the County of Suffex etc. * * * widdow the day of the date here of appeared Betore me william Clark deputy Regifter etc. * * * defiering to take out Letters of Adminiftracon of the Eftate of Henry Smith * * * deceafed Hufband * * * I doe therefore * * * Grant Letters of Adminiftracon unto the Said Sarah Smith etc. * * * Given * * * at Lewis the fifteenth day of the feaventh Moneth Called September in the year of our Lord etc. one Thoufand fix hundred and ninty.

Samuell Prefton Letter of Adminiftr on Georg Davids Eftate.

Whereas Samuell Prefton of the County of Suffex etc. * * * Appeared before me William Clark deputy Regifter etc. * * * defiering as Princable Craditer to take out Letters of Adminiftracon of the Eftate of Georg Davids * * * deceafed * * * I doe therefore etc. * * * Grant Letters of Adminiftracon unto the faid Samuell Prefton of all the Eftate * * * Given * * * at Lewis the Twentieth day of the feaventh Moneth Called September in the year of our Lord etc. one Thoufand fix hundred and ninty.

Copie Letters of Adminiftracon on John Bellamy Eftate.

The Court of the County of Suffex etc. * * * haveing ordered me William Clark deputy Regifter etc. * * * to Grant Letters of Adminiftracon unto Luke Wattfon Senr, Thomas Price Senr, and Luke wattfon Junr of the Eftate etc. * * * That John Bellamy * * * dyed poffeffed of * * * I doe therefore * * * Grant Letters of Adminiftracon unto them * * * Given * * * at Lewis * * * the Tenth day of the Tenth Month Called december in the year of our Lord etc. * * * one Thoufand fix hundred and nintye. WM: CLARK deputy Regifter.

Copie of Rebecka Draper &c and Henry Molifton Letter of Adminiftracon on Alex. Drapers Estate.

The three and Twentieth day of the firft Moneth Called March Anno: Dm 1691 * * * Then Came Rebecka Draper and Henry Moulfton Before me william Clark deputy Regifter etc. * * * And brought the Last will and Teftament of Alexander Draper Late of the aforesaid County of Suffex deceased, and before me made proof of the same; * * * I due therefore * * * Grant Letters of Adminiftracon unto the faid Rebecka Draper and Henry Moulfon of all the Eftate * * * In wittness where of * * * at Lewis the day and year ffirft above written.

Test. WM: CLARK dept Regfter.

Copie of Letters of Adminiftracon on ffrancis Cornwell Estate.

Whereas Mary Cornwell of the County of Suffex etc. * * * widdow * * * Appeared before me William Clark deputy Regifter etc. * * * defiering to take out Letters of Adminiftracon of the Eftate that her deceased Hufband ffrancis Cornwell * * * dyed poffeffed of * * * I doe Therefore * * * Grant Letters of Adminiftracon unto the faid Mary Cornwell of all the Eftate * * *. Given under my hand and feal at my office the Twelvth day of the ninth Moneth Called november in the year of our Lord etc. one Thoufand fix hundred nintye one.

WM: CLARK
deputy Regifter of Suffex & Kent.

Copie of Letters of Adminiftr on Ifaac Bowde Eftate.

Whereas Jane Scott of Lewes in the County of Sussex etc. * * * did * * * Appeare before me William Clark deputy Regifter * * * defiering to take out Letter of Adminiftracon upon the Eftate of her former Hufband Ifaac Bowde * * * deceafed * * * I doe therefore * * * Grant Letters of Adminiftracon unto the faid Jane Scott of all the Eftate etc. * * * Given * * * at Lewes * * * The fixt day of the feaventh Moneth in the year of our Lord * * * one Thoufand fix hundred nintye and Two, * * *. WM: CLARK, dept Reges.

Copie of Jopeth Booth Marriage.

Suffex County etc. * * * The Twenty Eight day of November 1690; Thefe may Certifie whom it may Concerne etc. * * *

Jofeph Booth did * * * take ffrancis Spencer to be his Lawfull wife * * * JOSEPH BOOTH [fealed]
FFRANCIS BOOTH [fealed]

John Hill, Juftice; Henry Bowman, Henry Molefton, Thomas Tilton, William Emmatt, Art A Johnfon Ver Kirk, The mark of Robert R Twelley, The mark of John + Draper, The mark of Wm × Collins, Mary Bowman, Margrett her M mark Molefton, Mathew his M mark ofborne, Grace her G mark Johnfon ver Kirk, Chatrine her × mark Draper.

Thomas Branfcomb will, June 30th, 1693.

* * * I Thomas Branfcomb * * * haveing a voyage to take in hand to Barbados it being my Care to fett my Buffnes in order in Cafe of Mortality, make this my Last will & Testament * * *

Item.—I give and bequeath unto Sarah Branfcomb my well beloved daughter * * * plantacon which I bought of Stephen whetman * * *.

Item.—I give and bequeath unto william ffootcher my fon in Law an Ifland * * * purchefed of John Johnfon negor by my pradefeffor william footcher deceafed * * *.

Item.—I give and bequeath unto my Two fons in Law Richard footcher and John footcher ech of them a gun etc. * * *.

And as for all the reft of my worldly Eftate etc. * * * I doe give and bequeath unto Mary Branscomb my well beloved wife * * *. THOMAS BRANSCOMB [fealed]

figned fealed and delivered in the prefents of us
CHARLES his × mark JOHNSON
ROBERT his × marke WALKER
THOMAS BESENT.

The 9th day of the Tenth Month 1693 then Thomas Befent and Charles Johnfon Cam before me and Attefted the above writing to be the Laft will and Teftament of Thomas Branfcomb deceased.

WM: CLARK.

Mary Branfcomb Letter of Aminiftracon.

The ninth day of the Tenth Moneth Called December in the year of our Lord etc. * * * one Thoufand fix hundred nintye three, * * * Came Mary Branfcomb of the County of Suffex etc. * * * and brought the Last will and Testament of Thomas Branfcomb etc. * * * and before me made proofe of the fame by the Teftimony of Thomas Befent and Charles Johnfon * * * I doe therefore etc. * * * Grant Letters of Adminiftracon unto the faid Mary Branfcomb of all the Eftate * * * In wittness whereof I have hereunto fett my hand and feal at Lewes etc.

WM: CLARK, dept Regifter.

Com Sufsex, *fs.*, on Dellaware. Whereas Banns of Matrimony etc. * * * By and Between Georg Ely late of Hopewell in the County of Burlington Batchelr And Jane Pettitt late of the same place Spinstr. Thefe are Therefore To Certifie That The Said Mariage Was Solemnly Confummated According to Law at the Houfe of

Mr. Jonathan Baily uncle of The Said Jane At The Town of Lewis in the County of Sufsex etc. * * * on The One and Twentieth Day of Augst Ano Domo 1705 In the psence of mee Philip Rufsell one of Her Majties Juftices of the Peace * * *.

Parties: GEORGE ELY
JEAN ELY

Witnefses: Philip Rufsell, Jonathan Baily, Hannah Baily, Mary Baily, Elias Baily, Thomas Harford, Edward Strecther, Preferved Coggeshall, William Coe, Jeremiah Claypoole, Martha Huling, Mary Rowland, Sarah Gray, Sarah Branscombe, Nehemiah ffield.

Registred The 23d Day of August 1705 per mee

NEHEMIAH FFIELD
Dpty Regr of the County of Sufsex Aforefd.

Edward Morgon Will.

* * * The 11th day of March in the year of our Lord one Thoufand fix hundred ninty & three the Laft will and Teftament of Edward Morgonie * * *; fecondly.—I doe give and bequeath to my Childe in Maryland * * *; Thirdly.—I doe give and bequeath to Mary Wattfon * * *; forthly I do give etc to Thomas Price Junr etc.; * * *. fiftly I doe give etc * * * to William Staplton etc.; * * * fixtly I doe give etc. * * * Messrs Bowman etc. * * *; feaventhly I doe give etc. * * * Wattfon * * *; Eightly I doe hereby Constitute and Appoint my ffriende Luke Wattfon Junr to be whole and fole executor of all my Estate * * *; Ninthly that after all my debts and Leagifis are paid etc. * * * that then the over plufe or remainer of my faid Estate I doe give etc. * * * unto my faid Executor Luke Wattfon Junr; Tenthly I doe hereby Revoke difanole and make void all former wills etc. * * *.

the mark of × EDWARD MORGON [fealed]

Signed fealed & delivered in the prefence of us:

Teftis CHARLES HAYNES
SUSANAH her S mark DAVIDS

Copie of the probitt of Edward Morgon will.

The five and Twentieth day of the Eight Moneth Called october * * * one Thoufand fix hundred nintye three * * * Executor & Teftis appeared before me William Clark deputy Regifter * * * Given * * * at Lewis.

Copie William Swetmans will.

* * * fixteenth day of feptember Anno: Dm: 1693 * * *. Item.—I give etc. * * * to wife Jean Sweatman all & fingular my Eftate perfonall & Reall * * * wife sole Executrix

WILLIAM SWEATMAN [fealed]

Witnesses:—
EDWARD GOULD
HENRY STRECTHER
JAMES PETERKIN

Copie the probitt of William Swetmans will.

The three and Twentieth day of the Eight Moneth Called october * * * one Thoufand fix hundred nintye three; Executrix & witnesses appeared before me * * * at Lewis.

WM. CLARK, dept Regifter.

Copie of Rich Patte will.

The Laft will and Teftament of Richard Patte son of John Patte the Land * * * when Mr Clark is fatiffied * * * daughter Lidey one heffer * * * rest of Cattle Equilly between my three gurls when daughter Ann Cometh to Age And my wife to InJoye if fhe doth not marry May 17th 1693. Names mentioned: Miney debter, William Woolfe, Timothy dongon, John oakey, Alburt Jacobs. Proved by the Teftamony of John & Elloner Tuxbury 11th 9 mo: 1693.

The 11th day of the ninth Moneth 1693 * * * Came John Patte of the County of Suffex etc * * * and brought will of Richard Patte * * * prooved by Teftimony of John Tuxbury and Elloner his wife * * *. Letters of Administration granted unto said John Patte. WM: CLARK, deputy Regifter.

Copie of Jane Hodgkins will.

* * * I Jane Hodskins of Lewis * * * to daughter Rebeckah Williams * * * Cloathes etc.; son Cornelius Wiltbanck six fhillings * * *. Refidue to fons Abraham and Ifaac Wiltbanck. * * * John Hill * * * sole exector * * * Husband Hermanis Wiltbanck deceafed * * *. Date Twenty third day of december 1693.

figned fealed & delivered in the prefence of

JOHN his X marke PYE,
NATHLL STARR,
NEHEMIAH FIELD.

Thomas and Mercy Willfon their Certificate of Marriage.

Suffex County etc * * * the Tenth day of febery 1694-5. Thefe may Certifie etc * * * That * * * Thomas Willfon Did * * * Take Mercy Milliner to bee his Lawfull wife ect. * * *.

THOMAS WILLSON [Seal]
MERCY WILLSON [Seal]

Jofeph Booth, William ffisher, Jofeph Hickman, Jenkin Smith, hendrick o Saverus or Varerus, Thomas Price, James his × mark Carpenter, Thomas I ffleming, John V Jones, John Bowman, John Milliner, Rebeckah × Draper, ffrancis × Hickman.

Copie of Nights Hawards will.

* * * I Knights Haward of Suffex County etc. * * * bequeath unto Luke Wattfon Junr * * * plantacon Lying and being in the great Kill * * * Bargaine with William Davids * * * debt due from William Dyer * * * also from John Mahon * * *. Item.—I give unto Elizabest Wattfon fister of

the faid Luke Wattfon Junr * * *. Luke Wattfon appointed Executor * * *. Item.—make over * * * Lands * * * sold to John Hill * * *. Item.—make over unto Capt. Thomas Pemberton all * * * Land that I fold unto him * * *. Dated * * * this fecond day of Janawary Anno: Dm: 1693.

the marke of KNIGHTS × HAWARD.

sealed figned and delivered in the prefence of:

NATH STARR
WILLIAM EMMATT
JOHN his IP marke PEY

The probitt of nights Hawards will.

The Eighteenth day of the Eleaventh Moneth Called Janawary etc. * * * one Thoufand fix hundred nintye three etc. * * * then Came Luke wattfon Junr * * * and brought said will * * *. prooved by the Testamony of William Emmatt John Pey and Nathaniel Starr * * *. Letters of Administracon granted to said Executor. WM. CLARK dept regifter.

Copie of Baptis Newcombs will.

* * * 13th Sept 1693 * * * I Baptis Newcomb of Suffex County etc. * * * friends John Hill and William Piles with my wife to be my Lawfull executors * * * unto my wife all my moveable Eftate * * * unto my three fons; William and Baptis and David this tract of Land whereon I live Called by the name of Whit oak neck * * * to John Hagifter a Certain point of Land * * * Adjoyning * * * Line of William Piles * * * also land to son Daniel. BAPTIS NEWCOMB [fealed]

figned fealed & delivered in the prefence of us:

BARNES GARRET
MARK his × mark MITCHELL.

Copie of the probitt of Baptis Newcomb will.

The Twenty fecond day of the Eleaventh Moneth Called Janawary * * * one Thoufand fix hundred nintye three * * * Then Came Ann Newcomb one of the executrix * * * of her deceafed Hufband * * * John Hill and William Piles * * * revoked there executorfhip Leaving it wholly to the faid Ann Newcomb * * * Letters granted to the said Ann * * * Given * * * at Lewes. * * * WM: CLARK, dept. Regifter.

Copie of Elizabeth Roades widdow will.

* * * Twenty fix day of febuary Anno: Dm 1694-3 I Elizabeth Roades widdow etc. * * * Item firft.—I give etc. * * * unto daughter Matha Tull * * * my Grandfon John Tull * * * unto daughter Mary Morgon * * * unto Rachel wife of Charles fofit my beloved grandaughter * * * unto Sarah Branfcomb daughter of Thomas & Elizabeth Branfcomb both deceafed * * * Elizabeth Roades & Pation Roads my grandaughters * * * to my grandfon John Wells * * * unto

my three grand Children Elizabeth Roades John Roades & pations Roades * * *. ffriends Robert Clifton and Jofeph Allif appointed truftees. ELIZABETH her E mark ROADES [fealed]
figned fealed & delivered in the prefents of us:
THO MIDGLEY,
SARAH CLIFTON,
THO BESENT.

Copie of the probitt of Elizabeth Roades Will.

The ninth day of the third Moneth Called May Anno: Dm 1694; then Robert Clifton brought the Last will etc. of Elizabeth Roades * * * Letters granted to the said Robert Clifton and Jofeph Allif of all the Eftate * * *. Given * * * at Lewes.
WM: CLARK, d Regifter.

Copie of Jofeph Booths Letters of Adminiftr on William Coudrey Eftate.

Whereas Joseph Booth of the County of Suffex, etc. * * * Brother in Law of *William Caudmes, Late of the William Coudrey* * * * appeared & desired to take out Letters of Administracon of the Eftate etc. * * * Letters were granted unto the said Jofeph Booth * * * Eleaventh day of the fift Moneth Called July * * * one Thoufand fix hundred nintye ffour.
WM: CLARK, dept Regifter.

Copie of Robert Hart Letters of Adminiftracon of his father Eftate.

Whereas Robert Hart of the County of Suffex fun and heire of Robert Hart * * * deceafed * * * appeare * * * defiering to take out Letters of Adminiftracon upon the Eftate * * * his mother Jone Hart Confenting there unto * * * Letters ware Granted unto the said Robert Hart * * *. Given * * * at Lewis the Tenth day of the forth Moneth etc * * * one Thoufand fix hundred Eightye five * * *. [The remainder of the letter is torn off.]

Samuel Gray His Laft Will and Testament.

I Samuel Gray of Sufsex County etc. * * *. 2ly.—I will and Bequeth This Tract of Land on which I now live * * * To my Wife and four Sons, viz, Ifaac and Jonathan, David and Thomas * * * after wifes death to be equally divided between the four sons. 3dly.—I will etc. * * * unto my two Sons, Samuel and John Gray that Tract of Land Called Grayes End * * * Equally divided * * * Children mentioned * * * Samuel, John, Elizabeth Rebeckah Ifaac and Sarah, Jonathan and David and Thomas * * *. The Remaining part of my Eftate my Wife have Dureing her naturall life and aftr her Death to bee Equally Divided between my nine Children Gerles To have a duble part * * *. Wife Sufannah Gray * * * Sole exxcetrix * * * friends Samuel Prefton and Luke Watfon Junr, To bee my overfeers * * * 23d of Octobr 1692.
Sined Sealed & deled in the Prsents of us: SAM GRAY [feal]
SAM: PRESTON
MARY LLOYD
MICHAELL CHAMBERS
JOHN his × mark CHAMBERS
ELES HERINGTON.

Inventory of the Eftate of Samuel Gray Deceased.

As It was Shown unto us the Sworne Appraifers * * * the Twenty Sixth Day of December 1694, By Sufanna Gray widow * * * Proved allowed and Regiftred * * * on the 5th day of March 1694 * * *.

NEHEMIAH FFIELD, Depty Regifter.

Appraised by us:

THO: PEMBERTON
THOMAS FFISHER

LEWIS, The 5th Day of March 1694.

Copy of the Probate of Samuel Grey Deceesed His will.

William Markham Esqr Leuit. Governor of the Province of Pennsilvania etc. * * * His Excell Benjamine ffletcher Capt. Genl: and Governor in cheife of Their Majesties province of New York etc. * * * [Names mentioned in the above Probate]. Given * * * this Eleventh Day of December Ano q Domini: 1694.

Signed Pr Order

NEHEMIAH FFIELD.

Jane Bembrick Letters of Adminiftr on her Hufband Eftate.

Whereas Jane Bembrick of the County of Suffex etc. * * * defiering to take out Letters etc. * * * Late Hufband Edward Bembrick * * * Given * * * at Lewis * * * The Seaventeenth day of the fift Moneth Called July * * * one Thoufand fix hundred Nintye four * * *.

WM. CLARK, depty Regifter.

Will of Roger ffretwell Deceesed.

Dorothea ffretwell widow and Relicte of Ralph ffretwell and Mother and Administratrix of Roger ffretwell of Barbadoes Merchtt. * * * John Edmondfon of Talbot County * * * Merchtt Attourney * * * chosen Administrator of said eftate by the mother of deceesed * * * Inventorie of all and Singular The Goods Chattells and Creditts of the Said Deceesed, and exhibiting the Same into ye Secretaries office at Lewis * * * at or before The Twenty Eigh Day of June next Enfueing which will bee in ye year 1695 Rendering a full & True Accompt * * * on The Twenty Eigth Day of December next Enfueing The above Date * * * Appointed on the Twenty Eigth Day of Decembr * * * Ano q Domini 1694.

Signed & Sealed Pr Order NEHEMIAH FFIELD.

Letter of Attourney sent to Barbados Island notifying that all just debts etc. be paid to John Edmonfon etc Dated 18th Day of the Second Month Called Aprill 1689. DOROTHEA FFRETWELL.

Witnefses:

ANTHON LYNCH
SAMUELL HOCKADAY

(Written on back of said Letter).

Know all men etc. * * * That I the within Named John Edmondfon etc * * * appoint * * * Samuel Prefton and Thomas ffifher * * * to collect a debt from Henry Bowman for said Dorothea ffretwell * * *.
December 28, 1694.
Witnefses: .

James Edmondson
Richard his R marke Dawson

Attested before us the 3th mo, 1694. Tho. Pemberton
Thomas Oldman

* * * To Sarah Paynter Widow and Relicte of Richard Paynter late of the Towne of Lewis etc. * * * Died Inteftate * * * wife given power of administration * * * fourth Day of March * * * Ano q Dom. 1694.

Signed & Sealed Pr Order Nehemiah Ffield.

To all To whom These Prsents etc. That on The ffifth Day of December 1694 The Nuncupative Laft Will etc. * * * of Charles Spooner Deceesed was in Open Court Proved Approved etc. * * * Letters of Adminiftration granted to widow Sufanna Spooner * * * the ninth Day of March * * * Ano q Dom 1694.

Signed etc. Nehemiah Ffield.

Witnefsed by Barnes Garrett and Anthony Haverley that all property etc. was left to widow. Annto Kerle?
Barrant Yerris.

Nehemiah Ffield Clerk.

This may Certifie etc. * * * That Peter Rayman of The County of Suffex etc. widr and Dina Pawling * * * Spinstr * * * were married on the 14th Day of Aprill 1697 At the houfe of Mr. John Gibb in The Town of Lewis * * *.

Peter Rayman
Dina her × mark Rayman

Witnesses:—Tho: Oldman Juftice, Simon his S mark Pawling, letebt [?] pocleut [?], Henry his × mark Strecther, James Peterkin, William Adams, William Clampitt, James Seattoon, Thomas Peterkin, John Croutch, James Walker, James Simpson, Thomas Maccandlis, Nehemiah ffield, Marie Gibb, Margarett M Simson, Jane her × mark Peterkin.

* * * This May Certifie That Major Edmund Howell of Cape May In West Jersey widower And Katharine Barwick late of Mary Land widow Did on The Twenty ninth Day of June Ano Domi. 1696 At the Towne of Lewis etc * * * Mutually Take Each other as Hufband and wife etc. * * *.

Edmund Howell
Katharine her K mark Howell

Consummated & Signed In The prsence of us:—Robert Clifton, Justice; Samuell Crowell, Henry Strecther, Thomas Clifton, Mongo

Clifford, William Dyre, John Croutche, John Paynter, Richard Crafford, William Orr, Nehemiah ffield, John Baron, Sufanna her SC mark Crowell, Marie Gibb, Mary Wolfenden.

* * * To Mary H Richards Widow etc * * * of John Richards of Suffex County etc. * * * Died Inteftate * * * Letters of Administration granted to widow * * * Given * * * at Lewis On the Ninth Day of March * * * Anoq Domi 1694.

Signed etc. NEHEMIAH FFIELD.

* * * att An Orphans Court Held * * * att Lewis for the County of Suffex etc. * * * On the ffifth Day of March 1694 The Nuncupative Laft will etc. * * * of Thomas Moalfon Deceesed * * * was Proved etc. * * * Letters etc. * * * Granted unto Mary Richards widow of John Richards ffather in law to the sd Thomas Moalfon both Deceesed * * * Given * * * this Ninth day of March * * * Anoq Domi. 1694.

Signed etc. NEHEMIAH FFIELD.

* * * Bryant Rowles and Thomas Coverdale Both of This County Being Present with Thomas Moalfon a little before his Death * * * Plantr * * * witnesses of the above will * * * Land given William Davies * * * situated upon the Broad Kill * * * Land * * * unto William Richards Son of John Richards * * * Cow unto Sarah Clarke * * * Barnes Garrett & Anthony Haverly Junr beneficiaries * * * debts due from John Putteet & John Hill.

BRIANT his B R mark ROWLES
THOMAS his Tc COVERDALE

NEHEMIAH FFIELD Clerk.

* * * To Jane Jones Widow etc. * * * of John Jones of Suffex County etc. * * * Plantr Deceesed * * * Died Intestate * * * wife made Administratrix * * * Letters granted * * * at Lewis on the ffourth Day of May * * * Anoq Dom. 1695.

Signed etc. NEHEMIAH FFIELD.

* * * Know yee That Before Luke Wattfon Senr and Joseph Booth Esqrs. * * * Juftices of the Peace for the County of Suffex etc. * * * The Laft Will etc. * * * of Thomas Price Deceesed * * * was proved etc. * * * on the Twenty ffifth Day of March 1695 * * * Letters granted unto his son Thomas Price Sole Executor. * * * This Twenty Sixth Day of Aprill * * * Annoq Domi. 1695.

Signed etc. NEHEMIAH FFIELD.

Thomas Price Senior his Laft Will and Teftament.

* * * 14th Day 1694–5 March. The Laft will etc. of Thomas Price Senior of Slater neck In the County of Suffex Planter * * *

Item.—to son Thomas Price my Plantation in Slater neck.

Item.—My well beloved wife Liveing with my son Thomas Price * * * he to take care of his mothers Chattells etc.

Item.—* * * unto William Price my Granfon one Cow etc. * * *

Item.—* * * unto Catheren Price my Grandaughter one Heffer etc. * * *

Item.—* * * unto Ian Price my Gran Daughter one black Cow etc. * * *

Item.—* * * unto Rachell Price my Grandaughter one * * * heffer etc. * * *

Item.—* * * unto wife Catheren Price all my Cattell * * * houfehold goods that Remains after my Debts and legyfes be Paid * * * after her Defef to be equally divided between Gran Children.

Item.—* * * Appoint my Son Thomas Price to be my Sole executor. THOMAS his T marke PRICE [Seal]

THOMAS PHELMON
The R marke of JEREMIHA BARTHELMY
WILLIAM FFISHER

Will sworn to by the two witnefses the 25th of March 1695 before Luke Wattfon Senr and Joseph Booth, Juftices of the Peace.

JOSEPH BOOTH
LUKE WATTSON

An Inventory of the Eftate of William Cowthry of Suffex County etc. * * * Deceesed * * * Shown unto us The Appraifers subnamed upon the 5th Day of September and 7th Day of December 1694, By Joseph Booth who att a Court Held att Lewis * * * On the Sixth Day of June 1694 was appointed Adminiftrator of the Same. Appraifed by

THO: PEMBERTON
THOMAS FFISHER

Sworn to by the above named appraisers before Nehemiah ffield Depty Regifter.

ST. PETER'S CHURCH.

ECCLESIASTICAL RECORDS.

A small village near Deal in England, called Sutton, had an ancient church dedicated to Saints Peter and Paul. The church was partly destroyed by an earthquake, April 6th, 1680.

It is possible that the town of New Deal may have had some people who were from Sutton, and as the destruction of Sutton parish church occurred about the time Sir Edmond Andross set apart the four acres, which were fenced in by St. Peter's Congregation before 1689, people from Sutton may have chosen the name St. Peter's to perpetuate the name of the church of their early affiliation. The Church burying ground was called the Public Burying Ground. An attempt was made to establish a Common Burying Ground.

This is the first record about the Church of England in Sussex County.

The land, the four acres fenced in at the above date is what is now St. Peter's churchyard, the church having been at the eastern corner at first. The present building is about in the centre of the yard and is the third building.

From 1689 to $170\frac{3}{4}$ we have no records of what the church people of Lewes were doing.

[KENT CO.] SUP. DELAWARE

We whose names are hereunto subscribed being Deeply sensible of the want of a Minister of God's Holy word and sacriments among us and the Duty incumbent on us to pay or cause to be payed to such Missionery as the Hon. So. for propagating the Gospell in foreign parts, shall be pleased to send to us Yearly and every year the severall sums annexed to our Respective Names, all which with the greatest sincerity of Heart we do humbly and freely offer to the service of Almighty God, and for the promotion of the Christian Religion in these parts. As Wittness our hands this 20 day of Feb. A. D. 1725.

John Parradee,
Henery Molleston,
John Tilton,
John Clayton,
Steven Parradee,
John Register,
Thos. Wells, Jr.,

John Bishop,
Wm Parvis,
Samuel Brady,
robert Howard,
William Hix,
Samuel Nichols,
Thos. Dixon,

John Greentree,
Mark Borden,
William Morgan,
Hugh Durborow,
John Wells,
Richard Hill,
John Newel,

Evan Jones,
Alexander Ponder,
Thos. Green,
George Hargrove,
Thos. Tarrant,
John Taylor,
Henry Shaw,
John Endsor,
Isaac ffreland,
Obadiah Voshall,
Philip Brady,
Thos. Slawtor,
Martin Turner,
Robert Wood,
John Tucker,
John ffisher,
George Green,
William Newel,
Ceasar Rodney,
Charles Hilliard,
George Nowel,
Samuel Berry,
Danl. Rodney,
Thos. Parke,
Timothy Oharon,
Edward Jennings,
ffrans. Alexander,
Thos. Wells,
John Pleasonton,
George Medcalf,
William Walton,
Samuel Hirons,
Nichs. Lookerman,
Michael Lober,
John Reynals,
Ezekiel Tomson,
Adam Latham,
John Evans,
Thomas Evans,
William Rodeney,
Richard Levick,
James Tryal,
Thos. Courtney,
Joseph Nickerson,
George Robison,

Certified Communicants In St. John's Parish of Kent County on Delaware.

This Indenture, made this Nineteenth day of November in the Year of Our Lord, One Thousand Eight Hundred and Sixty, between George R. Fisher, John Ponder and Nehemiah D. Welch, surviving Trustees of St. Matthew's Church, Cedar Creek Hundred in the County of Sussex, of the one part, and John Ingram of the same Hundred and County aforesaid, of the other part, Witnesseth, That the said George R. Fisher, John Ponder and Nehemiah D. Welch, surviving Trustees as aforesaid, for and in consideration of the Yearly Rents and Covenants hereinafter mentioned and reserved, on the part and behalf of the said John Ingram, his Executors, Administrators and Assigns, to be paid, kept and performed, have demised, set, and to farm let, and by these presents do demise, set, and to farm let, unto the said John Ingram his Executors, Administrators and Assigns, all that Messuage and Lot of Ground, situate, lying and being in the Hundred and County aforesaid, and commonly known as the Yard and Grounds of St. Matthew's Church, Cedar Creek, being the same piece and parcel of Land conveyed by David Thornton and Wife to the Trustees of said Church, by Deed made the Twenty Eight day of October in the Year A. D. Seventeen Hundred and Eighty Eight, 1788, and recorded in the Office of the Recorder of Deeds in and for Sussex County, in Libro B. No. 2, Folio 390, as by reference thereunto will fully and plainly appear, and containing Two Acres and Five and One Half Perches, be the same more or less, to have and to hold the said Lot or parcel of Ground, and all and singular the premises hereby demised, with the appurtenances, to the said John Ingram, his Executors, Administrators and assigns, for and during the full end and term of Thirty Three Years from and beginning at the First day of May in the Year of Our Lord One Thousand Eight Hundred and Fifty Eight, 1858, yielding and paying for the same unto the said George R. Fisher, John Ponder and Nehemiah D. Welch, Trustees as aforesaid, their Successors, Survivors, and Survivor, his Heirs and Assigns, the Yearly Rent or Sum of Two Dollars Lawful money each and every Year, the first of which to be paid on the first day of January next ensuing the date hereof, and on the First day of January each and every year hereafter during the Term aforesaid.

Provided, that the said John Ingram, shall not, either himself or his Executors, Administrators, or Assigns, they or either of them, erect or build, or cause or permit to be erected or built, on the ground or premises herein demised, or on any part of the same, any House, Tenement, Barn, Stable, Shop, Crib, Granary, Fold, Pen or Enclosure, or Shed for Cattle or other animals. Excepting, nevertheless, That the said John Ingram, may retain and use the Building at present standing on the aforesaid Lot, namely the Old Church, purchased by George S. Davis in the Year A. D. Eighteen Hundred and Fifty Eight of the said Trustees, and may repair and conserve the same to and for his own use, for the full Term of Years before mentioned. And also provided, that he, the said John Ingram, his Executors and Administrators and Assigns, they or either of them, shall not plow, till, dig, scrape or remove any earth, or break the soil, of such part or portion of said lot as has been occupied for a burial ground, but the same shall remain undisturbed and unbroken.

And the said John Ingram, for himself, his Heirs, Executors, Administrators and Assigns, doth covenant, promise, and agree to and with the said George R. Fisher, John Ponder, Nehemiah D. Welch, Trustees as aforesaid, their Successors, Survivors and Survivor, his Heirs and Assigns, that he the said John Ingram, his Executors, Administrators, and Assigns, shall pay or cause to be paid to the said Trustees, their Successors, Survivors, and Survivor, his Heirs and Assigns, that he the said John Ingram, his Executors, Administrators, and Assigns, shall pay or cause to be paid to the said Trustees, their Successors, Survivors, and Survivor, his Heirs and Assigns, the said Yearly Rent of Two Dollars lawful money, hereby reserved, on the several days and times hereinbefore mentioned, for the payment thereof, according to the true intent and meaning of these presents.

And the said George R. Fisher, John Ponder, and Nehemiah D. Welch, Trustees as aforesaid, for themselves, their Successors, Survivors and Survivor, his Heirs and Assigns, do covenant, promise, grant and agree to the said John Ingram, his Executors, Administrators and Assigns, paying the rents and performing the Covenants aforesaid, that he the said John Ingram, his Executors, Administrators and Assigns, shall and lawfully may, peaceably and quietly, under the limitations and provisions herebefore mentioned, have, hold, use, occupy, possess, and enjoy the said demised premises, during the term aforesaid, from the day and date aforesaid, without the lawful let, suit, trouble, eviction, molestation or interruption, of the said Trustees, their Successors, Survivors or Survivor, his Heirs or Assigns, or any other person by or under them.

In witness whereof the said Parties have hereunto set their Hands and Seals this Nineteenth day of November in the Year of Our Lord One Thousand Eight Hundred and Sixty.

Signed, Sealed, and Delivered in the presence of us		
	GEORGE R. FISHER.	[SEAL].
	JNO. PONDER.	[SEAL].
	NEHEMIAH D. WELCH.	[SEAL].
ROBT. C. HALL.	his JOHN INGRAM. mark	[SEAL].
A. H. TERRY.		

State of Delaware, Sussex County *Ss.* Be it remembered that on this Nineteenth day of November A. D. 1860, personally came before me, Nehemiah D. Welch, a Notary Public of the State of Delaware, George R. Fisher, John Ponder and John Ingram, and acknowledged the above Indenture to be their act and deed, (they being parties to the same and known to me personally to be such), and I, Nehemiah D. Welch do hereby acknowledge said Indenture to be my act and deed.

Given under my hand and Official Seal the day and Year aforesaid.

NEHEMIAH D. WELCH, N. P.

State of Delaware, }
Sussex County, } *Ss.*

In Testimony that this lease was lodged in the Recorder's Office in and for said County on the twentieth day of December A. D. eighteen hundred and sixty and stands recorded in Book No. 67, Folios 313 and 14, I have hereunto set my hand and affixed the seal of said office at Georgetown in the County aforesaid, the day and year aforesaid.

WILLIAM DAVIS, Recorder.

Beginning at a corner marked white oak by the east side of Draper's old mill pond, and running from thence N. 62 E. 31 perches to a stake in the field S. E. of said Church. Thence N. 28 West, 10½ perches to a stake on the N. E. side of said Church. Then S. 62 West 31 perches to a stake on the Hill near the said Pond. Thence South 28 East 10½ Perches, home to the first Beginning Corner, White oak. Surveyed and divided off for two acres and five and a half Square perches of land, on the 10th day of April 1770, by Caleb Cirwithin. Together with a Church house thereon, etc.

David Thornton and Elishe Thornton his Wife to Nehemiah Davis, Thomas Evans, Isaac Beauchamp, George Watson, Jacob Townsend, Bethnel Watson, and Mark Davis, Vestry.

Deed dated, 1788.

Docket No. 2, 1785. Page 390.

INSCRIPTIONS ON STONES IN CHURCHYARD OF ST. MATTHEW'S CHAPEL, CEDAR CREEK HUNDRED.

In memory of Reynear Williams, who departed this life April 2nd, 1773, aged 26 years and 7 months.

"How loved, how valued once avails him not
To whom related or by whom begot."

In memory of Abagail, wife of Sylvester Webb, who departed this life 17th December, 1785, aged 25 years.

In memory of Nelly Draper, who departed this life April 17th, 1790, aged 14 years.

All other tombstones are removed or destroyed.

Extracts from Journals of Society for the Propagation of the Gospel.

Sir Edmond Andros had ordered four acres of land to be set apart, in the centre of Lewes, for some public use. Previous to June, 1681, the Congregation of St. Peter's had fenced in this land and petitioned Governor Andross for it.

In 1689 a portion of this land was taken to build a Court House on. This Court House was used for services, provided the weather was not too cold, until the first church was built after the arrival of the Rev. William Becket.

17th Novr., 1704.—The Lord Bishop of London moved the Society in the Behalf of Mr. Crawford formerly appointed by ye Society a Missy. to Dover Hunder'd in Pensylvania:

Agreed that his case be refer'd to the Committee, and if they be Satisfyed he is an Object of the Society's Charity that he be forthwth sent over to the sd Place with the Usual Allowance.

15th Decr., 1704.—The Report of the Comtee. abt. sending back Mr. Crawford to the Place to which he was appointed & upon his first Establishmt was read & Agrd to by Socy.

Ordd that the 2nd half years allowance be advanc'd to the sd Mr. Crawford.

2nd March, 1705.—Agreed to give Mr. Crawford a large Com'on Prayer Book & a Book of Homilies, pursuant to a Motion from the Com'ittee.

16th March, 1705.—The Case of Mr. Crawford being represented to the Society from the Com'ittee, and it appearing that it has not been his fault that he has been so long detain'd from his Mission, Agreed that a 5th part of his second years Salary be advanced to the said Mr. Crawford, the better to enable him to pform his said Mission.

Copies of Letters from Mr. Thomas Crawford.

Mr. Crawford to the Secretary.

Honor'd Sir,

Not only your Station in the Society, but your Civility & Obligations conferr'd upon me, lays a tye on me to give you an Account of my circumstances from time to time as occasion offers.

Sir, after a long Fatigue at Sea I arrived here on the 24th. Instant, & waited on the Governor, who give me a very kind reception, & the Reverend Mr. Evans sustain'd me (as also my two Brothers along with me) with all Civility, for whom I preached on Sunday the 26 day, whose Congregation is numerous & still increasing. As for Kent County to which I go I can give no account of it (not having yet got there). But when I have certain knowledge of the place as opportunity offers I will write my circumstances & condition of the Congregation there. I know I shall not want Difficulties in the place, but not what I fear, but what I meet with, you shall have in the next. The ship is now fallen down the River, & the Captain is now going so that I have no time to add to this; or yet to pay my Respects to more of the Right Honble & Reverend Society, whose Comands shall still be a Law to me. I thought to have written to the Reverend Mr. Stubbs, to whom I am much obliged, and to Mr. Keith, to whom I hope you will have me excused, & give my service, kindly pardoning Presumption, and let me be honoured with a Line from your hand, with your councel and advice which shall be carefully observed by him who gives his humble service unto you, prays for your felicity, and rests

Honoured Sir
Your most humble Servant
THO. CRAWFORD.

PHILADELPHIA, August 27, 1705.

The directions are
To JOHN CHAMBERLAYNE, ESQRE. &c.

Mr. Crawford to ye Secretary.

SR.—After my coming unto this Province as soon as I had waited on ye Govr. I hasted to Dover Hundred ye Cure appointed me; Wch is a very sickly place, yea possibly one of the most sickly places in these parts of America; wch also I found so, for I had not been there but one Sunday, till I was most severely seized by a very high feaver, after that an Ague & as ye consequence of these with a Dropsie, & short windiness, of which I am not yet freed, & this is not only a seasoning to ye country, But fever & Ague does every year seize ye Inhabitants of the place. When I was first taken with ye fever I was crediby informed that there was not a Family in all the Shire, but that either ye whole or a part was sick: I leave it to ye Revd. Mr. Talbot to give an account how ill I was taken. Wherefore seeing the place is so sickly, & will not agree wth a constitution so weak as mine, I humbly desire the Right Honble Society may remove me to another place. If thought convenient to ye East side of Karaton River to Shrewsbury, or to Hopeswell so there be nothing pro'ded for, nor promised to a Minister there, yet the place is more healthy, & they want, & by the blessing of God I may do as great good there as in ye place I am ordered for, if I be not removed, in ye hot & sickly months of Summer I must remove & preach in a place more healthy, or then I shall soon be made incapable of doing service to God or his Church. This I hope you will take care to be laid before ye Society; wch with my humble Respects to your self is all from

Sr,
your most humble Servt,
THO. CRAWFORD.

BURLINGTON, Nov. 7, 1705.

The directions are
To MR. JOHN CHAMBERLAYNE, &c.

Mr. Crawford to the Secretary.

HOND. SIR.—Yours I received dated June 4th, 1707, of Mr. Talbot: wherein you desire frequent Letters, this I readily comply with, but I live in the country where no ships come, and under a hundred miles scarce can have a letter deliver'd or put on Bord of any Vessell and then some misgive, and many opportunities slip when I know not or cannot wait on them. Next you blame me (or seem to do so) because my Vestry wrote home some of their own circumstances, it was their own motion to do so, and to deny the people a request that is harmless you lose their favour, and again I did readyly comply with them because I thought their condition and circumstances might be as well received at their own hands as by my pen. Next you desire particular accounts from me, according to a Scheme laid down by the Society and to all the heads thereof, this I never saw, I never received any from any hand; I only conceive that those particulars following may be required, which I shall answer.

As to the number of Inhabitants in the county I know not, I never saw their Court Role.

As to the number of my hearers I sometimes have more sometimes have less according to the weather, I preach in the Church and two or three places more, the County being above fifty miles long, and those that are my hearers one day, not many are the next, and sometimes I have 30, 40, 50, 70, 100, 150, and upwards may be 200. A great many whereof (I think) have some good Tincture of Religion, at least of well meaning; But how many of them are (*in omnibus*) for the Church of England as by Law established there, I know not; some of them I know are of a dissenting temper in Government (which I do not admire there being at my entry not one man in the County that understood the Prayer Book, no not so far as to answer the Psalms or other parts of the service till I taught them privately) but all are satisfyed wth the Doctrine of the Church, so that they have no Grudge on that Account, only when some itinerant Presbyterian Preachers come amongst us some make breaches to go hear them, for all their sermons with us have been on Work days but many will not, so that I have none but a heathenish people called Quakers (several thereof are come over) that absent from the Worship of God as opportunity offers, other opinions make no debate to hear me, but how many Quakers there is I know not, but if we had the Governmt established we should have power.

As for the number of Communicants I have ordinarily above twenty or thirty odd, but never forty in one day.

For the number baptised by me in other places I know not, but in my own Charge I have young and old baptised 220 or 230, married 22 couple these three years of my residence here, our Justices do many frequently here because the Law allows.

As for my order in preaching I preach sometimes twice a week I have occasionally thrice, but I never fail four times in three weeks, one Sunday in the upper end of the County, another in the Church, the third in the lower end, and then a week days Sermon in some corner and then the following Sunday in the Church &c. I catechise the Children before the sermon all the Summer, cold weather I don't; this is as full a true and just account as I can now give of the place (this accepted) that many well meaning people want Prayer Books very much, there being none in the County but what I give them, nor can we have for money, and indeed many have not money to buy with, but of this I'le mind the Trea'r.

As to the order of the Society, to give an account of those of my hearers that have contributed to build churches, in a word, I know not any has given one farthing to any but to our own.

As for their names that subscribe to me, and their sums, I have not the catalogue, I have seen it, but the Church Warden has it, only I tell you that you have all in that address for a minister to Dover Hundred sent to my Ld. of London, which (if I remember) I deliver'd to the Society, and several of the best of those are dead, in whose place I have this year not before got some small Subscriptions; but our Subscriptions in America are larger than our Benefice: but whatever the Subscriptions be, this I can say upon the word of a Minister that these three years that I have been in this place, I have not had twenty pounds Pensylvania money p. ann; which is but a small Benefice, considering it is payd me not in Silver, but as people are able in corn, &c. T'is true there is more than £50 Pensylvania money subscribed,—but I can not have it, some are backward, many pretend they are not able the years are so badd, and to use the Law for it I never will, for that will frustrate my Mission and the designs of the Gospel of Jesus Christ, render my person odious to them, and so my Ministry and Preaching ineffectual, and I be look't upon as an hireling only; severe methods are not to be taken here, to gain converts by, so whatever is subscribed is to no advantage to me while it is not payd, but what I receive you shall have a yearly account.

As for the Society for reformacon of manners I have done and still do encourage it, and indeed at my request it was erected, and first by my Vestry whereof one Capt. Rodeny, Justice of Peace, was my principal assistant, the methods are most partly taken out of the Book of the Society for reformacon of manners wth some few variations, however we punished all that offended, but now our Work is easie; Our Meetings were once monthly, but now are quarterly, & then have little or no business, possibly not one found guilty in that time in all the County.

As for the Negroes I have been at pains, for I sometimes at the Church Porch teach 'em the Principles of religion, tho' many are very dull; and when I am not employed I catechize the children.

As for the Society's Instructions I shall be glad to receive them, none shall be more observant than I, and for writing often tho' I do, I understand my Letters do miscarry; so I hope if my Letters be not so frequent as other Missionaries' I shall be excused because I have not so good opportunities, and withall I have been sick Spring & Fall, not able to go abroad, but yet I understood that some of my Letters misgive, as also Letters from the Society (I fear) to me for I have not had a Letter these two years, but by Mr. Talbot. Nay my Attorneys Letters many of them never came to my hand, as I am informed by his last.

I have nothing new to suggest, but that I have nothing to intice me to this place, but the Sobriety of the People, this is all my Comfort others I have none, for many of the comforts of life are very farr withdrawn from me.

Sir, I trouble your Patience no more, only I begg your prayers on the Church here, & on me in particular that I may be serviceable therein, and I pray God to bless you and all those good and noble Spirits that are imployed in that Glorious Work of the Propagation of the Gospel of Jesus Christ, God himself strengthen you & incourage & bear you up in all difficulties; excuse the length of this from

Honor'd Sir
Your assured fr'd and humb' Serv't in
the Gospel of Jesus Christ.
THO. CRAWFORD.

1st FEBRUARY, 1706.—A letter from Mr. Crawford to the Secretary dated Burlington, 7, November, read.

28th MARCH, 1706.—Also two others [letters] from Mr. Crawford to Mr. Shibo & the Secretary from Burlington, 7 & 8 Novembr last;—Agreed to move the Society, that the said Mr. Crawford may be acquainted, that in case he continues to want his health in Dover hundred he shall be allow'd to remove to Hopewell or According to the Prayer of his said Letter. Agreed to.

14th FEBRUARY, 1707.—Also that having read a Paper from the Inhabitants of Sussex on Delaware River desiring a Minister may be sent 'em, and a Letter from Mr. Crawford the Minister appointed to Dover Hundred, near the above sd place, advising that the said Inhabitants are building a Church & want a Minister, they had Agreed to lay the Matter before the Society. Agreed that the Committee take care of this matter.

Also that having read two other Letters from the said Mr. Crawford (one to Mr. Stubs, t'other to the Secretary) dated April & June 1706, containing an Accot. of the said Mr. Crawford's Good Success in his Ministry, the poverty of the People & want of Com'on Prayer Books; they had Agreed to move ye Society that some numbers of Com'on Prayer Books be sent to the said Gentleman to be distributed amongst his People. Agreed to, & the No. to be ascertain'd by the Com'ittee.

15th APRIL 1709.—Also that they had read a Letter from the Lord Bishop of London to the Secretary dated 20th. Jan'ry last, containing a copy of a Letter from Mr. Crawford desiring a Pulpit Cloth, Surplice &c. and also an Original Letter from the said Mr. Crawford to the Secretary dated Kent County in Dover hundred Pensylvania 31st Augt. last containing the State of his Church there, the want of Common Prayer Books &c. which Letters they Agreed should be laid before the Society: then the said Letters were read;—Resolved that for the incouragement of the said Mr. Crawford ten pounds more (to commence from Lady day was twelve months) be added to his allowance so long as he stays in his present cure, and that it be referr'd to the Committee to send him such a number of Common Prayer Books as they think necessary, as also a pulpit Cloth and Surplice, the Charge of the whole not to exceed £10.

21st October, 1709.—A Petition from Mrs. Crawford wife of Mr. Thomas Crawford the Society's Missionary in Pensylvania was read, praying that some part of the allowance to the said Mr. Crawford may be paid to her the wife of the sd Crawford for her Subsistance till she can go over to her Husband: Order'd that the said Petition be refer'd to the Committee and that Mr. Lind, Mr. Crawford's Attorny have notice to attend at the same time.

18th November, 1709.—The Secretary reported from the Committee that they had considered the petition of Mrs. Crawford to them refer'd, and that the said Mrs. Crawford had fully made appear to them that she was the lawfull wife of Mr. Thomas Crawford the Society's Missionary at Dover Hundred in Pensylvania, and that she had not reced more than ten pounds from her Husband since he left England, which was about five years ago: That Mr. Lind, Attorny to the said Mr. Crawford, had also attended them, and being askt why he wou'd allow nothing to Mrs. Crawford to subsist and carry her over to her Husband, made answer, that he had no Orders from the Husband, nor any of his Effects in his hands, whereupon the Committee had Agreed to report the whole ffact as it appear'd to them, for the further Directions of the Society in the Matter: Then the Society having taken the above report into their consideration, and the Revd. Mr. Cook attending was call'd in, and gave the Society a farther Accot. of the Circumstances of the said Mrs. Crawford: Ordered that a stop be put to the Allowance from the Society to the said Mr. Crawford, till he give satisfaction to the Society about the Premises; and that the Secr'y do endeavour to inform himself from Mr. Evans and otherwise of Mr. Crawford's caracter &c.

30th December, 1709.—Also that they had read a Letter from Mr. Thomas Crawford late Missionary at Dover Hundred, dated London 26th Decembr. 1709, importing his desire of some money to put him into a Condition for to appear before the Society, and had thereupon Agreed to lay the said Letter before this Bord, and had also directed Mr. Middleton to attend on behalf of the Wife of the said Mr. Crawford: This matter being considered and the Society acquainted that Mr. Lind attended without on behalf of Mr. Crawford, and Mr. Middleton on behalf of the wife of the said Mr. Crawford, they were called in and acquainted that their business is refer'd to the Committee.

KENT COUNTY, DOVER HUNDRED IN PENSYLVANIA,
31st Augt. 1708.

SR.—I wou'd begg both your Letters & advice often if it be not too much trouble and none shall be more observant. Mr. Black is sick of the Ague, but his arrival has removed the charge of that place from my shoulders which I undertook willingly for the good of the Church.

Lord Bishop of London to ye Secretary.

FULHAM, 20 Jany. 1709.

SIR.—This is a copy of Mr. Crawford's Letter which I begg of you to lay before the Society, which seems to claim some charitable consideration from them. For my new Guest, as you call him, is so old an acquaintance, that I can't expect his departure so soon, as your good wishes wou'd have it. I am

Sir, Your most humble Servt.

H. LONDON.

Mr. Crawford to the Bishop of London.

MY LORD—After my dutyfull and most humble respects to yous Lo'p I presume to tell your Lo'p, that my health still continuer very uncertain, I am constantly sick Spring and Fall, and if it was not for my charge and office sake I wou'd by your Liberty leave the place, but my people, (tho' poor) have a particular respect for me as I have for them; and I thank God, they are as moral & Civil as any people I know in America, which I think is increas'd by a Society for a Reformation of Manners I have got erected here, so that now I believe one may live with us half a year and not hear one swear prophanely, or be catched drunk in the whole county: all I have to complain of is, that the people are not able to do much for me; I get but very little from them, and I have to preach sometimes twice and sometimes thrice in a week, the county is so large, and I think the congregation as numerous as any in America (Philadelphia excepted). Our Church is near finished, it is all Glazed and almost full of pews; only we want a Pulpit Cloth and Surplice and are not able to buy them. I pray God to bless your Lo'p, and long preserve you for an happy Instrument in his hand for good to his Church and our Encourager in Forreign parts. I rest

My Lord Your Lo'ps Son and Most humble Servant

THOMAS CRAWFORD.

KENT COUNTY ON DELAWARE IN PENSYLVANIA, 30th Augt. 1708.

Mr. Crawford to the Secretary.

LONDON, 26th Decr. 1709.

HONOR'D SIR.—After my humble service unto &c. by this know that I am once more return'd to London, I wou'd have waited on you but cannot be seen by any till I get cloaths, for I am all out of Order, wth my long absence and fatigue of my Voyage: wherefore I desire that my money that is due to me may be paid to my Attorny that I may get some mony to cloath me with, I have allowed none a Liberty to receive it but him, and since my return I have not recalled his power. I hope the Society will consider my condicon, that here I both want cloaths and money that what is due to me may be readily paid; that I may again appear before you and give you an account of my service abroad as also of the place and places adjacent thereto, and till then I for your satisfacon have sent the true copy of certificate from the Justices, that has the County Seal to it; I have more from the Wardens; as also from the Society for Reformation of Manners, with the County Seal to them that I cou'd not now coppy but the Originals shall be presented when you have paid my money to put me in any Order of appearing before you; this I hope you will communicate to the Committee and you will very much serve.

Honord Sir Your most humble Servt.

THOMAS CRAWFORD.

Mr. Crawford to the Secretary.

7th Jan'y. 1709.

SIR.—I presume yet to trouble you once more, to signify I am in strait for money, I cannot but admire that my money shou'd be denyed, seeing I am in want, and it justly due: as for Certificates of my diligence abroad and success in my office, I think I have been short of none that ever was sent by the Society (as what my Certificates will shew) one copy I have sent to you, and two other Originals I have order'd to be sent to my Lord of London; I have not only done as they certify but more in baptising several Negroes and Men & Women, some 60 years and downwards of all ages, I have opposed Schism,—preached publickly in Quakers meetings, disputed publickly, concerning which every one in the county can tell how well I acquit myself, silencing their Vagrant preachers; I supplyed Sussex in it, and at home frequently preaching thrice a week as opportunity and occasion offer'd, visiting the sick, burying the dead and all gratis, nay I have not only bought and bestowed Books on many, but also I have bestowed on the Church a Fine Pulpit Cloath and Cushion with a deep Silver Fringe, and none dare say but all my walk was suitable to my profession, and I think the glory of God and Good of Souls was my only design; tho' I labour'd under abundance of straits and troubles in that place: and now at my return I surely must say I meet with very hard measure for all my Labour; it is so great that I am forced out of Town for want of bread I being already indebted to Mr. Lind above £50 he will advance me no more: I know no reason why it shou'd be denyed or my Bills protested as he has done, since it is justly due by the Society; I am sure it will not redound much to your honor abroad: I can defy the World to tax me with an ill thing in my life time, but what has lately befallen me ignorantly, by the Hellish Contrivance of Elizabeth Watson and her base Mates and Associates she entertained: Mr. Middleton has had his own hand in it; he has been known to be no good man from his youth, nay for his uncleanness was turn'd out of the School of Edinburgh and not thought worthy to be Usher there, having appear'd in the Church in Pennance, among the ffornicators and unclean; whatever credit he has now wth you: worse than this I can say, and know this is matter of fact: and this Gentleman sent me word in a Letter which I have to produce, that Elizabeth Watson was not to be heard of; and by the mouth of Mr. Black she was dead, but wou'd not write the worst least he shou'd discourage me: as many in Dover hundred know and heard him say so and another Letter by another hand, as the Justices in the place know that she was dead, it was signed with her Brother's Name and hand; I taxed him upon it, he denyed it, but said he once believed she was dead; but his wife and he believed it was done by a fellow that was in the house with her whom all say she admitted to her embraces; But what I have to say of her uncleanness, that on oath I can get proved, and other villany to obtain her lust, & gratify her unclean desires as also a certificate of her former husbands death whom she trapann'd and sent to Sea, and then removed under the name of a Maid to a strange place, and things worse than these that I shall not mention: they lye not before you, nor are you Judges in such cases & therefore shall not trouble you with them: only I desire you not to pay my money to her but to Mr. Lind to whom I am indebted having received above £50 of him more than he has received; I have no way else to pay him, and it is a pitty he shou'd suffer on my account that has encourag'd so many missionaries; with all the last money I sent Elizabeth Watson, she laid it out to pay the Boarding of a Gentleman's Children, to whom she had been valet de chambre many a night till all the world took notice of her base carriage with him, and then when she had lost her fame she came after me: with all she does not want for money, she told me nine days ago she had a great deal at Interest in Scotland.

Sr. not troubling you farther since I cannot wait on the Society for want of money pray pay my money to Mr Lind and none else and in so doing you will oblige.

Sir,

Your humb' Servant

THOMAS CRAWFORD.

I design yet after this to see you all, till then let my misfortune be pityed and not enveyed against.

MR. WM. BLACK.

The Rev. William Black was the first Missionary in charge of Lewes and Sussex County. The following records are most interesting.

19th JULY, 1706.—The Secretary also reported from ye Committee that one Mr. Wm. Black a Layman recomended by the Lord Bishop of London had attended them and likewise offered his service for the Mission, and that he had produced a Letter from the Lord Bishop of Carlile to the Lord Bishop of London, together with a certificate under the hand and Seal of the late Bishop of Edinburgh, & another under the hands of the Lords of the College of Glasgow and ye comon Seal of the said College & all giving a very good character of the said Mr. Black, but the comittee had not yet come to any Resolution about ye said Person because he has not procured Testimonials according to Form.

16th AUGUST, 1706.—The Secretary acquainting the Bord that Mr. Black attended at the door.—Ordered that the Secretary do wait on the Lord A-Bishop & inform him that the Society does desire his Grace to direct what he thinks fit, in the case of the said Mr. Black.

20th SEPTEMBER, 1706.—Also that upon this occasion they had Agreed to move the Society that an application be made to the Lord Bishop of London that Mr. Wm. Black (who was some time ago recommended by the Lord Bishop of Carlile to the Society) may succeed Mr. Bridge as Assistant to the abovementioned Mr. Myles. The Secretary also reported that he had waited on the Lord Archbishop of Canterbury according to Order, & acquainted him with the case of Mr. Black, to whom his Grace had been pleased to give two Guineas for his p'sent support, & approved of his being sent to Boston. Agreed that the Secretary do wait on the Lord Bishop of London with the desire of the Society that Mr. Black may succeed Mr. Bridge.

18th OCTOBER, 1706.—The Secretary reported that he had waited on ye Lord Bishop of London with the Request of the Society at the last General Meeting that his Lordp would appoint Mr. Black to succeed Mr. Bridge at Boston, but that his Lordship was pleased to answer that Sr. Charles Hobby & some other N. England Gentlemen objected agt. the said Mr. Black as being too young; and that his Lordship did upon that occasion Recomend to ye Society the sending that Gentleman to Naraganset where a Minister is wanted. Ordered that the case of Mr. Black be Recomitted to ye Standing Committee.

15th NOVEMBER, 1706.—Also that the Committee had taken into their considerason ye case of Mr. Black, that the said Mr. Black had p.duced to them a Testimonial under the hand & seal of John Sharp of Hoddom one of the Justices of Peace in the Shire of Dumfries in Scotland & a Representative in Parliament there rectifying the said Mr. Black's conformity to all ye Qualificasons of the Society's Missionarys. That the Comittee had appointed the said Mr. Black to read prayers & preach, wch he pformed to the satisfaction of the Comittee. The said Report is Approved of & ye said Mr. Black was appointed to Naraganset with a Salary of £50 p. ann. for 3 years, comencing from Michas day last with the usual allowance of £10, & £5 for Books.

18th April, 1707.—Also that having considered of a Letter from ye Lord Bp. of London dated 29. March, together with an Address from the Inhitants of Sussex on Delaware River to his said Lop. bearing date 6. March, 1705/6 desiring a Minister for the said country the people of wch promise to do what they are able towards the maintenance of him; they had agreed to move the Society that Mr. Black who was appointed to Naraganset at the General Meeting of the Society 15. Nov. last, may be sent to Sussex as above, it being the desire of the Lord Bishop of London because Naraganset is already supply'd by Mr. Bridge; his Lop. having also in the said Letter, desir'd that Mr. Black may have some more advanc'd money upon the Acct. of his long stay here, they had agreed to move ye Society for their Directions in that matter. Ordered that Mr. Black be appointed to Sussex as above, and that the Treasurer do advance him his second half years allowance, on condition that he take the first opportunity of a Passage.

19th September, 1707.—Also that upon reading several Letters from Mr. Black & Mr. Jenkyns dated from Spithead on bord ye Ruby, 30. Aug. wherein they prayed the Advice & Assistance of the Comittee by reason of the said ship being appointed to Portugal, & complaining that they were reduced to great distress for want of money. The Comittee Agreed as their opinion that ye Secretary should write to the said Gentlemen & acquaint them that they should endeavour to pcure themselves a Passage in some other Ship bound to Virginia or Maryland forthwith, but if no such Opportunity offered that then they should return to London with their Effects. That the said Mr. Black & Mr. Jenkyns returned to London & attended the Comittee giving them Acct of their circumstances & Whereupon the Comittee Agreed to Report that ye Case of the said Mr. Black & Mr. Jenkyns is very compassionable, & Agreed to move the Society for their direction therein. This Report having been considered, and a Letter from Mr. Cordiner to the Secretary dated from Spithead 15. Sept. 1707, read. Agreed that the Treasurer be empowered to advance ye sum of Fifteen pounds to each of the abovemensoned Gentlemen out of their growing Salaries, to defray their respective Passages in the first Ships that are ready.

16th JANUARY, 1708.—A letter was read from Mr. Black to the Secretary dated 3. January, 1707, from Plymouth signifying his great Wants by being so long Wind-bound at the said Port & others, &c. Order'd that the Secretary do write to the said Mr. Black, and acquaint him that he may draw upon the Treasurer for Ten pounds to be advanced on the Credit of his growing Salary.

11th FEBRUARY, 1709.—Also that they had read two letters from Mr. Black dated 19. June & 19 July last, giving an Accot of his & Mr. Jenkyns Voyage, arrival &c. Ordered that the Secretary do write to the said Mr. Black, & desire him to give an Accot of the Behavior of Mr. Nicols, Ross, & Jenkyns, in relation to the leaving their respective Churches.

30th DECEMBER, 1709.—Also two Letters from Mr. Black to the Lord Bishop of London, & to the Secretary dated — Annapolis 7th June, 1709 importing that he and his people had been plunder'd & driven away by the ffrench; that he has received nothing from them, nor dos expect it now, and therefore prays he may be Lycensed for Maryland, & his Salary from the Society continued; Whereupon they had Agreed to report as their opinion that the said Mr. Black shou'd be appointed to Appoquiminink vacant by the death of Mr. Jenkins: Agreed to.

15th DECEMBER, 1710.—Also that they had read two Letters from Mr. Black to the Lord Bishop of London and the Secry. dated Accomake on the Eastern Shore of Virginia 8th & 9th March 1709 importing his removal from Sussex County, and the occasion thereof as mention'd in his former: that being invited by the Vestry of Accomake, he was to be Inducted the 14th of ye said month, and desires his Lo'p to confirm the same: That at Lewes Town in Sussex County there is no security for a Minister, it lying open to any Enemy and the people so divided they will not allow him any maintenance: that he offer'd to leave his Library, upon their giving Bond to be accountable to the Society for the same; but none of them willing so to do, he took it with him, and is ready to deliver it to the Society's Order: The Comee thereupon Agreed to lay these Letters before the

Society: Then the said Letters were read: Agreed that notice be given to Mr. Black that the Society is contented their Books should lye in his hands till further Ordr.

20th April, 1711.—Also another [letter] from Mr. Black dated—Accomake in Virginia 30th Septr. 1710 owning the Receipt of the Secretary's wherein he is ordered to remove to Appoquiminick, but prays to be excused being Instituted & Inducted into the parish where he is, and in which he will continue while he lives in America: That he has the Society's Library and prays it may be given his Parish; but if that can't be obtained will deliver it to ye Society's Order on the receipt of his Bond he gave for the same: and lastly desires what moneys are due to him from the Society may be paid to his Order.

Also another from the Vestry of Appoquiminick dated 15th Septr. 1710 importing Mr. Black's being settled at Accomake and his Resolution of continuing there; therefore pray to be supplyed with another Missionary: The Comee Agreed to lay this Letter before the Society and to move them that if Mr. Clubb appears to be qualifyed he may be removed to Appoquiminick and Mr. Humphrys to succeed him in Oxford in Pensylvania and that the Library in Mr. Black's hands be sent either to Appoquiminy or Oxford, if either of those places want the same: Agreed to, and that Mr. Humphrys have an allowance of fifty pounds p. ann: commencing from Ladyday last, and five pounds worth of small Tracts for the use of his people; and as to Mr. Black's demand, and the disposal of the Library abovemention'd it is hereby refer'd to the Comee to consider and report their opinion thereof.

10th October, 1712.—Another from Mr. Black at Accamick ye 7 July 1711.—says he has wrote several Letters but has had no answer—that ye Society is still in his debt a years Salary for serving at Sussex—and his bill protested tho' his removal was approv'd.—Thinks the reason may be because of his delay in Transporting himself from hence to Sussex which he says was impossible, or in not obeying the Orders of ye Society in removing to Appoquimick, which Letter did not reach him till a year after his being where he is, and where he contracted debts, and promis'd to stay.—That his circumstances are hard—prays the paymt of his mony & desires to be anointed ye Society's Missionary and that he may have some Common Prayer Books—Offers to serve ye Society in what they shall command him

Copies of Letters from Mr. Wm. Black.

Messrs Black & Jenkins to the Secretary.

Hond. Sir.—We presume from the Countenance and favour wherewith you and the rest of the honourable Society have entertained and employed us in this Mission, it might be your Expectation to hear from us before now; we therefore humbly crave your pardon for not writing to you sooner and at once do as humbly beg leave by you to acquaint the honble Committee with our ill success, having made no further progress in our Voyage than Torbay, where the whole Fleet now lye at Anchor in expectation of a fair and favourable wind; In the mean time nothing will be more grievous to us, than the pitifull treatment we get aboard, being in no respect better accommodated than the most ordinary Common Sailors, so much beneath and unbecoming the dignity of our profession, that we are loth, or indeed almost ashamed to trouble you with mentioning the Particulars of it, knowing not how it can be remedied; the whole provision which we made for our selves being now exhausted, and have not wherewith to get a new supply, without making further Intrusion upon the Societies bounty, however we only pray we may be considered as their Honours shall think fitt, knowing it is our duty (how necessitous and pressing soever our present circumstances be) to rest fully satisfyed with the will of God, and to continue unanimously in all due respects to yourself and all the Honble Society

Dear Sr

Your faithfull Missionaries & most obedt humble Servants,

Thomas Jenkins
William Black

Torbay, From on Board the Ruby.
Augst ye 13th, 1707.

We humbly beg your answer here or elsewhere as you can get Information of the Fleet.

Directions are
To Jno. Chamberlayne, Esqr.

Mr. Black to ye Secretary.

Spithead Aboard ye Ruby,
30th August 1707.

Hond. Sr.—Haying lately wrote to you conjunctly with Mr. Jenkins from Torbay, fearing then what is now to our grief come to pass; We were in great hopes that by this time we should have been proceeding with the rest of the Fleet, in our Voyage, but that very day we designed to have sailed, there came an Order that the Chester and Ruby shou'd return for Spithead. Wee have lived aboard these 14 weeks, and have endured such hardships as come little short of Captivity itself; the little money we had reserved for carrying us after our arrival at Virginia, to our respective places, we cou'd not possibly avoid the spending of; and being now destitute of every thing for to provide for our voyage, we are necessitate to request for assistance from the Honble Society, which otherways, considering their former bounty to my self in particular, I cou'd not without Chefhing desire. The sad treatment we have all of us met with has almost ruin'd our healths already, and if we be not supplyed and shou'd continue aboard may lay the foundation of sickness, which may make all our undertakings prove abortive; The uncertainty of the Admiralty in their Orders, has determined us (least we shou'd be disappointed a second time) to go aboard a Merchantman, but our money is at so low an Ebb, that we cannot come ashoare; hoping Sr. that your Answer will be suitable to my necessity. I am with all humility and duty

Yours and the Honble Societies Missionary & most humble Servant.

WM. BLACK.

Directions are

To JNO CHAMBERLAYNE, ESQR, &c.

Messrs Black & Jenkins to the Secretary.

PORTSMOUTH, 28th Octr. 1707.

SR.—The many misfortunes and discouragements we have met with, which seem still to be continued with the melancholy News of our Dear Brother Mr. Cr Cordiner and his family being carried into ffrance, and our present Disappointment here at Portsmouth, is the reason of our troubling you at this time. By the advice we had from the Gentlemen of the Admiralty office we came here. But the Oxford is not come yet to Spithead, and it being the opinion of many here that the Virginia fleet will not touch at Portsmouth, We humbly crave your and the Honble Society's advice what it is best for us to do in our present Circumstances. The Captain of the Bristol promis'd to take us both aboard his ship to the Downs where the Oxford lies, but he has to our great grief left us behind; Our being disappointed by him can't be imputed to any Negligence in us, for we waited upon him every day, and went once aboard his ship, we spake to him the night he sailed hence, at which time he told us he was not to sail for three days tho' he went off that very night; We add no more but that we are heartily sorry, and condole our disappointments from time to time and that we are very sensible of your own kindness, hoping that all the Dispensations of Gods Providence will teach us submission to him and Obedience and thankfulness to our Honorable Benefactors We are in all humility and Sincerity

Your and their faithfull Missionaries & humble Servants.

WM BLACK
THO. JENKINS

Superscribed

To JNO. CHAMBERLAYNE, ESQR., &c.

Mr. Black to the Secretary.

PLYMOUTH, 3rd Jany. 1707.

SR.—The Reason why I have not troubled you with an acct. of my Circumstances, since I was last at London is, because the last Letter that Mr. Jenkins and I wrote, (tho' we knew not the Spring of the bad resentmt of some of the Society,) had such an effect as to produce an ill understanding betwixt some particular Members and us, as if we had prodigally lavish'd away the money we had from the Honble Society. We are sure that we have done justly and candidly by representing things as they really were, for none of the money we have put to bad uses, as the accots of our disbursmts we have by us, if we may be believed can testify. Our whole dependance being upon the Honble

Society, and having no other way to unfold our Condition, but by representing the matter of Fact, we hope that the Honble Society will not take it ill that urgent necessity has again enforced us particularly myself again to address them. For Mr. Jenkins being Chaplain of the Oxford in which I am a Passenger has upon that accot had I suppose some money advanced him at Portsmouth which I cou'd not have. I confess that none of the Missionaries have been so troublesome as we, but if it be consider'd that our case is extraordinary having waited for Transportacon since the beginning of April, the Providence of God being also extraordinary wth respect to our Voyage for it is better to be here as we are, than to have been carried into France in the Ruby. We have used all means that human Industry cou'd Invent for saving money and attaining our end, but who can fight against the winds or resist his Will? I hope, all this consider'd, our humble desire for supply having no other Outgate, will appear by this time both reasonable and excusable, which that it may appear evidently I crave pardon to give a brief but true accot. of some of the Difficulties we have encounter'd since we left London. When we came to Portsmouth it was reported by all, that this Fleet then coming from the Downs was not to touch there, which laid us under a necessity of going aboard the Ipswich which was to meet the Fleet We thence went aboard the Oxford for which we had an Order, but she having run aground, went into the Dock, which cost us infinite Fateigue and trouble, then we went on Board the Guernsey where we were tormented by the ill treatment we reced and to sum up all our unhappyness, Capt. Huntington Commander set us a shoar; The Fleet being ready to sail, we went on Board a Merchant Man, then fearing We shou'd have lost our Passage We went aboard the Flagg Sr. John Norris Admiral who indeed of all that we met with pay'd us most respect and civility, what money this trouble from Ship to Ship cost us—can scarcely be believed by any but us who payd it. We have been universally hated because of our close adherence to the Honble Society their Orders to us in reproving the open and avow'd debaucheries of wicked and unreasonable men, being now reduced to our old Circumstances of Poverty, our engagement with the Honble Society puting us out of the way of all employment for our Sustenance. I humbly desire, Dear Sr, that you wou'd represent our Condition especially mine, upon the aforesd accot. that they the Honble Society may send us some assistance, for without it I am like to proceed no farther if the Fleet continue any time; Our treatment on Board is the same wth that of Common Sailors, which we wou'd never complain off if it were not Observ'd by others, who look upon us as ye veryest Wretches in the World being, as the world for the most part is, ready to measure a Man's happyness according to his Circumstances. Now if any of us shou'd miscarry, in this Mission, which God forbid, having done all and suffer'd all that Humane Nature can support, we cannot be chargeable of mismanagement. Wishing all happyness imaginable to your and your Family & an Imortal reward to each member of the Honble Society. I continue as ever

Your & their very humbe Servt WM. BLACK.

P. S.—DEAR SIR:—I hope you will honour me with an Answer, for our Necessities cry aloud for it, being never in such Circumstances as at present, not being able so much as to pay for a Boat from Shoar aboard. I am afraid that my Exigency will make me Contract debt wch I ever avoided as the last & worst of Shifts. I must tell you that both Mr. Jenkins and my Books reced from ye Honble Society are mightily damnifyed by being tossed from Ship to Ship. We are to be found on Board the Oxford riding in Plymouth Sound.

Mr. Black to the Secretary.

KICKATAN IN VIRGINIA
19th June, 1708.

HONOR'D SIR.—By the blessing of God we are now arrived here after a long and tedious Passage; there has bin such a Mortality on Bord our Ship the Oxford that we have buryed 30 men, & near 100 are dangerously sick. Mr. Jenkins was sick almost six Weeks, but is now recover'd and as well as ever, as for myself, I have not had one hour of sickness since I left England, and seem to be cut out by Providence for any Country. We are now using all means for geting as soon as possible to Pensilvania, where by the assistance of Divine Grace, I shall endeavour to be as usefull as I can that I may at the same time both discharge my Conscience & answer the expectations of so pious and Honble Society as our Worthy Patrons are. My most humble Service to yourself wishing you long life & prosperity. As for the Honble Society may they long florish & successfully go on in so good a Work, & when they are all to be translated to a better life, may they be succeeded by men of their own piety & care for our holy Religion. I am &c. WM. BLACK.

Mr. Black to the Secretary.

NEW CASTLE ON DELAWARE
RIVER 19th July 1708

HOND. SIR.—I wrote to you from Kickatan in Virginia about two weeks agoe since which time I am come so far in my Journey as this place. I have nothing to offer in this than what I said in my last Letter, but that I am hasting down Delaware to Sussex County, only I wou'd rather be guilty of Tautology in writing the same thing than of want of Deference and respect to so Venerable a Corporation as the Honble Society is. Mr. Jenkyns has now left me and is gone to his charge. I am inform'd his Congregation will be very small, the place being so wonderfully divided into Quakers, Independants and Presbyterians; But I hope that the place I am going to will prove less disturbed with Sectaries of any denomination; the contagion of Enthusiasm not having spread itself so far down the Country. I shall in every point, God enabling me, be observant of the Instructions I have already received or shall receive from the Honorable Society. I pray God to bless all my Benefactors and yr self & Family in particular. I am in all Sincerity

Honor'd Sr. Your most Obedt humble Servt
WM. BLACK.

Mr. Black to the Secretary.

ANNAPOLIS, June 7th, 1709.

HONOR'D SIR.—I rece'd a Letter from you wth an account of some of the Transactions of the Society, to which long ago I wrote an answer, since which time (May 7th) the ffrench have been among us, and have Pillaged the Town, and ruin'd the people; and I with great difficulty escaped: I was fain for my security to fly about 30 Miles upon Sunday the 8th May. The County in all places where 'tis inhabited lies open to the Sea so that there is no safety there. The Captain of the privateer is one Monsr Le Croix, the number of the Men is 120, with 4 Guns, and we are threatened by another Ship of the same force with a Man of War from old ffrance. The people have not contributed one farthing for my maintenance since I came; I've reced nothing from them, & those who subscribed are mostly ruin'd, so that now I cannot expect they shou'd give me any thing, since they were unwilling to subscribe when they were of Ability. I drew upon my Attorny my Salary for this year, before this encident happen'd, and indeed the £50 allowed me amounts to about £30 here, since ev'rything we buy is sold at the rate of 4 or 500 p. cent. I have been here now one year and am forced with the permission of my Lord of London to settle myself in our neighbouring Province of Maryland. I had my recourse to his Excellency the Governor of the Province who received me as he dos all clergymen, with great civility and has promised to provide for me, till such time as my Lord of London sends me a Lycence, at which time I am to be Legally establish'd, and since I cannot help my leaving Sussex, I hope that the Honble Society will not wthdraw their Bounty but continue it, as I shall to serve God & the Church according to my ability, where God in his providence shall cast my Lott. Mr. Crawford & Jenkins live on the same River but are far removed from Danger, but we lying at the very Capes become a prey to every Enemy that comes that way. The Quakers who are very numerous will neither resist themselves nor contribute to the maintenance of those that willingly wou'd. Wishing to yourself and all my very good Benefactors health and happyness here & hereafter I am

Your & their faithfull Missionary & humbe Servt.

WM. BLACK.

Mr. Black to Ld. Bp. of London.

ANNAPOLIS, 7. June. 1709.

MY LORD.—Having this Opportunity I thought it my duty to acquaint your Lo'p what has happen'd at Lewis Town in Sussex County, being that part of your Lop's Diocese in America to which I was sent. May 7th there arrived a ffrench Privateer of 4 Guns and about 120 Men on Monsr Le Croix being Captain, who pillaged the Town, and has laid wast all the parts adjacent; many of the people are fled back into the country, one Man only was kill'd, and it is thought that the dammage they have done to the place amounts to about £3000 the place is threatened to be burn't, for they inform'd the people that there was a Man of War from old ffrance and another Ship of equal force with themselves to be there very soon. I liv'd about one mile from the Town, and was chased from that place out of the County, and the people being mostly quakers, will neither fortify themselves agst their Enemies, nor contribute to the maintenance of such as wou'd, so that the whole County which is my charge is like to be ruin'd. The people also, as I have inform'd your Lo'p in a Letter of an older date than this, will contribute nothing to my subsistence, and the £50 I have from the Society amounts to above £30 here for nothing can be bought at the cheapest hand under 4 or 500 p. cent. and the Church not being establish't by Law in this Province of Pensylvania; no man can live here upon the precarious Contribution of a divided people upon this consideration I had my recourse to his Excellency the Governour of our neighbouring Province of Maryland who rather than that I shou'd return for Britain, has entertained me in Maryland upon condition that your Lo'p by sending me a Lycense to stay here shou'd approve of my removal; so that I beg that your Lo'p will send it me to Anapolis that I may serve God here, since your Lo'p was pleased to send me into these parts. This County of Sussex lyes so open to the Sea that there can be no safety in it; this is the 3rd time the people have been robbed, twice the last Warrs and onct this ; I hope that your Lo'p will prevail wth ye Society to continue my Salary since my removal is caused by meer & unavoidable necessity, wishing your Lo'p long life & health for the good of the Churches here & at home I am

May it please your Lo'p
Yor Lo'ps most dutyfull Son & humb Servant.
Wm. Black.

Mr. Black to ye Ld. Bishop of London.

My Lord.—I wrote to your Lo'p from Annapolis of the date of 16th or 20th of June 1709, and acquainted your Lo'p that I was necessitate to remove from Sussex County in Pensylvania to Maryland, where I was entertained by the Govr and permitted by him to Officiate in the Parish of Piscataway; But upon my return to Sussex to transport my Books to that place, The French who were the cause of my removal, and who had pillaged and laid wast the Town, were succeeded by another Privateer and prevented my return to Piscataway, I being to go up the River where they then rode: A little after I was invited by the Vestry of Accomake Parish on the Eastern Shore in the Colony of Virginia to officiate there, where I now am. I was directed by that Vestry to wait upon the President and your Lo'ps Commissary Mr. Blair which I did and was civilly accepted of by them. This parish for about fifteen years having been destitute of a Minister, that I might be the more encouraged to stay with them, addressed the President that I might be inducted into the said Parish, which he granted, so that I am to be Inducted into this Church the 14th of this instant. I told your Lo'p in my last that there is no security for any Minister to live at Lewis Town it lying open to any Enemy; and the people are so divided that they will not allow of any maintenance to a Minister, but willingly entertain Itinerant Enthusiasts and Straglers. Tho' I lived there a whole year, I never reced one farthing from any of them, and shou'd have been in very pityfull circumstances, if I had not had the Society's Salary allow'd me, which being £50 p. Ann: is too little by one half for a Minister who lives there: ffor while the Minister depends upon the precarious contribucon of a very poor people for the greatest part of his Salary, he is forced either to connive at many of their irregular actions, or to lose the next years subscription of every one he displeaseth by reproving their Vices. I carryed the Society's Books along with me, I offer'd 'em to be preserved for the Society's use, if they to whom

I shou'd commit the custody of them wou'd have given me their Bond to restore them to such as the Society shou'd give order hereafter to receive them: But none of the Chief men there wou'd releive my Bond whereby I am obliged to restore them in such condicon as I received them, reasonable use and other accidents excepted. The Books if the Society shou'd think fit wou'd answer the same design here as there, they being given us for our further encouragement. I humbly begg that your Lo'p would be pleased to confirme me in the Cure of the Parish where I now live, for having fforfeited my allowance from the Society by being forced to remove thence. If your Lo'p shou'd think fit to order me back again to Sussex, I shall have nothing to depend upon, so that my Circumstances will be so pressing that contrary to my Inclinations I shall be necessitate to return for Great Britain; that your Lo'p may long continue in life and health to the welfare of the Churches at home and abroad is the prayer of

May it please your Lo'p

Your Lo'ps most dutyfull son & humb servant.

Wm. Black.

Accomake, on the Eastern Shore of the Colony of Virginia 8. March. 1710.

Mr. Black to the Secretary.

Accomake, on the Eastern Shore in Virginia, 30th Septr. 1710.

Honor'd Sir.—I reced yours of the date of Janry 6, 1709, wherein I am ordered by the Society to remove forthwith to Appoquiminick; but I am now living in Virginia on the Eastern Shore about 200 miles from that place, the parish is very large, the people kind and I myself settled among them: I was here Instituted & Inducted into the parish as in a former Letter I have inform'd you. I have not received one farthing either from the Society (if they have not answered my Bill of £50 sterling) or the people of Sussex; for the truth whereof I appeal to the whole County where I lived a whole year; so that the Society is only owing me something more than one years salary. As for my removing, my Circumstances are such that I cannot, and the place and people where I am I like very well, and resolve if nothing prevent me to continue with them while I live in America. If my Bill shou'd be protested, 'tis what I fear'd and therefore was necessitate, tho' in great straits, not to make use of the money, which if God spare me, I will faithfully repay. I have served God and the Society in Sussex from the 26th of July 1708, to Augt 1709, since which time I've lived in Accomake in the Eastern Shore of Virginia. I hope Sr. if my money be not paid to my Attorney Mr. Law. Smith of Clifford's Inn that you will pay it according to my Order, for I am so afraid of Bills, that I shall be very Cautious in making use of that way; As for the Society's Books I carryed them with me; I earnestly desire Hond Sir that the Society would be pleased to appropriate them to the parish where I live, for I have very few Books of my own, and the Society will I hope attain their end in so doing. If they shou'd think fit to dispose otherwise of them, I am very ready to comply, as it is both reasonable and my duty, with their Orders, only I desire that my Bond may be sent to me whereby I obliged myself to restore them in as good case (ordinary use excepted) as I received them in; this was the reason. I carryed them to Accomake. I offer'd them to the Gentlemen of Sussex if they wou'd have given me their Bond to keep me harmless from that of the Society, if the Books shou'd have been lost or abused. I have had such an experience of the people of Pensylvania that I can never expect any better treatment than I have received, so that I desire that the Society wou'd let me serve God where I am, since God in his providence sent me to this place when I was in as great need of their Temporall, as they of my Spiritual assistance. May God long preserve the Honble Society and prosper their Designs and reward yourself for your kindness & civility to me when I was a Stranger. I am,

Honor'd Sir,

Your very humb and Obliged Servant. WM. BLACK.

A JOURNAL OF MR. ROSS'S LABOURS IN THE GOSPEL DUREING HIS SHORT STAY IN THE COUNTY OF SUSSEX UPON DELAWARE. (AUGUST 1717).

The zeal and affection of the People in Lewis Town for the church has appeared so great of late, that they have pitch'd upon a sober person an Inhabitant among them, to read prayers to them every Lord's day, which he does with so great applause that the congregation he supplyes as a Reader doth visibly increase every Sabbath. Mr. Brook collector there a good & zealous church man supplyes him with sermon books wherein the said Reader reads, much to the Satisfaction of the People. This method I could not but approve of, & recommend in their present circumstances.

The Hon. Colonel William Keith, with the Rev Mr. Ross and several other gentlemen, set sail from New Castle, Saturday, August 3d, 1717, for Lewes. They arrived Monday, August 5th. Tuesday, August 6th, Mr. Ross records: "I attended the Governor to the Court House of the said County where I read divine service, The Justice of the County with many others being present.

"Wednesday, August 7th, Service being read in the said Court House, I preached on these words, 'Thou shalt not bear false witness against thy neighbour.'

"The house was full of People and many hearkened at the doors and windows.

"They had not an opportunity of hearing a Minister of the Church a good while before, and therefore the diligent attention they gave to my discourse was the less surprising.

"I was obliged to dismiss the Congregation before I could proceed to administer Baptism to those many that came there to receive it, lest, by taking up too much of the Governor's time, I should prove a hindrance to him and the Justices in the dispatch of business.

"The number of Children and Infants baptized this day was thirty.

"Friday, August 9th, I preached again, the words I insisted upon were, 'and Behold one came and said unto Him Good Master, what good thing shall I do, that I may inherit Eternal Life;' the Governor and a greater auditory than I had formerly was present. I baptized one and twenty."

Abstracts from Deeds Showing Location of William Becket Property.

Deed from Samuel Davis of Somerset County in the province of Maryland, Gent.—to William Becket of the town of Lewes, in the County of Sussex upon Delaware, Gent.—

Dated sixth day of July in the eighth year of the reign of our Sovereign Lord George by the grace of God King of Great Britain A. D., 1722. Consideration—68 £.

Description.—One certain lott of Land Containing in breadth Sixty foot, & in length two hundred feet situate, lying and being in the second street of the Town of Lewes afs'd binding on the North West side with the lott that was formerly Philip Russell's but now in the Possession of William Godwin, and on the South East side with the Comon lotts and grave yard of the s'd Town. Together with the house that now is thereon and all and singular the appurtenances, privileges, proffits, Comoditys, ways, Easements, hereditaments, freedoms, Imunities whatsoever thereunto belonging or in anywise appertaining and all Deeds, writings & Evidences touching or Concerning the same or any part thereof.

Deed Philip Russell to Wm. Godwin, dated Aug. 8, 1723.—

All that lott or parcel of land lying and being in the Town of Lewes being sixty foot in breadth & two hundred feet in length and bounded on the South East with the lott of Wm. Becket and on the South West with a new street lately laid out and on the North West with knitting Street or Mulberry Street and on ye North East with the second Street.

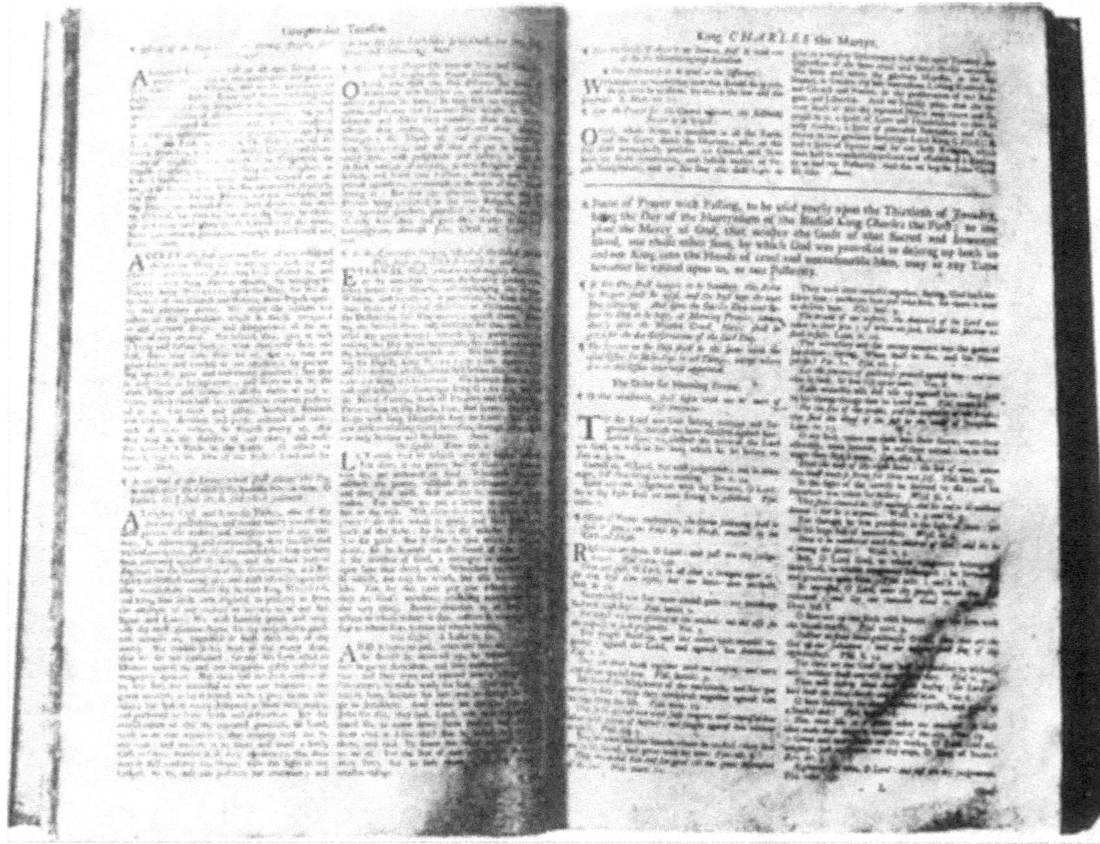

OLD PRAYER BOOK, 1722.

29 Sept., 1721.

MEMBERS OF THE CHURCH AT LEWES TOWN, PENSILVANIA.

The Rev. Mr. Beckett happily came amongst us on the first instant and after he had paid his respects to our worthy Govr Sir Wm. Keith made known to us the favorable disposition of the Hon. Society to this poor Congregation as they are set forth in a letter of the 31st of May wherewithal you have been pleased to favour us. We beseech you Sr to say for us to those Hon. persons that we shall always preserve in our minds a most gratefull sence of what they have had the goodness to do for us. And what we have hitherto seen of Mr. Beckett gives us the strongest hopes that in the Tenor of his Life & Doctrine he will both adorn his Profession & fulfill that good & great end to which he hath the Honor to be appointed so shall it be our lasting care as well as pay him that respect which is due to his character as to make such suitable provision for his better & more comfortable support as Himself could justly expect were he fully seen in the Circumstances of this People & we doubt not in a few months longer to make this good to his satisfaction & that of his Constituents. Do us the favour Sr to lay these things before the Hon. Board & we shall ever own ourselves to be

Sr Yor Most Humble & obliged Servants

HEN. BURKE,
WM. TILL.

LEWES ON MICHAELMAS DAY, 1721.

A. D. 1722. "The Reverend Mr. Beckett, Minister at Lewes-Town, &c., in Pensilvania; That he has three Places to officiate at, where he has Considerable numbers of Hearers; at two of which Places, the People have built Churches, before they had a Prospect of a Minister; & appointed sober Laymen to read the Prayers of the Church, to keep the people steady to their Principles; that Subscriptions are raising for building another Church; that he has baptized 55 Persons, nine whereof were adult; & there is a manifest change in the Lives & Manners of, & a very great Reformation among many of the People, since his Coming there; for which he has received the Thanks of the Magistrates & Gentlemen of the Church of England in that County."

1724. "From the Reverend Mr. Beckett, Minister at Lewes in Pensilvania, That the number of Persons baptized last year in his Parish are 82, eleven or twelve of which are Adults; that the Church of Lewes is almost finished; & tho' they have now three Churches in that County, yet none of them will contain the Hearers which Constantly attend at Divine Service; that in his Journey thro' Kent County he baptized in one day 6 adults, & 15 children, & had a numerous Congregation, where they have a large church, but no Minister."

QUERIES TO BE ANSWERED BY THE PERSONS WHO WERE COMMISSARIES TO MY PREDECESSOR (THE LATE BISHOP OF LONDON).

What Parishes are there, which have yet no Churches, nor Ministers?

Here being no publick Acts for a legal Establishment of the Church here; the Distinction of Parishes is yet unknown in this Government; but here are several large Tracts of Land inhabited, where there is neither Church nor Minister, and several Churches built in other Tracts, who are in great want of Missionarys; particularly those att Kent, Apoquiniminck, Bristol, Parkiomen, & White-Marsh.

We are My Lord

Yr Lo'p most obedient, most Dutifull Sons & Servants

ROBT. WEYMAN. GEO. ROSS.
WM. BECKETT. INS. HUMPHREYS.

(ANSWERS TO QUERIES ABT $172\frac{4}{5}$.)

Queries to be Answered by Every Minister, 1724.

How long is it since you went over? &c.

Three years in June last.

Have you had any other church? &c.

None, my Lord.

Have you been duly Licens'd by the Bishop of London? &c.

Yes.

How long have you been inducted? &c.

No Induction here.

Are you ordinarily resident in the Parish?

I have not been absent from my own care Two Sundays for the space of Ten Months pass'd.

Of what extent is your Parish?

I have the care of three churches in this County. One of them being 25 miles, the other 2 from the church in Lewes where I live. Number of Familys about Four Hundred.

1725. "From the Reverend Mr. Beckett, Minister at Lewes in Pensilvania, That tho' they have already three Churches, at which he officiates alternately, which are constantly filled with pretty regular Congregations; yet the People living in the Middle of the Country have raised a Subscription to build another Chappel in the Center of it; that the number of the baptized every year since his being there, has been never less than eighty; & on Easter & Whitsunday he had twenty-seven communicants."

1726.—Churches in Pensilvania, how supplyed with Ministers?

Lewes town & two more churches in Sussex County by Mr. Becket.

Are there any Infidels, bond or free?

Yes. A great many Negroe Slaves; Some whereof I have baptized since coming here. We have but few Indians & these seem obstinate to the means of conversion.

How oft is divine Service performed?

Thrice a week, viz Sundays, Wednesdays, & Fridays. On the Sabbath my Churches are full, & on Litany Days Several of the more Sober & devout duely attend on the Worship of God.

How oft is the Sacrament of the Lord's Supper administer'd?

Thrice a year viz: Easter, Whitsun, & Christmas. The number of communicants is about 20.

At what times do you Catechise?

Every Sunday in the Summer Season where I usually preach a catechetical Lecture in the Afternoon.

Are all things duly dispos'd & provided in the Church?

No, my Lord, Our Churches being none of them yet finished.

Of what value is your living in Sterling money?

Besides the Bounty of the Honable Society, I have but very little to depend on for subsistance. The People here have indeed subscribed towards my Support, but by reason of Poverty few are able to pay.

Have you a House and glebe?

No House nor glebe is provided for a Minister here.

Is due care taken to preserve your House in good repair?

Att my own.

Have you more cures than one?

I have 3 Churches in this county as before mentioned. Att one of which I officiate every Sunday alternately.

Have you in your Parish any Publick School?

None, my Lord.

Have you a Parochial Library?

I have the Library sent thither by the Honable Society For the due preservation of which I take a particular care myself. I am My Lord,

Yr Lordship's most obedt & most dutifull Son & Servt.

WM. BECKET.

Extract from Letter of Mr. Becket Writing in Favour of Peters.

May it please your Lordship.—The Congregation at Philadelphia, are desirous that the Reverend Mr. Peters, might be plac'd there, as Minister of that Church. And I beg with all Deference & Regard to remain,

My Lord,

Yr most Dutiful & obedient Son & Servant

Wm. Becket,
Missionary at Lewes.

Ussher's Letter Against Peters.

"I, Arthur Ussher missionary at Dover in the province of Pensilvania do solemnly declare, that I heard the Revnd Mr. Peters preach in Christs Church in Philadelphia on Whit Sunday in the present year 1737. The words of the text were these: He shall baptize you with the Holy Ghost. In his discourse he seem'd to extoll & establish natural religion, so far as to destroy the necessity of Divine inspiration; and farther said that *reason & Revelation alone*, were sufficient to enable a man to work out his salvation. The whole discourse seem'd to be calculated to establish natural religion. And I do farther declare, that the Revnd Mr. Peters, in the Revnd Mr. Cummings house on the sd Whit Sunday evening, just before he went into Church, & preached the sd subject he preached upon that evening, that he had given it, its due weight, & treated it in a different manner from our Modern Divine.

"Sept: 18th, 1737. "Arthur Ussher."

"Philadelphia, Sept. 4th, 1743.

"My Lord.—I am now all most seven years in the service of the venerable Society, and to the best of my knowledge and skill, have made use of all the possible means I could devise, to promote the glory of God, and the Salvation of the Souls committed to my charge, before the 26th of June last. I have baptized 510 grown persons and childeren, and since 45 childeren & 3 adults; The Mission of Lewes is now become vacant by the death of the late missionary Mr. Becket, the burthen of his charge lying upon me for these two years past (he being unable to officiate but a very short space of the above two years. After the strictest enquiry I coud make, I find a thousand and twenty men in the county of Kent, four hundred & eighty four of which number professing themselves of the Church of England, fifty six of the Quakers, three hundred and ninety seven Presbyterians, sixty two Papists, and above twenty who profess themselves to be of no religion, & seem to glory in it.

"I am, my Lord, with the greatest respect my Lord,

"Your most dutiful & obliged Son & Servant,

"Arthur Ussher."

Letter to Mr. Cummings.

March 13, 1727–8.

Revd. and Dear Bro.—I had the favour of your letter of Nov. 11, for which I thank you, & till that time did not hear tho' I did suspect what success our solicitations with respect to the licences, has met with. I will write to the Bishop & Society upon that head, by the 1st opportunity & shall be glad to hear what you will do in the case. Mr. Ross has not said one word about it in any of his letters to me, he only wanted one licence for himself and did not care what became of all the rest. Now he has sped himself he may perhaps have taken care for the rest. Mr. Campbell was here in the beginning of the year, he brought with him a paper of recommendation to whom it might concern cautiously worded & signed by Laymen signifying that since he was only yet accussed but not convicted he might be employed in the service of the church, I consented that some of the gentlemen here should sign it but would not do it myself tho' he pressed me much, I told him the clergy would do nothing but in conjunction & it would be a jest for me to sign it. Please to give my humble service to honest Mr. Peter Evans & all friends. Messers. Brooke & Pemberton are well and give their service to you we have no news here having been shut up with ice for many weeks. My service to Mr. Fenton's family.

I am Dr. Bror. yours most affectionately, W. B.

I take this opportunity to acquaint you the affairs of the churches which are under my care go on as usual, that is, I thank God for it, they are in the main in a prosperous condition. But there is a matter or two of some moment to the welfare of the Church as I conceive which I more especially crave leave and intend to lay before you at this time. Since Major Gordon's arrival here as Governor he has promiscuously granted licences to us and the Presbyterian ministers, a thing which was never done before (save only in the last year of Sir Wm. Keith's goverment when Doctor Welton nonjuror was minister at Phila.) He was not fit to grant them & indeed his fortune appeared Desperate, so yt he was willing to raise money by any means.) so yt a small perquisite is hereby in a great measure granted away from the Missionaries but what is more considerable is that it is depriving us of what is our Right. At our last Convention held at New Castle, the Missionaries did humbly represent this matter to the Governor desiring his Favour in the Case, which he hath denyed us. Perhaps a Letter in our favour from the Honrable Society to this Gentleman might bring him to reason & do the Missionaries a considerable kindness. There is another affair which I conceive of some moment which might lend much to promote the designs of the Honrable Society for propagating the Gospel in America which I must beg leave to lay before you & it is briefly this: Here is a large, good Tract of Land lying between Maryland & Pennsylvania called the 3 Lower Counties on Delaware about 100 miles long & in some places 20 or 30 wide. This land as yet has no Proprietor but his Majesty tho' both Lord Baltimore and Penn's Heirs are now contending for it in England, not because either of them has a Title to it but because it is convenient for both and each has a mind to it. It is generally believed by many of the best people here who know the weakness and insufficiency of both their claims that this Land when the dispute on both sides is fully heard will remain to the King. If his Majesty when it is so determined will bestow it on the Society, a good Sum of Money might easily be raised off of it towards the Support of a Bishop or Suffragan the maintenance of missionaries or to such uses as the Society should think fit. I am told by some of the Representatives of the people here who meet in Assembly for the making of our Laws, that here are about 200,000 Acres of Land cleared & improved, some of the Settlers have Titles from James, Duke of York, some from Penn the Quaker, some from Lord Baltimore, all it is believed good for nothing in Law. It would be of little value to the Crown to keep it but of great service to the Church to bestow it on the Society. It would be a popular act & make a noise in England. And the people here would be glad to have the Church their Landlord, I mean the majority who are members of the Church of England. Dissenters of all sorts here being not so numerous as the Church people. I am satisfied if this point could be carryed it would be of the greatest service to the Church here, I will write to my Lord Bp of London on the same subject. But I will trouble you with no more at present only desire you to lay this before the Honrable Society in obedience to whose Orders I will very soon send to you such an account of the Church History & of my Parishes as you require.

I remain Sr your most obedt Servt

W. B.

March 13, 1727–8 To Dr. Humphrey.

To the Bishop of London.

My Lord.—Tho' I have not the happiness of being known to your Lord'p, yet as I have been a Missionary to the Society for propagating the Gospel & in Pennsylvania near 7 years and have made some observation upon the state of affairs here, so I have something to offer to your Lordp's consideration which I conceive would (if it could be effected) conduce much to the Interest of Religion here. And this I humbly pray may be accepted as my Apology for giving your Lrp this present Trouble. Here is a good Tract of Land being on the West side of Delaware Bay & between the Two Provinces of Maryland & Pennsylvania commonly called the 3 Lower Counties (or Counties of New Castle, Kent & Sussex on Delaware about 100 miles in length & in some places 20 miles wide which as yet has probably no Proprietor but his Majesty tho' Lord Baltimore & the Heirs of Penn the Quaker are both now contending for it at Law in England, not so much because either has a good title to it as because each desires & it will be a good convenient addition to either of their Provinces could they recover or procure a Grant of it. But it is generally believed by many persons of the best credit & capacities here, who are most acqted with the case that the Land does yet belong to the Crown yt the claims of both the one & the other are weak and insufficient & yt, when is fully canvassed before the proper judicature in England it will be determined in favour of his Majesties claim who when at any time a Commission is passed to a Governor of Pennsylvania & of the 3 Lower Counties on Delaware has always a clause inserted to this purpose "Saving to ourself our Rights to the 3 Lower Counties on Delaware." Now should the case be so determined, if a Grant for this Land could be procured to the Society from his Majesty as a good Sum of Money might be raised from it not only at first but Annually so it might be a mean to enable them to carry on more effectually the good work for which they were incorporated I am informed by one of the most intelligent of our Assemblymen here as the Representatives of the people in Legislature are called) that here are about 200,000 Acres of Land cleared & settled, here some settlers having titles from James late Duke of York, some from Lord Baltimore & others from Penn & his Heirs all supposed to be void in Law, because the Title of these Grants of Land is its self precarious. The inhabitants at present are very anxious about their Titles but would be glad to be settled in their possessions on a good Foundation and to have the Church their Landlord. I mean the majority at least who are members of the Church of England. Could such a grant be procured here money might be raised toward supporting a Suffragan (much needed in America) to maintain Missionaries or to such Uses as the Society should judge most expedient. There is another affair which I also beg leave to lay before your Lordsp. Since Major Gordon's arrival here our present Governor, he hath Granted Marriage Licenses promiscuously to us & to the Presbyterian Ministers, a thing never done before in this Goverment except only in the last year of Sr William Keith his predecessor when his Fortune in a manner grew desperate and he was willing by any means to raise Money. Or as he alleged because Dr. Welton was then Minister at Philada. to whom it was by no means proper they should be granted. The Missionaries here did at our last Convention in September humbly lay this Greivance before our Governor but he has refused to redress us in this point tho' it is the only one wherein it is in his power to favour us. If your Lordship will be pleased to write to him about this it may perhaps be a mean to bring him to our Interest as he professes himself a Member of the Church & will be a great favour done to the Missionaries. My Lord, I humbly beg your pardon for this trouble and your prayers for me & those under my care and remain

May it please your Ldp.

Your most dutiful & Obedt Son & Servant

W. B., Missionary at Lewes.

PENNSYLVANIA, March 15, 1727–8.

To Bro. Jno. on the death of Bro. James.

DEAR BROTHER.—I recd that Sorrowful Letter of yours on the 5th day of July which was dated on March 16th at Ollerton. The sad news of the Death of my dear Brother James was a severe stroke to me, he was nearest to me in age & consequently the longest Acqtance of all my brethren. He had been my constant play fellow and bedfellow from my childhood till I grew up. We have spent a great many pleasant days and hours together but now that satisfaction is over and we must see each others face no more. And we were not only brethren but Friends. I have often experienced his Friendship to me & I thank God I had always a hearty & brotherly affection for him. A thousand endearing instances occur to my mind of our being together the thoughts of which melt me into tears so yt I can scarce see to write.

But what will perhaps greatly surprise you is this On Friday the second day of February last about four o'clock in the morning (as near as I can imagine) being in bed I dreamed that all the Teeth of my upper-jaw became loose upon which with my finger & thumb I took ym out & put them in my Pocket, immediately after which I thought I also felt all the Teeth in my under jaw loose & ready to drop out as the others upon which I also took ym out of my mouth & put ym in my pocket as I had done before with those of my upper jaw Upon which in my dream I made this reflexion to myself, What a great misfortune is this? That I who am now but 30 years of Age should loose all my teeth and be obliged to wear the face of an old man in the prime of my time. I then started and awoke out of my sleep in a great consternation & it immediately came into my memory that my Father has often told me that a little before his mother died (our Grandmother) he dreamed yt all his Teeth came out of his head, so yt I concluded with myself that my Mother or at least some near Relation was dead which I believed I should hear of in a little time. With the grief and trouble of this apprehension I arose out of my bed tho' it was before break of day in the morning not being able to compose myself any more & walked about the House very sorrowfully so great an impression the dream had made in my mind I put the time down in my Pocket Book & have ever since expected that the first Letter I should have from home would bring me Sorrowful News. Insomuch that when I recd your last it lay on the Table near an Hour before I had the Courage to open & look into it.

You tell me in your Letter that our Bro dy'd on Friday the twelfth of February about 9 a'clock in the morning But this must needs be a mistake for the twelfth of February last did not happen on a Friday but on a Monday so that I believe tis only a mistake in your letter and yt he dy'd yt day and minute when I dreamed yt my teeth came out for when it is 9 a clock in the morning with you it is 4 a clock with us here There being about 5 hours difference of meridian between you & us. That is, it is 9 a clock here 5 hours after it is 9 with you, and so of the other Hours and the second of Feb was on a Friday which the 12th was not.

I have been full & particular on this point because I look upon it to be extraordinary & surprising that I who was 4000 miles distance or near the matter at that very Instant should have notice that some great Calamity was fallen upon my Family, as I certainly concluded from the Dream I desire you will be exact when you write again & let me know whether I am any ways mistaken.

Could I have been present at his Burial & have mingled my Tears with yours it might have given some Relief to my Sorrow by giving vent to it. And I might have paid my last Respects to the memory of my Broer by preaching his Funeral Sermon if my grief would have suffered it, but I beleive I should not have been able to do it, & I so sensibly feel the weight of my misfortune at this Distance that I perhaps could not have born it better or it may be not so well had I been present. Had I been there with you my tears could not have prolong'd his Life as now those which I shed for him here are rain & fruitless & cannot redeem him from the grave, for we are as water split upon the ground & cannot be gathered up again as the Scripture speaks. It is our duty to submit to Providence in all its dispensertions tho' they may be bitter to us yet since they are according to the Will of God we must submit. When our Heavenly Father corrects us we may & must feel the smart, but we ought not to murmur & repine And this harsh Providence ought to be a sufficient warning to us the surviving brethren to consider our latter end and to live virtuous & good lives for if the strongest & likeliest to have lived to Old Age is cut off & taken out of the World in the Flower of his Time What Assurance have we of the continuance of our Life? Particulary I ought to apply this advice to myself who am his eldest Bror & according to Nature ought to have gone before him to the grave, especially considering what different sorts of air I have breathed wch naturally contributes to shorten human Life.

But God has been merciful to me & preserved me in good Health to this day, And I still hope to see you all before it be long I am exceedingly glad to hear of the safe recovery of my good mother and of the rest of you from your dangerous sickness & I pray for the continuance of your health I hope Bror John has well recovered of his Ague. You will give my duty to my dear Mother & love to Bros & Sister & my kind Respects to all Old Friends & neighbours, let me hear from you again as soon as may be & believe me ever to be

Your most affect. Bror Wm. Becket.

Lewes, Aug. 1, 1728.

To Dr. Humphreys.

Revd Sir.—I wrote to you the last Autumn acquainting you with the State of my Parish & giving you an Historical Account of it in Obedience to the Commands of the Honrable Society. I am uneasy till I hear whether you received that & my Letter in time. If it miscarry'd pray let me know as soon as may be that I may send you a second Copy and so at least it may get a place in the second edition. The State of my Parish is much as usual the Persons baptized in it for some years past having been more than 80 and less than an hundred per Annum. But here it must be remembered that I have not been able to compute the certain number either of Adults or Infants which I have occasionally baptis'd in my travells both in this & the Neighbouring Provinces of Maryland particularly in Kent County upon Delaware, where I have several Times baptis'd near 20 persons in a day and where there is both a very great want & desire of a Missionary.

The Number of Communicants in this County are increased considerably this year the Account in my book stands as follows.

1729.

At St. Peter's in Lewes at Christmas..............	19
At St. George's on Easter Sunday.................	20
At St. Matthew's on Whit Sunday.................	18
	57

Since the receipts of the Sermons sent over to me by the Hon. Society (I mean those of Bp. Beveridge and the distribution of my Lord Bp. of London's Letters to the Masters & Mistresses of families) I have with the Assistance & permission of their owners baptized seven negroes & have been apply'd to by some others who are not yet sufficiently instructed.

In my last I wrote to you to request of the Hm. Society that they will be pleased to give me leave to come over to England the next Summer with a continuance of my Salary that I may have an Opportunity of settling some Affairs of importance to me which cannot well be done in my Absence, and of seeing my Native Country once more & such of my Friends and Relations as the late Contagious Sickness in Cheshire hath yet left alive. Your favours in this Point will lay a great Obligation upon,

Sir your very hum. Servt W. Becket.

Lewes, May 29, 1729.

To A. Hamilton Esq.

Sr.—Several of my friends who have been at N Castle as members of Assembly the 2 or 3 last Sessions have been so kind as to tell me after what manner you thought fit to treat my Character behind my back, And as I am conscious to myself, & you know very well yt I never did you any injury or offered you any affront so I was surprized yt you should do anything so mean and so little becoming a Gentleman or a man in your Station.

If it be just Sir to speak ill of a man yt never wrong'd you nor any friend of yours & to attempt to hurt a man's Interest that never offer'd nor design'd any Injury to you, then you acted as became you. For my part I never was taught till now, that hard names & opprobrious language yt swearing and reviling at an Absent person befitted a Gentleman, I am sure that in the Country where you & I were bred these are called the language & manners of Porters & are thought to be very vulgar and indecent.

Is it fit that the Speaker of an Assembly, the Recorder of a City, a Magistrate & a professed Orator of no small Reputation should thus descend to the language of men of the meanest Rank & lowest breeding. For the sake of Justice treat me Sir with more Candor & good Nature and as we say, do as you would be done by, I had almost desired you to treat me as a Xn but since you seem to renounce yt name pray treat me fairly & I desire no more. Reputation is a Jewel yt no man cares to be robbed of, and I doubt not but you know men who had rather have a fair Attack made upon their Lives than an unfair one upon their Reputations And I should be glad to see yt you would be unwilling to take yt from another which you would not part with yourself.

If it be because of my Religion or Character yt you thus use me I am sure it is a way unsuitable to the King's or Wm. Penn's Government who would have no one ill used on these Accounts. And if you have imbraced principles different from mine I am of opinion yt they are not worth maintaining if they carry you beyond the bounds of Truth & Decency.

I have herein dealt plainly and severely with you & I know you cannot justly blame me for it I submit the whole to yor own Judgement & Reflection & remain

Sr. Your abused Frd & hum Servt

Wm. Becket.

Lewes, Nov. 26, 1729.
Mr. Hamilton.

To Hen Brooke Esqr.

THE HUM PETITION & ADDRESS OF WM BECKET IN BEHALF OF HIMSELF & SOME OTHER INHABITANTS OF THE TOWN OF LEWES. 1731.
SHEWETH:

That Providence hath placed your Petitioners in a sort of Retirement in a great measure separated from the noise & bustle as well as from the News & Politicks of this World.

That notwithstanding yor Sd Petitioners are pretty well content and do not greatly envy those who act in higher & more publick stations of Life when they consider among other things that the Audience in a Theatre have commonly greater pleasure than the Actors. That as yor Sd Petitioners desire no more yn to be lookers on & to observe how the Vim & the Busy part of mankind act their respective Parts so it is highly necessary that we should be furnished with the publick News both for our Instruction & entertainment.

That it hath been observed that several Persons in the fetres of London & Westmr & other places in his Majs Dominions have looked upon ymselves as great Wits & Politicans only from that Store of Learning & useful Erudition which they have collected from the Publick Papers.

That as yor Sd. Petitioners do not know when it may please the King to call upon some of them to act in great places of trust & profit which would be loath to refuse out of the great Zeal we have for his Maj's service & the welfare of his Subjects so we would not willingly be unfurnished with any sort of Learning & Knowledge yt might serve for so good a purpose.

That in Order here unto some of yor Sd Petitioners have for several years last past been at considerable charges to gratifie ymselves & have constantly taken in Mr. Bradford's Mercury at the expense of Ten Shill p Annum.

That besides the great Increase of necessary & useful Science which must have accru'd to ourselves upon this Account Great advantage must have arose from hence to the Publick Trade & Riches of this Colony in as much as we contributed our Share to employ many hands in the paper & printing Manufactures as by consulting learned Authors upon this Subject may more fully & at large appear.

That notwithstanding yor Sd. Petitioners cannot look upon their reading & studies as compleat for want of a certain paper printed Weekly by one Mr. Franklin of Phila. If therefore you w'd be pleased to give orders yt the said papers may be sent down to us We doubt not but you will soon be a Witness of our great improvements in many parts of Useful Learning.

And yor Sd Petitioners as in Duty bound shall ever pray &c.

The Rev. Mr. Bechet writes, September 25th, 1729, that one year ago he had taken charge of a fourth church, by name St. John Baptist.

The Rev. Hugh Neill to the Secretary of the S. P. G.:—"Dover, September 1, 1751.—I have since Mr. Ussher's departure, visited the County of Sussex several times, and find the two congregations in the country to be regular and numerous, but that in Lewestown appears to be small, I believe by reason of the Town going very much to decay."

1731. "From Pensylvania the Society have received the following Accounts: The Reverend Mr. Beckett, Missionary at Lewes, writes, That his Parish is much in the same State as when he wrote last. There are now in that Country 4 Congregations at 4 Churches, 3 of which Congregations are very numerous. He writes, that he lately officiated at St. George's Chappel, which tho' it hath been very considerably enlarged since his coming there, was not now able to contain above one half of the Hearers. He baptized that Day 5 White Children, & 3 Negroes. He remarks farther, that in about 6 Weeks time he had baptized in that Chappel, 10 White grown Persons, & 11 Negroes, besides a Considerable Number at the other Churches in this County. He adds farther, that he hopes it will appear from these Instances, that he hath been very diligent in his Mission, by promoting the Design of the Bishop of London's Letters, with regard to the Instruction of the Negroes in his Parish."

1732. "From Pensylvania, the Society have received the following Accounts: The Reverend Mr. Beckett, Minister at Lewis Town, acquaints the Society, That during the 11 Years which he hath been a Missionary, he hath constantly resided in his Mission, during which time, two new Churches had been built in that County, & two more which had been begun before his Arrival had been finished, so as to admit of the decent Performance of Publick Worship to Almighty God; that at each of these Places at times he hath constantly performed Divine Service upon all Sundays & Holidays, reading Prayers, Preaching, Catechizing the Children, Administring the Sacraments, & he can with Comfort say with Good Success, that during his Mission, above a thousand Persons, old & young, White & black, have been instructed in the Christian Faith & baptized, & many Persons are constant Communicants."

My Lord:—This is the first opportunity for London since I was honoured by your letter of September last. I never doubted but that my Commission was intended to be of the same extent with the Civil Government here, but then that it may be legally so, and is absolutely necessary that after the words Infra Provinciam Pensylvania should be added, Et Comitatus Novi Castri, Cantij & Sussesia Super Delaware, provided this be proper Law-

Latin for the Counties of Newcastle, Kent and Sussex upon Delaware. Our Lieutenants Governors Commission always mention these three Counties expressly after the province of Pensylvania, and by the Kings approbation they are appointed over the former Durante Beneplaicito, but over the latter without limitation. The right to these Counties is controverted not only between the Penn-family and Baltimore Ld. proprietor of Maryland, but the Crown (if I'm rightly informed) claims them as not granted to either of them, by their respective charters. Besides these counties have at present a different legislation, an assembly of their own, together with their own Judges & Courts of Justice. I'm sorry to give your Lordship so much trouble, but the design of the Commission can't be answered without the above addition, and some of the Clergy there at my last calling them together signified to me by their letters, that they did not think themselves obliged to meet me, seeing my Commission extended only to the Province of Pensylvania.

As to Mr. Hackets affair, our Governor did prosecute him, and though as I'm told there was no law in these Counties to found the action on, yet he being frightened submitted to the Court, and was fined 60 Lib. Ster. I can't, however, think the payment will be insisted on. I return your Lordship's most hearty thanks for the reasonable present of your excellent Pastoral letters. I distributed them according to directions, and hope they will have a good effect to preserve many from being infected by the profane principles of some here in public offices. I beg your Lordship's Benediction, and only add that I ever am with profound respect,

Your Lordship's Most Obedient servant,

ARCHD. CUMMING.

PHILADELPHIA, March 29th, 1732.

To the Honourable Society for propogating the Gospel in foreignn Parts.

THE HUMBLE PETITION OF WILLIAM BECKET THEIR MISSIONARY AT LEWES IN PENNSYLVANIA SHEWETH,

That your humble Petition hath been Missionary to the Hon Society for the Space of Eleven years and hath resided constantly in the place of his Mission Ten Years & a half in Lewes, in Sussex County, during which time (blessed be God), 2 new Churches have been built in this County & 2 that were raised before the arrival of yor Petitioner have been carried on so as to admit of the decent worship of A God in which places your Sd Petitioner hath given constant attendance alternately on Sundays & Holidays in preaching praying catichising administering the Holy Sacraments & other duties of his Function with good Success insomuch that above 1000 people Old and young white & black have been instructed & baptized in the Sd County by yor Sd Petitioner and many persons are Communicants of the Ch. of England. & that here are more people professing themselves members of the Sd Church than in any other County in the Government considered in proportion with Dissenters of all sorts that is to say, the Members of the Ch of England here are a great majority.

That there was a Presbyterian Minister & a Quaker speaker in this County at the time of your Sd Petitioner's Arrival but they have both now left the place without sending any one to succeed them so that now there is not any Preacher of any persuasion in this County except your Sd Petitioner.

That when your Petitioner had resided here for the space of 7 years or there abouts, being earnestly desirous to see his native Country once more and to settle some Affairs of his own there he did request the Hon Society for leave to that purpose which leave was kindly granted by the Sd Society.

But so it was that your Sd Petitioner could not as yet make use of the Indulgence granted him by the Sd Hon Society because yt no clergyman was to be procured to officiate in his absence & that upon many Accounts it would have been indiscreet & unsafe for yor Sd Petitioner to leave so great a Cure without any Pastor especially at such a juncture.

Upon this weighty Consideration your Sd Petitioner hath been content to set aside his own particular Inclination & Business at Present that he might the better serve the Ch of God & promote the good designs of the Hon Society.

That the labours & fatigues of yor Sd Petitioner have been very great in his Mission so yt some years besides performing the Offices of his Function he hath travelled at a moderate Computation 1632 miles to promote the good designs of the Sd Society & in other years when his Task has been the easiest no less than 1156 miles, so yt he was always obliged to keep 2 horses which are very chargeable to be maintained in a Town your Sd Petitioner having not any Glebe or Farm to Maintain them upon.

That the Parishoners of yor Sd Petitioner have been exceedingly kind to him during the whole time, by subscribing liberally towards his Support & maintenance (considering their poor circumstances) & by many other kind & good Offices, which has been a great encouragement to your Petitioner in the midst of his Labour. That besides what is already mencioned they have at this Time done an extraordinary Act of Kindness to your Petitioner A good Farm being offered to sale of about 400 Acres of Land with a good House on it a good Orchard of near 1000 fruit Trees, a good Barn Frame with a Kitchen & out Houses abt 7 miles from Lewes. They have advised him to buy it & promised to assist him unanimously to pay for it, that he may be enable to secure a more certain support for his Family.

And also yt no invitations from any neighbouring vacant Parishes in Virginia or Maryland (Many of which have been offered to him) may move him to leave them. Accordingly he hath joined them in a bargain with the Owner of the Sd Land &c the price to be paid for it is 270 pounds of this Currency. 160 pounds are to be pd down now, & 110 a year hence. Your venerable Board will see by a Copy of the Subscription which he has caused to be exemplified & sent over to you regularly attested how far the poor people of this parish were able to help your Petitioner in this Affair. A Testimony of their zeal for Religion & their Esteem for your Petitioner.

But as Lewes is a chargeable place being a small Sea Port on the Mouth of the great River Delaware where all European goods are generally sold at near 200 pr cent advance in Short & for as much as your Petitioner hath a numerous Family to maintain viz a Wife & 4 Children & hath been often times in Charity obliged to entertain

Ship wrecked & distressed people as well as in Civility to entertain Gentlemen & Strangers of the Communion of the Ch of England especially, who occasionally resorted to the place, and as a Clergyman must be given to hospitality as well as apt to teach Sr your Petitioner hath not been able to save any Money except only what may buy a Stock of Cattle & such Implements for Husbandry as are necessary upon a Farm & without wch it cannot turn to a profitable Account. Upon the whole your humble Petitioner desires the Hon Society to concur with his Parishoners in this Charitable Act that they will be pleased to bestow on your Petitioner something (whatever they in their wisdom & goodness shall think proper) towards paying for the Farm on which he is now settled, Or if not yt they will be so good as to advance a years Salary for him on the 25th of March next (when the Purchase Money is to be paid) and

Your Petitioner as in Duty bound shall ever pray &c.

APL. 15, 1732.

Letter to Dr. Humphreys.

REVEREND SIR.—I send you here with a Petition to the Hon Society which I must beg the favour of you to lay before the venerable board as also a copy of a subscription which my Parishoners have been so kind as to present me with, the better to enable me to buy a good Farm among them for my better settlement & support & that of my Family And I also shall send you a Map of Sussex County (my Parish) if I can get one truly and well drawn that so the Hon Society may the better judge of the inconvenience of my present situation with respect to the Several Churches here. When it is considered that the people here are generally poor, it will I doubt not appear to the Hon Society to be a very liberal Benefaction & yt I have not behaved myself ill among a people who are so desirous yt I should settle among them for life. If they could have raised money to have paid for the whole purchase ymselves, they did intend to have settled it as a Glebe for the use of the Societies Missionary for the time being. But money being exceedingly scarce here & they not able to advance the whole Sum, they have made me a present of what they could contribute. However if I die without issue (as God only knows what shall come to pass) I purpose in my last Will to bequeath it to the Hon Society.

The Purchase Money according to the Bargain made is to be paid as follows: 160 lbs. of this Country Currency is to be paid down now at my Entry on the Sd Farm (it being about 100 lbs Sterl) and 110 lbs Currency on the 25th day of March next being about 70 lbs Sterl.

You will be so good Sr as to lay these matters before the Hon Society and to let me know their pleasure herein with convenient speed that so I may know how to prepare myself for the latter paym't above mentioned.

The State of my Parish is much as usual so yt I do not need to trouble you with a particular Account of it at this time. Infidelity has spread much of late in some parts of this Government But (God be thanked) my Parish is pretty free from it. My Lord Bp. of London's letters &c have been of great use & service to Christianity in America, indeed every thing he writes is read here with great Esteem. We hear here yt some other of My Lds the Bishops & several other eminent Divines have employed their Pens in the Christian Cause, but being in this

Corner of the World I know not how to get any of them otherwise they would be of great use. My Parishoners are in great want of Ch Catechisms Prayer Books & Psalms of the New Version. That so they might bring up their Children more religiously. I remain

Revd Sir Your Most Obedt & Most Hum Servt,

LEWES, April 20th, 1732. WM. BECKET.

To the Hon Patrick Gordan Esqr Govr of Pennsylvania &c.

MAY IT PLEASE YOR HONOUR.—You have done me a great favour which you knew not of but which gratitude obliges me to acknowledge. The last year you were so kind as to recommend me in the handsomest manner to the late Governor of Maryland in order to procure me one of their best Parishes there. How I happen'd to be disappointed in that Affair I have already acquainted yor Honr. However your letter in my favour has at last had an effect more to my satisfaction & perhaps as much to my interest as if I had then succeeded—in the manner following.

My Parishoners observing that if they did not provide a Glebe or a Farm for me I should before long be obliged to accept of some vacant Parish in Maryland or Virginia where such a convenience might be had the better to support my growing family & knowing yt living constantly in a small Town was very chargeable to me, & being unwilling to part with me, they have unanimously joined with me in the purchase of a good Country House & Plantation to be settled on me & my Heirs. The plantation we have bought & to which I am now moved did belong to Mr. Davis (one of the Magistrates of this County) the quantity of land is about 400 Acres, abt 8 miles from Lewes. The Sum to be paid for it is £270. Of which my Parishoners have raised by contribution £150. Here is a good House Garden & Out Houses, & about a thousand fruit trees of several sorts, so yt I look upon myself now to be settled for life.

The situation of my new purchase is pleasant, & I hope will prove beautiful to my family, the Air is good & open in full view before my door lies Rehoboth Bay & the mouth of the Indian River well stored with excellent fish, cockles & Oysters Of which whenever you come down to Sussex I hope you will honor me so far as to take a taste.

And as I am much obliged to your Honr for several favours & kind Offices which you always did for me in the most cheerful & handsome manner so I did believe it would not be disagreeable to you to hear of the effect of your last years Letter in my favour & of my settlement under your Government. I remain Sr with the greatest gratitude & Esteem

Yor Honours most Obliged & Most Obedt Hum Servt

SUSSEX, May 9, 1732. WM. BECKET.

P. S.—My wife tells me there is a mocking bird sitting on 4 Eggs in a nest on a joyce in our Barn. If your Lady or any of your daughters will accept of a couple of the the young ones when they are feathered & fit to be carry'd, I will send them up the River by a careful Hand. But then I must desire you to order a Cage to be sent down by Mr. Stretcher or Mr. Willbank for there is no such thing as getting a handsome one here.

N. B.—Wm. Warrington pd 2s 6 the last year more than his due.

Letter to Revd. Mr. Cummings.

DEAR & REVD SIR.—Your Letters in my favour the last year to the Govr & Commissary of Maryland tho' they had not the Effect you intended have had a good one since here. The people of my Parish (finding yt if they did not provide for me I should ere long be obliged to move to some vacant Parish where my family might with more ease & less charge be supported have unanimously joined with me to purchase a good Plantation to be settled on me & my Heirs for ever, that so I may not be under any temptation to accept of any Maryland or Virginia Parish that may hereafter be offer'd to me.

We have purchased abt 400 Acres of good Land (abt 8 miles distant from Lewes) lying convenient enough for visiting the several Churches of this County. The purchase money is 270 lbs Currency. 110 lbs is to be paid down 60 lb to the Land Office & 100 lb a year hence. My Parishoners have given me by Contribution £150 pounds towards the purchase money (as you will see by a copy of their Subscription which I have inclos'd Upon this Plantation is a very good House & garden with good outhouses sufficient & upwards of a 1000 fruit trees of all sorts Rehoboth Bay, the Mouth of the Indian River and the Main Ocean lie in full view before my door. Here is plenty of fish of all sorts besides Shell Fish viz. Cockles Oysters & Crab Fish Abt 100 Acres of the land are cleared & improved the rest is all wood land, you may easily guess the late Owner is much in debt otherwise we should not have got such a bargain I mov'd my Family hither on the 30th day of March last and on the 25th of April all the Magistrates except a Quaker & a Presbyterian Justice (it being my Birth day) came to see me & wish me joy of my settlement among them for Life so yt you find that the Ch & State agree here very well. The leading men among them have pressed me to accept of the next Commission of the Peace but I have refused it & will not accept of it if you think it improper for indeed the proper business of my Function is more than enough for me. Pray let me know your Opinion when you write.

I leave it to your discretion whether it will be proper for you to let the Bp of London know of the generous present that my poor Parishoners have made me But pray let my good old Friend Mr Ross & Mr Hackett be acqted with the affair If you can excuse me from coming up the River to meet the Clergy (as usual) this Fall I shall take it as a great favour for I have a great sum to pay & none to Spend. If you have any papers to send home for the service of the Church let Mr Ross counterfeit my hand to them as he knows very well how I do and I shall be content. I remain Sr with the sincerest regard.

Yor Most obliged & Most affect Bror & Most Hum Servt

WM. BECKET.

PETTY PEOVER, May 10, 1732.

P. S. My Hum Service & my Spouses to Mrs. Cummings, to Mr. Moore & his Lady to Mr & Mrs Evans, Mrs Newmain & to that High Flyer Mr. Ammaud &c.

WEDNESDAY, July 28, 1736.

TO MY FRIEND DR. CHEW. A SYLLOGISM. 1736.

1. Whatsoever is asserted in the New Testament is undoubtedly true.
2. But the several Articles of the Athanasian Creed are derived from the N Testament.
3. Therefore every Article of the Athanasian Creed is undoubtedly true.

SR.—I promised you this Syllogism some years ago But did not think of it again till this Time Be so good as to pardon my forgetfulness You know Sir that most men are vain enough to imagine yt an Argumt that convinces themselves ought in Reason to convince others Whether this way of reasoning (as I call it) will have the same Effect upon you that it has upon me. I know not However let your own Reason judge for you, as it ought to do in all matters & believe me to be what I really am

Sir yor most Obedt Hum Servt WM. BECKET.

LEWES, July 28th, 1736.

MAY IT PLEASE YOUR HONOUR.—I heard but the other day the day the agreable news of your Recovery from your late dangerous Indisposition And tho' I live in so distant a Part of your Governmt yet give me leave to say that both Duty gratitude and Affection prompt me to congratulate with you upon your Recovery and to wish you a long continuance of your Health and yt we may long be happy under mild & just Administration. I have no notions of a good Governm but what suits with yours. My Tutors took care to instruct me that Honour & Honesty were the same Things That Truth & Candor are inseperable Companions of a Brave and a great mind That Falsehood & Lyeing proceed from Cowardice and meanness of Spirit. And that the refined Arts of Policy & Dissembling are built upon a rotten Foundation. They generally break out in Slander and Calumny And the Authors of them are attended with Scorn & contempt. If Truth and Justice and Generosity are Virtues, If a due & impartial Administration & Execution of Laws (without the utmost Rigor & Severity) render a Governmt easy & secure, then we have no Reason to be dissatisfy'd with yours. These Sir without flattery are my Sentimts of your Administration & if it had pleased God to have called you out of the World I shd have thought it my Duty as far as my Narrow Sphere extends, to have done the same Justice to your Memory which I now do to your character I beg leave with gratitude to remain

Sr yor Honrs most Obedt Most Hum Servt
WM. BECKET.

SUSSEX, August 4, 1736. GOVR. GORDON.

N. B. He dy'd the day Following.

Dy'd Aug. 5, 1736.

To The Memory of The Honourable Patrick Gordon Esqr late Govr of Pennsylvania & of the 3 Lower Counties on Del.

Plain Generous Honest Merciful & Brave
Each Good Man's Patron; Dread of every Knave
Wise without Craft; Corageous without Boast

With thee these Useful Virtues we have lost
Thy worth the British Hero Marlbro' knew
Under whose Care thy rising Genius grew
Tho' thou art gone thy Honour still remains
By valient Deeds in many long Campagnes
Our private thoughts thy Publick Virtues own
If envy rail; yet still let this be known
Thou brok'st no Promise sought no private End
Adieu! Thou Best of Governours & Friends.

Written Augt 14, 1736.

Verses to the Memory of Henry Brooke Esq. who departed this Life on Friday Feb 6 and was burried in the Church at Philadelphia on Saturday Feb 7th 1735–6—Printed in the *Mercury.*

Dignum laude virum musa vetat more.

Permit lamented Shade an humble Muse
In lowely Strains, thy worthy Name to Use
Thy Merit claim a Nobler Pen than mine
In lays polite & lofty like to thine
A Task so glorious Pope himself might try
And paint thy virtues fair before our Eye
In me my Grief supplies the want of Art
And gratitude sincere as was thy Heart
What useful Lessons did thy Virtues teach
Their Circle compassed all in human Reach
Thy Soul was uncorrupt, thy Genius strong
Thy Learning various in each different tongue
In thee the Greek & Roman Knowledge shone
Each Foreign modern language was thy own
No Science left unsearched, no Art could flie
Or scape the View of the discerning Eye
Each bright Idea printed on the Brain
Thy Memory Strong unerring did retain
From that clear fountain he whoever drew
Found all explained enforc'd improved anew
Each well chose thought in beuteous order lay
And clear Expression drove the Clouds away
Well chosen words so plain so sweet so strong
With Pleasure still we trac'd the Theme along
So when thick Fogs obscure the fall of Day
And men lament the absent Solar Ray
The pitying Sun breaks thro' with glorious light
And Hills and Plains restores to Mortal Light
Thy feet the paths of pure Religion trod
Thy Soul a living Sacrifice to God
No Affectation No abhorr'd Grimace
With which the Hypocrite obscures his face
Did 'eer thy Virtue or thy Honour stain
Twas all sincere & upright just & plain
Good Humour Manly Wit a generous mind
A Judgment strong a Fancy unconfin'd

A Friend to Virtue and a Foe to Vice
In all the conduct regularly nice
Happy the future Age that once shall see
In all respects a Parallell to thee
Thy great Contempt of Riches did we find
Give greater leisure to enrich thy mind
Knowledge & Virtue; these were all thy store
And to thy Talents still thou added'st more
O! couldst thou leave those Treasures to thy Friend
Than Gold more precious should the Gift descend
Yet still thy Bright Example shall remain
Our minds the great Impression long retain
From us thy Pattern never shall depart
Twill raise the Mind, and rectifie the Heart.

Written Mar 23d 1735–6

Henry Brooks Esqr was the Queen's Collector at Lewes in 1703—Vide Watsons Annals p. 258.

Letter to Dr. Humphreys.

REVD SIR.—1. It is a good while since I wrote to you concerning the State of my Parish my last I think was a Letter of thanks to the Hon. Society for their kind & generous Present of 20th The Reason why I have not wrote oftner is because the Circumstances of my Parish are much in the main as they us'd to be Except what I am going to relate to you If the Society had not been so good as to send me Relief so seasonably I knew not whether I should have been in the Church or the County Goal on Sundays But I do not blame my People for they are poor And tho' willing not able to do as they would. However now the danger is over I thank God and take Courage.

2d. The last time I went to the distant part of my Parish about a Month ago, I preached at the Ch of St. John the Baptist on Saturday 12 miles distant from my House And on Sunday the day following at St. Matthews Ch 25 Miles distant At the former Ch I baptis'd 11 Children and at the other Ch 10 and administered the Eucharist to 13 people. I visit those Churches about once a month and cannot do it oftner, they are at so great a distance.

It is necessary also that I not only tell you the Success of my Labours but also the discouragements that we meet with who are your Missionaries and I think this pretty common to us all. The Infidells or Deists (for they do not differ much here) under the Protection of a Quaker Influence have taught even the Common People, to call in Question not only the Reasonableness of Faith but the Truth of Fact in the O & N Testament So yt a great deal of our Conversation with them must necessarily turn upon proper Arguments to convince them of the Fallacy. You will easily guess by what I have wrote that our Task at this Time is as hard as the Infidells can make it.

P. S. Our Governour dy'd the 5th of this month. We have had very great Assistance from the Pastoral Lters of our Bishop among the the Few Learned & Well bred and discreet people that we have among us If there are any short and plain Treatises on the Subject published which are suited to the Capacitys of the meanest of the People (such as my Parishoners generally are) I would earnestly beg some Copies to be distributed among ym. I desire to remain always

Revd Sir Your most Obedt & most Hum Sert

WM. BECKET.

AUG 25 1736.

Great Good & Just could I but rate
My Grief and thy too rigid Fate
I'de weep the World to such a Strain
As it should deluge once again
But since thy loud tongu'd blood demands supplies
More from Brareus' hands than Argus' Eyes
I'le sing the Obsequies with Trumpets sounds
And write thy Epitaph with blood & Wounds.

Written by the Marquss of Montross on the Sands of Leith with the Point of his Sword 1648. Transcribed from Mr. Bickley August 25 1736.

MEMORANDUM.

The Revd Mr. William Black Rector of the Church in Accomack County in Virginia came the first Missionary to Lewes in Sussex Co. in Pennsylvania July 26 1708 and left the Mission in the Month of May 1709.

William Becket Missionary left London June 11 and arrived at Lewes Sepr 1st 1721 Born at Over Peover in Cheshire April 25 1697 The Son of John & Mary Becket.

Written Sepr 25 1736.

SIR.—I rec'd your very kind and handsome Lre some time ago, In answer of mine to the Govr who I heard was upon the Recovery I am sorry for the loss of your Family & yt of the Province. But he is gone and to speak in the Military language has march 'd off with Honour.

Or to express it in a graver Stile He is gone to the Spirits of just men made perfect I have sent you all the marriage Bonds I have by me (except one taken at the Marriage of Mr. Fenwick Stretcher which I have mislaid & cannot now find but will send it to you as soon as I light on it.) And I have sent you also 6 Blanck Bonds & Licences, the Bonds I have sent you filled up are in Number 17.

I have sent you my Account some Time ago, and I think that there are but 2 articles to be added to it viz £5 paid to Mr. Shaw March 12 1734/5 and paid also to him on your Acct. May 8 1736 £2 10s. 0d. which I have Receipts for, when you have added these to my Credit you will readily find how the Acct Stands.

I am sorry I had not the Opportunity of Granting the Blanck ones I send you back but the Govrs death prevented me.

The new Licences from our worthy President dont please me. They are not in the usual Stile nor directed to a Clergyman nor according to the Common Law and are lodg'd in the hands of Laymen. And we all know that it is but matter of Courtesy to make use of them. And I suppose the Clergy will bear it without complaining Home.

Because as the Scripture Sais, His Time is short. I beg the favour of you to make my Service acceptable to the Propr to your good Lady And all the Govrs Family and believe me to be

Sr. Yor most obliged & most hum Sert

DEC 14 1736. WM. BECKET.

MR. SECRETARY CHARLES.

Written on Thursday Apr 21, 1737 In a dangerous fit of Sickness.

I have taken several repeated bad colds the Winter past which occasioned a great constant Hoarsness so that I could scarcely be heard to read Prayers or preach, I took a journey to New Castle about New Years day which increas'd my Malady The Cold being very severe.

Mar. 19. I was wet to the Skin in a cold Rain after having felt a Pleuritic Pain in my right Side a Week whenever I cough'd.

Monday Mar 21. I was seiz'd with violent Vomiting & bleeding at the mouth the Shock having burst an Artery or a Vein Dr Fisher applied & administred several Remedies as Stypticks Emollients &c But on Tuesday Apl 19 Was oblig'd to take from me at least 24 oz of Blood. I am now under a Rule of Fasting, but in a weak Condition.

Misere mei domine & uxoris & liberorum & Jesum Christum Medicum Animae & Corporis maximum, Amen.

Written on St Georges Day Apl 23 being Saturday in the latter end of the 40 year of my age.

Me adhuc egroto & aere perfrigido

Non adhuc recit ver vix signum verio.

Written on my Birth Day Apl 25 1737 being exactly 40 years of age I was born at Over Peover in Cheshire on Sunday at noon St Marks day Anno 1697.

Written on Saturday Apl 29, 1738

I was 41 Years of Age 4 days ago, I recovered of my above menconed Malady in May last. Laus Deo soli. The Spring is forward The trees loaded with Leaves and Blossoms & the Earth cloathed with Grass this 29 Apl 1738 Nora. Penna.

Written on my Birthday Apl 25 1741 Aged 44 years Bona salute Laus Deo.

Address of the Clergy to Governor Thomas.

MAY IT PLEASE YOR HONR.—We the Clergy of the Ch of England licens'd for the Province of Pennsylvania beg leave to take this Opportunity of congratulating you upon your being appointed Governor of the Province of Pennsylvania & of the 3 Lower Counties on Delaware, and upon your safe arrival among us. We have no reason to doubt from your known Character of Justice & Integrity but yt you will encourage & protect us in the due discharge of our Sacred Function as your Worthy Predecessors have done to whose memory we owe all just gratitude and we doubt not of being happy under your wise and mild Administration as we have been under theirs We declare ourselves to be sincerely attatched to the British Constitution both in Church & State and to the present Happy Establishmt We have no private designs in view. No particular Faction to carry on. No party to promote in contradiction to the Laws, and the British Government and we hope those cannot be accounted the worst Subjects who readily embrace every part of our Happy Constitution. Our Duty is undoubtedly to pray for the King as Supreme, and for Governors as them yt are sent by him for the Punishment of Evil doers & the praise of them that do well. To promote the Xn Rel by serving God with discretion as well as zeal. To promote the Happiness of our Governor by teaching the people under our Care the duty they owe to those whom God has placed in Authority over them and to instruct them to live quiet & peaceable Lives in all Godliness & Honesty.

This Sr with the Devine Blessing and Assistance shall be the Constant care & Indeavor of

Yor Honours Most Obedt & Most Hum Servts

LEWES-TOWN, July 30, 1737.

Letter to Dr. Humphreys.

REVD SIR.—It is very fit that I give you an Acct of the State of my Parish not having troubled you with a letter for some considerable Time past. The Reason whereof is yt in general our religious Affairs are in a good measure in a Prosperous Condition Besides that in the beginning of the year I was visited with a dangerous Pleurisie which confined me to my house for 8 weeks and it was generally believed would have carry'd me off. But God was merciful to me & has restored me to my former State of Health, so yt I have been able for 2 months past to attend the duties of my Mission as usual. I contracted this disease by too adventerously exposing myself to the severities of a very Cold Winter Season in distant parts of the County where the Hon Society has placed me. We having 4 Churches & large Congregations yt zealously attend the Worship of God, I thought it would be a shame for the Priest to stay at Home notwithstanding the Rigor of the Season when the people show'd so much zeal & readiness to attend the Service of God.

To give you one Short Instance of the Success of my Labours thro' the Blessing of God, In the last Month (July) I baptis'd in the several Churches of this County 41 children which is no extraordinary number for the Time in a Summer Season. On the last Sunday but one I baptiz'd 12 children of the above Number On Whitsunday last at one of my Churches I had 21 Communicants. During the time of my Sickness for 3 Sundays I was utterly unable to do any thing the rest of the Sabbaths I was able to read Prayers & a Sermon of some Devine on that day when my Parishoners came to my House to visit me, During wch time I baptiz'd several Infants & 3 Adults.

There is no Missionary nor Clergyman of the Ch of England within 60 miles distant from Lewes so yt in my troubles, I have been called on in my journeys to baptize whole Families several Times. We labour under only 2 discouragements here, The first is (only) from our own People who tho' they freely attend Divine Worship yet are hardly induced to subscribe towards our Maintenance And (the second is) when they have subscrib'd they are hardly brought to pay us without a Law Suit which is a Remedy yt we apprehend might probably obstruct the good intents of our Mission & therefore is seldom made use of.

The second is Our Governmt is under the Influence of the Quakers, And as our President has taken upon him (as our Governors did formerly) to grant Marriage Licences so he has contrary to former usage lodg'd them in the Hands of Laymen of his own kidney or under his Immediate Influence To whom we are obliged to apply with much Ceremony and no small charge to our Parishoners to obtain a Marriage Licence I need to say no more on this Head than to desire to compare their avow'd Principles & Practices on this Point We find no Cause for this Evil but Patience. To prevent being further tedious I have no more to add but that I beg leave to remain

Reverend Sr

Your most Obliged & most Obed Servt

WM. BECKET.

LEWES, Aug 2d, 1737.

Letter to the Deputy Governor of New York.

MAY IT PLEASE YOUR HONR.—I have had several Letters from Mr. Harrison Missionary at Staten Island proposing an exchang of Mission between himself and me and yt we should join our Interests together to obtain leave of the Hon Society to grant & confirm the exchange As I have not the Honr to be of your Acqtance so I must beg leave before I ask a Favour to introduce myself to you by saying That I am Mr Brookes (your Kinsman's) Countryman That I was his most intimate Companion & Friend That he used humourously to call me his Confessor that he lodg'd & dieted in my House for some years, & yt he testified his Respect for me in his Last Will by leaving me his sole Heir & chief Extor.

When I have sd this I know yt I need to say no more to recommend me to some share of your Favour Mr. Abraham De Payster (the Tall) can assure you of the Truth of most of these Particulars.

And now Sr the favour which I would beg of you is That you would be pleased to Assist me with your Interest & Influence to promote the exchange of my Mission from Lewes to Staten Island I have no reason to desire it but that I live on a Country Plantation where I and my Family cannot have our Health as we have found by 5 years woeful experience In order to promote this Design I will wait upon you at N York as soon as the Spring opens if you are pleased to approve of it Be so good Sr as to Direct your Secretary to write me your Sentiments on the Subject for I shall not stir in it without your Consent & be pleased to acqt Mr. Commissary Vesey with the affair if you think proper Be pleased to give my Hum Service to your Lady & Miss Penelope tho' unknown (for they are both of my own Native Country Cheshire) and give me leave to say that I shall always remain

Sr Yor most Obedt & most Hum Servt W. B.

I will bring the Res of you & your Lady formerly wrote to Mr Brooke.

MAR 18, 1737–8

Lettr To the Rev. Mr. Harrison.

DEAR BROR HARRISON.—I was sick almost to Death when you wrote to me about the Exchange of our Parishes and cou'd not give you a satisfactory Ansr till now that I am got Hearty & strong again and now you may expect to see me at York very soon when the Spring opens if the Govr to whom I have wrote this day approves of the affair and my design is to act intirely in concert with you I met accidentally in Octr last at New Castle with the late Dean Berkley's Bror (the Dean is now Bp of Cloyne in Ireland) to whom I communicated the Affair He approves of the Exchange and has promised to facilitate it by writing to my Lord his Brother so yt we shall hardly meet with any difficulty in the fase For the remainder I beg leave to recommend you to the perusal of what I have this day wrote to your Governor. And as you will probably see me very soon so I need to say no more at prest but yt I am no Changeling But

Sr Yor old Friend & Bror & Hum Servt W. B.

MAR. 18, 1737–8.

Be pleased to write to me specially.

Letter to Dr. Humphreys.

REVEREND SR.—My last Letter to you contained in part an Acct of my Indisposition the last year which brought me very near the Grave This will bring you an account of my Recovery & yt I have been able thro' the Divine Blessing to perform the Duties of my Function the whole year past at the Several Churches of this County alternately as usual I have not laboured in Vain & thank God The 4 Churches of ys County have generally in good weather full Congregations I seldom baptize in one Sunday less than Three often six and sometimes more. I have at one Church 30 at another about 20 and at another 12 Communicants the last time I administred the Eucharist at the several Churches (For one of our Structures is a poor small Chappel lately built & inconvenient for that purpose.) The people are generally poor, willing but few of them able to contribute any thing to my support. But the Country-born as the People here call themselves are generally Professors of the Ch of England and are little inclined to either Bigottry or Enthusiasm. Quakerism decays strangely even in this Province the Nursery of it only for want of Opposition The Missionaries here are generally of Opinion That let it alone & it will die of itsself We study to be great & to mind our own Business. After having given you this brief Acct of the state of my Parish I must desire leave to lay before you and by your Means lay before the Hon Society a particular Case and beg leave yt it may be considered by way of Petition. The Revd Mr Harrison Missionary at Staten Island has often by letter desired me to sollicit from the Hon Society an Exchange of Missions between him & myself. The Reasons he gives me for it is some Uneasiness between himself & his Parishoners besides yt as this is a very private Corner of the World he desires to end his Days in Retirement being now about the Age of Sixty. The Reasons I have to beg leave to Accept of the Exchange are that I found by Eleven Years Experience that as Lewes was too changeable a place to support my Numerous Family so since I mov'd back into the Woods myself nor Family have never had our Health so well as usual. Tho' the Land be good yet it is situate among Swamps & Marshes Lewes Town which is a healthy place with the Hon Societies Salary will very well support a Single Person as He is But it is hard to subsist a Family. European goods being generally sold there at 300 ℔ Cent. The Church People of Staten Island as well as the Leiutenant Govr of N York are as I am well informed willing that the Exchange should be made if the Hon Society thinks fit. More especially because they want a man of Learning to assist in the Education of their Sons (*Absit arrogantia verbo*) the Parents being some of them rich and not only able but willing to be at the Expence of as good an Education as may be had for their Children. If the Hon Society judges that this Affair will be of any Service to Learning & Rel as well as to my Health & Interest I know they will grant the Prayer of my Petition. If not I must acquiesce. I desire always to remain

Revd Sir Yor Most Obliged & Most Obedt Hum Servt

WM BECKET.

LEWES, March 29, 1738

1738.—"The Reverend Mr. Becket, Minister at Lewis, writes April 22, 1738 That he was recovered from a very dangerous Illness; & through the Divine Blessing enabled to perform the Duties of his Function, & had not laboured in vain, the four churches in that County having generally full Congregations; and on Sundays he seldom baptizeth less than three, sometimes four, sometimes six; & hath at one Church thirty, at another twenty, & at a third twelve Communicants; that the Country-born People, as they call themselves, are generally Members of the Church of England; & Quakerism decays strangely, even in that Province designed to be the Nursery of it. He adds they have no Bibles but of the smaller Prints, & desires the Society to bestow on him one of the larger Print, & on his Congregation some Common Prayer-Books & Catechisms. The Society hath sent Mr Becket a Quarto Bible for himself fifty of Lewis's Exposition of the Church Catechism, to be distributed among his poor Parishioners."

PUBLIUS LENTULUS THE PROCONSUL FROM JERUSALEM TO THE SENATE OF ROME.—TRANSLATED FROM JEAN HUARTES.—Feb. 22d, 1724-5.

There has appeared in our days a man who is yet alive and furnished with the greatest Virtue called Jesus Christ whom the People name the Prophet of Truth and his disciples say that he is the Son of God. He raises the dead and heals the sick. His person is of a middle stature and strait & very agreable to sight. His visage is so venerable that those who look upon it are equally disposed to love & fear him. His Hairs are of the Colour of a Ripe Filbert and fall plain as far as his Ears and from thence to his Shoulders they are of the Colour of Wax but much brighter. From the middle of his forehead along the Top of his Head, his Hair is parted after the Fashion of the Nazarenes. His Forehead is smooth and most serene. His Face is without wrinkle or Spot of a Moderate Colour. For his Mouth and Nose there is no fault to be found with 'em. His beard is thick and like his Hair Its not overlong and grows forcke'd or parted in the Midst. His look is exceedingly sweet and Grave. His eyes piercing & very lively. When he reproves, he gives Terror, & pleases when he admonishes. He makes himself belov'd. He is gay with gravity. Never has he been seen to laugh but often to weep. His hands and arms are extremely handsome. He pleases much in conversation But uses it rarely. And when he appears with great Modesty. In a word in his whole air and behaviour he is the loveliest man that can be imagin'd.

Transcribed from Mr. Brooke's Translation, May 16, 1739.

To Mr. Whitefield.

REVD SR.—I rec'd your Pacquet & the Money & I thank you for your printed Pamphlets with the same degree of Sincerity which induced me to thank you for your Sermon. I am sorry Mr Grant pays his Debts with so ill a grace, to pay a debt and yet to use reviling language at the same time little [ ] of a Xn Spirit As to his accusing me before your Tribunal of Drunkenness I not only deny the Charge in General but his in a most particular manner. He is an open Lyar and I do assure you that I never drank a Bottle of Wine nor a Bowl of Punch (yt wicked Liquor as you term it) in company with him nor with any such paltry fellows in my Life, And us to himself I do certifie to you that he never was a common Drunkard to my Knowl' only he has a mind to creep up your Revd sleeve. But in these slanderous cases I always judge yt the Receiver is as bad as the Thief I heard a scandalous Storey of you in Lewes a fortnight before you arrived here publickly asserted yt you had kept a Girl in Man's Cloathes during your Travels to sleep with you & had now Shipt her off for England when you were blown. This Story was suprest'd as much as lay in us, by me & the rest of the Company out of Xn Charity a Doctrine wch I find you leave out of all your Sermons I have now done with being serious with you. But now to enter into the Rediculous part of your Doctrine & Conduct Your fathering Adams Sin upon us, your damning infants of a Span long, your accusing the Justice & Mercy of God by absolute Predestination, Your Inward feelings, wch are no evidence to any one (besides your self) your Faith without good works, your want of Xn Charity & damning like a Pirate (in the Xn Ch), all but yourself & your crazy followers. Your preaching against Xn Morality, your leaving my Church to go & preach in an open Balcony and to act the Mountebank when there was no occasion for it even after you had thrown about you Hell & Damnation Fire & Brimstone enough to have burnt a Wooden Frame As these and many more things were ridiculous, so I pardon you As to your empty censures, kicking about the Revd Dust of Dr. Tillotson above 40 years after his decease & your open abuses of our Revd Bishop yt now is. These things look like the highest Impudence. I conclude that Enthusiasm is a Sort of Wild fire yt leads men into Ponds & Ditches and for all yt the muddy fellows think they are in a good Road It will make men censorious & busy bodies and always disturbers of the publick peace & tranquillity. But this takes only with the Mob not by any means with men of a good understanding However when your beard is grown & your judgm't settled I still hope you will burn yor own works rather than Tillotsons & this I assure you will highly oblige.

Sr Yor Hum Servt WM BECKET.

JUNE 9, 1740.

P. S.—I cannot think you intended me an act of civility by yor Papers & Letters since you boasted to Capt Howell & your Crew concerning what you wrote to me &c. I rather take it to be the effect of your Spiritual Pride & Self.conceitedness.

Letter to Mr. Franklin in defence of Dr. Tillotson.

Sr.—As you have the Reputation of a man of candor, and do not make your Press the Engine of any particular Party you are desired to print these few lines in yor Gazette Which are a brief Refutation of what Mr. Whitefield has published agt A. B. Tillotson in his 3 letters.

The A. B. sais yt all yt the Gospel requires as necessary to these purposes (*i. e.* to mans justification & Salvation) is yt we perform the Conditions of the Gospel yt so we may be capable of Being made Partakers of the Blessings of it. And yet Mr Whitefield in a few Lines after in the same Lre sais, Here is not a Word menconed about the All-sufficient perfect & everlasting Righteousness & death of Jesus Christ as being the sole Cause & Condition of our being accepted by the Father Tis true indeed the A. B has not sd it in these very words but what He sais above is testamunt & comprehends it.

Is not Faith in Jesus Christ one of the conditions which the Gospel requires of us, in order to Salvation? The A B speaks in General & this Revd Gentleman only mencons one particular which is comprehended in his Grace's General assertion.

Is not believing in J C. one of the conditions of the Gospel? And does not he that affirms the whole affirm every particular part? So yt instead of refuting the A. B. he hath only refuted & exposed himself.

Faith is not all that the Gospel requires of us it is only one particular Condition of our Salvation.

This is the main Error that runs thro his Letters As to Dr Edwards, I have nothing to say of him He is dead, let him rest.

I am always concern'd at abusive language especially from a clergyman, But am still of Opinion yt the Reputation of Him whom he calls the Goliah of the Philistines But should have rather called the Great Champion of the Protestant Religion stands yet firm & unshaken,

I am Sr Yor hum Servt.

AUGT 26. 1740 B.

From the *Mercury* of Augt 14, 1740

The Congratulations humbly addressed to the Revd Mr Whitefield on his 68 preachments in 40 days, with the great & visible Effects of Meat & Money yt ensue'd therefrom.

Great Miracle of Modesty & Sense
Recount thy Prayers & recking up thy pence
Secure while these you tell & those you show
To meet yor great Reward, at least below
But waring lesser points for solid things
We find from whence thy Cash & Credit springs

How Pitious nonsense works on Knaves thy Tools,
When duely touched by corresponding Fools,
Scepticks no more contest thy pious Arts
Of crazing Noodles & of Cobbling Hearts,
When such amazing Prodigies arize
And Sin & Folly make us good & Wise
We see the Holy Proselytes expose
Their meekness Truth & Charity in prose
While in their Matchless Poetry is shown
Genius & Sense not much unlike thy own.

Letter to Governor Thomas.

May it Please Yor Honr.—I ought to ask yor Pardon for not waiting on you when I was in Philada The Reason was I heard you were very busy preparing to fit out the Troops. Your Assembly was sitting & other Matters & as for me I had but 4 days stay in Town. Pray Sr let these things and your good Nature plead my Excuse. There is another matter too in the case, I cou'd not sell my Bills of Exche & therefore cou'd not settle with your Secretaries Office for the Licences I had granted as I intended But this I think was rather a Misfortune than a Fault. But give me leave Sr to say that it was not Disrespect or Undutifulness that was the cause. I was well acquainted some years ago with your Character before you were my Govr from my Old Friend Mr. Brooke and I have lived to see what he said of you made good in your conduct since you were my Governor. A man must be very dull not to observe how much you were Supreme to an Obstinate Assembly by your Arguments And now by your Courage & Constancy maugre all opposition you fitted out your Quota of Troops for the Kings Service. And at the Same Time give me leave to say that I am glad that our Men of the 3 Lower Counties at least did their Part. Somebody has told me that our Great Men from Lewes as they call them, have given me a very bad Character to you. Men that rather insult than govern this County & that have turned all things upside down. Mr. Brooke is dead Mr. Till is moved and now the poor Parson is to be demolished. But not to meddle with Politicks wch is not my Province I am going to acqt you with the State of Rel here, Tho' my Churches are as full as ever yet Mr. Whitefield has dropt some of his Enthusiastic Venom at Lewes I have not been there this fortnight the Weather is so bad. But they have set up a Society in my absence I ask'd the Man that told me this what was the meaning of a Society. He told me they were to meet to sing Psalms & Hymns &c twice a week. There is no harm in the Affair, if there be no counter plot. But I cannot forbear suspecting that Whitefield & Tools have laid these Schemes all over America, to draw People to a dislike of our Church Doctrine Discipline & Government But Sr whatever Enthusiasts do or endeavor to do, let us stand fast to the Constitution convey'd down to us from our Forefathers both in Church & State. Let us not tear it to pieces but endeavor each Man in his Station to Support it. This is the sincere wish & shall always be the Endeavour of Sr

Yor most Obedt & Most dutiful Hum Servt

Jan 2, 1741 Wm Becket

As to News I beg leave to refer you to a Letter I have wrote to Mr. Till.

REVD SIR.—I was very sorry to hear from Mr. Commissary Cummings when I was at Phila in Oct last that the Letters & Parochial Acct of the Missionaries here were not come to your Hands. I never since I had your Orders neglected to write But tis probable My Letter came by some Vessel that fell into the Hands of an Enemy of which we have too many Instances here or Miscarry'd some other way. I find in my Note Book this Memm. Notitia Parochialis &c. Missa ad Philad Apl 30. 1740, Pro Anno precterito. It is scarce practicable that I should send to you so often as I ought being placed about 150 Miles from Philada our nearest Point yt trades to London but I shall not fail to do it as often as I can Mr. Commissary C. has my last Half Years Notitia &c to send to you.

The State of my Parish is somewhat changed from what it was, Tho' my Churches are as full on Sunday's as ever Mr. Whitefield having rambled over North America the last years, has with his Enthusiastic Notions very much disturb'd the minds of abundance of weak but perhaps well minded People by endeavoring to root out the respect which they had Entertained of the Church Service &c. He has Encouraged his Tools to set up Religious Societies as he calls them wherever he can. There is one at Lewes composed of some ch. People some Presbyterians & some Quakers, who meet twice a week, And many people are perpetually wrangling & disputing about Religion, I found his Industry this way had the same effect in many places where I preached the last Fall, for I travelled in Oct & Novr Last above 500 Miles & it was very visible in most places that where good seed had been Sown he had scattered Tares, so that what between Infidelity and Lukewarmness & Enthusiasm you may easily guess at the fluctuating State of Religion in many parts of our Colonies. I got but one copy of our Bishop's last excellent Pastoral Letter, but could heartily wish that I had some to distribute The Missionaries however are resolved to attend on their respective Churches carefully, and to wait the Event of these things with Xn patience We at first entertained him as a Bror. But when We perceived his design & looked upon him with an Air of Indifferency, he foresook both our Church & the Liturgy & has been a Field Preacher here as in England ever since.

I beg leave to remain Revd Sr yor most Obedt Hum Servt,

WM BECKET

LEWES, March 4, 1740-1.

It ought here to be remembered that our Govr & the Magistrates do not encourage Mr. W's unaccountable proceedings.

1740.—"The Reverend Mr. Becket, Missionary at Lewes in Sussex County, writes by a Letter dated June 11, 1740, That his People are constant Attendants on Divine Worship, insomuch that on Sundays more of them generally come to the Churches than they can contain: & that the Inhabitants of the upper Part of the County had petitioned the Society for a second Missionary, upon a most true allegation, that the four churches, each at a considerable distance from the other, in the County, are too much for him to attend; tho' he doth his best, & officiates once on a Sunday in every three weeks in three of them, & once in the middle of every week in the Church near the Center of the County. But by the great Fatigues resulting hence, he hath often contracted severe Illnesses, & begins now to grow in years; however, thro' the Blessing of God, he will go on chearfully to do what he is able in the Performance of his Duty in this great Cure, until the Society shall be pleased to appoint a second Missionary to it. It is not without very great Regret, that the Society hath found themselves obliged not to comply with this very reasonable Request for the present, thro' the very low Estate of their Cash. Mr. Becket hath baptized from the 30th of April 1739, to the 30th of April 1740, one hundred and eighteen Infants, & seven Adults, and the Number of his Communicants are generally about fifty."

Letter to the Secretary of the Society.

REVD. SR.—Accding to your instructions I now send you my Notitia But my Mission being 150 miles from any Sea Port trading to England it is impracticable for me to take a Sea Capts Receipt however I keep Copies of all the transactions you recommended.

I can with great Pleasure now inform you that we have lately finished the inside of our Church at Lewes with a good plain Wainscot the Roof is arched & we intend to paint it. This considering the Peoples poverty & the great scarcity of money is no small piece of work in this place. In the month of May last when I went to visit 2 of the most distant Churches in this County I baptized 57 children in two days time and in a corner of Maryland near me where I went to visit the people at their request in one day I baptized 9 children.

Thus Sr the good Designs of the Society by the Blessing of God prosper in our Hands. But not without opposition This puts me in mind of the Parable But when the Blade was sprung up & brought forth fruit yn appeared the Tares also. So the Servt of the Householder came & said to him Sr didst thou not sow good seed in the Field from whence then hath it Tares—To apply this—Mr. Whitefield hath done more mischief in America by reviling the Clergy & misrepresenting Xanity than all the Dissenters put together.

To tell you another Affair of Moment which tho' it ought by no means to be made publick so I think it ought not to be kept secret from you. The fine Church at Philada had undoubtedly been finished long ago had it not been for the pride & peevishness of our late Commissary whose groundless & needless jealousie of an English Clergyman threw the City into Parties put a stop to that great Work, & had almost made parties between the Clergy, But I hope all this died with him I know where he laid the blame but it was not right in him to do so. There is one favour I would beg of the Society if I may obtain it That they wou'd be so good as to bestow upon me or add to their Library here, Dr. Prideaux's Connection with the Map's? A Gent in this County has the Book, but the Map's are not in it nor to be had at Philada. You know how necessary they are to the clear understanding of that excellent History & how necessary for a Clergyman. My churches generally all the Summer Season have more people attending devine Service than they will hold so that I am often obliged to preach under the green trees. This notwithstanding all my difficulties in so extensive a Mission is no small pleasure, & encouragement to

Sr your faithful & Most Hum Servt WM BECKET.

LEWES, Octr 16, 1741.

P. S.—I am poor and so are my people so yt they are able to contribute very little to my support. The 20th part of the Ch. people dont live in Lewes, which are in this County, I must ride generally 40 or 50 miles every week sometimes over 60 or else I cannot do the duties of this County. A Horse lasts me a year or 2 and a suit of cloaths half a year. Bills of Exchd are lower'd & the price of goods much raised since the War. Can the Society afford to make me any addition for visiting distant Churches, Or must I be content to wear homespun Cloth as they call it here? Be it as it will I shall endeavour to be content I have not forgot the last Sermon I heard at St. Pauls by Dr. Maugey on these Words, No man having put his hand to the Plough & looking back is fit for the Km of God. I have faithfully distributed all the Books and small tracts sent by the Society here is indeed great want of more if they could be afforded.

1741.—"The Reverend Mr Becket, Missionary at Lewes, by a Letter dated October 16, 1741, writes, that the good Designs of the Society prosper there, but not without Opposition; however, all the Summer Season he hath more Persons attending Divine Service, than his Churches will hold; & he is often obliged to preach under the green Trees; & in the month of May, when he visited the most distant parts of his Mission, he baptized 57 children in two days; & stepping into a corner of Maryland to visit some People at their earnest Request, he baptized nine Children there. Mr Becket adds, that the Church of Lewes hath been lately wainscoted on the Inside in a plain decent Manner, & the Roof is arched, & will be painted"

Letter to the Secretary of the Society.

REVD SR.—On the other Half of this Sheet you will find my Notitia &c. By adding 52 persons & Children I baptized this half year to 86 baptized the last half year it appears yt I have baptized 138 in the last Twelve months. My churches are full every Sunday even at this Time of the year but in Summer they will not hold the people so yt I am often forced to preach in the Church Yard under a Shady Tree. But as to the people of the Town of Lewes in Particular who are a small mixture of all persuasions (Churchmen Quakers Presbyterians Whitefieldians i. e. Enthusiasts & Freethinkers) I must not conceal from you that they are for the most part a sad set of Mortalls I cannot give you a better idea of them yn to imagine yourself at Deal or Dover. They have lately beat the King's Coll. when in the Xn of his office almost blind and because at his request I read an Act of Parliament appointed to be read in Churches tho' they cannot for shame beat me yet they have not spared to ridicule me behind my back And have laid a Plot to starve me For tho' yesterday at the Church of Lewes, I had a full congregation yet when my Subscription was handed about for the Current Year Most of the People went out without signing a penny. Only Ten persons among them staid & subscribed Ten pounds Five Shillings currency among them equal to about £6 8s. 0d. Sterling But what is in the bottom of all this I am told by my Friends & I greatly suspected it is because when I was summoned before the Commissioners in Chancery above a Year ago in the Cause depending between Ld Baltimore & Mr. Penn I was obliged to declare upon Oath some Truths which it seem make against the Pennsylvanians, so that their creatures & Dependants have made a Party & laid this Scheme. I have kept my temper and I hope shall keep it not murmuring nor offering to return Evil for Evil. But shall study to be quiet & mind my own Business. When you write again be pleased to let me know what the Hon Society sais about my petition for some allowance for serving Distant Churches as menconed in my last. I remain Revd Sr Yor Most Obedt & Hum Servt WM BECKET.

MAR 29, 1742.

Letter to the Secretary of the Society.

REVD SR.—I acqted you in my last of March 29 with the State of my Parish (a whole County) and it is much in the same state as yet viz. My Churches are full on Sundays & Holidays & in the Summer my Churches (4 in number) will not hold the Congregations, so yt I am often obliged to preach under the green Trees for the want of Room & the sake of fresh Air & Shade

Pray Sr excuse me to the Treasuries for drawing quarterly this year. My Necessities urged me I carried my only Son to the Grammar School in Philada (a hopeful youth of 15) in May who dyed alass on the 4th of July of a Bloody flux, and I had no way to pay the necessary Charges but by trespassing on the Hon Societies goodness.—This is a sad Subject & my tears will not suffer me to write any more upon it. Be so good as to lay before the Hon Society my Petition to have something allowed for visiting distant Churches. There is no Clergyman yt lives within 50 or 60 miles of me and I sometimes every year am several days from Home on this very Acct. and have many times travelled from 60 to 100 miles as Reason & Necessity have required I have the pleasure to acqt. you now yt Enthusiasm abates as fast as it once increased here Mr. Whitefield's followers have recanted some of them (the most considerable, in Print. And the truth is your Missionaries have conquered & convinced them not so much by opposition as by Patience and by Studying to be quiet and to mind their own Business. You will find my last year's Notitia on the other half Sheet. So wishing yt all of us may be found worthy in Some measure of the Sacred trust reposed in us at the great Day I remain Revd Sr Yor most Obedt Hum Servt WM B.

LEWES IN PENNS., Sept 26, 1742.

1742.—"The Reverend Mr Becket, the Society's Missionary at Lewes, writes, that his Churches, (four in number) are full on Sundays, & in the Summer-season he is often obliged, for want of air & room, to preach under the green Trees; & now Enthusiasm abates as as fast as it did once increase there. The Truth is, as Mr. Becket well observes, that the Societys Missionaries have conquered it not so much by Opposition as by Patience, & a strict observance of the Apostolical Precept of *studying to be quiet & to do their own business*.

Subscription List to Buy William Becket a Farm.

We whose Names are here unto subscribed do promise to pay or cause to be paid to Wm Becket Missionary at Lewes or Order the several Sums annexed to our respective Names in Money or Country produce within the space of twelve months from the date hereof in Order to enable him to buy the Plantation of Mr. Samuel Davis in Angola Neck for his better settlement & support among us.

Witness our hands this 25th day of March 1732. Note of the said William Becket shall hereafter leave this County & accept of another Parish he doth oblige himself hereby to repay to the Ch Wardens the sums which the people respectively advance towards supporting the next Minister of the Ch of England which shall be his Successor in the Sd County.

Lewes & Rehoboth Hundred.

Henry Brooke	£5	0s.	0d.
Anderson Parker	3	0	0
Simon Kollock	5	0	0
Ryves Holt	3	0	0
Jacob Kolloch	5	0	0
John Jacobs	3	0	0
Richard Henman	5	0	0
Jonathan Baily	5	0	0
John Clowes	3	0	0
John Welbore (Parish Clerk)	1	0	0
Joseph Pemberton	3	0	0
Cornelius Wiltbank	2	0	0
Thomas Bluett (Attorney)	2	0	0
William Field	3	0	0
Henry Fisher	3	0	0
Jacob Willbank	2	0	0
Abraham Hood	1	0	0
John Aston	0	15	0
Comfort Jenkyns	1	0	0
Jane Hirons	1	0	0
Maria Kollock	2	0	0
John Hubrey	1	0	0
Robt Smith (a Presbyterian)	3	0	0
Jacob Phillips	4	0	0

Indian River Hundred.

John Prettyman	£2	0s.	0d.
Woodman Stoakly	2	0	0
William Warrington	1	0	0
Geo Parker	1	0	0
Wm Burton	1	10	0
Peter Robinson	1	0	0
Wm Williamson	0	10	0
Elias Hauzer	0	12	0
Wm Burton, Junr	0	15	0
Geo Venam	0	10	0
John Hill	0	10	0
John Smith	0	5	0
Robt Smith	0	5	0
Wm Woodstock	0	10	0
Richd Paremore	0	10	0
Saml Carey	0	18	0
Wm Waples	2	0	0
Saml Hauzer	0	10	0
Richd Poultney (a Quaker)	1	10	0
Wm Prettyman	1	10	0
Ben Stockly	1	5	0
Ann Burton (widow)	2	0	0
John Parsons	1	5	0
Thomas Leatherbury	1	0	0
Job Barker	2	0	0
Alexr Herring	1	0	0
Thomas Marriner	1	0	0
William Marriner	0	10	0
James Fox	0	10	0
Hen Brereton	1	0	0
Francis Wolfe	0	10	0
Cord Hazard	0	10	0
Thomas Warrington	1	0	0
Oliver Stoakley	1	0	0
Isaac Atkins	0	10	0
William Atkins	0	12	0
Joshua Stoakly	0	10	0
Charles Dogharty	0	10	0
Wm Hudson	0	5	0
Jno. Williams	0	10	0
Wm Butler	0	5	0
John Walls	0	10	0
John Price	0	6	0
Saml Hudson	0	6	0
Thomas Foster	0	10	0
Edwd Rickards	0	10	0
Cloud Fowler	0	10	0
Booth Jones	1	0	0
Daniel Nalwod	0	10	0
Jos Hazard	1	0	0
John Atkins	1	0	0
John Russel Senr	1	0	0

Wm Maccalley	£0	10s.	0d.
William Prettyman	0	10	0
William Day Junr	0	10	0
John Russel Junior	0	10	0
John Day	0	10	0
Wm Robinson	1	0	0
Thos Marriner Junr	0	10	0
Richd Burton	0	10	0
Thomas Bagwell	1	0	0
William Wolfe	0	10	0
Robt Burton	0	5	0
Thomas Lyrah	0	10	0
Rise Wolfe	0	10	0

Cedar Creek Hundred.

William Till	£5	0s.	0d.
John May	2	0	0
Abraham Wyncoop	2	10	0
Saml Watson	1	0	0
Thomas Davis Junior	1	10	0
Luke Watson	1	10	0
Nehemiah Davis	0	10	0
Saml Holburt	7	10	0
Joseph Hickman	0	10	0
Griffith Jones	0	10	0
Thomas Price	1	0	0
Isaac Watson	1	0	0
Caleb Cirwithen	0	10	0
Wm Carpenter	0	10	0
John Jones	0	10	0
Elizabeth Watson Wid	0	12	0
Mary Watson Wid	1	0	0
Daniel Bonler	0	10	0
Thomas Davis Senr	1	0	0
Henry Draper	1	0	0
Alexr Draper	5	0	0
John Hunter	1	0	0
Costen Townsend			
Joshua Hickman	0	15	0
Paris Chipman	1	0	0
Abraham Parseley	1	0	0
Thomas Goldsmith	0	10	0
Richard Jacobs	0	10	0
Ann May wid	1	0	0
William Darnley	1	0	0
Sarah Watson Widow	0	15	0
Christopher Phillips	0	15	0
Thomas Groves	0	15	0
Robert Caldwell	1	0	0

1743.—"The Reverend Dr. Jenney, the Commissary of this Province in the room of the late worthy Mr. Commissary Cummings, acquaints the Society by his Letter dated

Nov. 4, 1743, of the Death of Mr Beckett, the Society's Missionary in Lewes-Town in Sussex. This Gentleman had been fixed there by the Society in the year 1721; & from that year to the time of his Death, in the last Summer, he had laboured with great Diligence, & such Success in the Pastoral Office throughout that County, that according to the last letters received from him, the four churches in it under his care were so thronged, that in the Summer Season he was frequently obliged to preach under the green Trees for the Conveniency of Room & fresh air; he is much lamented by his congregations, & hath left behind him the character of a pious, faithful, & orthodox Pastor. The said congregations having petitioned the Society for the Reverend Mr Usher, the Society's Missionary at Dover in Kent County, who took care of & officiated to them during Mr. Becket's Sickness, as much as was consistent with his proper Care of the Church of Dover, to succeed Mr. Beckett in the Church of Lewes; & Mr Usher himself requesting it likewise, they have removed Mr Usher to the Church of Lewes, & appointed the Reverend Mr. Morris, lately employed by them in New England, at his own request, to succeed Mr Usher at Westchester."

Copy. Last Wil and Testament of William Becket.

In the name of God and of the Ever Blessed Trinity, I William Becket missionary of the Society for the propagation of the Gospel in foreign parts being sound in judgment and memory but weak in body do make and ordain this my last will and testament in manner and form following: I resign up my soul to God who gave it humbly hoping for pardon and forgivness thro Jesus Christ the Savior of me and of all that believe in him, and my body I commit to the earth to be decently interred by my executors according to the rites and usages of the Church of England, and desire it may be buried between my two wives in the Church Yard of St Peters, Lewis, in hopes of a joyful resurrection at the last day.

As to my worldly estate I dispose as follows; I will that my just debts be paid and discharged, and sence I have already given to my son-in-law William Futcher and his wife goods and chattles by building him a house giving him a negro and sundry other goods to ye value of £100 for which he and his wife are very ungratefull, I give each of them and english shilling and no more of my estate.

As to my house all my buildings my pattent and warrant lands amounting to about five hundred and fifty acres I give to be equally divided between my two daughters Elizabeth and Susannah to them and their heirs forever.

My negroes Jenny and Oxford I give to my said two daughters, but order that she that hath Oxford pay to the other a reasonable price of exchange and I leave my two said daughters executrixes of this my last will and testament.

I leave my priests habits to any of my reverend brethren that shall preach my funeral, I leave to my good old friends Ryves Holt Esq. a gold ring now on my ring finger, and to Capt. Cord Hazzard my best riding saddle that I may have at the time of my death.

I give my two daughters aforesaid, free leave to keep or dispose of my house land &c as they may see convenient but then I will that no deed of sale for the lands, till they have advised with the two Gentlemen above and the hand of one or both of them is to the deed be valid, and I desire them to be supervisors of this my last will and to advise my children for the best, I declare this to be my last will and testament having no other.

Signed sealed published and declared to be the last will and of the testator in the presence of us. WM. BECKET [SEAL.]

Tests I. P. PLASKETT
ANN PLASKETT
CORNELIUS BURTON

The words Acres, Funeral, and, be valid, were interlined before the sealing and delivering hereof.

I William Becket missionary of the society for the propagation of the Gospel in Foreign parts do by this codicil to my last will and testament give and bequeath to my son-in-law William Futcher my best suit of clothes,

In witness whereof I have hereunto set my hand and seal this 7th day of August Anno Dom. 1743.

Signed and sealed in presence of. [SEAL.]

1768.—"The Revd Dr Smith, Provost of the College of Philadelphia * * * incloses letters from the Mission of Trenton, backed by recommendation of the New Jersey clergy, in favor of Mr Thomson, who sollicits to be removed thither, as does Mr Andrews of Lewes, from Sussex on Delawar, on account of the unhealthfulness of the place, & would gladly accept of York County, & take care of Cumberland too till another missionary can be got. In this the Society have so far Concurred, that they have given Mr Andrews leave to remove to the Mission of York & Cumberland, provided he will take the whole duty upon him, as Mr Thomson did before, & promise to Continue in it without a prospect of having the Mission divided."

1769.—"By several letters from the Revd Dr Smith, Provost of the College in Philadelphia, the Society are made acquainted that due care has been taken by him of the Mission at Oxford. That Mr Thomson is settled at Trenton, & Mr Andrews at Cumberland. That Mr Lyon came to see the Gloster & Waterford Mission but not finding it answer the expectations given, & there being a greater necessity that the Lewes Mission vacated by Mr Andrews, should not be left destitute, he with the advice of the Philadelphia Clergy, removed thither, & having since earnestly sollicited to be placed there, the Society have consented to it, being in hopes of providing soon for the Gloster mission."

1771.—"Several letters have been received in the course of the year from the Rev. Mr Lyon. Missionary at Lewes, by which it appears that in one year he had baptized 267 white infants, 2 adult slaves, and 11 infant slaves; married 39; buried 18. That, he had been urged to go back often to the extremes of the County, where he has had large Congregations of grown persons, who never before attended public worship. That, his mission is growing & promises fair; & his health somewhat better; but at his first coming, he & his family suffered much by sickness, which proved fatal to his wife, & one other in the family."

1772.—"The Reverend Mr Lyon, Missionary at Lewes, writes that he officiates in three churches, & at other times, preaches in the remote parts, as far as to the borders of Maryland."

1774.—"Upon the joint recommendation of Dr Peters, Dr Smith, and Mr Duche, the Society have appointed Mr Tingley to the Mission of Lewes, vacated by Mr Lyon's acceptance of a parish in Virginia, And they have the satisfaction to hear that he is a diligent Missionary, & highly acceptable to his People."

"The Rev. Mr Lyon, late Missionary at Lewes, acquaints the Society that between Easter & November he baptized 129 white & 6 black infants, 1 black & 16 white adults; & recommends the forest part of the mission to the attention of his successor, the Rev. Mr Tingley, by whom the Society are informed that St George's at Indian River, though not mentioned in former Abstracts, is a part of his mission, that he frequently officiates in an old ruinous church in the forest to a considerable number of poor people, who have no other opportunity of public worship; & he does this often on Sundays, upon his return from St George's, with great fatigue to himself, that he may not take them off from their labour in the busy part of the year. During the Summer season he frequently reads prayers, preaches, & baptizes, on Mondays, in a private house, in Cedar-Creek Forest on account of it's distance from the Church. The three Churches of his mission are in general well filled, & the people very attentive. In each of them he administers the sacrament four times a year; his Communicants are about 110; he hath baptized 202 white & 43 black children & infants, 6 white & 13 black adults; marriages 36, burials 14. On every Friday afternoon he catechises the children at Lewes & hears them repeat portions of the Psalms, which he gives them to learn every week. After the Sunday's evening service he catechizes the negroes in the church; & explains the Catechism to them in the most familiar manner."

1775.—"By a letter of last June the Society have the first notice from Mr Tingley of his receiving his appointment to the Mission of Lewes. The delay, he says, was occasioned by the mis carriage of a letter from Philadelphia. He assures the Society of his constant attention to the duties of his office, & encloses the testimony of the church-wardens, which does honour to Mr Tingley, & induces the Society to believe that he may & will be very useful in those parts."

List of Subscribers to the building of St. Peters Church in the Town of Lewes which was raised on the 6th of October, 1722:

Name	£	s.	d.
Hon. Sir Wm. Keith, Bart. late governor	£5	0s.	0d.
Henry Brooke Esq	5	0	0
Capt. Jonathan Bailey	5	0	0
Mr. Richard Hinman	5	0	0
Mr. Simon Kollock	5	0	0
Wm. Becket, Missionary	5	0	0
Mr. Preserved Coggeshall	4	0	0
Mr. Ryves Holt	4	0	0
Mr. Jacob Kollock	3	0	0
Mr. Anderson Parker	3	0	0
Mr. Abram Wiltbank Senr	3	1	2
Mr. William Rodeney	3	0	0
Mr. Samuel Rowland	3	0	0
Mr. William White	2	10	0
Mr. William Asheton	1	3	8
Mr. Thos. Lawrence	1	0	7½
Mr. Robert Asheton	1	10	0
Doct. Thomas Graeme	1	3	7¼
Mr. Isaac Miranda	1	3	7¼
Mr. Thomas Sober	1	3	7¼
Mr. Peter Graeme	1	3	1¾
Mr. Richard Willing	1	3	7
Capt. Saml. Spofforth		11	11
Capt. Gruchee		11	8¼
Andrew Hamilton Esq	1	18	0
Berkley Codd, Esq	2	6	9
Col. St. Leger Codd	1	3	1½
Cornelius Wiltbank	3	0	0
Richard Paynter	2	0	0
Capt. Thomas James	1	3	5½

Mr. Ebenezer Empson	£1	0s.	0d.
Mr. Benjamin Godfrey	1	10	0
Mr. Woodman Stoakley	1	0	0
Mr. Samuel Lowman	1	3	6
Col. John French	2	10	0
Capt. John Price	1	0	0
Joseph Cord	1	0	0
Albertus Jacobs	1	0	0
Nicholas Maclander	1	0	0
Jeremiah Claypoole	1	0	0
Capt. Joseph Royall	2	0	0
William Godwyn	1	10	0
Mrs. Martha Johnson	2	0	0
John Russell	1	0	0
Thomas Stoakley	1	0	0
Robert Cornwall		5	0
	£96	6s.	5¼d.

and since the arrival of the Honourable Parrick Gordon, Esq. when he came to visit this part of his Government he gave five pounds towards finishing the gallery. Mr. Joseph Pemberton also has undertaken as a benefaction to this Church to cause the front of the Gallery to be wainscotted with black Walnut at his own proper cost and charge which work is now (1728) going on.

Account of the Building and state of the Churches in Sussex taken from a letter written by Wm. Becket Missionary at Lewes to the Venerable Society of England dated Oct. 11th. 1728. "The dimensions of the Church at Lewes is as follows, viz. 40 feet in length 24 broad, the height of the wall between the plate and sill is 15 feet. The Frame is of Wood the Roof is covered with Cypress Shingles and the wall with boards of the same wood. The inside of the Church is not yet finished, only the floor is laid, and the walls wainscotted with Cypress plank as high as the tops of the pews. The Pulpit, reading desk, Communion Table and Rail are handsomely built of black Walnut—and the pews are all made of pine plank.

The situation of this church is very pleasant standing on a rising ground in the middle of the town and having a view of Cape Henlopen grown over with cedar and fine trees which lies beyond the River of Lewes to the Eastward, sheltering the town in a great measure from the violence of the winds that blow off the great Atlantic Ocean. To the Northward and N. West we have a view of the great bay of Delaware. The greatest advantage of this situation is, that the N. West winds blow with full scope down Del. Bay and directly up Lewes river on the town which makes it perhaps one of the healthiest spots on the Globe—but I must not forget that I am writing an ecclesiastical not a natural history, pardon therefore this digression and we proceed——

The number of people frequenting this church I reckon at a mean computation about 150.

The first settlers of this County, were for the far greatest part, originally English, some few however there are of Dutch families, but of late years great numbers of Irish (who usually call themselves

Scotch Irish) have transported themselves and their families from the North of Ireland into the Province of Pennsylvania and have distributed themselves into the several Counties where Lands were to be taken up, many families are settled in the County of Sussex. They are Presbyterians by profession. They have a minister here of the same Nation whom they maintain by contribution and have two meeting houses in this County, one at the Cool Spring, 8 miles distant from Lewes, another in the town of Lewes, which being much decayed they have laid the foundation of another the last year close by the old one, the building is of brick, they are now carrying it on with dilligence so that the roof is likely to be raised, as I am told before the end of this present year. The numbers of people and their respective profession in my parish will be the best seen by inserting the copy of a Letter from Mr. Holt, High Sheriff of this County.

"SIR:—The Taxable inhabitants in Sussex are (at a mean computation) one year with another about 420, of which 350 are heads of families viz.

Churchmen	215
Presbyterians	120
Quakers	15
	350

and allowing 5 persons to each family the number of souls will be 1750. The above is as near the truth as I can possibly come, without a strict Poll was to be taken, I am

"Sr yr very humble Servt.

"JULY, 1728. "RYVES HOLT"

So that according to this computation, the number of souls is as follows:

Church people	1075
Presbyterians	600
Quakers	75
Whole number	1750

The Quakers have one meeting house in this County 7 miles distant from Lewes, but at present they have no teacher there, however they hold silent meetings, unless some travelling preacher or "friend" (as they call them) happen to come this way.

The inhabitants here live scattering generally at ½ a mile or a miles distance from one another except in Lewes where 58 families are settled together. The business or employment of the Country Planters is almost the same with that of an English farmer, they commonly raise wheat, Rye, Indian corn and tobacco and have store of Horses, Cows and hogs. The produce they raise is commonly sent to Philada 150 miles from here to purchase such European or West Indian commodities as they may want for their family use—or also to N. York or Boston. The people here have generally the reputation of being more industrious than they of some of the neighbouring counties; this last year there was a great scarcity of corn in Maryland and in this government except in this County which supplied them with large quantities in their necessity. This may be looked on as a mark of their care and diligence and an omen of their future Riches & success.

The distance of the Churches from each other is thus computed, from St. Peters at Lewes to St. Georges, South 9 miles, from St. Peters to St. John Baptists West 14 miles and from the said church to St. Matthews near N. West, 25 miles, again from St. Georges to St. John Baptists, 9 miles, from thence in a circuit Road to St. Mathews 12 miles.

But then we are a very great distance from any other churches that are supplyed with clergymen—for example my nearest neighbours of the clergy are the Revd. Mr. Fletcher of Somerset County in Maryland 60 miles distant, the Revd. Mr. Adams of the same County and Province 70 miles distant and the nearest Missionary to this place, is the Rev. Mr. Ross at N. Castle 115 miles distant.

The roads in my parish are very commodious for travelling, being level and sandy so that people usually come to church Winter and Summer, some 7 or 8 miles and others 12 or 14 miles which is no strange thing, but very common among the inhabitants of America.

As yet there have been no donations to the Church or Missionary here besides the annual contributions towards his support, which depend entirely upon the pleasure of the contributors; only one which I ought in gratitude to mention in this place which was a Legacy of ten pounds left me in the Last will of Berkley Codd, Esq. One of the Judges of the Supreme Court for this County, who died in the year 1724 and some other Legacies and gifts which have demonstrated, not so much the Riches, as the good will of the Donors. And that the circumstances of the people and their degree of zeal to promote the Christian Religion may be the better judged I have inserted a copy of the last Subscription towards the support of the Societies Missionary at Lewes."

Note.—This was omitted by Mr. Beckett in his copy of this letter. —D. R. K.

And now in answer to the remaining part of the queries, the truth is there is no house nor land provided for the minister nor any Library but that which the Hon. Socy. was pleased to allow, when they sent over the present Missionary, and there is no public school in all the County, the general custom being, for what they call a neighbourhood (which lies some times 4 or 5 miles distant, one part from another) to hire a person for a certain sum and term to teach their children to read and write English, for whose accommodation they meet together at a place agreed upon, cut down a number of trees and build a log house in a few hours, (as illustrious as that in which Pope Sixtus Quintus was born) whither they send their children every day during the term for it ought to be observed by way of commendation of the American Planters nowadays, that whatever pains or charge it may cost, they seldom omit to have their children instructed in Reading & writing the English Tongue.

The number of negros (Freemen & Slaves) in this county are 241 according to the exactest calculations that I can get having procured a particular list of them from a person in each hundred who could most commodiously take an account of them, several of them both bond & free I have baptized since my coming here, but far the greatest part of them do yet remain unbaptized, and (it is to be feared) uninstructed, however it is to be hoped those good sermons and discourses which have been sent over by the charity of the Honourable Society and that excellent letter which was lately transmitted to the Masters and Mistresses of families in America in order to persuade them to instruct and have their negros baptized (by the Ld. Bishop of London will in a short time produce a very good effect. St. John Baptists church was raised on Wednesday the 27th of March 1728. The frame is of white Oak, the dimensions are as follows viz. 30 feet long 20 broad & 12 feet between the plate and sill. It stands about the Center of the county in the forest of Sussex and is inscribed to St. John the Baptist.

The covering of the wall is to be of Cypress board and the roof of shingles of the same wood which is most used here for the like purposes as the rain will not cause it to Rot. The work is to be carry'd on by the voluntary contribution of the inhabitants as it has already been raised on that foundation—

Thus I have written to you every thing material that with any certainty I know or could learn concerning the state of religion here in answer to your queries. These matters here are in their infancy at present, but seem to grow and gather strength, and that they may still do so to maturity and long flourish to the honor of God and the increase of true Piety and Virtue is the ardent wish and Prayer of Sir

Your very humble servt. WILLIAM BECKET
Missionary at Lewes.

OCT. 11th, 1728.

REVEREND SIR:—In obedience to the commands of the Honourable Society I here send you a Historical account of my parish, which shall be as brief as will consist with what is requisite to make it full and clear, properties essentially necessary to a good history, and herein I shall exactly follow the method laid down in your letter to me in June last on this subject.

1. My Parish comprehends the whole county of Sussex, in the Territories of Penna (as it is commonly styled) or Counties of N. Castle Kent and Sussex on Delaware bounded on the East by Del. Bay, Somerset Coy, Md. on the South and west and Kent on Delaware on the North—in length about 30 and in breadth about 12 or 14 miles, Latitude about 39 degrees North.

In this County are 4 churches erected none as yet finished, but 3 of them so far carried on, as to admit of the decent performance of Divine Worship, every Sunday alternately, I shall give you a particular but brief account of each in the order in which they were raised.

1st. St. Matthews in Cedar Creek Hundred.
2d. St. Georges in Indian River do
3rd. St. Peters in Lewes & R. do
4th. St John Baptists in Broadkill do

The 2 first of these churches were erected before my coming here—the 2 last since my arrival here as the Societies Missionary.

Of the former I shall give as good an account as I can procure, from the inhabitants of the County. Of the latter upon my own knowledge.

St. Matthews Church Cedar Creek was raised in the year 1707 being the first building that was erected for the service of God and Religion in this Country according to the Rites and Usages of the Church of England. It is a Timber building, the wall covered with boards of Cypress, and the roof with cypress shingles, the floor has been laid, a pulpit, desk, Communion Table and some pews, were built about 4 years ago but the inside of the church is not yet finished.

The dimensions are as follows, Thirty feet long 20 wide 12 between joysts viz. between plate & sill The reason why the building was left unfinished was, because of the difficulty they had in getting a missionary, who had contributed towards the building of it, But why they have not gone on with the building since their church was supplyed, is not so clear. The work was begun and has been carried on by contribution, but as the subscription has for as much as I can learn been lost, so I cannot get any account of the Contributors names or of the sums they gave.

The congregation here is numerous being generally on Sundays when the weather is good to travel about 200 persons the church not being large enough to contain many more than one half of the number, though a small gallery has been raised across one end of the church. I am in hopes however to persuade them shortly to enlarge it. The first Missionary here was the Rev. William Black, now of Accomack County in Virginia, who staid near two years, after his departure the people had no minister settled among them for about 12 years, untill the year 1721 when the present Missionary arrived here. But they were sometimes visited by the Rev. Mr. Ross who came above 100 miles to preach to them & baptize their children and by the Rev. Mr. Adams who came nearly 90 miles during this long vacancy, whose Christian zeal and charity deserve to be mentioned with gratitude on this occasion.

St. George's Chapel in Indian River hundred, 9 miles distant from Lewes was raised in December 1719, The frame of Oak—the length of it was 25 feet the breadth 20 and the height 12 feet. The walls and roof were covered with red oak boards and thus remained till the year 1725 when a new addition of 15 feet was made to it; the older part of this building has a pulpit, gallery and floor, the new part is not yet floor'd, but we have agree'd with a workman this year to cover the whole roof with cypress shingles and to lay the floor of the new part, the congregation frequenting this chapel consist usually of about 200 people.

This Building was rais'd as all the churches in this Government are by voluntary contribution. The sum contributed towards carrying on the work at first was £34 15d. 8s. and the repairing and enlarging it since, has cost about as much more. The Contributors were about 66 in number to raise the first sum. The people here are constant attenders on the public service and annually contribute something of their small substance towards the carrying on the building of their yet unfinished chappel & the maintenance of their minister.

Oct. 11, 1728.

Petition of Arthur Usher.

TO THE VENERABLE AND HONY THE SOCIETY FOR THE PROPOGATION OF THE GOSPEL IN FOREIGN PARTS:

The Petition of Arthur Usher Humbly Sheweth That Your Petitioner being advised by Physicians to live in a warm Climate for the Recovery of his health, doth therefore offer himself as a Missionary and having already laid the Testimonials of his Good Life & Conversation before the Lord Bishop of London, is likewise ready to lay the same before the Said Society who he hopes will take him into their Consideration if there be a Vacancy.

And ye Petr (as in duty bound) Will Pray etc

ARTHUR USHER.

Mr. Ushers Testimonials.

HENRICUS Providentia Divina Clonensis Episcopus Dilecto Nobis in Christo Reverendo Arthurio Usher Cf.

JACOB HANNING, Reg's.

Ilen ■ Clonensis

Scriptum a Virgo Eptuno in Ordinaria [L. S.] Gyston en Virilaren Friend tent & Died blonen 21° die May A° D° 1736.

Visitaæ Die Clonentent
Vertio Die Septm ano Dome 1736°
JACOB HANNING, Rlgly.

Edv Lloyd
Reglius

OMNIBUS adquos, &c.

In Cujus rei Testimonum Singulorum Manus æt Publicum Collegii Sigillum apposunimus Decimo Sexto Die May anno Domini Millessimo Septengentessimo trigesimo Sexto.

JOHN ELWOOD
ROBT SHAW
HENY CLARK
H. GRAFTEN
CARL STEWART
SAML HUGHES
CA. CARTWRIGHT

RICHD BALDWIN Præptr.
[L. S.]

S. P. G. JOURNAL DECEMBER 17, 1725.

Beckett, dated 7-6-1725 would like to remove to Chester as the Rev. Mr. Humphries has gone to Annapolis.

Sept 16, 1742 has 4 churches & no clergyman within 50 miles of him Letter to Dr. (Rev) Jenney, Lewes April, 1744, from Reive Holt Trustee to the Rev. Mr. Becket's children. His estate settled & not enough to support children as Mr. Becket had not drawn salary since Xmas 1742 One of his daughters, about 19 yrs, has been a cripple for several years S. P. G. makes a small grant & pays back dues Rev. Mr. Usher, Sussex in Pa. Sept. 25, 1745 also in Kent Rev. Mr. Usher Missionary to Churches in Sussex March 25, 1745.

The Dissenters having no settled Teacher in them, & they behave decently & regularly when at church, and as soon as he is well settled at Lewes, he will enquire into, & send an account of all his churches.

A letter from Mr Usher dated L. 6-2-1745 acquainting that he has lately visited the four churches under his care, & can truly say that Religion flourishes in Sussex Co. & he has Baptized from the 25 of March preceeding 66.

Letter dated 12-26-1745 Sussex Co in Pa. The flourishing condition of the Church in Sussex, Dissenters attend & like service better than before, so that he expects a daily increase. The distance of the 4 churches in Sussex Co., & his attendance once a month at Dover during the vacancy there seem too hard for him, but he doth not grudge his pains, being determined to spend the remainder of his days in diligently performing the Duties of his station, & in enlarging the Kingdom of Christ in this world. He had lately Baptized 76 children, some of them born of Dissenting parents, who having no teacher in their own denomination applied to him to Baptize their children.

Lewes March 26, 1746 Since Dec. 26 has Baptized 42 Infants & 2 Adults after proper instruction. Number of Communicants 68 whose lives & conversations are agreeable to their profession After the death of Mr Morris he had attended the Churches in Kent Co. once every 5 weeks without so much as the allowance of traveling charges from the People of Kent County Hopes the Society will make allowance. They did.

Lewes Sussex Co. in Pa. June 26, 1746 Stating that all the Summer season he hath more hearers than the church will hold & therefore he Preaches sometimes under the shade of the large trees & Catechises on Sundays in the afternoon, after the 2d Lesson, generally about 20 children. Since 25 March has Baptized 58 White Children & 2 Blacks & 1 Adult person bred in Quakerism.

Rev Mr Arthur Usher Lewes June 26, 1747. The Members of the Church are assiduous & punctual in attending divine service all Parts of the year Since March 25 has Baptized 35 Infants & 3 Adults & his Congregations increase so fast that they have determined to make additions to two of his Country Chappels On Easter Day he had 18 Communicants at Lewes. Catechizes 18 or 19 Children at Ten of the Clock on Sunday Mornings before sermon. Had begun a Course of Lectures on the Ch. Catechism which he preaches on Sunday Evenings from March till September.

Rev Mr Arthur Usher Lewes in Pa. 3-25-1749 Acquainting that in February last the Rev. Mr. Bluet Missionary at Dover in Kent Co. had departed this Life not much lamented by his congregation. They had applied to him to serve their church as often as he could, which he had promised to do once in 5 weeks; & tho, by Mr. Bluet's indiscretion the church was reduced to a very low ebb, yet by God's Blessing he hoped to gather the scattered flock together again, & upon his preaching there after Mr Bluet's death he had between 2 & 300 Hearers who unanimously desired he might be restored to them again & which he would willingly accept if the Society should think proper He had Baptized, since last report, 26 White Children 5 Adult Negroes who could repeat the Creed, the Lord's Prayer & ten Commandments & 6 Negro Children Communicants at Xmas 18.

Copy of a Letter in Fulham Palace.

Rev. Sir:—This letter accompanies Mr. Hector Alison's, and Mr. John Erkine's, who are now in orders, according to the Rites and usage of the Church of Scotland, but do intend to conform and receive Episcopal Ordination, as soon as it shall please God to vouchsafe them an opportunity of waiting upon His Lordship the Bishop of London for the time being, or on some other of our Reverend Fathers in God, who are placed in the pastoral offices of the Church of England, or by Law established; and the aforementioned gentlemen having addressed themselves to us the subscribing wardens of St. Peters at Lewes, to give them a testimonial of their moral Characters and behaviour, we crave leave to say that we have been fortunately acquainted with Mr. Alison for near 3 years last Past, and do certainly know that his whole deportment among us hath been grave, regular and exemplary. And as to Mr. Erskine, we have heard as good report, and have also seen laudable Credentials of him with respect to his learning, Piety, Pasts, and conduct, from under the hands of Mr. Isaac Alison of Chester County, and Mr. Robert Cross of Philadelphia, the latter of whom as he lives in the same city with your Reverence, can (if applied to) give a more particular character of the said Mr. Erskine, Sir, we well know that to make suitable recommendations for most of the offices in life is no easy task, but the difficulty is much increased when it relates to so important a one as that of faithfully administering in the Church, and serving at the Christians Altar. However, we are all encouraged to solicit your favourable countenance towards the gentlemen first above named, not only from the Principles of Benevolence, but from a well-grounded hope, that if their desires are accomplished, they will walk worthy of that vocation whereunto they shall be called.

We conclude with sincere wishes for the peace & Prosperity of our Mother Church, and that those branches thereof, which by the favor of divine providence have been transplanted into this infant Colony, may flourish, increase, and grow up to such perfection, as to become the seminaries of real piety, virtue, and true Godliness; so devoutly pray

Rev. Sir, Your most obedient humble servant,

R. Holt
Jacob Kollick

Lewes, June 20th, 1749
Mr. Commissary of Pennsylvania.

Rev Mr Usher, Lewes in Pa., June 26, 1749 Since March 25 had Baptized 9 White & 3 Black Children & 2 Adult Whites after proper instruction, & received 4 new Communicants. It was near 12 years from the time of his admission into the Service of the Society & during that time he had not only discharged the Duties of his Function within his own Mission, but also occasionally supplied several neighbouring vacancies.

Had just received a letter from Ireland with an Account of the Death of an elder Brother which obliges him to ask leave of the Society to be absent six months from his Mission in Order to settle some affairs relating to his Deceased Brother's Estate.

Leave granted, Mr Usher taking care that the Church be duly supplied during his absence.

Rev. Mr Usher Lewes Pa. Dec. 26, 1749. Since last report had Baptized 36 Infants, two of which are Negroes, 2 White Adults & 4 Negroe Adults, after proper Instruction. That he had administered the H. C. four times in the year in the several Churches in Sussex Co. & he finds an increase of Communicants every time.

That the Masters & Mistresses are more inclined than ever to have their Negroes instructed in the Principles of the Ch. of England & Baptized.

He acquaints that the Congregation at Chester had a great loss in the death of their worthy Missionary Mr Backhouse. That he has drawn a bill for £15 Sterling & humbly reminds the Society for leave to return to his Native Country for Six Months.

Rev. Mr. Usher Lewes June 25, 1750. Acquainting that he can with great Truth assure the Society that his churches are so thronged in Summer that for conveniencey of Room he Preaches sometimes under a shady green Tree.

Since 25 of last March has Baptized 54 white Infants, 3 Negro Children & 2 White Adults, after previous examination. Within the year has received 10 new Communicants of regular lives.

Letter from the Rev. Mr Usher Missionary at Lewes in Sussex Co., Pa. Dated Lismore in Ireland, October 11, 1751, acquainting that when he left America he did not imagine that he should meet with so much Difficulty & Delay in the Settlement of his Deceased Brothers Affairs; but he thanked God, they would be brought to a conclusion in Novr Term, & he hoped he would embark for his Mission the first opportunity following. He desires leave to live in that part of the Mission which shall appear most convenient for the better care of the Whole, & not be confined to Lewes, as they have provided him neither House, nor Glebe, & yet expect he should Devote his Time to them to the Prejudice of the other Congregations.

Leave was given to settle in such Part of the Mission as may answer best for his taking Care of the Whole.

A letter from the Rev. Mr. Usher, Missionary at Lewes Sussex Co. in Pa. Dated Philada. May 11, 1752 acquainting that upon the Receipt of the Secretary's letter, he embraced the first opportunity of embarking from Ireland for Pa. & was just then happily arrived, & proposed to set out that evening for his Mission where by his Diligence in his Pastoral Office he would do his best endeavours to show his gratitude to the Society for all their Favours & Indulgences toward him.

Letter from the Rev. Mr Usher, Lewes October 18 1752 asking leave to resign his Mission for want of health, he purposing to return to his Native Country Ireland where he hopes in some measure at least to recover his health. The Congregation of Sussex Co. requested him to apply to the Society in their behalf, that no Missionary who had been bred a Dissenter might be sent to them, because such are seldom or ever Stedfast in Principles but comply too far with the Dissenters, which gives offence & renders them contemptible in the Eyes of the Church People.

The Rev Mr. Craig Itinerant Miss. in Pa in Letter dated Philadelphia Nov. 16, 1752, desires to be settled in first Vacant Mission.

Agreed to recommend Mr Craig to succeed Mr. Usher in ye Mission of Sussex Co. Salary same as Mr. Ushers & to commence from last Lady Day. He did not go to Lewes.

Letter from the Rev Mr Locke lately an Itinerant Missionary to Pa. Dated Nov. 6, 1752 acquainted that finding the People in the Itinerant Mission much attached to Mr Craig, he had consented to go, & administer to the Church of Lewes, & to Settle there, if the Society should approve thereof, & he was then at Lewes & had officiated several times & Baptized several Children & would be more particular, as to the Church of Lewes in his next, if the Society should think proper to fix him there. Agreed to fr the Society.

Agreed that a new Missionary be appointed for Sussex Co. provided it shall appear that Mr. Locke is dead.

Petition from St Peter's at Lewes, St George's Chapel in Indian River Hundred, & St Matthews in Cedar Creek Hd. all in the County of Sussex on Delaware, dated August 15, 1755 setting forth that the Mission to the said County hath either been vacant, or most Dishonourably & unwarrantably neglected, by the frequent non-attendance, & constant non-residence of Mr. Usher during the whole time of his Mission (of which the Church Wardens have given a particular account in the preceeding letter) now the Rev. Mr. Matthias Harris having of late preached several Sermons among them & performed the other Duties of His Holy Function with general approbation, it hath been moved by the Members of the above mentioned *Church & Chappels* to make such subscriptions towards his support as amount to upwards of £60 Sterling & on this consideration alone he is willing to officiate among them for the space of one year, or untill the Society's pleasure be known. The said Mr. Harris is a Native of Maryland, about 37 years of age, has a wife & 2 Children, was Ordained Deacon by the Bishop of London on March 18, 1753 & Priest on the 25th of the same month by the Bishop of Chester. Since his coming back to America he has served in the Cure of the Parish of All Hallows in the County of Worcester in the Province aforesaid for the space of 17 months, & has brought a certificate from the Parishioners of his Morals, Conduct, & Exemplary Behaviour among them, &c &c.

A letter from the Rev. Mr. Harris dated Lewes in Sussex Co., Nov. 15, 1755 refers to above & requests appointment.

Agreed out of regard to Mr. Cleveland Petitioner to be sent Missionary to the Church at Norwich, & in Compassion to his Numerous Family consisting of a Wife & 9 Children to recommend Mr. Cleveland to the Society to be appointed Missionary to the Churches of

Sussex Co. in Pennsylvania in the room of Mr. Locke deceased, if the Lord Bishop of London shall think him Worthy to admit him to Holy Orders.

A letter from the Rev. Mr. Cleveland Missionary to Lewes in Pa. dated Norwich Jan. 10, 1756 acquainting that after a long & tedious Voyage he is safely arrived in New England & should have immediately proceeded to his Mission were it not for the following reasons Viz. In his Passage from Halifax to New England, a violent storm cast them on the sands called *Nantucket* Shoals, but by the goodness of God, they all escaped unhurt except Mr. Cleveland.

The Vessel being but poorly manned he was obliged to assist the Sailors, & was struck by the Violence of the Sea against the side of the Ship, & was bruised in his head & other parts of his Body; that he was taken up for dead; of which he was not fully recovered when he wrote.

He proposed to embrace the first opportunity of a Passage to Lewes.

Letter from Mr Cleveland Missionary at Lewes &c &c Nov. 3, 1756 in which he writes of the Obstinacy of his Congregations still continues. They have of late locked up St. Matthew's against him, the only church he was permitted to preach in. They declare that no man but Mr. Harris should preach in it, though the Society shall discourage them ever so much. Mr Cleveland is in a most distressed condition, many miles off his family, & nothing to support him or them but the Society's allowance, & used with much indignity In this situation he craves the Society's assistance, that they would extricate him out of it by appointing him to succeed Mr. Brooke in Mission at New Castle. Agreed to &c.

Letter dated Oct. 11, 1756 Mr. Cleveland Missionary at Lewes &c. Mr. Harris leads the opposition, refuses to use all the Church Service, declares it is Romish &c. Mr. Cleveland administered H. C. to about 20 persons Baptized 29 Infants & 2 Adults. His Widow Mrs. Susannah Cleveland writes the Society Aug. 21, 1758 telling of the death of her Husband & asking aid for herself & children.

The Rev. Aaron Cleveland, son of Aaron and Abigail (Waters) Cleveland, was born in Cambridge, Massachusetts, October 19th, 1715, and died at Benjamin Franklin's house, Philadelphia, August 11th, 1757.

He was an ancestor of the late President Cleveland, and also of Bishop Coxe of the Diocese of Western New York.

In 1750 he was a Dissenting Minister in charge of a congregation in Halifax, Nova Scotia. In 1755 he was a Priest of the Church of England.

In 1752 Lewes and St. George's Chapel, Indian River, wish to have a clergyman who could give his whole time to these two churches.

St. Matthew's people objected and wrote August 1st, 1752:

"The Churchwardens and Vestrymen of St. Matthew's Chapel" that St. Matthews had "by much the largest congregation, who have been always zealous to embrace every opportunity of joining in the Divine Service, the Greatest number of Communicants, and many children Baptized, beside have subscribed the most freely to their Minister, and (God be thanked) always have kept up a good harmony, one with another."

The Secretary of the Convocation which met at Philadelphia May 2d, 1760, wrote to the S. P. G.:

"The Mission at Lewes is still vacant on account of the refractory conduct of the People, and one Mr. Harris, who intruded himself into it without the Society's Leave, and to the exclusion of the Missionary they had appointed some years ago.

"Mr. Harris did not offer to take his seat in Convention, but presented to their Committee a Submission on his own part and that of two of his churches, to be transmitted to the Society, praying to be reinstated in their favour.

"But as the Church of Lewes, which is the principal one, and the seat of the Mission, had not joined in this Submission, and as those who did join in it seemed still desirous of retaining Mr. Harris among them, the Committee did not chuse to have anything to do in transmitting their Papers, but ordered them to be returned to themselves to be transmitted in such manner as they should think proper."

The Hon. Ryves Holt, Chief Justice, writes from Lewes June 26th, 1762, to the S. P. G. for a pastor:

"And now, Sir, permit me to subscribe myself on behalf of the Congregations of St. Peter's Church, St. George's and St. Matthewe's Chappels in Sussex aforesaid."

In 1765 the Rev. Mr. Inglis of Dover (afterward Lord Bishop of Nova Scotia) writes: "Sussex County is to be twice as large, on account of the decision of the Lord Chancellor in favour of Penn, and two Maryland churches will be added.

"Separate St. Matthew's from Lewes, and attach it to St. Paul's Kent County."

He said St. Matthew's and St. Paul's could be worked together, as they were so near each other.

The Rev. Mr. Magaw, of Dover, writes, November 14th, 1767: "Cedar Creek (St. Matthew's) is at present connected with the Lewes Town Mission."

In a letter dated July 31, 1763, the parishoners of Sussex Co., St Peter's, St George's, & St. Matthews, agree to raise so much money & a glebe for such Missionary as the Society shall see fit to send them.

1765 Resolved that the Rev. Mr Quincy of Geddington Northampshire be appointed Missionary to Lewes in Sussex Co. Pa., with a Salary of £40 per annum &c. Mr. Quincy did not come to Lewes.

A letter from the inhabitants in Sussex Co. dated Lewes Co. on Del. Nov. 11, 1766 requesting that Mr. John Andrews who is perfectly well recommended by Dr. Smith, Mr. Peters & many worthy Clergymen, may be appointed the Society's Missionary to the Churches of St Peters, St. Georges & St. Matthews in that County. Agreed, if the Lord Bishop of London shall find him worthy of Holy Orders. Ordered that Mr. John Andrews be appointed to the Mission of Lewes in Sussex Co. on Del. with salary of £40 per annum to commence from Xmas last.

Letter from the Rev. Mr. John Andrews, Miss. at Lewes &c &c Cedar Creek dated Lewes 18 Nov. 1767. He met with a kind reception on his arrival June 1. His Mission includes St. Peters Lewes, St Georges at Indian River & St. Matthews at Cedar Creek, to each of which he gives an equal share of his labours Since his arrival he

REV. JOHN ANDREWS, D.D.
From a portrait by Sully.
St. Peter's, Lewes, 1767–1770.

has baptized 53 White, 7 Negroe & 2 Mulatto Children & has 67 Communicants. The three churches have jointly engaged to pay annually the sum of £75 Currency towards the support of a Miss. & to allow an equivalent for a Glebe till one shall be purchased, which will be as soon as a convenient place for that purpose shall be found, for which they have agreed to give £300. Currency. Mr. Andrews, with great modesty hopes that the Society will take into their consideration that his salary is reduced & his Duty expensive & Laborious & bestow on him a gratuity which he had some hope given him. Agreed to.

Letter from Mr. John Andrews Miss. at Lewes dated Philada Aug. 4, 1768 informing the Society that he lives in great harmony with his people, who are regular in their behaviour, but rather deficient in a proper sense of Religion, which cannot seem strange as they have been so long without the performance of Public Worship They are very illiterate owing to their great poverty Several attempts have been made in vain to establish a Grammar School at Lewes, because they could not furnish salary sufficient for a man duly qualified. At Xmas administer H. C. St Peter's Lewes to 16 at Easter at St. George's 34. Whitsun Day, St. Matthew's 21. Since last Nov. has Baptized 75 White & 2 Black Children & 1 Adult. The S. P. G. agreed to make an allowance for a Schoolmaster at Lewes.

Mr. Andrews at Lewes keeps his health so ill that he prays to be removed to his native hills of Pa. Sussex on Delaware is as it were the Fens of Essex & it is to be feared there will be no stable Mission there till a person can be procured who was born in the place & is naturalized to it, tho they well deserve notice as a numerous body of Churchpeople.

Letter from Mr. Andrews Lewes April 12, 1769. He continues to officiate at St. Matthew's whereat a neat & commodious church is at present building of 40 feet by 36, & high enough to admit of galleries & two tiers of windows. The Chapel at Indian River being found too small a new one is much talked of. The Church at Lewes has been considerably repaired, & it is to *the bounty of the ladies* that they are indebted for an elegant pulpit cloth cushion, a Desk cloth &c of crimson silk Damask. Among the benefactors were some of the Presbyterian denomination. On Xmas Day he administered the Lord's Supper at Lewes to 16 persons only, the weather being very cold. On Easter at St. Georges to 52. Since Aug. he has Baptized 70 white & 2 Negroe children, 1 White & 4 Negroe Adults. He mentions the unhealthiness of the situation & his constitution is greatly injured by repeated attacks of Agues & fevers.

Mr. Andrews desires to leave a Minister in his place in Lewes proposes Mr. Lyon.

The Rev. John Andrews, D. D. was the son of Moses and Letitia Andrews, and was born in Cecil County, Maryland, 1746. He graduated from the College of Philadelphia 1765. In 1767 he was ordained Deacon by the Bishop of St. David's, and Priest by the Bishop of London. In 1772 he married Mary Callender. He was Rector of York, Pa., at that time. In 1810 he became Provost of the University of Pennsylvania, in 1813 he resigned on account of ill health. He died at the age of 67 and was buried in Christ Church graveyard. He is described as being "tall and dignified and courteous, honest in opinions, of good judgement, benevolent, cheerful, and a fine conversationalist. He was an eloquent preacher, and a good theologian, and won the respect of his students."

Letter from Lewes July 24, 1769 is leaving Lewes for York & Cumberland. Speaks highly of the kindness of the people of Lewes & regrets leaving. On Whitsun Day had 24 Communicants. Since April 12, has Baptized 27 children. He arrived at York Dec. 16, 1769.

Agreed that Mr. John Lyon be appointed the Society Miss. at Lewes in Sussex Co. with the former Salary allowed to that Mission & that it may commence at Lady Day 1769.

Letter from the Rev Mr. Lyon, Miss. at Lewes dated Sussex Co Oct 24, 1770 acquainting the Society that in the course of the last year he had baptized 267 White infants—2 adult slaves, & 11 infant slaves. At Easter had 63 communicants—married 39 couples & buried 18. The people have bought a glebe, & are endeavouring to erect a house upon it, which will render his life more comfortable, provided he recovers his health.

Two letters from the Rev Mr Lyons Miss at Lewes one dated January 23, 1770, the other April 1, 1771 In the former he excuses himself for having incurred the displeasure of the Society so early, whom he means ever to respect. He hopes they will judge favourably of his removal & he will use more caution for the time to come. His duty has been very hard, as he has been urged to go back often to the extremes of the County, where he has had large Congregations of grown persons who never before attended public worship. He has visited them merely out of pity & regard, for generally speaking, he can expect no reward from them. He has been greatly indisposed, & since last July under the Doctor's care. His family, all sick, more or less. He came there 6 in a family, of whom his wife and one more are dead. He writes April 1, 1771 that the state of his Mission is growing, & promises fair, & his health is better. Since the 25th of Oct. 1770 he has Baptized 39 infants, married 24 couples, & buried 14 persons. Urged by necessity he has drawn a quarter's salary.

Rev Mr Lyon Lewes Miss. Letter dated New York Dec. 14, 1771 acquainting the Society that finding himself in a low & poor state of health last April, he had retired for a number of weeks to a Northern climate, where he has recovered equal to his wishes, & when he wrote this letter was upon his return home. He requests some Bibles, Prayer Books & pious Tracts.

Letter from the Rev Mr. Lyons Miss at Lewes dated April 28, 1772, in which he writes the same about the protested bills as Dr. Peters, adding that the charges on the bill will be suspended, till he hears from the Secretary. He encloses a copy of the Notary's Protest. Since Easter last he has baptized 2 White Adults & 181 infants, 1 Black adult & 8 Black infants, married 52 couples & buried 13 corpses.

Rev. Mr Lyon Lewes Oct. 25, 1772 acknowledges receipt of Secretary's letter of the 25 of March last, & the books. Wishes there had been some of Burkett's tracts, his help & guide to Xtian families, for those pieces have been of great use to the people who have been prejudiced against the Church. He gratefully mentions the Society's favor in answering his renewed bill for £70. but wishes to have some directions with regard to the damages of £14 19s- 3d. with interest, which he is liable to pay. The state of the Mission much the same. He has officiated in three churches on Sundays, & at other times preached in remote parts, as far as the borders of Maryland, to the number of 86 sermons since he came to the Mission.

Rev Mr Lyon Lewes April 12, 1773 states that his services have been as usual, having Baptized since last Easter 239 White, 27 Black infants & 4 Black adults. He intends in future, on every third Sunday in the afternoon, to give a Lecture in some part of the Forest among the poor people, which he humbly trusts the Society will promote by granting some annual encouragement.

Rev. Mr Lyon Lewes Nov. 22, 1773 acquainting the Society that the many fatigues of his Mission, together with his indisposition of body have determined him to accept of a parish in Virginia. The Rev. Mr. Tingley who will be recommended by Dr. Smith is ready to supply his place. The parish has purchased a piece of land for £190 Pa Currency, for a glebe, towards which he has contributed £10. He has been with the people entirely for 3 months after Easter, since which he has been with them occassionally. He has now but one petition to leave in favour of the Forest part of the Mission, whose lands are under water a great part of the year, they are therefore very poor He hopes that his successor will have special directions to visit them, at least one half of of the time at present allotted to St Georges, which is every third Sunday. He concludes with thanks to the Society for their last letter of the 4th of March & for the many favours received from them.

The Rev. John Lyon was born in New England, and was son of Mathew Lyon of Warrington, Lancashire, England. He matriculated 1743.

Bishop Meade speaks of the Rev John Lyon who came to St. Georges Accomac County Virginia, from Rhode Island. That is a mistake. Lyon went to Accomac from Lewes.

The Society agreed not to appoint the Rev Mr. Tingley until they should be better informed about him.

Letter from the Rev. Mr Tingley Miss at Lewes Nov. 10, 1774 that tho. no answer had been given to Dr Peters & the other clergyman's recommendation of him to succeed to the Mission of Lewes, he has officiated there from Oct. 14 1773, duly attending the several churches, which are one more in number than mentioned in the last Abstract, Viz. St Georges at Indian River. Besides the duties of his Mission, he has frequently officiated in an old ruinous church in the Forest, to a poor people, who are 8 miles distant from St Georges. In the Winter he has gone to them on Saturdays on his way to Cedar Creek, and in the Summer after evening service on Sundays. His churches are generally well filled & the people pay great attention. He has administered the sacrament 4 times in each church. Communicants 110. He has baptized 6 white adults, & 202 Children. 13 Black Adults & 43 children. Marriages 36. Burials 14. He catechises the children in town of Friday afternoons in the church, & hears them repeat portions of the Psalms. The Negroes he catechises on Sundays after the evening service. He hopes to prove himself a diligent Missionary if the Society should be pleased to appoint him. The whole Library delivered to him by the Church Wardens consists of the following books Burkett on the New Testament, Burnet on 39 Articles, Barrows Works, 2 vols. folio, Book of Homilies, Archbishop Tillotsons Sermon's 1 Vol. folio, Stanhopes Epistles & Gospels 3d &

4th Volumes. The Society directed the Rev. Mr. Tingley to use every means to recover the missing books.

Mr Tingley Miss at Lewes in a letter dated June 12, 1775 states that it was not until last Good Friday that he had the agreeable news of his appointment to that Mission, owing to the Miscarriage of a letter from Dr. Smith. He encloses a letter from the Church Wardens of Lewes expressing their thanks for his appointment & acquainting the Society that he has from the 23d of Nov. 1773 duly attended the duties of his Mission to general acceptance, besides occasionally preaching in the Forest. 25 Prayer Books to be sent to the Rev Mr Tingley whenever they can be conveyed with safety.

REV. SYDENHAM THORNE OF ST. PAUL'S KENT COUNTY.

Rev. Mr Thorne dated New York 5th Oct. 1778 which place he has obtained permission from those in power to visit, proposing to return to his Residence 200 miles off in the course of a week or two. About the beginning of Nov. 1774 he went to his Mission, where he was gladly received by the people, who did everything for him that his heart could wish for, both as to makeing his own situation easy, & also in repairing the churches. He continued to exercise the several Duties of his Calling for nearly three years, & never omitted praying for his most Gracious Sovereign, though frequently threatened with loss of life, if he did not desist. The Legislature of the State, as it is now called, then enacted a Treason Law by which praying for the King became a capital offence. In consequence of this he forbore preaching in the Churches; but as occasion required has preached at Funerals. He has lately prevailed upon a Religious Good Man to read Prayers in the churches, which he hopes may be a means of keeping the congregations together during the present times of confusion. He has been very happy in residing among a people distinguished for their Loyalty & Affection to the British Constitution; and he cannot recollect a single member belonging to either of his congregations who hath taken an active part against the Government. They still retain the highest affection for it, & are every day more & more sensible of the inestimable benefits resulting from it. Before these unhappy disputes, his congregations were large & continued growing during the whole time of his preaching. The number that commonly attended was between 7 & 800 at each church. The number of communicants about 100. Baptisms yearly between 4 & 500. Burials about 40. Marriages between 50 & 60.

His zeal for the British Constitution & the peculiar obligations he was under, as a clergyman of the Church of England, urged him to oppose the measures of Congress, Committees &ca as far as he consistly could. This soon rendered him obnoxious to the Resentment of that Party, who, at 4 different periods, summoned him before their Committee, & more particularly, for not attending church on a fast day appointed by Congress. He was, however, always fortunate enough to extricate himself from them, without receiving much more Injury, than a little personal abuse. He has drawn for £40 in favour of Capt. Henry Coupar. Allowed by the Society.

From the Rev. Mr. Tingley Miss at Lewes in Sussex Co., at Cedar Creek, & at St Georges at Indian River, dated New York 5th March

1782, apologizing for his long silence of six years, owing entirely to his situation, so remote & unconnected with New York, & the difficulties of the time which prevented his writing with any freedom. The fury of the persecution in his Mission is much abated. He has the satisfaction, however, of informing the Society, that during all their late, or present confusions, the members of the Church in his Mission have generally been loyal, two or three families excepted, who tho' Churchmen by profession are Presbyterians by trade. These joined with the hot-brained zealots among the Presbyterians, who have, almost without exception, been fiery advocates for Independence. Amidst the greatest fury, however, of the political storm, the church has been kept open; & in spite of threats of ill treatment he has persevered in the faithful discharge of his duty. After the Declaration of Independency, indeed, from a regard for the safety of his hearers, his family, or himself, he could not be so explicit, as he wished, in praying for the King. Unfortunately for him, his clerical Brethren of Philadelphia, far too generally, he thinks, made such compliance as are utterly repugnant to the principles, which must necessarily be interwoven in the very heart, soul, & mind of a Churchman; & so having none of great & established characters to consult with, he was left wholly to be directed by his own prudence. He verily believes it was by the merciful direction of Heaven itself, that, in this trying emergence, when he came to the petition, "O Lord save the King" it occurred to him at the moment to say, "O Lord, save those, whom Thou hast made it our especial duty to pray for," & this form he has continued to use ever since, making also a similar alteration in the Litany. He & his people can safely appeal to the Great Searcher of hearts for the integrity of their meaning; & thankful as they are for even so much indulgence, they trust they shall be forgiven for an apparent, but unavoidable, instance of duplicity. Some such management was absolutely necessary; as, had he been prevented altogether from preaching, his Flock must needs have been scattered. In so critical a situation, he was determined by all possible prudential means, to avoid the evil of having his church shut up, as foreseeing, that, if this were once done, he should never be able to have them opened again, but under the most humiliating & dishonourable circumstances. The same predential considerations determine him still to abide by the same form, tho' somewhat different from what he now finds is used by other loyal Missionaries, whose judgement he has the greatest respect for; inasmuch as the making any alterations now might lead to unfavorable suspicions; & he knows there are those who regard him with a jealous eye. Mr. Tingley's difficulties & Sufferings, he says, have been many & great; but, as the Society have already had many of a similar nature, he willingly spares them a circumstantial detail. Some comfortable refreshments for himself & his more distressed family were sent to them from their relations in New York; but these the Committees ordered to be seized; & armed multitudes were full ready, with many aggravating circumstances, to put their orders in execution; though his weak & dying wife begged a small part only of the things as medicine. It is a great consolation to him, that both she & his Mother, three years ago, were removed to that blessed place where the wicked cease from troubling & the weary are at rest. Ever since that time, he has been daily employed in travelling & preaching about the County which bounds his Mission; & sometimes by special invitation into the adjoining Province of Maryland; always & to the utmost of his power, strengthening & confirming the Brethren. In this duty, he has travelled at least 3000 miles a year. Notwithstanding his frequent preaching, such is the well-known backwardness of people in general in those countries to contribute, even according to their abilities, toward the decent support of Ministers; such have been the necessities of the times; such the rapid depreciation of their paper currency; he has been so pinched in his circumstances, that he may truly say, he has often scarcely had bread to eat, or raiment to put on. The opportunity he now enjoys of drawing on the Society, he is truly thankful for, as the expectation of it has been the chief support of his spirits, in the many years that he has had hardly any resources, but the little sums he could borrow from his friends. Two years ago, he had intended & endeavoured to obtain leave to visit New York, but could not. Nay, so jealous were they of him, that he was not even permitted to see two prisoners, on his return, who had been confined there; & from whom he hoped to have learned some tidings of his relations there. At length, however, Providence very unexpectedly raised him up a friend, Mr. John Dickinson, heretofore celebrated as the Pennsylvania Farmer, & lately chosen Governour of the new State of Delaware; who has procured him a permit to go & return from New York, unmolested. The weather has lately been more inclement that had been known for many years; & the roads also are particularly bad; so that he was eleven days on his journey from Lewes to New York, in which he had, when he wrote, been 16 days; but proposed to return in a few days to his family, his Mission, & his duty. He thanked God that he can now think of with less pain, as from a conviction either of the injustice, or the ill policy of it, that violent spirit, which, a few years ago, was so intolerant & intolerable, is now much abated. The inhabitants of Sussex Co. are remarkably subject to Ague & Fever, always in the Fall of the year; & Mr Tingley & his family have been & still are exceedingly afflicted with it. In the hope, therefore, that the good Providence of God, in compassion of both countries, may again restore their former happy connection, he takes the liberty now to entreat of the Society, to be appointed to any Mission near New York, his native & healthful climate. Being obliged, notwithstanding the better temper of the times, to set out on this journey, with some caution. Mr. Tingley had it not in his power to consult & take abstracts of the different Registers of his Mission so exactly as the Society requires. He is prepared, therefore, now to say only, that he has baptized several thousands since he wrote last; & among them many Blacks, from 60 years old to 2 months. This account may seem extraordinary to those who are not particularly well acquainted with the nature of the country, in which he resides, & who do not know that there is not now another clergyman in a district of an hundred miles in length; so that he has seldom performed public service without having at the same time 30, 40, or 50 Baptisms. People ride many miles, to enjoy the opportunity once more to worship God agreeable to the order of their own Church; & bring, with eager delight, their gift & heritage that cometh of the Lord, to Him, in the laver of Regeneration. He has, moreover, for these three years past, had to encounter with the enthusiastic notions of swarms of ignorant Methodists & Anabaptists, whose absurdities seem to him to have a direct tendency to overturn all order & decency in the Church, as the wretched principles of those who call themselves Whigs (a softer name for Rebels!) have to overturn the State. For the reasons above assigned, Mr. Tingley says, he has not drawn on the Society since May 24, 1776, so that now May 24, 1782 the Society owed him six years salary. For this viz. £240 he now draws in favour of Mess. Edward & William Laight; as it may be a long time before he has another opportunity of drawing.

Rev. Mr Tingley Lewes June 18, 1783 expressing great satisfaction & gratitude, on hearing, as he but lately has, that the Society have accepted & paid his bills He has again drawn for his salary to the 24 May 1783, which he should not have attempted without their express permission which he has been favoured with through Dr. Inglis. Since he last wrote to the Society he has been employed, as he has been for several years, in almost constantly traveling & preaching in different parts of the Country. He has baptized at least between 8 & 900 has married 40 couples & buried 40 corpses; but by no means all in his own Mission The number of Communicants has greatly increased.

July 1784 the Rev Mr Tingley had accepted a parish in Maryland In a letter dated May 11, 1784 Somerset Co. Maryland he informs the Society that he left the Mission in Sussex Co on Delaware, the middle of December 1783.

Mr Sydenham Thorne writes from Philadelphia 16th of September 1782 that it is now almost two years since he resumed the public exercise of his profession. A church is to be erected in St Johns Town in Sussex Co. about 12 miles from where Mr. Thorne lives. It is to be of brick, 50 feet by 35 & the work is now in such a state that he thinks the building will be finished in the course of next Summer. Has regularly officiated at Dover since Mr. Magaw left, although 21 miles away. Wishes to remove to New Castle.

In 1808 Parson (?) Weems was here. I do not think he was a clergyman, notwithstanding his story about the Bishop of London having ordained him. If he had been ordained, he could have shown his credentials, his Letters of Orders from the Bishop of London. He certainly was very clever.

The following was copied from Rev. Horace E. Hayden's "Virginia Genealogies:".

Fanny[4] Ewell, (Jesse[2], Charles[3], Charles[1],) b. Prince William county, Va., Aug. 28th, 1775; d. Aug. 28, 1843, ae. 68; m. cir. 1790–5. Rev. Mason Locke Weems, b. St. James Par., Ann Arundel county, Md., 1759; d. Beaufort, S. C., May 23, 1825, ae. 66, son of David and Margaret Harrison Weems.

Mason Locke Weems was educated in Edinburg, Dr. Allen says, "in the church;" was ordained Deacon pro. in Eng. by the Lord Bishop of London.

Returning to Md. he became Rector of All Hallow's Par., Md., 1784; had a Female seminary there; was Rector of Westminster Par., 1791; went to Va., 1793; he wrote and published "The Philanthropist," Dumfries, Va., 1799, 9th ed., Phila., 1809; "The Life of George Washington," 1800, reached cir. 50 editions; "The True Patriot," 1802; "The Life of Genl. Frances Marion," 4th ed., 1816; "The Drunkard's Looking Glass," 1816; "The Life of Benj. Franklin," 1817; "The Life of Wm. Penn," 1829; "The Old Bachelor," etc. All of these works passed through more than one edition.

His "Life of George Washington" was for many years a household work. It is the sole authority for the famous stories of "the hatchet and the cherry tree," and of the seed sown and growing in the name of Washington. These incidents which Weems records of the youth of Washington have in them nothing that is marvellous or even uncommon. They are ordinary events incident to the life of many a well raised boy. And yet, because Weems has been discredited by some writers, and was a man with noticeable peculiarities, and these incidents have no other recorder than Weems, they have been ridiculed and denied by even historical writers. Whatever may have been the character of Weems his pretty and natural anecdotes of the boyhood of Washington are much more easily ridiculed than disproved. It was the intention of the Rev. Philip Slaughter, D.D., Historiographer of the Diocese of Va., to write an historical sketch of the Rev. Mr. Weems, but his death prevented the completion of so desirable an undertaking.*

Bishop Meade knew Mr. Weems personally. He devotes two pages to him in "Old Churches," &c. (II., 234–5.) But he paints him in with such opposite colours that it is not easy to form an impartial estimate of his character. In order that some future writer may do Weems justice, a paper is reproduced here, from the Southern Churchman, (1888),

---

* The Weems family of Md. claim descent from David Weems, son of James, youngest son of the Earl of Wemys. James having been killed fighting for Charles Edward at Preston Pans, his son David was brought to Md. by Dr. Locke. He m. Margaret Harrison and had 5 sons, Capt. George, the youngest, b. May 23, 1784; d. Mar. 6, 1853; had—i. Thomas. ii. Margaret. iii. Mason Locke. iv. Gustavus. v. George. vi. Theodore.

Rev. M. L. Weems was of this line. Rev. Jno. Weems was ord. Deacon by Bp. White, June 24, 1787; d. 1821. Joannes Weems, Mary Landis, grad. M.D., Univ. Edinburg, 1792. Thesis "De Amenorhoea." Mason Locke is a common name in the family. Wm. Black Weems of Md., b. cir. 1730–5; m. Amelia Chapman, b. July 4, 1735; dau. of Nathaniel and Constance (Pearson) Chapman. (R. S., 4, 30, 81; 5, 7, 81.) David Locke Weems had Rachel, m. Jesse Ewell, No. 43, p. 340. Capt. William Weems, m. Nancy Ewell, No. 45, p. 340.

written by Mr. A. P. Gray, giving Dr. Jesse Ewell's recollection of his kinsman:

"Nestling close under the shadow of the Bull Run Mountains, in the extreme upper part of Prince William county, is 'Dumblane,' the quaint old fashioned home of Dr. Jesse Ewell, who, regardless of his eighty-six years, still attends his suffering neighbors night or day, sunshine or storm, rejoicing in the possession of all his faculties. His estimable wife, a most devout and staunch Churchwoman, is two years his senior, and for more than sixty years they have travelled earth's pilgrimage together, and now side by side are going down the hill, nearing the great river and in view of the Eternal City.

"Many a charming hour have I spent by their hospitable fireside listening to personal reminiscenses of Bishop Claggett, Dr. Walter Addison, Bishop Moore, the early days of Washington City, the war of 1812–15, and the noted men of seventy years ago. But the theme on which the Doctor most loves to dwell, and one which he always finds in me an attentive listner, is 'Parson Weems,' for the Doctor, being a nephew of the Parson's wife, lived for twenty years in his family, and knowing him well, loved and esteemed him for his piety, his benevolence, his earnest devotion to his work, his intelligence and his gentleness. Believing that others will be interested in one who has often entertained us in our childhood hours, I give what I could collect. The family seat of the Weemses, who came early to this country from Scotland (when the name was spelled Wemyss), was 'Billingsley,' Prince George's county, Md. The birthplace and early home of Mason Locke Weems was at Herring Bay, Anne Arundel county, on the Chesapeake. His mother's family name was Locke. He had two brothers, both older than he, David Locke and William Locke Weems, each of whom commanded trading vessels plying between the Old World and the New. Mason must have travelled with them occasionally, perhaps often, for he used to tell of his being on the Mediterranean in a turtle shell. He always had a great fondness for water and a roving disposition, both of which may be attributed to his early training.

"Says the Doctor: 'Even in his old age he never missed an opportunity for a plunge, and I verily believe he would soil his hands for the pleasure of washing them! Once in his later years when travelling from Leesburg back to Dumfries, just after a snow and a big thaw in early spring, finding a stream he wished to ford very much swollen, he deliberately disrobed and waded through to measure the depth and see if his wagon could cross without wetting his precious books.

"He first chose medicine as his profession and with this purpose went to Edinburgh to prosecute his studies, but while there determined to become a physician of souls, a minister of the gospel, and went to London to study theology, where he was ordained by the Bishop of London. Of course the Doctor could give no proof of his ordination, except Mr. Weems' own word, and also that Mr. Weems had a black silk gown, which he (Weems) said he had worn at his ordination and for which he had no further use. He left England at the breaking out of the Revolution, and returned to this country in his brother's ship in 1776.

"He married Frances, daughter of Col. Jesse Ewell, of 'Bel Air,' Prince William county, Va., who must have been many years his junior, for the family records show she was born in 1775, and died on her birthday, August 28th, 1843, aged sixty-eight. The 'Parson' died in 1825, at Beaufort, S. C., and was buried there.

"It was, of course, to the later part of Mr. Weems' life that the Doctor bears record. He describes him as of medium height, well-built figure, clad always neatly but simply in black, cut after the manner of the times, with a little horn of ink tied to the lapel of his coat and a quill pen in his hat. His eyes were dark (not black), his features regular and pleasant, his face clean shaven, his head, very bald on top, was surrounded with pure white hairs, giving him a most venerable and pleasant expression, true index of his character.

"Besides the lives of Washington, Franklin and Marion, he wrote or edited a number of other books and pamphlets, viz., 'Allan's Alarm to the Unconverted,' 'Dodd's Reflections on Death,' 'Davies' Sermons,' 'The Life of Conaro, a converted Italian,' 'The Drunkard's Looking Glass,' 'The Gambler's Looking Glass,' 'The Adulterer's Looking Glass,' etc.

"The life of Franklin was edited from Franklin's autobiography, and the manuscript of Marion's Life was given him by Major Horry (Marion's chief officer), to do with as he pleased. These he touched up in his own inimitable style to make more interesting and to teach a moral; for in every work he strove not only to interest, but to instruct in true virtue. Mathew Cary, of Philadelphia, was his publisher, and so successful was Weems in selling his own books that Cary gave him $50 per month to sell other books published by him. He had a two-horse Jersey wagon, covered, but without springs, except that the seat was swung on leather; into his wagon he had fitted a bookcase, so arranged it could be taken out, placed on the ground and opened to display the books without disturbing them.

"His home was at Dumfries, but he travelled continually from Philadelphia to Georgia and back again, attending the various courts along the route, selling his books to the crowds there collected, frequently giving them away to those who could not or would not buy, always having a word of exhortation for each; preaching every Sunday, or other day that opportunity offered, in church, court house or private residence, wherever he could get an audience, and generally having good ones. His long solitary rides gave him plenty of time for thought and meditation, and he seems to have used it well; for besides his numerous publications and frequent preaching, he memorized the most part of the Prayer-book services, Collects and Psalms and a large part of the Bible; so that at times he could go through the whole Morning or Evening Services, including Lessons and Psalter, without opening a book. He was always on the alert to pick up information, and prepared to note it down, and with his long experience as a traveller, his constant association with all classes of people, more especially the prominent men of his day, we may well conceive the fund he had to draw from, how entertaining he could be as a guest, and how welcomed he was wherever he went. Indeed, with what eagerness his books, his news, his company and his preaching must have been received, considering the scarcity of all these things in those days, and we can readily believe the Doctor's accounts of his immense popularity.

"Though he supported his own family comfortably, he gave freely and generously to the needy, and as at that time the country was full of French refugees (Huguenots), he found many an opportunity to act the good Samaritan, nor was he ever known to fail. One of those to whom he had been kind in adversity and sickness, being an artist, insisted on painting his portrait in return for his kindness. This portrait was kept for a long time in his parlor, but seems to have disappeared in the mutation of affairs. Another one, to show his gratitude, presented him with a violin, which, though plain, was a wonderfully fine one.

"The Parson was very fond of music, and a good violinist, but the Doctor repudiates with indignation the old story of his playing for a dancing party behind a curtain, etc., as altogether foreign to the nature and character of the man. He never carried his violin with him on his travels, but kept it carefully at home. Indeed it was difficult to get him to play anywhere but at home. He supposes the origin of the story to be in the fact that one evening while at a friend's house a party of young people returned from a wedding, and one of the young people having a violin persuaded the Parson to play a few Scottish airs, but there was no dancing.

"The Doctor has vivid recollections of the gentle admonitions he used to receive from the Parson, but says he never heard him utter a hasty reproof. It was his daily habit when at home to gather his family together morning and evening for family prayers, when they would sing a song or hymn, the Parson would recite a portion of Scripture and then offer prayer to the Heavenly Father.

"The name of Weems was early associated in my mind with the two books (Washington and Marion) which most fascinated me in my boyhood days and stirred my impressionable mind with admiration for noble and virtuous conduct, as well as pride in our countrymen, and I confess to being much disappointed with the brief and disparaging account given of the author by the venerable Bishop Meade.

"Now when, by the light of one who knew him well, I consider this historian of our infant republic, writing up its noblest men so as to stir the hearts of the rising generation to noble and virtuous conduct, this pioneer in American literature disseminating good seed broadcast over fallow ground, this missionary of the Church supporting himself at a time when many of the clergy were either deserting their posts or squabbling over their tithes, preaching and writing against drinking and gambling when many of the brethren were doing the same, speaking the word in season and out of season from Philadelphia to Georgia, burying the dead, baptizing the children, and ministering to the needy, laboring even unto the end, my opinion of the man is not only restored, but raised, and I can better appreciate his books. I hope this may be the case with others too, and that the name of a good man may be redeemed.

"Arthur P. Gray."

THE REV. JAMES WILTBANK,
Rector of St. Peter's Church, Lewes, Del., 1795.

ST. PETER'S VESTRY BOOK RECORDS.

At a meeting of the Trustees, incorporated persuant to law, for St. Peter's Episcopal Church at Lewes, in the County of Sussex; on Wednesday, the thirtieth day of June, in the year of Our Lord, one thousand seven hundred and ninety: Members present, Messrs. John Wiltbank, Esq., Reece Wolfe, John Russell, Phillip Kollock, Hap Hazzards and George Parker. Absent, Anderson Parker. When, on motion of Mr. Hap Hazzard, seconded by Mr. Reece Wolfe, John Russell was proposed to be appointed Chairman of the Trustees afrd; And thereupon the said John Russell was chosen and appointed Chairman, by the unanimous voice of the Trustees afrd. then and there present.

Ordered that the Chairman give notice by letter to Burton Waples, Esqr., and the other Trustees of St. George's Episcopal Church in Indian River hundred; requesting that the said Burton Waples with as many of the other Trustees as may by a majority thereof be appointed, attend a meeting of the Trustees of this Church, at Lewes, on Saturday, the twenty-fourth day of July next, and that they shall bring with them the deed said to be in possession of Peter Robinson, Esqr., and all other papers and accounts respecting the Glebe lands, that order may be taken for securing the title thereof; and that the accounts for rent in arrear may be settled and adjusted and such other orders taken therein, as may be thought right and most advantagious to the Churches afrd.

At which day a majority of the Trustees of St. Peter's Church met to wit: Messrs. John Wiltbank, John Russell, Anderson Parker and Philip Kollock, who together with Burton Waples, Esqr., proceeded to endeavor to settle and adjust the accounts of the rent of the Glebe, but for want of some of the vouchers for monies paid, could not finish and complete the same. Wherefore posponed the business until Monday, the twenty-sixth instant, when a majority of the Trustees met and on a motion appointed Messrs. Reece Woolf, Philip Kollock, Hap Hazzard, and George Parker, a committee, who, together with a Committee from St. George's

Chappel, are to settle with Burton Waples formerly appointed a Trustee for the Congregation of St. George's, and with Anderson Parker and John Wiltbank, also formerly appointed Trustees for the congregation of St. Peter's Church, at Lewes, for the purpose of renting out the Glebe and receiving and accounting for the profits thereof, and also ascertain each churches Coto of the Ballances due and likewise to consult and agree on such measures as may be by them though best for securing the title of the Glebe lands and plantation, for the use of the afrd. two churches.

At a meeting of the majority of the Trustees of St. Peter's Church at Lewes at the house of Mr. William Brereton, on Thursday, the ninth day of June, 1791, John Wiltbank, John Russell, Anderson Parker, Reece Woolf, Hap Hazzard and Phillips Kollock, absent George Parker, the Committee heretofore appointed for to settle and adjust the accounts of the rents and profits of the Glebe lands to the Churches of St. Peter's, at Lewes, and St. Georges, at Indian River, reported that they had settled the accounts, with the Trustees of St. George's, by which settlement it appears each church's coto of the rents of the Glebe, after deducting accounts for repairs, &c., was Sixty-four pounds two Shillings and Seven Pence half Penny, as may more particularly appear by an account stated and filed; and thereupon the afrd. Trustees proceeded to appoint a Treasuror for St. Peter's Church when John Russell was proposed and unanimously appointed. Afterwards Reece Wolfe, Hap Hazzard, Phillips Kollock, three of the four Trustees, (George Parker being the other who was absent) appointed to settle the accounts of the rents and profits of the Glebe belonging to St. Peter's Church with John Wiltbank, Esqr., and Anderson Parker, gentlemen, late Trustees for that purpose, who reported a balance due the church from the late Trustees afrd. of Four pounds Eight Shilling and one-half penny as may appear by an account stated and filed. Afterward it was considered and ordered by the Trustees that the execution of the deed from John Evans to Benjamin Burton and others dated the first day of December, 1769, for the Glebe lands be proved in Court by one of the subscribing witnesses thereto and that afterwards the said deed be recorded. And it was further considered and ordered by the Trustees that William Harrison with a sufficient number of advertisements giving notice of the sale of the Glebe at Public Vendue on the Wednesday of August Court next at Lewes. And it was further ordered that the Trustees of this Church meet on Saturday, the twenty-fifth of this instant, in order to settle and adjust any accounts which may be rendered against this church; and also with the administratrix or heir of John Road, decd., for and on account of the purchase money of a lott of land; by the said John Road sold and conveyed by a General Warrant, &c., to Daniel Nunez, Jun., decd., and by him devised to this Church; which lott of land was under a mortgage to loan office of Sussex County, and by virtue thereof sold; and it was ordered that John Russell, chairman of the Trustèes aforesaid, give notice in writing to the administratrix of the said John Roads to appear on the day afrd. before the said Trustees, and also to Thomas Mcham to render his account for repair on the Church, and to account for the rent of the Church lott and afterwards the Trustees adjourned to the day afrd.

At a meeting of a majority of the Trustees, to wit: John Wiltbank, John Russell, Reece Woolf, Phillips Kollock, and George Parker, at the house of Mr. William Brereton, in Lewes, on Saturday, the twenty-fifth day of June, 1791, Mr. Hinman Roads, son and sole heir of John Roads afrd. decd., in pursuance of the notice given to his mother (and on her behalf as well as his own) appeared before the Trustees afrd. and after some conversation had on the subject of the lott of land, by his father sold to Daniel Nunez, and by him devised to the use of this Church, he requested that the Trustees would give four weeks or thereabouts, to inform himself and consider the matter; to which requisition the Trustees agreed.

Mr. Thomas Mcham also appeared and rendered his account for repairs done on the Church, amounting to Seven Pounds, Ten Shillings and Seven pence, which amount was examined by the Trustees, but not fully settled and adjusted, after which said amount was filed amongst other papers belonging to the Church with inside of the lease for the Church lott. It was also considered and ordered by a majority of the Trustees afrd., that the four pounds, Eight Shillings and one-half penny, in the hands of John Wiltbank, Esqr., due for rent of the Glebe, be by him paid to Mr. Daniel Rodney in part of his amount, for materials by him furnished, for the repair of the Church. And afterward the Trustees adjourned without day.

August 3d, 1791, a number of the Trustees of St. Peter's and St. George's Churches met and agreed to adjourn the sale of the Glebe untill Saturday, the twenty-seventh instant. At which day pursuant to the afrd. adjournment, John Wiltbank, Esqr., John Russell, and Reece Wolf, the Committee heretofore appointed in behalf of St. Peter's Church, at Lewes, and Peter Robinson, Esqr., Robert Burton, and Woodman Stockley, the Committee for St. George's met on the Glebe and exposed all the right of the Churches afrd. in the same to public sale by way of vendue, when the same was purchased by the afrd. Peter Robinson at the sum of two hundred pounds under the incumberance of the lease of Mrs. Davises thirds—one half of the purchase money to be paid on the first day of January next ending the sale at which time the possession of the lands are to be given, and the remaining two-thirds parts thereof to be paid in one year with interest, from the afrd. first day of January; and that a deed be made to the afrd. Peter Robinson in fee, by the surviving grantees in the deed dated the first day of December, 1769, from John Evans. Mr. Robinson paid to Thomas Wilson, the Vendue Master, Seven Shilling and Six pence which is to be allowed him out of the purchase money.

At a meeting of a majority of the Trustees of St. Peter's Church, at Lewes, the fifteenth day of October, 1791, Road Shankland, Esqr., applyed to have his bond recd. by the said Trustees for the payment of £22 12s. 0d. for so much paid for and on account of Peter Robinson, Esqr., in part pay for the Glebe; also at the same time Mr. Daniel Rodney proffered to pay £27 8s. 1d. and give his bond for the payment of Fifty Pounds in full discharge of the said Peter Robinson, for and on account of this Churche's Cotoa of the money arising from the sale of the Glebe, which was considered and agreed to by John Wiltbank, John Russell, Reece Wolf, Phillips Kollock and George Parker, Trustees then present, and on the nineteenth instant the bonds were taken and the above sum of money recd. by J. Russell.

Do give and devise to the Wardens of St. Peter's Church in Lewestown and their successors forever, &c., adjoining lot of heirs of Wm. Piles and adjoining land of Rev. Matthew Willson "which lots I purchased from John Rhoads shall expend and apply rents issues and profits hereafter annually arising out of said lots towards keeping the said church of St. Peter's and the burying ground thereunto belonging, in good repair.

DANIEL NUNEZ.

At a meeting of a majority of the Commissioners or Trustees of St. Peter's Church at Lewes the seventeenth day of April, 1794, it was agreed that Samuel Paynter, George Parker, and Daniel Rodney, Esquire, be appointed managers to provide materials and employ workmen to put a new ruff on the Church and that they should draw orders on John Russell, Treasurer, for monies as so much thereof as may be in his hands for that purpose.

And at the same time, Mr. Elijah Cannon, junior, and Mr. Cornelius Wiltbank, Junior, was by the Congregation then present, chosen Trustees in the room of Anderson Parker, Gentleman, and John Wiltbank, Esqr., deceased.

And it was further agreed at the same time by the Trustees that Thomas Mcham's garden be taken on rent for one year, at the sum of Thirty-five Shillings.

At a meeting of the Trustees and Vestry of St. Peter's Church, at Lewes, on the eighth day of November, 1794, present Reece Wolf, Phillips Kollock, Cornelius Wiltbank, Elijah Cannon and George Parker. The Trustees afrd. went into the appointment of a Trustee in the room and stead of Philip Kollock, who was about to move to George Town, and Daniel Rodney, Esq., was unanimously appointed and chosen.

And Hap Hazzard, Esqr., was also nominated and appointed by the Vestry present to represent the Church of St. Peter's afrd. as a lay Deputy in the State Convention to be held at Dover the sixteenth day of December next.

"An account of the Revd. William Skilley the balance due as stated being £21 17s. 3d. for ministerial services for the year 1792 being laid before the board by Daniel Rodney, it was agreed that a sum of money should be raised by subscription to the amt. 10 or £15 which together with the sum due and not collected on the old subscriptions would be sufficient to discharge the above balance. Elijah Cannon was appointed to collect the subscriptions, and ordered to pay the overplus (If any) into the hands of the Treasurer of the Board.

At a meeting of the Trustees and a Number of the Congregation of the Church of St. Peter's, at Lewes, April 11th, 1795, it was agreed that the pews in the said Church should be raised one-third of the price they were formerly at. Also that the Congregation should receive the Rev. James Wiltbank as their minister and pay the sum of Sixty Pounds annually to commence at Easter past in consideration of his preaching in the said Church one sermon every third Sunday A. M. and one sermon once in every third Sunday P. M. during the summer season after he has preached at St. Georges in the fore-noon.

Also that Mr. Reece Wolf be and is hereby appointed to collect the pew taxes and subscriptions for paying the parson's salary to him and to settle with the committee heretofore appointed to repair the Church, to wit, Samuel Paynter, George Parker, and Daniel Rodney, Esqr., who are to approve of the delinquents (If any) and that he be allowed seven and a half per cent. on the sum collected.

1795, April the eleventh, being the Saturday after Easter, John Russell and Samuel Paynter, Senr., were chosen Wardens and John Woolf, Jacob Hazzard, John Maull, Senr., William Brereton, William Burton, Richard Howard, William Woolf, Burton Johnson, William Polk, William Cord, Joshua Burton, Cornelius Paynter, Walter Hudson, and Simon Marriner were chosen Vestrymen.

It was agreed at the same time that the price of the pews in St. Peter's Church should be raised one-third after which they would stand at the following rates, vizt:

No. 1–$3.	No. 11–$12.	No. 20–$2.
" 2– 6.	" 12– 6.	" 21– 4.
" 3–12.	" 13– 12.	" 22– 1.
" 4–12.	Parsons Pew 5.	" 23– 4.
" 5– 6.	Clarks Do. 3.	" 24– 4.
" 6– 6.	No. 14– 12.	" 25– 4.
" 7– 6.	" 15– 6.	" 26– 4.
" 8– 8.	" 16– 6.	" 27– 4.
" 9– 8.	" 17– 6.	" 28– 4.
" 10– 8.	Gallery " 18– 6.	" 29– 4.
	" 19– 2.	

"The whole number of pews at the foregoing rates will amt. to 160 Doll's or £60."

Thomas Martin was appointed at the same meeting to officiate as sexton, ring the bell, open and sweep the Church, &ca., for which services he is to be paid Ten Dollars pr annum.

January 22d, 1796. A meeting of several of the Trustees and Vestrymen of St. Peter's Church was held in Lewes, when George Parker and Daniel Rodney, were appointed to settle with the Rev. William Skilly and pay him the bal. due for ministerial services.

Also Messrs. Cornelius Wiltbank, and William Burton were appointed to settle with the Committee which were appointed the seventeenth day of April, 1794, to put a new roof and other repairs on the Church, the work having been completed some time and a bal. still remaining due and unpd. to George Parker one of the Managers.

Lewes, March 28, 1796, being Easter Monday: At a meeting of a majority of the Trustees, Vestry and other members of the congregation, Samuel Paynter, Senr., was unanimously elected a Trustee to supply the vacancy occasioned by the death of Hap Hazzard, Esqr., the former Trustees being reappointed are as follows, vizt.:

John Russell, Chairman; Samuel Paynter, Senr., Elijah Cannon, Senr., Daniel Rodney, Reece Woolf, Cornelius Wiltbank, Junr., George Parker.

Wardens and Vestry the same as last year, except Samuel Paynter, Junr., who was elected in the place and stead of Joshua Burton, decd, as a Vestryman.

Also, It was Resolved Unanimously to receive the Revd James Wiltbank as minister to Officiate in said Church every third Sunday and that he should be paid for his services Fifty Pounds Per Annum out of the monies raised by the pew tax.

Also, Reece Woolf appointed Collector and to be allowed 7½pr cent.

Also, Frederick Row, Clark and to be allowed Twelve Dollars pr Anm from the time he began to officiate until next Easter.

Also, Thomas Martin, Sexton, &ca., To be allowed Ten Dollars for the ensuing year and 11/3 for services done heretofore.

Also, That Cornelius Wiltbank be appointed Tax Delegate to represent this Church in the State Convention the ensuing year.

Also, That Reece Woolf, Daniel Rodney, and George Parker be appointed to let or rent the pews agreeably to the rates of Easter, 1795, and repair and cap the brick wall on the North West side of the Church Yard, And that Daniel Rodney may advance a sum sufficient for that purpose out of the money in his hands.

Agreeable to the order of January 22d, 1796, Mr. Daniel Rodney produced a receipt dated Oct., 1796, by which it appears he paid the Revd. William Skilly Twenty Dollars being the bal. of his acct in full.

Thursday, March 23rd, 1797, a majority of the Trustees, to wit, Samuel Paynter, Reece Wolfe, George Parker, and Cornelius Wiltbank, met, agreed to purchase one-fourth of a lott of Daniel Rodney and Revd James Wiltbank, adjoining the Church yard and to pay them for the same the sum of Twenty Eight Pounds out of the first monies that should be collected belonging to the Corporation in consequence of which appropriation, the said Daniel Rodney and James Wiltbank executed a deed to the Trustees.

April the seventeenth, 1797, being Easter Monday, at a meeting of the Wardens and Vestry it was agreed the Wardens and Vestry elected last Easter should be continued for the ensuing year except Simon Marriner, in whose place John Parker was elected as a Vestryman.

Easter Monday, April 17th, 1797, at a meeting of the Trustees, present, Saml Paynter, Elijah Cannon, Daniel Rodney, Cornelius Wiltbank, and George Parker, it was agreed to rent the old Court House to James Elliott, for one year at £25 to be paid quarterly, which the said Elliott agreed to, and Daniel Rodney was directed to draw a lease, to be executed when Elliott moved into the house, the rent to commence the 15th Apl.

October 16th, 1797, Daniel Rodney, George Parker and Cornelius Wiltbank, Junr., executed a bond for 73 Dollars and 23 cents, Amt due David M. McIlvaine for work done on the old Court House, and delivered the same to George Parker for safe keeping until the other Trustees to wit., Saml. Paynter, Senr., and Elijah Cannon should execute or sign the said bond.

Easter Monday, April 9th, 1798, at a meeting of the Trustees, present, Saml. Paynter, Senr., Elijah Cannon, Daniel Rodney, Cornelius Wiltbank, George Parker, and sundry others, the Wardens and Vestry of St. Peter's Church, the following persons were chosen as Trustees to said Church the present year, vizt.: Saml. Paynter, Senr., Elijah Cannon, Daniel Rodney, Cornelius Wiltbank, George Parker, William Burton, and Cornelius Paynter, of whom the said Daniel Rodney was elected Chairman, in the place of John Russell, who resigned in consequence of his removal to Georgetown.

Daniel Rodney exhibited an account for repairs, &ca., of the Court House for the use of St. Peters Church, to the amount of Twenty-seven Pounds 9/10, where-upon the Trustees agreed to discharge the said account by discount on his bond the balance thereof being Twenty-five Pounds 12/6 upon which the Trustees directed Mr. George Parker to deliver the said bond to the said Daniel Rodney. All the debts settled by mortgaging the old Court House and Church Lotts. Balances as settled this day for repairs of the Court House as follows:

	£	s.	d.
To John Parker	£3	18s.	9d.
" Saml. Paynter, Senr	14	5	4
" Mills McIlvaine a note (suppose)	27	15	0
" William Arnold, pd by C. Wiltbank (suppose)	23	12	6
" Robert Brereton pd	6	0	0
" Levi Oliver	6	0	0
" Hester McHams bond from James Wiltbank and Daniel Rodney, prinl	28	0	0
" George Parker	12	9	8
" Daniel Rodney	1	17	4½
" Caleb Rodney pd £10 by DB	8	12	6
" Richard Howards bill paid in part by rent of Church lott	3	13	10
" John Rodney £6 9s. 10d. Peter Robinson £4	10	9	10
Money due on Subscription papers	£143	0s.	11d.
Walter Hutson—paid by———	7	10	0

Wardens and Vestry elected for ensuing year, Vizt., Samuel Paynter and Cornelius Wiltbank, Wardens; and John Wolf, John Maull, Jacob Hazzard, Richard Howard, William Polk, Burton Johnson, Saml. Paynter, John Parker, Danl. Woolf, William Cord, and Levin Ennis, Vestrymen.

Whereas it appears to the Trustees, on settlement of the managers amts. to repair the old Court House that after applying all the money belonging to the Corporation towards discharging the bills there will be a deficiency of one hundred pounds and upwards as by the bills and bonds on the other side entered may be seen. Therefore the said Trustees do agree that if any of the members of the Congregation will advance the money or otherwise discharge the said demands they shall be repaid such sums together with legal interest thereon for the payment of which the said Trustees will mortgage or pledge the old Court House and appurtenances thereto. Adjourned and agreed to meet again at Lewes, on Wednesday the ninth of May, next.

January 1st, 1799. Three of the Trustees met. Vizt., Daniel Rodney, Samuel Paynter, and George Parker; there not being a Quorum adjourned till Saturday next.

Saturday, January 5th, 1799. Trustees met, present, the Rev. James Wiltbank; Trustees: Daniel Rodney, Samuel Paynter, Senr., Cornelius Wiltbank, George Parker, Cornelius Paynter, and William Burton, being all the Trustees except Elijah Cannon.

At said meeting the Trustees took into consideration the resolution of Easter Monday last relative to the debts due sundry individuals for the repairs of the Old Court House and other demands against the Corporation. Several of the members proposed to advance money for the discharge of said debts on condition the Trustees would mortgage the Old Court House and appurtenances together with the Church lot unto them as security and would apply the rents arising therefrom (till the whole principal and interest was paid) to discharge the same, which proposition was unanimously agreed to by the Trustees and other members of the Congregation present.

Whereupon Samuel Paynter, senr., paid in cash £5 14s. 8d. which with the sum of £14 5s. 4d. due him before made up the sum of £20 and George Parker also paid in cash £7 3s. 4d, which with the sum of £12 16s. 8d., due him before made the sum of £20. Daniel Rodney, James Wiltbank, and Cornelius Wiltbank each agreed to advance the sum of £20, Cornelius Paynter and Samuel Paynter, Junr, £20, John Cole and Daniel Woolf, £20, John Parker, William Burton, £10 between them and Woodman Stockley since agreed to advance £10.

And Daniel Rodney was requested by the Trustees to draw a mortgage deed by Saturday next to be executed and delivered to the persons above mentioned.

Saturday, January 12th, 1799. All the Trustees met and Daniel Rodney presented the deed agreeable to their request last meeting and the same was executed by Daniel Rodney, Samuel Paynter, Cornelius Wiltbank, George Parker, William Burton, and Cornelius Paynter, according to the above agreement. Elijah Cannon agreed to pay Peter Robinson's debt of £4 amount of his subscription to repair Court House which was for £6.

Cornelius and James Wiltbank produced receipts to the amount of £40 from William Arnell, Walter Hudson and Robert Brereton is in full for their shares as mentioned in the mortgage deed, £40.

Daniel Rodney also presented his amount for payment made to Frederick Row, as Clerk, for two years, one year at 10 and one at 12 dollars, £8 5s. 0d.; Do to Hester McHam on her Bond £15 9s. 3d., and a balance due him at settlement of his amount for repairing Old Court House last Easter, £1 17s. 4d., amounting in all to £25 11s. 7d.

Cr: being balance in his hands for rent of Lott £2 4s. 8d., which leaves £3 6s. 11d. due him over the sum of £20 he agreed to advance.

Daniel Woolf paid his share being £10 to Caleb Rodney per receipt shown the Trustees.

John Cole paid his share by taking up Bond from Jno. Woolf assigned by H. McHam balance £10.

There remains due from the persons to whom the mortgage was made the following sums:

C. P. pd. Jno. Rodney and Geo. Parker, Mar, 1800.

Pd viz—from Samuel and Cornelius Paynter	£20	0s.	0d.
Pd—from Woodn Stockley (pd Mills McIlvaine)	10	0	0
Pd—from Wm. Burton (appd to pay D. Rodney) from John Parker................	15	0	0
	1	1	3
pd from Elijah Cannon on Subscription pd D. R.	2	0	0
	£ 38	1s.	3d

Also the following debts remain:

Unpd. To Mills McIlvaine—£22 10s. 0d. paid.
pd To John Rodney £6 9s. 10d. pd by C. Paynter.
To Caleb Rodney, pd. £3 15s. 0d. bal due $2.35.
To Daniel Rodney as above £3 6s. 11d. £36 19s. 3d.

Trustees agreed to meet again February 16.

Agreeably to appointment the Trustees met February 16th, 1799, and agreed to meet again Easter Monday next.

Easter Monday, being the 25th March, 1799, the Trustees of St. Peter's Church, together with the Wardens and several of the Vestry, met at the old Court House in Lewes when the Trustees, Wardens, and Vestrymen that were appointed last Easter (no objection being made) were continued for the ensuing year.

March the 8th, 1800. The Trustees met this day agreeably to notice and agreed to rent the old Court House (and

Church lot at the expiration of Richard Howard's lease) to Simon Marriner for one year, he paying the thirty pounds rent, to bind himself not to suffer any person to play at cards or dice in said house during said term and to cause the chimneys to be clean swept at least once a month when fires are kept in them.

Also appointed Daniel Rodney and George Parker to settle with James Elliott—the former tenant.

Agreeably to appointment the committee met Monday the tenth of March, after crediting him with the following sums vizt.:

For paint, oil and Jug £2 17s. 3d. For pails in back yard, door &ca. as valued by Isaac Turner and Jno. Rodney pr their bill £4 18s. 3d. and Trustees Bond assigned to him by John Cole balance due thereon, £10 14s. 3d.

Also a deduction for the last years' rent the term for which he took it not having yet expired, £2 19s. 4d.

There was the sum of £19 4s. 10d. due the Trustees towards the last year's rent, which the said James Elliott has acknowledged under his hand.

By ten dollars January 23d, 1801 and twenty-four dollars August 10th, is thirty-four dollars.

James Elliott also paid George Parker 8/8 dollars, May, 1800.

Easter Monday being the fourteenth of April, Anno Domini, 1800, several Trustees, Vestrymen and other members of the Congregation met and proceeded to business when the following officers were appointed, vizt.: Samuel Paynter, Sr, Cornelius Wiltbank, Wardens; Jacob Hazzard, John Woolf, John Maul, Richard Howard, William Polk, Burton Johnson, Samuel Paynter, Junr., John Parker, Daniel Woolf, William Cord, Levin Ennis, and Elijah Cannon, Vestry for 1800.

Also at same time William Woolf, Esqr., was appointed lay delegate to represent this Congregation in the State Convention to be held in Dover the first Tuesday in May next, and that Eight Dollars be appropriated to pay in to the Treasurer of sd. Convention together with his expenses.

The Wardens and Vestry adjourned and agreed to meet again on Saturday the third of May next.

Saturday, third of May, 1800. The Wardens and Vestry met and continued the Rev. James Wiltbank as the pastor of this Church for the ensuing year.

Easter Monday, April 6th, 1801. The Wardens, Vestry, and Trustees met at the old Court House in Lewes.

The Wardens and Vestrymen appointed last Easter were continued and appointed for the following year.

At same time Samuel Paynter, Junr., was appointed lay delegate to represent the Church or Congregation in the State Convention to be held in New Castle, Tuesday, the fifth of May next, and case he should not be able to attend Cornelius Wiltbank should attend in his stead. And Daniel Rodney, Chairman of the Trustees was requested to advance to said delegate four dollars as the contribution of the said Church to the general Convention also his expenses in attending at New Castle.

Trustees for the year 1801: Daniel Rodney, Chairman; Samuel Paynter, senr., George Parker, Cornelius Wiltbank, William Burton, Elijah Cannon, Junr., Cornelius Paynter, were all present except Samuel Paynter, Senr., when it was agreed that Daniel Rodney and George Parker should be authorized to repair the Church wall and gate.

Also to rent the old Court House to Simon Marriner for the ensuing year for the sum of £27 10s.

April 6th, 1801. Simon Marriner paid £18 15s. and March the seventeenth 1802, he paid £10 18s. to Daniel Woolf for his share of the mortgage which is in full for his first year's rent and 13s. towards this year's rent which was due March the —, 1802.

Easter Monday, April 19th, 1802. At a meeting of the Wardens, Vestry, and other members of the Congregation, present the Rev. James Wiltbank It was agreed to receive him as pastor to officiate in said Church one Sunday in four weeks in the forenoon and one Sunday in four weeks in the afternoon.

It was also agreed to appoint John McCracken Sexton of the said Church, to give him Ten Dollars pr Ann. for ringing the bell, cleaning the Church, &ca., and two dollars extra if there should be preaching on other days besides Sundays. At same time Samuel Paynter, senr., was appointed a delegate to represent this Church in the State Convention to meet at Lewes the first Tuesday in May next.

Also Daniel Rodney, Chairman of the Trustees, is directed to advance four dollars to be paid to the State Convention towards defraying the expenses of the General Convention.

The Wardens appointed for the ensuing year are: Samuel Paynter, Senr., and Cornelius Wiltbank. Vestry: Jacob Hazzard, John Woolf, John Maull, William Woolf, Richard Howard, Burton Johnson, Samuel Paynter, Junr., Elijah Cannon, John Parker, Daniel Woolf, William Cord, Stephen Warrington. Trustees for the present year 1802: Daniel Rodney, Chairman; Samuel Paynter, Senr., Cornelius Wiltbank, George Parker, Elijah Cannon, Cornelius Paynter, and William Burton.

Simon Marriner Dr. To a year's rent due March 8th or 10th, 1802 (agreed at)		£27 10s. 0d.
Do By 13s. left or unpaid of the last year rent	£0 13s. 0d.	
By his account allowed for repairs at Easter 1803	3 14 1	
By cash at same time	20 12 11	25 0 0
Balance due Trustees March 1802		2 10 0
To one years rent due March 1803		27 10
		£30 0 0
By discounted with Parson Wiltbank towards his share of Mortgage		14 15 0
Balance due Trustees		£15 5 0

Due from James Elliott for principal and interest on his settlement April 10th, 1803, £6; which was assigned to the Rev. James Wiltbank towards his share of Mortgage.

Easter Monday, April 11th, 1803. The Trustees, a number of the Vestry, and others of the Congregation met this day and agreed to continue the Trustees, Wardens, and Vestry that were appointed last year, except William Woolf, Esqr., in whose place Thomas Warrington was appointed on account of Mr. Woolf's declining to serve.

Also Daniel Rodney was authorized to pay unto Sarah Stockley the amount of Woodman Stockley's share or part of the mortgage deed executed by the Trustees to the several persons therein mentioned in 1799, the principal being £10.

Also the said Daniel Rodney was authorized to pay unto John McCracken $6.33, amount being balance due him for the last year and out of the money he has received or may receive for rent. Also to continue the said John McCracken as bell ringer or sexton to open and clean the church, &ca., for the ensuing year.

It was further resolved that Daniel Rodney, Chairman of the Trustees, should pay unto William Burton his share of the mortgage given him and others by the Trustees in the year 1799, the principal of which is £5 and Interest according.

It was also agreed with Simon Marriner to rent him the Old Court House for the ensuing year at £25 10s. pr annum, commencing the eighth or tenth of March, 1803. The lot below the Church yard on Third Street, except a pound round the stable, is to remain in possession of the Trustees, and it is understood that in consequence of the rent being lowered since last year, they are at liberty to rent the aforesaid lower lotts to any other person.

And it was further agreed that Simon Marriner should have a credit towards the rent now due from him for any sum he should pay unto Parson Wiltbank towards his share of the Mortgage due from the Trustees and that Daniel Rodney is hereby authorized to pay the balance of said share of mortgages out of any money in his hands not otherways appropriated this day.

Statement of the sums due on Mortgage from the Trustees dated January 12th, 1799:

To Saml. Paynter Senr.	£20—In. 4 yrs	£4 4s.0d.		£24 4s.0d.
" George Parker	"	"		24 4 0
" Danl. Rodney	"	"		24 4 0
" Cornels. Wiltbank	"	"		24 4 0
" Saml. Paynter Junr. £10				
" Cornels. Paynter		10 is £20 & In.		24 4 0
" John Parker £5 and 4 yrs In at 6% is				6 4 0
				£127 4s.0d.

Paid to Revd. Jas. Wiltbank £24 4s. 0d. by a note assigned him by Simon Marriner, and a note by D. Rodney on James Elliott and cash. John Cole and Daniel Wolfe are paid.

Woodman Stockley and William Burton were paid their shares this day; Mr. Stockley was paid £12 8s. 0d. and William Burton £6 4s. 0d.

Easter Monday, April 2d, 1804. The Trustees, Wardens, and Vestry met agreeably to notice previously given when

John Wolfe was unanimously elected a Trustee to supply the place of Elijah Cannon, decd.

The Trustees for the ensuing year will then be: Daniel Rodney, Chairman; Samuel Paynter, Senr., George Parker, Cornelius Wiltbank, John Wolfe, Cornelius Paynter, and William Burton. Wardens elected or continued: Samuel Paynter, Senr., and Cornelius Wiltbank. Vestry for the ensuing year continued and elected: Jacob Hazzard, John Wolfe, John Maull, Thomas Warrington, Richard Howard, Burton Johnson, John Parker, Daniel Wolfe, William Paynter, and Stephen Warrington.

On the same day the following appropriation of money was made, vizt., which the chairman was authorized to pay: To pay John McCracken for ringing bell, &c[a], $10 and he was continued at same rate for ensuing year.

Also to pay the following persons in part of their Interest due on Mortgage, vizt: Danl. Rodney, $6; George Parker, $6; Saml Paynter, Jun., $3; Saml. Paynter, Senr., $6; Cornelius Wiltbank, $6; Cornels. Paynter, $3.

At same time Samuel Paynter, Senr., was appointed lay delegate to represent this Church in the Convention to be held in George Town in May next. Danl Rodney was directed to pay unto the aforesaid Samuel Paynter $4, as the contribution of this Church to the General Convention.

It was also agreed to continue the Revd. James Wiltbank as pastor of said Church the ensuing year to officiate as minister and preach every third Sunday and to be paid out of the pew tax that may be collected not to exceed one hundred Dollars.

Simon Marriner paid the sum of.........		£13 10s. 0d.
do To bal. due for rent Mar. 10th 1803	£15 5s. 0d.	
do To a year's rent due Mar. 10th 1804............	25 10 0	40 15 0
Bal. due from Simon Marriner...........		£27 5 0

The afrd. Simon Marriner was continued as tenant in the Old Court House for the ensuing year at £25 10s. per annum and to till the Church Lott in Corn and some potatoes for which he is to give one half the produce as rent.

Due the following persons on the mortgage each (exclusive of 6 Dolls. paid this day £24 5s 0d vize

George Parker, Samuel Paynter, Senr., Danl Rodney, Cornels. Wiltbank, Cornelius and Samuel Paynter, amt............................£121 15s. 0d.
To John Parker 6£ and 5 yrs. In. at 6%........ 7 10s. 0d.

£128 15s. 0d.

Simon Marriner by cash paid Daniel Wolfe towards Cedar Rails to fence the Church Lott this 22nd September, 1804..........................£ 7 10s. 0d.
Do By cash paid Saml Paynter, Senr.......... 7 10s. 0d.

£15 0s. 0d.

Easter Monday, April the fifteenth, A. D. 1805. At a meeting of the Wardens, Vestry, and other members of the congregation of St. Peter's Church, at Lewes, Samuel Paynter, Senr, and Cornelius Wiltbank were appointed Wardens for the ensuing year, and Jacob Hazzard, John Wolfe, John Maull, Samuel Paynter, Junr., David Johnson, John Parker, Thomas Warrington, Richard Howard, James Elliott, Daniel Wolfe, William Paynter and Sylvester Webb were chosen Vestrymen for the ensuing year. Also the following persons were elected Trustees for the ensuing year, vizt: Daniel Rodney, Chairman; Samuel Paynter, Senr, Cornelius Wiltbank, John Wolfe, Cornelius Paynter, George Parker, and William Burton.

The Wardens, Vestry and other members present agreed to receive the Revd. James Wiltbank as pastor to the said Church and pay him One Hundred and fifty Dollars for the ensuing year for officiating and preaching in said Church every other Sunday.

Mr. Daniel Wolfe was appointed Collector of the pew tax for which service he is to be allowed 5% on the sum collected.

John McCracken was appointed sexton and to ring the bell for which he is to be allowed 12 dollars per annum.

A subscription paper was drawn authorizing Messrs. George Parker and James Elliott to receive voluntary Contributions to be applied towards the payment of the Parson's salary.

All the accounts relative to fencing the Church Lott and the Potatoes received for rent were settled and paid off at this meeting, and C. Paynter paid 13/1½ for wood.

Simon Marriner agreed to Rent the House for the ensuing year, rent to commence March 10th, 1805, at the same rate he had it last year, vizt. £25. 10s. exclusive of the Lott. At settlement there appears to be £13 15s. 0d. due from the said Simon Marriner for arrears of rent the last year.

The Trustees having paid all the small bills and accounts against the Church out of the money received for the rent last year, the balance in their hands was £21 0s. 0d. which, with £5 11s. 0d. pd. Aug 17th, when it can be collected, will make £26 11s. 0d. was appropriated to the payment of the interest on the mortgage due to the following persons:

To Saml Paynter, Senr........................	£4 19s. 0d.
To Cornels Wiltbank £4 19s. 0d. Geo. Parker £4 19s. 0d..................................	9 18 0
To Danl Rodney £4 19s. 0d. Cornels & Saml Paynter £4 19s. 0d...........................	9 18 0
and to John Parker..........................	16 0
	£26 11s. 0d

After which there will be due on Mortgage to the above mentioned Mortgagees the following sums:	
To John Parker Principal with In. from Jan. 12th	£ 6 0s. 0d.
To Saml Paynter Senr & Danl Rodney each £20	40 0 0
To Cornels Wiltbank & Geo. Parker each £20.	40 0 0
and to Cornels & Saml Paynter Junr each £10.	20 0 0
due Jany 12th, 1805.........................	£106 0s. 0d.

Samuel Paynter, Senr., George Parker and Daniel Rodney were appointed a Committee to Sell the old brick and put up a Cedar fence on the northwest Side of the Church Yard, and to rent the pews for the ensuing year.

At a meeting of the Trustees, Wardens, &ca., August 17th, 1805; Simon Marriner paid £5 11s. towards last year's rent; Do paid $8.50 being the amount of one-third of 19¼ bushels of wheat raised on the Church Lott.

At same time Daniel Rodney was paid the sum of $8.50 towards repaying him an amount which he had paid to John Jeffreys for Carpenter's work on the Court House.

Also at said meeting the Trustees present, vizt, Daniel Rodney, Samuel Paynter, Senr, George Parker, Cornelius Wiltbank, and William Burton, authorized Simon Marriner to procure shingles and have a new roof put on the house which he agreed to do provided the expense did not exceed one year's rent.

See previous page for the manner the above sum of £5 11s. was appropriated, vizt, £4 19s. to Daniel Rodney and 12s. to George Parker which was left unpaid of their interest last Easter on account of the sum of £5 11s. not then collected.

November the 2nd, 1805. The Trustees, Wardens and some of the Vestry met and appointed Sylvester Webb to collect the pew tax and Subscriptions.

February the 22nd, 1806, at a meeting this day, present Daniel Rodney, Samuel Paynter, senr, John Wolfe, Cornelius Paynter, and William Burton and several of the Vestry and other members of the Congregation, Simon Marriner presented Isaac Turner's account which he had paid amounting to $35.04 of which $6.75 appeared to have been settled in 1803, balance will be........................ $28.29

he also agreed to pay Jos. Coutter $1 and for shingles to Mr. Long amounting to $61.................. $62.00

James Holland's bill for work.................... 6.25

Thomas Warrington's do. for do. after deducting $2 for his subscription........................ 12.10

for boarding the Carpenters...................... 4.00

$112.64

do. to his subscription......................... $4.00

To one year's rent due March 10th................ 68.00

To balance due for rent March, 1805.............. 36.67

$108.67

$112.64
108.67

There will be a bal of $3.97 cents due Simon Marriner March 10th, 1806........................ $3.97

Also the amounts for repairing the Church wall, the kitchen, cellar, and putting a new roof on the Old Court House were brought in amounting to $162.28, exclusive of Mr. Carlisle's bill for Oak board, $112.64, of which Simon Marriner assumed to pay, for which he is credited above, and $49.64

paid out of subscription money except Caleb Rodney's account of $13.86. T. Carlisle's bill for board was not brought in with the others and is yet unpaid. Thomas Carlisle's bill amounting to £4 10s. 9d. paid by Sylvester Webb.

Easter Monday, April 7th, 1806. This day a meeting was held at the house of Simon Marriner; present George Parker, Daniel Rodney, William Wolfe, James Elliott, Daniel Wolfe, and Sylvester Webb, when it was agreed on account of the small number present to adjourn the meeting till this day three weeks.

On the twenty-eighth day of April, 1806, agreeably to adjournment, several of the Trustees, Vestry, and members of the Congregation met and appointed Samuel Paynter, Junr, and Sylvester Webb lay delegates to represent this Church in the State Convention to be held at Milford the first Tuesday in May.

Also the Wardens, Vestrymen and bell ringer appointed last year were continued for the ensuing year.

At a meeting held the twenty-sixth day of July, it was agreed to recommend raising the pew tax for the last year so as to make up fifty dollars more than the tax amounted to before, which was $100; the aforesaid fifty dollars to be paid to the Rev. James Wiltbank in addition to the sum collected for the pews at the old rate.

It was also resolved to receive the Revd. James Wiltbank as pastor of this Church for this year, 1806, and to pay him the same salary and in the same manner as he was paid before Easter, 1805, vizt: out of the pew tax that could be collected and voluntary subscriptions.

1807. At a meeting of the Wardens, Vestry, Trustees and other members of St. Peter's Church, at Lewes, this thirtieth day of March, being Easter Monday, the Wardens, vizt. Samuel Paynter, Senr. and Cornelius Wiltbank, appointed last year, were continued for the ensuing year.

The Trustees are Daniel Rodney, Samuel Paynter, Senr., Cornelius Wiltbank, George Parker, John Wolfe, Cornelius Paynter, and William Burton.

The Vestry for the last year were John Wolfe, Jacob Hazzard, Thomas Warrington, Daniel Wolfe, Samuel Paynter, Junr., David Johnson, John Parker, Richard Howard, James Elliott, Sylvester Webb, and John Maull, Senr.; who were continued for the ensuing year and Charles M. Cullen was also appointed a Vestryman for the ensuing year.

At same time Simon Marriner paid £30 for his rent due the tenth of this month in the following manner:—A Bill for

Latches, plank, &ca.	$2.93
A bill over paid by him last year	3.97
	$6.90
And cash	73.00
	80.00

Also Samuel Paynter, Senr., and Daniel Rodney were appointed lay delegates to represent this Church in the State Convention to be held the first Saturday in June, and Daniel Rodney was directed to pay four dollars as the Contribution of this Church to the General Convention.

It was agreed by a majority of the members present that the Trustees should sell that part of the Church lott which lays between the public ditch and Fourth street and that the same should be advertised to be sold on Saturday week next.

Also Daniel Rodney was authorized to pay John McCracken for his services in ringing the bell, &ca., $12 for the last year; and the above mentioned lott was sold, at the time appointed, unto Caleb Rodney who gave a note for one-half the purchase money payable in three months for the sum of £25 and the residue being £25 more payable next Easter.

The first of the above notes were paid and applied by the Trustees towards getting timber and materials for building the new church.

1808, August 29th, the other note from Caleb Rodney was discharged by his account for nails and other articles furnished for the new Church.

Easter Monday, April the 18th, 1808. At a meeting of a number of the Vestry and other members of St. Peter's Church, at Lewes, the Wardens and Vestry appointed last year were continued for the ensuing year.

At same time Simon Marriner paid cash	$40.00
Also his bill for repairs	9.81
Jno West, Isaac Turner & Jos Coutters do	9.87
	$59.68
To his rent due last month	80.00
due St. Peter's Church from Simon Marriner towards last year's rent	$20.32

The above was settled by bill for porch and cash April 3d, 1809.

August 29th, 1808, the Wardens, Vestry, Trustees and other members of the Congregation of St. Peter's, at Lewes, having agreed to build a new church of the same size of the old one and to set it about thirty or forty feet to the south and west of the old Church, which was so much decayed that the carpenters and others considered it would not bear repairing, the new Church was raised in June, and was so far ready and prepared for the congregation to meet in and hear a sermon delivered by the Revd James Wiltbank, yesterday.

September the fifteenth, 1808, the new Church was this day completely finished and the workmen discharged; being about three months in building from the time it was raised.

Easter Monday, April 3d, 1809. This day the Wardens, Vestrymen and other members of the congregation of St. Peter's, at Lewes, met at Simon Marriner's and re-elected Samuel Paynter, Senr., and Cornelius Wiltbank, Wardens. Vestrymen elected this year are: John Wolfe, William Wolfe, place of Jacob Hazzard, decd., Samuel Paynter, Junr., David Johnson, John Parker, Senr., Thomas Warrinton, Daniel Wolfe, Richard Howard, John Maull, Senr., Sylvester Webb, Charles M. Cullen and James Elliott—12. Also Charles M. Cullen and John Parker, Senr., were appointed to represent this Church in the Convention to be held at Milford this year.

Daniel Rodney, Chairman of the Trustees, was also requested to pay the delegates $4 for the annual contribution to the Convention, and to pay John McCracken the sexton $12 for his services in ringing the bell, &ca., for the year past.

At same time a full settlement was made between the Vestry and the Revd. James Wiltbank in which it was agreed by the Vestry to release any claim they had against him for arrears of subscriptions and by the Parson to release any claim which he had for arrears of salary, &ca.

Simon Marriner settled his rent due the tenth of last month in the following manner:

By a note of James and Thomas Prettyman due in July, which was assigned to Thomas Warrington.....	$25.00
Another note on do due in March next..............	25.00
And cash paid to Daniel Rodney....................	30.00
	$80.00

ST. PETER'S, 1808
(Second Building)

St. Peters Church at Lewes. Dr.

Date		£	s.	d.
1808.				
Octr. 6.	To amt Brot. over	£122	4s.	4d.
18th.	To candles to light Church for Parson Weems		1	10½
	To paid Isaac Turner the bal. of his bill	4	15	6
	To do John Parker (Farmer)			
	To do John Orr the bal. of his bill	7	11	10
	To pd John McCracken for ringing bell &ca	4	10	0
1809.				
April 3rd.	To pd John Little Junr		15	
6th.	To pd Thos. Warrington 26.71	10	5	4
June 2d.	pd. Charles M. Cullen Esq for the Annual Contribution of this Church to the Convention	1	10	0
	John M. West for Cedar	4	8	11
1810.				
Jan. 18.	Gave Isaac Turner an order on Wm Steel Senr for his subscription amtg. to $6.00			
	Mr. Wiltbank pd. Mr. Carlisle for 2808 feet of Laths £4. 14s. 4d.			
April 23d.	To Cash paid Chas. M. Cullen the bal. of his bill for Boards for Church	1	6	3
		£156	19s.	1d.
27.	Paid Wm Harris the bal of his Bill for work on the Church.	3	15	1
July 13.	Paid Sylvester Webb for the Annual Contribution of this Church to the State Convention	1	10	0
	Paid Richd Enos for cleaning Pulpit &c		8	5
Sept. 19.	Cash paid Thos. Rodney for Oil & Paint for the outside of the Church $40.00	15	0	0
		£177	12s.	6d.

1811.					
May	20.	Cash paid Caleb Rodney for Well Sweep &c............		11s.	3d.
		" Isaac Turner for putg. it up..................		3	9
June	1.	Cash paid John Milby for 1500 Bricks & Lime............	7	17	6
	11.	To a hhd of Lime $6, porterage &c 3s. 9d.................	2	8	9
Aug.	20.	Paid Wm. Wolfe Esq. $14 the balance of his act. for Timber & hauling for Church yard after deducting $10 which he subscribed........	5	5	0
Sept.		To pd. Scipio and George for Sawing Timber for capg....	1	1	2
			£194	19s.	11d.
1812.					
May	29.	To 1s. 6d. pd Postmaster.....		1	6
Sept.	7.	To Cash paid Mrs Bell admr of the Rev. Hamilton Bell towards his salary 49.50....	18	3	9
			£213	3s.	2d.

Easter Monday, April the 23rd, 1810. At a meeting of the Wardens and several others of the Congregation of St. Peter's this day, it was agreed to appoint Thomas Rodney and James Long as Vestrymen in the stead of James Elliott and Richard Howard and to continue the other Vestrymen and Wardens that were appointed last year for the ensuing year. Also Charles M. Cullen and Sylvester Webb were appointed as lay delegates to represent this Church in the Convention which is to meet in Milford the first Saturday in June next.

At same time Samuel Paynter, Senr., Daniel Rodney, George Parker, Cornelius Wiltbank, and John Parker, Senr., agreed that the mortgage given to them and others by the trustees in 1799 for the Church lotts and buildings should be discharged and that satisfaction should be entered thereon and on the margin of the Record.

Simon Marriner also paid his rent for the last year in the following manner:—

Cash paid to Daniel Rodney C of Trustees.......... $64.00
and bills for repairs &ca allowed.................. 16.00

$80.00

This year, 1810, we have had no stated preaching the Revd. James Wiltbank having removed to Holmesburgh in Pensylvania.

Easter, April 15th, 1811. At a meeting this day the Wardens and the Vestry for the last year were continued and appointed for the ensuing year.

Hamilton Bell was ordained Deacon on Sunday, September, 1747, in the Chapel of Fulham Palace. He was born in Dumfries, Scotland.

The Wardens and Vestry agreed to receive the Revd. Hamilton Bell as their Pastor to officiate in this Church every other Sunday, or once in two weeks during the year from the third Sunday before Easter and to pay him for said service one hundred and fifty dollars which sum they propose to raise by pew tax and subscription.

Simon Marriner paid in cash....................... $65.30
do by a bill for steple & repairs.................. 4.70

$70.00

leaving a bal of $10 due....for last year.
March 1812 By cash $10 by Mrs Marriner in full for
1810.................................... 10.00

$80.00

The Revd. Hamilton Bell died the twenty-sixth of November, 1811, at his house in Dagsbury Hundred and was buried the twenty-eighth at Broad Creek Church.

So read the entries in the minutes of St. Peter's Vestry.

The Rev. Hamilton Bell was called to "officiate in Lewes, every other Sunday, or once in two weeks during the year from the third Sunday before Easter." This was Easter Monday, April 15, 1811.

The Rev. Hamilton Bell left two children, Elizabeth Hamilton Bell, and Mary Eleanor Bell. Mary Eleanor was under fourteen years of age at the time of her father's death. John Polk, merchant, of Little Creek, became their guardian.

The Rev. William Wickes was here in 1816. He was ordained Deacon by Bishop Seabury. Deposed, 1825.

The Rev. John Forman became Rector of St. Peter's parish August, 1817. November 27th, 1820, he resigned.

At a meeting of the Vestry, Easter Monday, April 4th, 1836, the Rev. C. E. Pleasants acted as chairman. He had resigned before March 27th, 1837.

At a meeting of the Vestry, Monday, March 31st, 1834, the Rev. Nathan Kingsberry was present as Rector.

At a meeting of the Vestry, Easter Monday, 1835, a communication from the Rev. Nathan Kingsberry stated that he had given up his charge in Sussex County on account of ill health, and had removed to New York.

At a meeting of delegates from five churches (Georgetown, Laurel, Dagsboro, St. Peter's, and St. George's) it was agreed to receive the Rev. Daniel Higbee as their Pastor.

December 10th, 1821, Daniel Higbee gave a receipt for \$20$\frac{00}{100}$ towards his services as Rector of St. Peter's Church. St. Peter's was to pay \$180$\frac{00}{100}$ a year, and the other churches \$120$\frac{00}{100}$.

At a meeting of the Vestry April 20th, 1829, there is no mention of the Rev. Daniel Higbee.

Simon Marriner died July 2nd, 1811.

Simon Marriner Dr. to a year's rent from March 10th, 1811, to March 10th, 1812		$80.00
By bill for repairs	$ 6.00	
By cash	50.00	56.00
Bal due Trustees		$24.00

Sarah Marriner, the widow of Simon, agreed to rent the Old Court House the ensuing year at £30 per annum, the rent to commence the tenth of this inst. March, 1812.

September 7th, 1812, paid Mrs. Bell $49.50 cents, which, with $50.50 paid to the Revd. H. Bell in his life time, amounts to $100, leaving a balance of $50 yet due him.

September 28th, Mr. Webb left $30 which he had collected, Octr. 7th Mr. Webb left $10 which he had collected for Mrs. Bell, and $10.50 pd her by Daniel Rodney, at Georgetown, or to Mr. Cooper for her use, is in full of her husband's salary.

Easter Monday, March the 30th, 1812. At a meeting of a number of the congregation this day the Wardens, Vestry and Trustees heretofore appointed and elected were continued for the ensuing year as follows: Wardens: Samuel Paynter, Senr., Cornelius Wiltbank. Vestry: John Wolfe, Samuel Paynter, Junr., James Long, John Parker, Senr., David Johnson, John Maull, Senr., Sylvester Webb, Daniel Wolfe, Thos. Warrington, Thomas Rodney, Charles M. Cullen, and Wm. Wolfe. Trustees: Daniel Rodney, Chairman; Samuel Paynter, Senr., Cornelius Wiltbank, George Parker, John Wolfe, Cornelius Paynter, William Burton.

At same time it was resolved that Daniel Rodney should prove the account against Simon Marriner, decd., for balance

of Rent due March 10th, 1811		$10.00
for a years rent due do 1812		80.00
for balance of his subscription to New Church		5.00
for his pew tax for 1811		3.50
		$98.50
By repairs in the lifetime of S. Marriner		3.00
		$95.50
By do made by the widow	$3.00	
By cash paid do.	60.00	
By discounts for pew tax and subscription	8.50	
By cash received for balance	24.00	
	95.50	
Recd for Rent in May, 1813		$70.46
in repairs as settled		9.54
		$80.00

Easter Monday, 1813, in consequence of the war between the United States and Great Britain, and the Town being filled with Militia no meeting of the Wardens and Vestry took place.

1814, April 11th. George Parker was appointed a Church Warden vice Cornelius Wiltbank deceased. Recd for rent in cash $71.93, repairs $8.07.

1815. At a Stated Annual Meeting, Easter Monday, March the 27th, A. D. 1815, at the house of Mrs. Marriner, in Lewes, of the Wardens, Vestry, Trustees, and part of the Congregation, for the purpose of appointing and continuing the Trustees and other Officers, George Parker, Senr., was continued and appointed one of the Church Wardens; Cornelius Paynter appointed Church Warden in the place of Samuel Paynter, Senr, decd. Vestry continued:—John Maull, Senr., John Parker, Senr, William Wolfe, Daniel Wolfe, Thomas Rodney, James Long, David Johnson, and Thos. Warrington; Wm. Futcher, appointed; also William Paynter, Wm. Burton, John Milby, Anderson Hudson, appointed; David Paynter and John Parker, Junr. Trustees continued and appointed, vizt: Daniel Rodney, Chairman; George Parker, Senr, Cornelius Paynter, William Burton, William Wolfe, Samuel Paynter, and Thomas Rodney.

It was also resolved that the Trustees should lay out a part of the money received for rent in repairing the Court House putting up a partition, painting the roof of it, and the Northeast side of the Church, pointing the cap of the Church Wall, &ca.

Received this year in cash	$61.42
in repairs	18.58
	$80.00

Easter Monday, 1816. The Wardens, Vestry, and Trustees appointed last year were continued for the ensuing year.

Sarah Marriner to one years rent	$80.00
By her acct as settled for repairs	$12.21
By cash paid D Ry.—C. of T.	67.79
	$80.00

At a meeting of several of the Vestry, Wardens and Trustees the twenty-seventh of May, 1816, Thomas Rodney, and John Parker, Junr., were appointed the delegates to represent this Church in the State Convention, to be held at Milford, on Saturday the first of June next. Four dollars were sent by them as the contribution of this Church and $3.22 paid to them on their return for their extra expenses, by Chairman of Trustees.

Easter Monday, April the 7th, 1817, at a meeting of the Wardens, Vestry, and Trustees, the officers appointed in 1815 and continued last year were continued for the ensuing year.

Also it was agreed that the Chairman of the Trustees, should contribute and pay Thirty dolls. to the Missionary

Society of the State of Delaware and four dollars to the Convention.

Thomas Rodney and Daniel Wolfe, were appointed to represent this Church, as lay delegates in the State Convention, to be held in Milford, the first Saturday in June next.

Sarah Marriner paid $80 for a year's rent due tenth of last month; her amount for repairs to be taken out of this year's rent.

Mrs. Sarah Marriner died on Sunday the thirteenth of April, 1817.

The Wheat on the lott was cut and not taken off till August.

"16th February 1818 Received of Daniel Rodney, the sum of fifty dollars, on account of my services as Rector of the Parish of St. Peters at Lewes.

"JOHN FORMAN."

The Revd John Forman was received by the parishes of St. Peter's and St. George's as their Rector in August or September last, at which Churches he was to preach once in three weeks, at one in the forenoon and the other in the afternoon, for the annual compensation of two hundred dollars or one hundred for each Church, as it was understood, and perhaps one-third of fifty dollars, may be expected from the above mentioned Churches.

Easter Monday, March 23d, 1818. A meeting of the Wardens and Vestry of St. Peter's took place at the house of Thomas Warrington, at which it was resolved or agreed that all the officers appointed in 1815 and since continued, (except John Parker, Jun., and David Paynter who have moved out of the Parish), should be continued for the ensuing year; also that George Parker and Thomas Rodney should be a committee to rent the pews; also that Thomas Warrington who moved into the Old Court House in December last should have the house at the same rate Mrs. Marriner had, vizt., Eighty dolls. per annum. The rent was to commence at November Court, about the twentieth of November.

The Trustees agreed to take the stable and carriage house of Reece Marriner, the admc, at the appraisement, $12, which, deducted from $35 left $23 due for last year's rent.

Charles M. Cullen and Daniel Wolfe appointed to attend the Convention to be held at Dover in June next. Delivd M.

Cullen $4 as the annual contribution from this Church, also $4.75 for his expenses.

The Revd John Forman, Rector; Easter Monday, April the 12th, 1819. At a regular Stated Meeting of the Wardens, Vestry, Trustees and Congregation of St. Peter's, at Lewes, held at the house of Thomas Warrington, or the old Court House this day, the following officers were continued and appointed, vizt: Wardens: George Parker and Cornelius Paynter: Trustees: Daniel Rodney, Chairman, George Parker, Cornelius Paynter, William Burton, Samuel Paynter, Junr., Thomas Rodney, and Charles M. Cullen, appd. Vestry: John Maull, Senr, Daniel Wolfe, John Parker, Senr, James Long, William Futcher, Thomas Warrington, John Milby, Anderson Hudson, William Paynter, David Johnson, John Wiltbank, Burton Stockley, Kendle Batson, Reece Woolfe. Also Charles M. Cullen, Daniel Wolfe, and John Wiltbank were appointed to represent this Church as lay delegates in the State Convention to be held in Dover on the first Saturday in June next.

February 20, 1776.

The bonds put into Mr. George Parker's, Jr., hands this day, April 21st, 1836:

Thomas Coleman	$227.48
Henry Myers	83.00
John M. West	115.00
Christopher Lekats	90.00
John Sweney	112.50
Gideon Burton	200.00

The following gentlemen were continued Wardens, viz.: George Parker, Sr., and Daniel Rodney.

The following persons were elected vestrymen for the ensuing year, viz.: William Fletcher, George Parker, Jr., George Hickman, Gov. Samuel Paynter, Robert Burton, Thomas Coleman, Kendal Batson, William Marshall, Sr., William Paynter, Albert Burton, John Marshall, John H. Burton, John Rodney, Jr., David J. Marshall, and Henry F. Rodney.

The following persons were appointed to represent this church in the State Convention to be held in this church in June next, viz.: George Parker, Jr., Henry F. Rodney.

Easter Monday, March 27th, 1837.—At a meeting of the

Wardens and Vestry, & others, this day the s^{d} officers app^{d} last year were Continued for the ensuing year.

At the same time Saml. Paynter, Senr, and Henry F. Rodney were app^{d} lay Delegates to Represent St. Peter's Church in the State Convention to meet at Milford.

The Committee app^{d} in April last with the same power then given were Cont^{d} except John H. Burton in whose place John Marshall was Chosen for the ensuing year. At the same time Governor Paynter, John Marshall, and John Rodney, Jr., were app^{d} to meet other delegates of the different Congregations, to Consider the propriety of procuring a Pastor to Officiate in the Churches lately under the charge of the Rev. Mr. Pleasants.

January 10th, 1838.—At a meeting of the Wardens and Vestry, it was Resolved that three Delegates be appointed to meet the Delegates from the other parishes at George Town on Tuesday next, to take measures for procuring the services of a Clergyman.

Col. Samuel Paynter, George Parker, Jr., and Henry F. Rodney were appointed.

Resolved that the Treasurer of this parish be authorized to pay its quota of the expense of the present Visit of the Rev. Mr. McKim.

The Delegates above app^{d} met others from Indian River, Dagsboro and George Town, and agreed to receive the Rev. Mr. McKim as their Minister, and make up a reasonable, or adequate compensation for him.

Easter Monday, April 16th, 1838.—There being but a small meeting the officers app^{d} for last year will be continued this year, viz.: Daniel Rodney and George Parker, Wardens. Vestry:—George Parker, Jr., George Hickman, Thomas Coleman, Albert Burton, John H. Burton, John Rodney, Junr., Robert Burton, Samuel Paynter, William Marshall, Sr., William Paynter, John Marshall, David J. Marshall—12. Trustees:—Danl. Rodney, Saml. Paynter, Thomas Coleman, George Parker, Senr., George Hickman, Cornelius Paynter, Rev. Mr. McKim, Pastor.

March the 9th, 1839.—Several advertisements were put up in public places for the Election of a Trustee in the place of William Burton, Esq., dec^{d}. Elect^{n} to take place Thursday, March 21st.

March 21st.—Trustees present as below, also Vestry W^{m}. & John Marshall, Albt. Burton, John H. Burton, Thomas

Norman, S. John Rody, &c., at which time it was resolved that an action of Trespass be brought ag[t]. Ferdinand Schey, for encroaching on the Church yard or Burying Ground of St. Peter's, Lewes.

GEORGE PARKER,
DANL. RODNEY,
SAMUEL PAYNTER,
ROBERT BURTON.

Easter Monday, April 1st, 1839.—Officers continued in office Samuel Paynter and Robert Burton were appointed Lay Delegates to represent Saint Peter's church in the State Convention to be held at Seaford in May next.

September 26th, 1839.—At a meeting of the Wardens, Vestry, &c., of Saint Peter's Church, held pursuant to a Public Notice, it was resolved unanimously to call the Rev. Mr. Whitesides, who has lately paid a visit here from Philada. as Rector of Saint Peter's Church, and guarantee the sum of two hundred dollars, certain—and any further sum that can be raised beside the said \$200$\frac{00}{100}$ as our part of his salary for one year.

2d. Resolved that this meeting request that each of the parishes, viz.: Dagsboro, George Town & Saint George's Chapel should act upon the proposition as soon as possibly convenient, and say what certain sum each Congregation would give for the support of the said Rev. Mr. Whitesides and forward the same to the Wardens of Saint Peter's Church at this place, to be by them forwarded to the Rev. Mr. Whitesides. Provided that those Parishes should agree to call the said Clergyman, and in case a union can not be made with the said Parishes (as has been heretofore) then it is recommended that this Parish try to effect a union with Milford.

Easter Monday, April 20th, 1840.—The same Wardens, Vestry, and Trustees continued in office.

Samuel Paynter and Robert Burton were appointed to represent this church in the Convention to be held in Milford—and John Rodney and John H. Burton also appointed in case either or both of the other delegates could not attend. At the same time John Rodney was appointed the Treasurer of Saint Peter's church in the place of George Parker, Jr., who was not in attendance at the meeting this day.

Wednesday, October 28th, 1840.—At a meeting then held pursuant to regular notice given with regard to the calling of a Minister, it was then agreed after due deliberation, to call the Rev. John Reynolds, now living in Milford, Kent County, Delaware, provided a full majority of the Vestry & Wardens should sign a call of invitation to the said Rev. John Reynolds for said purpose. A letter of Invitation was then agreed to be made out and a copy recorded below, viz.:

"LEWES, SUSSEX COUNTY, DEL.
"Nov. 2, 1840

"REV[D]. JOHN REYNOLDS

"DEAR SIR:—We the undersigned wardens, and a majority of the Vestry men of Saint Peter's church in Lewes Sussex County Del[ar] are desirous of having regularly preformed in said Saint Peter's church —The divine services of the Protestant Episcopal Church. Do hereby respectfully offer to your consideration the following proposition, Namely, that you take into your charge the said Saint Peter's Church and perform Episcopal services in the same every other Sunday for one year.

"For which we do agree to pay you the sum of One Hundred and Seventy Five Dollars, certain per annum, and do Further promise to increase that sum to two Hundred Dollars provided that it can be raised by subscription.

"DAN[L] RODNEY
"GEORGE PARKER
Wardens
"JOHN MARSHALL
"ALBERT BURTON
"WILLIAM PAYNTER
"GEORGE PARKER JR.
"JOHN RODNEY
"JOHN H. BURTON
"WILLIAM MARSHALL
"ROBERT BURTON
"DAVID J. MARSHALL"
Vestry Men

N. B.—This above call of invitation was accordingly accepted by the said Rev[d] John Reynolds.

Feb. 23d, 1841.—Capt. W[m]. Brock Dr. for Burying his child in the yard this day $1.50.

March 27th, 1841.—Capt. Wm. Brock gave bond to Saint Peter's Church for Ninety two & $\frac{80}{10}$ Dollars, for property on Market St.

Easter Monday, April 12th, 1841.—At a meeting held this day in Saint Peter's church Albert Burton was called to the Chair and John Rodney appointed Secty.

Owing to the unfavorable state of the weather there were but few persons present, no business transacted and no election.

Resolved to adjourn until Saturday afternoon next at 2 Oclock.

Saturday afternoon, two Oclock, April 17th, 1841.—The members of the church met pursuant to adjournment Daniel Rodney was called to the Chair and John Rodney appointed Secretary.

Present at this meeting, Vizt. Daniel Rodney, John H. Burton, Joshua S. Burton, William Skellinger, David J. Marshall, Albert Burton, Robert Burton, George Hickman, Thomas Norman, Richard Paynter, Peter Warrington, John Rodney.

The following persons were appointed as lay delegates to represent this church in the State Convention to be held at George Town in May next, Vizt. Col. Samuel Paynter and Robert Burton, and George Parker Jr. was also appointed in case either of the other delegates could not attend.

On Motion Resolved that this meeting go into the election of a Vestry by Ballot, whereupon the following persons were elected Viz. George Parker Jr., John H. Burton, David J. Marshall, Albert Burton, John Marshall, Robert Burton, William Skellinger, John Rodney, Wm. Paynter, Nicholas R. Rodney and George Hickman.

Samuel Paynter and William Marshall were also chosen. The Wardens, Daniel Rodney & George Parker Senr.

Easter Monday, March 28th, 1842.—At a meeting held this day in Saint Peter's Church Rev. John Reynolds took the chair, and John H. Burton was appointed Secretary.

The Wardens and Vestry were continued with the addition of Dr. William Harris as Vestryman.

Col. Samuel Paynter and John Rodney were elected Delegates to attend the Diocesan Convention to be held at Wilmington in next May—and Robert Burton and John Marshall were elected as substitutes.

April 7th, 1842.—At a meeting of the Trustees of St. Peter's church held this day, Present Daniel Rodney, Samuel Paynter, George Hickman, and Robert Burton. It was unanimously that the Treasurer of the Trustees of this church shall not pay out any monies without a written order signed by a majority of the Trustees.

Easter Monday, April 17th, 1843.—At a meeting of the Congregation of Saint Peter's church held in said Church this day, Daniel Rodney Esq. was called to the Chair, and Dr. William Harris appointed Secretary.

On motion it was resolved that the meeting go into an election for a Warden to supply the place of Mr. George Parker Sen[r] decd., by ballot.

George Parker Jr. was duly elected in his place. Daniel Rodney was re-elected for the other Warden.

It was resolved to reduce the number of Vestrymen from 12 to 8.

The following persons were elected: Samuel Paynter, William Marshall, sen[r], John H. Paynter, John Marshall, John H. Burton, William Paynter, Albert Burton, John Rodney.

Col. Samuel Paynter and Robert Burton were appointed delegates to the Diocesan Convention to be held in Smyrna in May next and George Parker and John Rodney were elected as substitutes.

Saint Peter's church, Wednesday, January 3d, 1844.—At a meeting of the Vestry pursuant to a notice being given. Col. Samuel Paynter, Daniel Rodney, William Marshall, sen[r]. John H. Burton, Albert Burton & John Rodney, also, the Sexton of the said church, Thomas Norman. The object of the meeting being stated, vizt. for the consideration of the calling of a regular minister, and fixing on some sum of money (certain) for his support &c $150\frac{00}{100}$ was promised (certain) for the services of the Rev. Walter E. Franklin, the present Missionary of the Parish, or for the services of the Rev. John Linn McKim, who is shortly expected to come into the County of Sussex and take charge of some Parishes in the same; for the selection of either we do hereby leave to the Direction of the Bishop, the Rt. Rev. Alfred Lee, D. D., or to the Bishop and the said Clergyman, as it may best seem for the good of the Church in our said County, trusting that it will be so arranged that peace and good will may again dwell amongst us.

The meeting then adjourned to Wednesday the 24th after arranging to have a new fence on the Northwest side of the Church yard.

Easter Monday, April 8th, 1844.—At a meeting of the congregation held in the church this day Daniel Rodney was called to the Chair and John Rodney chosen Secretary.

John Rodney was elected a Trustee in the place of George Parker sen[r] dec[d] and John H. Burton was elected Trustee in the place of Thomas Coleman. Col. Samuel Paynter was elected Warden in the place of George Parker Jr. decd.

The Wardens are considered as Vestrymen.

Col. Samuel Paynter and Robert Burton were appointed Lay Delegates to represent this parish in the Diocesan Convention to be held in this town of Lewes in May next.

John Marshall and John H. Burton were appointed as substitutes.

Easter Monday, 1845.

"RESPECTED FRIENDS

"This being the day observed by the Church for a hundred years past to make appointments and fill up vacancies &c. I think it is proper to inform you, that I am from age, and personal infirmities, unable to attend our meetings a Chairman, of the Trustees, and Wardens. I do therefore resign the aforesaid offices, the first of which I have held since 1795 when Mr. John Russel removed from Lewes.

The Books, Papers, &c I have delivered over to Mr. John Rodney, to lay before you. There will be several vacancies of Trustees, which you know will require ten days notice to the Congregation

"I am yours most affectionately

"DAN[L] RODNEY

"TO THE WARDEN, VESTRY AND CONGREGATION OF ST. PETER'S."

By resolution the above was not accepted.

Easter Monday, March 23d, 1845.—The following were continued in office : Wardens Daniel Rodney and Col. Samuel Paynter. Vestry: Daniel Rodney, William Marshall sen[r]. John Marshall, Albert Burton, Col. Samuel Paynter, John P. Paynter, John H. Burton, John Rodney.

William P. Orr was elected in the place of William Paynter dec[d] who departed this life March 19, 1845.

May, 1845.—A meeting was held in Saint Peter's Church according to notice. A request of the Rector the Rev. John A. Childs who has been duly received.

Delegates to the Convention to be held in Wilmington the last Wednesday of this month, vizt Col. Samuel Paynter and Robert Burton. Substitutes John Rodney and John H. Burton.

April 11th, 1846.—At a meeting of the Congregation of St. Peter's Church Lewes, held according to notice given as the Law directs, the Hon. Dan[l] Rodney was called to the Chair, and John H. Burton was appointed Secretary. On motion it was Resolved to fill the vacancies in the Board of Trustees occasioned by the nonacceptance of John Rodney, and the death of the Hon. Samuel Paynter. Whereupon they proceeded to ballot for two Trustees, and on counting the ballots

William Marshall and William P. Orr were found to have an unanimous vote and declared to be elected.

The Hon. Daniel Rodney having left the chair it was on motion Resolved that the resignation of the Hon. Daniel Rodney be not accepted, and that he be continued in office.

Easter Monday, April 13th, 1846.—Delegates for the Convention to be held at Milford in May, Robert Burton and John Rodney.

John H. Burton and William P. Orr as substitutes.

On motion, Resolved that liberty be given to inter in the Burial Ground of Saint Peter's Church, the remains of the late Nathan Kingsberry, without charge, on account of his former connection with this church as Rector.

"Easter Monday, April, 1847.—Congregational meeting, the Rev. John A. Childs, Rector, in the chair. Alfred P. Robinson was appointed Secretary. Warders: Robert Burton, William P. Orr. Vestry: William Marshall, John Marshall, Alfred P. Robinson, Joshua S. Burton, John Rodney.

"Robert Burton and W^m^. P. Orr were appointed Delegates to represent this church in Convention to be held in Georgetown May next.

"The following was offered and adopted:

"'Whereas it hath pleased Divine Providence to remove from our midst the Hon. Daniel Rodney, for many years and at his death Warden and Chairman of the Trustees, be it Resolved

"'That while expressing due resignation to the Divine Disposal of events, they are deeply sensible of the loss they have lately sustained.

"'Resolved That a copy of this preamble and resolution be presented to the family of the deceased.'

"ALFRED P. ROBINSON Secty."

. At a special meeting May 10, 1847, the following preamble and resolution was read and offered:

"Whereas by an act passed Feb. 25, 1843 the words Rectors, Wardens and Vestrymen are said to be taken and applied to the word 'Trustees' in the former act of incorporation, and all the lawful powers in them vested, be it Resolved, That the powers of the said Trustees are hereby vested in the Wardens and Vestry of this church."

On motion it was Resolved

"The the Wardens and Vestry of this Church, be and are hereby elected Trustees of the same."

November 6th, 1847.—Called Meeting. Whereas by a change of the powers heretofore vested in the Trustees, into Rector, Wardens, and Vestry, the office of Treasurer is now vacant. William P. Orr was appointed Treasurer.

At the meeting Easter Monday, April 24th, 1848, a letter from the Rev. Aaron Freeman recommending the Rev. John Colhoun, was read.

"At a meeting of the Wardens and Vestry Nov. 3, 1848, steps were taken towards raising money for a new church. The present building is the result of that resolution. The Vestry & Congregation of St. Peter's Church met Saturday, May 15, 1852, in accordance to previous public notice. Whereupon John Marshall was called to the Chair and W^{m}. M. L. Richards appointed Secretary.

"The object of the meeting being to take the sense of the Congregation in regard to the sale of the old church building which was about to be effected under a resolution of the Vestry at a previous meeting, was fully stated. A letter was then read from Mary King to the Vestry offering to purchase the building for $300.00; to be paid in sums of $100.00 annual payments by means of public fairs for that purpose; or $400.00 if an additional year be allowed for the payment.

"This proposition having been considered of no importance toward the attainment of the object designed, no action was accordingly taken upon it.

"Afterwards a motion was made by W^{m}. M. Hickman that the meeting approve of the course of the Vestry and Committee touching the matter of the church building, which was negatived.

"Additionally to the above motion, it was resolved that the church building be retained and be repaired by enlarging and modernizing its construction in the manner deemed most advisable to the committee formerly appointed by the Vestry and that the congregation will approve the course of the committee in the matter.

"WM. M. L. RICHARDS, Secty.

CAPE HENLOPEN LIGHTHOUSE.

MISCELLANEOUS RECORDS.

A LOST SETTLEMENT OF THE DELAWARE.

PLOCKHOY'S COLONY, WHICH THE BRITISH WIPED OUT. RESEARCHES OF THE PENNSYLVANIA HISTORICAL SOCIETY THROW LIGHT ON PLOCKHOY'S ATTEMPT—THE SITE OF THE SETTLEMENT WAS NEAR LEWES, DEL.

(By Dr. George G. Groff.)

In making a report to the British Ministers in 1664, Sir Robert Carr, Governor of New York, wrote that he had "destroyed the quaking colony of Plockhoy to a nail." We know that the Dutch and English were then at war; that Carr visited the Delaware river to destroy the Dutch forts, and that it was on this river that he found and destroyed the colony of Plockhoy. But who was this Plockhoy? Who were the colonists? Where was the colony planted? For 200 years there was absolutely no answer to those queries. Now, through the researches of members of the Pennsylvania Historical Society, and especially of the Honorable Samuel W. Pennypacker, the archives in Holland have been made to yield their hidden secrets, and we know the purpose and end of Plockhoy's colony, and of the man himself.

In the various Government documents of the New Netherlands possession of the Delaware or South river is claimed from "primitive times," "ancient times," for "many years," the earliest date for the establishment of any Dutch trading station being given as 1598 by adventurers of the Dutch Greenland Company, who, it is claimed, built forts both on the North (Hudson) and on the South (Delaware) rivers. From this date, until finally driven out by the English, the Dutch seem to have maintained stations on the river, and since there often were married men, with their families, in the stations, they may be considered permanent settlements.

In 1609 Henry Hudson visited the Delaware and in 1610 Lord Delaware. Cornelius Mey made his settlement in 1624; DeVries founded his first colony in 1630 and the second in 1631. New Albion, by Lord Clowden, was founded (if any settlements were ever made) in 1634. In 1635, and again in 1640, 1641 and 1642 the Connecticut people made determined efforts to found settlements on this river. In 1638 the Swedes made their first settlements. Then there is a mysterious Minesink settlement, which is claimed to have been made "shortly after 1609."

PETER CORNELIUS PLOCKHOY.

In 1662 Peter Cornelius Plockhoy, a Mennonite, of Zierik Zee, Holland, after unsuccessful applications to Cromwell, Lord Protector of England, 1658, and to the English Parliament in 1659, obtained from the States General of the United Netherlands and the Magistrates of Amsterdam permission and aid to establish a colony, or community, in New Netherlands. On June 6, 1662, he entered into an agreement with the Burgomasters of Amsterdam to take twenty-five Mennonites to the South river. One hundred guilders were advanced to each colonist, and the colony was to be free from taxes for twenty years.

The settlement was made on the Hoorn Kill, near the town of Lewes, Del., on the same site on which had been planted the first unfortunate colony of DeVries, 1630, which was totally destroyed by the Indians. The place was called Swanendael, or "Valley of the Swans," by the first colony. In Plockhoy's prospectus the place is referred to as "Swanendaél, where Osset had his throne." Osset being the Governor of DeVries colony when it was destroyed by the Indians. The prospectus says:

> "New Netherlands 's the flower, the noblest of all lands.
> The birds obscure the sky, so numerous in their flight;
> The animals roam wild and flatten down the ground,
> The fish swarm in the waters and exclude the light,
> The oysters there, than which no better can be found,
> Are piled up heap upon heap, until islands they attain.
> And vegetation clothes the forest, mead and plain."

"No Lordship or Servile Slavery."

It was on the bank of the Delaware that the Declaration of Independence was promulgated. It was here that the first treaty was made with the Indians which was never broken. It was here that the first united protest against African slavery was made, while the English and Dutch were actively engaged in the slave trade. And here, only three years after a Massachusetts court decreed that the Quakers, Daniel and Provided Southwick, should be sold into slavery in the Barbadoes, Peter Cornelius Plockhoy established his colony in which "no lordship or servile slavery" should ever burden the people. It endured but two short years, and was then destroyed by Carr, as above stated. Plockhoy's colony was a community settlement, and his ideas, published in two letters to Cromwell, an address to the English Parliament and in the prospectus for his colony, show him to have been a man far in advance of his age, the forerunner of Robert Owen, Charles Fourier and Robert Bellers. Two fundamental ideas were at the basis of his community, namely, equality and association. He advocated unity in the Church. "In the Church differences of opinion can be permitted, but brotherhood and unity possess them all." He urged complete separation of Church and State, and that "the common life must again rest upon righteousness, upon love and upon brotherly union."

Plan of the Community.

The title page to Plockhoy's prospectus, taken from the Hon. Samuel W. Pennypacker's history of Germantown, reads:

"Short and clear plan, serving as a mutual contract to lighten the labor and anxiety and trouble of all kinds of handicrafts men by the establishment of a community or colony on the South river, in New Netherlands, comprising agriculturists, seafaring men, all kinds of necessary tradespeople and masters of good arts and sciences, under the protection of their High Mightinesses, the Lords-State-General of the United Netherlands, and particularly under the favorable auspices of the Honorable Magistrates of the City of Amsterdam, depending upon the privileges of their Honors, as hereinafter set forth, granted for the purpose. Brought together by Peter Cornelius Plockhoy, of Zierik Zee, for himself and other lovers of New Netherland. Amsterdam, 1662." This prospectus provided that members might dwell in their own homes and improve them as they saw fit: each one was to labor six hours each day in some useful occupation; profits were to be divided to each person over 20 years of age; officers were to be elected by ballot each year, but no officer could succeed himself. The only officers provided for were a director and two bookkeepers. The funds of the community were to be kept in a strong box, with three different locks, each officer having a key to a single lock, so that the funds could be handled only when all three were present, a plan now pursued by the Friends with church funds. Only those goods were common which were produced by the six hours of required labor. Children were all required to attend the common school half of each day, and to work at some trade the other half of the day; in this school no human formulas of religion, but only the Holy Scriptures, natural sciences and similar instruction enabling them to rightly use their reason, were to be taught. No foundation of sect or partisanship was to be laid in their hearts. (It would almost seem that Girard drew his rules for his college from Plockhoy.) Those who could not conscientiously bear arms in self-defence were to pay a contribution, in case the same were needed for the defence of the community. In matters of religion there was to be full freedom of conscience. No member of the community should be servant or servant maid, yet strangers could be employed at a wage. No lord or slave was to be tolerated in the community. Members were free to withdraw at any time and receive their share of the profits. Members were permitted to marry in the community or out of it, as they saw fit.

The Tragic Ending.

The colony was planted at Swanendael. Two years later it was totally destroyed. There is absolutely no record of what became of the colonists, except the founder and his wife. Of them Judge Pennypacker says: "In the near 1694 there came an old blind man and his wife to Germantown. His miserable condition awakened the tender sympathies of the Mennonites there. They gave him the citizenship free of charge. They set apart for him at the end street of the village, by Peter Klever's corner, a lot twelve rods long and one rod wide, whereon to build a little house and to make a garden, which should be his, so long as he and his wife should live. In front of it they planted a tree. Jan Daeden and William Rittenhouse were appointed to take up a 'free will offering,' and to have the little house built. This is all we know, but it is surely a satisfaction to see this ray of sunshine thrown upon the brow of the hapless old man as he neared his grave. After thirty years of untraced wanderings upon these wild shores, friends had come across the sea to give a home at last to one whose whole life had been devoted to the welfare of others. It was Peter Cornelius Plockhoy. What recognition may hereafter be awarded his career cannot be foretold. His efforts resulted in what the world called failure, and for 200 years he has slept in the greatest obscurity. Yet when we compare him with his contemporaries, with the courtiers, Sir Walter Raleigh and Sir William Berkeley, with Cotton Mather, inciting the magistrates to hang old women for imaginary crimes, and see him wrestling with Cromwell, not for his own gain, but for the help of the downtrodden and the poor, teaching the separation of the Church and the state, protesting against the injuring the minds of children by dogma, and with so clear a sense of justice that even the vicious, when driven from the community, were to receive their share of the possessions, we cannot help but recognize his merit and intelligence, and feel for him that sympathy that makes us all akin. When we find him, first of all the colonizers of America, so long ago as 1662, announcing the broad principle that 'no lordship or servile slavery shall burden our company,' he seems to grow into heroic proportions. Whatever else may happen, certain it is that the events of the life of one whose work marks the very beginning of the literature and history of the ten millions of people who now live in the States along the Zuid river must always be of keen interest to them and to their descendants."

LEWISBURG, PA.

THE BOMBARDMENT OF LEWES BY THE BRITISH

APRIL 6 AND 7, 1813.

March 13th, 1813, the Bay was blockaded by three frigates of seventy-four guns each and smaller vessels. The frigates Poitiers, Belvidere, had been sent from Norfolk.

One of the papers speaking of arrival of the fleet says:—

"Our inhabitants are in a great state of alarm. On Saturday a British seventy-four came into the Delaware, and is now about ten miles within the Capes. On Monday a frigate anchored alongside. Last night, at twelve o'clock, two of the Cape May Pilot-boats were driven in Maurice River and captured by the enemy."

The militia was assembled on the coast.

In a letter to a friend in Baltimore dated March 20th, General Green says:—

"We have a British fleet at the Capes of the Delaware. They have burned several vessels and taken others. We have had an engagement with them from the shore. Our ammunition gave out, or we would have prevented from burning the Charleston packet. They had four large boats full of men, and came within two hundred yards of the shore. I am now on my way to Lewistown, where there are one thousand men under arms. We have men sufficient to prevent them from landing, but we are in want of ammunition, which we shall be supplied with in a few days."

Shortly after the arrival of the British fleet, its commander, Commodore J. Beresford, sent the following letter "to the first magistrate of Lewistown."

"SIR:—As soon as you receive this, I must request you will send twenty live bullocks, with a proportionate quantity of vegetables and hay, to the Poitiers, for the use of his Brittanic Majesty's Squadron, now at this anchorage, which shall be immediately paid for at the Philadelphia prices.

"If you refuse to comply with this request, I shall be under the necessity of destroying your town."

If the first magistrate of Lewes had sent the supplies, it would have cost him his life. It, the letter, was sent to Governor Haslet at Dover. He immediately left Dover and came to Lewes. In a letter to the British Commodore dated March 23d in a reply to the letter sent to the first magistrate, Governor Haslet says:—

"As Governor of the State of Delaware, and as commander of its military force, I improve the earliest time afforded me, since my arrival at this place, of acknowledging the receipt of your letter to the chief magistrate of Lewes.

"The respect which generous and magnanimous nations, even when they are enemies, take pride in cherishing towards each other, enjoins it upon me as a duty I owe the State over which I have the honor at this time to preside, to the government of which this State is a member, and to the civilized world, to enquire of you whether upon further and more mature reflection, you continue resolved to attempt the destruction of this town."

Beresford replied the same day as follows:—

"In reply to your letter received today, by a flag of truce, in answer to mine of the 16th inst., I have to observe, that the demand I have made upon Lewistown is, in my opinion, neither ungenerous nor wanting in that magnimity which one nation ought to observe with another with which it is at war. It is in my power to destroy your town, and the request I have made upon it, as the price of its security, is neither distressing nor unusual. I must therefore persist, and whatever sufferings may fall upon the inhabitants of Lewes must be attributed to yourselves by not complying with a request so easily acquiesced in."

Not until April 7th did Beresford make the attack. One of the newspapers of that day says:—

"Commodore Beresford would seem to have suddenly altered his mind with respect to burning down Lewistown, to make a fire to roast the Delaware oxen by. It would be too offensive to suppose a British officer would threaten without meaning to make good his word. But certain it is that the Commodore has fallen into a dilemma, which 'his friends' at the coffee house have not explained. Delaware beef is highly seasoned, and if served up with forced meat balls, might not prove as palatable to this nautical hero as the beef of old England."

At last the attack was made. Colonel Davis' despatch to the Governor says:—

"This evening the Belvidere and two small vessels came close into Lewes and commenced an attack by firing several thirty-two pound shot into the town, which have been picked up; after which a flag was sent, to which the following reply was returned :—

"'SIR:—I reply to the renewal of your demand, with the addition for "a supply of water," I have to inform you, that neither can be complied with. This, too, you must be sensible of; therefore I must insist the attack on the inhabitants of this town is both wanton and cruel. I have the honor to be your most obedient servant

"'S. B. DAVIS
"'Colonel Commandant.'"

One Captain R. Byron seemed deputed by Beresford to continue the correspondence for supplies. He says:

"No dishonor can be attached in complying with the demand of Sir John Beresford to Lewes in consideration of his superior force. I must, therefore, consider your refusal to supply the squadron with water, and the cattle that the neighborhood affords, most cruel, upon your part, to its inhabitants. I grieve for the distress of the women and children are reduced to by your conduct, and earnestly desire they may be instantly removed."

Colonel Davis answered that he had already taken care of the ladies.

The attack was made immediately, "and continued till near ten o'clock. The fire from our battery silenced one of their most dangerous gunboats, against which I directed the fire from an eighteen-pounder, for which I request you (the Governor) will immediately send me a supply of shot and powder, as it is uncertain how long the bombardment will continue. They have not succeeded with their bombs in reaching the town, and the damages from their thirty-two-pounders and canister cannot be ascertained until daylight."

A letter sent from Dover, April 7th, to the Baltimore *Federal Gazette*, says:

"When the bombardment began, two eighteen-pounders were serviceable, but without ball; two nine-pounders, ball too large; there were but fifteen casks of powder.

"One of the eighteen-pounders mounted on the 6th played on a sloop and silenced its guns.

"Our men behaved well; the women and children left the garrison; the Belvidere came within two miles of the town, too close for her shot to fall in it; the smaller vessels sent balls flying over the town.

"On the fifth of April there were 286 men, 418 muskets complete; 8000 cartridges; 25 bags of grape-shot; 15 kegs of powder; 2270 flints; 41 twelve-pound balls; 88 nine-pound ball; 167 six-pound ball; 216 four-pound ball; 434 kegs of lead; 2 eighteen-pounders, one mounted; 2 nine-pounders, badly mounted; 4 six-pounders, badly mounted; 3 four-pounders, mounted."

The Baltimore *Patriot*, April 7th, read:

"This morning a very steady smoke was seen in the direction of Lewistown, supposed to be occasioned by throwing rockets into that place.

"The enemy fired eight hundred cannon balls on shore,which were picked up by the brave people of Lewes, and 'returned to the enemy with interest.'

"A spectator describes the scene as follows: 'He was just above the town and have a clear view. The British ships were ranged in line of battle; the fire ceased about two o'clock, when he visited the earth-works. The weather was threatening, wind easterly. Captain Byron drew off his squadron at four o'clock, a few miles, where he remained until sailing for the Capes.'

"About five-hundred shots were fired. A collection was made of one hundred and fifty of small sizes and a few bombs. Houses were injured, chimneys cut almost in two, the corner-posts, plates, and studs cut off in several houses. The foremast of a schooner was cut away, and another received a shot in her hull.

"Of two particular rockets thrown, one fell on a lot, another in a marsh.

"A fire was directed at the breastwork, where more than thirty men were stationed. Shot struck the battery and broke the pine logs. Two shots entered by the guns.

"A further account mentions that one bombshell fell in the town, likewise the shots of the Belvidere, and fell some distance beyond. The loss by destruction of property was estimated to be $\$2000\frac{0}{100}$.

"On the tenth of April a letter reached Philadelphia from Dover, dated the 8th inst., written at quarter past 8 o'clock, saying: 'Lewes is yet safe, Mr. White left there at eleven o'clock yesterday, and says the enemy cannot, in his opinion, destroy the place unless they land, which he thinks they would probably do in the course of the day. The barges, to the number of five, were full of men. The house of Peter Hall (a tavern on the bank) was demolished, and several others damaged; the bombs and rockets fell short of the town.'"

The same paper concludes:

"The British withdrew from Lewistown on the eighth, after bombarding and cannonading it incessantly for twenty-two hours, without doing any material injury to the place, most of their shot and shell falling short of their object."

Another paper says:

"The militia fired but few shots, as they had only one eighteen- and one nineteen-pounder and but few shots for them, and of which they endeavored to make the best possible use, and have reason to suppose they gave one of the sloops the contents of the eighteen-pounder, as she was obliged to haul out of the line soon after it was seen to strike her.

"We are assured the inhabitants of Lewis and Pilot-towns, the volunteers and militia under the command of Colonel Samuel Davis, behaved in a cool and determined manner. The pilots who were stationed in the fort deserve the highest praise, and the whole was so judiciously stationed by the commanding officers that had the British landed they would have been able to give a good account of themselves.

"Powder from Dupont's Mills in Wilmington was rapidly sent forward to Lewes, and ball was hurried there, too.

"The general government had furnished Delaware one hundred and fifty stands of arms, part of its war quota; these were distributed among the volunteers at Lewes. The British made an attempt to land on the 8th; a number of small vessels with armed men approached the shore, the militia and volunteers hastening to the beach to receive them.

"The British were called back by a signal from their squadron. Col. Davis resorted to a ruse. He marched the militia and volunteers along the water front up to where, unseen by the enemy, they could enter a back street of the town, countermarch to the water front and along it, go and return; thus deceiving the British into believing that an advancing army was flooding Lewes with troops."

The old inhabitants say that many of the marchers carried cornstalks to represent guns.

"On the 8th, the fleet was at its anchorage at the capes, foiled and dispirited, without bullocks, vegetables, hay, or so much as a cup of cold water.

"April 28 the Belvidere put to sea, sailing for the Chesapeake with a few prisoners."

William Marshall, pilot, and lieutenant-commander during the bombardment, left a diary in which is recorded the following persons who were in the battery:

John Gauns, Second Lieutenant, Commander; Job Cornell, Sr., Job Cornell, Jr., John Rowland, Richard Poynter, Samuel Rowland, Arthur Pointer, Charles Baker, William Edwards, Thomas Norman, John Saunders, Moses Nichols, Jacob Art, P. Davis, Samuel Thompson, Simon Edwards, George Orton, Joseph Ort, Jerry Shillenger, John Clampitt, Samuel West, William Jeffries, J. W. Batson, William Johnson, J. W. Norwood, Thomas Virden, William Masters, James Nicholson, B. Atkins, David Hall, Nathaniel Neuman, John Davis, Simon Edwards, Jr., John Norman, William Lewis, Cook Clampitt, Gilbert McCracken, William West, William Art, Privates.

There were 500 men encamped at Block House Pond.

One ball from the British ships made a hole in the door of Caleb Rodney's store.

Gilbert McCracken, whose name appears in the list of soldiers, had also served in the Revolutionary army. Being taken prisoner by the British, he was carried to New York and imprisoned in the "Jersey," prison ship. At that time he was only twelve years of age.

The people were in a great state of excitement when the firing commenced and many wished to flee, some did so. Thomas Rowland said to his wife: "Put your trust in God; bury the tool-chest in the garden, and set your face for Copes'." Mr. Cope lived seven miles from Lewes.

A sloop called "Black Duck," loaded with cotton, was captured by the British just before the fight, but was recaptured by the Americans.

While Henry McCracken was standing near Colonel Davis a musket ball grazed the latter. Turning to McCracken he said, "Henry, an inch more and that ball would have fixed me."

Niles' Register of April 24th, says:

"The people of Lewistown are making themselves quite merry for the late bombardment of that place. They enumerate their killed and wounded as follows: one chicken killed, one pig wounded—leg broken. It was a ridiculous affair on the part of the enemy. We have nothing new from this quarter except that Sir John Beresford has captured five oyster-boats, and, after a severe engagement, caused these whole cargoes to be devoured."

After the battle the British made another attempt to obtain water. They dropped down the river seven miles and sent men in boats with casks for water, and halters for bullocks. Colonel Davis had suspected such a move and had sent Major George H. Hunter with one hundred and fifty men, to prevent the landing of the British. Major Hunter drove the enemy back to their ships, minus water and bullocks.

Copies of Old Letters Found in Lewes.

Fort Cumberland Dec. 9, 1756.

"Sir:—I hear you have been at Annapolis lately and would have been glad to hear ye news,—

"We have erected a sort of Ravelin on the north side the fort one face fronting the Hill, the other, that of the Valley on the East Side Wills Creek. The Rampart is brought almost to a Level with the Hill, is about 20 foot thick, The parapet six foot high and of the same thickness; In the angle of the Ravelin I have built a magazine proof against small shells, and has out a way under ground to the Water of Wills Creek. Govr. Denwiddie has given orders to Continue the work.

"I expect news from the Ohio Daily—a small Detach^{mt} has been out about twenty days and I am sorry have had very severe weather —I am

"Sir Your most ob^{t} hub^{l} Servt,

"ADAM STEPHEN.

"P. S. I wish you and Mrs. Dagworthy the Compliments of the Approaching Season, We have had some diversion on the Ice already."

"Mr. Nunez pay unto Jacob Kollock, John Rodney and John Wiltbank of Sussex County in Delaware Esq^{rs} whatever Monies you as Administrator of a certain Henrietta Sims late of the said County deceased, may have recovered or shall recover as belonging to the said Henrietta at her death and since to me as Governor of the Three lower Counties she having died without any relations or known kindred, which Monies I expect when paid by you to those gentlemen they will apply to the use of Christ Church in the Town of Lewis and the receipt of them or any two of them shall be your discharge for the same from yo^{rs}

"I am Sir Your very hble servant

"JOHN PENN

"NEW CASTLE ye 24th March 1770.
"To MR. DANIEL NUNEZ
"of Lewis Town."

"Dr. Franklin presents his Thanks to Mr. Hill for the opportunity given him of perusing this Manuscript which has afforded him much pleasure by refreshing his Memory of things and Places that he had formerly seen. Dr. F. would be glad to have also a sight of the Drawings particularly that of the Marble Mill at Bakewell, having lost one he made himself when there, It is to be wished that all our young Men who travel had the same spirit of observation and Diligence in noting down what might be useful to their Country.

"JAN. 18, '87."

"PHILADELPHIA, Oct. 16, 1780.

'MY DEAR GENERAL.

"I received your favour of the 29th of Septr. last, and have taken the liberty of publishing to the World, tho' not as coming from you, the perfidy, villainy & meaness of the Wreck Arnold—This man appears to me to be Phenomenon of Human Depravity, and were I certain you would not conceive it arrogance in me, I should suppose that Omnipotence itself could not form so complicated yet so complete a Character of every thing that is base and injurious—

"Inclosed I send you a number of late News Papers, from these you will learn how great & how important a Change has taken place, in our legislature. Will you believe me? Our honest friend Delaney is a Member—Sam Penrose Mr. R. Morris Christian Sam, (would we had more christians) Geo. Gray, Geo. Campbell, &c. &c. in the same stile—however, by these papers & the inclosed Lists you will see the Change that has been affected, & I thank God, I have been instrumental, in some small degree, in this business, having like a Freeman given my vote for men who pleased me.

"Pray what think you of the Principle established in the Report of the Committee of the late House, respecting their making up on Depreciation? However, as the Scale of Depreciation is the chief thing, whenever that is agreed on by the New House we shall transmitt you the same for your Observations thereon and approbation.

"Your family Dr General are all well, some of your friends are not, among the number I am one; I have been persecuted with a villianous fever which at length left me, but in a feeble and weak State indeed—It has proved fatal to many, 20 having been buried of a day for months past—

"I have nothing new to communicate therefore shall bid you adieu.

"Subscribing myself your sincere friend & Servant

"F. JOHNSON"

CORRESPONDENCE OF WILLIAM HILL WELLS, ESQ., DAGSBOROUGH, DEL.

PHILADA: 9 March, 1794.

MY DEAR SON:—Tho' I have nothing worth Postage to communicate, except the pretty general Welfare of the Family, yet I thought a Line might remove any Anxiety that might arise from our Silence, for tho' it is near 9 & the Post goes off to morrow neither of thy scribbling Sisters have prepar'd a Letter—thy last ℔ Post proved very pleasing, and I hope thy new Arrangement of Businefs will be ultimately more to thy Advantage, for great Undertakings require great Stock; I wish thou had not quite so much locked up in Leather but I suppose it was the best that could be done—If you get the Papers regularly you will perceive that we are on the Brink of a War—the late outrageous Proceeding of the British Cabinet in directing the Seizure of all Vefsels going to a French Port whether beseiged or not has exasperated all Clafses of Citizens, & altho' we must certainly suffer more by War than even by the Restrictions aimed against us by England, yet the Spirit of the People & the Idea of the Honor of a Nation will precipitate us into a War unlefs a Peace in Europe should speedily take Place—Congrefs have resolved on the Measure of providing Ships of War, and to have all the great Sea Port Towns immediately fortified,—perhaps the Mornings Paper by the Post will furnish the Acct. of the Evacuation of Toulon which took place on the 18 Decr. & all the french Fleet burnd but 2 Frigates—the Accot came from Carthagena to N York the Harbour was a noble one but the Town could not be retained—the surrounding high Ground commanding it, they embarked in such haste that it is said numbers of the Citizens who wished to fly rushed into the water after the Boats & were drownd the Harbour is somewhat thus [map]

Our Friend Charlotte is in Town & likely to *have occasion* to stay here a few Months—I fear a War will make it difficult to find money for the great Canal her Husband is engaged in tho' it may furnish a number of idle hands—our dear Love to Bettsy & the Tiney ones and thyself B W

PHILAD July 17 1794

MY DEAR SON:—Having wrote by last Post, I should not write again so soon, but as the present Conveyanc will cost nothing, a Letter worth nothing ought not to be so much complained of—however I am sure *some Value* will be given to it, for bringing only 4 Days later Accot. of our being well & I hope I may add that Hannah walks stronger every Day—This Afternoon Benny, Polly & Rachel go off for the Sea Shore if Rain does not prevent of which there is some Probability—we have had a more rainy Season spring & Summer than I ever remember—though my Books will not hand down so true a History of it as I fear thine will—at least it will be a negative History of Work *not done* in the Swamp;—what a Pity it is that when the Shingle Businefs stands still, the Saw Mills cannot be turned to Accot.—I formerly used to please myself with the Thought that when there was too much Water in the Swamp the Mills wod dance up & down more merrily—but this I am disappointed in.

Capt. Derrickson has brought up a Cargo of young Blacks—B Morris has one Anth' Morris 2—G Wells I believe one, & I am just now going to look at a 7 year old Boy—perhaps to prove a Plague they are all to be bound to 28, but we are going to bring on in our Supreme Court the important Question, "whether any Man can *constitutionally* be held to Service either for Life or beyond 21"—Lewis, Rawle Ingersol & Bradford, have all undertaken to plead for general Freedom, & a Case is prepared—the 2 former are standing Counsellors of the Abolition Society & wod take no Fee—the other Gentlemen hesitated & have it ad referendum whether they will not return the 50 Dollars each which we we have given them—whether we succeed or not. I shall not hold my Boy (if I get him) above 21—Love to Bettsey & the young ones.

Thy affect Father R W

WILMINGTON July 27th 95.

SIR:—In consequence of the communications made from your county, respecting arrangements for the election of Governor; a number of Gentlemen met at this place on Saturday last. They fully agree with you in sentiment, that union is most important, & more likely to be obtained by a conference & mutual communication of sentiments, than in any other way. On the part of this county we have therefore appointed Mr. Grantham, Mr. Bayard & Mr. Frazer, to meet the commifsioners from Kent & Sufsex at Dover at the time mentioned in your letters. I sincerely hope we may get such a chief magistrate, as will do honor to the State; & who by patriotic & conciliatory measures, may unite us all in sentiment & exertions for the interest & happinefs of our common country—rescue us from those factions which prevail, & which are so enemical to the peace order & dignity of government.

I am with much respect Your obedt Hbble Servt

GUNN'G BEDFORD JNR

Willm Hill Wells Esqr

THE GROVE, December 24th, 1795.

DEAR SIR:—I hope before now you have received a letter from me refpecting some of your bufinfs in the Law—I have not as yet taken any Steps in your suit against Leven Miller as it waill be proper to Confult you refpecting the plase you wan to have prosefs ifsued, should you Conclude to Commence profeedings in Sufsex I have no doubt but you wanto be succefsful in the collection of your debt there—but should you Conclude to profeed against him in Maryland it would be best I think to remove the Judgment as it is and ifsue Si Fa there againft him which must be done when evere it is moved, tho' I am sure the money Can be got without this mode of profeeding—I suppose you must have had all the news from the City. the difagreement of senate to the appointment of the Chief Justice of the United States is Confidered a damn'd good thing The involved situation of this man and the disreputable means which he was practiseing to extricate himfelf from embarrafsment in my Judgment ware reasons suffecant to warrant the measure of the Senate. but added to this thay I am told had other strong ones.

I inclose you here a speach of the Kings the attack made on him as Stated there is gainsaid in other papers and that he only had a Stone discharged against him.

The introduction of the governor to the general afsembly of this State for is qualification is to be vastly grand, I am sorry to tell you that he is now confined to his bed with the Gout.

You have underftood I make now doubt the situation you are in withregart to Sherriff—I am told that the two next highest on the return in Sufsex and Kent are to be appointed—I hope it will be no harm to say thank God for our Dear Moleston in Kent he is a fine fellow indeed.

Mrs Botson is yet in the City she desiered me when ever I wrote you to make her affectionate regard to yourself & Mrs. Wells

Davd Nixon has lately pranced off to the other World, and the Porson is in good Sperits of being Clark to the House of Representatives. Will you Spend a Night with me on your way to the Legeslature. it will give me much pleasure for you always to Consider the Grove as a second Home be pleased to make my sincere Refpects to Mrs Wells, your Dear little Son & Daughter

God bless you adieu JNO W. BATSON

P. S.—finding the Kings speach in the papers I have omided sending it. J W B.

THE GROVE, SEPT. 19th, 1796

DEAR SIR:—Your interesting letter of the 20th Ulto never made its appearance before last Evening owing to my unfortunate detention in Philadelp. with a Shocking illness. The late Tour you and Mrs. Wells have taken through the moft healthy parts of Maryland, Virginia, Pennsylvania, and Delaware, was a Circumftance of some little supprise to me" it being altogether a novel excurfion for any of our Gentlemen. I hope the journey will Tend to the reeftablishment of Mrs. Wells and Mifs Rachel's health and Totally baffle any defign the Dagsborough atmosphere might have had against yours. I am sure you have made your observation on the Federal City. I wish much to have some Converfation with you on that Subject: it was my intention some ago, to have Visited it this Summer but the destruction of my health from about the 15th of august to the present period, give a stab to that and every other pleasure. "The extreem lafsetude in which the deseas have left me I fear will make this letter too dull for my Friend" I remember that one of King Charles's Golden Rules, was to repeat no grievances, and amongst people that pity a greatdeal I am Cautious of doing it—I know the magnanimity of your mind on Such Occafions Seours to the proper Standard "a Bumper to my recovering health of your Salubrious Wine will do me the greatest honor and you the most good. I have Since Yestorday got to drinking same good wine but am obliged to dilute it [in consequence of my liver being much affected by the Malignant bilious fence which I have been Just Confined with in the City].—I will now make a glass as potent as I dare and drink it to your health, and your late Traveling Party, and Succefs to the Federal Ticket. if the situation of my health will admit of it I will unquestionably be with at your Ellection! mourn with me at the departure of Gods best [earthly] likenefs, from our Government—I am much flattered with the present prospect of our Kent Ellection. Heaven grant You Succefs in Sufsex and all will be right. I am much Obliged to you and Mrs. Wells for your interestednefs for Mrs. Batson & little Ann's Health they are now in the City but was tolerably well when I left them about three days ago. We shall undoubtedly expect you & Mrs. Wells &c in the winter—Honour me in making my most profound refpects to Mrs. Wells and believe me your very Sincere friend & most aff. St. JNO W. BATSON.

D SIR:—I anticipated the pleasure of Seing you before this time but my indisposition has been such Since you came home that I have not been out of my house till within two days paft. I am now upon the Recovery and hope in a few day to git out. the Election businefs I am apt to think as it Regards myself has been turning against me fom what on account of my Confinement and Robinsons activity—but if my friends dont forsake me I hope to bring that up. I think I am asking the voice of the public in a more proper manner than my aponant is as I was put in the General Tickett agreeable to the form of making ticket in our party—if I had not have been put in the Tickett I should not have thought myself so much intituled to the Interest of the party neither should I have offered myself in the manner that Robinson has but should have felt myself bound to push the Tickett (as I had declared before a Tickett was formed) but a free people will think for themselves and act for themselves and I hope they will in this instance—but as a friend to party I shall always feal my self bound to stand to what my party shall do. from what I have had the pleasure of hearing you Say on the Subject I hope I have your Interest and good wishes &c—if so I am not afraid of my Election.

I am with great Esteeme your friend, &c KENDLE BATSON

Geo: Town Septr 24th 1796.

WM. H. WELLS Esqr.

PHILADA. 25, Jany. 1798.

DEAR SIR:—You will excuse the liberty I take of begging you to consider how far it will be proper for the Legislature to interfere in fixing the allowance which each County shall pay to the Atty General. I presume you know the fact to be, that the Levy Court of NCastle County refused to make the Atty any compensation for his services. The consequence is that Kent & Sufsex support a State officer, and NC is equally benefitted by his services without paying any thing for them. A strong reason why the salary should be fixed, is that the Atty might always be placed beyond influence. At present the Levy Court is liable to indictmt. & if the Atty does his duty he loses the emoluments of his office.

There is no foreign intelligence of late date & no dispatches have yet been recd by our Governmt. The House of Reps. is still occupied in debates on the foreign intercourse Bill. We have used each other with very little ceremony. We have been charged as Monarchists and it has been returned with the charge of Anarchifts. the question which will follow the debates is the more important as it will go far in deciding the strength of the Parties. It is calculated that we have a small majority, but accident may occasion the lofs of the question.

I am with great regard my dear Wells, Your Obt Sert

JAMES A. BAYARD

GEO: TOWN August 27th 1798.

DEAR SIR:—Yours of the 17th instant came to hand Some days ago and I have to aske your pardon for not answering it before this time which neglect was owing to my receiveing your Letter just as I was leaving home and being gone three days. I forgot to answer yours as I intended upon my return. You will receive herewith 30 Stamps of 4 Cents each. I would have sent you a quire But have not got them by me but I expect Some down in a few days and if you want I will send some down. I have also inclosed you the Law Respecting Stamped paper &c, which you will please to Return after you have perused it &c. I expect to see you at Geo: Town Tomorrow as that is a day appointed by our friends to have Some Consultation Respecting our Election &c.

I will forward you a Copy of my account with you in a few days.

I am with esteeme your Sinseare and very devoted friend

KENDLE BATSON

W. H. WELLS ESQ

THE GROVE Sept 23rd 98

DEAR SIR:—From the contrariety of opinions circulated here relative To the Politics of Sufsex, I have felt anxious to have yours. The federal party in Kent is pretty well united; and I think we have reafon to calculate on a Majority of one hundred and 50 at least for Governor, and reprefentative; this with the ordinary superiority of Sufsex, I trust will counteract the democratical fetes of N. Caftle County. which by the bye I prefume will meet with a rub from the rage of the fever in Wilmington. Tho it is a calamity I very much lament, and most ardently wish a speedy period to its ravages.

I must Confefs my supprise in the Changes that has taken place with the Officers in Sufsex, that of the Prothonotary is an extraordinary Case indeed; and I doubt whether there is more than one more character, in the federal Party, cloathed with the same power, refulting from the People, as the Senate, that would at this time have braved the same act. all intimacy between the former Officer and my self, appears to have subfided: Yet I am not so much bereft of the feelings of Propriety as it regards the Public, and the individual, as to have no senfibilities on the Occafion.

Mrs. Batson unites with me in Sincere efteem for you, and Mrs. Wells. believe me your devoted friend and Hub Sert

I. W. BATSON

WILLIAM HILL WELLS Esquire

The Grove Febry 24th 1799.

DEAR SIR:—As the Conclufion of this Sefsion of Congrefs may take place, before the Refignation of Mr. Bassett as Commifsioner of the Fore may be Known in its proper department of Government; I have thought it not improper to resume the Subject at this time; and Observe to you that such is the Supposition here. The Confidence I feel in your political management, and favourable wishes for my happiness, Saves here the Communication of any further ideas on the Subject.

It is a pleasing circumftance to your friends in Delaware, to find the Federalists so Universally rejoiceing in your Ellection to the Senate of the United States. I have often blefs'd my Stars that not one d——n democrat voted for you. As I mean this for your own Eyes alone You can make such mention of me to Mefsrs L. & B. as you may deem proper.

I am your much devoted friend & Sincere Humb Sert

JOHN W. BATSON

GEORGE TOWN.

DEAR SIR:—I recd your last ℘ mail, & as an apology for not writing you on the return of the Mail I would observe that I was engaged with the Board of Property which was sitting at that time.

I am informed that the Court of Apl will sit at Dover on the 2nd Tuesday in August.

If you have found the Whip which I left at your house please to send it by the Stage. If not be so kind as to look about the Garden or yard. It is a loaded whip Silver mounted & battered on the head. It belongs to Mr Batson & may probably have some mark on the head.

I send by Stage the Plate of Buonaparte, Koskiusko &c.

I am Dr Sir sincerely yours &c J. M. BROOM

GEO: TOWN 17. July '99.

DEAR SIR:—I understand that Broad Creek & Lewis Town are about to follow the worthy example of Dagsborough in establishing a public library. Geo: Town too I am sure will make the attempt. But I fear while these intended institutions are so seperated, and remain on the extremities of the County, neither can florish or be of that public benefit, for which they may be designed. But if they with the Dagsborough Library could be united and placed at Geo: Town, the most central spot, and where people from all quarters of the County resort at least once in two weeks, I should imagine we could not fail to have a good library. For it is highly probable that people from all parts of the County would subscribe, seeing it so easy of accefs. One of the leading gentlemen of the library at Broad Creek was yesterday talking with me on the subject, and observed he thought there would be no difficulty in supprefsing theirs, provided the one at Dags. could be moved to Geo: Town.

At the instance of that gentleman I have taken the liberty to addrefs you on the subject and to ask if you think it probable the Dagsborough library could be moved to Geo: Town in case the Gentlemen of Broad Creek, Lewis and this place will give up their design and join in promoting the one institution.

I remain, dear sir, with much respect your mo. obt hble Servt

OUTERBRIDGE HORSEY

GEO: TOWN 29. July '99.
MONDAY.

DEAR SIR:—Tuesday the 20th of Aug. has been mentioned as the time for our meeting to form the County ticket, but as yet no time is absolutely fixed upon. You will please to pardon me for not answering yours sooner as I have been waiting for the time to be ascertained.

Our next election is certainly a very important one. I dread the effects of it. The obstinacy wth which the two candidates seem to contend, and the great zeal, to frequently accompanied with slander, displayed by the friends of each, I fear, will tend to encrease that discord wch unhappily has too long subsisted between the eastern and western friends, and which there is too much reason to apprehend, without great care and cercumspection will one day or other be fatal to our federal majority. But while we are apprehensive of so dreadful an event, let us think how we shall prevent its taking effect, and especially on the present occasion. As to my own part I have too little experience to suggest any ways or means, by which harmony could be restored; but I think if yourself with some of the leading friends of both the candidates could have an interview previous to the general meeting, and talk the matter over seriously, something might be done towards a compromise, or at least to put the election on such a footing that the contest between the two candidates should not effect the ticket in any other respect than that of sheriff. And even in this respect, I think it desirable, should a compromise not take place, that something could be done, that would induce the candidates and their friends to electioneer in a candid, fair and liberal manner. For it is the false electioneering stories that irritate, & do most of the mischief of which the Demos. will not forget to avail themselves. These no doubt they will industriously circulate to set us by the ears.

Tomorrow is meeting day here if you can conveniently come perhaps an earlier time might be fixed on than before mentioned and some arrangement could be made preparitory to the general meeting that might be of happy effect.

With much regard I remain, Sir, your very obt & hble fervt

O. HORSEY

P. S.—I regret the death of Doc. Lacos. Isaac Davis is appointed to succeed him in the registers office. Cap. White I understand has marched to Elizabeth Town. The federalists in Kent I hear are likely to have considerable difficuly about their sheriff, or rather about the person to run with Brinkly Wear.

N. B.—As soon as the time of meeting is fixed I will drop you a line, but am in hopes you will be here tomorrow & that it will then be concluded upon.

GEO: TOWN 9. Sep. '99.

DEAR SIR:—You will not be a little surprised at my addrefsing you again on the subject of the election. It is doing what I did not expect to do when we parted last. But knowing the allimportance of our party, I could not reconcile it to my fealings, not to make one effort more, at least, to afsuage the impending storm.

If you adhere to the ticket you made out on tuesday last you drive the friends of Mr. Batson to a measure, in my mind, highly alarming. To a measure which nothing but the kind of policy used by the friends of Mr. Robinson in forming their ticket could ever induce me to consent to adopt. I mean that of forming a seperate ticket. My dear sir shall we thus divide and destroy ourselves and suffer the common enemy to take the field, in wch they have been so often and so long defeated. They have already began to rally, and I am told, should we divide, mean to make a desperate effort. They care nothing about the Sheriffs. The representatives are their aim. But I yet indulge a faint hope they will be disappointed.

I understand you mean to meet us again tomorrow. Can't something be done to unite us in forming the ticket as it regards senators, representatives, and Levy Court, if not as to Sheriffs. To attain this object I would propose that we meet and form the ticket in all respects excepting sheriff but about these *say nothing*. After we have formed the ticket in this way, the friends of our candidate can retire to another room and complete the ticket and those who remain can do the same. I do not know that Mr. Batson's friends can be brought into this measure. But I flatter myself if the friends of Mr. Robinson would cordially acquiesce, it might be effected. As one of Mr. B's friends I declare I wish it from my heart and will do all in my power to bring it about, and I am authorised to say Gen. Mitchell will do the same, altho' it's relinquishing a right Mr. Batson is entitled to, and may operate against him. But any thing to disappoint and Shagrin the Jacobins. If something of this kind can't be done where is the use of our meeting? We had better not meet at all. For our meeting will only tend to exasperate and widen the breach.

I was at Little Creek on saturday last. I there saw a number of different tickets. But Batson's name in all. There was a large meeting, three companies, wch were for Batson *Nemine Cont.* Old Townsend has started the *Union Ticket*, headed himself Senator &c. Should this ticket be pushed with as much succefs at it was at the last election, I should think it very probable, if we should run separate tickets, that some of the Demos. would get into the Legislature. But I trust federalism has too many friends in this County thus to be wounded.

With sincere regard & esteem I am, dear sir, Your Most Obt & hble Servt O. HORSEY

GEO: TOWN 18 Sep. '99.

DEAR SIR:—I should have been one of the last persons to attack Mr. Robinson's character in any shape, but especially in so serious a point as that of religion. But when he and his friends have made the afsault. When I see them labouring to degrade Mr. Batson, and to destroy his reputation, not only as a politician, but as a private man, I can't help emotions of resentment, and fealing a disposition to retaliate. It was no longer than monday last, Mr. Sam. Williams, *in the presence of Mr. Robinson*, as I am told by unquestionable authority, in a speech he made to the people, declared Mr. Batson was a damned rascal, a poor deceitful scroundrel, not to be trusted with the public money, *and every man that voted for him was a damned rascal.* Is it, my friend, to be expected that speeches of this kind are to pafs unnoticed? Is it to be expected that Mr. Batson's character is to be tourn in pieces with, what we shall make appear, unfounded accusations and the most unprovoked slander, without recrimination? We have testimony in our hands completely to refute all the charges made against Mr. Batson, even the big story that is made out of what Mr France has said. Doc. Robertson conversed with Mr. France on this subject yesterday was a week, and from what Mr: France told the Doc. I am most fully satisfyed that there has been a misconstruction on what Mr. Batson said to France.

It is to be regreted that any accusations have been made, but as Mr. Robinson & his friends gave the first blow, they must expect to receive the last. And let it be remembered that all Mr. Batson has said & done or may say and do, is nothing more than Mr. Robinson's own strokes recoiling upon himself.

We collected several of Mr. Batson's friends last evening. I read to them your letter. The determination was that the affidavit of Mr. Houston should be put into print.

I remain, dear Sir, with much regard your hble Servt

O. Horsey

N. B.—I think when we saw each other last, it was understood that when we intended any part of our correspondence on the subject of the election, to be in confidence, it was so to be expressly mentioned. I hope I did not do wrong in reading your letter.

Geo: Town 16. Oct. '99.

Dear Sir:—I forgot to speak to you about the clerkship of the house of representatives. I understand Tho: Clayton has it in view. Should you give me the preference, will you be so good as to speak to Mr. Burton & Doc. Wolf on the subject & such other of the members as you may have an oppy. to speak with.

When I talked of offering there was no person who made any pretention excepting Mr. Fisher, whether Mr. Clayton knew I ment to apply I cannot tell, but should think it probable he did, as it was known by a number of gentlemen in Dover. As to the appointment itself I feel quite indifferent but do not wish to give it up before I can develop the mistery of Clayton's standing.

If I find Mr. Clayton did not know I intended to offer and that he stood simply in opposition to Fisher perhaps I shall relinquish. But wish to be prepared for the event of his *opposing me*.

White tells me I can certainly get four of the Kent members and if I can get sufsex there can be no doubt of my succefs. I should think it probable that New Castle will vote for Clayton. Your afsistance in this businefs will be greatfully acknowledged.

I remain as ever with Sincere regard your hbl Servt

O. Horsey

I was informed yesterday by Mr. John Robinson that a Mr. Young of Cedar Creek declares that Mr. Rodgers told him that he Mr. Rodgers heard Mr. Bayard say "that the people of Delaware were not half taxed." This story this Young and Mr. Haygalett are making great use of and do not hesitate to make it known that Mr. Rodgers is the author. I am sure it is impofsible that Mr. R. could have made any such declaration and that this story must be a mere creation of Youngs or some other Democrats brain.

Would it not be advisable for you to write to Mr. Rodgers and obtain a cerfificate on the subject. This story I understand is the most formidable Weapon against us. O. HORSEY

HON. SIR:—Although nearly a stranger, yet from the parental affection displayed by you to the people of your neighbourhood, I am emboldened to Addrefs you on the present occafsion.

I have been informed by our Poftmaster (Capt Frisbee) that at the expiration of the present quarter [Aexpires in April] he shall relinquish the Poft Office and as I have been accustomed to conduct a P. O. I have to beg the favor of your intercefsion for me with the Poftmafter General as his Succefsor. If Sir thro your means I may be so happy as to get the Appointmt I shall consider myself under a lasting obligation.

With the profoundest respt I am, Sir, your obdt Servt

W. BLACK

DOVER Feb. 25th 1800

☞ If Security or a recommendation is wanted I can procure the first from my friends and I make no doubt Mr. Nining would give me the latter tho' I have not asked him.

SIR:—I have recd your Letter of ye 25th of last Month relating to the Post Office. I do not know what may be the Intentions of the Post Mastr Genl, but I should suppose he would be much influenced in his Selection of a Person to succeed Mr. L. if [illegible] by a Recommendation from ye Inhabitants of Dover. You will pardon me for saying that I cannot support your Application under any other Circumstances. As You have so lately become a Citizen of our State your Pretensions to this office ought to be maintained in the most unequivocal Manner by those among whom you reside—& more particularly so seeing yt they are the Persons.

GEO: TOWN 19 June 1800

DEAR SIR:—A number of gentlemen, both of Mr. Robinson's & Mr. Batson's friends having met on tuesday last to make some arrangements for the fourth of July, the subject of representatives to congress was mentioned;—and tuesday the 15th of July was agreed on as the time of meeting, at this place, to appoint the conferrees to meet at the Court of Appeals.

The conferrees are appointed in New Castle. I am happy to say we met on both sides as if no differences had existed.

We calculate on the pleasure of your company the fourth of July.

Accept my thanks for the loan of De Lome. I have sent you the Journal of the Senate & House of Representatives.

The Deed you sent me I have not been able to acknowledge owing to neither of the Witnefses attending to prove the excon of it which is required by the practice of the Court. Mr. Tunnel & Isaiah Long are the Witnefses. You had better get one of them to come in the next Court.

I remain as ever with great regard Your Obt Servt

O. HORSEY

GEO: TOWN 11. June 1801.

DEAR SIR:—If you have any of the bills containing Genl. Washington's Certificate published at Mr. Bafsetts election to refute the charge that he was a tory, I'll thank you to send me one or two. Will you also be good enough to State if you recollect whether the bill *verbatim* or in substance was not printed in the Delaware & Eastern Shore Advertiser, or if you have the paper containing it be so good as to send it.

Have you heard of the letters Mr. Hargis lately has written to several of our friends in Little Creek.

For this two weeks past this place has been more sickley than it was ever known to be—I have been confined about a week but am now getting up.

In haste Yours with regard & esteem O HORSEY

GEO: TOWN 11. Sep. 1801.

DEAR SIR:—The following is the arrangement concluded on with regard to our meetings—Baltimore, at the Widow Waples' on Thursday 17th inst.; Dagsborough at Tho: Wests on Friday the 18th; Indian River at the Chapel on Saturday the 19th; Ceder Creek at Eli Williams on Thursday the 24th; North W. Fork at Bridge Branch on Friday the 25th; Little Creek at English's on Saturday the 26th; Nanticke at Wm. Jones' on Friday the 2d October and at Isaac Short's on Saturday 3d. We were forced to have meetings at both these places on account of both having been spoken to & expecting it before the places of meeting were concluded on.

Will it be in your power to send word to the Widow Waples to make some proviscon for our dinner & liquors.

Yours very sincerely O. HORSEY.

GEO: TOWN 13. Oct. 1801.

DEAR SIR:—I received yours containing the hundred dollars which you were pleased to return. As yet none of the gentlemen have come down but Mr. Johns & *Mr. Vandyke.* It was thought best by Mr. Johns & myself to postpone giving you an answer upon the subject of the invitation you were so obliging to make, till thursdays mail, that we might know the disposition of the other gentlemen.

I remain as ever yours O. HORSEY.

GEO: TOWN 23. Sep. 1802. Thursday

DEAR SIR:—I send you the document by the driver and please to accept my thanks for the use of it. I am not able to give you a precise account of the little elections. The general result tho' is we are beat in 3 Hds. and have beat in 7. The Majority in Broad Creek and L. Rohoboth are something greater against us than they weer the last year, but the Majority in N. W. Fork is considerably lefs. All the rest have terminated much as usual.

Our first meeting is at Isaac Shorts on tomorrow. The next day it is at Mrs. Wests the widow of Tho: Wests. The Thursday succeeding at Eli Williams in Ceder Creek and next day at Bridge Branch. And the next day at English's. If your health will admit of it your attendance will be very material. I calculate on a bold opposition from the other party. They will no doubt send their oritors round with us.

We have taken great pains to draw our conferees out next tuesday and I am persuaded we shall have a full meeting. The Com. of Con. are to meet that day Mr. Rodney is written to and will no doubt attend. My expectation is great upon the good effects of this Meeting. We must here afsign some of the most active to ride from house to house in each hundred and we must endeavour to devise ways & means to get those out who have not conveyances of whom I am told there is a great number in Ceder Creek.

In hase Yours sincerely O. H.

GEO: TOWN 31. July 1803.

DEAR SIR:—I have recd another duning letter from Black for his $20. This letter is dated the 22d inst. What has become of your remittance? It must have miscarried. I did not think to ask you when here if you had ever recd the ten dollars I enclosed you, but I take it for granted you did. I sd be glad to here from you on this subject.

I have just got about after a weeks confinement by an inflamation in my face occasioned by an unsuccessful attempt to extract a tooth.

Yours truly &c O. HORSEY

GEO: TOWN 17. Sep. 1803

DEAR SIR:—In Leues & R. we have lost our Inspector but have carried our Afsefsor C. Wiltbank by a majority of 5. This our friends consider a great victory & the demos. are completely downd. Every exertion was made on both sides. The election was as large as the last year & the year before. We have beat in N. W. Fork handsomely Laws & Handy are elected by a majortty of 31. In short we shall have all the little elections except Brad Creek where I am told we did not intend to make opposition. Indian R. Little Creek & Nanticoke I have heard from they are ours. We shall certainly attend to the Levy Lists. As Laws is elected I take it for granted that Sordein continues. I am unable to answer as to David Smith but will endeavour to send you word tuesday next. We have upwards of £20. subscribed to the Library.

Yours truly. O. H.

WASHN, 28th Nov. 1811.

MY DEAR FRIEND:—I but this moment recd·enclosing the note yours without date. I fear its too late. But I have guarded against [illegible] by sending my note endorced by Mr. Ridgely to meet yours in Bank. So there can be no protest. I have tho endorced the note you enclosed & sent it to Mr. Worrell & have directed him to return it to me in case it should not be in time.

Your prize shall be attend to. Harrison has been surprized & severely handled by the Prophet. The U. S. Troops lost in killed & wounded 179—out of about 700—Numbers engaged nearly equal on both sides. Harrison was surprised by a piece of the most refined treachery. The Prophet on the day of the morning before he made the attack, sent about forty men to Harrison of a tribe supposed to be most averse to the war with the U. S. who afsured Harrison that they were the friends of the U. S. & ubraided him for having shewn such a want of confidence in them—, that they did not mean war & would intercede with the Prophet & that a White flag should be sent the next day. The next morning about 4. oclok the Indians killed the centinels with arrows & got into the midft of the camp of our troops before so unexpectly that many were tomihocked before they could drefs themselves. Our men as soon & as well as they could abandoned the camp & rallied & formed at some distance. When the action afsumed a lefs promiscuous & more regular form & continued till about sun rise, when upon the appearance of the horse the Indians gave way. I saw a letter from a Capt Wells who was in St. Clairs defeat & had fought with Waine & been in many Indian fights but says this was the hardest & best maintained on both sides. Our troops followed the Indians & burnt the Prophets Town wch was in about one mile of the camp, & on returning to the frontiers. They were about 100 Miles in the Indian Territory from the settlements, and it is apprehended, may suffer much on the retreat for want of provisions as the Indians destroyed nearly all their provisions while they had pofsefsion of t camp & sd the Indians attack them on the retreat, wch is apprehended some suppose we must suffer very severely, if not be destroyed.

A very serious riot has lately happened at Savannah. Two French Privateers were burnt, & the [illegible] were obliged to fly to the Jail as an asylum agst the fury of t mob. It or [illegible]—a banditti of French sailors had stabbed two americans, sailors, who it seems were buried a la [illegible] Pearce, I mean in solem procefsion. Our tars as soon as they had paid their last tribute to thir brothers resolved to be avenged. They were Joined by the Citizens & immediately pofsefsed themselves of one of the Privateers & burnt her. In the mean time the other was armed by French & a body of Mareens belonging to U. S. who were ordered to protect the vefsel. [illegible] they got another vefsel & loaded her with combustable material & were laying her along side of the privateer to blow her up. Our marines seeing the fury of the afsailants abandoned the privateer to her fate. She also was burnt.

This is news enough for one letter, in case you have not seen or heard it before. The documents are not printed yet.

O. Horsey

Wilmington 24. Aug. 1814.

My dear Wells:—The cashier of the bank at Laurel has informed me that the rules of the Bank require that persons residing out of the County should have two indorcers residents of the County. I had a note for one thousand dollars discounted at that Bank some time ago which runs out the 27th of next month wch was indorced by two gentlemen of this town and to bring it within the rules of the Bank Mr. Bull and Mr. Polk were good enough to volunteer their indorcements. As I do not wish to impose on the goodness of Mr. Bull I have taken the liberty to send the enclosed note for your indorsement and will thank you to indorse the same and take it with you if you are a director, or otherwise send it to Mr. Polk the cashier in due time, to whom I have written. If it should be convenient to you I should be very glad if you would attend the Senate on the first day of the Sefsion, on account of my brother in law A. L. who is an applicant for the secretaryship, for whom I am sure you will vote on my account, if there be no other applicant of higher claims to your preference.

Yours as ever truly & sincerely O. HORSEY.

Remember me to my friends in your neighbourhood & in Geo: Town.

WIL 24. Apl 1817.

DEAR WELLS:—I have recd yr communication & the duplicate but our gentlemen are so scattered that I find it impofsible to get their signatures at present. I am this moment on the point of starting for my farm & when I return I shall devote myself your business.

In haste. God blefs & prosper yr undertakings O. HORSEY

WIL. 26. Aug. 1817.

MY DEAR WELLS:—I was not at home when your letter arrived, but had I been it would not have saved the protest as the notarial seal had been affixed to it before your letter was mailed or at least before the date of the post mark. The truth is, tho the officers of the bank growl and snarll, you are very popular with the notary & so long as your custom enables him to buy his bread he will praise you for your absence of mind & wish you forgetfulness. It is however well enough. Your forgetfulness operates as a benevolence. The notary is a worthy revolutionary officer & like most of his surviving compeers, poor and needy. He is worthy of your charity & may your memory fail you while his wants continue.

Every other blessing I wish you with all my soul. O. HORSEY

N. B.—Please sign the note enclosed "twice" & send it without delay to y cashier of the bank at Laurel & request him to procure Mr. Polke's endorsement. Also please send y check with y note.

Yr letter being 3ble I had to pay 25 cents additional postage & will balance y a/c by putting y postage of this letter upon you.

Letter to The Honorable Gunning Bedford, Esq., New Castle.

DAGSBOROUGH 10 June 1795.

SIR:—Having been summoned to attend the Circuit Courts, as a Grand Juror, and it not being in my Power to obey this notice, I think it my Duty to communicate to the Court the occasion of my not attending. At the Time I received the Marshall's Summons, it was fully my Intention to have complied with its Requisition. I had, but a few Days, returned from condoling with the Friends of my honor'd, deceased mother, when it became necessary for me to leave Home, again, in pursuance of the Summons I have mentioned. Notwithstanding the considerable Inconvenience of undertaking another long Journey under these Circumstances, I resolved to discharge my Duty, & accordingly did set off; but I had scarce proceeded twenty Miles before my Horse became fick & I was compelled to return. Thus, Sir, I shall be prevented from attending, not, I beg Leave to assure the Court, by a Disposition to treat its orders without proper

Respect upon all occasions whatsoever, but by Circumstances not within my control.

I have the Honor to be Sir, yr most obed hble Sv

WM. HILL WELLS

The HONBLE GUNNING BEDFORD ESQ.

Letter from S. White to Outerbridge Horsey, George Town.

DOVER Octr 8th 1802

The Democracy of Delaware has done its utmost—it has trampled on tallents and merrit and disgraced our State—Bayard is beat and that too by only *fifteen votes*—R' majority in N. C. was 957 Bayard in this county had 219 and in Sufsex it seems 723. We are down—the irishmen of N. C. are to govern Kent & Sufsex. fare well.

S WHITE

Letter from Daniel Rodney, Esq., to Commodore Murray.

LEWES Feb 24th 1814

SIR:—The app of a Ship of the Line, two frigates, and a Sloop of War off the Cape on Saty and Sun last having caused an alarm along the Shores of Delaware, and in the Creeks where they were preparing to fit out and load their Shallops for Philada I addd a Letter to A Genl Duane on Tues y last—Sollicitg him* to send us some military aid if within his power, there being no force of any descripn organd here or indeed in the State except abt 40 of the inhab of this Town chiefly Pils witht any Compt officer yet they are cald U. S. volunteers.

Persuad that a part of the Flotilla, could be advantageously employed in the Western or Shallop Channel, to protect and convoy the trade to Phila, and believing the Naval force in the Del. to be under your direction Permit me to request your attention to this measure—if the G B and Gs should be ordered on this Service, tho' it is early in the season they will be perfectly secure from the N and E winds as they can make a harbour in any of the Creeks from Bomb H to Lewes when the Wind is on Shore,* if necefsary good Pilots for the Creeks can be obtained here or at Milford—I need not say to you who has such a perfect knowledge of the Bay, thay the Enemy cannot approach them the flotilla in this Channel except in their Barges—* while the Shears, Boyds Shoals, and the long Western flat, secures them from an Attack from the Enemy except in their Barges.

I am Sir with great respect Your Obt Servt D R

· COME MURRAY.

Letter from William Hill Wells, Esq., to The Hon. William Hunter.

DAGSBOROUGH, June 25th, 1817.

MY DEAR SIR:—I forward you herewith a more succinct Sketch of the Estate, than that which I transmitted you previous to your embarking for England. I should prefer receiving the payment, to be made, in Cash:—but if it be a *sine qua non*, I agree to receive a part, say a moiety of the whole amount or, if indispensably necefsary, the whole in Manchester, Sheffield Birmingham and Leeds manufactures suited for the Philadelphia Market, at the same Prices for which they are Shipped there on orders. Sixty thousand Dollars, clear of all

Expences, is the very lowest sum I will take: and the more I think of sacrificing a moiety of this immensely increasing Estate which promises so fairly to be in so short a Period, a Principality for my Family—if I can keep it—the lefs I like to do it. Let me hear from you on your Receipt of this Communication.

With the sincerest wishes for your Health and Happiness and Succefs believe me truly and affectionately Your's

WM. HILL WELLS.

P. S.—I am content to receive for my share of the sixty thousand dollars the sum of fifty thousand—and to divide with you all that can be got above sixty thousand—I do, on my conscience believe that one hundred thousand dollars for a moiety—is but a small Price.

Bill of Sale, James Maull to Tho. Rodney, for Negroe Boy Cyrus, Aged 11 yrs or Thereabouts.

Know all men by these presents that I James Maull of George Town in the County of Sufsex and State of Delaware for and in Consideration of the sum of Two Hundred Dollars Lawful money to me in hand paid by Thomas Rodney Esquire of Lewes Town in the County and State aforesaid at and before the sealing and delivery of these presents, the receipt whereof the said James Maull do hereby acknowledge, have granted bargained sold and confirmed and by these presents do grant bargain sell and confirm unto the said Thomas Rodney Esqr. his heirs Executors Administrators or afsigns a Certain Negro or Mulatto Boy named Cye or Cyrus about the age of Eleven years at the date of these presents. To have and to hold all & Singular the Negro or Mulatto Boy afsd. by these presents granted, bargained sold and confirmed unto the only proper use benefit & behoof of him the said Thomas Rodney his heirs Executors administrators and afsigns forever, freely, quietly, peaceably and entirely without any Contradiction, claim, disturbance or hindrance of any person or persons whatsoever and without any account to me, or to any other whatsoever to be made, answered or hereafter to be rendered, so that neither I the said James Maull, nor any other for me or in my name, ought to exact, challenge, claim, or demand at any time or times hereafter, any right, interest, claim or demand of, in to or for the afsd Negro or Mulatto Boy, but from all action, right, title, estate, claim, demand, pofsefsion and interest thereof, shall be wholly based and excluded by force & virtue of these presents, and I the said James Maull for myself my heirs Exors & Admrs shall & will warrant & forever defend the afsd. Boy unto the said Thomas Rodney his heirs Exors Admrs & afsigns against me the said James Maull my heirs Exors Admrs & afsigns & against all & every other person or persons whatsoever of the before mentioned Boy I the said James Maull have put the said Thomas Rodney in full pofsefsion of the afsd. Negro or Mulatto Boy Cyrus, In witnefs whereof I have hereunto set my hand and seal this Twenty third day of January in the year of our Lord one thousand eight hundred and Nineteen.

JAMES MAULL [SEAL]

Signed, Sealed & Delivered
In the presence of
JAMES P. W. KOLLOCK

Recd January 23d 1819 of Thomas Rodney for the use of James Maul in Cash One Hundred Dollars & his Bond for One Hundred Dollars which when paid will be in full for the Consideration Money of the Boy within Mentioned JAMES P. W. KOLLOCK

Test. DANL RODNEY

Muster Roll of the First Company of Delaware Light Artillery attached to the First Battalion Eighth Regiment Third Brigade Delaware Militia.

1 James P. Barker.............................Captain
2 John E. Parker.............................1st Lieut.
3 Caleb R. Layton.............................1st Lieut.
4 James M. Rench.............................2nd Lieut.
1 Short W. Vincent.............................Orderly Sergt.
2 Thomas B Sipple.............................2nd "
3 Levan B Day.............................3rd "
4 Elisha Gothard.............................4th "
5 James Dunning.............................5th "
1 William Short (of G).............................1st Corpl.
2 Nathan Mefsick.............................2nd "
3 James S Chase.............................3rd "
4 Thomas W Hatteld.............................4th "
1 Adams Isaac.............................Private.
2 Barker Robinson............................. "
3 Chase George B............................. "
4 Conaway John............................. "
5 Conaway Jefse............................. "
6 Davis Henry............................. "
7 Dodd George............................. "
8 Ellegood William............................. "
9 Ewing Adolphus P............................. "
10 Elwell Charles............................. "
11 Fisher Isaac M............................. "
12 Greenley Thomas............................. "
13 Houston John W............................. "
14 Hastings Luther............................. "
15 Hunter Joseph............................. "
16 Jefferson Job............................. "
17 Kollick Jacob M............................. "
18 Mefsick John............................. "
19 Marvell Joseph H............................. "
20 Morris Joseph B............................. "
21 Morris Elihu............................. "
22 Maxfield Elias............................. "
23 McCalla John W............................. "
24 McCalla Daniel............................. "
25 Pettyjohn Rowland D............................. "
26 Pettyjohn Theadore............................. "
27 Pettyjohn William............................. "
28 Pettyjohn Purnall............................. "
29 Parker James A............................. "
30 Pride Job............................. "
31 Pepper Edward G............................. "

32 Pepper Peter.................................Private.
33 Pepper Levan.................................. "
34 Pepper Nutter.................................. "
35 Prettyman Burton C............................ "
36 Pafsionters John.............................. "
37 Reynolds William.............................. "
38 Short John M.................................. "
39 Short Samuel.................................. "
40 Windsor Philip................................ "
41 Wolfe James A................................. "
42 Wolfe Wm P.................................... "
43 Walls George.................................. "
44 Wilson Major.................................. "

I Certify on Honor That this Muster Roll exhibits the true state of the First Company of Delaware Light Artillery and the above named persons are fully equipped with the Uniform of the Company

JAMES P BARKER
Captain Commanding

GEORGETOWN DEL. September 22nd 1846

FOR THE GAZETTE OF THE UNITED STATES.

To the

PEOPLE OF THE UNITED STATES

No. 12.

FRIENDS & COUNTRYMEN:—I quit the Farmer in my last Number just as he was boasting that the Innocence of the Federalists, with regard to the Charge against them of embezzling the public Money, had been made as clear as the Sun at Mid-day. As I mean to reserve myself until he has done, I shall not at this Moment, trouble you with any Comments of mine upon this extraordinary Production of his; but proceed to give it to you as he has given it to me.

THE FARMER'S LETTER

to

RICHARD FALSTAFF,

continued.

"Be so good as to tell me, Mr. Falstaff, why Congress does not call up the List of "*black stocking*" Gentry, that have made away with the public Money during the administrations of Mr. Jefferson and Mr. Madison? For a very plain Reason they do not, because the People would then see the damning Proofs that their own Party had been guilty of the very Offences that they falsely charged the Federalists with.

I confess to you, upon this Subject, I can not restrain my Indignation. Such Villany ought not to go unpunished—a Whip ought to be put into the Hand of every honest Man to lash it through the World. Twenty two thousand dollars given to one Favourite!—and a hundred thousand stolen and run away with by another!—two very pretty little Items in the account of Virtue and Patriotism!

Yes, Sir, the Federalists were honest men; and after your Party had slandered them—vilely slandered them out of the good opinion of their Fellow Citizens, your Leaders thought it wise to make a Merit of Necessity, and candidly acknowledge them honest Men. You, and the whole of you, have now had nearly twelve years for Enquiry and Investigation, and, I repeat, there is not a single Federalist, employed in the Government of the United States, upon whom you have been able to fix the Charge of Peculation. All the Instances of Corruption, and Knavery, and Falsehood, and Deceit and Treachery that have happened in the Affairs of the United States Government, for now nearly four and twenty Years, have been on your Side of the House.

You seem to think the Villany of Brown of New Orleans a trifle. Sir, was it a Trifle to run away with more than a hundred Thousand Dollars of the public Money? That Sum would have defrayed the govermental Expenses of some of our smaller States for nearly ten years. The Embezzlement of about the like Sum by one of your leading Republicans, formerly of New York, now of New Orleans, you pafs over with the same nonchalance. I suppose you would consider as a Trifle the Present made by Mr. Jefferson, at the very threshold of his Administration, out of the public Money to Mr. Callender: not only contrary to Law, but in violation of the Constitution which he was sworn to support. The princely Present of Twenty two thousand Dollars to Mr. Erving you skipped over: knowing, perhaps, that the least that was said upon that Topic the better —because an Investigation of it would implicate your Idol *Jefferson*— his Deputy *Madison*—and their myrmidons in Congrefs who assisted in throwing the Veil of Authority over that shamelefs Transaction. You may say that *Mr. Jefferson* and Mr. Madison ought not to be responsible for the malconduct of their Agents. I am fully aware, I acknowledge, that bad Men will get into office sometimes notwithstanding all the Foresight and Vigilance that can be exercised: but both of those Gentlemen ought to be responsible when they have been in the Practice of confiding important Trusts to notorious Swindlers and blackstocking adventurers. Mr. Madison, most especially, ought to be answerable when he acknowledges that he recommends men to the Senate whom, he knows at the Time, are unworthy of the Appointments he nominates them for.

You will [must] excuse me for not dismissing the Subject of Money Affairs so soon as you may wish to get rid of it. Your Leaders were wont formerly to dwell a good deal upon this Subject: but, in this Respect at least, they have entirely failed to fix any Stigma upon the poor Federalists, who have come out of the Furnace you heated for them unhurt. I am not going [disposed] to throw you into that Furnace, much as you deserve it: but you cannot surely blame me for wishing to put you, and your Friends to some little Trial. We will say nothing more of the TWENTY TWO THOUSAND DOLLARS made a Present of to Mr. Ervine: but, if you please, we will turn our attention from the civil to the military Department. Your Idol professed to have a great Regard for the "*Mouth of Labour;*" and you shall see what pretty, nice, sweet little Things he reserved for the mouths of his Friends.

From the 7th of December 1803 to the 24th of April 1804 (just four Months and seventeen Days) Governour Clairborne and General Wilkinson were employed, as Commissioners, in taking Possession of New Orleans, and their TABLE EXPENCES, for that Period, amounted to SIX THOUSAND, SIX HUNDRED AND NINETEEN DOLLARS AND SEVENTY TWO CENTS. I shall not trouble you with more than a few Items from the List of Particulars such as 844 Bottles of Claret (*a very costly wine*)—nine hundred and twelve Bottles of Madeira (*the Farmers of Lancaster County in Pennsylvania know what Madeira costs*) 144 Bottles of Champaign (*a very nice and delicate Wine & comes confoundedly high*)—fifty Bottles of white Wine (*I don't know much about that*) 100 Bottles of Hermitage (*old Hermitage, I suppose, that must cost I should guefs three or four Dollars, at the least, a Bottle*) 558 Bottles of red wine (*this, I suppose, must be Tokay—it comes all the way from the Dominions of Bonaparte's Father in Law, and they say it is a most charming wine—rich, luscious and aromatic in the highest Degree—I'll set this down, as the Farmer does not tell us how much it costs, at half an Eagle a Bottle—and I wish to gracious I had some of it this moment at Hand to drink General Wilkinson, & Governor Clairborne & Mr. Jeffersons healths:—but I beg your Pardon, Mr. Farmer, go on again if you please with your Bill of Fare*) 81 Bottles of Porter (*we all know what this is, and if I had been Mr. Jefferson's Accomptant I would have allowed him for 81 Hogsheads instead of 81 Bottles—for it looks ashamed resting on the Ground under the "huge Legs" of the other Items.*) 258 Bottles of Ale (*surely the Ale & Porter Brewers of New Orleans must have brought themselves under the Displeasure of our noble General*) 67 gallons of Brandy (*this is worse than all—67 gallons of Brandy!—this was not more than enough to have made Fog slings for the General & the Governor—which, for four months and feventeen Days was just half a gallon a piece for every morning. Lord if our poor foldiers that died there like rotten sheep could have had enough of this they would still have been alive to help us take the Canadas from the British.*) and ELEVEN THOUSAND THREE HUNDRED AND FIFTY CEGARS. (*In New England here, I admit that eleven thousand three hundred & fifty Cegars (Spanish Cegars too I suppose) would be a pretty good Allowance for a couple of hearty fellows and a few Friends for four months & feventeen Days: but the Farmer does not consider that the gingling of Glasses & the Smoke of Tobacco are absolutely necessary, at New Orleans, to keep off the Musquitoes: and besides, too, he totally forgets that Mr. Jefferson sent those Gentlemen to take possession of New Orleans and it would have been a pretty story if they had surrendered themselves Prisoners to the Musquitoes, as the Southern People have the Impudence to say some of our Yankey officers did to the Bullfrogs during our Revolutionary war.*) I omit the Cakes, the Mackaroons, and the Sugar Plumbs (*Lord why would you leave them out? You don't consider how much good they may have done? Would you have had our Republican General and Governor to have gone about among the Women and Children, like old Elves, with hard boiled Eggs in their Pockets? You can't suppose that two fuch old Fellows could have been liquorish enough to have eaten those things themselves:—no—no—they made better use of them, they distributed them to the Women and Children: and when the General gave to the Men of this new Country some of his rich, luscious Tokay, they, no Doubt, exclaimed with Calaban,*

This is a brave God, and bears celestial Liquer;

We will kneel to him.) When the People add to this modest account the Pay of their General, they will find that their Presidents of New Orleans, for the Time being, cost them more than their President at Washington.

From the 13th of September 1806 to the 24th of May 1807, General Wilkinson was allowed for Rations 2033 Dollars and fixty fix Cents, notwithstanding it was exprefsly declared by an Act of Congrefs, passed on the 16th of March 1802 that his Pay of 225 dollars per month should be "his full and entire Compensation, without a" "Right to demand, or receive any Rations, Forage, travelling Ex-" "pences, or other Perquisite or Emolument whatsoever, except such" "Stationary as might be requisite for the use of his Department." In the eight months then he recived for Pay & Rations 3900 Dollars. You will please to add to this, his Salary of Governor of upper Louisiana, for the said eight months, about 1700 dollars, and you have for your republican Brigadier General 5600 dollars; which is at the Rate of 8400 dollars per year.

In 1802 and 1803 he received, for his personal Expenses, 2715 dollars and 29 Cents:—as Indian Commissioner 4898 dollars:—and as Brigadier General 5400 dollars, total 13913 dollars and twenty nine Cents, or Six thousand nine hundred and fifty six dollars and fixty four Cents per annum.

I make no account of 3879 dollars & 79 Cents paid him by John Wilkins; nor of 7891 dollars the amount of Money and Supplies furnished him by public agents; for, I suppose, he has rendered, or will render, his accounts thereof; in which it is but Charity to hope that there are no more Charges of Claret and Madeira, and red wine and white wine & Champaign & Hermitage, and Mackaroons, and Preserves and Sugar Plumbs, seeing there was enough of them, to surfeit us all, in the other accounts. Nor do I say any Thing about 11000 dollars secret Service Money paid him, as that account was Settled with Mr. Jefferson himself who deemed *"the Specification of its Disbursement inexpedient."*

Mr. Falstaff you will remember that, during one of the last year's administration of the Federalists, Mr. Tracy, a member of the Senate of the United States, was sent by the the Secretary of War, in the Recess of Congress, upon Businefs of the Public, to the Westward. I think he was allowed six dollars per Day for his Services: and there was a Washerwoman's Bill, and perhaps a Barber's Bill in the List of his Expences. Have you forgotten the Noise you exclusive Patriots made about this thing at the Time? Mr. Tracy was a poor Man, and very probably travelled with his Saddle bags behind him : and his Six dollars per Day enabled him to lay by something for his Wife and Children at Home, who lived in plain republican Simplicity. My God! what would have been said if Mr. Tracy had sent in his Bill of Hermitage, and Madeira, & Champaign, and Cegars, and red wine and white wine, and macaroons, and Sweet meats, and Sugar Plumbs? Where is the Difference in the Case? Was not Mr. Tracy made of the same Flesh and Blood as General Wilkinson? In Point of understanding there was no Comparison—it was Silenus to Apollo. No Doubt he would have liked a Glass of sparkling old Hermitage as well as the General: but not having such a Bank to draw upon he was obliged to say, with Horace, (a)

——mea nec Falernœ
Temperant vites, neque Formiani
Pocula colles.

Yes I venture to say that either the Sugar Plumbs or Mackaroons would have been Ratsbane to him. He would never have drank any more Tokay or Burgundy or Hermitage or Champaign, as long as he lived, at the public Expence. How you impartial—and honest —and virtuous—and honourable—and mouth of labour saving Patriots would have hopped about with the account and blazoned it to all the world! How you would have rung it in our Ears! One would have given us the account under the biting Head of "SOBER HABITS." Another would have dished it up to us under the Cover of "FEDERAL FRUGALITY!!!" Here would have stared us in the Face "A FEDERAL NABOB:"—there we should have feen "LOOK AT IT FAIRLY:" and here would have been "SIGNS OF THE TIMES!!" —"MONARCHY MEN"—and the Lord knows what.

Yes, yes, I see Mr. Falstaff I am taking Pains for nothing—YOU WILL NOT DARE TO PUBLISH THIS LETTER: and the poor silly Dupes of your Party will glue their Eyes together—and stuff their Ears— and turn their Heads away. *You* will not DARE to publish it, and yet you need not fear, for *they* will not DARE to read it. Go on good Folks—step high over the stumbling Blocks that Truth and Wisdom lay in your Path—proceed; you will save your *Faces* by it—but you [balance missing.]

WHEN EDWD.

When Edward left his native plain,
He heaved a sigh he dropt a tear,
Ere spring returns thy Constant Swain
Thy faithful Edward will be here
Tho Edward vowd and I believed
Ah! blooming flowrets why so fair
Alas ye prove that I'm deceived
for faithlefs Edward is not here.

The early lark proclaims the Spring
The Thrush delights with notes so clear
The flowers will bloom and birds will sing
Tho faithlefs Edward is not here.

Had Edward been true oh how blest I'd been
Each flowret more sweet and more gay every seen
If he had been true so had I been too
But if with another he seeks for delight
To be true to myself I his falsehood requite
Young Henry is true so will I be too
At the dance on the green at the wake or the fair
I'll be happy and Merry tho faithlefs Edward's not there.

MY SWEET VILLAGE MAID

When I quitted the cottage that stands on the Moor
Round the which play'd the breezes of Health
'Twas to gain for fair Anna the nymph I adore
Abroad a snug portion of Wealth
I told the sweet girl when preparing to part
Of my constancy ne'er be afraid
Tho distant your Image will dwell in my heart
For there reigns my sweet Village Maid.

2

Fortunes prosperous gales had now wafted me back
  And I hasted my Anna to meet
While fancy pourtrayed while I followed the track
  With what Joy I my Anna shall greet
How her bright eyes will sparkle approaching to view
  When of present my store I displayed
And touching her lips, whisper these are for you
  Yes all for my Sweet Village Maid.

3

I trudged smiling thus with pleasure my guide
  When a shriek onward did urge
I flew to the spot saw drove down by the tide
  An angel embraced by the surge.
I dashed thro the stream brought her safe to the shore,
  On the bank where she gently was laid
Reviving I saw the dear girl I adore
  Ah me twas my sweet Village Maid.

Presbyterian Records.

"At the Court of Common Pleas held in Lewes, Sussex County May 6th 1707 before Thomas Fisher, Joseph Booth, Jonathan Bailey, James Russell, and William Bagwell Esqrs. Justices of said court Thomas Fenwick appeared in open court and acknowledged and made over for the use of the Presbyterian professors for a Meeting House, School House and burial place a parcel of land in the town of Lewes between the county road that goes to Mr. Samuel Davis' plantation, on the Hill, containing one hundred foot square according to a deed of settlement bearing date May 6″ inst."

The Pennsylvania Magazine, Vol. 8, 1884, has a very interesting article by the Rev. Edward S. Neill about the Rev. Matthew Wilson, D.D., of Lewes, Delaware. He says:—

"Among the prominent men in the State of Delaware, during the formative period of the Republic, was Matthew Wilson, D.D. of Lewes.

"As a scholar, civilian, physician, educator, and divine, he was surpassed by few in America. His parents settled in Chester County, Pennsylvania, and in East Nottingham Township, on the 15th of January, 1731, he was born."

During his boyhood, a man of remarkable talent and versatility, Francis Alison, D.D., afterwards Vice-Provost of the College of Philadelphia, now the University of Pennsylvania, was settled over a congregation at New London in Chester County.

As a Scotch-Irish Presbyterian, Alison was imbued with the idea that the school was as necessary as the church, as the anvil to the blacksmith, and that Christianity must advance by employing keen-eyed science as her servant.

He was among the first to agitate for a college in Pennsylvania and Delaware.

The Presbytery of Lewes, in 1738, sent a memorial to the Synod of Philadelphia, in which they use this language:—

"That this part of the world where God has ordered our lot, labours under a grievous disadvantage for want of the opportunities of universities and professors skilled in the several branches of useful learning, and that many students from Europe are especially cramped in prosecuting their studies, their parents removing to these Colonies before they have an opportunity of attending the college, after having spent some years at the grammar school; and that many persons born in the country groan under the same pressure, whose circumstances are not able to support them to spend a course of years in the European or New England colleges &c. &c."

In 1744 a school was established. Mr. Alison was "chosen Master of said school, with privilege of choosing an usher under him to assist him."

Matthew Wilson was pupil under Alison in the school at New London.

Alison was succeded by the Rev. Alexander McDowell.

Under McDowell Wilson became a teacher in the school.

By the Presbytery of New Castle, Wilson was ordained as a minister October, 1755.

One of Wilson's pupils was Dr. John Neill, of Snow Hill, Maryland.

Dr. John Neill was the son of John Neill, lawyer, of Lewes, and the brother of Col. Henry Neill, of Lewes. After the discussions relative to the Stamp Acts, on February 21st, 1769, a son was born to Wilson, and was named James Patriot Wilson.

When ships with tea, arrived at the mouth of the Delaware River, upon which a duty of three pence per pound was to be paid for the benefit of the East India Company, he resolved that his family should use no more of the article. To reconcile the ladies, he published a paper in the newspapers, which afterwards appeared in the February, 1775, number of the American Magazine, showing the enervating effect of tea, and giving the names of seventeen herbs or vegetables which were good substitutes. In the midst of this discussion his wife's sister came from Philadelphia on a visit, and brought

OLD PRESBYTERIAN CHURCH, 1727.

down some of the prohibited article. She claimed that she was a patriot, but saw no good reason why she should not drink "old tea" upon which no duty had been paid, and "tea she would drink." The good Doctor, always diffident, and dreading "a tempest in a tea-pot," quietly submitted.

When, in 1774, the news reached Lewes that the British government had closed the port of Boston, he was one of the committee to send help to the distressed inhabitants of that city.

After the Declaration of Independence there was an increase of the Tory feeling in Sussex County, and those in favor of separation from Great Britain were in the minority.

The following letter throws a great deal of light upon conditions prevailing in Sussex County:—

"LEWES TOWN, July 30th, 1778.

"SIR: Inclosed you have a letter from the Rev. Mr. Wilson, soliciting your interest for the liberty of a certain James Cooper, one of the Reffugees from this State, now in your Gaol; the young man, I believe, was corrupted by some persons of the disaffected class; but they have ever acted so cautious, and ever so true to each other, that no positive proof could be had against them.

"I should be glad that you would not let Mr. Wilson's Letter be made public, as it will of consequence create him some enemies, that may have it in their power to injure him. Should it be in your power and not too much Trouble to obtain liberty for the young man to come down, I will pay any expenses for his imprisonment.

"I am Sir Yours

"HENRY NEILL.

"To Col. William Bradford
"At the London Coffee House
"Philadelphia."

Dr. Wilson's Letter.

"To Mr. William Bradford, and other members of the honourable Board of War in Philadelphia. Favoured by Henry Neill, Col.-Lieut. of Sussex.

"GENTLEMEN: We are informed that some few of our Sussex Tories have fallen into your hands, and are justly confined in Jail, where they are much much more likely to have an Impartial Trial, than here, where at least two-thirds of the County, by the Influence, Lies, Falsehoods, & base insinuations of your Joshua Fisher, and about a score of leading Men, who at that Time, held all Offices and Places of Trust in this County, are really disaffected to the American Cause, yet, by their numbers will soon be elected to fill their places again; so that if this State can do any harm to the Cause of America, by betraying the French, our Friends, or any of the Whig Colonists trading here, or by assisting, supporting, or encouraging our enemies, as well as persecuting forever the Whig Colonies here 'who have borne the burden and heat of the day,' there are more honors than I can now foresee, must come from Tories ruling the Delaware State.

"To remedy these dangerous evils I can see only 2 plans that appear practicable, either to disfranchise the Delaware State, and divide it between Maryland and Pennsylvania, which appears more necessary, because the State is too weak to bear the expense of its present Government, and also because of its smallness: any contention here between a leading Whig and a leading Tory would immediately divide the whole State into two parties, when Justice and Peace would be excluded from the State.

"The other remedy would only be partial and temporary, *i. e.*, The Congress fixing such Resolves, by such accurate Descriptions of Characters as would exclude all Tories and disaffected persons from holding any Offices in the State during this Generation at least.

"This would, indeed, incapacitate a great number from doing the highest injuries to the Country, Yet the most artful and dangerous Tories who stirred up the rest, and use them as Catspaws, would be still at the helm. They have veer'd all around the Compass, give the Whigs no positive proof against them, and have secured the Tories, to give no Information.

"The most probable Way to come to the Truth, would seem by pardoning some Tory or two on condition of becoming a true Witness against the Rest. There is one, Couper (James), I think, who would perhaps turn evidence on these terms. He kept Merchants' accounts formerly for Col. Simon Kollock, a staunch Whig, when this unhappy Couper was thought a good Whig, but going to live with Philip Kollock, he became such a Tory, as to go voluntarily, with others, to the English.

"Would you take the trouble to have him sounded apart from the rest, whether he would, in order to be restored, & pardoned, & admitted to Protection in Col. Kollock's house again, honestly inform you who were his advisers to prompt Him to go to the Enemy, whether he knows and can prove enough to convict Lawyer Moor, Isaac Smith, John Wiltbank, Philip Kollock, Esquires, Peter Robinson, late Sheriff, Anderson Parker, Ben. Burton, Esquires, &c &c.

"If you should find that he will make a good State Evidence, perhaps you could send him down in Col. Neill's vessel, who is Lieutenant of the County, and would take proper Care of Him, that he might not be enticed by the Tories.

"I am, with great respect, Gentlemen,

"Very much at your Service "Mat. Wilson.

"Lewes, July 29, 1778."

Henry Neill, son of John Neill, of Lewes, lawyer, married Mary, daughter, of Col. Simon Kollock. He was made, in September, 1775, Adjutant of the First Delaware Battalion, of which David Hall was Colonel. In May, 1778, he was elected Lieutenant of the County of Sussex. In June, 1780, he was Acting Colonel of the Fourth Delaware Regiment, being the second regiment of Delaware in the Continental service.

In 1803 he died, childless.

His friend, Dr. Wilson, prepared the following inscription, which is cut on his tombstone in the Presbyterian graveyard, Lewes:—

"In memory of Col. Henry Neill who died Nov. 10, 1803, aged 61 years, who valued independence, who dared, scorning submission to a foreign yoke, to force deliverance from the oppressors rod."

Dr. Wilson died March 31st, 1790.

GRANT FOR COOL SPRING CHURCH.

SEPTEMBER 13, 1737.

To ye Minister & Congregation of Presbiterians near Cold Spring in Sussex for 10 Acres to enclose their Meet'g House.

FORT CUMBERLAND, April 9th, 1757.

SIR:—We esteem ourselves obligd to you for the kindness shown by you & Mrs. Dagworthy to Old Ross &c. &c.

We are alive here. I have ordered the Volunteers to be informd that none are to proceed [torn] this Expedition, but [torn] as Sure them for me, and Mr. Ross by the first Occasion will Send them to Maidstone. My Complimts to Mrs. Dagworthy. I am

Your most obt hule Sert.

ADAM STEPHEN.

FORT CUMBERLAND, Feby 14th, 1757.

SIR:—John Fraser Complains that Some of the Detachmt from Fort Frederick has Carried off a gang of His Horses brought in by the Cherokees & taken privately away from them & stabled at Cressops plantation untill the Cherokees were gone out of the Way. William Ross has a Gray Lame Mare Carried down by the Same party.

The Cherokees are gone, & their return, in my Opinion [torn]. The Catabaws carried home at the Rate of £30 a man among which was £20 in Silver & £50 of Wampum & yet disatisfy'd. Fear is the strongest bond of an Indian they love & despise. Nothing but hard fighting & Success will recover the Indian Interest.

I am Sir, Yr most Obt huble Serv

ADAM STEPHEN.

SIR:—I have made what Enquiry I Could Relating to Mr. Fraziers Horses but do not find the Party from & his has taken them they Brought an old Lame Horse which was turn'd loose as being Useless which very Probably belongs to Mr. Ross & I suppose is Returned. all the News we have here is that Lord London Meets the Governors from the Differant Province this Day at Philada. the Result it is Probable we shall heare in a few Weeks.

SIR:—In Return for your [torn] Inclosed Some English [torn] to Pass off an Hour or two, this Dismal Weather, I am &c.

SIR:—Your Letter of the 11th Inst. I have received & in Answer thereto am to acquaint You that the Governor approves of Your Agreement with the Mason concerning the Building of the Chimnies & plaistering the Officers Barracks, but He says You must not enter into any such Engagement with the Soldiers who are employed as Sawyers, or into any with those that profess themselves Carpenters; Such as are employed in those Capacities will be considered & have an allowance [torn] unless You will enter into a particular Engagement with them His Excellency desires You will find them Business on the Allegany Mountains for a time or take any other method to bring them to a right Understanding. The Governor desires to know how much plank Mr. Waugh will want to finish the Soldiers Barracks that are already set up & those of ye Officers; & as the Assembly is to meet next Monday Sennight His Excellency desires You will as soon as possible send him Muster Rolls of the three Companies specifying for what time each man first enlisted or has since engaged to serve that he might try the same before the House if it shall be thought Necessary. I have writ to the Agents & presume they will forthwith send up the Cloathing for the Recruits as well as Money to pay the several Companies.

I am Sir Your most humb. Servt

J. RIDOUT.

ANNAPOLIS, The 13 Jan'y. 1757.

SIR:—This will be presented by John Linton the Recruit whom I mentioned to You in a former Letter. He comes with the Waggon & as He is to go by the Way of Elk Ridge I have given him a Dollar to bear his Expenses to the Fort. He was enlisted the 27th of Jany. so for his Board in Town since that time I must [torn] five Shillings which with the Bounty [torn] advanced him & the Dollar above mentioned makes £1. 15. 0. to be remitted me by any Opportunity of Conveyance that shall offer.

I am Sir Your most humb. & obed. Servt.,

J. RIDOUT.

ANNAPOLIS, the 1st Feby. 1757.

SIR:—The Governor desires that those Officers & Men that brought William Johnson from Plummer's to Fort Frederick may be part of the Detachment that You shall order hither with the Covered Waggon for Powder; His Excellency wants to ask them some questions but You need not mention it to them. You will let me know by a Line who the Persons are.

I am Sir Your most humb. & obedt. Servt.,

J. RIDOUT.

ANNAPOLIS, the 1st Decr. 1756.

P. S.—We have an Account that Adl. Hawke has had an Engagement with the French Fleet & taken & destroyed 7 of theirs with the Loss of three of his own Ships. Many Circumstances that are mentioned give us room to believe the Account ought to be depended on. We are also told that Bing has shot himself.

The Governor would not have You take any of Capt. Joshua Beall's Men into ye Company till farther Orders.

PRELUDE.

Altho Capt Daggworthy is a bad Correspondent And has not thought proper to favor me wh a Line these six Months nevertheless to shew him there is one at Fort Cumberland does not forget the many agreable Hours he has spent this time twelve Month whose name will be at the Bottom of this Scrawl & wh Capt. Daggworthy when he calls back past time may chance to recolect amongst the many less Animals in ye Creation to be known to Nature however Sc. to throw off the Disguise. Harry Woodward now speaks to you Wishing you & Mrs. Daggworthy Health happiness & success in all your Undertakings for the Present Year and at the same time cant help wishing you up at Fort Cumberland where you could See Tamorlane Exhibited in a very pretty Play-House. And as Mrs. Daggworthy I am sure woud ask who were the Actors I shall now set them down wh the Parts they Acted.

Tamorlane performed by....Capt. Peachy.
Bajazet..................Lieut. Hall.
Mokeses..................Mr. Hubbard.
Lama.....................Mr. Lawson.
Morvan...................Mr. Kennedy.
Stratocles...............Mr. Peachy.
Haly.....................Mr. Thompson.
Prince of Tanais ....Mr. Brockenbrough.
The Derveze..............Mr. De fierre.
Axalla...................Humble Servant.
Omar.....................Mr. Peachys Man.
Selima...................my Servant (who Acts very well.)
Aspasia..................Myself.

There was an Occassional Epilogue wrote by Hubbard in which my Actor was taken off and spoken by him.

N. B.—Brockenbrough was so touchd by it so that he will never never Act Again.

Æsop was the Farce and De fierre was the fine Lady by wh you may judge if it was a Farce or not. I am just Summoned to a Genl Court Martial wh obliges me abruptly to Conclude wh my respts to Mrs. Dagworthy.

Your most Obedt Humble Servt.,

H. WOODWARD.

FORT CUMBERLAND.

ANNAPOLIS, Septr. 12th, 1755.

SIR:—You are hereby directed to repair to Fort Cumberland & reassume the Command of the Mary [torn] with Your Co [torn] receive Instructions from me for that purpose, or unless the Virginia Troops find themselves strong enough & are ordered to march over the Allegany Hills to annoy the Enemy or construct some place of Defence there, in such Case You are to act as shall be judged best for his Majesty's Service

HORO SHARPE.

TO CAPTAIN JOHN DAGWORTHY.

To Captain John Dagworthy.

[Torn] Apl. 7, 1757.

SIR:—The Assembly is now sitting at Baltimore County & I understand Colo. Stanwick & Governor Sharpe are to have the Command of the Forces upon an Expedition to the Ohio which are to be those raised in Pennsylvania Virgini to be joined to one Batalion of the Royal Americans & the Governor desired me to [torn] an Express down as soon as either Daniel or the Indians should arive that he might make provision for Encouraging them & such Voluntares as shoud join them & I believe it would not be disagreable to him to let as many Soldiers [torn] Garrison go Voluntares I have dispatched a Messenger to the Governor yesterday who I imagine will Arive Today I apprehend by The Governor that he will be up soon in Order to have a Fort built at the Old Town, There is an Act. of the Fleet's sailing from Britain with the Forces & since I came from Town I heard that there had abt 10 or 12 Thousand Men arived at Hailifax & 20 Men of War who are to be joined by the Forces from new York & New England It's said that there is to be 500 Men raised in Maryland & that the Pennsylvanians have passed a Bill for [torn]

Your Friend &

THOS. CRESAP.

To Captain John Dagworthy.

SIR:—Inclos'd is the whole Instructions I Receiv'd the 23d Ult. hope you'l Lett Corpl. Love come Down to Join Mr. Beall in Charles County, Shall use all Endeavours to Raise what men I can while Down & Shall be at the fort by the Middle of March at Farthest, hope you'l Excuse the sending Barrickman Back Again, As we are in hopes of Stopping those person's Deserted.

I am with all Respect Your Humble Servt

ALEX. BEALL.

P. S. —Have Sent Mrs. Dagworthy A pair of Stockings price 6/6 if Dont think proper to keep them I will take them Again at my Return & as there was no more here shall Endeavour to serve her Lower Down.

FRED TOWN, Feby 24th, 1757.

SIR:—In the Governor's Absence I Received your Letter to him and Inclosed, you a Coppy of that part of the Act of Assembly that relates to the Affair You Mention'd & to Which I Refer.

I am, Sir Your Very Humbl Servant

BENJ TASKER.

ANNAPOLIS, 12th of Feby. 1757.

R CREEK GEORGE TOWN, Feby. 14th, 1757.

SIR:—His Excell. Sett out for Philadelphia the Day Before I Gott to Annapolis I Apply'd to Esq. Tasker and he thought it Requisite to Raise the Company's Again as Fast as possible, Which he Gave the Agent Order's to Lett me have One hundred & Eight pounds for that use, he Likewise has sent you A paragraph of the Last Act of Assembly, Wherein Directs how we are to proceed in Recruiting, we are to Inlist men till the 10th of Aprill, But if the Wise Assembly shall think proper, they Are to be Continued for Six Months Longer, No News here, All Freind well, & shall continue at R Creek, till such Time as I see or here from you Agreeable to Your Order's, I believe that I shall Gett Recruits Very fast I have Inlisted one, and am to Meet Several's at Bladenburgh this Week and am Sir your

Very Humble Servt to Command

LEUT. COLO. BEALL.

To Captain John Dagworthy.

FORT CUMBERLAND, March 1, 1757.

SIR:—Pursuant to an order from Governor Dinwiddie, I have sent down William Ross and two sons, Trotter & Slater who resided at this Garrison ever since the Fort was built—They have behaved honestly as far as I know, & have been very serviceable to the Garrison, Slater a Butcher & salter, Trotter as Guide & Labourer. William Ross and sons have resided here, ever Since plummer Left old tow [torn] have observed the Rules of the Garrison, and has lived upon his stock of Cattle having Supplyd us w' Butter & other little things which you know to be very necessary & agreeable at Such a distance from the Inhabitants.

Upon a Complaint from Colo. Cressop Sometime ago I had an Enquiry made by the officer of this garrison, into the reason of said Complaint. Ross can let you see the proceedings. He brought up two steers of Cressop's which he could not Easily separate from his own Cattle, but immediately informed me of it, and in Cosequence of a letter from Cressop I had them killed for the use of the garrison; and orderd the Commissary to send Cressop an act. of them & several others killed for the same purpose.

The old man brought up some Sheep of Plummer's which he said he did out of friendship to him; and informed the officer of it, saying plummer told him he should have Payment for them when he came up again but William Ross seeing that the place was a thorough fare for country people and Indians as they went up & down, thought he did a kindness to Mr. Plummer, & meant to oblige him by bringing up the sheep with some others which he drove to this Fort, and intended to Acct with him for them.

I inform'd him of my orders to send him down & the old-fellow never thought of moving out of the way and I had none of them Confined before the party came on.

It seems to me to be owing to an Old grudge between Ross & Cressop; and as you will have his sons in pledge espically I shall take it as a favour that you let him go About to do his Business, & make Friends. If I imagin'd that he would, or had reason to Attempt as Escape, be assurd I would never request the favour. I am obliged to you for the news p [torn] Indians were down on the Bran [torn] young men, burnt two plantations.

We are big with hopes [torn] the governors. I offer my [torn] Dagworthy and am

Sir, Your [torn] humble Sert

ADAM STEPHEN.

P. S.:—Since writing the Above I am informd that you are in the Commission of the peace, and one of the Magistrates to try these people. It is needless to request you to act w' the discretion which is so common & natural to you, in this affair, & weigh the Characters of the Evidence if there are any, because the affair will be canvessed, and make a great Noise, if the people are long detaind & harassd.

The lighthouse at Cape Henlopen is supposed to have been erected in 1725. The Hon. John Penn, November, 1763, had two hundred acres of land, or sand, surveyed and set aside for the benefit of the lighthouse. The lantern or top is said to have been burned by the British during the Revolution.

On the twenty-eighth of July, 1774, Thomas McKean, afterwards signer of the Declaration of Independence, made an address in Lewes, urging the people to make common cause with the Boston people in their stand against the imposition of unjust taxation.

This was after the Boston people had thrown the tea overboard.

In 1779–80 when the British frigate Roebuck was lying in the Bay, a number of men were sent ashore to obtain supplies. They seized Thomas Fisher, a boy of 17, on his father's farm near Lewes, and carried him and a negro slave back to the Roebuck, sending word to the parents that Thomas and the negro could be ransomed for one hundred bullocks. The terms were hastily complied with and Thomas was released.

Jerome Bonaparte was a guest in the old Peter Maull house. He had been recalled to France by his brother, Napoleon.

On account of the British blockading the Bay the French vessel could not leave. In the meantime a furious storm drove the ship ashore on the point of the Cape. Jerome with others escaped drowning and he was cared for at the Peter Maull house.

From Watson's Annals.

Nathiel Lukens, pilot of the "ketch 'James' (whereof Capt. James Risbie was owner) was put ashore at Cape Henlopen by Ely Lush, Wm. Rawlings, Charles kemarr, Robt. Lindsay, peter Goss, mariners. By reason of the bad weather the sailors could not get on the Ketch again." February 169_3.

January 18th, 1733. Great snow at Lewes; ice driven ashore by a north-east storm.

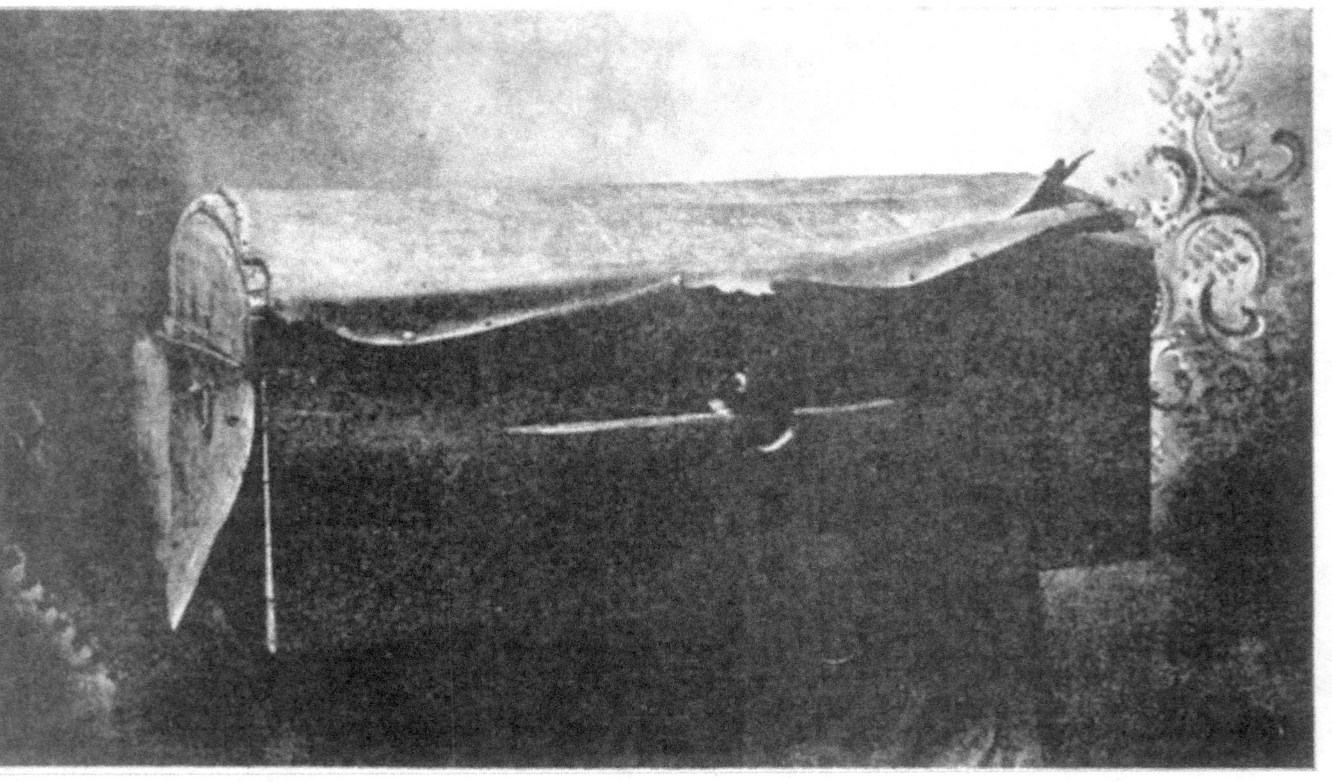

CAPT. DREW'S TRUNK.

January 8th, 1741. "Our river has been fast some time, and we heard from Lewes that 'tis all ice towards the sea as far as the eye can reach."

"At this early period of time (1733), so much had the little Lewistown at our southern cape the pre-eminence in female tuition, that Thomas Lloyd, the deputy governor, preferred to send his younger daughters from Philadelphia to that place to finish their education." (*Watson's Annals*).

Joshua Fisher, of Lewistown, afterwards of Philadelphia, merchant, first tried the quadrant in the bay of Delaware.

Joshua Fisher, of Lewistown, Delaware, made the first known Bay-chart of the Delaware. The one from which all our subsequent ones have been copied. It bears the imprint of London, 1756.

1703. The Grand Jury (Philadelphia) present Henry Brooks, the Queen's Collector at the Hore-kills, and three others, for raising a great disturbance and riot in the city at the dead of night.

Captain Drew and the De Braak.

James Drew was commissioned lieutenant in the Royal Navy, July 29th, 1775; master and commander, December 1st, 1787, and took rank as post-captain in 1790.

He commanded in order, the Echo, Fly, and De Braak, sloops-of-war.

The De Braak was a Dutch national ship detained at Falmouth by the Fortune (F. Wooldridge), August 20th, 1795.

The De Braak was commissioned, 1798, under the command of Captain James Drew, and attached to the fleet "off the Western Islands."

The following report was received in London, July, 1798:—

"Philadelphia, May 31, 1798—His Brittanic Majesty's sloop-of-war De Braak, Captain Drew, was overset in Old Kiln Roads about 4 O'clock last Friday afternoon. She was at the time under mainsail and reefed topsail, just about to cast anchor, a mile from the lighthouse, her boat alongside, waiting for the Captain, who intended to go on shore at Lewes Town; a sudden slew of wind laid her on her beam ends; she immediately filled and went down, with Captain Drew, his Lieutenant, and thirty-eight officers, seamen, and marines.

"The rest of the ship's company, about twenty-five, including the boatswain, escaped in the boats, and several were taken up by a pilot-boat.

"The De Braak parted with the fleet off the Western Islands in chase of a strange sail and was unable to join the convoy.

"About twenty-five days ago she fell in with and captured a Spanish ship from La Plata, bound to Spain, with a very valuable cargo, consisting of 200 tons of copper, a quantity of cocoa, &c. The prize is arrived in the Delaware. Twelve of the prisoners were lost in the sloop-of-war. The surviving Spanish prisoners have been brought to Philadelphia and given to the agents of Spain.

"The crew of the De Braak consisted of eighty-three persons in all, about half of whom were saved, including those who were in the prize.

"The officers left alive are the boatswain, a midshipman, and the prize-master.

"This melancholy accident is heightened by the Captain's lady being so near as New York, where she was every hour in anxious expectation of meeting him. The prize lies at the fort."

When the De Braak sunk three Spanish prisoners took the Captain's trunk and used it as a raft to get ashore.

Randolph McCracken, great grandson of Gilbert McCracken, pilot on the De Braak, let the present rector have the trunk. It is in the Sunday-school room of St. Peter's church.

BIBLE RECORDS.

FOOTCHER.

Wills, Administrations, Marriages. Kent and Sussex Counties, Delaware, 1683-95.

"William footcher son of William and Mary footcher was borne the Tenth day of the moneth called February one Thousand Six hundred Seaventy four, five;

"Sarah footcher daughter of William and Mary footcher was born the thirteenth day of the Second Moneth called April One Thousand six hundred Seaventy Seaven;

"Elizabeth footcher daughter of William and Mary footcher was borne the Eight day of the Moneth called February one Thousand Six hundred Eighty one, two;

"Richard footcher son of William and Mary footcher was borne the first day of the forth moneth called June one Thousand six hundred Eighty four;

"John footcher son of William and Mary footcher was borne the first day of the Second Moneth called April one Thousand six hundred Eight Seaven;

"Henry footcher son of William and Mary footcher was borne the Thirty first day of the Eight Moneth called October, one Thousand six hundred Eighty nine."

Judge John Wiltbank departed this life, 1792.

Mary Wiltbank, wife of John Wiltbank, departed this life, 1795.

Cornelius Wiltbank, son of Judge John and Mary Wiltbank, died November 9th, 1813.

Ann Wiltbank, wife of Cornelius Wiltbank, departed this life April 9th, 1801.

Esther Wiltbank, wife of Cornelius Wiltbank, departed this life November 1st, 1802.

John Wiltbank, son of Cornelius and Ann Wiltbank, was born January 23d, 1795; married Eliza Paynter, A. D. 1817; died February 13th, 1830.

Cornelius Wiltbank, son of John and Mary Wiltbank, departed this life November 9th, 1813.

Ann Hudson, wife of Henry Hudson, and daughter of Cornelius and Ann Wiltbank, departed this life January 24th, 1812.

Mary Metcalf, wife of Thomas Metcalf, and daughter of Cornelius Wiltbank, departed this life October 29th, 1814.

Thomas Metcalf, son of John and Esther Metcalf, departed this life November 1st, 1814 (He survvived his loving wife only two weeks).

Robert Wiltbank, son of Cornelius and Ann Wiltbank, departed this life on Sunday, January 22d, 1815, at the house of his grandfather, Judge John Wiltbank, "Dover," Delaware, was buried at the family burial ground on Wednesday, January 25th, 1815 (at Tower Hill Farm near Lewes).

John Wiltbank, son of Cornelius and Ann Wiltbank, departed this life on Saturday morning, February 13th, 1830, age 35 years and 21 days. Sermon delivered by Rev. John Mitchell, from Luke 12: 37. Buried in family ground near Lewes.

John and Eliza Wiltbank's first son was born September 5th, 1818, and departed this life fifteenth of the same month.

Samuel Paynter Wiltbank, son of John and Eliza Wiltbank, was born April 19th, 1820.

John Cornelius Wiltbank, son of John and Eliza Wiltbank, was born on Tuesday, July 15th, 1823.

Alfred Stockley Wiltbank, son of John and Eliza Wiltbank, was born on Saturday, September 12th, 1829.

John Cornelius Wiltbank departed this life September 9th, 1829.

Alfred Stockley Wiltbank and Hannah Richards Wolfe were married by Rev. John L. M'Kim, January 28th, 1852.

Samuel Rowland, John Paynter and Alfred Stockley, children of Alfred S. and Hannah R. Wiltbank, all died in infancy.

Frank Comly Wiltbank, son of Alfred and Hannah R. Wiltbank, was born July 9th, 1859.

Alfred Stockley Wiltbank, M. D., son of John and Eliza Wiltbank, departed this life August 7th, 1860.

Comly J. Wiltbank, M.D., departed this life December 23d, 1886.

Samuel Paynter, Senr., was born October 20th, 1736.

Samuel Paynter, son of Samuel Paynter, Senr., was born August 25th, 1768.

Elizabeth Rowland was born December 9th, 1779.

Samuel Paynter, Junr., and Elizabeth Rowland were married by the Rev. James Wiltbank, at the house of Mr. Cornelius Wiltbank, on Wednesday, March 16th, 1796, at 4 o'clock. That and the next day were remarkably stormy days, but it is hoped that prudence and economy may render the married life a happy one.

Mary Paynter, daughter of Samuel and Elizabeth Paynter, was born.

Mary Paynter and Simon K. Wilson, M.D., were married.

Samuel I. Wilson, son of Simon K. Wilson and Mary Paynter, was born July, 1820; died in 1849.

Mary P. Wilson, wife of Simon K. Wilson, M.D., and daughter of Samuel and Elizabeth Paynter, departed this life November 12th, 1820.

Eliza Paynter, daughter of Samuel and Elizabeth Paynter, was born December 8th, 1798; died November 14th, 1857, at Lewes, Delaware.

John Wiltbank and Eliza Paynter were married by the Rev. James Wiltbank, on Thursday, August 7th, 1817.

Samuel Rowland Paynter, son of Samuel and Elizabeth Paynter, was born.

Sarah Paynter, daughter of Samuel and Elizabeth Paynter, died August 10th, 1820.

John Parker Paynter, son of Samuel and Elizabeth.

Alfred Stockley Paynter, son of Samuel and Elizabeth Paynter, died, age 5 years.

Elizabeth Paynter, wife of Samuel Paynter, departed this life November 10th, 1820, aged 40 years.

Samuel Paynter departed this life on October 2d, 1845, in the 78th year of his age.

"With unfeigned regret that we announce the death of Ex Governor Samuel Paynter at his residence at the Dracot Bridge, Sussex County, Delaware, on the 2nd inst. in the 78th year of his age."—*Delaware Journal*, October, 1845.

Comly I. Wiltbank was baptized by the Rev. Walter Franklin at St. Peter's Church, Lewes, Delaware, August 4th, 1844, making the seventh generation baptized in that church, Sponsers his great-grandfather, Ex Governor Paynter of Delaware and grandmother, Eliza P. Wiltbank. He was born May 12th, 1844.

J. Comly Jones married, September 10th, 1821, by the Rev. Mr. Meyer, Mary Mary Hillborn, daughter of Joseph and Rachell Roberts.

Rachell Roberts Jones, daughter of Comly and Mary H. Jones, was born May 7th, 1824.

Samuel Paynter Wiltbank was married to Rachell Roberts Jones August 4th, 1842, by the Right Reverend Bishop H. M. Onderdonck.

Mary Elizabeth Wiltbank, daughter of Samuel Paynter and Rachell Roberts Wiltbank, was born August 1st.

Died at Philadelphia on the tenth day of June, 1845, J. Comly Jones aged 49 years.

Died on February 23d, 1850, Charles B. Jones, in the seventeenth year of his age.

Died on June 17th, 1860, Mary R. Jones, in the nineteenth year of her age.

Died in Philadelphia on August 7th, 1860, Dr. A. S. Wiltbank, of Lewes, Delaware.

William Manlove, Senior, was born December 25th, 1691. William Manlove departed this life on the fifteenth day of March in ye afternoon, about one hour before sun setting A. D. 1761. (William Manlove. His book bought in Philadelphia in ye year 1729. The price of this book is £1. 15. 0.)

Ruth Manlove departed this life the fifth day of April, 1746.

Sarah Masten, the wife of William Masten, departed this life February 27th, about one o'clock in the afternoon, 1776.

Mary Mason, the wife of Joseph Mason, departed this life November 5th, about one o'clock in the afternoon, 1779.

The ages of the children of William Manlove and Mary, his wife:

Nathaniel Manlove was born the sixth day of January, 1717, and departed this life April 27th, 1729.

William Manlove, Jr., was born April 29th, 1721, about midnight.

Mary Manlove was born the twenty-seventh day of October, 1723, about 4 o'clock in the afternoon.

Ruth Manlove was born December 10th, 1726, about 11 o'clock in the evening.

Sarah Manlove was born September 28th, 1830, about 8 o'clock at night.

Edmund Bibbe was married to his wife, Mary, October 1st, 1709.

William Manlove was married to his wife, Mary, December 6th, 1716.

Mary Manlove, daughter of Mark Manlove and Ann, his wife, was born April 18th, 1712.

Elizabet Manlove, daughter of Mark Manlove and Ann, his wife, was born October 7th, 1716.

Thomas Manlove, son of Mark Manlove and Ann, his wife, was born June 27th, 1714.

Esther Bibbe was born November 16th, 1710.

Matthew Bibbe was born January 19th, $17\frac{12}{13}$.

Mary, wife of William Manlove, above, departed this life December ye 1st day about 5 o'clock in the afternoon Anno. Dom. 1757.

John Masson Brown was born August ye 5, 1728, about two o'clock in the afternoon.

Sarah Chipman was born the thirtieth day of October, A. D. 1757.

William Shaw departed this life the twenty-fifth day of May, A. D. 1758.

Elizabeth Polk, daughter of Ephriam and Mary Polk, was born the twenty-ninth day of March, 1739.

William Borroughs, the son of John Borroughs & Ester Borroughs, was born the second day of January, $173\frac{8}{9}$.

The above William Borroughs departed this life on the fourteenth day of April, 1797.

Esther Borroughs, the daughter of John and Esther Borroughs, was born the eighth day of January, 1739 or 40.

William Masten, the son of W. M. Masten and Sarah, his wife, was born the seventh day of February, about 10 o'clock in the morning, A. D. $175\frac{0}{1}$.

Thomas Broxson was born in the year 1736 on the 27th December.

Joseph Broxson born, 1741, on the seventeenth of November.

An account of the birth of the children of Joseph Mason and Mary, his wife:

Sarah was born April 7th, 1744;

Mary was born March 13th, 1748;

Jacob was born December 19th, 1754;

Charles and Elias were born March 24th, 1760;

Joseph was born December 24th, 1763, and died April 16th, 1851. Age 57 years and 4 months.

William Masten, son of John Masten and Hannah, his wife, was born January 15th, 1711.

John Masten departed this life December, twentieth day, 1771.

William Masten, son of William Masten and Sarah, his wife, was born February, seventh day, 1751.

Mary Masten was born November 17th, 1754;

Sarah Masten was born January 25th, 1756;

Deborah Masten was born October 8th, 1760;

John Masten was born November 1st, 1763;

David Masten was born February 6th, 1767.

Charles Mason and Catherine Stayton, his wife, were married May 6th, 1815.

Jacob Mason, son of Charles Mason and Catherine, his wife, was born April 20th, 1816.

James L., son of Charles Mason and Catherine, his wife, was born April 1st, 1818.

William S., son of Charles and Catherine Mason, was born October 16th, 1821.

Joseph H., son of Charles and Catherine Mason, was born February 20th, 1823.

Catherine, only daughter of Charles and Catherine Mason, was born July 4th, 1830.

William S. Mason departed this life October, 1876.

James H. Mason departed this life ——, 1852.

An account of the times of the births of the children of Charles Mason and Betty, his wife:

Mary was born upon Sunday, the eleventh day of May, 1783.

Rachell was born upon Sunday, the thirty-first day of October, 1784.

Jacob was born upon Friday, the twenty-eighth day of December, 1786.

Charles was born on Saturday, the thirteenth day of September, 1788.

The above Betty Mason departed this life upon Saturday, the nineteenth day of November, about 8 o'clock in the morning, 1791.

The above Charles Mason, Senior, departed this life upon Sunday, the thirtieth day of September, 1810, being aged 50 years, 6 months and 6 days.

The above Jacob, son of Charles and Elizabeth Mason, departed this life January 20th, 1825.

Charles, Junior, son of Charles and Elizabeth Mason, departed this life August 21st, 1858.

Elias Mason was married to Magdelan Owens on the sixth day of March, 1783.

The births of the children of Elias Mason and Magdelan, his wife, are as follows:

Joseph was born October 23d, 1785;

Elias was born November 30th, 1787;

Elizabeth was born January 28th, 1790.

The above Elias Mason, Senr., departed this life December 17th, 1793.

Stephen Sturgis was married to Sally Mason October 12th, 1807.

The above Sarah Mason departed this life June 9th, 1847.

An account of the times of the births of the children of George Cullen and Sarah, his wife, is as follows, vizi:

Margin of leaf missing.

John Cullen was born June 7th, 176—;

Charles Mason Cullen was born January 9th, 176—;

Piercy Cullen was born September 17th, 1773;

Sarah Cullen was born September 14th, 1—;

Jonathan Cullen was born ——— 31st, 17—.

Piercy Cullen departed this life May 24th, 178—.

Sarah Cullen, younger, departed this life December 8th, 1794.

The above named Charles M. Cullen was married to Elizabeth Dickerson on the twenty-sixth day of January, 1797.

Elisha D. Cullen, son of the abovenamed, Charles and Elizabeth, his wife, was born April 23d, 1799.

An account of the children of Thomas Kellam and Mary Mason, his wife:—

Thomas Kellam and Mary Mason were married the fifteenth day of December, 1802.

Elizabeth W. Kellam was born the twenty-fourth day of April, 1804.

Joseph Mason and Mary, his wife, were married the twentieth day of November, 1807.

"(James W. Mason M.D. one among the decendants of those whose births and marriages are recorded in this book will be 38 years of age the twenty-seventh day of this present month, February, 1835.

"Cincinnati Ohio
"February 5th, 1835.

"The Widow Cullen gave me this book when I was in Lewistown Del in ye year 1832. J. M. M.)

"James W. Mason departed this life (margin destroyed) Cincinnati, Ohio, at 7 o'clock in the morning.

"This bible was presented to me by Sarah Mason widow of Joseph Mason (the younger): she resided in Cincinnati, Ohio, where she died April 14, 1843, age 74.

"Joseph Mason, her husband, died April 16th 1821, aged 57 years.

"JAMES W. MASON
"Son of Charles Jr."

Inscription of fly page of Bible:—

"Printed & Sold by Richard Ware at ye Bible & Sun in Amen Corner."

MARRIAGES.

Thomas H. Carpenter, Margaret M. Staton; March 4th, 1826; Philadelphia.

Thomas H. Carpenter, Catharine F. Marshall; September 3d, 1850; Lewes.

BIRTHS.

Thomas Howard Carpenter, son of Joseph and Mary Carpenter, born March 28th, 1804, Lewes.

Margaret M. Staton, daughter of Warrington and Hester Stanton, born Accomac County, Virginia, April 12th, 1806.

Mary Quinn, daughter of Thomas H. and Margaret Carpenter, born April 7th, 1827, Philadelphia.

Thomas Howard, son of Thomas H. and Margaret Carpenter, born December 10th, 1829, Philadelphia.

James Henry, son of Thomas H. and Margaret Carpenter, born October 9th, 1838, Lewes.

John Dorman, son of Samuel Dorman and Elizabeth Staton, born June 24th, 1818, Baltimore.

Louis Marshall Carpenter, son of Thomas H. and Catherine F. Carpenter, was born in St. Louis, Mo., September 24th, 1863.

Mary Quinn Carpenter, daughter of Thomas H. and Catherine F. Carpenter, was born August 26th, 1861.

Annie Eliza Carpenter was born St. Louis, Mo., September 24th, 1863, daughter of Thomas H. and Catherine F. Carpenter.

Thomas H. Carpenter, son of Thomas H. and Catherine F. Carpenter, was born St. Louis, Mo., August 19th, 1866.

James Carpenter was born May 15th, 1775.

Mary Dean was born January 16th, 1781.

Comfort H., married a Brown, Philadelphia, daughter of James and Mary Carpenter, was born June 12th, 1799.

Nancy, daughter of James and Mary Carpenter, was born January 28th, 1801; died March 24th, 1808; age 7 years, 1 month, 26 days.

Elizabeth, daughter of James and Mary Carpenter, was born November 13th, 1802.

Thomas H., son of James and Mary Carpenter, was born March 28th, 1804.

Robert Howard, son of James and Mary Carpenter, was born April 18th, 1806; died September 14th, 1808; age 2 years, 5 months, 16 days.

Mary Rodgers, daughter of James and Mary Carpenter, was born February 13th, 1808; died December 24th, 1842; age 34 years, 10 months, 11 days.

John Dean, son of James and Mary Carpenter, was born April 13th, 1810; lived in Philadelphia; died, age 49 years, 4 months, 18 days.

Jane, daughter of James and Mary Carpenter, was born July 8th, 1812; died, age 34 years, 11 months, 17 days.

Lydia, daughter of James and Mary Carpenter, was born June 28th, 1815. Married a Conwell.

Elizabeth, daughter of James and Mary Carpenter, was born January 24th, 1818.

James, son of James and Mary Carpenter, was born August 15th, 1820; died February 25th, 1842, age 21 years, 6 months, 10 days; pilot.

Margaret, daughter of James and Mary Carpenter, was born April 2d, 1822. Married H. Long.

Benjamin, son of James and Mary Carpenter, was born September 22d, 1825; emigrated to South; married, and supposed killed on railroad.

Marriages.

James Carpenter and Mary Dean were married February 15th, 1798.

Deaths.

Nancy, daughter of James and Mary, died March 24th, 1808, age 7 years, 1 month, 26 days.

Robert Howard, son of James and Mary, died September 14th, 1808; age 2 years, 5 months, 16 days.

James, son of James and Mary, died February 25th, 1842; age 21 years, 6 months and 10 days; pilot.

Mary Rodgers, daughter of James and Mary, died December 24th, 1842; age 34 years, 10 months, 11 days.

Jane Sweeney, daughter of James and Mary Sweeney, departed June 25th, 1847; age 34 years, 11 months, 18 days.

Thomas H., son of James and Mary, departed May 20th, 1858; age 54 years, 1 month, 32 days.

Mary, wife of James Carpenter, departed July 3d, 1858; age 77 years, 5 months, 17 days.

John Dean, son of James and Mary Carpenter, died September 1, 1859; age 49 years, 4 months and 18 days; lived in Philadelphia.

Lydia Coverdale, daughter of James and Mary Carpenter, died December 15th, 1859; age 44 years, 5 months, 17 days.

James Carpenter, departed January 7th, 1861; age 85 years, 7 months, 22 days.

James H. Carpenter, son of Thomas H. and Margaret Carpenter, died at Corning, Arkansas, November 13th, 1877.

Mary Q. Marshall, wife of J. A. Marshall, daughter of T. H. and Margaret Carpenter, died January 16th, 1886, Lewes, Del.

Catherine F. Carpenter, wife of Thomas H. Carpenter, and daughter of D. J. and Eliza A. Marshall, died June 29th, 1869; age 33 years, 6 months, 3 days.

[Inscriptions on Tombstones in St. Peter's Church Yard, Lewes, Delaware.]

Margaret Huling, widow of James Huling, died February 16th, 1707, in the 76th year of her age.

Daughter of Margaret Huling, February 1st, 1708, in the eighth year of her age.

Jacob Kollock, died March 30th, 1760, aged 63.

Mary, the late wife of Jacob Kollock, died September 30th, 1741, aged 95 years.

In memory of Mr. Rives Holt, Esq., who departed this life May 8th, 1765, in the sixty-seventh year of his age.

Here lieth interred the body of Ryves Holt, Jr., who departed this life March 17th, 1760. In the twenty-second year of his age.

In the memory of Daniel Nunez, Esq., who departed this life the twenty-second day of June in (Stone broken) fourth year of his age.

In memory of Mary, the wife of Daniel Nunez, who departed this life October 24th, 1746, aged 53 years.

Here lies interred Sarah, the late wife of Mr. Reese Wolfe, who departed this life January 15th, 1771, aged 33 years, 8 months and 1 day. Also infant, Daniel Nunez Wolfe, son of Sarah and Reese.

In memory of Hens Octs son of Daniel Nunez, who died July 27th, 1753, aged 21 years.

In memory of Daniel Nunez, Esq., who departed this life May 28th, 1775, in the forty-fifth year of his age.

Susanna, daughter of Jacob and Margaret Kollock, died ye 8th of October in the sixteenth year of her age.

In memory of Moses, son of Daniel and Mary Nunez, who departed this life February 24th, 1744, aged 23 years.

In memory of Esther, daughter of Daniel Nunez and Dianna, his wife, died January 8th, 1763, in the sixteenth year of her age.

Mary Becket, wife of the Rev. William Becket, departed this life August 15th, 1732, aged 46 years.

William Byron, born in Malta, naturalized in Boston, October 18th, 1849, died.

Henry F., son of the late Henry G. and Mary A. Dearborn, of Salem, Mass., died on U. S. Ship Saratoga, July 4th, 1863, aged 18 years.

Sarah H. Paynter, died September 19th, 1829, aged 55 years, 9 months, 23 days.

James J., son of William and Jane Paynter, died April 19th, 1836, aged 37 years.

Mary S. Paynter, died September 15th, 1830, aged 21 years, 9 months, 3 days.

Albert J. Paynter, died June 10th, 1828, aged 28 years, 6 months, 15 days.

Jane, wife of William Paynter, died August 10th, 1813, aged 30 years, 9 months, 20 days.

William Paynter, died March 19th, 1845, aged 71 years, 1 month, 25 days.

Elizabeth Jacobs, died December 24th, 1783, in the twentieth year of her age.

Albert Jacobs, died March 4th, 1786, in the twenty-eighth year of his age.

Thomas Truxton, son of William and Elizabeth Truxton, died March 9th, 1861; born May 17th, 1802.

Ann Green, departed this life June 10th, 1830, aged 23 years, 5 months, 15 days.

Jane Eliza Green, departed this life December 15th, 1829, aged 2 years and 3 days.

Jane Paynter, departed this life December 9th, 1832, aged 27 years, 9 months and 2 days.

Jane C. Thompson, daughter of John M. and Sarah Thompson, departed this life October 11th, 1813, aged 13 months.

James, son of John M. and Sarah Thompson, departed this life October 18th, 1845, aged 5 years, 5 months.

Marriages.

Thomas R. Norman and Miriam Bennett were married June 7th, 1798.

Thomas R. Norman, son of John and Anne Norman, was born October 22d, 1774.

Mariam Bennett, daughter of Pernal and Mariam Bennett, was born February 20th, 1779.

John B., son of Thomas R. and Mariam Norman, was born November 18th, 1799.

Mills R., son of Thomas R. and Mariam Norman, was born August 4th, 1801.

Joshua L., son of Thomas and Mariam Norman, was born December 10th, 1803.

Patience, daughter of Thomas and Mariam Norman, was born February 20th, 1806.

Annes, daughter of Thomas R. and Mariam Norman was born September 30th, 1808.

Eliza, daughter of Thomas R. and Mariam Norman, was born September 22d, 1810.

Mary, daughter of Thomas R. and Mariam Norman, was born April 8th, 1813.

Purnal Norman, son of Thomas R. and Mariam Norman, was born January 8th, 1816.

Mary Norman, daughter of Thomas R. and Mariam Norman, was born April 29th, 1818.

Thomas L. Judge Norman, son of Thomas R. and Mariam Norman, was born March 18th, 1821.

Mary, daughter of Thomas R. and Mariam Norman, died September 13th, 1814.

Thomas L. Judge, son of Thomas R. and Mariam Norman, died July 11th, 1823.

Thomas R. Norman died March 27th, 1863.

Mariam B. Norman, died September 27th, 1857.

George Orton, son of William and Hannah Orton, died 2–5–1830.

John Bennett Norman died 9–24–1853.

William Shankland, son of Mills and Sarah Shankland, was born October 10th, 1768.

William and Patience Shankland were married October 6th, 1789.

William Shankland died October 21st, 1819, aged 51 years and 11 days.

Patience, the daughter of Rhoads and Ann Shankland, was born January 11th, A. D. 1771.

MRS. ANN ELIZA MARSHALL,
Aged 96.

Patience Shankland, the wife of William Shankland, died September 20th, 1790. Born of this marriage one daughter, Ann May, September 7th, 1790.

Ann May, daughter of William and Patience Shankland, was married to John H. Burton, November 30th, 1808.

John H. Burton died January 15th, 1822.

Ann May Burton and Dr. Joseph Marsh were married August 28th, 1822.

Ann May Marsh died April 12th, 1847, aged 57 years, 7 months, 5 days.

ANN MAY'S CHILDREN.

Burton's.

William Shankland Burton, born January 15th, 1810.

	Born.	Died.
Mary Ann, ...	Feb. 3d, 1812—	Sept. 3d, 1812.
Eliza Ann, ...	Feb. 20th, 1814—	
Theophilus, ...	May 8th, 1816—	June 22d, 1825.
Caroline, ...	Aug. 9th, 1818—	
Mary Vaughan, ...	Nov. 22d, 1820—	Dec. 21st, 1822.

Marsh's.

James P. W. Marsh, born August 23d, 1823.
John A., born June 29th, 1825.
Sarah Ann May, born August 23d, 1829.

Nehemiah Maull, son of John Maull II. & Mary Marsh married 1st, Mary Keen; 2d. Mary Marrott.

Issue by second wife: Jane, born 1791; Ann Jane, born 1796; Margaret and Hannah.

Nehemiah died October 23d, 1817.

John Maull his Bible brought from Londen by Capt. Budden.

John Maull born November 28, 1714.

Mary Field, born August 1, 1719.

John Maull and Mary Field were married October 12, 1736.

Issue:

Nehemiah, born October 15th, 1737.

Elizabeth, born November 27th, 1739, died June 3d, 1753;

John, born October 9th, 1742;

James, born October 3d, 1744, married Jane Moulder, October 16th, 1766;

Henry, born April 9th, 1747, died August 9th, 1748;

Mary, May 4th, 1749;

William, born May 6th, 1752.

John Maull, Senr., died July 27th, 1753.

Mary Field, widow of John Maull, Senr., married Luke Shields.

Peter Maull, son of John Maull and Mary Marsh, his wife, was born March 29th, 1773, married Mary Allen, daughter of Moses Allen; Mary Allen was born August 4th, 1774.

ISSUE:

Mary born August 26th, 1795;

Joseph born September 15th, 1797.

Eliza born November 21st, 1799;

Jane born January 16th, 1803;

Peter born September 27th, 1804;

Margaret born October 26th, 1806;

Hetty born September 11th, 1809;

Lydia Marsh born November 6th, 1811;

Matilda born May 25th, 1814.

Nehemiah Maull, son of John Maull and Mary Field, his wife, was born October 15th, 1737; married Mary Moulder March 19th, 1763

ISSUE:

John, born August 23d, 1764, died October 8th, 1765;

Robert, born July 19th, 1766.

Elizabeth, born August 1st, 1768.

Mary, born September 6th, 1770;

Nehemiah, born February 9th, 1774;

Rachel born ——————;

William, born August 10th, 1778.

James Maull, son of John Maull and Mary Field, his wife, was born October 3d, 1744; married Jane Moulder October 16th, 1766.

John Maull II., born October 9th, 1742;

Mary Marsh, daughter of Peter Marsh and Esther, his wife, was born December 7th, 1752;

John Maull and Mary Marsh were married March 24th, 1768.

ISSUE:

Peter, born April 9th, 1769, died August 11th, 1771;

Peter Marsh, born April 10th, 1771;

Peter, born March 29th, 1773;

John III., born February 22d, 1775, died October 9th, 1843;

Nehemiah, born April —, 1777;

Samuel, born April 10th, 1779;

Hetty, September 25th, 1783.

John Maull III., married Sarah

ISSUE:

James R., born October 3d, 1797;

Dedrouh, born January 14th, 1800;

John IV., born September 25th, 1802, died November 15th, 1842;

Samuel, born April 22d, 1805;

William Stette, September 29th, 1807.

William Maull, born May 6th, 1752.

William Maull and Leah Burton were married December 21st, 1777.

Hetty daughter of William and Leah Maull born ———, 1778;

Catherine, born October 23d, 1779, married William Marshall.

Henry, son of John Maull, II., and Mary Marsh, his wife, was born September 25th, 1783;

Mary Bedford Webb, daughter of Jacob and Hannah Thompson Webb, was born at New Castle, Del., December 25th, 1778;

Henry Maull and Mary Bedford Webb were married December 19th, 1804.

ISSUE:

Hetty, born November 10th, 1806;

Charles, born November 22d, 1808;

Henry, born November 30th, 1811;

Edward, born September 22d, 1813;

George, born December 23d, 1815;

John, born December 10th, 1817;

Hannah, born September 11th, 1819;

Mary Ann W., born October 17th, 1821;

Sarah R., born August 21st, 1823;

Deborah, born October 10th, 1825;

Maria Louisa, born October 10th, 1827;

William, born February 5th, 1829.

From the Clowes Bible

1783. Catherine Clowes within mentioned, now the widow of John Young has but one child living (viz) John Young born 28 July 1772.

Mary Clowes within mentioned, now the wife of John K. Dorman, has living four children (viz) 3 boys and 1 girl. Gerhardus Dorman born 23d of Aug. 1772, Nehemiah born 31 July, 1774, Elizabeth Dorman born 29 July 1776, John Dorman born 22d May 1779.

Meirs Clarke was married to Aletta Clowes in the year 1785. Meirs Clarke was born the 2 of May in the year 1761. Mary Clarke daughter of Miers & Aletta Clarke was born August 28 about 3 Oclock in the afternoon, on Sunday in the year 1786; was Baptized by the Rev. Sydenham Thorne. Miers Clarke departed this life December 17, 1810.

1792, May 9, Wednesday about 9 oClock was born Sarah, daughter of Miers Clarke and Aletta, his wife.

Sept. 7, 1758, John Clowes, Jr., was married to Mary Draper by the Rev. Matthias Harris at John Spencer's Esq., about 1 in the afternoon. Mary Draper, daughter of Isaac & Sarah Draper, was born the 10th day of November, 1739.

On frayday the 17th day of Aug. anno Domi. 1759 Between the Hours of 12 & 1 in the morning was born Sarah Clowes Daughter to John & Mary Clowes and was Baptized Munday Privately by the Reverend Matthias Harris. On thursday the 1st day of July 1761 about 2 Oclock in the afternoon she was Siezed with a choaking fitt which ended with her life in about 9 or 10 hours afterwards and she was buried at John Havelaves on Saturday following.

1808, May 12th, at 4 Oclock in the afternoon, James Walker was married to Mary Clarke by Revd. Mr. William Hickman.

1794, Sept. 10, on Wednesday about 9 o'clock at night was born Hannah daughter to Miers Clarke and Aletta his wife.

1798, Oct. 24, on tuesday was born Elizabeth, about 11 in the morning, Daughter to Miers Clarke and Aletta his wife.

1800, July 18, about 5 in the morning, on Friday, was born Lidia, Daughter to Miers Clarke and Aletta his wife.

1803, febbruary the 1st, about 2 in the afternoon, was born, tuesday, Ester Daughter to Miers Clarke and Aletta his wife.

1805, febbruary 6th, on Wednesday morning about 1 o'clock was born Anna, Daughter to Miers Clarke and Aletta his wife.

1807, April 30, between 12 in the morning, was born Aletta, Daughter to Miers Clarke and Aletta his wife.

Mary Clowes Died the 6th of August, 1813, aged 73 years, 8 months, & 26 days.

1809, Aug. 16, on Monday, was born James Miers Walker, son of James & Mary Walker. He died March 10, aged 27 years, 4 months, 8 days.

1815, Joanna Truitt March 17, on Friday, Daughter to John and Sarah Truit.

Sarah Pinner daughter of Miers Clarke and Aletta his wife died in North Carolina Jan. 3, 1871.

1733, September 16th, at 5 in the morning, their third son David Clowes was born at Lewes and Christened there by Mr. Beckett 28 April, 1734. His sponsors were Mr. Ryves Clowes & Mrs. Comfort Clowes.

1736, July 9th, at 9 in the morning, Catharine Clowes, second daughter of John & Mary Clowes, was born at Lewes aforesaid & there Christened by the aforesaid Revd Wm Beckett on the 5th of Sept. following. Her sponsors were Mr. Daniel Nunez, Mrs. Mary Nunez & Mrs. Eliza Price.

1737, Dec. 31st, at 6 in the evening, their fourth son, Samuel Clowes, was born at Lewes & there Christened by Mr. Beckett on the 5th of March following. His sponsors were Mr. Simon Kollock, Mr. Edward Naws & Mrs. Comfort Kollock. He lived untill the 19th March, 1758, on which day being about 9 in the morning he Dyed much regretted by his friends. He was buried at Broad Kill in the burying ground of his Mother's relations there.

On Monday the 22d of March, 1762, between one and two in the afternoon was born Samuel Clowes, son to John and Mary Clowes, and Baptized on Saturday, the second of October, following, by the Rev. Matthias Harris at Pilot Town.

On Sunday, the 7th of October, 1764, at 2 Oclock in the afternoon, was born John Clowes, son to John & Mary Clowes, and was Baptized on Sunday the 29th of September, 1765, at St. Georges Chappel by the Rev. Matthias Harris, and on Sunday the 21st of September, 1766, departed this life at half after four in the afternoon with a flux of four days' continuance.

1767, on Thursday, the 7th of Aprill, at half after nine in the morning, was born Aletta Clowes, Daughter to John & Mary Clowes, and was Baptized on Wednesday, the 13 of May, at home by the Rev. Matthias Harris.

"He Baptized 85 Children here this day 46 girls & 29 boys."

1769, On Monday, the 12th of June, at half after eight in the morning, was born Sarah Clowes, Daughter to John & Mary Clowes, and on Monday, the 18 of Sept., following, was Baptized by Rev. John Andrews.

1771, on Tuesday, the 16 day of July, at eight in the morning, was born John Clowes, son to John & Mary Clowes, and on Monday, the 5 of August, following, was Baptized by the Rev. John Lyons; and the next day at ½ after one in the afternoon it pleased God to take his soul, and on the 7th inst. his body was intered in the Vault at John Heavcloe's.

1780, Nov. 21, their first son, Samuel, was lost in Delaware Bay in a violent storm, wind S. E., together with all the others and the vessel. Heard on the 3d of June following that he was buried on Murder Kill Beach, and on diging down to the body believe it to be the remains.

1772, On Thursday, the 20th of Aug., at ½ after three in the afternoon was born Isaac Clowes, son to John & Mary Clowes, and was Baptized by the Rev. John Lyon the 28 of Nov. following.

1775, Thursday, 2d day of February, at Twelve Oclock was born Peter Clowes, son to John & Mary Clowes, & on the 29th of May following was Baptized by the Rev. Mr. Samuel Tingle at our own house. He died with a bilious fever leaving one son Ezekiel Williams Clowes.

1777, Friday, Sept. 7, at 1 Oclock in the morning, was born John Clowes, son to John & Mary Clowes, & was Baptized by the Rev. Samuel Tinley on Saturday, May 28, 1778, at our own home. The reason why he was so long unbaptized was the times. Toryism prevailed & it was dangerous to go to church & the Parson seldom called on us.

1780, Friday, May 19, at 11 Oclock in the morning, was born Mary Clowes, Daughter to John & Mary Clowes, and was Baptized by the Rev. Samuel Tinley on Saturday, the 26 of August, at our own house, myself from home. July 17, 1781, she was taken with a purgeing which continued till the 3d of September when she gave up the Gost. On the 4th her remains was buried in the Vault.

1784, January 27, Our third son, John, left this life of trial & probation of a malignant quencey or the putrid ulcerous sore throat, of only three days continuance. On the 29th we laid his remains in the Vault, in extreme cold.

1789, December 9, their 2d Daughter, Sarah, wife to John Clarke, died the 4th day of her sickness, on Wednesday, at 10 Oclock in the morning, with a violent head plurasy or inflamation of the brain; 11th we laid her in the ground at the south end of the Vault. Mr. Wilson preached her funeral the 14th. Aged 20 years & 6 months lacking 3 days. Left 2 children.

Printed and Sold by Richard Ware at ye Bible & Sun in Amen Corner. Just Published fitted to Bind up with all sorts of House Bibles a Brief Concordance for the more easy finding out of the useful Places therein Contained. by I. Downame B. D. [No Date].

Anno Domini, 1727, August 25th, at 5 afternoon, John Clowes was married unto Mary his wife at Lewes Town, in the County of Sussex on Delaware, by the Rev. William Beckett, Missionary from the Society for Propagating the Gospel.

1728, June 28th, at 4 in the morning William Clowes, eldest son of them, the said John & Mary, was born at Broad Kill, in the aforesaid County of Sussex, and was christened by the abovesaid Missionary Beckett, privately at Lewes Town, on the 28th Aug. following. Said Wm. Beckett, Jonathan Bayley, Jr, & Mrs Becket his sponsors.

1730, November 5th, at 11 in the morning John Clowes, their second son, was born at Lewes Town, and there christened by the said Mr. Beckett the 11th December following. His sponsors were Mr. Ryves Holt, Mr. John Welbor & Mrs. Holt.

1732, August 28th, at 1 in the morning their first daughter, Alletta Clowes, was born at Lewes Town, & on the 5th September following she was Christened by Sd Mr. Beckett privately (being very ill) & on the 6th inst. at 8 in the morning she Dyed & was buried in the Church yard at Lewes.

1739-40, February the 7th, at 5 in the morning, their third Daughter, Mary Clowes, was born at Lewes & there Christened by Mr. Beckett, on the 27th of April following. Her sponsors were Mr. Cornelius Wiltbank Mrs. Margaret Kollock, & Mrs. Hester Philips.

1742, May 19th, at 7 in the morning, their fourth Daughter, Lidia Clowes, was born at Lewes, & there Christened by Mr. Beckett on the first of August following. Her Sponsors were Mr. Ryves Holt, Mrs. Catherine Holt & Mrs. Mary Nunez.

1747-8, March 12, at 10 in the morning, their fifth son, Gerhardus Clowes, was born at Parktown on the Broad Kill, in Sd County of Sussex, and was Christened by the Rev.

Mr. Usher, a Missionary at Lewes, on the 18th September following. His sponsors were the said Mr. Usher, Mr. Daniel Nunez & his own Mother.

1766, Oct. 26th, their eldest son, William, departed this life of a plurafie. He was Interred at Eliza Staytons at Broad Kill, where his former wife was buried.

1768, March 19, their son, Gerhardus, perished to Death in a Most Violent Storm of Snow on Apoquimini Creek, on Delaware River, being Drove in a Vessel there, & was there Desently Buried in an old burying ground Much lamented by his friends.

1766, Oct. 26, the foregoing William Clowes, died of a pluracy. He left 4 Children, Two by each Wife:—1st, Catherine, born ——; 2d, Mary, born ——; 3d, Lydia, born 15 Nov., 1762; 4th, John, born 18th March, 1765.

1770, June 18, John Clowes, the second son mentioned in the foregoing Catalogue of Births, got this old Bible new Bound at Philadelphia, and Proposeth to enter hereunder the famely Deaths till God shall call him hence.

1769, April 24th, at 12 oClock in the day, John Clowes, esq., father of the forementioned, departed this Life in the ninth day of a plurasie, aged sixty six years and nine days; the Corps was laid in an open grave the 27th inst. and on the 5th of June was Intered in a New Vault built since his death at Mr. Heavelo's Landing. Mr. Andrews preached his funeral.

1770, May 25, at 9 oClock in the morning, David Clowes departed this Life of a disorder that had raged on him near four years, and on the 27 inst was Intered in the aforesaid Vault. Mr. Lyons preached his funeral sermon. He left only one child, a daughter; she was born at Nanticoke, 22d day of April 1767, 1783, the 9th day, the above Hannah died of a quency at 12 last night and was intered in sd vault.

1781, Nov. 25, on Sunday, at 3 in the morning, Lydia Clowes, the wife of Lot Clark, departed this Life of a Nervers Fevor; and on the 27th her Remains was laid in the Vault. On the 4th of Dec. Mr. Tillney preached her funeral sermon. She Left six Children three by first, and three Girls by her Second Husband, viz., Shepherd Conwell, born 23d July, 1765; Gerhardus Conwell, born 12th Nov., 1767; John Conwell, born 29th January, 1770; Melicent Clark, born 24th Sept., 1776; Anna Clark, born 27th April, 1778; Charlotte Clark, born 12th Feb., 1780.

1790, Feb. 24th, at 5 oClock in the morning, on Wednesday, the above mentioned John Clowes, Esq., & Judge of the Court, Died the 9th day of his sicknefs, with a violent Plurasie & inflamtion of the lungs, Aged 59 years 3 months & 18 days, & was buried at the South Corner of the Vault. Mr. Willson Preached his funeral. He objected being laid in the Vault; left his beloved wife; & Mary Clowes died 6 of August, 1813. Only 3 children out of ten survived him.

From a Bible Owned by Miss Lydia Conwell.

1783. Catherine Clowes, within mentioned, now the widow of John Young has but one child living, viz.: John Young born 28th July, 1772.

Mary Clowes, within mentioned, now the wife of John K. Dorman, has living four children, viz. three boys and one girl.

Gerhardus Dorman, born 23d of August, 1772;
Nehemiah, born 31st July, 1774;
Elizabeth Dorman, born 29th July, 1776;
John Dorman, born 22d May, 1779.

Miers Clarke was married to Aletta Clowes in the year 1785; Miers Clarke was born the 2d of May, in the year 1761.

Mary Clarke, daughter of Miers and Aletta Clarke, was born August 28th, about 3 o'clock in the afternoon, on Sunday, in the year 1786, was baptized by the Rev. Sydenham Thorne.

Miers Clarke departed this life December 17, 1810.

1792. May 9th, Wednesday, about 9 in the morning, was born Sarah Clarke, daughter to Miers Clarke and his wife.

1794. September 10th, Wednesday, about 9 o'clock at night, was born Hannah Clarke, daughter to Miers Clarke and Aletta, his wife.

1798. October 24th, on tuesday, was born Elizabeth Clarke, about 11 in the morning, daughter of Miers Clarke and Aletta, his wife.

1800. July 18th, about 5 in the morning, on Friday, was born Lidia Clarke, daughter to Miers Clarke and Aletta, his wife.

1803. February the 1st, at 2 in the afternoon, was born, tuesday, Ester Clarke, daughter to Miers Clarke and Aletta his wife.

1805. february 6th, on Wednesday morning about 1 o'clock, was born Anna Clarke, daughter to Miers Clarke and Aletta, his wife.

1807. April 30th, between 12 in the morning, was born Aletta Clarke, daughter to Miers Clarke and Aletta, his wife.

Mary Clowes died the 6th of August, 1813, aged 73 years, 8 months, and 26 days.

September 7th, 1758. John Clowes, Jr., was married to Mary Draper by the Rev. Matthias Harris at John Spencer's, Esq., about 1 in the afternoon.

Mary Draper, daughter of Isaac and Sarah Draper, was born the tenth day of November, 1739.

On frayday, the seventeenth day of August, anno Domi. 1759, between the hours of 12 and 1 in the morning, was born Sarah Clowes, daughter to John and Mary Clowes, and was baptized Munday, privately by the Reverend Matthias Harris. On thursday the first day of July, 1761, about 2 o'clock in the afternoon, she was siezed with a choaking fitt which ended with her life in about 9 or 10 hours afterwards, and she was buried at John Havelaves on Saturday following.

1808. May 12th, at 4 o'clock in the afternoon, James Walker was married to Mary Clarke, by Rev. Mr. William Hickman.

1809. Aug. 16th, on Monday, was born James Miers Walker, son of James and Mary Walker. He died March 10th, aged 27 years, 4 months, 8 days.

1815. Joanna Truitt, March 17th, on Friday, daughter to John and Sarah Truitt.

Sarah Pinner, daughter of Miers Clarke and Aletta, his wife, died in North Carolina, January 3d, 1871.

Aletta Clarke's Book, April 28, 1789.

1789. Our family has the measles. In July, Polly, my little daughter, had a gathering in her head.

August 24. I was taken very sick. Lidia Hall stayed with me.

September 15. Sister and I went to fathers.

September 16. Came home. Parted with the two old ladies from New York, my father's cousins. We may never see them again in this world.

September 19. I went to see my sister.

October 10. About 10 o'clock at night as I was returning home, I saw a strange light in the house, that I could not account for, the house being fastened up, and no one in it.

October 31. I went to see my sister. She told me of two dreams she had dreamed. In one she was dressed in white, and her company told her she did not look as if she belonged to this world. In the other her child was born, and she was to die three days afterwards.

November 5. My sister and I went to the store at the bridge.
November 7. We went to warp at Mrs. Russels, neither of us very well.
November 14. Went to see my sister. She was poorly.
November 25. Went to see my sister and stayed all night. A most violent storm came on, the wind in the East.
November 29. Polly Draper came here.
November 30. Monday. Went to my father's. As it was snowing and very cold I stayed all night.
December 1. I came home, and went to my Sister's, to get help about sizeing up a web.
December 2. I got the piece out that I had in the loom, and got it to work.
December 4. I wove on it all day. Just at night Mrs. Russel sent for me. I went over to see her. About 10 o'clock at night she was delivered of a daughter. About 12 I got home. My Brother Isaac Clowes came down this afternoon for sister and me to go to see our Dadda and Mamma.
December 5. In the morning my Brother came over and said that Sister Sally was taken with an ague, and was very sick. I went right away to see her, and found her sickness most violent. Mamma came down in the afternoon. About 9 o'clock at night I sent for Grandmamma. Her violent sickness brought on her labour. On Sunday the 6th at sunrise she was delivered of a son. Not being well I went home. In the afternoon I went back. I found my sister in a sleepy condition. I walked home.
December 7. This morning she complained of a sharp pain in her head, and about 9 o'clock she had a convulsion. She would frequently cry out: "Oh my head! my poor head!" About 2 in the afternoon she was taken with another convulsion, and that left her speechless. She lay in this distressing condition until the 9th day about 3½ o'clock it pleased God to take her into His safe keeping. She was 20 years and 6 months old this day lacking 3 days.
December 11. The burial—but the Parson could not come. Parson Willson preached her funeral Monday the 14th.
December 23. A violent pain in my head and eyes.
December 24. Some better.
December 25. Christmas Day. Go to see my Dadda and Mama.
December 26 & 27. My sister's little baby had the measles, and Comfort Staton's child is sick.
December 28. My father very sick. We send to the Doctor.
December 29. Comfort's child died, and Comfort exceeding bad. My Dadda got better, thanks be to heaven.
December 30. I came home from my Dadda's.
December 31. Negroes a Christmasing.

1790.

January 1. Negroes gone.
January 2. Mr. Watson and his wife here.
January 3. Watson and his wife and Mr. Cade and his wife here Sunday. Some people make the holy day a day of visiting.
January 4. Negroes at home.
January 5. Miers from home.

January 6. I go to my father's. He is at Lewes town.

January 7. Came home and went to see Mrs. Heveloe. She was very sick.

January 8. In the morning she was some better.

January 16. Go to my father's.

January 17 & 18. Came home. Comfort was some better.

January 20. Mrs. Heaveloe died, after a long tedious spell of sickness.

January 22. I was at her burying. She was a very kind neighbor. She lived one mile from me.

January 23. Charles Conwell died. A young man, married about three months. His widow with child. He lived two miles from me. Abner Lamb died the same day. He lived about five miles away.

January 30. Was at Conwell's burying. From there rode to my father's about 3 o'clock at night. We thought my sister's little son was dying. Sent word for its father about 10 o'clock. It got better by the next morning.

February 1. On Monday my Dadda came here. He gave me an Almanack and a paper of pins. From here he rode to Lewes-town.

February 2. Wove all day.

February 3 & 4. Wove on my piece.

February 8. Wove some but was not well.

February 13. Should have gone to my father's but was not well.

February 14. Harry Fisher and Sarah Truit were buried. Fisher lived 7 miles from here, and Sarah Truit 5 miles.

February 16. On Tuesday mama sent me word that Dadda was very sick. I rode to see father as soon as I could and found him in a sleepy condition. We had means from the Doctor.

February 17. My father was very sick.

February 18. A little better. Sat up some.

February 19. We thought him a great deal better. He walked out of his room. I ventured to go home, brother Isaac with me. We stopped to see two sick neighbors. Jonathan Lewis died 1 mile from here.

February 20. Mary Miller died 1 mile from me.

February 21. Miers gone to Lewises. On Sunday Mama sent for me to go and see my father. He was worse than ever before. I rode up there as fast as I could and found him exceeding bad. He had a piercing pain in his breast and side, and the worst cough that I ever saw any person have. We sent for the Doctors on Monday.

February 22, 23. There were two Doctors with him but they were of no manner of service. Everything was done for him we poor creatures could do, but it was of no service.

February 24. At 5 o'clock in the morning it pleased God to ease his body by taking his soul into His safe keeping. Thus my dear and tender parent is gone. A most violent pleurisy has ended his life the 9th day of his sickness. He is this day 59 years, 3 months, and 18 days old. He lived 32 years, 5 months, and 17 days with my Mama, and I never knew them to have any anger the time of his life. He was an affectionate husband, a loving father, a kind good master, and a kind neighbor in sickness or in health. His greatest anxiety was to love mercy, justice, and truth. In doing justice towards God and man, his parents saw his young mind improve in every virtue.

February 26. Mr. Willson preached his funeral. Yonder like a faded flower lies the dust he has abandoned. Sarah Claypool died. Lived about 2 miles from me. Patience Coverdale died the same day, 6 miles from me.

February 28. Mary Lewis died. her husband died nine days before. They lived about 1 mile from me. The sickliest time that I ever knew, there is hardly an individual without complaint. Wm. Chace died the same da 9 miles. I was at Sarah Claypool's burying.

March 2. Dorman Cade died 6 miles from here.

March 3. A sister of Chace's died, 9 miles from here.

March 10. John Clifton died, about 8 miles, and John Caddy died about 7 miles from here.

March 11. Another of the Chace family died, 9 miles, and Sarah Heavelo died just in her 17 year, 1 mile.

March 17. I hear there are 4 more of the Chace family dead, I am told that out of 10 there are but 3 left. Lord have mercy. Thy arrows fly not at random.

March 17. Elizabeth Jeams died 6 miles off, and Mr. Hinmon died, 6 miles off.

March 19. A child of Chaces scalded to death. Rachel Heaveloe died in her 19th year. Mrs. Heaveloe, her 2 daughters and a negro child have died since this day 2 months, just 1 mile from me.

March 21. Reece Rickets died about 4 miles from me.

March 24. John Fisher died. About 3 miles off.

March 25. Luke Watson's wife died. Lived 6 miles away. George Wiltbank and one of his children died. 7 miles.

March 30. One of Mr. Russel's children died. Mrs. Russel left the child in bed when she got up in the morning. About breakfast time, on going up to get it, she found it was dead. Her surprise was very great. I was out back of our garden and heard great lamentations. I could not imagine what it could be. I walked up to the house and found what was the matter.

March 31. Parson Wilson died about 7 miles from me. He was a very fine Parson and an oblidgeing Doctor. He died in the 60th year of his age, greatly missed and lamented.

April 4. Sarah Corwidda died. She lived 4 miles from me. She was a great loss to her children and family.

April 8. Sarah Finley died. 4 miles.

April 9. Nelly Draper died 7 miles. Both young women.

April 19. Mary Russel died very suddenly, only a few hours' sickness. Lived about 1½ miles.

April 24. My Grandmama was here.

April 25. Sunday, the old lady went home, well and hearty. Miers went to church at Cedar Creek. (St. Matthew's.)

April 26. Very cold wind. E.

April 27. Wind N. W. very cold

April 28. Snow a good part of the day. The green wheat was covered with snow. Very cold.

April 29 & 30. Still very cold.

May 1. Middling warm. Mama & Grandmama came here.
May 2. On Sunday they went home.
May 3 & 4. Miers cut his knee middling bad.
May 9. Mr. Luker & his wife here on Sunday. All middling well.
May 10. Fine weather. I go to see aunt Polly Dorman. She was very sick.
May 11 & 12. My Brothers came here.
May 13. The Boys went home. My knee is swollen, and it hurts me to walk.
May 14, 15, & 16. Miers knee upon the mend, & my own some better.
May 17, 18, 19, 20, 21, 22, & 23. Whitsun Day. I came home from Mamma's, my Brothers, & Cousin Sally Draper with me.
May 24. A great meeting on the Beach, Cakes, Raisins, Meat, Bread, Rum, Wine, & all such things there to sell.
May 25. The Boys & Sally went home.
May 26, 27, 28, 29, & 30. Trinity Sunday. All middling well.
May 31. The last day of May.
June 1, 2, 3, 4, 5, & 6. Sunday. People more healthy.
June 8, 9, & 10. Philis sick.
June 11, 12, & 13. Philis very sick Sunday.
June 14. Some better.
June 15. I went to Mamma's. Philis some better, and came home the same day. Betty sick, keeps her bed.
June 16, 17, 18, 19, & 20. Betty still sick.
June 21 & 22. Some better.
June 23, 24, & 25. Still keeps about.
June 26. Taken down again to her bed.
June 27, 28, 29, & 30. Some better.
July 1. Very warm.
July 2. Went to Mamma's.
July 3. Saturday.
July 4. Sunday. Went to quarterly meeting. There was a great fright among the people. A crazy man threw an axe up at the meeting house windows. It struck somebody, but I did not see the person. The second preaching was under the trees, a very great number of people, and the same man, they said, got a gun and was going to fire it through the crowd. The first thing I knew the people were screaming and halloing, and rushing almost over one another. I could not imagine what could be the matter; such a noise in the time of the sermon, when all should have been peace, and quietness. Some said the Devil appeared; some one thing, and some another. When I found out the truth, that it was the crazy man, with his gun, I came back to Mamma, and from there home with a very bad pain in my head. The dust and heat almost overcame me.
July 5. Billy did work here.
July 6. Brother Peter, Sarah & Polly Draper came here.
July 7. Went to the harvest at John Clark's.
July 8. They went home.
July 9 & 10. I was at the bridge.
July 11. Sunday.
July 12, 13, 14, & 15. Abby Fleetwood lives here.

July 16. Am sick & fainty.

July 17. Some better. Mamma and Brother Isaac came here. I had 3 of the neighbour's women here the same day, to see me.

July 18. Sunday. Very dry weather. A smart shower this afternoon.

July 19. Mamma & Brother Isaac rode home.

July 20 & 21. Hannah and Liddy Russell here to see me. I am better.

July 22, 23 & 24. I went to Mamma's.

July 25. Came home on Sunday.

July 26, 27, 28 & 29. Mamma here. Still very dry.

July 30. My Brothers came here. Almost 4 weeks since we have had a good rain.

July 31. Mamma & the Boys went home. A fine rain this afternoon. Thanks be to the Great Providence. Our corn is in a manner burnt up, and the grass is dying.

August 1. Sunday. Very likely for rain. I should have gone to Church.

August 2, 3, 4, 5, 6 & 7. Very seasonable weather; everything takes new life. Sally Draper & Peter Jackson & his wife here. Rain this afternoon.

August 8. Sunday. Very showery all day.

August 9. They went home. I went to see Mrs. Russel this afternoon.

August 10, 11 & 12. Not very well. Very warm. A pain in my head.

August 13. Sarah Draper came here & we were at the singing school.

August 14. She rode home. I with her. From there to Mamma's.

August 15 & 16. We came home from Mamma's. Very warm.

August 17, 18, 19 & 20. I was at the singing school at Mr. Russel's.

August 21 & 22. Sunday. Rainy this morning. Could not go to church.

August 23, 24, 25 & 26. A bad pain in my breast.

August 27 & 28. We started for Philadelphia. The tide being very low we could not go out.

August 29. Still could not get out.

August 30. The wind being in the East we came home.

August 31. We rode down to the boat again.

September 1. About 1 o'clock we got out of the mouth of the Creek. About 4 o'clock we struck on the Shears, a very dangerous place. The wind blew fresh & the waters were in a great rage. Everybody was very much frightened, but the Blessed Preserver of all poor mortals preserved us through all danger. Next morning we were up against New Castle. About 4 o'clock we arrived at Philadelphia. Got up to Mr. Irwin's about 5 o'clock.

September 3. We walked about a great deal in the afternoon. Mr. & Mrs. Irwin & the young —— Cousin & myself drank tea at Mrs. Ashmead's.

September 4. We drank tea at Mrs. Stretcher's.

September 5. Sunday. I stayed out almost all day. We walked to church and heard a very fine sermon.

September 6. I walked down to Mrs. Stretcher's and dined there & drank tea nowhere, not being well.

September 7. After dinner I walked down to Mrs. Snoud's, and drank tea there. The old lady was very glad to see me. Stayed all night at Mrs. Stretcher's.

September 8. Walked home to Mrs. Irwin's. Her two daughters and myself walked down to Mrs. Ashmead's. From there we walked to Major Moore's where my Brothers lodged, to know when the vessel was to go. We found it was to go the next morning at 5 o'clock.

September 9. We took leave of our friends and made sail.

September 10. We anchored about 7 o'clock just without the mouth of the river.

September 11. About 2 o'clock we found ourselves on a shoal, but it was very calm and smooth. We lay there until flood tide. About 10 o'clock we made sail again. Got down against Mushmillion and there anchored. About 2 o'clock made sail again.

September 12. We anchored off Slaughter Creek, the weather very stormy and wind from the East, so that we could not get into the Creek. When the tide made, we turned about and ran into Mushmillion. There we got ashore, and tried to put her off but could not. My two Brothers, my Cousin and myself walked down to Cedar Creek, 7 miles, and there we hired horses and got home the same night. Our people were very glad to see us, being very uneasy about us.

September 13, 14, 15, 16, 17 & 18. Not very well. Caught a great cold on board the vessel. Rode up to Mamma's.

September 19. Sunday. Rode home.

September 20. Not very well.

September 21. Miers sick.

September 22, 23, 24, 25 & 26. Sunday. Miers Clark still very sick. Not well myself.

September 27 & 28. Still poorly.

September 29. Poorly.

September 30. Polly sick. Her Dadda some better. Myself not well.

October 1. Polly and her Dadda some better, but very poorly. Myself a very bad pain in my head. I did not sit up.

October 2. A great deal better.

October 3. Came home from Mamma's. Polly sick.

October 5, 6, 7 & 8. Rode up to Mamma's. Little Johnny, the child, very sick. Intended to go home on the 9th, but there came up rain so that I could not get home until the 11th.

October 12, 13, 14, 15, 16 & 17. Sunday. Middling cool weather. We heard of Polly Jackson's being (sick) sometime back, but had got some better.

October 18, 19, 20, 21, 22, 23 & 24. Sunday. Middling cold weather. 8 months to-day since my Dadda left this troublesome world.

October 25, 26, 27, 28, 29, 30 & 31. Rainy weather. Family middling healthy.

November 1, 2, 3, 4, 5, 6 & 7. Sunday.

November 8, 9, 10, 11, 12, 13 & 14. Singing school at Wessel's and Coolspring the last days of the quarter, but I did not go.

November 15, 16, 17, 18, 19, 20 & 21. Cold weather.

November 22, 23, 24, 25, 26, 27 & 28. Sunday. Moderate weather.
November 29 & 30. The last days of November.
December 1 & 2. Henry Vessels came from the backwoods.
December 3 & 4. Singing school at Russel's. Our corn gathered.
December 5. Sunday. Sally & Polly Draper go home. Very cold.
December 6, 7, 8, 9, 10 & 11. Philis moves away. I rode up to see Mamma. Came home on Monday, the 13, Brother Isaac with us.
December 14, 15, 16, 17, 18 & 19. Sunday. Polly has ague and fever.
December 21, 22, 23 & 24. Great shooting at the bridge. Brother came here from me to go up to Mamma's.
December 25. Christmas Day. We go to Mamma's. Foggy and wet.
December 27. Came home. Brother Peter with us.
December 28, 29, 30, & 31. The last day of the year.

1791.

January 1. New Year's Day. Very cold. We were to go to Mr. Draper's today to take dinner with them, but it is too cold.
January 2, 3, 4, & 5. Today we go to my Uncle Draper's. From there to Mamma's.
January 6. Came home. Mamma with us. John Clarke taken sick this night.
January 7. Send for Doctor Hall. Mamma, Miers, and myself stay all night.
January 8. A great deal better. Mamma rode home.
January 9. Sunday. This day 13 months ago my dear sister died.
January 10, 11, 12, & 13. Mrs. Hazzard died. She lived about 2½ miles from here.
January 15. This day I walked over to see my Aunt Polly Dorman. She is very sick. I don't think she will recover.
January 16. Sunday. I went to see my Aunt again. Stayed and minded her. I had not been home very long the next morning before they sent for me. I went back again and stayed with her until she died. She departed about 3 Oclock Tuesday morning.
January 18. Of the month she was born the 7th day of this same month 1739. I have but one Aunt alive, and not one Uncle on my Dadda's side.
January 20. The funeral sermon was preached by Dr. McKee.
January 21, 22, & 23. A great many people sick.
January 24, 25, 26, 27, 28, & 31. The last day of the month.
February. Mrs. Waller died and 2 of her daughters lie sick 2 miles from me.
February 7. She is buried. Grandmamma came here from the burying. Shepherd Conwell is taken sick and could not get home. Caught cold at the funeral.
February 12. We go to see Betty Jackson. We heard she was very sick. William Hazzard died. He lives about 2 miles from me. A great many sick, Edward Ross.
February 15. He lives 2½, Sally Rowland, the widow Rowland's daughter.
February 18. Griffith Jones died, about 7 miles, & Andone Willkins, he lives about 7.

February 19. Lot Clark's Mother was buried. 3 miles.
February 24. This day 12 months my dear and tender parent left me.
February 27. A very sickly time in this neighborhood.
February 28. The last day of this month.
March 1. Middling warm weather.
March 2, 3, 4, 5, & 6 to 13, Sunday, to 20, Sunday.
April 1 to 10. Sunday. Sally Paynter here.
April 11 to 17. I was at John Clark's and Lydia Hall came there, and came home with us.
April 18. Polly taken very sick.
April 19 & 20. We hardly expect her to recover. Polly Draper came down. Mamma came down to see the child. She bleeds at the nose.
April 21. Grandmamma came to see the child. She is rather worse this afternoon.
April 22 & 23. The child some better. Grandmamma goes home. Miers goes after Sam and brings him home with him, and they go a fishing.
April 24. Easter Day. Polly a great deal better. Betty & Polly Heaveloe here, and Aunt Caly Young, and 3 more people today.
April 25 & 26. The child seems quite well, thanks be to God for His mercy.
April 27, 28, 29, & 30. We all ride up to Mamma's.
May 1. I go to Coolspring meeting. Mr. McKee preached there.
May 2 & 3. Milla Clarke came to stay awhile with me. Sally Draper came today.
May 4. Sally went home. I am not well.
May 5, 6, 7, & 8. Not very well.
May 15. Rode up to Mamma's. They are all well there.
May 16. I came home and met Brother going home. He has been seeing to the cutting of his corn, and to haveing it put on the vessel. Polly has a large red place on her hand and has ague and pains in her head and back, and high fever.
May 22. Still sick and the spot remains.
May 29. We ask the Doctor about it. He thinks it is scurvy. Gave her a warm purge, and it made her very sick.
June 1 & 2. Mamma came down & Polly very sick.
June 3. A fine rain.
June 4. Mamma goes home. Good rain this morning.
June 5. Sunday. I am poorly, and the child also.
June 6–10. Rode up to Mamma's. The Doctor came down with me to see Mr. King's negro with small pox.
June 12. Whitsun Day. So unwell that I cannot sit up. The child still has ague and fever.
June 13. A great day of frolic on the beach. I hear there were a great many there and a great disturbance. Many were hurt. Thompson finishes the ditch.
June 14 & 15. Sally Painter and Betsy & Polly King here.
June 16 & 17. King's negro dies with the small pox.
June 18, 19. Sunday. A very fine rain this afternoon.
June 22. Mamma came down to see us. Polly sick.

June 23. Mamma goes home. She carried my poor Sister Sally's clothes home with her, to keep them for the child she left. My Sister's marseilles coat was given me, because my Sister was buried in a white one of mine.
June 24. Mr. & Mrs. Jackson here and their two little boys.
June 25. We all go over to John Clarke's. Miers and the child sick.
June 26. Mr. & Mrs. Jackson went home. Miers and the child go to Mamma's. I went to quarterly meeting and came round by Mamma's. Was very tired, the weather very warm and crowds of people.
June 27. Came home and commenced preparations for harvest.
June 28. We have our harvest. The greatest part of the wheat cut.
June 29 & 30. Finish whitewashing the house and am very tired. Brother Peter goes home.
July 1 & 2. Milly goes home sick. Polly sick.
July 3. Sunday. All middling well.
July 4. Hessy began to work.
July 8. Rode to Mamma's, and came home Sunday the 10.
July 17. Sunday. Polly still sick.
July 24. We rode up to Mamma's. There was singing. Came home on Sunday and went to meeting at William Conwell's.
July 30. Mamma came here. I was at the bridge. Mamma went to John's.
July 31. Sunday. Went home the 1st day of August, and Grandmamma came down.
August 6. Grandmamma goes home. Hessy went home today.
August 7. Sunday. We went to hear Livy Hall preach.
August 14. We went to see Gerhardus & Nancy Conwell.
August 21. We went to Jonathan Heaveloe's and to hear Livy.
August 25. Sheldron Dorman married Tabitha Parmore [Palmer].
August 27. I go up to Mamma's, & from there to Uncle Isaac Draper's and stayed all night. Came home on Sunday the 28th.
August 30. My Grandmamma, Mamma, Aunt, Brother, 3 Cousins, husband, and child, all went down to the beach, together with others. I suppose as an extraordinary company that has gone down for years. There was my Grandmamma, & her Daughter, her Daughter's Daughter, that is myself, and her Daughters Daughter's Daughter, that is my Polly, and she was 6 years old day before yesterday.
August 31. They all rode home in good health, only a little fatigued.
September 1. Hessy gets her hat. Costs 26s.
September 3. Polly very sick. Miers goes to John Hazzard's. Rained. I send for Betsy Dorman to come and stay with me.
September 4. Sunday. Betsy went home after the rain was over.
September 10. Hannah Russel very sick yesterday. Sunday the 11th we go to her funeral. We got wet.
September 18. Mamma & Brother Isaac came her. Polly and I not well.
September 25. I went to meeting at Coolspring and heard a very fine sermon. Brother Isaac came home with me. I saw Mamma there. She said that Granny was sick. When I came home Miers and Polly were both sick.
September 26. Miers still sick. Polly is about today.

September 30. Miers some better today.
October 1. We go to Mamma's. Miers goes out to the election.
October 2. We came back. Brother Peter with us. Miers very poorly.
October 9. Miers very bad with his pains.
October 16. Miers still in great pain.
October 23. Miers some better.
October 27. Grandmamma came here. I am not very well.
October 30. Grandmamma goes home today. Miers very poorly.
October 31. A little better today.
November 1. Mamma came here today, & Doctor Hall advised Miers to try brimstone water. Nancy Conwell is very sick.
November 4. Mamma went home today. Very cold weather.
November 6. Brother Isaac came. Miers a great deal better. He went out today for the first time this 5 weeks.
November 8. Miers well enough to ride out. Weather warm. I go to see Nancy Conwell. She is still very poorly.
November 10. Miers in much pain.
November 13. Miers still down. I suppose he caught cold.
November 19. Doctor Hall came here today. He says that Miers' leg will break, or must be lanced. I rode up to Mamma's this afternoon and back again. They are all middling well. Mamma gave me 10 yards of Calico.
November 20. Middling cold today, and windy.
November 27. Miers is poorly.
December 3. Brother Isaac came today.
December 8. Nancy is sick and goes home, leaving the piece not woven.
December 9. Brother Isaac & Brother Peter came today.
December 10. They trod out our wheat.
December 11. The Boys went home today.
December 15. Mamma came today.
December 18. Sunday. Very warm for the season.
December 23. Brother Isaac & Brother Peter came, & went to the shooting match at Dick Star's.
December 24. Brother Peter went home. Brother Isaac went to the bridge and got a bad fall. Miers is sick.
December 25. Christmas Day. I went to Church, and from there I went to Joseph Watson's. The horse started, throwing me and hurting me very badly.
December 26. Mrs. Watson carried me to her father's Mr. Draper's.
December 27. They sent me in a carriage to my Mamma's.
December 31. Nancy Conwell came here.

1792.

January 1. Very wet weather.
January 3. I let Gerhardus Conwell have 6 geese.
January 4. I hired Ainee Fowler today.
January 7. Middling cold weather. There are a great many frolics this Christmas.
January 9. A frolic at John Conwell's. John Hazzard got drunk, and John Clarke got to dancing, so I was told.
January 15. Brother Isaac came today.

January 18. Polly Draper is to be married today. Brother Isaac sat up a little while ago, for the wedding. Is sick. Snowing hard today. Bill Coverdale is married today to Nance Rida.
January 22. Snowing all day and very cold. The snow was so deep that people could not pass the Causeway. There were three lodged here all night.
January 23. Dreadfully cold weather. The wind N. W.
January 26. John Clarke has a frolic at his house.
January 27. Brother Peter and Sarah Draper went home.
January 29. John Clarke and Brother Isaac went to church.
January 31. Still very cold.
February 2. I went to Mrs. Russell's to warp my web.
February 5. Sunday. Middling cold weather.
February 7. Cold rain. Wind Easterly.
February 9. Mamma and Brother Peter came here.
February 11. Mamma and Brother Peter rode home. Miers, myself, Polly, and Anne rode up to Gerhardus Conwell's. We left the children all night.
February 12. Miers brought the children home. Drizzling weather.
February 14. Miers went to Fergus's and from there to John Hazzard's, and did not get home until today. Mrs. Russel's girls stayed with me.
February 15. John Heaviloe and his wife came along and would have Miers and me go to David King's with them.
February 16. David King and wife, John Heaviloe and wife, and several others were here until night. After they left we put the horse to the sleigh and rode up to Mamma's. It was quite dark when we got there, and we were very cold.
February 17. Came home. Left Polly at Mamma's sick.
February 18. Miers went after the child. She would not come, and Miers left without her. On the way home the horses ran away with the sleigh and broke it.
Februray 19. Miers and myself went over to the bridge.
February 20. Very cold weather.
February 23. Mrs. Blount sends for me. Sarah Draper brings Polly home. She has fever again. Sally went home after dinner. Mrs. Russel and I went to see Mrs. Blount.
February 26. Sunday. Polly is sick today.
February 28. Sally Painter, Mrs. Dorman, came to see me.
February 29. Hannah Russel and David Pennewell are married.
March 3. I and Polly went to Mamma's.
March 4. We came home. Grandmamma with us. The horse threw Grandma and hurt her middling bad.
March 6. Philis is delivered of a girl.
March 9. Grandma went home.
March 11. Sunday. Brother Isaac came.
March 12. Polly sick. Brother Isaac went home.
March 15. Snow storm from the E. Quilting at Mrs. Russel's and at Uncle Isaac Draper's. I was not invited to my Uncle's.
March 16. Miers went to the bridge to see about his plank.
March 17. Carting plank from the vessel. Brother Isaac is here.
March 18. Sunday. Drizzling weather. Wind S. E.

March 19. Betty Russel came to weave for me.
March 23. Warm, damp weather.
March 25. Sunday. Middling cool today. Maud Draper is here.
March 29. Sally Draper came.
March 30. Betty Russel got her piece out. I and Polly went home with Sally, and from there to Mamma's.
March 31. I came home. Brother Isaac with me. Middling cool.
April 1. Brother Isaac and John Clarke went to Coolspring. Aunt Katy came. We all went to John's after they came back from meeting Katy wanted to see the painting.
April 2. Brother Isaac went home. Mrs. Russel sent for me to go to David King's with her, but I did not go. Mrs. Dorman went.
April 3. Betty came and put in my blankets.
April 4. Mrs. Dorman came to see me.
April 5. Lydia Russel came to see us.
April 6. Betty got out her other piece.
April 7. I and Polly went to Mr. Heaviloe's.
April 8. I went to church. Sacrament was given to a great many people. All the weaving that Betty has done came to 13s. 6d.
April 13. Brother Peter came to see us.
April 14. Brother Peter went home and John Clarke with him.
April 15. Meeting at Mr. Ellits. John Hill preached.
April 17. Warm with lightning, and thunder and showers.
April 18. Damp and cool. Aunt Caty came, and carried Polly to Nancy Conwell's.
April 19. Mrs. Blount, Sarah Painter, Aunt Caty, and Nancy Conwell came to see me. Rain and very cold.
April 20. Nancy went home. Still very cold. Wind E.
April 22. Brother Isaac came here from meeting.
April 23. Brother Isaac went home. Pleasant weather.
April 25. A great deal of rain fell this evening.
April 27. Nancy Conwell came this evening.
April 28. Gerhardus and Nancy started from the bridge in Heavileo's vessel. I walked down with them. Walked over to Mrs. Russel's this afternoon and met Grandma and Mamma. They went home with me.
April 29. Middling cool. Aunt Caty came. Hear that Dorman is drunk, it being such a fitting day to be that way, Sunday.
April 30. Rain all the morning. Mamma went home.
May 1. Damp weather.
May 4. Anne hurt her face with a fence log, Polly went over and stayed all night. The greatest rain this morning, perhaps for several years.
May 5. Brother Isaac came here. Mrs. Russel came this afternoon.
May 6. Sunday. I was walking and saw Dorman just going home from the Justice's meeting. He had remained all night.
May 7. Middling pleasant weather.
May 8. Rainy weather. Very busy with my goslins. Brother Peter came.
May 9. My little girl Sarah was born. Grandma and Sally Draper went home.

May 11. Brother Isaac came down and brought Polly home. Mamma and Brother went home this afternoon.
May 12. Sally Draper came down.
May 13. Sacrament at Coolspring. Mrs. Dorman here, and several others.
May 15. Sally went home. Bubba Russel broke his thigh.
May 17. Mamma came down.
May 19. Mamma went home. Mr. and Mrs. Hooker, Mrs. Hook and Betty Dorman here.
May 20. Sunday. They went home. Uncle Isaac and Aunt Betty came to see me.
May 21. Lydia Hall went home with her poor cross child.
May 27. Mamma and Sally Draper came down and brought me some pease. The child is very cross.
May 28. Whitsun Monday. A great many people going to the beach. They have a frolic at John Hazzard's. Sally Draper and Brother Isaac went there.
May 29. Mamma and Sally went home. Sally not well.
May 31. Brother Isaac and Miers went up to Milford. They took Jack to Mamma's.
June 1. Miers came home. Very warm. Jack went back.
June 7. Very cool. Wind E. Miers went fishing and caught a fine lot.
June 10. The worst spell of weather that I ever remember for this time of year.
June 11. Betty Dorman went home. Still cold and damp.
June 14. I walked out of doors for the first time. Brothers Isaac and Peter, and little John Clarke came down.
June 15. I moved out of the room and had it washed out. Sally Painter here. A great fog.
June 22. Mr. & Mrs. Jackson came down, their 2 sons, a hired man, and a negro boy and girl.
June 23. Brother Isaac came down for me to go home with him, but I could not go. Mrs. Jackson and Brother Isaac went to John Clarke's. Miers and Mr. Jackson went down the Creek. Brother Isaac went home this afternoon, and took the girls with him.
June 24. Sunday. Warm. Musquitoes very thick.
June 25. I went as far as Mamma's with Mrs. Jackson, and a dreadful time I had of it. From there I went home.
June 26. Harvesting at Mamma's, and Washy's.
June 27. Grandmamma and I went to Uncle Isaac's. A very warm afternoon.
June 29. We begin our harvest. 4 hands hired. There came up a cloud just before sunset, as I stepped in the door there was one of the loudest peals of thunder I have ever heard. Mr. Tull's house was struck, and part of the chimney fell.
June 30. I went to see Mrs. Russel. John Clark, Brother Isaac, and Mr. Simpler here. We rob our bees tonight.
July 1. Sunday. Wm. Painter here. He eats some honey.
July 2. Peter came down. Mrs. Russel & Mrs. Pennewell here. Brother Peter went home. Aunt Caty here.

July 7. Finish harvesting this afternoon.

July 8. I go to meeting at Elliots. Bevy Hall preached. They expected Aydelott. I went to Uncle Isaac's and came home in the afternoon, Cousin Sally with me. Very warm.

July 9. Cousin Sally went home. Very warm and dry.

July 11. Lidia Russel came to see me. John Clarke from home.

July 12. Brother Peter came down. He took Polly home with him.

July 13. Brother Isaac and Doctor Wilson came down down.

July 14. Brother Isaac and a great many went to the beach. I went to John's to eat oysters.

July 15. A great many people went to meeting today. I see Brother Isaac riding alongside of Hannah Conwell.

July 16. Very warm, windy, and dry.

July 18. Brothers Isaac & Peter, Mrs. Ashmead & Benny Draper went down to the beach, Miers with them. Came back in the afternoon and went home. Little Sally very poorly.

July 22. Went up to Mamma's. Looks like rain, Child still has a bad purgeing. Polly not well.

July 28. Polly Hook and Lidia Hall came.

July 29. Rainy weather. Toby's funeral preached today. Polly Hook went home. John Clarke & Hazzard here.

July 30. Lidia Hall went home. Mamma and Brother Isaac here. He is not well.

July 31. Brother Isaac middling today. They go home. Mrs. Russel and Aunt Caty here. Aunt Caty is not well.

August 5. I hear that Mamma is sick.

August 6. Brother Isaac came. I go with him to see Mamma and find her very sick with Rose (?)

August 7. Mamma very sick this morning. Did not sleep. Mamma some better this afternoon. I came home, Brother Peter with me.

August 8. Brother Peter went home. He bottomed Polly's chairs.

August 11. Roderick Heaviloe here. They have a frolic at John Hazard's. Roderick looks very poorly.

August 12. Sunday. Very warm. Nat Wright came here. Lidia Hall and her son here, & Shepherd Conwell.

August 13. Lidia gone. Brother Isaac here. He says Mamma is middling again.

August 15. I went to Mr. Heaviloe's to warp.

August 16. John Clarke went to town. He heard that James Wilson was married yesterday.

August 17. John came back. Wilson was married 7 weeks ago and noone knew of it except the Parson and his Brother.

August 18. Miers went out and got our sugar & coffee from on board. Brother Peter came. Very warm weather.

August 19. Sunday. Brother Isaac and Sally Draper, & John Clarke came this morning to bid us farewell. They went to Philadelphia. From there John & Isaac are to go to New York. Brother Peter went home and took Polly & Anna with him.

August 21. Ruth has been sick since Sunday.

August 22. Got my piece and wove more than two yards. Ruth better.

August 23. Brother Peter brings Polly home and says that Mamma and several of the family are sick. Aunt Caty came she wanted me to go to Mr. Russel's with her, but I could not go.

August 24. A smart shower of rain today.

August 25. Thomas Clarke came this evening.

August 26. Sunday. Little Sally very cross.

August 27. I am not well. Brother Peter came.

August 29. Brother Peter went home. Aunt Caty here. She is not well.

August 30. Aunt Caty and I walked over to Mrs. Russel's.

August 31. Very warm and dry.

September 1. Miers had such a bad fall that he thought he had broken two of his ribs, but I think they are not broken. Miers had a letter from John Clarke today. He says they did not arrive in town until Thursday, the 23d and are to leave there Sunday the 26th. They are well.

September 2. Looks like rain. John Conwell here.

September 3. Mamma came down to see us. Mrs. Russel sent for me. I was there when she came.

September 4. Mamma goes home. Mrs. Pennewell and Lidda Russel here.

September 6. Wm. Coffin's wife is dead. Left a young baby.

September 8. Brother Peter came down this afternoon.

September 9. I went to meeting at Wm. Conwell's, and heard a fine sermon. Coming home it was very warm. It hailed, the stones very large. Brother Peter went home.

September 10. John Young here.

September 11. Polly sick, and Sally.

September 13. Polly still very sick, but determined to go to Grandma's.

September 14. We took her there.

September 15. Brother Isaac came back from New York by land. John Ashmead came with him. They left John Clarke in Philadelphia, to come by water.

September 16. It rains. Polly some better. We ride over to Mr. Draper's. Sally came back with us. Mrs. Martin's child very sick.

September 17. John Clarke came up to Mamma's. He came back yesterday. We came home. Polly a great deal better. Brother Isaac with me.

September 19. Lidia Hall came to stay with me until the children are better.

September 20. Lidia & Philis picked the geese. Wm. King's child died.

September 22. Mrs. Young came to see us.

September 23. My Brothers, Sally Draper and myself went to Wm. King's to the funeral. David King's wife very sick.

September 24. The boys and Sally went home. Lidia went to see her children.

September 30. Polly still poorly. Mamma & Brother Isaac here.

October 2. Miers goes to vote. Very rainy and cool.

October 6. Miers very sick. Lidia goes to see her child.

October 9. Miers still sick. Mamma & Brother Peter came down. Aunt Caty is sick & Mamma went to see her. It is a very sickly time. Brother Peter went to work on the cherry tree, with Philip. He worked until he nearly fainted, then got John's Frank. Mamma & Brother Peter went home and left the negroes at work. Miers is better. Fillis is sick. Sue and Mos sick, & Ruth gone.

October 13. The negroes still sick. Miers better.

October 16. I am not well. Filis middling. Her children still sick.

October 20. Brother Peter came after me to go up there.

October 21. We came home, Brother Peter with us. Left Polly at her Grandma's.

October 22. Brother Peter went home.

October 23. He came down to go gunning on the great marsh. Sue sick & Filis gone to mill.

October 24. Betty Dorman brought Polly home.

October 28. Joseph Russel is dead.

October 29. Sally very cross, she has one tooth just out. , Polly not well.

October 31. Middling warm weather.

November 2. James Vent buried. Miers went to the funeral. Our folks are at a goose picking. Somebody has picked a good many of them for me. I understand it is Mrs. Dorman.

November 3. Mamma came down after little Johnny. I understand he is at his dadda's.

November 4. We went over to John's. The boys came down and we all ate dinner there. Brother Isaac went to John Hazzard's, Mamma came home with us.

November 5. Brother Peter came down. Old Whorten hewed his tree. Brother Peter & Mamma went home and took Anna with them.

November 9. Sally is 6 months old today. Sally Draper is here.

November 10. Brother Peter came down and took Polly home with him. Miers gone to the great marsh. Fisher Conwell is here.

November 11. Miers & Fisher went to Elias Conwell's. Thomas Clarke came. Mrs. Russel went to Mrs. Hazard's to see Mrs. Cade. We got back in the evening.

November 12. Brother Isaac came.

November 13. Clarke went home. Brother Isaac went to Milford.

November 14. Went to Mrs. Russel's to warp my piece.

November 16. Brother Peter came down for me to go there.

November 17. I went to Mamma's.

November 18. We came home, Brother Isaac with us.

November 19. Jerry Claypool & George, Miers, Brother Isaac, & John out gunning. I am a good deal afraid that Claypool will carry off Ruth.

November 21. Miers, Brother Isaac & John went to Burton Robison's.

November 22. John sends in Mamma's name for Uncle Isaac's mare. He and Brother Isaac went to Milford to a wedding.

November 24. Rainy weather. Brother Isaac & John came back, and went off again. I do not know where. Fillis is sick.

November 25. Sunday. Anna sick. Her Dadda not at home. Miers gone to the great marsh to look after his cattle.

November 30. Middling cold weather.

December 1. John Heaviloe here. Shepherd Conwill & Sue Coverdale here.

December 2. I went up to Mamma's. Very cold.

December 3. Came home not very well. I saw a man with his nose bit off.

December 4. Brother Peter went home.

December 6. Hessy came back from Charles Connerly's.

December 8. Hessy went to see her Brother with his nose bit off. The boys came here. Isaac went to Hazzard's.

December 9. Sunday. Joshua Clarke, his wife and child came. John & Anna here. Peter went home. Very cold.

December 10. Aunt Caty here. Clarke & his wife went away, Hessy got home. Her Sister Feeby came after her to go and weave.

December 15. I and the child not well.

December 16. Brother Isaac came. Have a very bad pain in my head.

December 17. Brother Isaac asked me to go and see him married. Feeby came home, and Hessy with her.

December 18. John Hazzard married to Mrs. Hosman in Lewes town.

December 19. Brother Isaac married to Hannah Conwell, John Hazzard's first wife's daughter about 1 o'clock. The weddeners came from town. There being so many spectators Brother Isaac and Hannah were married privately up stairs. None but the Parson, the groomsman, the bridesmaid, and John Clarke saw it. About 10 o'clock at night we got home, Sally Draper with us.

December 20. Sally and I set off very early to Mamma's that all of Hazzard's guests were to come there about 1 or 2 o'clock. Grandma & Ma welcomed their new relation. They all left about 10 o'clock.

December 21. Brother Isaac and Hannah came home with me. Feeby was still here. When we were at supper she wanted Ruth to get some shad for her. Ruth said No. She said take the key and go, they are at supper, they will not know it. The poor creature would have been as much deceived as Cain when he slew his brother and thought that no one knew it, for his Maker knew it, she was going to her Brother's that night and wanted to carry the fish with her.

December 22. Brother Isaac and Hannah went to Hazzard's to see them.

December 25. Christmas Day. Aunt Caty came. Miers not at home.

December 26. Clarke went to the forest. Annie is here.

December 27. Brother Isaac and several neighbours came for dinner.

December 28. John & Brother Peter came. I was to go up the Neck, but did not go. All went to Russel's to a frolic. Paid ¼ of a dollar a piece. Got back about 2 o'clock.

December 29. We went to Mamma's, and from there to Mr. Collin's, Brothers Isaac & Peter, and Hannah with me.

December 30. Mrs. Collins and I went to Mrs. Jackson's. We dined upon rockfish. Mr. Collins, Brother & his wife, and Brother Peter went to Meeting.

December 31. Coming home Hannah fell out of the carriage. The wheel ran over her and hurt her very much. We stopped to see Polly Jackson. She is very poorly. When we came to Mamma's, Mr. Hazzard and his wife were there. They went away, and we went to Uncle Isaac Draper's. I wished Sally much joy as she and John were married privately last Thursday at Georgetown. Only two or three knew of it.

1793.

January 1. I came home. Brother Isaac, Hannah & Sally went to meeting.

January 2. They went home. John went to see his wife last night.

January 6. We went to John's. He said he would bring his wife home this week.

January 11. John came for me to go there. I went. Fillis went and made some bread.

January 12. I went over very early before John had his breakfast. He got ready as soon as he could. Brother Peter and Sam Painter went with him. I was there until about 2 Oclock, and then went home to get clean clothes on, and to get my child. But John and the guests got back before I did. We had a very agreeable evening of it, and all went home in peace about 10 o'clock.

January 13. Sunday. Brother Isaac & his wife, Brother Peter & Polly Wiltbank came in the afternoon. John sent for us. We stay until after tea. They went to John Hazzard's, and we came home.

January 20. Mr. Hazzard, his wife, and myself went to John Clarke's.

January 22. Sally Clarke came and we passed a pleasant evening together. Miers and John having gone to the vendue.

January 23. I went to see Sally. Middling cool weather.

January 25. Brother Isaac and Hannah, Brother Peter, John and Sally came. They stayed until bedtime. After much laughter they went home, Peter and Shepherd with them.

January 26. We go up to Mamma's. The men value the land today.

January 27. Isaac, Hannah, Brother Peter, and I walked to Luker's. Came by Mr. Tull's. He and his wife very sick.

January 28. We came home, Brother Peter with us.

January 29. Miers away. Weather fine. Grandmama, Aunt Betsy, John, Sally, and Annie came.

January 30. Dreadful snow storm came on about 1 o'clock in the morning. I could not hear whether the vessel went out. It is now almost night and Miers not at home. I am afraid he is out in the storm. About 8 o'clock he came home. I think I was never so glad to see him in my life, for I did not know what might happen.

January 31. Aunt Betsy went home. Polly Wiltbank married.

February 1. Miers not well. Grandma and I insisted that he should not go out, but he said he would go to the vessel and get his clothes. About dinner time I expected him back, and kept his dinner by the fire until almost night, and his supper also until bedtime, but he did not come. I heard the vessel went out about 1 o'clock. Mrs. Russel came today.
February 2. Very rainy. Miers not returned. I hear that Ma is sick.
February 3. Sunday. Fine moderate weather. Mr. Cary is buried today.
February 4. Grandma went home. Lidia Russel came here. John, Sally, & Annie here.
February 5. Lidia went home. I got her to stay all night. Betty and Polly Heaviloe and Sally Clarke came. Sally stayed all night.
February 6. I went home. Sally stayed all night.
February 7. I expect Miers at home, the wind being fair all day.
February 8. Brother Peter came.
February 10. Brother Peter went home. Brother Isaac and Hannah came here from meeting. John, Sally, and Lidia Russel came over. Miers back from Morris River.
February 11. We all went over to John's, and came back in the night. It snowed and blew so that we could not see our way.
February 12, 13, 14. Very cold weather.
February 16. Mama came to see us.
February 18. Mama went over to John's and stayed all night. Lidia Hall came.
February 19. Mama went home.
February 21. Lidia went away.
February 24. It is three years since my father died.
March 2. Brother Isaac & Hannah here.
March 3. They went home.
March 9. The boys here. Very cold weather.
March 15. Lidia Russel here.
March 16. Polly Hook here.
March 17. I went to meeting at Wm. King's.
March 22. I went to Mama's.
March 24. Mama came back with me.
March 25. Mama and Aunt Caty went to John's.

Joshua Fisher of Lewes went to Philadelphia, 1745.

Inscriptions on Tombstones in the Ancient Cemetery in Pilot-town.

In memory of Hannah Baily who died January 16th, 1732, aged 72 years.

Here lies the Body of Hannah Jacobs, Born May 11th, 1734; Departed this life December 18th, 1767.

In memory of Albertus Jacobs, who died April the 28th, 1748, aged 53 years.

In memory of John Jacobs, who dyed ye 19th March, 1741, aged 45 years.

In memory of Jacob Art, who departed this life September 13th, 1769, aged 48.

In memory of Sarah Art, the wife of Bailey Art, who departed this life October 1st, 1797, aged 26 years

John Naws.

Benjamin Naws.

INDEX.

www.ingramcontent.com/pod-product-compliance
Lightning Source LLC
Chambersburg PA
CBHW060958280326
41935CB00009B/755